The meanings of Timbuktu

EDITED BY

Shamil Jeppie and
Souleymane Bachir Diagne

HSRC PRESS

CODESRIA

Published by HSRC Press
Private Bag X9182, Cape Town, 8000, South Africa
www.hsrcpress.ac.za

In association with CODESRIA
Avenue Cheikh Anta Diop, X Canal IV, BP3304, Dakar, CP 18524 Senegal
www.codesria.org

First published 2008

ISBN 978-0-7969-2204-5

Copyedited by Lee Smith and Mary Starkey
Designed and typeset by Jenny Young
Print management by comPress

Distributed in Africa by Blue Weaver
Tel: +27 (0) 21 701 4477
Fax: +27 (0) 21 701 7302
www.oneworldbooks.com

Distributed in Europe and the United Kingdom
by Eurospan Distribution Services (EDS)
Tel: +44 (0) 20 7240 0856
Fax: +44 (0) 20 7379 0609
www.eurospanbookstore.com

Distributed in North America by Independent Publishers Group (IPG)
Call toll-free: (800) 888 4741; Fax: +1 (312) 337 5985
www.ipgbook.com

Algiers
Tunis
TUNISIA
Tripoli
MOROCCO
LIBYA
Cairo
EGYPT
ALGERIA
MAURITANIA
MALI
S
Boutilimit
ouakchott
Walata
Awdaghust
Kumbi Saleh
Boudjebeha
Timbuktu
Gao
Mangabera
Ségou
Mopti
Bamako
NIGER
NIGERIA
G
C
SOMALIA
KENYA
TANZANIA
MOZAMBIQUE
MADAGASCAR
STATES AT THEIR HEIGHT
Ghana c. AD 1000
Mali c. AD 1230
Songhay c. AD 1460
MAJOR TRADE ROUTES
Local trade routes 1200–1600
European trade routes 1450–1600
MINERAL DEPOSITS
G Gold
C Copper
S Rock salt

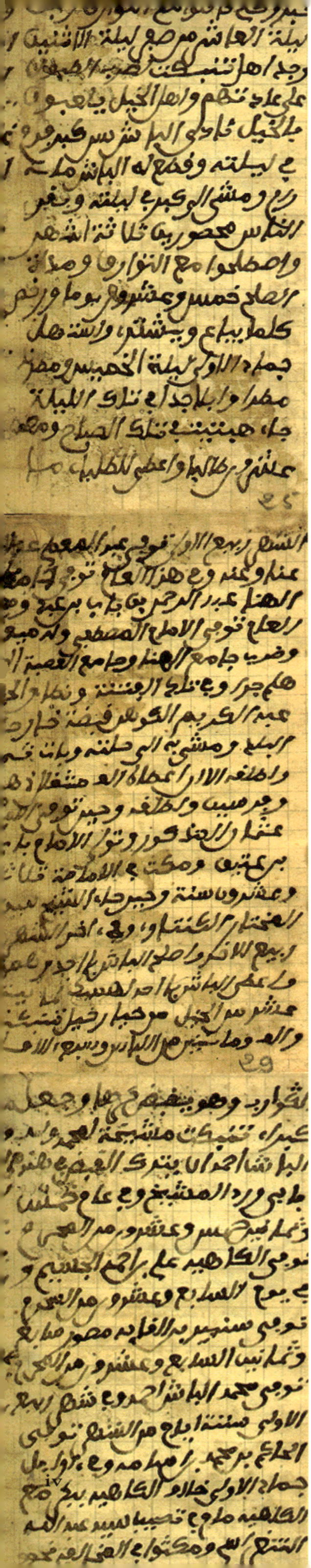

Contents

Part III: Scholars of Timbuktu

Part IV: The Timbuktu libraries

Part V: Beyond Timbuktu

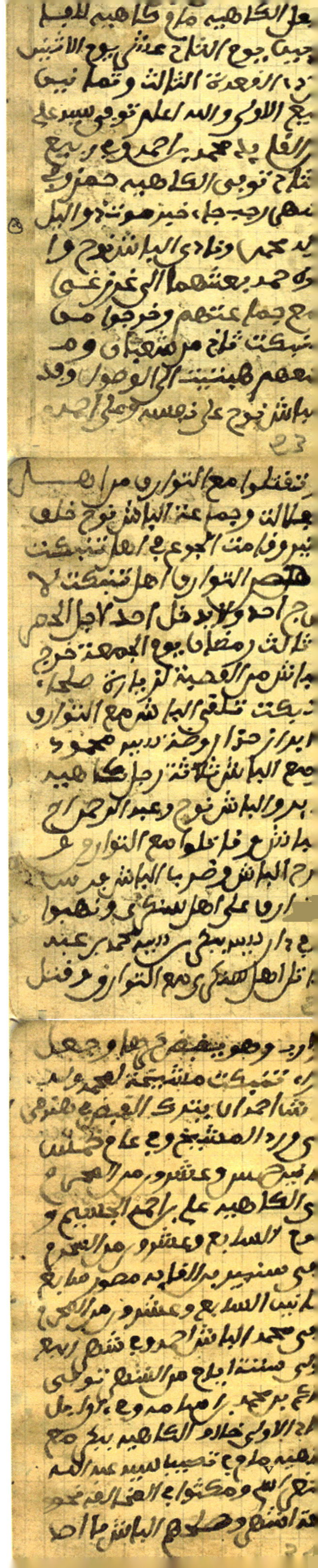

Preface

We are pleased finally to be able to present this volume of essays to the reading public in South Africa and elsewhere on the continent. The essays were, with one exception, all originally read as papers at a conference of the Tomb*ouct*ou Manuscript Project of the University of Cape Town in August 2005. On that occasion, they were prepared and presented in one of three languages – Arabic, English and French – and we are delighted to give English-language readers the opportunity to now read them all in one volume. Simultaneous translation was available at the conference, and publication of the papers in all three languages in separate volumes was our original and rather idealistic ambition, but funding for such a publishing project was unfortunately, if understandably, not obtainable; Furthermore, the logistics of editing a single volume has been a sufficient challenge: with the two editors living at great distances from each other, and authors who are spread across three continents, and many of them often away from desk and classroom. Simultaneity in this case was a most fanciful idea, but it is hoped that now that this collection of essays is in the public realm, the resources will be found to translate the volume into the other languages. We are confident that we have original essays of value here that deserve to be widely read in South Africa, Africa and beyond. It is our hope that, in the near future, readers other than those within the normal reach of the market of this Press – French and Arabic speakers, if not other regional languages – will have the book to hand.

The African traditions of scholarship, articulated in the Arabic language, and in African languages written in the Arabic script (the so-called *ajami*), that most of the chapters in this volume address, have to date been studied by a very small group of scholars – Arabists and historians or anthropologists, very largely, of course, trained to research and focus on the western regions of the continent. Modern scholarly research on this African Islamic tradition of learning has a presence in a few scattered places in Africa, Europe and the United States of America. While there is a colonial tradition of scholarship particularly focused on translating key texts relevant to the colonial policy-makers, later, 'scientific' research about African pre-colonial writing has grown steadily if lethargically since the 1960s.

This world of African scholarship before the appearance of European colonialism is, however, generally not as widely known or incorporated into school or university curricula about Africa as, say, aspects of the continent's archaeology or oral traditions. Yet the corpus of materials to study is vast and, excluding North Africa above the Sahara, extends across West Africa and down the East African coast and there even exists a small body of materials in Cape Town, South Africa. In recent years some intermittent international media attention to these traditions of writing has led to a popular focus on them; but like so much that is pursued by the media there is instant, intense and often sparkling light thrown on the subject, only for it to be soon relegated to make way for the next big scoop.

The written heritage of 'mysterious Timbuktu' has attracted this kind of attention from time to time for a short while until 'the next big thing' came along. So that desert town has had its 15 minutes of fame. However, we believe that Timbuktu's recent fame should be kept alive for a bit longer among scholars interested in the past of books and libraries; it should remain prominent among those concerned with at least a part of Africa's last few hundred years of written history. An ongoing scholarly investigation across disciplines, and a broadening of the present narrow base of specialists concerned with this rather neglected aspect of the history of Africa, remains imperative. We hope that this volume reaches a wide audience with an interest in this fascinating aspect of African history.

This collection is a selection of over twenty studies, which combine specialist expertise and accessibility about the extensive institutions of scholarship spread over parts of the Sahara and the Sahel – that region on the edges of the Sahara stretching from the Atlantic Ocean to the Red Sea, also known as *Bilad al-Sudan* since the medieval period. We also include two essays on the regions beyond, which is by no means comprehensive but merely an indicator of what exists outside the focus area of this collection. Altogether, these studies should whet the appetite of any educated reader or student interested in the transmission of learning and book production. We do not make any claim to comprehensiveness or definitiveness but cumulatively the essays provide concise introductions that are solidly researched and reliable and offer multiple perspectives on the worlds and meanings of scholarly reading and writing in Timbuktu and beyond.

This is not a collection of essays composed only of the work of scholars from universities outside the regions under study. We have scholars from within the region who continue to work in, manage or own the libraries under discussion. We also have scholars whose style of composition still has something of the classical modes of expression still taught in some tutorials and classes in the Sahel. Even though the book does not contain essays on the aesthetics of the written materials themselves, except for one on aspects of calligraphy, there are enough images in the following pages to give an impression of what future research is possible in fields such as West African arts and design, for example. It was therefore a conscious decision to include a generous selection of images of texts and their contexts from the regions addressed in this volume.

Outline of the volume

The Prolegomena has two essays by the editors providing a background and context to the collection. The first sets the current South African initiatives on the conservation of Timbuktu's manuscripts in context; the second examines the meanings of an intellectual history of the region and why Timbuktu is a symbol of a much more extensive African scholarly tradition.

Part I, an Introduction to the Timbuktu region, offers a historical perspective and a geographical frame central to an understanding of the region but broader and wider than the manuscripts alone provide. In his chapter, Roderick J. McIntosh systematically unravels the deeper archaeological past of the Timbuktu region and its immediate surrounds, the Azawad. The issues of paper and calligraphy are foundational to any discussion of Timbuktu's written heritage; chapters by art historians Jonathan Bloom and Sheila Blair look, respectively, at the history of paper and its introduction into the region, and at Arabic calligraphic styles in relation to the older West Asian and North African calligraphies. The last essay in this section is by Timothy Cleaveland on Timbuktu's tradition of higher education and its regional setting. He stresses the importance of attending to the unique features of 'traditional' forms of schooling and individual student–teacher relations, while pointing to the role and importance of the often forgotten town of Walata. He also offers insight into the genealogies of certain families and their broader scholarly networks over wide parts of the region.

Part II explores various kinds of Arabic writing from Africa as sources for the writing of African history. In his chapter, Paulo Moraes de Farias compares various genres of historical representation from the region and calls for a critical re-examination of the *tarikh* (chronicle), a genre which forms the foundation of most of the historical writing about the Mali and Songhay states. He sets the well-known chronicles beside the rather under-studied epigraphic evidence and invites scholars to see the authors of the chronicles as more than merely recording disembodied 'facts' about the past. Two essays follow on the use of Arabic script in the writing of African languages. Moulaye Hassane offers a survey of the issue within the broader question of the Arabic transcription of African languages and discusses the relationship between Islamic and pre-Islamic cultures in West Africa. Hamid Bobboyi surveys the *ajami* library of the nineteenth-century Sokoto Caliphate of northern Nigeria. Murray Last's chapter looks at the book economy of the Sokoto state, opening up, in a most fascinating way, an array of questions related to the circulation of written materials in nineteenth-century West Africa. Writing on the same period and region, Beverly Mack focuses on the canon of Arabic sources used by women scholars; she also goes beyond Sokoto to look at women writers from Morocco. The last essay in the section is by Mohamed Shaid Mathee and Aslam Farouk-Alli, who address the way that legal texts (more specifically, legal *responsa* or *fatawa*) could be used as a source of historical inquiry; they introduce us to a few of the cases currently being studied as a way into the social history of Timbuktu.

Part III is almost exclusively devoted to the influential family of Kunti scholars of the late eighteenth and mid-nineteenth century. It is an expression of their scholarly authority and contribution to the intellectual life of Timbuktu and the region, that three essays cover the lives and works of Shaykh Sidi al-Mukhtar al-Kunti (1729–1811) and Shaykh Sidi Muhammad al-Kunti (d.1826). Yahya Ould el-Bara and Abdel Wedoud Ould Cheikh offer two readings of the careers of the elder and younger Kunti. The essay by Mahamane Mahamadou, a leading scholar and resident of Timbuktu, who has been trained in the traditional Islamic sciences, was originally written in Arabic and follows traditional Arabic rhetoric and style. Somewhat similar in style is the chapter by Muhammad Diagayete on the twentieth-century scholar Shaykh Abu al-Khayr al-Arawani.

Mali has dozens of private manuscript collections and Part IV of the volume focuses specifically on Timbuktu's the libraries and private manuscripts collections. The chapters in this section were written by people who work, own or curate these libraries; thus their first-hand knowledge of the manuscripts provides invaluable information on Timbuktu's written heritage. Abdel Kader Haidara, of the Mamma Haidara Memorial Library, presents an overview of the history of the manuscript collections in Timbuktu, dealing more specifically with the private libraries under the Society for the Preservation of Manuscripts in Timbuktu. This is followed by an overview of the different libraries in Timbuktu with a specific focus on the Fondo Ka'ti private library written by Ismaël Diadié Haidara and Haoua Taore. The next chapter focuses on one of the great scholars of Timbuktu, Shaykh Muhammad Baghayogho al-Wangari, and the library he founded, the Wangari Library for Manuscripts. The chapter is written by one of his descendants, Mukhtar al-Wangari. The next chapter, written by Muhammad Ould Youbba, on the Ahmed Baba Institute, gives an overview of the history of the archive, the challenges it faces, as well as of the kinds of manuscripts it conserves. John Hunwick, one of the pioneers of the study of Timbuktu's history, then gives a crisp and comprehensive overview of the Arabic literature of the region, while Charles Stewart describes an initiative undertaken by the University of Illinois at Urbana-Champaign, where a database of West African manuscripts has been developed that could become a universal, on-line resource for Sahelian Arabic-script manuscript identification.

The last part of the volume goes beyond Timbuktu and the West African region to consider the written legacy of the eastern half of Africa – a good comparison to Timbuktu and its surrounds. Sean O'Fahey gives an overview of the Arabic literature in the eastern half of Africa, including Sudan, the Horn countries and finally Swahili literature written in the Arabic script. The last chapter, by Norwegian scholar Anne Bang, concentrates on the manuscripts found at the Zanzibar National Archives in Tanzania.

Acknowledgements

Many individuals and institutions deserve our thanks for supporting us in the publication of this work. Dr Pallo Jordan, the Minister of Arts and Culture, apart from regular queries as to its progress, provided a publication subvention that allowed this book to take its present form. Dr Essop Pahad, the Minister in the Presidency, has also been a keen supporter of this work as is to be expected given his role, on behalf of President Mbeki, in championing the building of the new premises for the Ahmed Baba archives in Timbuktu. The Malian Ambassador in South Africa, Mr Sinaly Coulibaly and the South African Ambassador in Bamako, Dr Pandelani Thomas Mathoma have assisted through their offices and personally with transport arrangements of participants in the conference and the regular visits of researchers between the two countries. John Butler-Adam, and before him Ahmed Bawa, at the Ford Foundation (Johannesburg) have been keen supporters of this and the larger project.

When John Daniel was Chair of the Editorial Board at the HSRC Press, he enthusiastically agreed to look at our proposal and urged us to get it all going; and the team at the Press that has worked on turning an unwieldy collection of papers into this more-or-less coherent collection has demonstrated their customary professionalism and good humour throughout. Mary Ralphs has been a wonderfully tolerant editor; but she also quietly makes demands and has pursued us and our authors all over the world for responses on the tiniest and thorniest questions of translation and transliteration, among other problems we gave her! Garry Rosenberg plotted the bigger game plan for this work and has helped to shape a new series of titles, of which this volume is the first. Utando Baduza chased us with paperwork, and Karen Bruns has been imagining and then working hard on marketing this collection for many months already. Designer Jenny Young and copy-editors Lee Smith and Mary Starkey all gave us the benefit of their professionalism and care.

The team of Timbuktu researchers all crammed into one office in the Department of Historical Studies at the University of Cape Town have been wonderful in their eager responses to being mobilised into assisting with multiple aspects of this work – from assistance with translation to sourcing images and so much more. They have certainly gained much insight into various aspects of publishing; without them this collection would have had to wait even longer. Susana Molins-Lliteras has been an energetic assistant and a committed and cheerful intermediary between the editors, the Press and the authors. Mohamed Shaid Mathee, Ebrahiem Moos, Nurghan Singh and Naefa Kahn all generously gave of their time. Present and former colleagues in the South–South Exchange Programme in the History of Development and the Council on the Development of Research in Africa, with which we have long-established ties, have been supportive of this project throughout. Members of the broader South Africa–Mali Timbuktu Manuscripts Project also played their part; they are Dr Graham Dominy, Nazeem Mahatey, Alexio Motsi, Mary Manicka and Riason Naidoo.

All the authors in this volume have been cordially co-operative and most patient when they could easily have given up on this project. Their forbearance gives us faith in those scholars in and outside the continent who have a commitment to seeing work on Africa actually published and circulating on the continent; one of the reasons why this is so important is the cost of important books into the continent, so at least with this collection there is no need to convert from euros or dollars!

This work is founded on the historic legacy laid down by the peoples of Timbuktu. Contributions in this collection by library owner–scholars from Timbuktu are but a small reflection of this heritage. Furthermore, this work would not have been possible without their co-operation and collaboration, and we are ever thankful for opportunities to work at various locations in their town. Many of them play a vital role in assisting visiting researchers; the names of Abdel Kader Haidara and Dr Muhammad Dicko deserve special mention; our gratitude to them also for allowing us to photograph and publish images of manuscripts in their collections.

Our families suffered through yet another bout of our obsession with books and handled calls by editors, copy-editors, designers and others. As ever, I, Shamil, thank Gigi, Mazin and Haytham and I, Souleymane, thank Mariame, Sijh, Mouhamadou, Abdallah and Moimouna for their patience and support.

Shamil Jeppie
Cape Town

Souleymane Bachir Diagne
Chicago

Key dates in the history of the western Bilad al-Sudan

covering present-day Senegal, Mali, Mauritania, Niger, Burkina Faso and parts of northern Nigeria

300 BC	Jenne-jeno is a growing settlement.
c.AD 600	This century witnesses the early development of the state of Ghana known as Wagadu.
c.600	The Songhay set up markets in Koukaya and Gao on the Niger River.
c.950	Around this time the Arab geographer Ibn Haukal provides a depiction of Ghana and its then capital of Koumbi.
c.990	Awdaghust, an important trading centre, is annexed to the expanding state of Ghana.
c.1000	Ghana is believed to have reached its zenith.
c.1079	The once-prosperous Ghana begins to crumble and in about 1087 devolves into three states.
c.1100	The city of Timbuktu is founded by the Tuareg Imashagan also known as the Kel Tamasheq.
c.1230–1240	Sunjata Keita becomes the king of Mali and in about 1240 conquers and subsequently destroys what is left of the state of Ghana. The state of Mali is then established.
1307	Mansa Musa becomes the new ruler of Mali and successfully extends the reach of the state.
1324	Kankan Musa brings his state to the attention of a much wider Muslim world with his famous pilgrimage to Mecca. He arrives in Cairo with vast quantities of gold and spends lavishly in Egypt.
1325	On his return journey, Kankan Musa stops in Timbuktu and is so impressed with the settlement that he appoints Andalusian architect Abu Ishaq al-Sahili to design Sankore's first mosque, the Jingere-Ber Masjid, as well as a palace for Musa to stay in when visiting. During this period the Malian state also reaches the height of its success and prosperity.
1400	Mali begins to decline.
1465	Sonni 'Ali Ber accedes to the position of ruler of the Songhay state and under his leadership it prospers.
1493–1528	Under Askiya Muhammad Timbuktu becomes a centre of Islamic study and scholarly pursuits while Songhay continues to expand.
1591	The Moroccan army conquers and destroys the Songhay state – chaos and decay ensue.
1660	The Arma, descendants of the Moroccan invaders, sever loyalty to Morocco and begin to rule from Timbuktu.
1712–1755	Rule of Biton Coulibaly over the Bambara kingdom of Ségou.
1766	N'Golo Diarra succeeds Biton after a decade of instability after the latter's death.
c.1800	Diarra conquers Timbuktu.
1810–1844	Chekou Hamadou reigns as head of Masina and establishes a religious state.
1857	Al-Hajj 'Umar Tall invades and conquers the Kaarta state which had been established by Massassi Bambara in the 1400s. Al-Hajj 'Umar conquers the Bambara kingdom of Ségou and Hamdullahi, the capital city of Masina.
1870s–1880s	During this period Senegal assumes the position of France's key African possession.
6 April 1890	Ségou captured by French colonel, Louis Archinard. Later in the same year, the Tukulor army in Kaarta is also defeated.

1897	Timbuktu conquered by the French. The establishment of the Institut Fondamental d'Afrique Noire. The institute is based in Dakar and produced significant research covering what is today known as Senegal, Mali, Mauritania, Burkina Faso, Cote d'Ivoire, Guinea, Republic of Benin and Togo.
May 1957	Attacks directed at 'Wahhabis' in Bamako. Most of their property is destroyed. The year of independence: Senegal, Mali, Upper Volta, Mauritania, Niger and Chad all achieve independence from France.
Jan. 1961	Modiba Keita becomes head of government of the newly independent Republic of Mali.
Aug. 1967	Keita introduces the 'cultural revolution', effectively seeking to rid the party of dissenters.
19 Nov. 1968	A coup d'état ends Keita's reign and the Comité Militaire de Liberation Nationale is established, headed by Lieutenant Musa Traoré.
19 June 1979	Elections are held, and Musa Traoré, the only contender presented for the presidency, is subsequently elected president.
1984–1985	Northern Mali experiences severe drought and it is estimated that the Tuareg lose about 70% of their livestock.
9 June 1985	Traoré re-elected.
Dec. 1985	War breaks out between Mali and Burkina Faso over the Agacher Strip. In 1986 the International Court of Justice makes a ruling dividing the strip between the two states.
1990–1991	These years are marked by Tuareg attacks and military reprisals, often on Tuareg civilians. They are also marked by pro-democracy demonstrations.
Mar. 1991	Traoré removed from power through a coup d'état led by Lieutenant Colonel Amadou Toumani Touré.
Aug. 1991	The Swiss are able to confirm that Traoré and his close associates had embezzled $2 billion.
Mar. 1992	A peace agreement is signed between the government and Tuareg rebels although skirmishes persist.
24 Feb. 1992	Marks the beginning of the electoral process, and on 22 May 1992 Alpha Oumar Konaré is officially declared president.
May 1994	Fearing further attacks by Tuaregs, the Songhay in northern Mali form a militia group.
1995	Peace agreement signed between government and the Tuareg, and thousands of Tuareg refugees return to the country.
May 1997	Mali's second multi-party national elections take place with President Konaré winning re-election.
1998–2002	Konaré wins international praise for his efforts to revive Mali's faltering economy. His adherence to International Monetary Fund guidelines increases foreign investment and helps make Mali the second-largest cotton producer in Africa.
Nov. 2001	President Thabo Mbeki's official visit to Mali and first trip to Timbuktu.
June 2002	Amadou Toumani Touré elected president of Mali. Konaré retired after serving the two five-year terms permitted by the constitution.
2005	A severe locust infestation and drought threatens about 10% of the population with starvation.
June 2006	The government signs a peace treaty ending a Tuareg rebellion earlier in the year. The president promises a significant development and anti-poverty programme for the Tuaregs.
April 2007	Touré is re-elected, winning 68.3% of the vote; his opponent, Ibrahim Boubacar Keita, gets 18.6%.

PROLEGOMENA

CHAPTER 1

Re/discovering Timbuktu

Shamil Jeppie

In November 2001 President Thabo Mbeki travelled to the Republic of Mali on an official visit accompanied by a large South African delegation. Travelling statesmen, government officials and businessmen usually live very comfortably in respectable hotels and meet their counterparts in air-conditioned boardrooms in capital cities, then they head back home. Bamako, the capital of Mali, where the South Africans landed and held all their meetings, is a sprawling African city along the Niger River. It has its share of high-rise air-conditioned hotels with swimming pools where visitors with the right budgets can stay. It is a product of late nineteenth-century French colonial encroachment into the interior of West Africa. It had no significance before this.

One has to go far from the capital city, to the historic centres of learning to the north – to Jenne and Ségou, to Timbuktu and Gao – to witness more clearly the residues and vestiges of 'pre-modern' styles of schooling. There one can easily stumble upon children sitting around teachers under trees in the sand, or reading under a street lamp at night, or catch the cacophony of noise as groups of boys or girls practise their lessons prescribed for memorisation.

There is nothing to show in the capital that the modern Malian state inherited successive traditions of state formation dating back centuries. There is certainly no evidence, on the surface at least, of Mali's older traditions of education, under the sharp sun and amidst the bustle of urban Bamako – the potholed and dusty streets filled with rusty, ageing vehicles, the occasional four-wheel drive, agile scooters, makeshift markets where everything is traded from imported bright fabrics and a variety of local textiles to animal fetishes, and improvised housing stretching out in all directions in seemingly unplanned fashion. If this is the physical experience of the city which hides and forgets older traditions of urban organisation, then there are also the limits of overstretched government educational and cultural budgets that inhibit the realisation for an ordinary visitor that Mali is also heir to an extensive tradition of indigenous scholarship.

Unfortunately for the South African delegation, the place where they may have found some faint reference to the earlier traditions of urban life, state-building and traditional learning was closed. The Musée National du Mali was undergoing renovation and its impressive local collections were stacked away; an attractive new building was in the last stages of completion. This would be a modern, western Sudanic-style structure – a mix of modernist minimalism and local forms and colour. The museum is located en route to the country's presidential palace which is perched high above the rest of the capital. It is a naturally elevated spot in the urban landscape with power inscribed in it since the official residence of the president is there and one has to literally look up to it. Maybe this then is all that remains from earlier forms of statehood, a special space symbolising authority.

One has to hang around in Bamako for a long time and befriend those with local knowledge to get introductions to students and marabouts[1] who still practise and value those older conventions of reading, writing and memorisation. These marabouts may also be specialised in the more esoteric arts of numerology and geomancy, and engage in some healing with this knowledge. They may also be leading members within Sufi orders. One can still find the instruments of this kind of learning in the city's main market – printed copies of classics used for centuries but in handwritten form; clean wooden slates for writing down lessons; and vast numbers of *tasbihs* or rosaries, some beautifully crafted from local woods, others made of plastic, possibly in China. These are not meant specifically for students but marabouts and pious students will certainly be in possession of them and use them daily in the prescribed fashion.

'Traditional' learning has, of course, not been passed on unchanged and without ongoing negotiations between parties with divergent interpretations of that legacy. The French came and imposed their language and secular education in the course of the twentieth century. Some local elites took to this; others took to it while maintaining one foot in the more traditional Arabic Islamic schools. The French also created their own *médersa* which attempted to combine the teaching of Arabic and French but under their supervision and control. Then from the years just before independence in 1960 there were steadily growing numbers of young intellectuals who came back from the Middle East with new ideas of what local education should look like.[2] The contestations over learning and the most appropriate way of life for Malians are not readily transparent. One has to go far away from the capital city, to the historic centres of learning to the north – to Jenne and Ségou, to Timbuktu and Gao – to witness more clearly the residues and vestiges of those 'pre-modern' styles of schooling and how to become an educated man or woman. There one could easily stumble upon children sitting around teachers under trees in the sand, or reading under a street lamp at night, or gathering in the homes of teachers from after sunrise, writing lessons on wooden slates, or catch the cacophony of noise as groups of boys or girls practise their lessons prescribed for memorisation. Timbuktu is still alive with a whole range of educational activities with origins in pre-colonial, colonial and post-colonial ideas and planning.

For a president to take his delegation to Timbuktu, some 750 kilometres from the capital, is rather unusual. Indeed, given that 'going to Timbuktu' means in so many languages to go to an unreachable or extremely distant location, and still has currency as a figure of speech, putting that destination down on the official itinerary may have appeared as a belated April Fool's joke on the part of the Presidency. From the perspective of urban Mali, from Bamako in other words, Timbuktu is a dust-covered and unexciting backwater. You pick this up in the blank looks and responses of people you meet in Bamako when you say you're on your way to Timbuktu. You can get transported there but never with impressive efficiency or undiluted enthusiasm. Nobody in Bamako tells you it's a great place to visit with interesting monuments and rare artefacts. To get to Timbuktu is indeed a tedious trek. There are two scheduled flights per week on small aircraft – as well as an exotic airline offering the service – otherwise you travel overland for two days in ancient but resilient Landcruisers over some really rough terrain. There is no conventional road connecting Timbuktu with any other major town. There's also the longer river option, of course, which can take anything from two to five days depending on the season and where the boat leaves from. So, you have to be an authentic adventure traveller, keen on the human and geographical diversity of the continent, or a researcher – say an anthropologist concerned with nomads or a historian working with African Arabic writings – on a fieldwork trip if you go there these days. Or, you can be the president of South Africa.

The South African president was accompanied by the then president of Mali, Alpha Oumar Konaré, who is now a senior statesman in the African Union based in Addis Ababa. Konaré was Mali's first democratically elected president from 1992 onward, after a long period of dictatorial rule over the country by Lieutenant-General Mousa Traoré who seized power in 1968. Konaré is a historian and archaeologist by training and a former minister of culture. The then first lady, Madame Adamé Ba Konaré, is also a historian. With two history PhDs occupying the hill in Bamako, the subject of history when meeting Mbeki would always be on the agenda. Their invitation to the South African delegation to make a trip to the historically significant town of Timbuktu was therefore to be expected. As historians serving in the higher education institutes of Bamako in the 1970s, they had been concerned with the pre-colonial history of Mali – with the states and societies which were located in and just beyond the space that the nation state now stretches across. For them, Timbuktu is a repository of history, a living archive which anybody with a concern for African history should be acquainted with. Timbuktu may be hard to get to but it played an essential role as a centre of scholarship under the Songhay state until the invasion from the rulers of Marrakesh in 1591, and even thereafter it was revived.[3] In its previous incarnations then, Timbuktu was a centre of trade and scholarship, a magnet to people from far and wide coming to exchange goods and ideas. Furthermore, in this dusty settlement – which young people with computer skills and knowledge of French now want to leave for the employment possibilities and energy of Bamako – there was a lively circuit of writers and their audiences, of visiting traders and sometimes diplomats and travellers from the remote corners of the Mediterranean world, long before Bamako was founded. The capital may now be the regional magnet by virtue of being the national capital but Timbuktu definitely played that role in a previous period of the vast region's history.

Timbuktu remains off the beaten track and any trip there for an outsider is a kind of trek from the centre to the margins of the state. But the Malian president saw the entirety of the land as his concern. The official Timbuktu Region, numbered seven in the country's administrative layout, was especially in need of central government attention. There had been increasing hardship followed by unrest during and after the droughts of the 1970s – when the term 'Sahel' came to be synonymous with arid and barren landscapes and human hardship – which transformed local communities there. Then in 1990 a sustained rebellion began that lasted until 1996 when, under the Konaré administration, a civil accord was signed leading to peace in the region. There had been a sense among large sections of the population living in that vast terrain sharing borders with Algeria and Mauritania that it was purposely neglected. The rebellions of the 1990s took the form of a regional ethnic/linguistic Tamasheq and Moor 'nationalism'.[4] Timbuktu was on the margins of this conflict but it did reach the town too. This otherwise sleepy settlement was the site of protest marches and political unrest. But a peace accord had been signed and a monument to peace constructed on the northern edge of the town. The inhabitants of Timbuktu, who had only recently again become used to tourists, were rather unused to the level of the South Africa state visit so the whole town was focused on the appearance of the South African head of state. This was also, of course, the first visit to Timbuktu by President Mbeki and his large delegation.

South African media has historically been, and remains, more intimately linked to the dominant northern sources of information; and apartheid education and politics kept the population cut off from the rest of the continent. London and Amsterdam, Paris and Hamburg, Tel Aviv and New York were seen as more important points of political and cultural connection. The vast land mass north of the country's border was a large fly-over zone to be missed and dismissed. Nothing of aesthetic value had come from there; there were no great works of art and literature, it was asserted or implied. Since 1994, part of the continuing post-apartheid struggle has been to reorient the attention of the media and of intellectuals, and to steer education and cultural institutions to look with greater interest and concern to the continent (and other parts of the global south) as a location for collaborative possibilities and not as a miserable space to pass over.

Understandably, not many heads of state, even from the continent itself, take the time to go to Timbuktu even when they are in Mali. The Brother Leader Muammar Gaddafi has gone, of course, and pitched his tent there. After Mbeki's visit there were rumours of the German then the French presidents planning visits; indeed, other statesmen landed there too.

The town has attracted numerous other visitors of note since at least the time of Ibn Battuta, the great North African globetrotter who arrived there in 1353.[5] He left his native land across the Sahara and travelled for many years through parts of Africa and went as far as China. Timbuktu has become a destination for travellers like Ibn Battuta: those who incessantly travel and explore and are animated by the search for fresh human experiences and challenges; those who will go to the ends of the earth to find something new and try to learn from those they encounter there; those who simply take pleasure in the journey itself and in the experiences along the way. There are many other

The bustling modern city of Bamako, capital of Mali, gives little hint of the treasures of the country's ancient heritage.

well-known travellers who arrived in Timbuktu and left behind impressions of the town. There was the Andalusian émigré, writer and diplomat al-Hasan al-Wazzan (Leo Africanus), who went there on a diplomatic mission for the sultan of Fez in 1526.[6] Despite the mythic status that Timbuktu achieved by the sixteenth century through Portuguese and English imaginings of a location with immense wealth deep inside Africa, the European explorers did not reach that illusive place until the nineteenth century. They competed to arrive there first and some like Heinrich Barth, who reached there in 1853, produced important observations on the town and many of the people he encountered along the way.[7]

So President Mbeki's arrival in Timbuktu at the start of the new millennium was as part of a long line of travellers led there by its now near mythic status. For many, imaginary gold was the force attracting them; for others it was the availability of books and savants. Some had the noble intentions of learning and communicating with those whom they met there; others were intent on producing images to feed the appetites of conquerors. There were the cosmopolitan travellers prepared to share and discover and then there were the colonising surveyors, writing to inform their sponsors in the industrial capitals of the north.

There is much to learn in that old city of mud brick buildings on the edge of the desert. The fact that various communities had been living there for centuries and managed to establish a growing settlement is in itself a cause to engage with its inhabitants. But it had also become over the centuries a renowned centre of learning in north-west Africa and was also known in learned circles in Cairo and Mecca. The town as an emblem for a regional centre of reading and writing was remarked upon by various travellers from the time of Ibn Battuta. Barth settled there for a while and engaged with local scholars. Timbuktu was always a distant place even in its own regional setting yet it was linked by trade and scholarship to other locations in the region. Salt, slaves, gold and other goods were exchanged. But so were books. Expert readers and writers, paper and copyists, books – originals and copies – were circulated between Timbuktu and its regional counterparts.

The mud brick buildings of Timbuktu, built on foundations many centuries old.

It was during his 2001 visit that the South African president was introduced to the manuscript collections at the Ahmed Baba Institute. A confusing web of buildings set around what must have been planned as a courtyard is located off the main thoroughfare into the centre of town. These buildings hold the most significant traces of the scholarly world of which Timbuktu was once a part. It is very easy to overlook them and even on entering them there is nothing to lure the visitor in, to seduce you to stay on and linger over the paper and ink, the crafted leather bindings and other remains from the past. The exhibition space consists of two small tables with glass cases filled with texts, none of which is wholly visible because there is too little space so they lie on top of each other in the cases. On top of them are slips of modern white typed paper describing the respective texts – titles, authors, dates and so on. This exhibition is like an afterthought, yet what is on display is stunning. These texts are mere snippets of the wealth of material available in this institute. The items are beautiful and important documents of a living intellectual past but far too little attention has been given to the methods of their presentation. No wonder most visitors to Timbuktu and most guidebooks appear not to capture the importance of what the institute stands for.

This institute was founded on the recommendation of the United Nations Educational, Scientific and Cultural Organisation (Unesco) in 1970 to collect and conserve the written heritage of the region. It was born during a period of great excitement about the possibilities of writing a new kind of African history and using newly uncovered sources from Africa itself to write this history – written and oral sources were to be collected and made available to the new generation of African historians.[8] President Mbeki – like other African intellectuals and leading figures of resistance of his generation – has always had a keen interest in African and world history and had of course known of the legacy of Timbuktu. But the impressive manuscripts that remain as traces of a long, complex and fascinating intellectual tradition in Timbuktu were a revelation to the South African president. This, and the larger African written heritage, still remains relatively unknown except to a rather small group of scholars and professionals concerned with matters of conservation and libraries in Africa. Some of the leading scholars concerned with this heritage are represented in this volume. On the continent itself, except in the communities where these manuscripts were produced and still circulate, there is much ignorance about the pre-European traditions of reading and writing.

The media paid little attention to the president's 2001 Malian trip. The fact that he went to Timbuktu was even less noteworthy. As a result, it is almost impossible to find press images of the trip or of the president pressed into the little exhibition room, poring over the glass cabinets and listening to translated explanations about their content and authorship. There is precious little visual coverage of this inaugural South African visit to Timbuktu. Is this a sign of the significance that the media gave either to Mali, a distant and poor African country, or to Timbuktu, that mythical place that was not supposed to exist? But since then, there has been notable change in the coverage. This happened because it became impossible to ignore the announcements and fund-raising activities of the South Africa–Mali Project in its efforts to build a new archive in Timbuktu.

President Mbeki promised his Malian counterpart that his government would assist the government of Mali to conserve the thousands of manuscripts held in Timbuktu at the Ahmed Baba Institute. The number of manuscript items is large – running into 20 000 items – but the storage and conservation facilities and the human capacities to conserve them for posterity were questionable. The tiny exhibition room had a semblance of order, but a room meant to be the conservation studio was in disarray and disuse and equipment looked rusty and outdated.

Timbuktu is far from the capital and the central state has many pressing priorities to address; texts largely from another era of scholarship come far down the line on the list of the state's financial priorities. The choice appeared to be between clean water and sanitation and investing in the conservation and display of thousands of old, dusty books. This much Konaré told the South African president. The central government, however, had been stretching its own resources to at least keep the basic functions of the archive in Timbuktu – there was electricity, a measure of security for the archive, and a rudimentary management structure. Bamako had also been facilitating outside assistance, from a few donor agencies in Europe and the United States, to keep the institute in Timbuktu afloat. A growing number of collections in the hands of various families had also come to light and individual attempts have been made by representatives of these families to conserve their family heritage (see the chapters in this collection by representatives of various private libraries).

In its previous incarnations, the dusty settlement of Timbuktu was a centre of trade and scholarship, a magnet to people from far and wide coming to exchange goods and ideas. For many, imaginary gold was the force attracting them; for others it was the availability of books and savants. Some had the noble intentions of learning and communicating with those whom they met there; others were intent on producing images to feed the appetites of conquerors. There were the cosmopolitan travellers prepared to share and discover and then there were the colonising surveyors, writing to inform their sponsors in the industrial capitals of the north.

Timbuktu is located where the Niger flows north into the southern edge of the desert, making the town a place where 'camel meets canoe'. From at least as early as the eleventh century, Timbuktu has been an important port for trade between West and North Africa.

However, there was clearly a need for more resources and skills development. In terms of contemporary standards of conservation there was a huge and growing gap between what was required as the ageing paper record deteriorated, and the very little that was being done to protect this precious legacy.

The promise of assistance from the southern tip of Africa to a Sahelian town at the bend of the great Niger River was an expression of the commitment to what Mbeki has called 'the African Renaissance'. In 1996 he gave his famous 'I am an African' speech while he was still deputy-president. In 1998 he convened a conference with a range of South African intellectuals on the subject of the 'renaissance' of Africa. He was aware of the challenges facing the continent but solutions could not be proposed or implemented without the simultaneous reclamation of a complex 'African identity' and the resolve to act as Africans in the interests of the continent.[9] Despite all the crucial challenges, the continent is not a lost cause and the possibilities that exist to transform it from within have to be harnessed. This is in direct opposition to the so-called 'Afro-pessimist' case, which asserts that the continent is on an ever-downward path of economic and political decay. Mbeki's argument is that the revival of the continent is clearly necessary and this is not possible without Africans engaging in regional and continent-wide coordination and exchanges to transform their conditions. The intellectual and cultural exchanges are as important as the political and economic collaboration needed to strengthen African capacities. It was out of this commitment to a vision of renewal on the continent that a South African project on the Malian manuscript heritage was initiated. This project began immediately after the president's return from Mali when a delegation from the Department of Arts and Culture was sent to make an assessment of the archival, conservation and research situation at the Ahmed Baba Institute, then known as Cedrab (Centre de Documentation et de Recherches Ahmed Baba), later renamed IHERI-AB (Institut des Hautes Etudes et de Recherche Islamique – Ahmed Baba) in 2001.

A 'technical team' – as the bureaucratic language would have it – of professionals constituted by the Department of Arts and Culture left for Mali in early December 2001, two weeks after the presidential trip. Their purpose was to advise the Presidency and the minister of arts and culture on what, in practical terms, needed to be done in

Timbuktu and what South Africa could offer. They went to meet with their counterparts in the capital and investigate the state of the facilities at Cedrab in Timbuktu.[10] Beyond the presidential gesture, this team had to work out the finer details of any future project in the town. South Africa then still had no official representation in Bamako – an embassy would be opened only in 2004 – and so the team had no official welcome, no vehicles, no hotel, nothing. In those days trips from South Africa to Mali went via Paris, so it was a very weary group of South Africans that arrived in Bamako via Paris late at night. They waited about at Senufo airport for a welcoming Malian official but ended up having to negotiate the cost of a ride into town with local taxi drivers and decide on a hotel. Malian officials had no idea that the South Africans were sending a team so soon after the Mbeki visit.

The next day they went from ministry to ministry, announcing themselves, until they found that the relevant ministry was education, not the Malian national department of culture. Officials there looked suspiciously at this band of awkward South Africans who informed them that they were there in response to Mbeki's promise of assistance. For this team the whole trip – from arrival in Bamako, through the two-day road trip to Timbuktu (accompanied by two sullen *gendarmes* from some point before Douenza), the time in Timbuktu and the flight back on the morning when the locals were to celebrate the end of the month of Ramadan – fell into the 'adventure travel' category rather than the hassle-free diplomatic kind their colleagues had experienced two weeks earlier. It was a rediscovery of Timbuktu the hard way; more like backpacking student travellers on a low budget than officials used to air-conditioned boardrooms and chartered jets.

The team's recommendations remained filled with passion despite the bureaucratic prose advising on what was to be done. Many trips followed, long meetings were held to work out details, and reports were submitted urging urgent measures. Finally work began in Mali. The conservation studio was brought back to life as Cedrab nominated young men to go for training at the National Archives of South Africa, which would be the engine room of the project. Training also took place at the institute itself when South African trainers went annually on two-week training stints to Timbuktu. 'Conservation' became an exciting field among a section of Timbuktu's young people. A 'building team' was constituted in South Africa and a design was developed, together with Malian experts, for a new archival centre in the town. Later on, access was provided to digital copies of manuscripts selected from the existing catalogues. The minister in the Presidency, Essop Pahad, cracked the whip to keep the whole multifaceted project focused and in line and, importantly, to get South Africans with deep pockets to give generously to this initiative. In Timbuktu itself, the idea of welcoming South Africans had moved beyond the event of a major presidential visit to welcoming all kinds of South Africans from various backgrounds – first those associated with the project, then others who had learned about Timbuktu and the logistics of getting there because of growing publicity evoked by the project. The linguistically gifted young touts who awaited new tourist arrivals in the town soon picked up Afrikaans, Xhosa and other South African words and expressions from these new visitors – so making it easier to sell them their wares.

Ahmad Baba (1556–1627), the venerable son of the soil, became a frequently invoked name as those associated with the project came to learn more about the rich materials deposited in the archives founded in his name, and promoted this newest effort to conserve an African heritage and see it listed on the Unesco 'memory of the world' register of humankind's most significant documentary heritage.[11] Baba was prolific, authoring more than 50 works. We know of 23 titles that are still accessible. His *Nayl al-ibtihaj bi-tatriz al-dibaj* is a biographical dictionary of the leading scholars of his time.[12] It lists around 800 scholars, including his teacher Muhammad al-Wangari Baghayoho. Baba left a strong intellectual imprint in Timbuktu and his legacy is still remembered, thus the recurrent references to him. There are numerous copies of his works in Timbuktu and beyond.[13]

Just as Baba's name was frequently cited as the premier example of local scholarship, so the word 'manuscript' came to hold magical qualities as if it were in itself something extraordinary.[14] At times there were the usual overstatements and mis-descriptions in the media, such as referring to the collections as 'ancient scrolls' or as holding 'the secrets' to 'the African past' – as if the putative 'secrets' would solve our problems or there was one Africa with a single past. This was especially the case with references to the still unstudied astronomy and astrology texts and items of a numerological nature in the archives. In a time of 'new age' searching for alternatives to consumerism and materialism it has ironically become easy to in turn commodify other people's ways of living – their ideas, values and practices, whether from the Andes, Timbuktu, the Karoo or Tibet – and such finds were useful materials to turn into products to sell. Fortunately, it appears that not too much of this kind of 'new age' usage of the Timbuktu heritage has so far occurred. But the overstatements and ideas of 'secrets' from Timbuktu were, in some way, part of the feverish excitement of discovery, of unearthing an African written tradition to set beside the oral tradition always invoked as an expression of African historical memory. It was yet another reflection of a country coming in from the cold and discovering a culturally rich and diverse continent far beyond its borders.

The manuscripts have also been described as 'ancient', which they are in the sense that many of them were produced many generations ago, hundreds of years back, but not meaning that they go back to before, say, AD 900 or 1200. Indeed, the earliest item shown to various teams of visitors was a Qur'an dating back to the thirteenth century. These 'ancient' materials are mostly in such a fragile state that handling them – for conservation or digitisation, for instance – has been out of the question. Materials for digitisation and research have had to be limited to those items from more recent periods – the eighteenth and nineteenth centuries, and through the colonial twentieth century.

Dating the manuscripts and attribution of authorship have been major challenges of the research project at the University of Cape Town (called the Tomb*ouct*ou Manuscript Project), for it would appear that many authors were not in the habit of dating their works and neither were many of them keen to sign them. This absence of information on authorship, provenance and date of composition for so many of the manuscripts so far studied is most probably linked to the esoteric world in which the scholars produced their work. Historians such as Louis Brenner have noted the deep Sufi or mystical roots of the pre-colonial style of education in which individuality, personal worldly achievement and recognition were not of any significance. A scholar was simply a vehicle for conveying already established knowledge and esoteric learning, irrespective of the subject. The source of knowledge was not the individual writer but went beyond him to the divine, to God.[15] While this argument is plausible given the widespread influence of various bodies of Sufi ideas in the region, the question still requires further study. Some of the manuscripts contain debates and individual opinions, especially the legal materials. There is also criticism and personal invective within the scholarly community. So a quasi-idyllic esoteric consensus among writers was not the norm. It remains to be studied whether in certain fields of writing there was greater effort to 'hide' the identity of an author, whereas in others an author had to assert his identity, and if over time there was a greater movement from anonymity to declaration of an authorial role. It does, however, seem clear that the idea of the autonomous creative agent was not known there (in Europe it had been a construct since early modern times and not an essential attribute of scholarship), but neither was all literary output the product of a 'culture of anonymous writing'.[16] A similar set of issues is involved in the question of copying and collecting of manuscripts, for a writer–copyist–collector complex constituted the 'scribal culture' of Timbuktu.

The word 'manuscript' has come to hold magical qualities as if it were in itself something extraordinary. There are the usual overstatements in the media, referring to the collections as 'ancient scrolls' or as holding 'the secrets' to 'the African past' – as if the putative 'secrets' would solve our problems, or there was one Africa with a single past. But the overstatements and ideas of 'secrets' from Timbuktu were, in some way, part of the feverish excitement of discovery, of unearthing an African written tradition to set beside the oral tradition that is always invoked as an expression of African historical memory.

The officials of the Ahmed Baba Insititute and Abdel Kader Haidara, in charge of his family's collection of manuscripts and more recently the coordinator of a consortium of similar private libraries, have been particularly generous and forthcoming in their collaboration, facilitating research and study of the wide array of materials held in the archives. There are only two sets of catalogues available as research aids and while they have been most useful as a starting point, they are not without their limitations and problems.[17] They do not cover the whole corpus of materials held at either the Ahmed Baba or the Haidara archive, and often the catalogue descriptions of items are either incomplete or misleading. They also suffer from the general problems identified above, that is, gaps in attribution and dating. The experience of looking at piles and piles of manuscripts without a finding aid describing what is held in an archive is daunting. The catalogues were therefore a great help but, even so, it was intimidating and overwhelming to be confronted with the approximately 16 000 titles listed in the catalogues.[18] Then there are the many thousands of items in other private libraries for which there appears to be no cataloguing project under way at all. Convinced that a conservation project should unfold with a parallel research project, we had to almost instantly decide on subjects to pursue in the research project. Once again collaboration with scholars from Mali – and with other established scholars in the field such as John Hunwick – was the only way to proceed. Dr Mahmoud Zouber, the former director of Ahmed Baba Insititute, was forthcoming and supportive from the outset, as have been the rest of our colleagues in Timbuktu, some of whom are represented in this volume.

Though the focus of the project is on the manuscripts of Timbuktu there is in fact also another purpose at the core of the South Africa–Mali project that goes beyond the preservation of this body of invaluable manuscripts in a historic African town. For the South African and Malian governments it is also a project of continental and global importance that speaks to the future. There is the comradeship that grows out of the practical and logistical aspects of government officials and citizens from two African states, thousands of kilometres apart, collaborating on a common cultural project. This collaboration is not mediated by an international agency or foundation or by northern powers. It has grown directly out of a common sense of purpose; it was not imposed but has emerged organically with all the usual and sometimes comical misunderstandings borne out of the understandable strains and headaches of working across such distances, across bureaucratic styles and language barriers. More significantly, the area of cooperation is a vastly underestimated literary heritage that is potentially a symbol of a much wider continental heritage of creativity and a written tradition in particular. This, of course, is the very opposite of what Timbuktu has come to stand for in popular culture almost across the globe: a most distant and unreachable place. Timbuktu, through the international attention generated by this and other projects, could well become a symbol, at least in the African context, of any place with large quantities of written materials. It is a place of paper and books, emphatically not a non-place.

✣ ✣ ✣

Timbuktu persists as a subject in the travel-writing genre. The 'mystery' of Timbuktu can always be relied upon to attract readers.[19] That Timbuktu has become synonymous with a place of remoteness and myth is not fortuitous. It is a sign of the way in which the idea of Africa was represented in discourses on the continent since at least antiquity by writers from the other side of the Mediterranean and the Red Sea. Ignorance and prejudice became transformed into empirical fact and philosophical principle during the eighteenth-century Enlightenment. Ideas became powerful supports as European companies and armies began to penetrate the continent, and thus were cast the standard modern prejudices against Africa. Popular representations of the continent reflected ignorance and arrogance, but some of the most sophisticated European thinkers also advanced the same kind of representations. These most eminent of thinkers, whose legacy we still live with, produced subtle discourses on moral philosophy and aesthetics but, when the subject of Africa came up, they reverted to truly unscholarly and nasty prose. Thus the still influential philosopher Immanuel Kant (1724–1804) wrote: 'Humanity reaches its greatest perfection in the white race...The

Negroes are lower and the lowest are some of the American peoples.'[20] Similarly, Hegel (1770–1831) infamously wrote that Africa was a continent without history: 'Africa is no historical part of the world; it has no movement or development to exhibit.'[21]

This view of the continent would have a long and enduring legacy and shape the language of conquest and domination. Implicit in and integral to the European colonial project was a denial of history and the agency of African subjects, their cultures, social values and practices. As Frantz Fanon wrote:

> ...colonialism is not simply content to impose its rule upon the present and the future of a dominated country. Colonialism is not satisfied merely with holding a people in its grip and emptying the native's brain of all form and content. By a kind of perverted logic, it turns to the past of the oppressed people, and distorts, disfigures and destroys it.[22]

Thus, in the view of the colonial rulers of the twentieth century, history began with the arrival of the white man, wherever he may have set his foot on the continent. Whatever else went before or was contemporaneous with the conquests was derided, denied and denigrated. The exception lay in the way in which the great architectural and artistic works of the continent were seen: while they were recognised and preserved, they were attributed to people from outside the continent. No indigenous intelligence was possible. Even in the case of the written legacy of Africa in Timbuktu, the popular view is that the authors of the works were 'outsiders', 'Arabs'.

Timbuktu in particular has a long pedigree in European imaginings of the continent. In these traditional framings, in the case of West Africa and Timbuktu, all that is relevant is the harshness of the landscape, the martial character of certain peoples, the prevalence of slavery, the futility of productive engagement with it and so on. Thus the natives had first to be subjected to imperialist rule as a precondition for civilisation before they could be treated as equal human beings.

Throughout colonialism, this inherently racist perspective permeated the very history which began to be taught in Europe and the colonies. Thus, in the West African French colonies, schoolchildren were taught to remember: '*nos ancetres, les Gaulois*' (our ancestors, the Gauls).

Yet, the impact of the colonial moment cannot easily be disavowed; it is impossible and undesirable to ignore the impact of colonial education, for instance. No African country that has experienced colonialism can ignore its impact and imprint and wish it away. This applies to Mali with its French colonial imprint as much as to South Africa with its Dutch and British marks of conquest. Adamé Ba Konaré's observation, writing about Mali, is apposite here: 'Malian historiography, indeed African historiography, cannot be understood outside of the colonial domination from which it came and in relation to which it is defined.'[23]

Throughout the northern parts of the continent, across the Sahara, and along the whole of Sudanic Africa – from Senegal to Ethiopia – and down the East African coast as far as northern Mozambique, we can find rich and copious examples of Africans engaged in reading and writing as far back as the earlier centuries of the previous millennium. They unambiguously reveal the sophisticated use of a wide diversity of Africa's languages in high-level intellectual pursuits, demonstrating African peoples' capacities to express themselves in complex forms and African intellectual capabilities over the centuries. Intellectual and scholarly endeavours are an integral part of African history.

The teaching of history in South Africa has not been spared the influences of colonialism and apartheid, right into the 1990s after the end of apartheid. In 2002, then Minister of Education Kader Asmal instituted a wide-ranging process to review the curricula being taught in South African schools. The History and Archaeology Panel found that Africa's place in the world was being taught with an 'overwhelmingly Eurocentric' conception of the continent as 'mostly inert, and treated within the context of European impact through colonization'.[24]

Initiatives such as those in the history curriculum in South Africa are therefore fundamental. The overall project on Timbuktu – building, conservation, research – is part of this reorientation of South Africa as an integral part of the continent. Thus the Timbuktu Project came to illustrate that there were places of scholarship and learning with long histories on the continent. Timbuktu was an important centre of learning whose history goes back almost a thousand years, with its intellectual high point sometime in the sixteenth century. Many of the products of this scholarship still remain, either in original form or as copies made over the years. We also know that these places were well connected through intellectual engagement and trade routes with other places of learning spread throughout the world. Thus, the author Leo Africanus wrote in the sixteenth century, 'In Timbuktu there are numerous judges, scholars and priests, all well paid by the king. Many manuscript books coming from Barbary are sold. Such sales are more profitable than any other goods.'[25]

There were other towns across the Sahara which became known as centres of intellectual pursuit, although Timbuktu has in more recent times come to stand as a kind of symbol for these African literary activities because so many scholars spent time in it, or copies of their texts have found their way there. Furthermore, with all this attention on Timbuktu there is now also a growing enthusiasm among Malians in a number of towns – such as Jenne and Ségou – that it is possible to conserve their manuscripts without having to lose them to collectors from overseas. Thus a whole series of new projects has been established to collect and conserve papers in various locations of Mali. In Timbuktu many new family collections have been brought to the notice of researchers in the last five years.

Other places in Africa, such as Abyssinia, also had thriving centres of reading, writing and knowledge production.[26] Throughout the northern parts of the continent, across the Sahara, and along the whole of Sudanic Africa – from Senegal to Ethiopia – and down the East African coast as far as northern Mozambique, we can find rich and copious examples of Africans engaged in reading and writing as far back as the earlier centuries of the previous millennium. They unambiguously reveal the sophisticated use of a wide diversity of Africa's languages in high-level intellectual pursuits, demonstrating African peoples' capacities to express themselves in complex forms and African intellectual capabilities over the centuries. Intellectual and scholarly endeavours have been an integral part of African history since the development of writing on the continent.

Yet within the historiography of Africa, attempts to argue for an intellectual history of Africa have often been met with the argument that Africa only has an oral tradition. This historical untruth cannot be sustained. The Timbuktu libraries contain materials that can illuminate various aspects of the intellectual pursuits of the literate elites of the region, in addition to offering other materials for historians concerned with relations of domination and slavery, among others. This new history will no doubt have to correct the hitherto most neglected aspects of the study of Africa's past, including the written legacies from the period before European colonialism. Modern scholarship and research necessarily have to deal with the disagreeable aspects of African histories; the scholars and researchers working on the manuscripts are among some of the leading specialists in the world and have in no way avoided these. On the contrary, the manuscripts serve as repositories of important historical data for virtually all aspects of life in the region and beyond.

The vast collections of manuscripts and papers that still remain in Timbuktu and its surrounds decisively confound the view of Africa as a remote, mythical entity devoid of history and of the practices of reading and writing. Moreover, the views of many historians who wrote off a whole continent – as of no consequence to humanity, as having no history, who stated that intellectual history is not a field for African historians – can no longer be sustained what with this mine of information (the basic materials in the craft of writing history) which still remains to be analysed and written up.

Adamé Ba Konaré, with all the insight of a historian and a woman close to the sources of political power in her country, has criticised the misuses of the powers of historical narrative in African nationalist historical writing. Her insight, which has also been formulated in similar terms by other scholars familiar with the crafts of history and heritage in Africa, should signal a note of caution against any new nationalist orthodoxies or 'nativist' intellectual enterprises built on the edifice of the Timbuktu manuscripts or other similar initiatives of reclaiming African pasts inside Africa and in the diaspora. She reminds us that Malian post-colonial historiography replaced colonial nationalist history with its own narrow, uncritical and unreflective nationalist history and the 'historians fell into a trap'. What happened in Mali was in keeping with so much of the history that was produced elsewhere on the continent from the 1960s onward:

> ...official history, directed from above and without nuance, became a true prison almost everywhere in Africa. It could not be corrected in public or even in private. When it came to the heroes, a critic ran the risk of offense, even blasphemy in relation to the warrior heroes of the past. The problem is even more complicated in Mali where it is difficult to develop an objective history when the descendants of the heroes are still alive, jealous of what they consider to be their family heritage, and sensitive to the honor due to their ancestors.[27]

These words from a former Malian first lady who was instrumental in the programme that initiated South Africans into the heritage of Timbuktu should be heeded by Malians and South Africans who are engaged in working on the manuscript tradition of Timbuktu, and indeed more generally in the fields of heritage and the craft of historical writing. A key word to embrace in the quoted passage is 'nuance', for so much of it is needed when attempting to deal with any aspect of the continent's past and present. While this project was without doubt established 'from above' – two presidents met and agreed on an initiative – it did not come with a historical narrative prescribed 'from above'. This collection of essays, which is hopefully only the first of many publications to emerge from this project, is not official history and hopefully demonstrates some of the nuance that Adamé Ba Konaré points to as an absence and a shortcoming in some African historiography.

NOTES

1 A marabout is a religious teacher or spiritual guide. It is derived from the Arabic word *murabit.*

2 See Brenner (2001: esp. Chapters 1 & 2) and Bouwman (2005: Chapters 2 & 3).

3 See Hunwick (1999: introduction).

4 On this see Lecocq (2002).

5 For an abridged account see Mackintosh-Smith (2002: Chapter 18).

6 Africanus (1738); see also Davis (2006: Chapter 1).

7 Barth (1857).

8 See Unesco (2003).

9 Speech by the deputy president to the Constitutional Assembly on the adoption of the 1996 Constitution, on 8 May 1996, in Debates of the Constitutional Assembly, Vol. 3 (29 March to 11 October 1996, cols 422–427). The 'I am an African' speech appears to have been influenced by ANC founder Pixley Ka Seme's 'The regeneration of Africa', a speech that was later published in the *Journal of the Royal Africa Society* (1905–06). See Mbeki (1998).

10 This team was led by Mr Themba Wakashe and consisted of Dr Graham Dominy, Mr Douwe Drijfhout, Mr Alexio Motsi and the author.

11 See www.unesco.org/webworld/mdm/register.

12 Baba (2000).

13 See Mahmoud Zouber's (1977) biography of Ahmad Baba.

14 The term 'manuscript' is derived from post-classical Latin *manuscriptus*, meaning handwritten (*manu* = hand; *scriptus* = to write), used in European languages since the early sixteenth century. One definition is: 'A book, document, etc. written by hand, *esp* one written before the general adoption of printing in a country; a handwritten copy of an ancient text' (*Oxford English Dictionary Online*, Oxford University Press, 2005).

15 See Brenner (2001).

16 The phrase is from Robert Alter, 'Committee speak', *London Review of Books*, 19 July 2007.

17 Ahmed Baba Institute (1995–98); Mamma Haidara Library (2000).

18 I must also mention the invaluable catalogue, which covers a much wider area, of Hunwick and O'Fahey (2003).

19 Recent titles include Salak (2004) and Freemantle (2005).

20 Kant (1802: 15).

21 Hegel (1872: 95–103).

22 Fanon (1963: 210).

23 Konaré (2000: 15–22).

24 DoE (2003: 44–45).

25 Africanus (1738).

26 Tamrat (1972).

27 Konaré (2000: 18).

REFERENCES

Africanus L (1526) *The history and description of Africa and the notable things therein contained.* English edition translated by J. Pory (1600, reprinted 1896) London: Hakluyt Society

Ahmed Baba Institute (1995–98) *Fihris makhtutat markaz Ahmad Baba li'l-tawthiq wa'l buhuth al-tarikhiyya bi Tinbuktu / Handlist of manuscripts in the Centre de Documentation et de Rechercher Historiques Ahmed Baba* (5 Vols). London: Al-Furqan Islamic Heritage Foundation

Baba, Ahmad (2000) *Nayl al-ibtihaj bi tatariz addibaj.* Annotated by Dr Abdelhamid al Harrama. Tripoli: Dar Al Katib

Barth H (1857) *Travels in north and central Africa.* London: publisher

Bouwman D (2005) *Throwing stones at the moon: the role of Arabic in contemporary Mali.* Leiden: Research School CNWS

Brenner L (2001) *Controlling knowledge: religion, power and schooling in a West African Muslim society.* Bloomington: Indiana University Press

Davis NZ (2006) *Trickster travels: a sixteenth-century Muslim between worlds.* New York: Hill & Wang

DoE (Department of Education, South Africa) (2003) *Report of the History and Archaeology Panel.* Reproduced in the *South African History Project progress report 2001–2003.* Pretoria: Department of Education

Fanon F (1963) *The wretched of the earth.* Translated by C Farrington. New York: Grove Weidenfeld

Freemantle T (2005) *The road to Timbuktu: down the Niger on the trail of Mungo Park.* London: Constable & Robinson

Hegel GWF (1872) *Lectures on the philosophy of history.* Translated by J Sibree. London: Bell & Daldy

Hunwick JO (1999) *Timbuktu and the Songhay empire: al-Sadi's Tarikh al-Sudan down to 1613 and other contemporary documents.* Leiden: Brill

Hunwick JO & O'Fahey RS (Eds) (2003) *Arabic literature of Africa. The writings of western Sudanic Africa* (Vol. 4). Leiden: Brill

Kant I (1802) *Physische Geographie* (Vol. II). Königsberg

Konaré A (2000) Perspectives on history and culture: the case of Mali. In RJ Bingen, D Robinson & JM Staatz (Eds) *Democracy and development in Mali.* East Lansing: Michigan State University Press

Lecocq B (2002) That desert is our country: Tuareg rebellions and competing nationalism in contemporary Mali (1946–1996). PhD thesis, University of Amsterdam

Mackintosh-Smith T (Ed.) (2002) *The travels of Ibn Battutah.* London: Picador

Mamma Haidara Manuscript Library (2000) *Catalogue of manuscripts in the Mamma Haidara library* (3 Vols). Compiled by Abdel Kader Haidara and edited by Ayman Fuad Sayyid. London: Al-Furqan Islamic Heritage Foundation

Mbeki T (1998) *The African renaissance.* Johannesburg: Konrad-Adenauer Stiftung

Salak K (2004) *The cruellest journey: 600 miles by canoe to the legendary city of Timbuktu.* London: Bantam

Tamrat, T (1972) *Church and State in Ethiopia, 1270-1527.* New York: Oxford University Press

Unesco (2003) International scientific committee for drafting a general history of Africa, various editors, *General History of Africa* (8 Vols), abridged edition. Cape Town: New Africa Books

Zouber M (1977) *Ahmad Baba de Tombouctou (1556–1627). Sa vie et son oeuvre.* Paris: Maisonneuve et Larose

CHAPTER 2

Toward an intellectual history of West Africa: the meaning of Timbuktu

Souleymane Bachir Diagne

Cheikh Anta Diop, the well-known Senegalese historian, once wrote that centuries before Europe colonised the continent and questioned the primitive character of African 'mentality', Aristotelian logic was being discussed by local African scholars in places like Timbuktu. Here are Diop's exact words: 'Four centuries before Levy-Bruhl wrote his *Primitive Mentality* [also known by the title *How Natives Think*] Black Muslim Africa was commenting on Aristotle's "formal logic" and was devoted to dialectics.'[1] I shall question Diop's affirmation later in the chapter, but let me just, for the moment, comment on its general meaning. What Diop was saying is that it is impossible to give a proper account of the history of philosophy in the African continent while ignoring totally the significance of the penetration of Islamic knowledge in Africa. Because of this ignorance (and I take this word to mean both 'lack of knowledge' and 'dismissal'), the intellectual history of Africa in general, beyond the particular case of philosophy and logic, is still a widely open field to be studied. And this needs to be done in the light of the Islamisation of many African regions, a process that became an important factor in sub-Saharan Africa around the eleventh century. Such a study would put an end to the preconceived notion that African cultures are oral cultures in essence; that Africanity is, at its very core, orality. What Timbuktu and other places where Islamic scholarship was developed teach us is to have a sense of history that opposes this identification of Africa with orality, a generalisation which is just not accurate. Of course orality is important in all cultures and especially in Africa. But we should not ignore that the graphic rationality of Islam has meant, in many areas, the adoption of Arabic, or rather Arabic script, by populations who, among other consequences of their conversion to the Muslim religion, literally rewrote who they were and created a written intellectual tradition that we need to study. Wolof, Fulfulde, Hausa and Bambara ceased to be oral languages at the very moment when some people, trained in the Arabic script in Qur'anic schools, started writing chronicles, myths and praise

It is impossible to give a proper account of the history of philosophy on the African continent while ignoring the significance of Islam in Africa.

Throughout West Africa, Qur'anic schools associated with mosques educate children and youth in Muslim philosophy and the art of calligraphy. Characters written in ink or charcoal are easily washed off the wooden boards, providing a fresh surface for additional exercises.

poetry in these languages. And a new era of African intellectual history was opened when scholars such as those who authored the manuscripts in Timbuktu and elsewhere started writing didactic poetry and prose on jurisprudence, theology, Sufism and other areas, both in the Arabic language and sometimes in their native tongue.

This chapter will consider three points in relation to Timbuktu, the best testimony and symbol of this written tradition: the first is what I have called the significance of Islamisation as self-rewriting; in the second part the focus is on the discipline of philosophy in order to show how ignorance of the written tradition represented by Timbuktu has led to the ill-posed question of African philosophy as a debate between ethno-philosophers and euro-philosophers; in the third part I study one example of a work that represents the intellectual atmosphere of Timbuktu – *Tuhfat al-fudala bi ba'di fada'il al 'ulama* (The Gift of the Noble Ones Regarding Some of the Virtues of the Scholars). I conclude with a short lesson that we can draw from that work by the most prestigious Timbuktu scholar: Ahmad Baba (1556–1627/963–1037).

Conversions: Islamisation as self-rewriting

Conversion is not only entering a new religion with its creed, dogmas and rituals. As the Latin etymology indicates, to convert is to get totally turned around. That means a new self-reappraisal following the adoption of a new cosmology. One visible aspect of conversions has been a radical change in the discourse of identity. This is the case with the Islamised rewriting of certain epics, for example that of the Mande. Seydou Camara, in a lecture given in Timbuktu on Islam and West Africa and titled 'Islam and the historical tradition in the Mande' (*Islam et tradition historique au Manden*),[2] has indicated that the Jabate from the centre of Kela have a written version of a narrative that presents the new Islamic cosmology of the Mande people as constituted by the following phases:

The creation of the universe and the origins of Humanity.
The conquest of Khaybar
The beginnings of the *mansaya* [monarchy] in the Mande
The saga of Sunjata
The mottos and genealogies of the heroes of the main Mande clans
The list of the thirty Mande 'families'
The settlement and hegemony of the Keyita Kandasi in the Niger valley.[3]

What we see in this succession of episodes, mixing myths of origins and historical facts such as the conquest of Khaybar or the beginnings of the Mande *mansaya*, is what I call – using a word coined by French orientalist and philosopher Henry Corbin – the projection of 'hiero-history' on the plane of history. By this I mean that the Mande people rewrite their own history in continuity with a sacred narrative (hiero-narrative) within which it acquires a totally new sense. In this case we see how Mande identity is linked to an event that functions as a founding myth in Muslim faith and from which it now derives its reality and meaning: the battle and victory of Khaybar. That battle was one of the great military victories of the early Muslim community during which 'Ali ibn Abi Talib, especially, distinguished himself as the hero who overtook the reputed inexpugnable fortress of Khaybar. Now, in the rewriting of their origins, the Mande present themselves as the descendants of the royalty from Khaybar who converted to Islam after the episode of their military defeat. The function of this narrative is quite clear. First, it transforms the conversion of the Mande to Islam and its cosmology into an epic which took place at the very beginning of the Muslim religion as part of the Islamic early saga in the Arabian Peninsula. Second, it legitimises the *mansaya* as the continuation of an ancient tradition of royalty in Khaybar (a process of legitimisation which is the usual role of myths). This kind of self-rewriting is not limited to the Mande people. The same pattern is to be found also in the written chronicles of the Fulani people in Futa Jallon or Futa Toro: a new origin Islamised by its linkage to the dawn of Islam in Arabia. Seydou Camara and others have read this kind of self-rewriting as a sign that the people who converted were ashamed of their pagan origin and therefore

Now, in the rewriting of their origins, the Mande present themselves as the descendants of the royalty from Khaybar who converted to Islam after their military defeat. The function of this narrative is quite clear. First, it transforms the conversion of the Mande to Islam and its cosmology into an epic which took place at the very beginning of the Muslim religion, as part of the early Islamic saga in the Arabian Peninsula. Second, it legitimises the *mansaya* as the continuation of an ancient tradition of royalty in Khaybar (a process of legitimisation which is the usual role of myths). The same pattern is to be found in the written chronicles of the Fulani people in Futa Jallon or Futa Toro: a new origin Islamised by its linkage to the dawn of Islam in Arabia.

It is important to look at the global meaning of a radically new cosmology where the beginning of the world itself is different and demands a different narrative to account for the way in which the community now fits in a totally different space and time. The self-rewriting process is a deep reorganisation and reappraisal of the social imagination. The importance of the manuscripts we are dealing with is that they bear witness to such a process.

invented new ancestries when the literate among them decided to fabricate oriental connections.[4] I do not think that that is the whole story. It is more important to look at the global meaning of a radically new cosmology where the beginning of the world itself is different and demands a different narrative to account for the way in which the community now fits in a totally different space and time, that of the *umma*, the Muslim global world. The self-rewriting process is a deep reorganisation and reappraisal of the social imagination that occurred in West Africa. The importance of the manuscripts we are dealing with is that they bear witness to such a process, to which a good intellectual history of the region must pay careful attention.

One crucial aspect of the new cosmology which calls for particular attention is a new philosophy of time that marks a turning point in the intellectual history of the Bilad al-Sudan (land of the black people), as the region was called. This philosophy of time can be perceived in the famous Sudanese chronicles emblematic of the Timbuktu manuscripts: the *Tarikh al-Sudan* by ʻAbd al-Rahman al-Saʻdi and the *Tarikh al-fattash* by Mahmud b. Mutawakkil Ka'ti. Beside their immense value as sources for the history of Mali and the Songhay, these narratives about the societies of West Africa – weaving together dynastic evolutions, collective movements, sociological considerations, the philosophy of history, biographies or genealogies – express a philosophy of becoming, a thought of time as creative movement. In the *Tarikh al-fattash*, for example, we read that 'what led God to cast the Songhay state into chaos, what brought to its citizens the punishment they were laughing about until then, was the inobservance of the laws of God, the injustice of the servants, the arrogance of the elite'.[5] And that:

> during the time of Ishaq, the city of Gao had reached the extreme limit of immorality; the worst crimes, the most disagreeable actions to God's sight were openly committed while the ugliest misdeeds were on display. The situation had reached the point where a[n] officer had been designated to attend to issues of adultery, with a drum specially made for him, and the different parties would present to him their cases against each other. Many other things were going on that would bring dishonor to those who would dare mention them. To God we belong, and to Him we will return.[6]

'Inna lillahi wa inna ilayhi rajiun' – this Qur'anic quote by which al-Saʻdi concludes his lament summarises the underlying philosophy of time and history pervasive in his chronicle: the course of human events carries with itself, as by some immanent justice, its divine sanction and the inobservance of the laws of God inevitably leads to decline and chaos.

The question of African philosophy

I consider my second point by first raising the question of the way in which African philosophy has now become an academic discipline. First there was GWF Hegel, the German philosopher, who decided that historicity and philosophy were the distinctive, specific characters of Europe and only Europe. As a consequence, he wiped Africa out of history and denied any possibility that the black continent could have produced anything comparable to a thought. Exiled from reason, civilisation, true monotheistic religion and philosophical thinking, Africa, according to Hegel, was barely the primitive stammering of humanity, enveloped, as it was, 'in the dark mantle of the night' – a spiritual night, needless to say. This did not apply to all of Africa, though – only to what he called 'Africa proper', namely sub-Saharan Africa. Egypt and its civilisation were of course excised by him from the rest of the continent and linked to Asia while North Africa, the Maghrib, was also to be detached from it and linked to Europe – where it truly belonged albeit in a derived way – through the promising event of colonialism (Hegel saw its promise when in 1830 the French took control of Algiers, an event he saluted). The only good thing that could then happen to Africa proper was, on the one hand, European slavery, an evil per se but still a way of putting the uprooted African populations in the new context of civilisation where they could develop beyond any possibility available in the 'dark continent'; and, on the other hand, another possible civilising influence was seen by Hegel to be Islam.

After Hegel, the stage was dominated by the ethnological paradigm. The 'mentality' of the Africans (their mental activities could not be dignified with a word like 'thought') was studied in some continuity with Hegelianism given the premise that this mentality was considered to function as the 'other' of reason and philosophical spirit. Lucien Lévy-Bruhl distinguished himself in the enterprise of characterising the natives' mentality as foreign to 'our' logic, 'our' rationality and 'our' capacity to think and live by a consistent system of sound principles. In a third phase, around World War Two, still within the ethnological paradigm, this Lévy-Bruhlian line of thought was challenged by Africanists who claimed that African customary law, customs, ethics and so on were to be fully understood only if seen as stemming from a coherent set of philosophical principles expressing an original ontology. The notion of African philosophies was not an oxymoron any more. *Bantu Philosophy*, the well-known and loudly acclaimed book by Father Placide Tempels, appears as the model for all the works that were later published with titles such as *The Moral Philosophy of the Wolof*, *Akan Philosophy*, *Yoruba Philosophy* and so on. This phase was followed by another, when the ethnological paradigm itself was questioned. Ethno-philosophy, as it came to be disparagingly called, was criticised and dismissed as the wrong way of considering philosophical activity in Africa. Philosophy must be the written (not oral), individual (not collective), rational and critical thinking of a person presenting himself or herself as a philosopher, according to those who denounced ethno-philosophy. They were in turn accused of

Euro-philosophers versus ethno-philosophers established the debate on African philosophy in total ignorance of the written tradition of the kind that is revealed by the Timbuktu manuscripts.

having uncritically embraced a Eurocentric definition of philosophy, thus begging the question of what philosophy is. Euro-philosophers versus ethno-philosophers – they established the debate on African philosophy in total ignorance of the written tradition of the kind that is revealed by the Timbuktu manuscripts.

The philosopher Kwame Anthony Appiah is right when he writes about philosophy in Africa: 'Muslims have a long history of philosophical writing, much of it written in Africa, so that the study of philosophy can be seen as traditional (and therefore holy) and endogenous (and therefore nationalistic).'[7] Recalling this simple fact, which was overlooked in the very terms of the debate about ethno-philosophy and African orality, is crucial when it comes to establishing the *history* of philosophical thinking on the continent. Appiah's words echo the statement by Cheikh Anta Diop that I quoted at the beginning of this chapter and that I am now going to examine. The remark must be made that although Timbuktu and other similar intellectual centres were quite comparable to the best places of learning in the Islamic world at large in the same period, philosophy as a distinct discipline, the tradition known as *falsafa* among the Muslim sciences, had almost disappeared from the curriculum. *Falsafa* is what Greek philosophy became once it had been appropriated by Muslim scholars such as al-Farabi in the ninth century AD, Ibn Sina in the tenth, al-Ghazali in the eleventh and Ibn Rushd (Averroes) in the twelfth, to name but the most famous. These philosophers contributed to the universal history of the discipline by pursuing a fruitful dialogue with the likes of Plato, Aristotle and Plotinus from their own perspective, which is their Qur'anic culture. The tradition they created can be said to have declined after Averroes's death in 1198. So one should not expect the Timbuktu manuscripts to reveal ground-breaking philosophical treatises about, say, crucial aspects of Aristotelism. This type of work was nowhere to be found in the Muslim world (at least the Sunni part of it) during the intellectual golden age of Mali or the Songhay. But that being said, one must not forget either that philosophy is an all-encompassing way of thinking which goes far beyond the disciplinary boundaries. If *falsafa* as such was not taught in the curriculum as we know it from the manuscripts and other testimonies, *kalam* (theology) was taught, as were *fiqh* (jurisprudence) and Sufism (mysticism) – and in all these sciences philosophical thinking is present – not to mention *mantiq* (logic), the science of valid reasoning, a foundational discipline among the *ulum al-din* (sciences of the religion), considered by the peripatetic followers of Aristotle as the *Organon*, the instrument for all knowledge in general.

Let me mention here the work of 'Abd al-Qadir b. al-Mustafa al-Turudu, a nineteenth-century philosopher that we know of thanks to John Hunwick's patient task of digging out the written intellectual heritage of Timbuktu. He was a nephew and student of the well-known scholar Muhammad Bello. Al-Turudu died in 1864. According to Hunwick's compilation,[8] his is an example of philosophic work in the pure tradition of *falsafa*, in particular his *Futuhat al-rabbaniyya* written in 1828–29 in which he proceeds to a 'critical evaluation of the materialists', naturalists' and physicists' perceptions of

Opposite: a manuscript discussing the celebration of the of the prophet Muhammad's birthday, *Milad al-Nabi*.

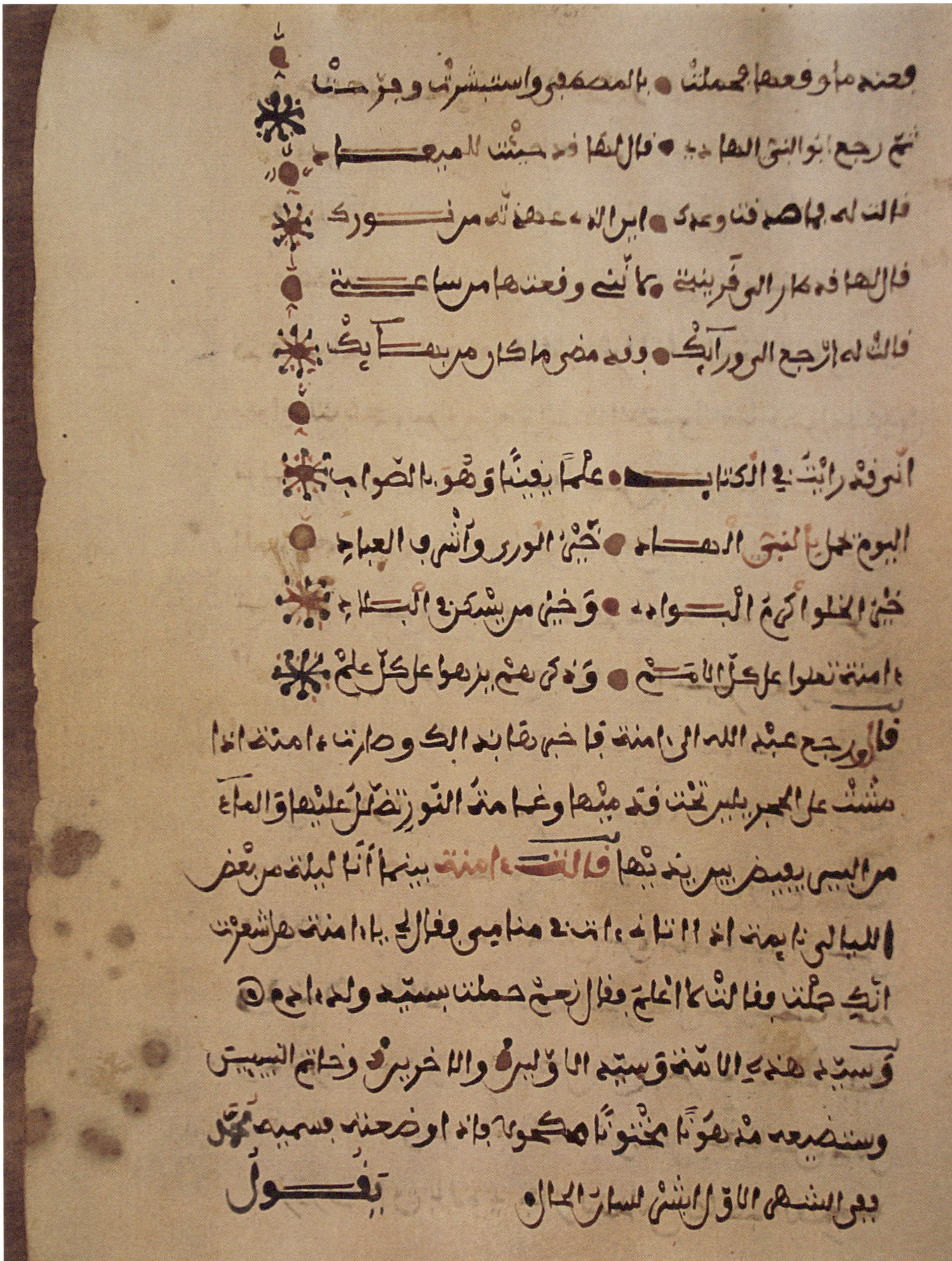

The first lesson on the importance of knowledge is that the manuscripts must of course be preserved and catalogued, but turning them into sheer museum objects is not the ultimate goal. Meditation on African sciences and knowledge requires that the manuscripts, in Timbuktu and elsewhere, be published and made accessible to today's scholarship. The second lesson is a prophetic saying, quoted by Baba in *Tuhfat al-fudala*: 'The ink of the scholar is more precious than the blood of the martyr.'

life', considering also 'matters related to the transient nature of the world, existence or non-existence of the spirit and the nature of celestial spheres'.[9]

Conclusion: a few lessons from Timbuktu

I conclude this chapter by simply enumerating what I consider important lessons from Timbuktu. The first lesson is the one to be drawn from the fact that science and scholarship in Africa have a history prior to colonialism and prior to the introduction of European languages. The manuscripts are not only in Arabic. They are also in local languages using Arabic script. When African philosophers, for example, discuss questions of translation or the transformation of African languages into philosophical languages, they should first remember that this is a process that happened at different periods in the history of this discipline to many different languages through their contact with Greek philosophy: Latin with Cicero, Arabic with the Nestorian translators of Aristotle and Plato, French with Descartes, and so on. They should also be fully cognisant of the African tradition of the so-called *ajami* literature, that is, literature using Arabic script in a non-Arabic language.

Other lessons are to be drawn from the works of the most prominent representative of the elite of scholars from Timbuktu, Ahmad Baba. His importance has been highlighted in many chapters. I would like in turn to insist on the position taken by this great African philosopher in the face of racism, when he replied unambiguously to interlocutors who implied that enslavement of black people was the natural consequence of some cosmic curse against the descendants of Ham, son of Noah: 'There is no difference between one race and another,' he wrote in his *Mi'raj al-su'ud*,[10] dismissing unequivocally any idea of a 'natural' character of slavery that could lead to disparagingly calling black people *'abid* (slaves), as is even today sometimes the case.

I also consider that Ahmad Baba's work titled *Tuhfat al-fudala*[11] encapsulates the meaning of Timbuktu's and of West Africa's written tradition in general. At the centre of its topic is Baba's citation of a prophetic saying (*hadith*) that summarises perfectly the argument made in the book: 'One hour of a scholar laying on his bed but meditating on his knowledge is more valuable than the worship of a devout person during seventy years.'[12] Ahmad Baba insists on the value of knowledge with the precision that knowledge is authentic and complete only when it is a way of life, when beyond the mastery of a science there is scrupulous attention to what a good life means, when the accomplished *faqih* (jurist) is also the fully realised *'arif* (sage).

The reason I mention the importance of *Tuhfat al-fudala* is that it conveys a double lesson for us today. The first lesson about the importance of knowledge is that the manuscripts must of course be preserved and catalogued, but turning them into sheer museum objects is not the ultimate goal. The meditation on African sciences and knowledge requires that the manuscripts, in Timbuktu and elsewhere, be published and made accessible to today's scholarship. The second lesson is another prophetic saying, also quoted by Baba in *Tuhfat al-fudala*: 'The ink of the scholar is more precious than the blood of the martyr.'[13] Although we live in a time when ignorance speaks in the loud voice of bombs and assassins pretend that they are martyrs, we are reminded by one of the greatest African philosophers of the past that the patience of education has incomparably more value than any other form of combat.

NOTES

1 Diop (1960: 133).
2 In Publications de la Fondation Temimi (1997). See also Diagne (2000).
3 Publications de la Fondation Temimi (1997: 117).
4 Publications de la Fondation Temimi (1997: 116).
5 Ka'ti (1913: 272).
6 Ka'ti (1913: 272).
7 Appiah (1992: 144).
8 Hunwick & O'Fahey (1995: 222).
9 Hunwick & O'Fahey (1995: 222).
10 Hunwick & Harrak (2000: 35).
11 Sami & Zniber (1992).
12 Sami & Zniber (1992: 29).
13 Sami & Zniber (1992: 16).

REFERENCES

Appiah KA (1992) *In my father's house: Africa in the philosophy of culture.* London: Methuen

Diagne SB (2000) Savoirs islamiques et sciences sociales en Afrique de l'Ouest. In *Mélanges d'archéologie, d'histoire et de littérature offerts au Doyen Oumar Kane.* Dakar: Presses Universitaires de Dakar

Diop CA (1960) *L'Afrique noire précoloniale.* Paris: Présence Africaine

Hunwick J & Harrak F (annotated and trans.) (2000) *Mi'raj al-su'ud. Ahmad Baba's replies on slavery.* Rabat: Institute of African Studies

Hunwick JO & O'Fahey RS (Eds) (1995) *Arabic literature of Africa. The writings of Central Sudanic Africa* (Vol. 2). Leiden: Brill

Ka'ti M (1913) *Tarikh al-fattash.* Edition of Arabic text and translation by O Houdas & M Delafosse. Paris: Leroux

Publications de la Fondation Temimi (1997) *La culture Arabo-Islamique en Afrique au sud du Sahara: cas de l'Afrique de l'Ouest, actes du colloque international tenu a Tombouctou.* Zaghouan, Tunisia: Publications de la Fondation Temimi

Sami S & Zniber M (est. and trans.) (1992) *Tuhfat al-fudala bi ba'di fada'il-al-'ulama. Des mérites des 'ulama.* Rabat: Institute of African Studies

PART I

INTRODUCTION TO THE TIMBUKTU REGION

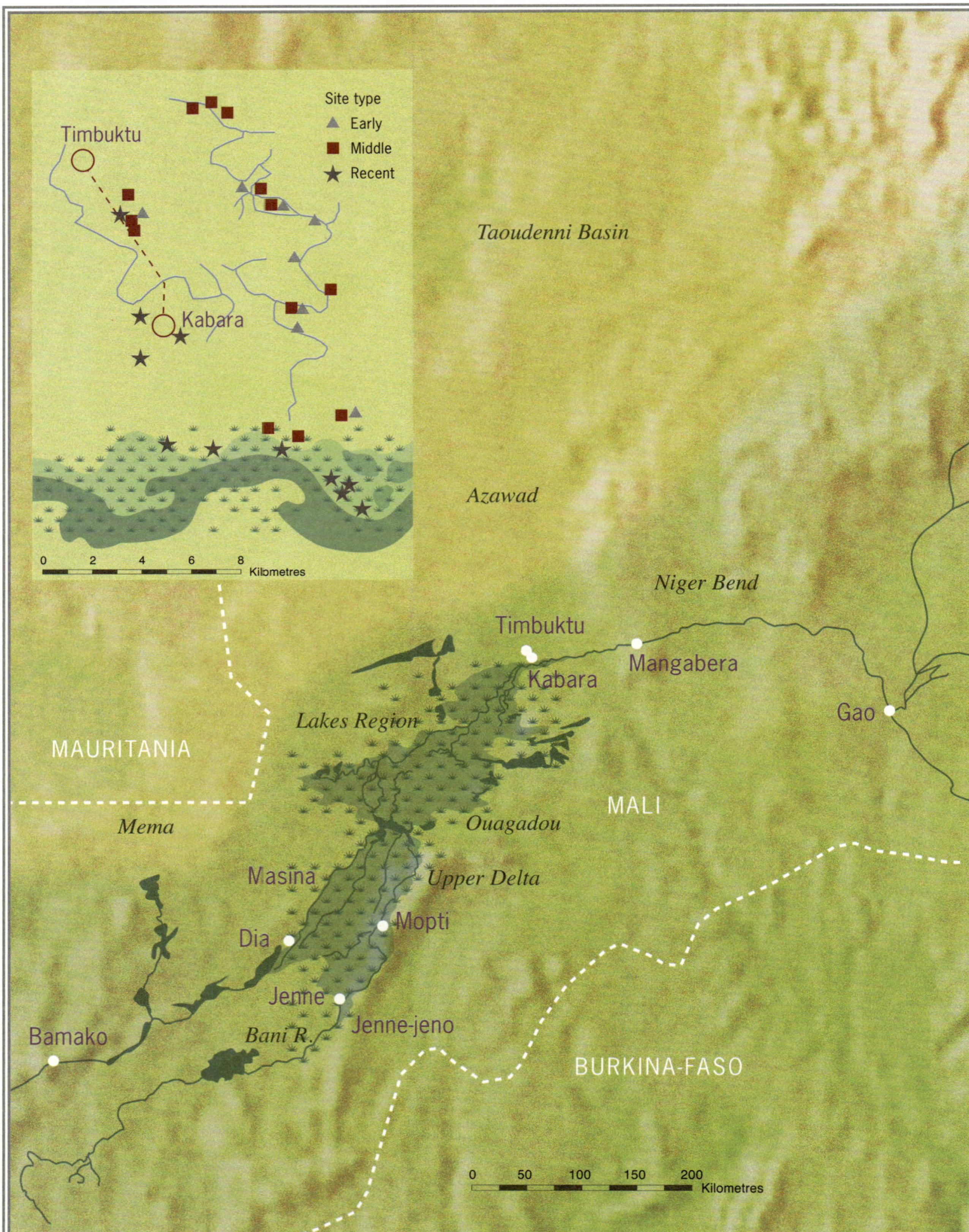

Site type
Early
Middle
Recent
Timbuktu
Kabara
0
2
4
6
8
Kilometres
Taoudenni Basin
Azawad
Niger Bend
Timbuktu
Kabara
Mangabera
Gao
Lakes Region
MAURITANIA
MALI
Mema
Ouagadou
Masina
Upper Delta
Dia
Mopti
Jenne
Jenne-jeno
Bani R.
Bamako
BURKINA-FASO
0
50
100
150
200
Kilometres

CHAPTER 3

Before Timbuktu: cities of the Elder World

Roderick J McIntosh

The received foundation date of the early second millennium AD for historical Timbuktu now seems far too late. The archaeology of 'sister cities' elsewhere in the Middle Niger reveals an indigenous urbanism dating to the first millennium BC and there is no reason to think that the Niger Bend should have been excluded from this explosive, pervasive process. Excavations within today's Timbuktu have been few and inconclusive; survey within the immediate hinterland, however, reveals an ecology vastly different from that of today – and a quite unexpected settlement history. Timbuktu, the trans-Saharan trade terminus, appears to be a vestigial and much transformed remnant of an earlier, a very different 'Elder World'.

Excavations within today's Timbuktu have been few and inconclusive; survey within the immediate hinterland, however, reveals an ecology vastly different from that of today – and a quite unexpected settlement history. Timbuktu, the trans-Saharan trade terminus, appears to be a vestigial and much transformed remnant of an earlier, a very different 'Elder World'.

'A very different Elder World'...Alfred Tennyson, the Cambridge first-year, would surely have been dumbstruck by his own prescience when he penned the famous lines of his winning entry to the 1829 Chancellor's Competition for English Verse:[1]

Then I raised my voice and cried, 'Wide Afric, doth thy Sun
Lighten, thy hills enfold a city as fair
As those which starr'd the night o' the Elder World?
Or is the rumour of thy Timbuctoo
A dream as frail as those of ancient time?'

One can only imagine the reaction to results of archaeological survey around Timbuktu of an older Tennyson, icon and poetic voice of an optimistic and expansionist England (although he surely would have bridled at that particular characterisation of his national role). Would he have accepted our current understanding of the numbers, size, importance and precocity of the cities 'starring' the ancient landscape of the Niger Bend during what we here will label its Elder World? Would his conception of the world have been able to transform so radically as to encompass not the 'argent streets' of his romantic idyll, the 'tremulous domes' and 'obelisks of ranged chrysolite' of his frail dream city, but an urbanism in Mali's Middle Niger as dense and expansive as those

Around 8 500 years ago, the Azawad was an enormous 90 000-square-kilometre marshy (paludal) and lake (lacustrine) basin, probably with permanent flooding at the present locale of Timbuktu. In the present time, the Niger River is over a kilometre wide in places during the rainy season.

of Mesopotamia or the Nile Valley – and apparently owing nothing to those urban cradles for the birth of a citied landscape?

We have long relied on just six case studies to understand the emergence of such features of sociocultural complexity as state formation and urbanism. These are Mesopotamia and Egypt (*c.*3500–3000 BC), the Indus Valley and north China (*c.*2500 BC), and Mesoamerica and the Andes (*c.*0 AD). In recent decades it has become apparent that sub-Saharan West Africa must be added to this list, specifically the Middle Niger. Not only did this region experience indigenous development of complex cultural features, it did so in a way that offers a challenging perspective on generalisations about urbanism developed elsewhere.[2] The Sahel of West Africa offers, in particular but not exclusively, new opportunities for comparative research on responses to climate change and regional abandonment in arid lands.[3] Just as the aforementioned six cases must now open the table to a Middle Niger seventh, those same six complex cultural traditions all experienced episodes of collapse and/or regional abandonment (not the same thing) that may be better understood with the comparative study of regional abandonment in West Africa.

Why this emphasis on regional abandonment? A basic premise of this chapter is that the familiar Timbuktu of the past several centuries is a vestige of a spectacular regional abandonment process and that hidden just beneath its present duned hinterland is a very different, dynamic fluvial and lacustrine ecology of a not-so-very-ancient Elder World. This Elder World of the Niger Bend may have been as city-dominated and certainly seems to have been as dense in demography as the Lakes Region of the Niger's interior flood plain and, indeed, as urbanised as the other basins comprising the Middle Niger. Those basins are, from south to north, the Upper Delta dominated by Jenne, the

An aerial view of the Niger River. The Niger Bend supported urban centres and long-distance commercial activity substantially earlier than dates allowed by traditional historical reconstruction.

Masina boasting ancient Dia, the Erg of Ouagadou just north of Lake Debo, the now-desert Méma abutting the Mauritanian frontier, the Lakes Region and Niger Bend and finally the Azawad dunelands north of Timbuktu.[4] What I intend to do here is first briefly to describe the wind-dominated landscape of today's Timbuktu, arguing that perhaps as recently as the eleventh to thirteenth centuries AD a very different biophysical environment prevailed. Indeed, the familiar desert dominance may only have been in place since the seventeenth century, with the end of a minor pluvial coincident with the end of the 'Little Ice Age' of the upper latitudes. I show that the earlier lake and river environment extended far north into the present Sahara and, on analogy with archaeological settlement patterns known from better researched basins of the Middle Niger, almost certainly supported a denser network of towns, villages and temporary hamlets. I then summarise archaeological surveys conducted in the Timbuktu hinterlands, and the all too brief excavations in Timbuktu itself. I end with a suite of questions about whether some memory of this Elder World might subtly have conditioned the vision of the world (and of causation in human affairs and in human–land dynamics) expressed in the manuscripts of Timbuktu.

Timbuktu is a town at the frontier of the Niger's dead and live deltas, at the frontier between the Saharan Azawad and the Sahelian, annually inundated Lakes Region and Niger Bend. To the natural scientist, the Azawad sand plains (and the related Taoudenni palaeolake depressions further to the north) tell of the eventual triumph of wind over rain and flood. Barren though it may appear to some, the Azawad is nevertheless a mosaic of river, swamp, lake, and wind-borne deposits. So, too, are all six Middle Niger basins. Layered transformation is the best description of the cumulative effects of alternating agencies of rain, river and desiccation that caused the complex interweave of microenvironments throughout the Middle Niger. However, whereas once the inundated area of the Middle Niger was up to 170 000 square kilometres, with the desiccation of the Méma and Azawad basins, the 'live' (annually inundated) Middle Niger today represents only some 55 000 square kilometres.

In the palaeolake region of Taoudenni, dunes trail downwind from tall columns of eroded lake deposits. South, in the Azawad proper, ancient shallow lakes (playas), permanent streams and once-generous rains left behind carpets of freshwater shell mixed with bones of massive perch, catfish and crocodile. However, for five millennia, the wind has tended to dominate. Each basin of the Middle Niger is a tight clustering of microenvironments, each rapidly shifting in potential with a volatile climate. The peoples of the Middle Niger have risen to the challenge of that environmental volatility by producing a web of specialised but articulated occupations,[5] resulting in a reciprocity relationship that allowed an admirable resilience when responding to strong, abrupt climate oscillations. Thanks to a small number of innovative, multidisciplinary research projects in the Taoudenni and Azawad, we have detailed descriptions of the regions' climate, local environment and modes of adaptation.[6] We therefore have a much-refined appreciation of the local and regional effects on local populations of Holocene wet periods (pluvials) of 8 500–3 000 BP that alternated with periods of sharp desiccation.[7] The last such full pluvial period ended some 4 000–3 000 years ago. The familiar Sahara has been gaining in ascendancy ever since, although there have been significant periods (decades and even centuries, from 700 to 1100, for example) of annual rainfall at 120 per cent or more of the 1930–60 standard (the baseline average of temperature, rainfall or other climatic variables against which scientists assess deviations).

The environmental history of the Azawad has been the overlapping transformation of distinct local ecologies and micro-niches. By 8 500 years ago, the Azawad was an enormous 90 000-square-kilometre marshy (paludal) and lake (lacustrine) basin, probably with permanent flooding at the present locale of Timbuktu. In the deepest parts of the Azawad there were large permanent lakes (some over 500 km^2 in area). Some were fed by rainfall; some were recharged by groundwater exposed by low relief. Niger overflow fed most of the seasonal Azawad lakes and creeks (marigots) and especially the vast network of interdunal corridors between the massive late Pleistocene (longitudinal) dunes covering most of this basin. During the best of times, the lakes were home to abundant perch, tilapia and catfish, to several species of water turtle, crocodile, hippo, and a water python that could grow to an alarming four metres.

Lake and swampland temperature, salinity and oxygen levels can be recorded by silica-shelled algae (diatoms), molluscs, and bivalve crustaceans (ostracods).[8] These tiny organic documents demonstrate that long periods of fresh, well-oxygenated water were periodically interrupted by high evaporation. Particularly affected by dry episodes were the backswamps, vast low-lying regions inundated each year by flooding (ultimately from the Niger). The annual floods probably extended north of Hassi el-Abiod only during exceptional years. These swamps and interdunal ponds served as nurseries for great shoals of fish that thrived upon the abundant vegetation of marshes. Hippo, crocodile and at least two species of water-dependent antelopes (*Tragelaphus* and *Kob*), as well as African water buffalo (*Syncerus caffer*), roamed the swamps. The shallows would have been prime environments for wild, edible grasses, some of which were ancestral to domesticated sorghums, millets, fonio and African rice (*Oryza glaberrima*). The annual flood was spread throughout the Azawad by a network of palaeochannels extending over 180 kilometres north–south by 130 kilometres east–west. Most channels served to distribute Niger flood water brought into the Azawad by a great palaeochannel, the Wadi el-Ahmar, 1 200 metres wide at its southern end (at the Niger Bend, just east of Timbuktu).[9] The channel's 70–100 kilometre northward meandering is clearly traced on satellite images and aerial photos, as are the great, long interdunal depressions (framed by the Pleistocene longitudinal dunes that, reanimated, visually dominate the landscape today) recharged year after year by the floods and by local rain.

The archaeological richness of the banks of these palaeochannels is essentially untapped. The revealing exception was a total survey of the proximal (southern) 13 kilometres of the Wadi el-Ahmar. The survey began at its point of departure from the Niger flood plain, about three kilometres east of Timbuktu.[10] This survey provides the basic data for the conclusions about first millennium AD urbanism in the southern Azawad wastes and at the Niger Bend–Azawad interface, to be presented below. Let us end this discussion of the geomorphology, hydrology and environments of Timbuktu's Elder World by offering the stark image of a dune-dominated, trans-Saharan, trade-dependent Timbuktu and of its wilderness hinterland...with, just beneath the shifting blanket of saltating sand, a radically different palimpsest landscape of lakes, swamps, channels, and steppe-lands. This was the Elder World. Just as the diverse plant, fish and mammal resources of that Elder World supported a high Late Stone Age and Early Iron Age population, so too the Timbuktu–Wadi el-Ahmar survey demonstrated that, perhaps as recently as 700–800 years ago, Timbuktu's hinterland was indeed 'starr'd'.

But before turning to the results of the Timbuktu region survey (and of excavations within the city itself), let us see what research elsewhere in the Middle Niger suggests might be the patterns of settlement associated with the rich, aquatic and mosaical ecologies just described. The other basins of the Middle Niger share the same geomorphological features as the Azawad and Lakes Region and Niger Bend (longitudinal dunes, backswamps, playas, channel levees, etc.) – but in different proportions and, for each basin, in different signature arrangements. In the other 'dead' basin, the Méma, for example, the Pleistocene dunes forming the defining geographical structure are hidden much deeper under a maze of lake and swamp deposits.[11] Overlaying those aquatic deposits are the archaeological remains of cities (dating back at least to the end of the first millennium BC[12]) and villages (first appearing around 2000 BC[13]). The cities are classic *tells*, mounds built up to 10 or more metres in height, sometimes 50 or more hectares in area, constructed over the centuries by the melt of mud-brick houses, the

Overlaying those aquatic deposits are the archaeological remains of cities (dating back at least to the end of the first millennium BC) and villages (first appearing around 2000 BC).

The grand mosque at Jenne. Jenne-jeno, or old Jenne, is probably the oldest of the settlements in the area and the present mosque at Jenne is built on the site of one of the earliest mosques in West Africa.

accumulated garbage of the inhabitants – everyday debris of everyday lives. Clearly the Saharan–Sahelian ecology of the Méma could not today support cities, or the dense network of associated villages in the hinterland of each.

Large-scale, multidisciplinary research has only just begun in the Méma. But it seems certain that, when the end to urbanism came, it came very quickly. When one finds similar cases of rapid regional abandonment elsewhere in the world it usually means that the climate or hydrology changed precipitately, or that population size or its concentration in large groupings became unsupportable, or that exploitation habits were unsustainable leading to a moment of collapse – or a tangle of all of these. In the Méma, the end came by the thirteenth or fourteenth centuries AD – but the mass abandonment of these towns should not make us forget that a sustainable, resilient, citied landscape was the rule in this highly changeable Sahelian Middle Niger basin for a thousand years or more. And during much of that period, the flood-plain ecology of the Méma must have been no more aquatic, no less mosaical, no more resource rich (and no more subject to the notoriously oscillating precipitation patterns [interannual, interdecadal, intercentury] and shifting river regime of this northern fringe of the West African monsoonal system) than the southern Azawad and Niger Bend. Lesson number one to extrapolate to the Elder World of Timbuktu's hinterland: we can come with an expectation of an earlier, wetlands-adapted historical ecology, in which high densities of population could be supported – sustainably for a millennium or more – by a deep-time adaptive pattern of ecological resilience.[14] All good things, however, must end.

Less radical forms of regional abandonment, too, ended ancient Middle Niger patterns of urbanism in the two 'live' Middle Niger basins to have received sustained archaeological attention, the Macina (Dia and its hinterland) and, especially, the Jenne and Jenne-jeno region of the Upper Delta. After some 30 years of excavation at these city mounds, combined with dedicated surveys in the cities' hinterlands, we begin to know something of the chronology and patterning of indigenous Middle Niger urbanism. The first point to make is that this appears to have been an indigenous process. When excavations at Jenne-jeno began in the late 1970s I was as surprised and delighted as anyone by the lack of evidence for contact, colonisation or 'stimulated directionality' from across the Sahara. Cities begin by the third century BC in the Jenne region,[15] and arguably some centuries earlier at Dia.[16]

These earliest cities grew out of (again, without intrusions of peoples or ideas from the outside) the aforementioned wetlands-adapted environments that characterised the Middle Niger since the Late Stone Age.[17] One of the signal aspects of urbanism in each of the Middle Niger basins in which adequate regional coverage has been attained is that of multiple, non-primate, urban centres. In other words, each basin individually and, to judge from the homogenisation from Timbuktu to Jenne of the ceramic assemblages covering some 1 600 years, the whole of the 55 000-square-kilometre (or more) Middle Niger was a peer heterarchy – a vast field of interacting population centres with none of the oppressive regional settlement hierarchy that characterised other indigenous urban arenas in which the politics of despotism prevailed (such as post-Uruk-period Mesopotamia, or later Shang China). From this we can take lesson number two to extrapolate to the Elder World of Timbuktu's hinterland: ancient Middle Niger urbanism, regionally, describes a field of multiple, non-primate, urban centres.

Lastly, taking to heart the classic definition of a city as a larger settlement of heterogeneous population that provides a range of services to a larger hinterland,[18] the laborious process of digging through the metres upon metres of *tell* deposits had to be linked to hinterland surveys. In order to test the true urban nature of those settlements, there is no substitute for month after month of trudging over every landform of the hinterland, locating sites of all sizes and types, systematically recording the dateable ceramics on their surfaces, noting features and artefacts that might speak to the occupations and affinities of the inhabitants, and eventually excavating into the stratified deposits of those sites as well. This survey, first at Jenne-jeno, then at Dia and eventually at the Méma cities as well, provided a great surprise: clustered urbanism! Jenne-jeno is surrounded by no fewer than 70 satellite sites, all within very close proximity. After several seasons of surface recording, and now after excavation at 10 of the 70 sites, we are convinced that the entire assemblage of settlements (with a 4 km radius) comprises the city.

The mass abandonment of some of the towns should not make us forget that a sustainable, resilient, citied landscape was the rule in this highly changeable Sahelian Middle Niger basin for a thousand years or more.

Is this conclusion backed up by the results of several cycles of hinterland survey?[19] Whereas evidence of all corporate activities are found at Jenne-jeno, at 29 other sites one finds only one, two or at most three represented. These activities may be subsistence based (fishing) or artisan (metallurgy, weaving) or 'miscellaneous' (ritual or symbolic, funerary). Apparently specialists were drawn together, yet resisted final absorption into a unitary city. Let us attempt an analysis of the clustering rationale: the clustered city was a stable solution (for greater than 1 000 years) to the complementary ecological problems (physical and social) confronting Middle Niger communities of the Elder World in the past. Firstly, this was a superbly productive environment, but one marked by highly variable rain and flood regimes. Secondly, to combat climatic unpredictability, artisans and subsistence producers grew increasingly specialised, yet must have been linked together into a generalised economy. Yet, thirdly, this was a highly complex society organised horizontally, a heterarchy with multiple sub-components representing overlapping and competing agencies of resistance to centralisation. (In over 30 years of excavation at Jenne-jeno and elsewhere around the Middle Niger, we have yet to find convincing evidence of kings, or even of clear elites, at these cities.) The dispersed clustered city was an instrument of that resistance. Such a view calls up profound and deep-time Middle Niger views of roughly equivalent, highly occult-charged power places distributed in a power grid across the landscape, an argument I make fully in my 2005 *Ancient Middle Niger: Urbanism and the Self-Organizing Landscape*. For our purposes here we can take lesson number three to extrapolate to the Elder World of Timbuktu's hinterland: the venerable Middle Niger pattern of urbanism created non-nucleated congeries of specialised parts, urban clusters, very different from the walled, citadel-dominated agglomerations with a depopulated near-hinterland that we associated with urbanism in other Old World flood plains such as Mesopotamia.

When survey began in the Timbuktu region in 1984, we never for a moment believed that these expectations about *flood-plain-adapted* Middle Niger urbanism might be applicable there as well. To summarise: i) an earlier wetlands-adapted historical ecology, in which high densities of population could be supported – sustainably – by a deep-time adaptive pattern of ecological resilience; ii) ancient Middle Niger urbanism, regionally, describes a vast field (over more than today's 55 000 km^2) of multiple, non-primate, urban centres; and iii) individual cities here became non-nucleated congeries of specialised parts – urban clusters. How, then, do the archaeological settlement patterns of the Timbuktu hinterland fit with these expectations, or not as the case might be? And what of present Timbuktu itself, that desert-oriented wreck, foundering on the Sahelian shore of the great desert, washed onto a prevailing environment very far from the wetlands of the 'live' Middle Niger, terminus to the trans-Saharan trade and, if we believe the great *tarikhs*, dependent upon southern sister-cities such as Jenne even for the provisioning of its population.

In a word, the results of excavations at Timbuktu itself have been inconclusive. In 1998 a University of Cambridge student, Tim Insoll, excavated at three localities around the city (at the 'Casbah Morocaine', next to the Sankore Mosque, and in the western Azalai area).[20] In the former two areas, digging stopped at around five metres depth, with AMS (high precision radiometric) dates still only in the eighteenth century. In the latter, archaeological deposits upon natural soil still yielded tobacco pipes (that is, still post-dating the very end of the sixteenth century). All Insoll could conclude was that '...the "mysterious" nature of Timbuktu still persists, and the *Tarikh al-Sudan* appears to be correct in stating that the building of Timbuktu, and the joining of all its parts together was only completed in the mid 16th century AD [mid-tenth century *hijri*]'.[21] Perhaps the Timbuktu we know now really was an artefact of a world, and of the trans-Saharan commerce, post-dating the Middle Niger's Elder World. Archaeological surveys, however, tell a different story.

There were highly complex societies organised horizontally, heterarchies with multiple sub-components representing overlapping and competing agencies of resistance to centralisation. We have yet to find convincing evidence of kings, or even of clear elites, in these cities.

In 1984, Téréba Togola, Susan Keech McIntosh and I conducted a preliminary reconnaissance of the Timbuktu hinterland and that of Mangabéra, some 90 kilometres further downstream along the Niger.[22] Not knowing anything of the environmental logic of potentially early sites, this survey was entirely geomorphologically driven. Judgementally, we opted for thoroughly walking irregular transects, testing various Azawad and Niger Bend landforms – dunes, the recently constructed flood plain of the Niger itself, with its scoured fluvial deposits, and more interior palaeochannels. Much effort was spent on testing the banks of the Wadi el-Ahmar. Many new data were recovered and the work might be said to have altered our understanding of the human landscape of the Timbuktu hinterland. We covered roughly 50 per cent of the region, but in a way that was entirely judgemental and not strictly systematic in a probabilistic sense.

Frustrating data, too. Our initial (history-driven) expectation was that present Timbuktu would be a rather late (second millennium AD) desert outlier of the Middle Niger, flood-plain-oriented urban civilisation, an artefact of the trans-Saharan trade and, frankly, a parasite on older, indigenous cities to the south. Rather, we found a far denser network of sites oriented to the (constricted) flood plain and the dune-traversing palaeochannels. Briefly, in a 260-square-kilometre survey area in Timbuktu's vicinity, we found 43 sites. Curiously, no Late Stone Age sites remained on the surface and any Iron Age sites dating to before around AD 300–500 were quite ephemeral. Spectacularly, by AD 500 there was a dense network of villages and fully urban *tells*, in a pattern that closely recalls the classic Middle Niger urban clustering described above. The majority of these sites were abandoned by 1500 (how many centuries before, only proper excavation will tell) in a regional abandonment, the completeness (and abruptness) of which echoes that of the Méma.

Are any of these mute cities the lost localities of the Niger Bend mentioned, but still unidentified, in the Arabic sources – Awqham, Safanku, Tirekka, Bughrat?[23] Clearly an artefact of wetter times, was this an urban network anterior and independent of any historical settlements, such as Timbuktu? Or is that fabled town a vestigial – representing just a sad rumour, a residual of an earlier, denser settlement pattern? There, far up the palaeochannel, the Wadi el-Ahmar, was an enormous town-size site (50 ha), apparently with a ring of satellites, abandoned most probably between 900 and 1200. An antecedent Timbuktu?

Thinking about the survey results in terms of hydrology, geomorphology and land use combined, it is clear from the numbers and positions of the sites dating to c.500–1500 that the Niger flood stage and/or local precipitation was significantly higher, such that the Wadi el-Ahmar (and other Azawad palaeochannels?) ran stronger seasonally, if not permanently. The shocking evidence of voluminous iron production in the hinterlands suggests that Niger flood alone was not responsible for the more dynamic hydrology. Indeed, the marigot of Kabara linking the Niger to Timbuktu (and the Badjindé ponds) may very well have held water year-round – further hinting that some occupation was likely at least by the first millennium AD at the present location of the town. However, when the Sahara triumphed and regional abandonment took place, a significant regional population either declined entirely, consolidated into the 'primate' situation at Timbuktu, or moved deeper into the 'live' basins of the Middle Niger.

And then there is the shock of discoveries at Mangabéra. We surveyed two small transects (50 km^2 total area) at a point 90 kilometres further downstream along the river, where the Pleistocene dunes pinch the river quite narrowly, selected at random. Never really expecting to find much in such desolation, there we stumbled upon a curious number of large, perhaps clustered *tells*. Was every stretch of the river bank and near dune landscape downstream of Timbuktu as heavily invested with substantial occupation? Our judgemental survey simply will not allow us to say. Does the history of urbanism in the Niger Bend parallel that of the broader flood-plain basins to the south? Our judgemental survey will not allow us to say, but that does appear to be the case in general. All we can say is that the Niger Bend supported urban centres and long-distance commercial activity substantially earlier than dates allowed by traditional historical reconstruction.[24]

I end, then, with a series of interlocking questions. These questions have to do with the relevance of the Elder World to 'our' Timbuktu of scholars, merchants and the faithful. These questions come out of a recent development in archaeology and historical geography, called historical ecology.[25] Beyond the recognition of long-term recursive, back-and-forth impacts of environment (including climate change) upon humans and of humans upon the land, historical ecology takes this two steps further. The first step is the realisation that people act upon their *perceptions* of landscape and perception is moulded by all the beliefs and 'para-scientific' insights that go into any group's social construction of reality. The second is that, just as the landscape we see today is a palimpsest of multiple past human actions on the land (that is, results of multiple, cumulative past decisions about where to live, where to farm, what locales have their own vital forces, etc.), so too are beliefs about landscape a palimpsest of multiple past experiences with or about the landscape. I have made the argument elsewhere that an unequal mapping of power localities over the Middle Niger landscape is a feature of a very ancient perception of that landscape and that the persistent Mande practice of *dalimasigi* (knowledge pilgrimages by specialists) relates directly to that particular perception of the land.[26] Now, archaeologists who scrounge around in other people's garbage have only a tenuous link to the thoughts in those people's minds! Perhaps those with a command of the Timbuktu manuscripts can play with three questions that came to mind as I thought about the relevance of Middle Niger urbanism to a post-Elder World Timbuktu:

- By the time Islam penetrates Timbuktu, has the memory of the Elder World been so thoroughly effaced that no vestiges remain in the world view expressed in the manuscripts?
- Or, can an understanding of the antecedent landscape and settlement logic one day help us to understand the particular moral logic of West African Sufism that constructed a landscape of high-value pilgrimage sites?[27]
- Might, therefore, archaeologists, historical geographers, historians (and peripatetic epigraphers such as Paulo de Moraes Farias) *together* have access to a palimpsest, written upon the Azawad and Niger Bend landscape, that is vital to our understanding of the progress of Islamic enculturation and to the evolution of the moral sciences in Timbuktu?

Asking such questions, then, is the ultimate utility, for archaeologists and historians alike, of concepts such as landscape (all physical, biological and cultural phenomena interacting within a region) and historical ecology (an appreciation of how humans, individually and as communities, acted according to their culturally conditioned perceptions of the biophysical world and of causation in that world) for giving an overall methodological and interpretive structure to research into the deep-time history of vital places such as Timbuktu.

Can an understanding of the antecedent landscape and settlement logic one day help us to understand the particular moral logic of West African Sufism that constructed a landscape of high-value pilgrimage sites? Might, therefore, archaeologists, historical geographers, historians, etc. together have access to a palimpsest that is vital to our understanding of the progress of Islamic enculturation and to the evolution of the moral sciences in Timbuktu?

NOTES

1 Tennyson (1829).
2 McIntosh (2005a).
3 McIntosh & Tainter (2005).
4 McIntosh (1998).
5 McIntosh (1993).
6 Petit-Maire (1986; 1991); Petit-Maire & Riser (1983); Petit-Maire et al. (1983); Fabre & Petit-Maire (1988); Raimbault (1990). The radiocarbon determinations reported by this project convincingly date the range of time for prehistoric occupation from 7000 to *c.*3500 BP. However, there are too few samples to convincingly date any one individual site, or determinations were run on materials such as shell that yield very large error factors.
7 Commelin et al. (1993); McIntosh (1994); McIntosh (2005b).
8 McIntosh (2003).
9 Rognon (1993); Risier & Petit-Maire (1986); McIntosh & McIntosh (1986).
10 McIntosh & McIntosh (1986).
11 DeVries et al. (2005).
12 Togola (1993).
13 MacDonald (1994).
14 McIntosh (2005c).
15 McIntosh (1995).
16 Bedaux et al. (2001).
17 McIntosh & McIntosh (2003); McIntosh (2005a).
18 Trigger & Pendergast (1972).
19 McIntosh & McIntosh (2003); McIntosh (2005a: Ch. 4).
20 Insoll (1998; 2000).
21 Insoll (2000: 484).
22 McIntosh & McIntosh (1986).
23 Levtzion (1973).
24 McIntosh & McIntosh (1986).
25 McIntosh et al. (2000); Ashmore & Knapp (1999).
26 McIntosh (2000).
27 Such as that, among many other generators of identity and sacrality, analysed by Paulo de Moraes Farias (2003) for the Niger Bend, from Timbuktu to Gao and Bentia and, recently, by Edmond Bernus et al. (1999) for the 420 000 km^2 Azawagh palaeochannel basin in eastern Niger, where they look at the archaeological landscape's role in the development of southern Berber history and identity, as well as specifically at In Teduq, a multi-component Sufi pilgrimage site, itself probably just one highly charged element within the larger sacred landscape.

REFERENCES

Ashmore W & Knapp AB (1999) *Archaeological landscape: Contemporary perspectives.* Oxford: Blackwell

Bedaux RMA, MacDonald K, Person A, Polet J, Sanogo K, Schmidt A & Sidibé S (2001) The Dia archaeological project: Rescuing cultural heritage in the inland Niger Delta (Mali). *Antiquity* 75: 837–876

Bernus E, Cressier P, Durand A, Paris F & Saliège J-F (1999) *Vallée de l'Azawagh (Sahara du Niger).* Editions Nigériennes No. 57. Paris: Editions Sépia

Commelin D, Raimbault M & Saliège J-F (1993) Nouvelles données sur la chronologie du Néolithique au Sahara malien: *Comptes Rendus de la Académie des Sciences* Série 2(317): 543–550

De Vries E, Makaske A, McIntosh RJ & Tainter J (Eds) (2005) *Geomorphology and human palaeoecology of the Méma, Mali.* Wageningen: Alterra

Fabre J & Petit-Maire N (1988) Holocene climatic evolution at 22–23° N from two palaeolakes in the Taoudenni area (northern Mali). *Palaeogeography, Palaeoclimatology, Palaeoecology* 65: 133–148

Insoll T (1998) Archaeological research in Timbuktu, Mali. *Antiquity* 72: 413–417

Insoll T (2000) The origins of Timbuktu. *Antiquity* 74: 483–484

Levtzion N (1973) *Ancient Ghana and Mali.* London: Methuen

MacDonald K (1994) Socio-economic diversity and the origin of cultural complexity along the Middle Niger (2000 BC to AD 300). PhD thesis, Cambridge University

McIntosh RJ (1993) The Pulse Theory: genesis and accommodation of specialization in the Middle Niger. *Journal of African History* 34(2): 181–220

McIntosh RJ (1998) *The peoples of the Middle Niger: The island of gold.* Oxford: Blackwell

McIntosh RJ (2000) The Mande weather machine. In RJ McIntosh, JA Tainter & SK McIntosh (Eds) *The way the wind blows: Climate, history, and human action.* Historical Ecology Series. New York: Columbia University Press

McIntosh RJ (2003) Climate change and population: history. In P Demeny & G McNicoll (Eds) *The encyclopedia of population* (Vol. 1). New York: Macmillan Reference

McIntosh RJ (2005a) *Ancient Middle Niger. Urbanism and the self-organizing landscape.* Case Studies in Early Society Series. Cambridge: Cambridge University Press

McIntosh RJ (2005b) Chansing Denekejugu over the Mande landscape: making sense of prehistoric and historic climate change. In R McIntosh & J Tainter (Eds) *Climates of the Mande.* Special section of *Mande Studies* 6: 11–28

McIntosh RJ (2005c) Two thousand years of niche specialization and ecological resilience in the Middle Niger. In RJ McIntosh & JA Tainter (Eds) *Climates of the Mande.* Special section of *Mande Studies* 6: 59–75

McIntosh RJ & McIntosh SK (2003) Early urban configurations on the Middle Niger: clustered cities and landscapes of power. In ML Smith (Ed.) *The social construction of ancient cities.* Washington DC: Smithsonian Institution Press

McIntosh RJ & Tainter JA (Eds) (2005) Climates of the Mande. Special section of *Mande Studies* 6: 1–85

McIntosh RJ, Tainter JA & McIntosh SK (Eds) (2000) Climate, history and human action (Introduction). *The way the wind blows: Climate, history, and human action.* Historical Ecology Series. New York: Columbia University Press

McIntosh SK & McIntosh R (1986) Archaeological reconnaissance in the region of Timbuktu, Mali. *National Geographic Research* 2(3): 302–319

McIntosh SK (1994) Changing perceptions of West Africa's past: Archaeological research since 1988. *Journal of Archaeological Research* 2(2): 167–173

McIntosh SK (Ed.) (1995) *Excavations at Jenne-jeno, Hambarketolo and Kaniana: The 1981 season.* University of California Monographs in Anthropology. Berkeley: University of California Press

Moraes Farias PF (2003) *Arabic medieval inscriptions from the Republic of Mali: Epigraphy, chronicles and Songhay–Tuareg history.* Oxford: Oxford University Press

Petit-Maire N (1986) Homo climaticus: vers une paléoanthropologie écologique. *Bulletin de la Société Royale Belge d'Anthropologie et de Préhistoire* 97: 59–75

Petit-Maire N (Ed.) (1991) *Paléoenvironnements du Sahara, lacs holocène à Taodenni.* Paris: CNRS editions

Petit-Maire N, Celles JC, Commelin D, Delibrias G & Raimbault M (1983) The Sahara in northern Mali: Man and his environment between 10,000 and 3500 years BP. *The African Archaeological Review* 1: 105–125

Petit-Maire N & Riser J (Eds) (1983) *Sahara ou Sahel? Quaternaire récent du bassin de Taoudenni (Mali).* Marseille: CNRS editions

Raimbault M (1990) Pour une approche du néolithique du Sahara malien. *Travaux du laboratoire d'Anthropologie et de préhistoire des pays de la Méditerranée Occidentale*: 67–81

Risier J & Petit-Maire N (1986) Paléohydrologie du bassin d'Araouane à l'Holocène. *Revue de Géologie Dynamique et de Géographie Physique* 27(3/4): 205–212

Rognon P (1993) L'Evolution des Vallées du Niger depuis 20.000 ans. *Vallées du Niger,* 49–51. Paris: Réunion des Musées Nationaux

Tennyson A (1829) Timbuctoo. *Prolusiones academicae.* Cambridge Prize Poems. Cambridge: Cambridge University Press

Togola T (1993) Archaeological investigations of Iron Age sites in the Méma, Mali. PhD thesis, Rice University, Houston, Texas

Trigger B & Pendergast JF (1972) *Cartier's Hochelaga and the Dawson site.* Montreal: McGill-Queen's University Press

ثم رجع الا لضرورة فيتحاصان عتق المريض

ومعتق غيره وجزم في المريض اشتراء من

يعتق عليه بثلثه ويرث لا ان اوصى بشرائه

ابنه وعتق في ثم الابن على غيره وان اوصى

بمنفعة معين او بما ليس فيها او بعتق

الثلث

عبده بعد موته بشهر ولم يحمله الوارث

أن يجيز أو يخلع ثلث الجميع ونصيب

CHAPTER 4

Paper in Sudanic Africa

Jonathan M Bloom

Paper was invented in China in the centuries before Christ and was first used as a writing material there about the beginning of the first millennium AD. Within a thousand years, thanks to the agency of Islam – which united a vast swath of western Asia and northern Africa in a single cultural sphere – paper and papermaking technology were carried from the deserts of Central Asia to the Atlantic shores of Morocco and Spain. From Spain and Italy, where paper and papermaking were also introduced from the Arab world, they spread to the rest of western Europe, spurred in the mid-fifteenth century by Gutenberg's development of printing with movable type. Thanks to the availability of this flexible, strong and relatively cheap writing material, printing made mass-produced books more common and accessible than manuscripts laboriously copied onto parchment.[1]

By the beginning of the second millennium AD, paper was known and used across all of Muslim North Africa from Egypt to Morocco, enabling its diffusion northwards into Christian Europe.

By the beginning of the second millennium AD paper was known and used across all of Muslim North Africa from Egypt to Morocco, enabling its diffusion northwards into Christian Europe. Its diffusion southwards across the Sahara into the region known as Bilad al-Sudan, however, was quite different from its route north. As Christians came to control larger areas of the Iberian Peninsula after the year 1000, papermakers in these areas improved and surpassed their former masters in the Muslim regions of the south, exporting paper and ultimately papermaking techniques to other regions of western and southern Europe. In contrast, while paper and paper manuscripts must have been exported across the Sahara to the Muslim centres of West Africa, papermaking technology did not reach this region until the colonial period. This long delay meant that in Bilad al-Sudan paper remained for centuries an expensive, imported luxury item rather than the engine of intellectual and cultural transformation it was elsewhere in the Islamic lands.

Paper seems to have been first used in ancient China as a textile material for wrapping, but by the beginning of the first millennium AD it began to replace the heavy bamboo tablets and the costly silk cloth that the Chinese had used previously for writing and drawing. Paper and papermaking techniques were carried by Buddhist monks, mission-

Papermaking technology did not reach West Africa until the colonial period. In the Bilad al-Sudan paper remained for centuries an expensive, imported luxury good rather than the engine of intellectual and cultural transformation it was elsewhere in the Islamic lands.

aries and merchants from south-eastern China, the region where it was invented, throughout East Asia. They found it a useful medium on which to collect and transmit Buddhist scripture. Buddhists brought paper and papermaking to Korea and Japan in the east, Vietnam in the south, and Central Asia in the west, where travellers stopped on their way around the Himalayas to India, the homeland of Buddhism. Oddly enough, while many Chinese Buddhists travelled to India, there is no evidence that they introduced papermaking to India at this time, perhaps because Indians already had a satisfactory writing material in the form of palm leaves, which were trimmed and gathered together with cords to form books.

Paper is a mat of cellulose fibres that have been beaten in the presence of water, collected on a screen, and dried. Cellulose is present in varying quantities and qualities in virtually all plants and in materials made from them, such as textiles, old rags, ropes and nets. While the Chinese logograph for paper suggests that they initially used plant and textile waste fibre to make paper, they soon came to make it from bast (plant) fibres, particularly the inner bark of such plants and shrubs as bamboo, paper mulberry, rattan and ramie, which grow abundantly in the warm and moist climate of south-east China. These fibres would have been collected, moistened, pounded to a pulp, suspended in water, collected in moulds, and dried. As papermaking technology was taken to other regions with other climates, technical adjustments had to be made. In the extreme and arid climate of Central Asia, for example, where plants such as bamboo and rattan did not grow, papermakers used such materials as rags and old ropes to supplement bast fibres derived from flax and hemp plants. Much of our knowledge of early paper comes from archaeological finds in the deserts of Central Asia, where the extremely dry climate has preserved fragments that would otherwise have disappeared. Among the most famous are the more than 30 000 paper rolls sealed in a cave in the early twelfth century at Dunhuang in Gansu Province, China. Some of the paper was surely imported, but other paper must have been made locally.

Following the revelation of Islam in early seventh-century Arabia and its spread throughout West Asia after the death of the Prophet Muhammad in 632, Muslim armies began to make forays into western Central Asia, establishing a permanent presence there in the eighth century. They defeated the Chinese at the Battle of Talas in 751, theoretically opening the way to the Muslim penetration of eastern Central Asia, but the Muslims decided not to expand further east. Instead, men and ideas from Khorasan (north-west Iran) and Central Asia began to play critical roles in the Islamic civilisation developing in Iraq. At this time, Muslim bureaucrats, who had previously used only papyrus and parchment, the two flexible writing supports known in the Mediterranean region in antiquity, learned of Central Asian paper and papermaking. While papyrus was cheap, it could only be made in Egypt where the papyrus plant grew; parchment, made from the skins of animals, could be made virtually anywhere, but it was expensive because it entailed killing an animal. Paper combined the best of both: it was relatively cheap and could be made virtually everywhere. Within an extraordinarily short time, paper technology had been carried from Central Asia to Iran and Iraq. By around 800 rag paper was being made at Baghdad, the new Abbasid capital, as well as at Damascus, the old Umayyad one. A century later paper was being made at what is now Cairo in Egypt, causing the 4 000-year-old papyrus industry to collapse, and by the year 1000 it had been carried across North Africa to Spain.

The first Spaniard to mention paper was the Muslim poet and encyclopaedist Ibn 'Abd al-Rabbih (860–940). In his encyclopaedia *al-'Iqd al-farid* (The Unique Pearl), he discusses the different kinds of reed pens most suitable for writing on parchment, papyrus and paper. Considering the early date at which he wrote, he probably encountered paper on his pilgrimage to Mecca rather than in Spain itself.[2] By the middle of the tenth century, however, substantial quantities of paper must have been available for the tenth-century lexicographer Ibn Hani al-Andalusi to give his students paper on which to copy books from his private library. The library of the Umayyad caliph and bibliophile al-Hakam II (reigned 961–76) was said, perhaps incredibly, to contain 400 000 volumes, but only one manuscript (copied in 970) from al-Hakam's library is known to survive.[3] Papermaking in the Iberian Peninsula soon became a major business, not only among the Muslims but also among the Christians of the newly conquered provinces of Valencia and Aragon, where the great need for legal documents spurred an unusually great demand for the material. Although Iberian papermakers were soon exporting their product to France, Italy and elsewhere in Europe, documents show that even as late as the fourteenth century, Fez still shipped some fine paper to Majorca and Aragon.[4] In the thirteenth century Italians began making paper near Genoa, having learned it from the Catalans, but the major centres of Italian papermaking were to be located either in central Italy at Fabriano, where paper was made from the mid-thirteenth century, or in the north at Treviso, Florence, Bologna, Parma, Milan and Venice, where it was made from the mid-fourteenth century.

Italian paper was distinguished from Arab and Spanish paper by the introduction of watermarks, a faint design – often figural – imparted to the sheet during the manufacturing process, which served as a trademark. Dated documents on watermarked paper have allowed scholars to catalogue and chronicle their evolution. Undated documents can often be dated by their watermarks. In contrast, paper made in the Islamic lands was never watermarked, which makes dating undated documents difficult. Early Spanish paper bears characteristic zigzag lines that are poorly understood. They may have been meant to mimic the marks found on parchment sheets.

In the central and eastern Islamic lands, where paper was adopted earliest, its introduction had a transformative effect on all aspects of administrative and intellectual life, as people from bureaucrats to scholars and writers on all subjects – from the religious sciences to astronomy, belles-lettres, cookery and popular literature – began to use it. For the first few centuries, however, Muslims appear to have been reluctant to

Parchment as shown here, made from the skins of animals, could be made virtually anywhere, but it was expensive because it entailed killing an animal. Very few of the Timbuktu manuscripts are made of parchment, but many are encased or covered in leather.

transcribe the Qur'an onto paper, preferring to use the traditional medium of parchment sheets or folios formatted horizontally or in 'landscape' format, and gathered together or bound into books. By the middle of the tenth century, however, copyists in Iran began copying the Qur'an onto sheets of paper, thereby engendering two transformations: first, Qur'an manuscripts with a vertical or 'portrait' format became standard; and second, calligraphers developed new, more fluid scripts from the old scribal hands for copying the Qur'an.

Nevertheless, writers in the western Islamic lands continued to use parchment when elsewhere it had been abandoned in favour of paper, and they continued to use the older scripts and their variants rather than the new ones that had become *de rigueur* elsewhere. The major reason for this seems to have been that the region was somewhat isolated by its great distance from Islamic cultural centres in West Asia. This tendency may have been exacerbated by the political and cultural situation: the neo-Umayyads ruled in al-Andalus until the eleventh century, and in North Africa the advent of the Shi'ite Fatimids in the early tenth century meant that the region became increasingly isolated from developments elsewhere. By the eleventh century, when strong relations with the east were re-established, the die had been cast. Furthermore, the provinces of Ifriqiya (corresponding to modern Tunisia) and Sicily were great centres for sheep raising, and the manufacture of leather and parchment, as well as the export of hides, remained an important industry. Many surviving Qur'an manuscripts on parchment are attributed to ninth- and tenth-century Qayrawan, although none is dated. One of the most famous Tunisian manuscripts, the 'Nurse's Qur'an', is a manuscript copied and illuminated by 'Ali ibn Ahmad al-Warraq ('the stationer') for the wet-nurse of the Zirid ruler al-Mu'izz ibn Badis in 1020, a date by which calligraphers anywhere else would have transcribed any book, including the Qur'an, onto paper. The oldest surviving Maghribi Qur'an manuscript on paper dates from a century later in 1139–40,[5] but scribes continued to use parchment well into the fourteenth and even fifteenth centuries. Maghribi scribes also continued to use parchment for other types of manuscripts long after paper had become common elsewhere. For example, one Muhammad ibn Hakam ibn Sa'id transcribed a copy of Abu Hatim al-Sijistani's *Kitab al-nakhl* (Book of the Palm) in a distinctive North African (Maghribi) script on 27 small parchment folios; he completed his work on 26 March 1004, a date by which such a book produced elsewhere would surely have been copied on paper.[6] In addition, while Egyptian letter writers had made the transition to paper about a century earlier, private letters and accounts sent from Tunisia found among the Cairo Geniza documents (which relate to the medieval Jewish community) were written on parchment well into the middle of the eleventh century. Geniza documents also indicate that Tunisians got their paper from Egypt.[7] Nevertheless, paper is said – perhaps somewhat wishfully – to have been known in North Africa as early as the ninth century.[8]

Italian paper was distinguished from Arab and Spanish paper by the introduction of watermarks, a faint design – often figural – imparted to the sheet during the manufacturing process, which served as a trademark. Dated documents on watermarked paper have allowed scholars to catalogue and chronicle their evolution. Undated documents can often be dated by their watermarks. In contrast, paper made in the Islamic lands was never watermarked, which makes dating undated documents difficult.

Papermaking was surely practised in North Africa from the eleventh century, since the only medieval account of Arab papermaking to survive anywhere is the treatise on bookmaking by the Zirid prince Tamim ibn al-Mu'izz ibn Badis (1031–1108), who ruled in what is now eastern Algeria and Tunisia.[9] Oddly enough, he makes no mention of the preparation of parchment, although he does give recipes for making special coloured inks to use on it. According to Ibn Badis, to make paper:

> you soak the best white flax repeatedly in water and quicklime, rub it with your hands, and then dry it in the sun until the plant stalks release the fibers. Next you soak the fibers in fresh water to rinse away the lime and then pound it in a mortar until it is very fine. You then dissolve the pulp in water and make it into sheets on molds. These are made from straw used for baskets, nails, and the walls are collapsible. Under it is an empty rib. The flax is beaten with the hand vigorously until it is mixed. Then it is thrown with the hand flat in the mold so that it will not be thick in one place and thin in another. When it is evened, then its water dries away. It is found proper in its mold. When the desired [result] is attained, it is adjusted on a flat tablet. Then it is bound to a wall and straightened with the hand. It is left until it is dry. It separates and falls off.[10]

Taken as a whole, Ibn Badis's text is remarkably out of date, for he neglects to mention the use of rags, which papermakers actually used, and he describes making paper with a floating mould that most papermakers in the Muslim world had long abandoned for production with a two-piece dip-and-drain mould. Ibn Badis's book is therefore comparable to many medieval Islamic 'how-to' manuals: long on theory but short on practical advice.

In the absence of dated manuscripts, the suggestion that North Africans produced paper during Ibn Badis's lifetime is confirmed by the report of the fourteenth-century writer Ibn Abi Zar', who said that by the end of the twelfth century the city of Fez had

At the same time that Muslims were bringing paper and papermaking technology across North Africa to Spain, they were also bringing Islam from the Maghrib to the Bilad al-Sudan. In the western Sudan, Islam was initially a simple badge of social status like the luxury goods – such as horses, salt, fabrics and glassware – that were also imported from the north. Islam gradually took root among African merchants in the cities and in the courts of local chiefs, who might encourage their subjects to convert, but it took many centuries before Islam would spread from the cities to the countryside, from the elites to the peasantry, and from the inhabitants of the cities on the fringes of the desert to the villages of the deep interior.

472 paper mills.[11] Whatever the accuracy of his number, the paper industry in Fez was encouraged by the swift stream that flows through the industrial centre of the city, which still supplies dyers and tanners with plenty of fresh water and could also have powered hammer mills for processing pulp. Documents show that even in the fourteenth century, Fez still shipped some fine paper to Majorca and Aragon.[12]

By the middle of the fourteenth century, however, Arab chanceries in North Africa started to use Italian paper. Having learned the art of papermaking from Muslims, European Christians were able to make it better and cheaper by harnessing copious supplies of running water to power their paper mills. In addition to their technical advantage, European merchants 'dumped' their product below cost in North African and West Asian markets, thereby destroying local paper industries, in an attempt to corner the market. By the middle of the fourteenth century, a letter from the sultan of Tunis to King Peter IV of Aragon–Catalonia, dated 8 December 1350, was written on paper bearing a griffin watermark that had probably been exported from Italy to Tunis as part of the trade carried out between the two regions.[13] Another paper document dated 23 February 1360 is written on a sheet bearing both a watermark and a zigzag, the distinctive mark of Spanish papers. It was probably made in Italy especially for the North African or Catalan markets.[14] Meanwhile, the Egyptian writer al-Qalqashandi (d.1418) claimed that the European paper imported into Egypt was of the 'worst' quality.[15] Egyptians continued to make some paper – known as *waraq baladi* – into the seventeenth century, but the Mahkama court in Cairo was already using European paper by the middle of the sixteenth century, as the earliest watermarked paper there was made in Genoa in 1524.[16]

Muslims were initially troubled about using these European products, especially because some of them bore watermarked images such as crosses or animals, which particularly conservative people found objectionable. Common watermarks included a hand (or glove) and anchor, which are typical of Genoa; a bull's head and a pot, which are typical of France; three tiers of bells topped by a cross; and a crown, star, and crescent. A watermark with three crescents appeared in the early sixteenth century and enjoyed wide popularity from the seventeenth century to the nineteenth. It was known in Italy as *tre lune* and in the Arab world as *waraq hilali*.[17] In Tlemcen, a city now in western Algeria, the noted jurisconsult Abu 'Abdallah ibn Marzuq (d.1439) delivered a long *fatwa*, or legal decision, on 21 August 1409. Entitled *Taqrir al-dalil al-wadih al-ma'lum 'ala jawaz al-naskh fi kaghid al-rum* (Decision Concerning the Permissibility of Writing on Paper Made by Christians), it shows that by the beginning of the fifteenth century Italian paper had entirely supplanted local production. According to the document, paper had once been made in Tlemcen as well as in Fez and in al-Andalus, but it no longer was. Pious Muslims were therefore forced to write on European paper bearing watermarks that they found offensive, since the designs often contained a cross or an image of some living being. According to Ibn Marzuq's decision, which saw the problem in terms of ritual purity, the act of writing in Arabic over the idolatrous designs rendered them invisible. Writing God's name (and message) on such papers, Ibn Marzuq argued, replaced falsehood with truth. He argued that the situation was comparable to the way Muslims had been able over the centuries to transform Christian churches into mosques.[18] In short, by the fifteenth century the North African paper industry had vanished in the face of European competition.

The introduction of Islam and paper to the Bilad al-Sudan

At the same time that Muslims were bringing paper and papermaking technology across North Africa to Spain, they were also bringing Islam from the Maghrib to the Bilad al-Sudan. Islam closely followed the caravan routes from the Maghrib across the Sahara. Thanks to the domestication of the camel, merchants were able to cross the desert from Sijilmasa to Awdaghust and Ghana in the west; Tripoli, Ifriqiya and Wargla to Tadmakka and Gao in the centre; and the Nile Valley in the east. Different routes came to the fore with the rise and fall of such northern powers as the neo-Umayyads in the Iberian Peninsula and Morocco, the Fatimids and Hafsids in Ifriqiya, the Almoravids and Almohads in north-west Africa, and the Ayyubids and Mamluks in Egypt.

For Muslims, who first mentioned the western Sudan in the second half of the eighth century (for example, the geographer al-Fazari), the region represented not primarily a locus for new converts but a source of high-value merchandise such as gold, ivory, precious woods and slaves. With the exception of a few expeditions, the historical caliphates of North Africa never attempted to occupy any part of the region, and schismatic Kharijites may have made up most of the initial Muslim presence. Even the Almoravids, who traced their origins to southern Mauritania in the eleventh century, based their power in the north. Although they attached great importance to the control of the gold routes across the Sahara, they soon lost interest in the region's politics, and their role in the Islamisation of West Africa has remained controversial.[19]

The slow pace of cultural contact and interaction is partially explained by the absence of a strong centralising power that drew its legitimacy from its profession of Islam. In the western Bilad al-Sudan, Islam was initially a simple badge of social status like the luxury goods – such as horses, salt, fabrics and glassware – that were also imported from the north. Islam gradually took root among African merchants in the cities and in the courts of local chiefs, who might encourage their subjects to convert, but it took many centuries before Islam would spread from the cities to the countryside, from the elites to the peasantry, and from the inhabitants of the cities on the fringes of the desert to the villages of the deep interior. Apart from Mauritania, where the settlement of the Banu Hilal tribes in the eleventh century led to an early and significant degree of Arabisation and Islamisation, the initial Islamic penetration of the western Sudan did not lead, as it did in other regions of the Islamic world, to the rapid spread of the Arabic language, except in a few educated circles and in the adoption of some Arabic loan words for the days of the week, commerce and personal names.[20] Rulers seem to have been able to profess Islam while maintaining all of their traditional practices.

In the first centuries of Islam in the region there would have been, therefore, limited call for books and paper for writing. Most Muslims – as they did elsewhere – would have learned parts or all of the Qur'an and the traditions of the Prophet orally rather than by reading from books, and this would have fitted perfectly with local African traditions of orality. Although Muslims might have built mosques for their communal worship, there was no fixed plan or design necessary for a mosque, so local traditions could be adapted. The relatively shallow level of Islamisation at this time did not lead to the adoption of other aspects of contemporary material culture in the Islamic lands of south-west Asia and North Africa, such as architectural decoration with *muqarnas*, arabesque ornament, glazed ceramics or papermaking.

Apart from the figure of Ibrahim b. Ya'qub al-Dhakwani al-Kanemi (d. between 1211 and 1213), who 'appears like a comet in the late twelfth century', no other local writer in Central Sudan is known by name before around 1500. The founding of the Madrasa Ibn Rashiq in Cairo for the benefit of Kanemi's students in the mid-thirteenth century suggests that they would have returned to their homeland with some level of scholarship, and a letter of Mai 'Uthman b. Idris of Borno to the Mamluk sultan al-Malik al-Zahir Barquq demonstrates the presence of 'sophisticated' scribes in Borno in 1391–92.[21] In western Bilad al-Sudan, the arrival of larger numbers of books and scholars can be dated from the period following the pilgrimage of the Malian ruler Mansa Musa (1312–37) to Mecca in 1324.[22] While on the pilgrimage, he is said to have met the Andalusian poet Abu Ishaq Ibrahim al-Sahili (d.1346), who accompanied him back to Mali. The poet, known as al-Tuwayjin (the little casserole), was the son of the head of the corporation of perfumers in Granada.[23] He was the most notable of several scholars from North Africa or the Saharan oases known to have settled in Timbuktu in the period after 1350,[24] but apart from their names there is little evidence for a broad-based culture of writing that would have demanded supplies of paper greater than those that could be brought in by trans-Saharan caravans.

Some authors have also suggested that al-Sahili played a decisive role in the development of Islamic architecture in Mali, but more reasoned analysis suggests that his role, if any, was quite limited.[25] The architectural crafts in Granada had reached their zenith by the fourteenth century, and it is extremely unlikely that a cultured and wealthy poet would have had anything more than a dilettante's knowledge of the intricacies of contemporary architectural practice.[26] Similarly, as Sudani written culture expanded in the fourteenth and fifteenth centuries, few – if any – Muslims from Egypt or the Maghrib would have been able to teach local residents how to make paper, because the paper industry in those regions was already in sharp decline in the face of strong European competition. Thus, most Sudani manuscripts were written on European – specifically Italian – paper, which had been trans-shipped via such entrepôts as Cairo and Tripoli.

Egypt established early trade relations with western Bilad al-Sudan because it was on the route to the Holy Cities. In 1635 Santo Seguezzi, the Venetian merchant whose account is among the *Relations veritables et curieuses de l'isle de Madagascar et du Bresil…et trois relations d'Egypte et une du royaume de Perse* (True and Curious Accounts of the Island of Madagascar and of Brasil…and Three Accounts of Egypt and One of the Kingdom of Persia), reported on the gold brought from the *pays d'Acrouri* that was exchanged for 'silk stuffs from Italy, coral, paper, lead, copper, tin, and quicksilver'.[27] About this time, a Cairene merchant stored paper – presumably Venetian or Genoese – for a party of West African pilgrims while they journeyed on to the Hijaz and back.[28] Earlier sixteenth-century export paper might have included French or Italian paper watermarked with hands, pots or bulls' heads.[29]

In the seventeenth century, Tripoli became a market for Euro–African exchange, and the major trade routes linking western Bilad al-Sudan with the Mediterranean world shifted. The French never succeeded in gaining a commercial foothold in Tripoli, and almost all reports of the paper trade from the seventeenth century onward refer to Italian imports, particularly paper watermarked with the *tre lune* or three crescents. The French consul Le Maire reported at the end of the seventeenth century that the trade between Fazzan and Borno of glass beads, bracelets, cloth, paper, copper wire and sheets was mostly from Venice. Eighteenth-century accounts confirm the Venetian dominance of the paper trade, much of which was re-exported 'to the blacks'. A 1767 British report on the trade of Tripoli listed among imports from Venice: 'paper stamped with three moons' (800 reams), 'writing paper' (200 reams), 'outside quires' (300 reams), 'another kind of the same' (150 reams). The Venetians (but not the Genoese, the Livornese or the Marseillais) were so entrenched that the British toyed with the idea of making 'three half-moon' paper at Mahon (in the Balearics) to cut into their share.[30] In seventeenth-century Morocco, French paper made in Provence sold well and some was undoubtedly shipped south. Hunwick noted the 'raisin' watermark on a Timbuktu manuscript dated 1715 with a heart and the initials FS.[31] By the eighteenth and nineteenth centuries paper often ranked only after cloth as the most important article of trade among European exports to the Middle East and North Africa, and the profit earned in selling it was as high as that earned on the sale of any European-crafted product.[32]

The German explorer Henry (Heinrich) Barth (1821–65) wrote in his *Travels and Discoveries in North and Central Africa* that 'Common paper, called on the coast "tre lune," is imported in great quantity, being used for wrapping up the country cloth; but it is a bulky heavy article, and in large quantities is sold at a very cheap rate.'[33] Gustav Nachtigal (1834–95), another German explorer, wrote in *Sahara and Sudan* that 'Paper is also a not unimportant article of commerce in Kuka. It is very coarse...[and] shows its Italian origin by its watermark of three crescents with the legend, tre lune.'[34] Their observations are confirmed by surviving Sudani manuscripts, which were written on paper produced in Pordenone and Friuli, now in north-east Italy. Foremost among them are the products of the Galvani firm, those of Giovanni Berti, and an unidentified

A watermark with three crescents, known as the *tre lune*, appeared on handmade paper from Italy in the early sixteenth century and enjoyed wide popularity from the seventeenth to the nineteenth century. There are several variants on the basic design. The top row above shows the typical form. The centre row shows a variant with one of the crescents slightly tipped. The last row shows a variant with faces.

Watermark of Beniamino Arbib inscribed in Arabic, *ya nasib* (O Fate!) found on several dozen manuscripts from the western Sudan produced in the late nineteenth and early twentieth centuries. The image in the centre may represent a charging horse and rider with flying robes and a gun. The location of this paper mill has not yet been identified, but the prominent Arbib family had branches across North Africa and in Livorno, Italy.

papermaker who marked his sheets SSB. Other papers included those manufactured by the Venetian firms of Bernardino Nodari, Isidoro Mori, Niccolo Berlindis, Niccolo Raccanelli, and Luigi Trentin, as well as the Austrian papermaker Franz Thurn.[35] Paper made by the British firms Waterlow & Sons Limited, John Dent & Co., TH Saunders, and CMS Bookshop (Lagos) probably dates from the time of the British occupation of Nigeria (protectorate in 1901 and colony in 1914).[36]

The situation was similar in the eastern Bilad al-Sudan. WG Browne visited Darfur in 1796–98 and found that 'writing paper' was a 'considerable article [of trade]'.[37] In 1801, Girard noted that of the 20 000 reams of Venetian paper imported to Egypt, part was consumed there, part exported to Arabia and part exported to the interior of Africa.[38] Paper was re-exported to eastern Bilad al-Sudan by long-distance merchants travelling to Sinnar (Sennar) and Darfur and to western Bilad al-Sudan by long-distance merchants and pilgrims travelling the caravan routes via the Libyan oases.[39] The Swiss traveller and orientalist John Lewis Burckhardt (1784–1817) provides some explicit details for the early nineteenth century: 'Paper [*papier de trois limes*, from Genoa and Leghorn] is rather a heavy article here; it is more in demand in the western countries, to which it is carried by the Darfour caravans: it is, however, always found in the warehouses of the Egyptians.'[40] Some nineteenth-century travellers report on a trade in 'Turkish paper' or 'paper dressed in the Turkish fashion', but this seems to refer to Italian paper that had been glazed in Egypt and bore crescent watermarks. After the establishment of the Turco–Egyptian regime in 1821, large quantities of paper must have been shipped from Cairo to Khartoum for the use of the bureaucracy; supplies may have also reached Khartoum from Jidda.[41]

In the mid-nineteenth century, the French consul in Cairo, Delaporte, estimated that the eastern Sudan trade amounted to 750–2 400 reams (each of 500 sheets) of 'Frioul' (that is, Galvani) paper a year, no more than 5 per cent of Egypt's paper imports. By the 1870s, paper imports from Italy into Darfur had increased significantly, and paper was no longer rare. At the end of the nineteenth century, a thick brown (perhaps cream-coloured) paper called *abu shibbak*, presumably referring to its weave or even texture, was also imported from Europe.[42]

It is beyond the scope of this chapter to explore the attempts to revive papermaking in the Islamic lands. Suffice to say that Muhammad 'Ali, the ruler of Egypt from 1805 to 1849, established a paper factory in 1833. In 1834 he ordered his soldiers (and in 1836 the shaykhs of the town quarters) to send their old clothing to the factory to serve as raw material. The paper, produced sporadically until 1870, wasn't very good.[43] By this time, however, European and American papermakers had discovered that they could make paper from trees, and the virtually inexhaustible supplies of cellulose in that raw material, quite apart from all sorts of other factors, meant that Egypt was in no position to compete.

Conclusion

The history of paper in Sudanic Africa differs sharply from its history in most other parts of the Muslim world. Elsewhere, the spread and growth of Islam was closely paralleled by the spread and growth of institutions and practices associated with Islamic society, particularly a culture of writing, reading and ultimately papermaking. The ready availability of paper in turn reinforced the culture of writing and reading. While raw materials for papermaking were available in Sudanic Africa, several centuries intervened between the first introduction of Islam and the growth of Islamic societies, and during that time the practice of Islam was largely limited to merchants and some rulers. By the time that sufficient numbers of African Muslims needed a quantity of paper for writing sufficient to support local production, their co-religionists in Egypt and the Maghrib, who might once have been able to teach them to make paper with local materials, had long forgotten how, and the production of paper had fallen entirely into European hands.

The closest parallel to the situation in Africa might be India, another land where Islam appeared at about the same time. Already in the centuries after Christ, Indians should have learned of papermaking from Chinese Buddhist missionaries, but curiously there is no evidence that they did so. Although some Muslims settled in Sind as early as the eighth century, about the time when paper first became known in the eastern Islamic lands, the first permanent Muslim presence in northern India dates from the late twelfth century, and the first manuscripts that can be ascribed to India date from the fourteenth century, just about the time that Europeans were beginning to manufacture and export paper. India, however, was much further from Europe than Africa, and until the sixteenth century there was little chance that European paper would be exported that far. Instead, under the tutelage of Central Asian and Iranian papermakers, Indians began making paper in the early fifteenth century and they were ably to supply the needs of a wide range of writers and artists through the seventeenth and eighteenth centuries. Indeed, as late as the eighteenth century paper was exported from Dawlatabad to Iran, although by the nineteenth century most Iranian paper was being imported from Russia.

The history of paper in Sudanic Africa, therefore, is inextricably tied to the history of Islam in the region as well as to the varying fortunes of papermakers in the Muslim lands to the north. The nature of conversion to Islam and its relatively late date meant that paper, unlike elsewhere in the Islamic lands, was comparatively unimportant and that locally made paper did not play the transformative role in African Islamic society that it had played elsewhere.

NOTES

1 Bloom (2001).

2 *'Iqd al-farid* (Cairo, 1904/1322), 2:183, quoted in Pedersen (1984: 62). On Ibn 'Abd al-Rabbih's pilgrimage, see Shafi (1922).

3 Lévi-Provençal (1934).

4 Burns (1985: 174–176).

5 Sold at Christie's London, 9 October 1990, sales catalogue pl. 46. See Khemir (1992: 117).

6 The manuscript, now in Palermo, Biblioteca Regionale della Sicilia Ms. III.D. 10, is discussed in Curatola (1993: 180–181).

7 Goitein (1967–94: 1:112).

8 According to 'Abd al-Wahhab (1956), there is a manuscript on paper copied at Qayrawan in 884 and the manufacture of paper began in the tenth century at Qayrawan, Tunis and Mahdiyya. The oldest dated paper made at Qayrawan is from 1154.

9 Levy (1962: 39–40).

10 Levy (1962: 43–44).

11 Le Léannec-Bavavéas (1998: 111).

12 Burns (1985: 174–176).

13 Valls i Subirà (1970: 11).

14 Valls i Subirà (1970: 12).

15 Ashtor (1977: 270).

16 Walz (1988: 30).

17 Walz (1988: 31).

18 The decision, recorded by the Fassi jurist al-Wansharisi, is summarised in Lagardière (1995: 42). I am most grateful to David S Powers of Cornell University for bringing this reference to my attention.

19 Gibb et al. (1960), s.v. 'Sudan, Bilad al-' 9: 752.

20 Gibb et al. (1960), s.v. 'Sudan, Bilad al-' 9: 753.

21 Hunwick (1995: 16–17).

22 Gibb et al. (1960), s.v. 'Sudan, Bilad al-' 9: 756a.

23 Morris & Preston Blier (2003: 190).

24 Hunwick (2003: 8).

25 Gibb et al. (1960), s.v. 'Mansa Musa' 6: 421–422; Ibn Battuta (1994: 958); Aradeon (1989); Hunwick (1990).

26 Aradeon (1989).

27 Walz (1988: 40).

28 Walz (1988: 40).

29 Walz (1988: 40).

30 Walz (1988: 40).

31 Walz (1988: 47 n.46).

32 Walz (1988: 29).

33 Walz (1988: 47).

34 Walz (1988: 47).

35 Walz (1988: 41).

36 Walz (1988: 41–42).

37 Walz (1988: 40).

38 Walz (1988: 39).

39 Walz (1988: 39).

40 Walz (1988: 46) quoting Burckhardt (1822: 302).

41 Walz (1988: 39).

42 Walz (1988: 40).

43 Walz (1988: 38).

REFERENCES

'Abd al-Wahhab HH (1956) al-Bardi wa al-riqq wa al-kaghad fi Ifriqiyya al-tunisiyya. *Majallat Ma'hid Makhtutat Arabiyya* 2: 34–45

Aradeon SB (1989) al-Sahili: the historians' myth of architectural technology transfer from North Africa. *Journal Des Africainistes* 59 (1/2): 99–131

Ashtor E (1977) Levantine sugar industry in the Later Middle Ages – an example of technological decline. *Israel Oriental Studies* 7: 226–280. Tel Aviv University

Barth H (1857) *Travels and discoveries in North and Central Africa.* New York: Harper & Brothers

Bloom JM (2001) *Paper before print: the history and impact of paper in the Islamic world.* New Haven: Yale University Press

Burckhardt JL (1822) *Travels in Nubia* (2nd edition). London: J Murray

Burns R (1985) *Society and documentation in Crusader Valencia. Diplomatarium of the Crusader Kingdom of Valencia: The Registered Charters of its Conqueror Jaume I, 1257–1276.* Princeton: Princeton University Press

Curatola G (1993) *Eredità dell'Islam.* Venice: Silvana Editoriale

Gibb HAR et al. (Eds) (1960) *The encyclopaedia of Islam* (new edition). Leiden: Brill

Goitein SD (1967–94) *A Mediterranean society.* Berkeley/Los Angeles: University of California Press

Hunwick JO (1990) An Andalusian in Mali: A contribution to the biography of Abu Ishaq al-Sahili, c.1290–1346. *Paideuma* 36: 59–66

Hunwick JO (1995) *Arabic literature of Africa: The writings of central Sudanic Africa* (Vol. 2). Leiden: Brill

Hunwick JO (2003) *Arabic literature of Africa: The writings of western Sudanic Africa* (Vol. 4). Leiden: Brill

Ibn Battuta (1994) *The travels of Ibn Battuta, AD 1325–1354* (Vol. 4). Edited and translated by HAR Gibb & CF Beckingham. London: The Haklyut Society

Khemir S (1992) The arts of the book. In JD Dodds (Ed.) *Al-Andalus: The art of Islamic Spain.* New York: The Metropolitan Museum of Art/Harry N Abrams

Lagardière V (1995) *Histoire et société en occident musulmane au moyen-age: Analyse du Mi'yar d'al-Wansharisi.* Collection de la Casa de Velázquez. Madrid: Casa de Velázquez

Le Léannec-Bavavéas M-T (1998) *Les papiers non filigranés médiévaux de la Perse à l'Espagne: Bibliographie 1950–1995.* Paris: CNRS editions

Lévi-Provençal E (1934) Un manuscrit de la bibliothèque du calife al-Hakam II. *Hespéris* 18: 198–200

Levy M (1962) Medieval Arabic bookmaking and its relation to early chemistry and pharmacology. *Transactions of the American Philosophical Society* 40: 3–79

Morris J & Preston Blier S (2003) *Butabu: Adobe architecture of West Africa.* New York: Princeton Architectural Press

Nachtigal G (1879/1987) *Sahara and Sudan.* Translated from the original German with a new introduction and notes by AGB Fisher & HJ Fisher. London/Atlantic Highlands, NJ: C. Hurst/Humanities Press International

Pedersen J (1984) *The Arabic book.* With an introduction by Robert Hillenbrand, translated by Geoffrey French. Princeton: Princeton University Press

Seguezzi S (1651) *Relations veritables et curieuses de l'isle de Madagascar et du Bresil...et trois relations d'Egypte et une du Royaume de Perse.* Paris: Augustin Courbé

Shafí M (1922) A description of the two sanctuaries of Islam by Ibn 'Abd Rabbihi (†940). In TW Arnold & RA Nicholson (Eds) *A volume of oriental studies presented to Edward G. Browne.* Cambridge: Cambridge University Press

Valls i Subirà O (1970) *Paper and watermarks in Catalonia.* Monumenta Chartae Papyracea Historiam Illustrantia. Amsterdam: Paper Publications Society (Labarre Foundation)

Walz T (1988) The paper trade of Egypt and the Sudan in the eighteenth and nineteenth centuries. In MW Daly (Ed.) *Modernization in the Sudan.* New York: Lilian Berber Press

سورة فاتحة الكتاب مكية وهي سبع ايات
بسم الله الرحمن الرحيم
الحمد لله رب العلمين الرحمن الرحيم
ملك يوم الدين اياك نعبد واياك نستعين
اهدنا الصرط المستقيم صرط الذين
انعمت عليهم غير المغضوب
عليهم ولا الضالين
سورة البقرة مدنية وهي ماتان وخمس
وثمانون اية بسم الله الرحمن الرحيم
الم
ذلك

CHAPTER 5

Arabic calligraphy in West Africa

Sheila S Blair

The history of Arabic calligraphy in West Africa is a story that is beginning to unfold. Scholars are just uncovering the extraordinary richness of local libraries in Timbuktu which preserve large caches of hitherto unknown manuscripts, some made there in the last few centuries. Most of these discoveries are so recent that they have been described only briefly on the internet.[1]

These written documents cover a variety of subjects, as shown by a recent exhibition of manuscripts from the Mamma Haidara Memorial Library held at the Library of Congress in Washington DC in 2005.[2] Some, such as an astronomical text dated 1733, contain scientific texts, often embellished with diagrams to aid in understanding. Others, such as a chronicle of the Songhay Empire dated 1809, are historical. Most of these texts are in prose, but a few contain poetry, such as one with the laws of commerce written in verse to aid memorisation. Still other manuscripts deal with religious affairs, including a Sufi treatise dated 1858.

But of all manuscripts produced in the region, the finest in terms of both quality of materials and carefulness of execution are copies of the Qur'an. At least two dozen are known, of which a generous handful have been published with colour illustrations (see Figure 5.1).[3]

Like the others, these Qur'an manuscripts show a range of writing styles, but in general they are all well executed, with colour enhancing both text and illumination. Each manuscript is written in a controlled, practised and uniform hand closest to the 'ideal' script, which could be executed with varying levels of competence and performance.[4]

Figure 5.1 (opposite): The opening page of text from a typical manuscript of the Qur'an made in West Africa.

Of all the manuscripts produced in the region, the finest in terms of both quality of materials and carefulness of execution are copies of the Qur'an.

Characteristics of West African Arabic script

Using these published manuscripts, especially copies of the Qur'an, our first task then is to outline the salient characteristics of the 'ideal' Arabic script used in West Africa. This script is often dubbed 'Sudani', a name coined in 1886 by Octave Houdas in a seminal article on Maghribi script, the style used in the Maghrib, or Islamic West.[5] He distinguished four subtypes of Maghribi, all sharing certain characteristics. Some relate to the alphabet. Arabic speakers (or, more precisely, writers) in the Maghrib use a different (and older) system of alphanumerics, in which the positions of *sin* and *sad* are reversed from the positions they hold in the (newer) eastern system. Other differences are orthographic. In the Maghrib, for example, *fa* and *qaf* are pointed differently than they are in the East, with a single dot below *fa* and above *qaf*. Final *fa*, *qaf*, *nun*, *ya* and *ta marbuta* are often dotless or unpointed.

Still other differences relate to the ways that calligraphers pen their strokes. The strokes used in the Maghrib have softer, more curved edges than the tauter, sharper-edged strokes used in the round hands known as the Six Pens that have been popular in the eastern Islamic lands since medieval times. Such a difference in *ductus* is probably due to the difference in pens: although calligraphers everywhere in the Islamic lands traditionally use a reed pen, calligraphers in the Maghrib slice the reed into flat slats whose tips are trimmed with a blunt or rounded end that gives a round outline. They control thicks and thins through the amount of ink on the pen and the speed with which they move it.[6] By contrast, calligraphers in the East use a pen cut from the full circumference of the reed and trimmed, since the time of Ibn Muqla (886–940) and the introduction of round scripts, with an oblique cut.[7]

Differences in materials and technique seem to have engendered differences in aspect. Maghribi script is posed on a flat baseline, with diacritical marks added in complementary horizontal strokes. In the East, by contrast, single words are often written on a slope, as are the small strokes indicating short vowels. Maghribi calligraphers typically draw only one or two letters at a time, and thus within words there are often tiny spaces or overlapping strokes. In contrast, flowing strokes and ligatures between unauthorised letters such as *alif* to *lam* are characteristic of the Six Pens used in the East, notably *thuluth*.

In addition, the shapes of individual letters in Maghribi script show more variation, as a single letter can assume four or five different shapes on the same page. The shapes also differ from those typical of the round scripts. In Maghribi script the vertical strokes for *alif*, *lam* and *ta/za* are often curved, not rigidly straight, and have a large dot or serif that faces left. The connected final *alif* descends below the baseline. The bodies of *sad* and *ta/za* are elliptical rather than triangular, as is typical of round scripts, and smooth, lacking the final notch typical of eastern scripts. In addition, Maghribi calligraphers typically exaggerate the ends of the letters, especially *sin*, *sad*, *lam*, *mim* and *nun*.

These features characterise all four subtypes of Maghribi script, but Houdas distinguished the subtype Sudani by its heaviness. Its letters are thicker and blacker. They also show greater variation between thick and thin, with thinner vertical strokes set next to thicker horizontal and diagonal ones, achieved by using the pen along its vertical chisel edge. Houdas distinguished this heavy Sudani script from three other subtypes that he designated as Qayrawani (from Qayrawan, the city now in Tunisia), a smooth, even script that resembled the round scripts used in the East; Andalusi (from Andalusia), a small, compact and jerky script; and Fasi (from Fez in southern Morocco), a large, round and elegant script. Houdas's choice of names was in many ways unfortunate, for these styles of script, while different, are not distinct to the geographical locations to which he assigned them, and two styles were sometimes combined in the same manuscript, as in a copy of a work on traditions, *Shihab al-akhbar* (The Meteor of News), transcribed in 1172–73.[8] Such intermingling of styles in any one centre of production is not surprising given the movement of both people and manuscripts throughout this region.[9] Scholars such as Ibn Rushd or Ibn Khaldun moved about Andalusia and North Africa, not always by choice. They often took manuscripts with them. Thus, the copy of *Shihab al-akhbar* produced in Valencia was read 16 years later at the Great Mosque of Cordova and is now preserved in Rabat, Morocco.

Houdas's choice of Sudani for the fourth subtype of Maghribi script was also confusing. It seems to have been predicated on the use of the term 'Sudani' as in Bilad al-Sudan (literally, the land of the black people), traditionally used to designate the broad swath of Saharo–Sahelian land across middle Africa from the Atlantic to the Red Sea, a region that today is often divided into east and west.[10] This chapter concentrates on the Arabic script used in the western half of this broad belt, and one of my goals is to set out methods to distinguish manuscripts of the Qur'an and other texts made there from manuscripts made in the eastern Bilad al-Sudan. Such regional traditions may be established on the basis of not only script, but also format and decoration as well as, in the case of the Qur'an, the specific reading of the text. I shall work from the few dated and localised manuscripts outwards to the larger group of similar but undated examples in order to delineate characteristics of the 'ideal' script and typical codex from West Africa and to establish a chronological and geographical framework about when and where this script was popular. Finally, I shall conclude with more general considerations about the cultural significance of writing in West Africa. Along the way, I shall also suggest the kinds of information that still need to be gathered to test these preliminary hypotheses.

Characteristics of Qur'anic manuscripts

Let us begin with the finest and best published manuscripts that can be assigned to West Africa, copies of the Qur'an. The image in Figure 5.2, dated 8 Rabi' I 1250 (15 July 1834), for example, was penned by a scribe named Sayrallah for Malam al-Qadi ibn al-Husayn of Borno.[11] Many of the same features, with some variations, can be seen in a

Figure 5.2 Loose-leaf manuscript of the Qur'an copied by Sayrallah for Malam al-Qadi ibn al-Husayn of Borno and completed on 8 Rabi' I 1250 (15 July 1834).

handful of similar manuscripts, most of them undated, including copies in the Nour and Ghassan Shaker collections (numbers 6 and 73, respectively). All are loose-leaf manuscripts held in a tooled leather wallet that is not attached to the text block, but rather wrapped around it, with the flap folded on the outside (see Figure 5.3). The flap is often pointed or ogival and can be held in place by a cowrie shell and leather thong wrapped around the binding. The wallet, in turn, is held in a leather satchel, said to preserve the manuscript from impurity and protect it from the evil eye, but also used to enhance portability.[12] Made of goatskin, the satchel usually has a shoulder strap and a flap secured by plaited leather thongs.[13]

The text in a typical Qur'an manuscript made in West Africa (see Figures 5.1 and 5.2) is copied on some 400 to 500 separate sheets of hand-trimmed paper, each measuring approximately 23 by 17 centimetres. The written area varies, but an average surface measures on the order of 15 by 10 centimetres. Each page typically contains 15 lines of writing, although the number can vary anywhere from 14 to 20, even within the same manuscript. The text, identified in at least two cases as the reading transmitted by Warsh from Nafi',[14] is penned in brownish-black ink, with vowels, *sukun* and *shadda* marked in red and *hamzat al-qat'* marked with a yellow dot. Green is used sparingly for *hamzat al-wasl*, as on opening pages of the Qur'an manuscript seen by Nadia Abbott.[15] Chapter titles are typically written in red, with markings in brownish-black (see Figure 5.1).

Certain letter forms are distinctive. The letters themselves are squat, and the written height within the line is almost uniform, such that *fa'/qaf* is almost as tall as *alif* or *lam*,

Figure 5.3 Typical binding and satchel from the copy of the Qur'an in Leeds University. In West Africa, many loose-leaf manuscripts are held in a tooled leather wallet that is not attached to the text block, but rather wrapped around it, with the flap folded on the outside. The flap is often pointed or ogival and can be held in place by a cowrie shell and leather thong wrapped around the binding. The wallet, in turn, is held in a leather satchel, said to preserve the manuscript from impurity and protect it from the evil eye, but also used to enhance portability. Made of goatskin, the satchel usually has a shoulder strap and a flap secured by plaited leather thongs.

the same height as the initial *ba* in the *basmala* that begins all but one chapter in the Qur'an. '*Ayn* is large. *Sad* is a smooth, toothless lozenge that is sometimes quite large, as in the Nour manuscript Qur'an (no. 7). It can also be elongated to fill out the line, as in the Leeds Qur'an (see Figure 5.1). Medial *ha* is written flat on the line like a bow on a package. Unwritten *alif* is added as a thin red slash.

These Qur'an manuscripts from West Africa are typically decorated with illumination of simple geometrical shapes painted in the same earth colours used to copy the text: brown, red, yellow, and occasionally green. Examination of the manuscript in Leeds suggests that the yellow is probably orpiment (Arabic *zarnih asfar*), an arsenic sulphide used elsewhere in the Maghrib and mentioned by Ibn Badis.[16] Further testing on the red would be useful as different substances were used in various regions to produce red: vermillion (*zanghafr*) was typical in the East, whereas cochineal was common in the Maghrib, not only for manuscript illumination but also for dying skins.[17] Individual verses in these West African manuscripts of the Qur'an are typically divided by pyramids of three yellow circles outlined in red. Groups of five and ten verses are indicated by various types of filled circles. Similar marginal ornaments indicate the division of the text (see Figure 5.2) into sixtieths (*hizb*), further subdivided into eight parts, indicated with rectangular panels containing the letters *ba* (one-fourth), *nun* (for *nisf*, one-half) and *tha* (for *thumn*, one-eighth). Divisions of the text into the seven parts known as *khatam al-ahzab* are sometimes indicated by circles inscribed with the word 'seven' (*al-sab*'). Places of prostration are marked with similar designs containing the word *sajda*. In the manuscript examined by Abbott, for example, 10 of 11 prostrations accepted by the Maliki school are thus marked.[18]

Several manuscripts also contain marginal notes in the same red script as the headings. Some supply supplementary information about the numbers of verses, words and letters in each chapter. Other notes give alternate readings and instructions on recitation techniques, a topical subject in a region with a strong oral tradition. In the manuscript examined by Abbott, the marginal notes consist of a word or phrase that is to be repeated as many as 11 times, with the added instruction that this word or phrase should be repeated in recitation each time that it occurs in the Qur'an.[19] According to Abbott, this type of recitation is said to be characteristic of Sufi sects in North Africa.

Most of these small-format, loose-leaf Qur'an manuscripts can be attributed to the eighteenth or nineteenth century. At least one is dated: the copy made for the *qadi* of Borno in 1834 (see Figure 5.2).[20] In most cases we can date the manuscripts by the materials: they are copied on paper watermarked with the distinctive *tre lune*, paper that was manufactured by the firm of Andrea Galvini since the seventeenth century.[21] Some manuscripts may even date from the seventeenth century. A composite codex in the Bibliothèque Nationale containing fragments from different manuscripts (see Figure 5.4) includes a final folio dated Ramadan 1100 (June 1689).[22] The oldest Qur'an manuscript that can be attributed to the area is one examined by ADH Bivar at Maiduguri in Nigeria (see Figure 5.5).[23] It has interlinear glosses in a form of Kanembu, a dialect of Kanuri still spoken by parts of the Borno population around Lake Chad. The margins are filled with several commentaries, including a lengthy one by al-Qurtubi, whose colophon says that it was completed on 1 Jumada II 1080 (Sunday 27 October 1669). Bivar concluded that this bilingual Qur'an manuscript and three similar ones that he had seen in northern Nigeria were produced in Birni N'gazargamu, the former capital of the Borno Empire destroyed by the local Fulanis in 1808.

In format, the bilingual manuscript differs from the typical West African examples perhaps made in later centuries. It is larger (32 x 23 cm). Each page is therefore twice the area of the smaller manuscripts and has eight widely spaced lines of text written in a hand that shares many features with the Maghribi style. Letters are posed on a flat baseline and share the classic Maghribi pointing and shape, with swooping – though shorter – tails, horizontal diacritical marks, unusual pointing for *fa'* and *qaf*, and typical letter shapes such as *alif* often with a club foot, flat *sad*, *kaf* with a diagonal bar, and *dal* like pursed lips. Verses are marked with a pyramid of three balls. Like the smaller examples, the decoration is added with simple geometric shapes in earth colours, used on folio 1b to fill the bottom of the page, space that would have been occupied by the eighth line of text on regular text pages.

Colophons suggest further that the scribal tradition existed in West Africa at least from the turn of the fifteenth to the sixteenth century. The colophon to the bilingual Qur'an

with Kanembu gives the genealogy of the calligrapher, whose family had lived in Borno as early as the last quarter of the fifteenth century.

Sites of production

Localising the place of production of these manuscripts is difficult, for few contain a colophon and those that do are somewhat confusing. Some of the Qur'an manuscripts can be connected with Borno and the region around Lake Chad where the bilingual manuscripts with Kanembu would have been used. The Qur'an manuscript dated 1834 (see Figure 5.2) was made for the *qadi* of Borno, but the colophon reports that the scribe was in Tunis near Bab Suwayqah, which can be identified as a gate in the north wall in the medina there. The colophon adds that the scribe wrote it in the village (*balad*) of *w-z-k*, repeating the name of the settlement, the village of *w-z-q*, with a different spelling. Tim Stanley has suggested that the scribe might have moved to Tunis or was en route from his home in West Africa to Tunis.[24]

Figure 5.4 (left) Composite codex containing fragments from different texts including a final folio dated Ramadan 1100 (June 1689).

Figure 5.5 (right) Manuscript of the Qur'an with interlinear glosses in Kanembu and marginal commentary by al-Qurtubi. Several manuscripts also contain marginal notes in the same red script as the headings. Some supply supplementary information about the numbers of verses, words and letters. Other notes give alternate readings and instructions on recitation techniques.

Two signatures in the manuscript examined by Abbott state that it was written in the city of Qariyan or Qariya. Abbott found that al-Bakri mentioned Qariya as a small hill-city with many springs near Tunis. Marginal notes give the name of the calligrapher as Muhammad ibn Muhammad ibn Mika'il ibn Fatima, whose name once includes the unexplained letters *ta-sin* after the second Muhammad and twice contains a non-Arabic phrase describing him as a craftsman who paints or draws (*yasawara*). Abbott concluded that the manuscript was a copy of an older one penned by the above-mentioned Muhammad, whose signature was then copied by someone in the southern Bilad al-Sudan, whence the manuscript made its way to Lagos, where it was purchased in 1935.

The distinctive script used in these West African manuscripts clearly derives from Maghribi, but scholars have debated which other subtype was the immediate source. Bivar designated the West African script *'ifriqi*, meaning from Ifriqiya, the Arabic name for the region comprising modern-day Tunisia and western Algeria.[25] As evidence, he cited the statement by the great North African historian Ibn Khaldun, writing *c.*1375, who reported that Muslim calligraphers fleeing from Andalusia introduced a more delicate and flowing hand which had replaced the styles used earlier in North Africa, notably at Qayrawan and Mahdiyya.[26] The old scripts, Ibn Khaldun continued, were preserved only in a few towns in the Jarid, a word literally meaning palms and a term designating the region of south-western Tunisia in the Sahara. Bivar argued that the old style of script was also preserved south of the Sahara in the Sahel, brought there by the Almoravids during their conquests of the Upper Niger region. He distinguished this heavy angular *'ifriqi* script from a thinner and more flexible hand that he, like Houdas, called Andalusi.

Though ingenious, Bivar's arguments are ultimately unsatisfactory for a variety of reasons, ranging from historical to palaeographic.[27] The Almoravids, who introduced Maliki Islam and many other features to the Sahel, never controlled Ifriqiya, the presumed home of the *'ifriqi* script, although they might have imported manuscripts from there.[28] Furthermore, the style that developed in tenth-century Tunisia was different, more closely related to developments in the East.[29] A legal text copied in 1015, almost certainly in Qayrawan, shows many characteristics of eastern scripts, such as *sad* with a bump and medial *ha* shaped like a figure 8 that descends below the baseline.[30]

The script used in the Qur'an manuscripts from West Africa, by contrast, shares many, many characteristics with the western Maghribi style used in Morocco and Andalusia.[31] *Sad* is written without a final tooth, as in the Maghribi style, and medial *ha* also follows the Maghribi rather than the eastern style. To see this, we can compare typical pages from Qur'an manuscripts made in West Africa (see Figures 5.1 and 5.2) and Morocco, specifically a copy transcribed in 975 (1568) for the Sharifan sultan of Morocco, Mawlay 'Abdallah ibn Muhammad (see Figure 5.6).[32] Both scripts are distinguished by swooping tails and flat diacritical marks, *alif* with a club foot, *dal* like pursed lips, *kaf* with a diagonal bar. Both have a medial *ha* that sits on the baseline like a bow and a very large

بسم الله الرحمن الرحيم
انا فتحنا لك فتحا مبينا ليغفر
لك الله ما تقدم من ذنبك وما تاخر ويتم
نعمته عليك ويهديك صراطا
مستقيما وينصرك الله نصرا
عزيزا هو الذي انزل السكينة في
قلوب المومنين ليزدادوا ايمانا مع ايمانهم
ولله جنود السموات والارض وكان
الله عليما حكيما ليدخل المومنين
والمومنات جنات تجري من تحتها الانهار
خالدين فيها ويكفر عنهم سياتهم
وكان ذلك عند الله فوزا عظيما ويعذب
المنافقين والمنافقات والمشركين والمشركات
الظانين بالله ظن السوء عليهم دائرة
السوء وغضب الله عليهم ولعنهم واعد
لهم جهنم وساءت مصيرا ولله

Figure 5. 6 Manuscript of the Qur'an copied in 975 (1568) for the Sharifan sultan of Morocco, Mawlay 'Abdallah ibn Muhammad.

Figure 5.7 Copy of Bukhari's *Sahih* dated 1419.

initial *ba* in the *basmala*. Neither of these features is found in a Qur'an manuscript endowed by the Hafsid ruler Abu 'l-Faris to the Qasba Mosque of Tunis in Ramadan 807 (March 1405).[33]

Features of layout used in West African manuscripts of the Qur'an also continue those used further north in Morocco and Andalusia. The commentary in the bilingual Qur'an (see Figure 5.5) circles around the text, the epistolary tradition used in Andalusia as shown by a rare cache of 162 letters written by various Muslim rulers of Spain and North Africa to the kings of Aragon–Catalonia.[34] The text on one dated 10 Sha'ban 745 (17 September 1344) that was written by Yusuf I, Nasrid ruler of Granada, to Peter IV (the Ceremonious) of Aragon, for example, begins in the horizontal lines but then continues in a circle to fill the page, the same kind of circular format as in the Kanembu bilingual Qur'an manuscript. Similarly, religious manuscripts from West Africa, such as a book of litanies and prayers with the names of Muhammad and litanies to be recited on Saturday,[35] use the small square format that remained common in the western Maghrib long after it had been abandoned in the west. Such a format is used, among many other examples, for a well-known Qur'an manuscript made at Cordova in 1143,[36] and it continued to be used until the nineteenth century, as shown by copies of the *Dala'il al-khayrat* in the Berlin Museum and the Shaker collection.[37]

The decoration of West African manuscripts of the Qur'an also shows features of the style used in the western Maghrib. The pyramid of three balls, for example, is part of a long tradition there, found also in the Cordovan Qur'an of 1143. The illumination in West African Qur'an and other manuscripts also relates to traditions further north. The decoration of the larger panels resembles textile patterns seen on Berber rugs from Morocco. We can compare, for example, a page from the Leeds Qur'an manuscript with the last verse of Chapter 6 (folio 81b) to a Zemmoura flatweave from the Middle Atlas.[38] Such patterns of diagonals, zigzags and strapwork arranged in rectangular panels are standard on *bogolanfini*, the discharge-dyed mud cloths made in Mali, traditionally by sewing together narrow strips.[39]

Western Maghribi script had long been the model in the area. The earliest examples of Arabic calligraphy to survive from western Africa comprise a group of tombstones found near Gao.[40] At least four seem to have been carved at Almería in Andalusia and shipped to West Africa where they provided the models for local copies. Moroccan manuscripts were also imported to West Africa. The oldest codices in the Kati collection, for example, were made in Morocco, to judge from the style of a copy of al-Bukhari's *Sahih* (Authentic) transcribed in 1419 (see Figure 5.7).[41] Similarly, a copy of Iyad ibn Musa's *al-Shifa bi-ta'rif huquq al-mustafa* (Healing by the Recognition of the Rights of the Chosen One) in the collection of Malam Nagwamatse of Sokoto was probably transcribed at Fez in the sixteenth or seventeenth century.[42]

The development of Arabic calligraphy in West Africa

We can therefore pose the following outline for the development of Arabic calligraphy in West Africa. Arabic manuscripts were clearly read and appreciated there since the conversion of rulers to Islam. The Moroccan globetrotter Ibn Battuta, who visited the area in 1353, mentioned that the people of Walata regularly studied religious law and memorised the Qur'an.[43] He also tells us that for the feast held in his honour in the Malian capital, Qur'an cases were brought and the whole Qur'an was read.[44] The construction of mosques throughout the region may well have been accompanied by the endowment of Qur'an manuscripts for public reading.

For practical reasons, notably the lack of paper, it is likely that in these earlier centuries the manuscripts were imported, probably from Morocco. Ibn Battuta noted that the kings of Mali sent members of the *'ulama* to Fez and exchanged embassies with the Marinid ruler Abu al-Hasan. These embassies may well have brought back books, long popular as official gifts. Illustrations show us, for example, that Safavid embassies often presented books to their rivals, the Ottomans.[45] Scholars also brought manuscripts from North to West Africa. A note in one manuscript in the Fondo Ka'ti Library states that it was purchased in the Saharan oasis of Tuwat in 1467 while the purchaser was en route from Toledo to West Africa.[46] Pilgrims too probably brought home copies of the Qur'an and bestowed them on family and friends.[47]

With the increasing prevalence of a written – rather than an oral – tradition and the increased availability of materials, West Africans began to produce their own manuscripts. Production may have begun as early as the sixteenth century, and increased gradually in the seventeenth century due to an increase in both demand for written works, notably new chronicles, and the availability of European watermarked paper from Pordenone and elsewhere in the Veneto. Arabic manuscripts became common in the eighteenth and nineteenth centuries such that we can talk of a distinctive West African style of script. This scenario bears comparison with what occurred at another borderland in the Islamic lands: India. The sultans of Delhi established Islam as the state religion in the opening years of the thirteenth century, but a distinctive style of script, known as *bihari*, dates only to the very end of the fourteenth century and became widespread in the fifteenth and sixteenth.[48]

Looking at the manuscripts themselves shows us that production in West Africa was very much a local affair. The materials were expensive. The imported paper was often cut from larger sheets, with various kinds combined in the same manuscript. The Leeds Qur'an (see Figure 5.1), for example, uses three different types of paper.[49] The one examined by Abbott is copied mainly on paper watermarked with the Arabic phrase *ya nasib*, the name Beniamino Arbib written in Roman characters, and the figure of a horseman, but the manuscript also has two folios of heavier paper watermarked with the *tre lune*. The expense of the paper is clear from layout as well. Scribes such as the one who copied the Kanembu Qur'an were anxious to use every surface available. Pens too were expensive. Brockett's close examination of the copy in Leeds shows that the nib became increasingly blunt over the pages, showing that the scribe wanted to preserve the nib for as long as possible. The inks and pigments for text and illumination are also local, and there is no use of gold, a hallmark of fancier manuscripts produced elsewhere in the Maghrib. Such an absence is somewhat ironic, given that gold was a major export of the region.

Various features of format and decoration also indicate that production in West Africa was more a matter of home production than a formal school with set rules. The pages are not ruled, and the number of lines varies within a single manuscript. Marginal notes are added in various directions and places. There is no indication of a division of labour between scribe and illuminator, and indeed the note in the Qur'an manuscript examined by Abbott suggests that both were the same. In contrast, these became specialised tasks in Iran and the East from the twelfth century and in the Maghrib shortly thereafter, as shown by both signatures and pigment analysis.[50] The illumination of these West African manuscripts also comprises simple designs, often drawn from the textile repertory, patterns that could be worked out directly on the surface. In contrast, the elaborate floral arabesques typical of eastern manuscripts require cartoons or templates that were part of the workshop practice.[51] In the East, canons of calligraphy were passed from master to pupil by instruction in organised schools, written manuals, and albums with specimens of specific scripts. The codification of a tradition there makes it difficult if not impossible to identify individual hands.[52] In West Africa, by contrast, learning – even Arabic script – was often oral and visual (rather than written and kinetic), often

Figure 5.8 Manuscript of the Qur'an copied by al-Hajj Ahmad Muhammad ibn Ahmad Musa in the eastern Bilad al-Sudan in 1879.

taught through the use of writing boards.[53] Hence, it is no surprise that there is greater deviation from any 'ideal' West African script and more variety of individual hands.

Despite the variety of hands used to copy Qur'an manuscripts in West Africa, we may be able to distinguish them from manuscripts copied further east in what is now the Republic of the Sudan, as in a copy in Leeds dated 1881 (ms. 619) and one in the Shaker collection dated 17 Ramadan 1296 (August 1879) (see Figure 5.8).[54] One major difference is the reading: the Leeds manuscript contains that of the Basran Abu 'Amr, a reading that was widespread only in the eastern Bilad al-Sudan.[55] This text can be distinguished from that of Nafi' via Warsh, a reading that is popular in Libya and West Africa.[56] Identifying the reading in an individual manuscript is therefore essential information in publishing a Qur'an manuscript, particularly one from these later centuries.

The script in these two Qur'an manuscripts from the eastern Bilad al-Sudan is also different. It derives from the regular round script known as *naskh*. It shares certain letter shapes with eastern styles, notably medial *ha* written as a figure 8 rather than a flat bow. The script slants distinctly to the left, a feature also found in a Qur'an manuscript dated Shawwal 1162 (September–October 1749) and once in Zanzibar.[57] Like the example in the Shaker collection (see Figure 5.8), the one associated with Zanzibar is larger (33 x 22 cm). It also shares features with manuscripts in the distinctive *bihari* script used in India, such as an upper and lower line in larger script and illuminated pages in the beginning, middle and end.

In short, the script used in manuscripts from West Africa forms a distinct subgroup of the Maghribi script used in North Africa. Copyists in West Africa used a more formal variety of the 'ideal' script for manuscripts of the Qur'an, but the same style can be seen in other manuscripts with historical and scientific texts. It is often written more hurriedly, with a decided slant to the right, but has the same letter shapes and position on the line. Though less polished than the scripts perfected in the East and somewhat rough around the edges, the Arabic script typical of West Africa is energetic and lively, a testament to the vigorous tradition of Islam that has flourished there in the last centuries. West African scripts deserve more detailed study, especially given the existence of numerous substyles of calligraphy.

NOTES

1 See, for example, the article on the Kati Library at http://www.saharanstudies.org/projects/kati/ or one by the University of Oslo on the libraries of Timbuktu at http://www.sum.uio.no/timbuktu/index.html.

2 For the exhibition 'Ancient manuscripts from the libraries in Timbuktu', see http://www.loc.gov/exhibits/mali/.

3 There are, for example, two Qur'an manuscripts from West Africa in the Nour collection, London – see Bayani et al. (1999: numbers 6, 7). Tim Stanley's essay there, 'The Qur'anic script of Western Sudan: Maghribi or Ifriqi', note 1, gives a list of other similar manuscripts. The best published manuscript is the copy in Leeds' illustrated in Figure 5.1, for which see Brockett (1987). One of the earliest to be published was examined by Nadia Abbott (1949) in Chicago in the 1940s. The Chester Beatty Library in Dublin, one of the largest repositories of Qur'an manuscripts outside the Islamic lands, owns five: see Arberry (1967: numbers 131 and 239–242), but illustrations of only one double page (ms. 1594) and one binding (ms. 1599) have been published; James (1980: numbers 94, 115). The Bibliothèque Nationale in Paris has 10, but no illustrations have been published – see Déroche (1985: numbers 334–343). Colour reproductions of others include manuscripts in the Ghassan Shaker collection (Safwat 2000: number 73) and one in the Russian Academy of Sciences, St Petersburg (number C-1689; Petrosyan et al. [1995: number 67]).

4 By script, I follow the definition given by Michael Gullick in the introduction to his article on script in Volume 28 of Turner (1996: 303) – 'system or style of writing. Scripts are identifiable and their particular features enumerated, as a consistent graphic representation of notations or letters of the alphabet.' A script is therefore a hypothetical model; it can be distinguished from a hand, what a particular individual writes. Gullick used the example of italic: Michelangelo and Queen Elizabeth I both wrote italic letters, but they had very different hands. On the terms 'competence' and 'performance', developed by Noam Chomsky for linguistics, as applied to Arabic writing on papyri from the early period, see Khan (1993: 19).

5 Houdas (1886). For an appraisal of his work, see Déroche (1994).

6 My thanks to Muhammad Zakariya who supplied this lucid description of the pens used in the Maghrib today. On this, as on many other aspects of contemporary Arabic calligraphy, he remains a master of traditional styles.

7 For examples of the pen, see Déroche (2000: 114–115 and figure 34); Guesdon & Vernay-Nouri (2001: number 6), also reproduced in Blair (2006).

8 Rabat, Bibliothèque Royale 1810; illustrated in Dodds (1992: number 77). The text is transcribed in the larger, looser Fasi and the marginal notes in the smaller Andalusi.

9 On this point, see Blair (2006: chapter 6).

10 See for example Gibb et al. (1960), in which the article 'Sudan, Bilad al-' is subdivided into eastern and western.

11 Quaritch Catalogue (1995: number 21). The manuscript was formerly in the Newberry Library, Chicago (Or. Ms. 235), which acquired it from the collection of Henry Probasco; his bookplate is dated 1 December 1890.

12 See also Déroche (2000: 309 and figures 86, 87).

13 James (1980: number 115); Safwat (2000: number 73).

14 This is the case with the manuscript in Leeds (see Figure 5.1); Brockett (1987: 45); and the one in St Petersburg (Petrosyan et al. 1995: number 67).

15 Abbott (1949: 63).

16 Brockett (1987: note 23).

17 Déroche (2000: 155–156).

18 Abbott (1949: 64).

19 Abbott (1949: 64).

20 Quaritch Catalogue (1995: number 21).

21 Walz (1988). See also Jonathan Bloom's chapter in this volume.

22 Déroche (1985: number 334). Smaller than the typical West African example (20 x 15 cm) and copied on 'oriental' paper, it is probably from the eastern Bilad al-Sudan.

23 Bivar (1960). As in south-east Asia, the cataloguing of collections in this region will undoubtedly bring to light more early manuscripts. In 1987, CC Stewart at the University of Illinois at Urbana-Champaigne initiated a project known as the Arabic Manuscript Management System (AMMS) to provide an online catalogue of manuscripts in the West African Sahel. AMMS version 2 database included 19 000 records from 6 collections in Boutilimit, Mauritania, Niger, Paris, Timbuktu, and Evanston, Illinois. The newer third version, described at http://test.atlas.uiuc.edu/amms/ammsinfo.html#acks, will allow for easier addition of new material, internet access to these collection entries, and an opportunity to finally reunite an impressive quantity and range of Arabic writing representative of a broad sweep of West Africa in, mainly, pre-colonial times. On the Mauritanian collections, see also Werner (2003).

24 Quaritch Catalogue (1995: number 115). See also Stanley's essay in Bayani et al. (1999: 32).

25 Bivar (1968); Brockett (1987) accepted Bivar's argument.

26 Ibn Khaldun (1967: 2:286).

27 See the criticisms by Stanley in Bayani et al. (1999: 33–34).

28 On the Almoravids and this area, see the entries for 'Murabittun' and 'Maritanniya' in Gibb et al. (1960).

29 For the origins of Maghribi script and the difference between that used in Tunisia and those used further west, see Déroche (1999).

30 Reproduced in Bayani et al. (1999: 32).

31 Bivar's identification of this script as *'ifriqi* on the basis of Ibn Khaldun's use of the name poses the same problem that scholars have encountered in trying to identify early Arabic scripts on the basis of references in Ibn al-Nadim's *Fihrist*: without dated and identified examples, it is difficult, if not impossible, to match names mentioned in texts with extant examples.

32 London, BL 1405; Lings & Safadi (1976: number 50); Lings (1976: 108–110); Safadi (1978: figures 79, 80); Blair (2006: figures 12, 13).

33 Paris, Bibliothèque Nationale, ms. 389–92; Déroche (1985: numbers 305–308).

34 Alarcón y Santón & García de Linares (1940); Valls i Subirà (1978).

35 Paris, Bibliothèque Nationale, ms. arabe 6869; Guesdon & Vernay-Nouri (2001: number 39).

36 Istanbul University Library ms. A6755; Dodds (1992: number 75).

37 Kröger (1991); Safwat (2000: number 71). The text, a collection of prayers for Muhammad composed by the Moroccan Sufi al-Jazuli, was popular from the Maghrib to south-east Asia. See Blair (2006: chapter 12).

38 Many examples of these flatweaves are illustrated in Fiske et al. (1980); Pickering et al. (1994).

39 See Turner (1996), Mali (3) Textiles.

40 Sauvaget (1949).

41 FK 36, Hofheinz (2003). The manuscript is illustrated on the projects page of the Saharan Studies Association: http://www.saharanstudies.org/projects/.

42 Bivar (1968: plate III).

43 Ibn Battuta (1993: 4:951).

44 Ibn Battuta (1993: 4:957).

45 See, for example, the double-page illustration showing the presentation of gifts, notably books, by the Safavid ambassador Shahquli to Selim II in 1567, from a copy of Loqman's *Shahnama-yi selim khan* done in 1581; Istanbul, Topkapi Palace Library ms. A3595, fol. 53b–54a; reproduced in Blair & Bloom (1994: figure 308).

46 The Fondo Ka'ti Library, available at http://www.saharanstudies.org/projects/kati/.

47 See, for example, a small standard Ottoman copy of the Qur'an that was presented to 'Abd al-Kader by his father when he had returned from the pilgrimage in 1827; Paris, BN ms. 7252; Guesdon & Vernay-Nouri (2001: number 1); Déroche (2004: figure 3).

48 Blair (2006: chapter 9).

49 Brockett (1987: 48).

50 Spectrographic analysis showed, for example, that a Qur'an codex copied in the Maghrib in the thirteenth or fourteenth century (BN, ms. 6935; Déroche [1985: number 302]) had diacritical marks done in blue made from azurite, but marginal decoration in blue from the more expensive lapis (Déroche 2000: 152–153).

51 On the use of paper cartoons and the different types of designs, see Bloom (2001).

52 This is the case, for example, with the various Mubarakshahs who worked in the early fourteenth century. From calligraphic style alone, it has been impossible to tell how many separate individuals used this name.

53 See, for example, the writing board illustrated in Porter and Barakat (2004: number 104) or the various examples in the National Museum of African Art, Smithsonian Institution (2001-16-1 and 2001-16-1), available through their website http://www.nmafa.si.edu/.

54 The Leeds manuscript was acquired in the Sudan just after the death of the Mahdiyya (see Brockett 1987). The Shaker manuscript contains several notes by people with the *nisba* Hilwani ('of Hilwan'), referring to the town on the Egypto–Sudanese border (see Safwat 2000: number 72).

55 Identified in Cook (2000: 74–75 and figure 12).

56 For the various readings, see Dammen McAuliffe (2001), Readings of the Qur'an; Brockett (1988).

57 Nour collection QUR706; Bayani et al. (1999: number 5).

REFERENCES

Abbott N (1949) Maghribi Koran manuscripts of the seventeenth to the eighteenth centuries. *American Journal of Semitic Languages and Literatures* 55(1): 61–65

Alarcón y Santón MA & García de Linares R (1940) *Los documentos arabes diplomáticos del archivo de la corona de Aragón.* Madrid: Estanislao Maestre

Arberry AJ (1967) *The Koran illuminated: A handlist of Korans in the Chester Beatty Library.* Dublin: Hodges, Figgis & Co.

Bayani M, Contadini A & Stanley T (1999) *The decorated word: Qur'ans of the 17th to 19th centuries.* The Nasser D Khalili collection of Islamic Art. London: The Nour Foundation in association with Azimuth Editions and Oxford University Press

Bivar ADH (1960) A dated Kuran from Bornu. *Nigeria Magazine* June: 199–205

Bivar ADH (1968) The Arabic calligraphy of West Africa. *African Language Review* 7: 3–15

Blair SS (2006) *Islamic calligraphy.* Edinburgh: Edinburgh University Press

Blair SS & Bloom JM (1994) *The art and architecture of Islam, 1250–1800.* The Pelican History of Art. London/New Haven: Yale University Press

Bloom JM (2001) *Paper before print: The history and impact of paper in the Islamic world.* New Haven: Yale University Press

Brockett A (1987) Aspects of the physical transmission of the Qur'an in 19th-century Sudan: Script, decoration, binding and paper. *Manuscripts of the Middle East* 2: 45–67

Brockett A (1988) The value of the Hafs and Warsh transmissions for the textual history of the Qur'an. In A Rippin (Ed.) *Approaches to the history of the interpretation of the Qur'an.* Oxford: Clarendon Press

Cook M (2000) *The Koran: A very short introduction.* Oxford: Oxford University Press

Dammen McAuliffe J (Ed.) (2001) *Encyclopaedia of the Qu'ran.* Leiden: Brill

Déroche F (1985) *Les manuscrits du coran, du Maghrib à l'Insulinde.* Paris: Bibliothèque Nationale, Département Des Manuscrits, Catalogue Des Manuscrits Arabes

Déroche F (1994) O. Houdas et les écritures maghrébines. In A-C Binebine (Ed.) *Le manucrit arabe et la codicologie.* Rabat: Faculté des Lettres et des Sciences Humaines

Déroche F (1999) Tradition et innovation dans la pratique de l'écriture au Maghreb pendant les IVe/Xe siècles. In S Lancel (Ed.) *Afrique du Nord antique et médiévale: Numismatique, langues, écritures et arts du livre, spécificité des art figurés (Actes du VIIe colloque internationale sur l'histoire et l'archéologie de l'Afrique du Nord).* Paris: Editions du CTHS

Déroche F (2000) *Manuel de codicologie des manuscrits en écriture arabe.* Contributions by A Berthier, M-G Guesdon, B Guineau, F Fichard, A Vernay-Nouri, J Vezin & MI Waley. Paris: Bibliothèque Nationale de France

Déroche F (2004) *Le livre manuscrit arabe: Préludes à une historie.* Paris: Bibliothèque Nationale de France

Dodds JD (Ed.) (1992) *Al-Andalus: The art of Islamic Spain.* New York: Metropolitan Museum of Art

Fiske PL, Pickering WR & Yohe RS (Eds) (1980) *From the far west: Carpets and textiles of Morocco.* Washington DC: The Textile Museum

Gibb HAR et al. (Eds) (1960) *The encyclopaedia of Islam* (new edition). Leiden: Brill

Guesdon M-G & Vernay-Nouri A (Eds) (2001) *L'art du livre arabe: Du manuscrit au livre d'artiste.* Paris: Bibliothèque Nationale de France

Hofheinz A (2003) Goths in the lands of the blacks: a preliminary study of the Ka'ti Library in Timbuktu. In S Reese (Ed.) *The transmission of learning in Islamic Africa.* Leiden: Brill

Houdas O (1886) Essai sur l'écriture maghrébine. In *Nouveaux mélanges orientaux.* Paris: Ecole des langues orientales vivantes

Ibn Battuta (1993) *The travels of Ibn Baṭtuta.* Edited and translated by HAR Gibb, 1958–71. New Delhi: Munshiram Manoharlal

Ibn Khaldun (1967) *The Muqaddimah: An introduction to history.* Translated by F Rosenthal, 1958. New York: Bollingen Foundation

James D (1980) *Qur'ans and bindings from the Chester Beatty Library: A facsimile exhibition.* Exhibition catalogue. World of Islam Festival Trust

Khan G (1993) *Bills, letters and deeds: Arabic papyri of the 7th to 11th centuries.* Edited by J Raby. The Nasser D Khalili collection of Islamic Art. London: The Nour Foundation in association with Azimuth Editions and Oxford University Press

Kröger J (1991) Ein weit gereistes buch: Zu einer Neuerwerbung. *Museum Für Islamische Kunst: Berlin, Staatliche Museen Preussischer Kulturbesitz, Museums Journal* 5(1): 56–57

Lings M (1976) *The Quranic art of calligraphy and illumination.* London: World of Islam Festival Trust

Lings M & Safadi Y (1976) *The Qur'an.* London: World of Islam Publishing Company for the British Library

Petrosyan YA, Akimushkin OF, Khalidov AB & Rezvan EA (1995) *Pages of perfection: Islamic paintings and calligraphy from the Russian Academy of Sciences, St Petersburg.* Exhibition catalogue. Essays by ML Swietochowski & S Carboni. Lugano: ARCH Foundation/Electa

Pickering B, Pickering WR & Yohe RS (1994) *Moroccan carpets.* London/Chevy Chase: Hali Publications/Near Eastern Art Research Center

Porter V & Barakat HN (2004) *Mightier than the sword: Arabic script: Beauty and meaning.* Contributions by C Bresc. Kuala Lumpur: The Islamic Arts Museum Malaysia

Quaritch Catalogue (1995) *The Qur'an and calligraphy: A selection of fine manuscript material.* Bernard Quaritch Catalogue 1213. London: Bernard Quaritch

Safadi YH (1978) *Islamic calligraphy.* Boulder, CO: Shambala

Safwat NF (2000) *Golden pages: Qur'ans and other manuscripts from the collection of Ghassan I Shaker.* Oxford: Oxford University Press for Azimuth Editions

Sauvaget J (1949) Les épitaphes royales de Gao. *Al-Andalus* 14: 123–141

Turner J (Ed.) (1996) *The dictionary of art.* London: Macmillan Publishers

Valls i Subirà O (1978) *The history of paper in Spain (X–XIV centuries).* Madrid: Empresa Nacional de Celulosas SA

Walz T (1988) The paper trade of Egypt and the Sudan in the eighteenth and nineteenth centuries. In MW Daly (Ed.) *Modernization in the Sudan.* New York: Lilian Berber Press

Werner L (2003) Mauritania's manuscripts. *Saudi Aramco World* 54(6): 2–16

CHAPTER 6

Timbuktu and Walata: lineages and higher education

Timothy Cleaveland

On 25 November 1961, Kwame Nkrumah inaugurated the University of Ghana with a speech that drew upon the history of education in Africa and specifically cited the West African centres of Islamic scholarship, Timbuktu and Walata. Nkrumah praised Walata and Timbuktu for their contribution to medieval African education and singled out what he called the 'University of Sankore' in Timbuktu. He argued that 'if the University of Sankore had not been destroyed, if the University of Sankore as it was in 1591 had survived the ravages of foreign invasions, the academic and cultural history of Africa might have been different from what it is today'[1]. Nkrumah's statement referred to the scholars associated with the Sankore Mosque, and the plight of those scholars under the Maghribi (Moroccan) occupation of Timbuktu that began with the invasion of the Songhay Kingdom in 1591. In this speech Nkrumah seems to have used the word 'African' to mean sub-Saharan, as he did not refer to the al-Azhar school, founded in Cairo in the tenth century, as part of the history of African education, and he referred to the Moroccan expeditionary force as 'foreign invaders' even though they were also African, at least in the continental sense of the word. A few years later the Nigerian scholar JF Ade Ajayi contradicted Nkrumah in his introduction to a short biography of Samuel Ajayi Crowther (the first black Anglican bishop), writing that in 1827 Crowther was the 'first student to register at Fourah Bay College in Freetown, now the oldest institution of higher leaning in West Africa'.[2]

In this chapter I will argue that Ajayi was not quite correct, but neither was Nkrumah. Fourah Bay College was not the oldest institution of higher learning in West Africa. However, Nkrumah was also not quite right in suggesting that the Sankore Mosque and similar institutions in towns such as Timbuktu and Walata were African while al-Azhar was not. Nor do these West African institutions resemble the original meaning of the Latin word *universitas*, which means 'corporation'. The scholars of Timbuktu, like those in many other West African towns, did achieve a high level of Islamic scholarship by the sixteenth century, the point at which they began to produce their own scholarly

Opposite: Sankore Mosque, centre of higher learning in Timbuktu from the sixteenth to the eighteenth century.

The scholars of Timbuktu, like those in many other West African towns, did achieve a high level of Islamic scholarship by the sixteenth century, the point at which they began to produce their own scholarly literature. But these scholars did not acquire their skills in universities, according to the modern or the medieval European model. Instead, they acquired their knowledge through informal institutions that may have been in many ways distinctively West African, and were also clearly multi-ethnic and multiracial.

literature. But these scholars did not acquire their skills in universities, not according to the modern model, nor to the medieval European model. Instead, they acquired their knowledge through informal institutions that may have been in many ways distinctively West African, but were also clearly multi-ethnic and multiracial. It is not unreasonable that many people, from Nkrumah to Henry Louis Gates, have expressed their admiration for this scholarship by attributing it to a 'university' in Timbuktu. After all, Nkrumah was trying to inform a European or European-influenced audience, and attract international students to Ghana's new, modern university. And besides, there was no convenient English word or phrase to describe the informal institutions of West African Muslim scholarship. The problem with the term 'university' is that while it conveys status and achievement, it also obscures much that was distinctive and admirable about Muslim scholarship in towns like Timbuktu.

Now that nearly 40 years have passed since Nkrumah's speech, and institutions like the University of Ghana have uncovered so much more of the African past and rendered colonial versions of African history obsolete – now it is time to replace the flattering but misleading caricature of Muslim education in late medieval and early modern West Africa.

Many of the medieval European universities were similar to the earlier monastic schools, as they were created and controlled by the Catholic Church, and are sometimes called 'cathedral schools'. The University of Bologna, founded in 1088, was an exception as it was primarily secular. But even the curricula of the cathedral schools were generally secular, specialising in law and medicine. These early European 'universities' were called *universitas* because they started as small corporations of students or teachers. When the Church and the various states recognised these corporations, they regulated them and granted them privileges. The Church granted the privilege of teaching, which had previously been reserved, and the states granted the teachers and students exemptions from financial and military services.[3] By contrast, higher education in medieval and early modern West Africa was always explicitly religious, though religious scholars and teachers had never been subject to higher Islamic authority. There was never an Islamic counterpart of the Catholic Church. Nor did students and teachers in towns such as Timbuktu and Walata form corporations in the European sense. The state of Songhay, in the person of the ruler (*askiya*) and his governors, did confer gifts and privileges on important scholars in Timbuktu and elsewhere in the kingdom, but these were directed to individuals or families, not a corporation of teachers or students. And many towns, such as Walata, stood outside the borders of states for most of their history, and guarded their autonomy jealously.

I argue that although higher education in late medieval West Africa did not take place in corporations as such, there was a corporate aspect to production and reproduction of scholarship in the region. I will also argue that one should resist the temptation to describe the scholarly institutions in Timbuktu and Walata as 'black', as they clearly were multi-ethnic and multiracial, though they derived a substantial portion of their vitality from scholars of southern origin. The institutions of West African higher education were not mosques, but rather extended families or lineages. Elias Saad, in his excellent book *A Social History of Timbuktu*, described how these families maintained reputations for scholarship over centuries, and referred to them as patrician families. Saad was right to marvel at the long-term persistence of these families or coalitions of families, but in many respects they were highly dynamic despite their great longevity and continuity. Two of the most prominent families in the history of Timbuktu apparently had their origins in Walata, the Aqit family and the family known as the Banu al-Qadi al-Hajj. Elements of these families emigrated back and forth between Walata and Timbuktu several times over a period of about 300 years. In the 1700s those that had moved back to Walata seem to have disappeared. But I argue that their disappearance is explained by the formation of a political coalition that included these families and various Walati families, the most prominent of which were the families of Baba Masir Biru and 'Ali Sila – two families who bore apparently Soninké or Mande names. These and other families coalesced into a group that became known as the Lemhajib, and after a few generations of intermarriage within the group they effectively became a great extended family.

Walata and Timbuktu

The towns of Timbuktu and Walata almost certainly began as small black settlements, Songhay or Sorko in the case of Timbuktu and Mande in the case of Walata. However, by the thirteenth or fourteenth century AD both towns were multi-ethnic, multiracial centres of commerce and Islamic scholarship.

Many of the early scholars of both towns were of sub-Saharan origin, although the evidence for this is much stronger for Timbuktu than it is for Walata. That is because although Timbuktu is not nearly as old as Walata, it developed a lively literary production before Walata. However, as time passed, fewer and fewer scholarly families in both towns claimed a West African ethnic identity, and some that did nevertheless also claimed to be patrilineally Arab and therefore Bidan (white). By 1800 there were no scholarly families left in Walata that claimed anything other than an Arab identity, and the only people who considered themselves to be Sudan (black) were marginalised people whom the elite 'Arabs' defined as slaves or people of slave origin. In Timbuktu the situation was similar but not nearly so stark.

Over the course of the last millennium Walata has been dominated by three successive cultural groups. Accordingly, it has been known by three different names: Biru, Iwalatan, and Walata, each name marking a period of a particular cultural dominance in the town. In its earliest period the town was known by the Mande name 'Biru' and was located on the periphery of the Ghana Empire. Later it was drawn into the Mali and then the Songhay Empires, and began also to be known by the Berber name 'Iwalatan'. By the end of the Songhay period in the late sixteenth century, the town began to be referred to as 'Walata', the Arabised form of 'Iwalatan'. 'Biru' is the plural form of the Mande word *bire* meaning 'a roof made of straw supported by wooden sticks', which suggests a market.[4] Similarly, the Malinke word *wala* means 'shady spot'. The name 'Iwalatan' is the Berber form of this word, and 'Walata' is the Arabised version.[5] This and other evidence suggest that the original inhabitants of the town that later became known as Walata were Mande agriculturists.[6]

Walata was built on a slope descending from an escarpment varying in height from about 60 to 80 feet above the valley. The oldest sections are the highest on the escarpment's slope, quite near the edge. As the town grew, it expanded down the slope.[7] New houses and groups of houses were grafted onto the town so as to preserve its enclosed outer wall, for defensive purposes. Today the general division of the town into upper (*vogani*) and lower (*tahtani*) sections is a part of everyday life. For example, a woman from the upper part of town might refer to a friend from the lower part as her *tahtaniyya* friend.[8] The upper and lower sections of town also reflect the town's cultural history in their place names. Upper sections of the town still bear place names from a non-Arabic language that my informants described as 'Azayr', such as Gidinu, Karavolé, Kamrankani, Gumbusinya and Dnayda. Lower sections of town tend to bear Arabic place names, such as Rahba Lahbib, Luqmayd, Rahba Il-bir Buya, Rahba Libel and Rahba Lemlid.[9] Walata is a labyrinth of narrow streets and small, closed-in spaces, and in this respect it is a highly urban environment (similar to Timbuktu).

Timbuktu grew rapidly in the thirteenth or fourteenth century and eventually replaced Walata as the premier trading town in the southern Sahara, drawing away many of its traders and scholars.[10] Despite this shift in trade, Walata survived and even served as a haven for scholarly families of Timbuktu that opposed the expansion of the Songhay Empire in 1465 and the invasion of a Maghribi expeditionary force in 1591. While most of the families fleeing Timbuktu bore Berber or Mande names, some may have been Songhay, or at least culturally Songhay. Leo Africanus, writing from the Mediterranean in the sixteenth century, asserted that Songhay was spoken at Walata.[11] Both floods of refugees temporarily revitalised Walata, and the refugees of 1591 probably helped Walata to start its own literary production. Azayr, a mixture of Mande and Berber, was an important language in Walata at the end of the sixteenth century, despite emigration from Timbuktu and the growing presence of Arabic speakers in the southern desert. But the emigration of nomadic Arabs and later sedentarised Arabs from northern Saharan oases began to transform Walata's Mande/Berber culture.[12] By the early seventeenth century individuals and families from the locally dominant Hassani groups began to sedentarise in Walata and by the mid-seventeenth century Timbuktu historians began to refer to the town as Walata, the Arabised form of Iwalatan. Yet, of the three names, Biru was still the most widely used. [13]

Walata's relative importance as a centre of trade within Takrur was apparently eclipsed by the growth of Timbuktu in the fourteenth or fifteenth century. Al-Sa'di, writing from Timbuktu in 1655, provided information about Walata in the context of Songhay history. He described the decline of Biru and the rise of Timbuktu and made strong statements about the cultural heritage of both. He asserted that Timbuktu and Biru drew their culture almost exclusively from north-west Africa. This assessment closely resembles al-Bakri's description of Awdaghust. Al-Sa'di wrote:

> The commercial center [of the region] used to be Biru. There flowed caravans from every land, and great scholars, and pious persons. Wealthy people from every race and every country settled there, including people from Egypt; Aujela Fezzan; Ghadanies; Tuwat; Dra'; Tafilalt; Fez; the Sus; Bitu; and others. All of that was transferred to Timbuktu little by little until they were concentrated at Timbuktu. Additionally, all the tribes of the Sanbaja rejoined their elements [which had moved to Timbuktu]. The prosperity of Timbuktu was the ruin of Biru. Its [Timbuktu's] civilization came to it exclusively from the Maghrib, in matters of religion as well as trade. In the beginning, homes of the [indigenous] residents consisted of enclosures of sticks and straw, then they were replaced by small houses of clay.[14]

Timbuktu grew rapidly in the thirteenth or fourteenth century and eventually replaced Walata as the premier trading town in the southern Sahara drawing away many of its traders and scholars. Despite this shift in trade, Walata survived and even served as a haven for scholarly families of Timbuktu that opposed the expansion of the Songhay Empire in 1465 and the invasion of a Maghribi expeditionary force in 1591.

Although al-Sa'di asserted that the most prominent citizens of Biru/Walata were originally from North Africa, and that Timbuktu derived its civilisation from the Maghrib, other sources, and even al-Sa'di's own work, suggest that this was an exaggeration.[15] Among the origins of Biru's immigrants, al-Sa'di mentioned only one place south of the Sahara, Bitu.[16] Nor did he mention in this passage the local and sub-Saharan scholars of Biru. But this characterisation of Biru and Timbuktu is contradicted by al-Sa'di's own detailed account of Songhay history. It is true that Islam spread from North Africa to Biru and Timbuktu, and most of the early development of Maliki law, the dominant school of Islamic law in West Africa, took place in north-west Africa. But al-Sa'di and other West African scholars recorded the development of West African scholarship, which included many important sub-Saharan scholars. One of the earliest scholars in Timbuktu was Muhammad al-Kabari, who came from a town in the Niger flood plain near Dia. Additionally, the regional trade towns supported several large families that enjoyed a scholarly reputation, among them the Gidadu, Gurdu and Baghayogho.[17]

Al-Sa'di also stated that the transfer of citizens and commerce from Biru to Timbuktu began in earnest at the end of the ninth century of the *hijra* (*c*.AD 1490) and was fairly complete by the middle of the tenth century (*c*.AD 1540).[18] The testimony of Leo Africanus, who wrote in the early sixteenth century, corroborates al-Sa'di:

> When the people of Libya dominated the region [of Walata] they established the seat of their royal government there, and in consequence many Barbaric merchants used to come there. But since the reign of Sonni 'Ali, who was a powerful man, the merchants have gradually abandoned Gualata [Walata] and gone to Tombutto [Timbuktu] and Gago [Gao], hence the chief of Gualata has become poor and powerless. The people of this country speak a language called Songai. These men are

Timbuktu's reliance on trade meant that it was constantly attracting emigrants and, at the same time, generating its own diaspora, as sons left town to extend their families' trade network. This economic dynamism, along with regional political instability, probably created many periods of decline and growth over the years.

> extremely poor and base, but very friendly, especially with foreigners. The chief who governs them pays tribute to the king of Tombutto because he came once into the land [of Walata] with his army. The chief of Gualata fled into the desert, where his kinsmen lived. The king of Tombutto realized that he could not occupy the territory because the chief, aided by his desert kinsmen, caused him a lot of problems, therefore he made an agreement with him which established the payment of a fixed tribute. The chief returned to Gualata and the king returned to Tombutto.[19]

There were no doubt many factors in the fifteenth-century rise of Timbuktu and decline of Biru, but despite the corroborating accounts of Leo Africanus and al-Sa'di it seems that they exaggerated the transfer of commerce and citizens to Timbuktu and the 'ruin' of Biru. Certainly many prominent families emigrated to Timbuktu during this period, but Biru survived. Indeed, because of the town's reliance on trade it was constantly attracting emigrants and at the same time generating its own diaspora, as sons left town to extend their families' trade network. This economic dynamism, along with regional political instability, probably created many periods of decline and growth over the last 800 years. The scholarly families of Timbuktu had come from various towns throughout the region in the fourteenth and fifteenth centuries. Among the many Biru families that moved to Timbuktu during the fifteenth century was that of a scholar known as al-Hajj who became *qadi* and who came to Timbuktu in about 1430. Both he and his brother had moved to Timbuktu from Biru. Several of al-Hajj's descendants were prominent Timbuktu judges and scholars.[20]

Emigration did not always flow from Biru to Timbuktu. Scholars living in Timbuktu fled in numbers to Biru (or Walata) on at least two occasions. The first came in 1468 soon after Sonni 'Ali took power in Timbuktu and came into conflict with several groups, including the scholars. According to the account provided by al-Sa'di, prominent members of two scholarly families fled from Timbuktu to Biru at this time. These were the families of Muhammad Aqit and Andag Muhammad, which were connected by marriage ties. The scholar 'Umar b. Muhammad Aqit left with three sons, all of whom became scholars. Two years after this first episode another group of scholarly families abandoned Timbuktu for Biru, but many of these people were tracked down and killed by Sonni 'Ali's army before they could reach Biru.[21]

The second occasion came in 1591 when the Songhay Kingdom was invaded by the Maghribi expeditionary force. The scholars who fled to Biru after the Maghribi invasion were particularly important and their presence is recalled in biographical dictionaries and chronicles produced in the nineteenth century. Most of the scholarly families that emigrated from Timbuktu to Biru probably did not consider themselves to be Songhay, but they undoubtedly took Songhay culture with them. The emigrant families whose names are known seem by their names to be Berber and Mande. Prominent among them was 'Ali Sila, whose ancestors had migrated from Biru to Timbuktu in the fifteenth century. 'Ali Sila became a prominent judge in Walata and a close associate of the local leader 'Umar al-Wali al-Mahjub, one of the Lemhajib. The evidence suggests that the Sila family, as well as the Misir family to which 'Ali Sila was related through maternal kin, were Soninké.[22]

The arrival of Timbuktu scholars in Walata in 1468 and 1591 and the corresponding improvements in trade due to political problems in Timbuktu helped bring Biru (Walata) into its period of full literary production, and sped its transformation into Walata. The earliest known documents from Walata date to the first quarter of the seventeenth century. The scholar who produced the oldest surviving Walati documents was Anda 'Abd Allah (d.1628), the nephew of 'Abd Allah al-Mahjub, the eponymous ancestor of the Lemhajib. Further, the two known chronicles of Walati history begin their accounts with the events of the Moroccan invasion. Indeed, Ahmad Baba's biographical dictionary, *Nayl al-ibtihaj*, completed in 1596, did not list a single scholar identifiable as a Walati. Ahmad Baba gave none of the scholars in his study a Walati *nisba*, although he gave one a Tizakhti *nisba*. Neither did any of the scholars have a Biri *nisba* or the *nisba* of an identifiable Biru/Walata family.[23]

Muhammad al-Timbukti al-Daysafi and the Lemhajib

One of the most important sources on the origins of the Lemhajib is a mysterious poem that was probably written in about 1800. According to al-Daysafi's poem, the Lemhajib consisted of at least three families or patrilineages among which was divided the inherited offices of *qadi* and *imam*. The first was the Bani (or Banu) al-Faqih 'Uthman; the second was identified only as the family of the *qadi* 'Ali b. 'Abd Allah; and the third family, from which the *imam* was chosen, was not identified at all. However, a preface, which was not written by al-Daysafi and may be much more recent, supplements the information presented in the poem. The preface translated below identifies the family of imams with the lineage of Andag Muhammad al-Kabir, who was a famous late sixteenth-century refugee from Timbuktu. It also adds the name 'Muhammad' to the lineage of 'Ali b. 'Abd Allah. Other versions of the preface, which are not translated below, describe the lineage of 'Ali b. 'Abd Allah as the Awlad Nda 'Ali, which is a name found in other accounts of the Lemhajib's origins.[24]

> In the name of God, the Merciful and Beneficent, the desire of their lords. Peace be on the noble Prophet and on his family and his companions. And from the best of what is said in praise, Muhammad b. Muslim al-Daysafi al-Imyari discussed the merit of Bani [the families of] al-Faqih 'Uthman b. Muhammad al-Ghayth b. Muhammad al-Fath b. Yahya al-Kamil, and the family of the *qadi* Muhammad b. 'Ali b. 'Abd Allah, and the family of the *imam* Andag Muhammad al-Kabir the Mahjubi *imam*, who came to them visiting from Timbuktu, may God bless us through them and their progeny. Amen.

> If you are wandering in the countryside
> desiring the abode of some of the renowned righteous [folk],

Go to Faqih [the scholar] 'Uthman the regenerator and his sons,
most distinguished and noble ancestor of the Fihr.[25]
They are the best forbears [in terms of their] customs,
ancient and good origins in the most civilized societies.
Muhammad al-Ghayth son of the Pole of his time,
Muhammad al-Fath the leader in affairs.
Muhammad al-Ghayth, whose generosity used to take the place of rain
in times of hardship.
And his noble father al-Fath Muhammad,
with whom was victory over difficulties throughout all times.
And he was the son of Yahya al-Kamil, who was wholly good.
And he is the son of the progeny of the Khalifas and scholars.
And from the progeny of him whom Quraysh held in awe
and devoted themselves to in private and public [the Prophet Muhammad].
Shuayb b. Idris b. Musa b. Ja'far, worthy of being traced back
to the best sons of Nadir.
Husayn, son of the daughter of al-Mustafa [the Prophet] and his nephew ['Ali].
What a splendid fallen one [martyr] of lofty glory and rank.
And Yahya, through whom God revived his town [religiously].
When it was sunk deep in Mazdaism and disbelief
Its people became loyal to God and his religion,
as did everyone who was in the walled town.
And he was for them an invulnerable fortress and a place of refuge.
And for them he was like the stars and the sun and the full moon.

And do not forget the *qadi* of the walled town, the ancestor of its Qadis,
'Ali b. 'Abd Allah. What a splendid honored brother,
He was noble and descended from a noble and illustrious people,
companion of the friend of God, our lord Khadir.
He was of the progeny of the son of Khawla, Muhammad,
who was famous for his gentleness and mildness,
Descendant of the nephew of the Prophet and his executor 'Ali,
father of the two grandsons, possessors of knowledge and diffusion.

And their leader, who led the group in virtue, just as he led them in purity of origin.
Imam selected from among the pure *imams*, the *imams* selected [?] him [?] greatly.[26]
Indeed the Chosen [the Prophet] was the most just judge of their ancestors,
the first among the Arabs.
Sa'id son of the offspring of al-['As], the best of his companions,
may God's peace be on him to the end of time.[27]

And from all of them came powerful men, just as they are the source
of power and victory.

And they became a tribe [Qabila] and intermarried,
such that all of them were rooted in the glory of Fihr.[28]
They were in greatness unequaled by anyone in terms of
goodness, character, and glory.
Indeed, they are also from the best of ʻAdnan [still] existing,
and from close kinship from those who possess goodness.
Among them are those who ascend the pulpit, and among them
there are judges in the government who are vigilant.
And among them are *qadis* who are just, and among them
leaders in the science (*fiqh*) in verse and prose.
And they taught the people leadership and piety,
and before the paths were rough.
They assumed the name 'Lemhajib' as a group,
and the scholar is the one concealed (*mahjub*) and learning is what is prominent.[29]
Men of energy, white, possessed of splendor,
conquerors, successors to all the righteous men worthy of mention.[30]
And even if I made up my mind to count their virtues,
I would tire of counting and enumerating.
Greetings on them from Noble God, and from them and on them
the best of them for all times.
And then on al-Mukhtar [the Chosen] a more fitting greeting,
with the family and his noble companions, possessors of gratitude.

The most significant aspect of this poem is the way it conceptualises the formation of the Lemhajib 'tribe' or alliance as forged from three different clans or sets of families. But before dealing with the conceptual aspects of the poem, the more material details need to be examined. Information about the Lemhajib drawn from al-Bartayli's biographical dictionary and the Walati chronicles provide some solid clues as to the identities of the three sets of families described in al-Daysafi's poem and the preface. The identification of the Faqih ʻUthman and ʻAli b. ʻAbd Allah is an important element in the analysis of al-Daysafi's poem, because the families or lineages that derived their identities from them, the Bani al-Faqih ʻUthman and the Awlad Nda ʻAli, clearly predated the formation of the Lemhajib. Similarly important, but somewhat easier, is the identification of Andag Muhammad al-Kabir, who is described as the ancestor of the family of the *imams* in the preface of al-Daysafi's poem, though not in the poem itself. Andag Muhammad al-Kabir (the Elder) was the *qadi* of Timbuktu in the mid-fifteenth century, and several of his descendants took refuge in Walata from the oppression of Sonni ʻAli in 1468, and it is quite likely that some did again after the Moroccan expedition's conquest of Timbuktu in 1591. The Faqih ʻUthman described in the poem seems to refer to a distant ancestor of the families that later formed the Lemhajib, though this cannot be clearly determined from the poem or any available pre-twentieth-century evidence. Faqih ʻUthman was the grandson of Yahya al-Kamil, the earliest ancestor listed in the Mahjubi biographies of the *Fath al-shakur*, but because families often named children after recent ancestors, there were later 'Faqih 'Uthmans among the Lemhajib.[31] However, subsequent evidence, which the next section describes, suggests that the Faqih 'Uthman in al-Daysafi's poem referred to the distant ancestor. Finally, it is impossible to identify 'Ali b. 'Abd Allah from the evidence presented so far, as the two names were very common and no previous source mentions a clan or lineage called the Awlad Nda 'Ali.[32]

Evidence from the various Walati sources regarding the Lemhajib is only sufficient to suggest a very general period for the composition of al-Daysafi's poem. On first examination it seems that the poem was written no later than the middle of the seventeenth century, because the families he identified as controlling the offices of *qadi* and *imam* lost those offices to the families who descended from Faqih 'Uthman in about 1650 or shortly thereafter.[33] But such a date is at variance with the evidence from the *Tarikh al-Takrur* and the *Fath al-shakur*, which suggests that the descendants of 'Abd Allah al-Mahjub had only produced a few families by 1650, and that the Mahjubi *nisba* probably did not begin to represent a politically significant corporate identity until the late seventeenth or early eighteenth century. What is more, the poem marginalises the families it describes as controlling the offices of the *qadi* and *imam* much more than one would expect if those families still controlled those offices. No member of the family of the *imam* is even named in the poem. The preface corrects this deficiency, but cannot compensate for the fact that most of the poem is devoted to the families claiming descent from Faqih 'Uthman. All these factors suggest that the poem was actually written after the control of the offices of *qadi* and *imam* had passed to the families of the Bani al-Faqih 'Uthman. The timing of the poem's composition is significant because it is suggestive of its function. If the poem was produced substantially after the formation of the Mahjubi alliance (as it purports), then it would have served as a rationalisation and a reinforcement of a political process, but if it was written during the process it would constitute a mechanism for social and political change.

In addition to the strong evidence that al-Daysafi's poem was not written before 1650, there are good reasons to suspect that it was written after 1700. The whole body of written evidence from Walata and the region strongly suggests that the Lemhajib did not become an important corporate identity before 1700. The earliest evidence for this assertion comes from the regional literature produced in the seventeenth century. Ahmad Baba's biographical dictionary *Nayl al-ibtihaj*, which he completed in 1596, did not include a single scholar identified by the Mahjubi *nisba* among its 830 biographies. Nor was the *nisba* mentioned in any of the three main chronicles produced in Timbuktu: al-Sa'di's *Tarikh al-Sudan* (c.1655), al-Ka'ti's *Tarikh al-fattash* (c.1665), and the anonymous *Tadhkirat al-nisiyan* (c.1751). Early nineteenth-century sources describing the descendants of 'Abd Allah al-Mahjub also suggest that the Lemhajib was in the early stage of formation in 1650. While no source provides dates for the life or death of al-Mahjub or any of his sons or grandsons, the *Fath al-shakur* includes a short biography of one of his great-grandsons, and reports that he died in 1689–90. The *Tarikh Bilad al-Takrur* and the *Fath al-shakur* both provide information on the careers and deaths of several of al-Mahjub's great-great-grandsons, whom they describe as dying between 1710 and 1758, though most died around 1725. If each generation was divided by about 25 to 30 years, then al-Mahjub would have died some time between 1600 and 1625. The formation of the Lemhajib no doubt began as a small clan during the lives of his grandsons and began to grow into a larger, more diverse alliance a generation or two later, perhaps around 1700.

In 1641 the *qadi* of Walata, Sidi Muhammad b. Muhammad b. 'Ali Sila, died and was eventually replaced by Ahmad al-Wali, a descendant of Faqih 'Uthman and al-Mahjub. Sidi Muhammad was the last *qadi* from a group of families that had previously dominated the qadiship, and Ahmad al-Wali was the first *imam* and *qadi* from among the Lemhajib. When Ahmad al-Wali died in 1683 he was replaced by 'Abd Allah b. Abu Bakr, a paternal cousin. At this point the Sidi Ahmad branch of the Bani al-Faqih 'Uthman seems to have been subordinate to the descendants of al-Mahjub, who controlled the offices of *qadi* and *imam*. After the death of 'Abd Allah b. Abu Bakr, the qadiship and imamship was split between two men, though both were descendants of al-Mahjub. But when this third Mahjubi *imam* died in 1715, the office of *imam* passed to a descendant of the Sidi Ahmad branch for the first time, and there it stayed for the next 150 years. The office of *qadi* remained under the control of the descendants of al-Mahjub, and thus the two branches of the Bani al-Faqih 'Uthman shared power on a more or less equal basis. It is unlikely that the Sidi Ahmad branch became assimilated into the broader Mahjubi identity before this power-sharing arrangement had become institutionalised.[34] When the first *imam* from the Sidi Ahmad branch died in 1732 he was replaced by a paternal cousin, so at this point the arrangement between the two branches of the Bani al-Faqih 'Uthman was becoming secure.[35]

Talib Bubakar's last statement on Mahjubi identity

The *Minah* was Talib Bubakar's final statement about Walata and its history, which he completed around 1915. Talib Bubakar devoted a special section of the *Minah* to the Lemhajib and their origins, though he did not provide an actual account of Yahya al-Kamil's arrival at Biru/Walata or any information about the early history of the town. In this section he presented al-Daysafi's poem, but did not endorse its principal message: that the Lemhajib were actually three separate patrilineages that unified through intermarriage, and that the primary lineage (of Faqih 'Uthman) was descended from the Prophet Muhammad through Fatima. Neither did Talib Bubakar assert directly that al-Daysafi was wrong. Instead, he stated that the Lemhajib was a patrilineage descended from Yahya al-Kamil, and that though there were several theories about his origins, no one knew for sure, except God. This, Talib Bubakar explained, was because Yahya al-Kamil successfully hid his origins, apparently even from his own family.[36] However, by presenting the claim without endorsing it, Talib Bubakar effectively supported the claim without technically doing so, although he also mentioned the Kunta story of 'Uqba ibn Nafi'. Talib Bubakar did provide information about the origins of the woman who married Yahya al-Kamil's son, Muhammad, and gave birth to the lineage of al-Faqih 'Uthman. Likewise, he also provided information about the mother of al-Mahjub and Sidi Ahmad, the two sons who actually started the expansion of the lineage. Talib Bubakar wrote:

> Al-Mahjub and Sidi Ahmad were full brothers (*shaqiqan*), and they are the ones from whom branched the Lemhajib. Their mother was the daughter of Baba Misir Biru, of the progeny of the *Wali Allah* [friend of God], Anda 'Ali, the ancestor of the 'Ali al-Qadi [family of the *qadi*] of the progeny of Muhammad b. al-Hanifiyya, son of our master 'Ali ibn Abi Talib. May God be pleased with him. Al-Mahjub and Sidi Ahmad were the sons of Muhammad al-Ghayth b. Muhammad al-Fath b. 'Abd Allah al-Qutb b. Muhammad al-Faqih b. al-Faqih b. al-Faqih 'Uthman b. Muhammad b. Yahya al-Kamil. Our great ancestor is the one who came to Walata with his son Muhammad in the fifth century. Then his son Muhammad married the daughter of the friend of God almighty, Anda 'Ali, the family of the *qadi*, which has completely vanished away. They are the progeny of Muhammad b. al-Hanifiyya, son of our master 'Ali b. Abi Talib. May God be pleased with him. She [the daughter of Anda 'Ali] gave birth to al-Faqih 'Uthman and Anda 'Ali is his ancestor by his mother. And Muhammad al-Ghayth is the father of al-Mahjub and Sidi Ahmad, and their mother is the daughter of Baba Misir Biru of the progeny of Anda 'Ali also. As for our great ancestor Yahya al-Kamil, he never mentioned his *nasab* [origins]...Our great ancestor Yahya al-Kamil was a contemporary of Shaykh 'Abd al-Qadir al-Jilani the Sharif, and I think there was some relationship between them, but I do not know what it was.[37]

This passage reveals that Talib Bubakar was well informed about the Lemhajib's matrifilial kinship with some very old and powerful Walati families. It was important for him to show the Lemhajib's matrilineal connection to Baba Misir Biru and Anda 'Ali because they belonged to Walata's 'Ali al-Qadi, the family of the *qadi*. Several sources suggest that it was from this group of families that the Lemhajib obtained the qadiship, though they provide relatively little information about the 'Ali al-Qadi. One apparent member was a Walati scholar named Muhammad b. Muhammad b. 'Ali Sila, whose ancestors lived in Biru/Walata, then migrated to Timbuktu in the fifteenth century, and finally returned to Walata in the seventeenth century. Muhammad, the grandson of 'Ali Sila, was the earliest recorded *qadi* of Walata, and died in 1640. The *Fath al-shakur* describes 'Ali Sila as a close associate of 'Umar al-Wali al-Mahjubi, who was the grandson of 'Abd Allah al-Mahjub. 'Ali Sila was part of the family of 'Ali b. 'Abd Allah (or Anda 'Ali), which al-Daysafi and Talib Bubakar described as dominating the office of *qadi*.[38] It seems that Sidi Ahmad al-Wali (d.1683–84) became the first *imam* and *qadi* of the lineage of Bani al-Faqih 'Uthman immediately after the death of Qadi Muhammad b. Muhammad b. 'Ali Sila, or possibly after the death of Muhammad's son Atiq some time after 1667. Given the emphasis that al-Daysafi and Talib Bubakar placed on intermarriage, it seems likely that Muhammad b. Muhammad b. 'Ali Sila was Sidi Ahmad al-Wali's maternal grandfather, or perhaps his maternal uncle.

The connection between the lineages of Anda 'Ali and al-Faqih 'Uthman is particularly historic because the Anda 'Ali appear to have been Soninké. Elias Saad, a modern historian, has argued that both Baba Misir Biru and 'Ali Sila were Soninké, or at least descended from Soninké families. His assertion is supported by the *Tarikh Walata-I*, which described the Walati scholar Sidi Muhammad b. al-Hajj Sila (d.1727–28) as Sudani or black. Similarly, the *Tarikh al-Sudan* described the Songhay dynasty of Askiya Muhammad as 'Silanké'.[39] Talib Bubakar's claim that the Anda 'Ali were descended from the Prophet's cousin does not preclude them from being culturally Soninké.

It is not clear when the unification of the families of Anda 'Ali and al-Faqih 'Uthman took place, but it is likely that the Anda 'Ali retained their separate identity for some time after their political and social assimilation. Nevertheless, by the time Talib Bubakar wrote the *Minah*, the Walati descendants of 'Ali Sila, Anda 'Ali, and Andag Muhammad and the other families that became Mahjubi were no longer socially identifiable, as they had been completely absorbed or assimilated into the Lemhajib. The assimilation of the lineage of 'Ali Sila into the Lemhajib is particularly significant because the families of Baba Misir Biru and 'Ali Sila were Soninké, or were of Soninké origin. The assimilation and disappearance of these families provides an explanation for the apparent disappearance of the original Mande inhabitants of Biru/Walata. They were absorbed, through intermarriage, into the town's dominant 'Arab' social groups.

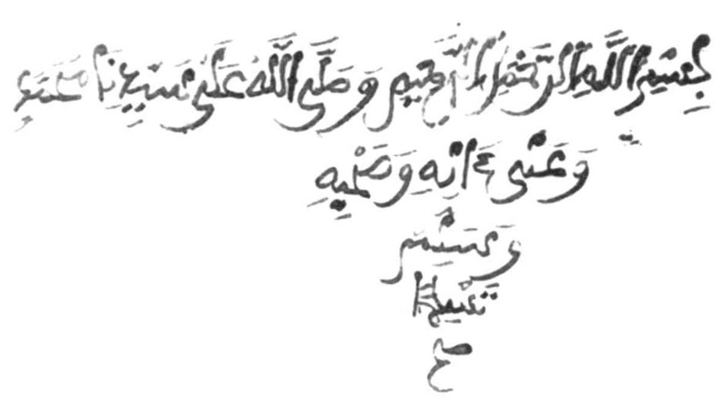
بسم الله الرحمن الرحيم وصلى الله على سيدنا محمد
وعلى آله وصحبه
وسلم
تسليما
صح

NOTES

1 Nkrumah (1967: 7–88).

2 Ajayi (1967: 290).

3 See for example the websites http://www.csupomona.edu/~plin/ls201/medieval_curriculum.html and http://www.answers.com/topic/medieval-university.

4 Bathily (1975: 16). See also Hunwick (1985: 15) and Meunié (1961: 72).

5 Trimingham (1975: 58) and Bathily (1975: 16). Bathily hypothesised that the name 'Biru' was 'indicative of the provisional character of the settlement there'. Even if this were true, it would not necessarily imply that the settlement still retained this 'provisional' character at the time of the arrival of the Masufa. In late sixteenth-century Songhay the Mande name seems to have been more commonly used than the Arabised Berber name. See also al-Sa'di (1964). His work contains 17 uses of the name 'Biru', but only 7 uses of 'Walata' and 'Iwalatan' combined.

6 Trimingham (1975: 58) and Lucas (1931: 154–160). Lucas collected oral accounts of the arrival of the 'Maures' in the Adrar. Most of the 'Maures' he interviewed in 1931 believed that their ancestors met and conquered an Azayr-speaking Sarakolé people when they moved into the Adrar and Tagant. Generally, the Bidan consider the Sarakolé to be the ancestors of the people whom they now most often refer to as the 'Suwanik'. Some of the Bidan that Colonel Modat interviewed in 1919 reported that a people called the Bafur had settled in the Adrar before or at the same time as the proto-Mande (Modat 1919: 378).

7 Interview with Neh Wuld 'Abd al-Rahman. Research notes available from author (page 91).

8 Certain crafts are associated with Haratin, such as basket and mat making, whereas Bidani women more often sew and make pottery.

9 Interview, several Lemhajib. Research notes available from author (pages 128, 131).

10 Ibn Khaldun (1981: 339). Ibn Khaldun stated that Arabs, apparently the Hassan, 'molested caravans between Tuwat and Walatan [*sic*]'. See also Levtzion (1994: 159).

11 Africanus (1956: 463–464).

12 In the mid-nineteenth century, Heinrich Barth stated that Azayr was spoken at Walata, though he did not visit there. See Barth (1965: 696).

13 Al-Sa'di (1964). Compare index entries for Biru and Walata.

14 Al-Sa'di (1964: 21; trans. 36–37).

15 Elias Saad (1983: 32–33), a modem historian of Timbuktu, suggested that al-Sa'di did not intend the name 'Maghrib', as it appears in this passage, to refer to north-west Africa, but rather to the lands *west* of Timbuktu, that is, Biru, Kumbi and Tishit. However, the context of al-Sa'di's statement does not support this interpretation. After all, al-Sa'di's statement on Timbuktu immediately followed his assertion that the most prominent citizens of Biru/Walata were originally from North Africa. According to the *Tarikh Tishit*, the town was established in 1153. See Monteil (1939: 284).

16 Wilks (1982).

17 Saad (1983: 7, 243–246).

18 Saad (1983: 22).

19 Africanus (1956: 463–464).

20 Africanus (1956: 27–28).

21 Al-Sa'di (1964: 65–67; trans. 105–108).

22 Saad (1983: 130, 278). This is particularly significant for the history of the Lemhajib, who dominated Walata in the nineteenth century. The pre-eminent Mahjubi scholar linked the earliest remembered Mahjubi patriarch to Baba Misir Biru through marriage to his daughter. The family name of 'Ali Sila may have also been pronounced by some as 'Sili'.

23 Baba (1989: 587).

24 See the preface of the more recent copy of al-Daysafi's poem from the library of Bati Wuld Baba, which is translated from Arabic to Spanish in Corral (2000: 225–226).

25 Ancestors of Quraysh, the eponymous ancestor of the Prophet's tribe or tribal confederation.

26 The translation of this line is very much in doubt.

27 This refers to Amr b. al-'As, the conqueror of Egypt.

28 Fihr was supposed to be the ancestor of the Quraysh, the 'tribe' of the Prophet Muhammad and 'Uqba ibn Nafi'.

29 This is a clever play on words (al-'alim al-Mahjub [the hidden knower] of 'ilm al-badr).

30 The use of the word 'white' here probably is intended to symbolise purity or nobility.

31 There was a later Mahjubi scholar named Faqih 'Uthman, who died in 1715–16 and was the son of 'Umar al-Wali b. Shaykh Muhammad 'Abd Allah. Faqih 'Uthman b. 'Umar al-Wali was a prominent patriarch of the Awlad al-Faqih 'Uthman. Al-Bartayli introduced 'Uthman as 'Sidi' in his biography, but he also called him a '*faqih*'. His biography is one of the longest in the *Fath al-shakur*, and al-Bartayli praised his scholarship and his ability to intimidate bandits and those who

would impose tribute on Walata. 'Uthman's father, 'Umar al-Wali, received a similarly laudatory notice, and today the Lemhajib visit his tomb more than any other ancestor. See al-Bartayli (1981: 191–195).

32 Even though there is a man named 'Ali b. 'Abd Allah in the Sidi Ahmad branch of what became the Mahjubi lineage, this is apparently only coincidence. There is no evidence that anyone from the Sidi Ahmad branch was ever *qadi*, the office that the Awlad Nda 'Ali is supposed to have dominated, and later evidence suggests that the 'Ali b. 'Abd Allah that al-Daysafi named did not belong to the lineage descending from Yahya al-Kamil.

33 Al-Bartayli mentioned that Sidi Ahmad al-Wali al-Mahjubi (d.1683–84) was the first member of Faqih 'Uthman's family to hold the office of *imam*. This suggests that al-Daysafi wrote his poem before 1680 because he attributed the office of *imam* to the family that the preface identifies as the descendants of Andag Muhammad (al-Bartayli 1981: 41–42).

34 The evidence for this argument is drawn primarily from the *Tarikh Walata-I* and the *Fath al-shakur*, especially al-Bartayli's biographies numbered 23, 55, 160 and 163. For 'Abd Allah al-Mahjub's great-grandson, Talib Bubakar b. 'Ali b. al-Shaykh b. al-Mahjub, see al-Bartayli (1981: bio. 55).

35 See the death notices for Imam Ahmad b. Bubakar (d.1732) and Imam Sidi 'Uthman b. 'Abd Allah (d.1744) in the *Tarikh Walata-I*, 562, 564.

36 Al-Mahjubi, *Minah*, f.270–278, Ms 699, Ahmed Baba Institute, Timbuktu.

37 Al-Mahjubi, *Minah*, f.275–276, Ms 699, Ahmed Baba Institute, Timbuktu.

38 For the biography of Muhammad b. Muhammad b. 'Ali Sila and his ancestor, see al-Bartayli (1981: 114, 197). 'Umar al-Wali al-Mahjubi was also the father of Faqih 'Uthman (d.1715), who was named for the eponymous ancestor of the Bani al-Faqih 'Uthman (al-Bartayli 1981: 41, 191). For a brief discussion of these relationships see Saad (1983: 130, and footnote 23 on 282).

39 'Ali Sila (or Sili) was the son of Baba Misir Biru's daughter. For his biography see al-Bartayli (1981: 197). For the race of Muhammad b. al-Hajj Sila see *Tarikh Walata-I*, 560. See the analysis of Saad (1983: 110, and fn. 93 & 94 on 278). For the Sila or Silanké origins of Askiya Dawud, see Hunwick (1999: 102, 112).

REFERENCES

Africanus L (Jean-Leon l'Africain) (1956) *Description de l'Afrique*. Translated by A Epaulard. Paris: Adrien Maisonneuve

Ajayi JF (1967) The narrative of Samuel Ajaya Crowther, In P Curtin (Ed.) *Africa remembered*. Madison: University of Wisconsin Press

Baba A (1989) *Nayl al-ibtihaj bi tatriz al-dibaj*. Tarabulus, Libya: al-Jamahiriyah al-'Arabiyah al-Libiyah al-Shabiyah al-Ishtirakiyah al-Uzma

al-Bartayli TM (1981) *Fath al-Shakur*. Beirut: Dar al-Gharb

Barth H (1965) *Travels and discoveries in North and Central Africa in the years 1849–1855* (Vol. 3). London: F. Cass

Bathily A (1975) A discussion of the traditions of Wagadu with some reference to ancient Ghana. *Bull. de 1'IFAN* 28 sér. B1: 16

Corral JJ (2000) *Ciudades de las caravanas: itinerarios de arquitectura antigua en Mauritania, 1978–1981*. Granada: Legado Andalusi

Hunwick JO (1985) *Shari 'a in Songhay: The replies of al-Maghili to the questions of Askia al-Hajj Muhammad*. Edited and translated with an introduction and commentary by JO Hunwick. London/New York: Published for the British Academy by Oxford University Press

Hunwick J (trans.) (1999) *Tarikh al-Sudan*. In *Timbuktu and the Songhay Empire*. Leiden: EJ Brill

Ibn Khaldun (1981) *Kitab al-'ibar*. In *Corpus of early Arabic sources for West African history*. Translated by JFP Hopkins; edited and annotated by N Levtzion & JF Hopkins. Cambridge/New York: Cambridge University Press

Levtzion N (1994) *Islam in West Africa: Religion, society and politics to 1800*. Aldershot: Variorum

Lucas J (1931) Considerations sur l'ethnique maure et en particulier sur une race ancienne: Les Bafours. *Journal des Africanistes* 1(2): 152–194

Meunié D (1961) *Cités anciennes de Mauritanie, provinces du Tagannt et du Hodh*. Paris: Librairie C. Klincksieck

Modat C (1919) *Les populations primitives de l'Adrar Mauritanien*. BCEHS 4: 372–391

Monteil V (1939) Chroniques de Tichit. *Bulletin de l'Institute Fondamental d'Afrique Noire* I: 284

Nkrumah K (1967) Ghana's cultural history. *Présence Africaine* 13/14: 7–8

Saad E (1983) *A social history of Timbuktu*. Cambridge/New York: Cambridge University Press

al-Sa'di (1964) *Tarikh al-Sudan* (Texte arabe édité et traduit par O Houdas, avec la collaboration de E Benoist). Paris: Adrien-Maisonneuve

Trimingham S (1975) *A history of Islam in West Africa*. Oxford: Oxford University Press

Wilks I (1982) Wangara, Akan and Portuguese in the fifteenth and sixteenth centuries. I. The matter of Bitu. *The Journal of African History* 23(3): 344–349

PART II

AFRICAN ARABIC LITERATURE AS A SOURCE OF HISTORY

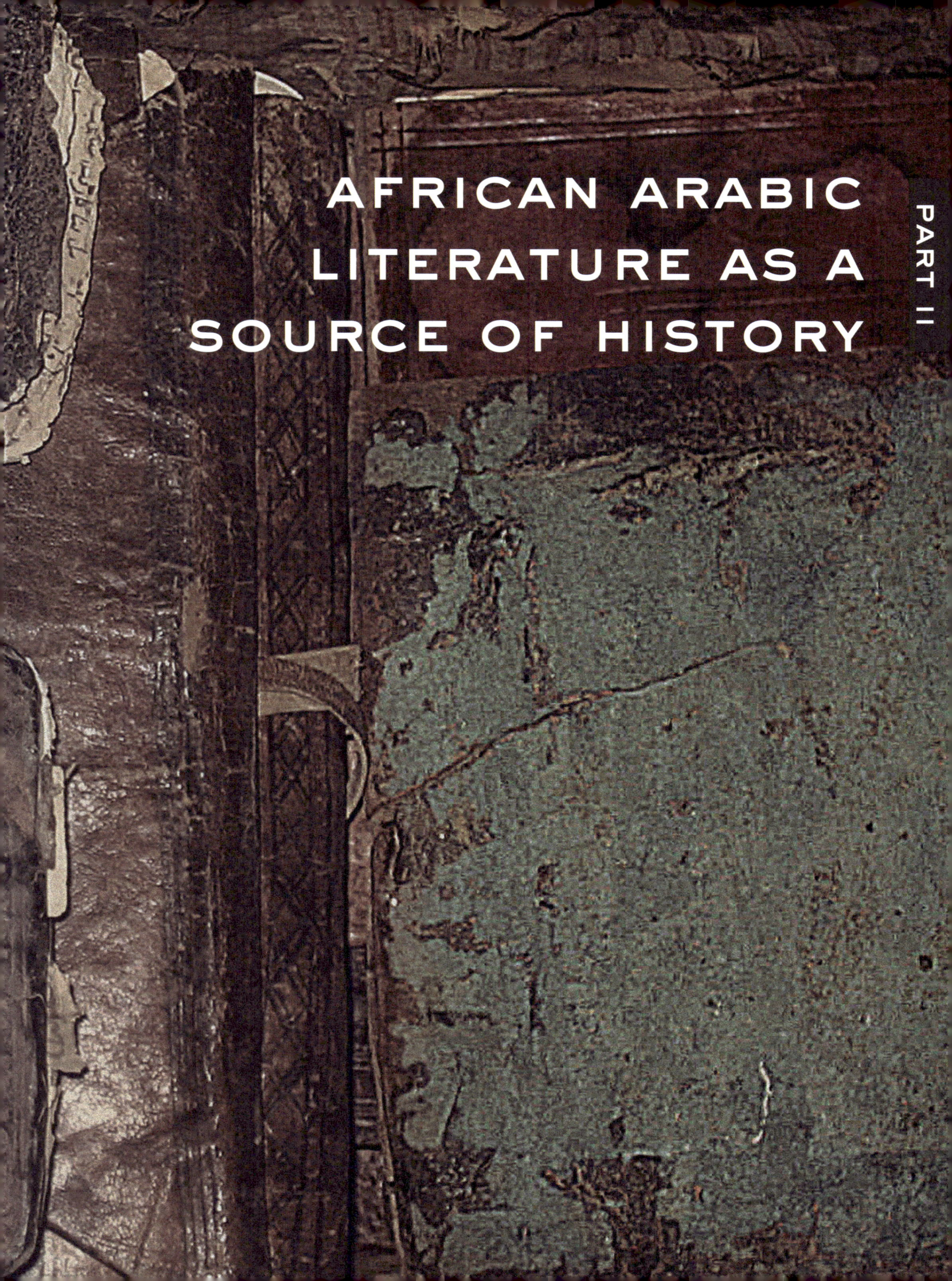

Site N°12

CHAPTER 7

Intellectual innovation and reinvention of the Sahel: the seventeenth-century Timbuktu chronicles

Paulo F de Moraes Farias

The properties of Timbuktu's *tarikh* genre

Something special happened in Timbuktu in the second half of the seventeenth century AD/eleventh century *hijri*: the emergence of a new literary genre. This was the Timbuktu *tarikh* genre.

The Timbuktu works which share *tarikh* properties are the *Tarikh al-Sudan* (Chronicle of the Sudan)[1] of al-Sa'di (completed in 1653 but updated in 1656); the *Tarikh al-fattash* (Chronicle of the Researcher)[2] of Ibn al-Mukhtar (completed in 1664 or soon after); and the anonymous, so-called *Notice historique*[3] (which began to be written some time between 1657 and 1669). Another work that appears to have belonged to the same genre, the *Durar al-hisan fi akhbar ba'd muluk al-Sudan* (Pearls of Beauties Concerning What is Related About Some Kings of the Sudan), by Baba Goro, has been lost. It may have been written earlier than the others, still in the first half of the seventeenth century, though it is also possible it was composed after the *Tarikh al-Sudan*, which fails to mention it (by contrast, the *Tarikh al-fattash* quotes from the *Durar al-hisan*).[4]

Those who practised the *tarikh* genre aimed at producing a unified narrative of various areas of the Sahel (Sahil) region – a narrative ranging from the earliest centuries to the time of the writers. At the present state of knowledge, it seems that this was the first time their kind of overarching narrative was attempted in the region. Indeed, except for the introduction and some other passages in the *Tarikh al-fattash*, all of which are believed to be nineteenth-century forgeries,[5] there is so far no evidence suggesting that historical syntheses comparable to the extant *tarikh* works in scope, or in intellectual

Opposite: Examples of inscriptions at an epigraphic site north of Timbuktu.

and ideological orientation, had existed before them. No work of this kind, dated from before the seventeenth century, has been found among the manuscripts rediscovered in Timbuktu in recent years.[6]

Actually, the *tarikh* writers themselves underline this difference. They did draw on inherited knowledge. And they incorporated in their texts accounts provided by oral traditionists, and quoted from earlier Timbuktu writings. One of them (the author of the *Tarikh al-Sudan*) also mentions oral discussions of historical topics held by their own Timbuktu-elite ancestors. However, the two *tarikh* writers whose original prefaces survive (the authors of the *Tarikh al-Sudan* and the *Notice historique*) present their works as new syntheses and new investigations of the discrete and fragmentary strands of tradition available to them, not as a simple prolongation of integrated visions of the past already in existence. The *Notice historique* states that the available historical records were inadequate with regard to even the most recent of the Songhay dynasties, the Askiya dynasty. The *Tarikh al-Sudan* calls attention to issues not covered by the existing accounts of the origins of the Zuwa dynasty. The *Tarikh al-fattash* explicitly declares that no *tarikh* whatsoever was available about the Kayamagha dynasty of medieval Ghana.[7]

These remarks by the authors themselves should not be dismissed as self-serving, boastful, rhetorical devices. They were not unwarranted claims to originality. Rather, they reflect an intellectual dissatisfaction with earlier accounts – a dissatisfaction that could not but be felt by writers who wanted to address new historical and intellectual issues, but who found that the collection of the evidence required for this purpose had not been at the forefront of their ancestors' preoccupations. The *tarikh* writers were in fact inventing a new idea of the Sahelian past.

However, despite the statements to the contrary by the *tarikh* writers, we modern historians have insisted on assuming those writers had at their disposal a wealth of reliable historical records transmitted from generation to generation and reaching back several centuries. The accumulated weight of this supposed heritage is deemed to be the force that made those writers write – no other possible spur to their endeavours has been considered. Therefore the chroniclers are misrepresented as more or less passive conduits of tradition, while in fact they were intellectual innovators and politico-ideological doers. The *tarikh* writing done in the seventeenth century was a literary genre that had no precedent and no succession in Timbuktu. Sadly, the *tarikh* genre was short-lived.

The post-*tarikh* period in Timbuktu yielded works like the anonymous *Tadhkirat al-nisiyan fi akhbar muluk as-Sudan* (Reminder for Forgetfulness Regarding What is Related About the Rulers of the Sudan),[8] completed in 1751 and essentially a biographical dictionary of Pasha rulers; or the (also anonymous and still unpublished) *Diwan al-muluk fi salatin al-Sudan* (Royal Records of the Rulers of the Sudan),[9] also a history of the Pashalik during most of the period covered by the *Tadhkirat al-nisiyan*; or yet the *Dhikr al-wafayat wa-ma hadath min al-'umur al-'izam* (Recollection of Deaths and [Other]

Grave Events)[10] by Mawlay al-Qasim b. Mawlay Sulayman, which offers information on events in the Timbuktu–Jenne area from 1747 to 1801. None of these later works is comparable to the *tarikh* writings in geographical, chronological or conceptual scope. As far as we know, the *tarikh* genre had no continuation in the two centuries that followed its short golden age.

The reasons why this genre was born so suddenly, as well as the reasons for its equally sudden demise, are inscribed in the intellectual and political issues that were at the core of their texts.

It is clear, from the *tarikh* texts, that they were centred upon the task of making historical sense of the political and social upheavals brought about by the Moroccan invasion of 1591. Obviously, none of the writing genres existing before that invasion could have paid any attention to such a task, which is one of the defining specificities of the *tarikh* genre and which unmistakably provides this genre with a *terminus a quo*, or limit for its possible starting point in time.

But the *tarikh* works were also implicitly centred on a novel political project, which expressed a will to power. Their distinctive characteristics were clearly geared to this project, which is the only thing capable of explaining 'oddities' in the *tarikh* texts that otherwise would remain impossible to understand.[11] It was political aspirations that set the new genre in motion, not the accumulated weight of earlier manuscripts from which *tarikh* historical writing actually differs in kind.

That political project would have been not only unnecessary, but in fact unthinkable, in earlier centuries – and was still unthinkable just a few decades before the *tarikh* works were composed. It only became possible under the conditions obtaining after the Moroccan invasion. It would have been nonsensical at any earlier stage. Moreover, it only became imaginable after a high degree of integration with local society had been achieved by the Arma (the descendants of the Maghribians, Spaniards and Portuguese, brought into the region by the Moroccan invasion and its aftermath).[12]

It was a project of reconciliation between three elites, aimed at a closer, less unequal political integration of each of them with the others.[13] These three elites were the Arma military and political class themselves (who needed definitively to legitimise their power), the Askiya lineages (now deprived by the Moroccan invasion of independent sovereign power over the region, but still playing significant political roles in it) and the urban patriciate of Timbuktu and Jenne (to which the *tarikh* writers belonged, and which had suffered much from the invasion but still retained considerable influence and literate skills useful to the Arma administration). Modern historians have long overlooked this project of a new social pact and its pertinence to the emergence of the *tarikh* genre.[14]

Unfortunately, not long after the *tarikh* works were produced, the politically and conceptually audacious project that inspired them became unfeasible, given increasing

The *tarikh* writing done in the seventeenth century was a literary genre that had no precedent and no succession in Timbuktu. Sadly, the *tarikh* genre was short-lived. It is clear, from the *tarikh* texts, that they were centred upon the task of making historical sense of the political and social upheavals brought about by the Moroccan invasion of 1591. Obviously, none of the writing genres existing before that invasion could have paid any attention to such a task, which is one of the defining specificities of the *tarikh* genre and which unmistakably provides this genre with a *terminus a quo*, or limit for its possible starting point in time.

factionalism among the Arma and among the Askiya lineages as well, to which was added increasing political pressure from Tuareg confederations. The *tarikh* genre perished together with that project, without literary posterity.

New textual genres are directly or indirectly sponsored into existence by new audiences equipped with new sensibilities, expectations and worldly interests, though these new audiences themselves are also constituted and shaped by the new genres that address them. The process is reciprocal. Hence, if audiences' expectations radically change, the vitality of the textual genre they sponsored may be fatally undermined. *Tarikh* writing went out in Timbuktu when *tarikh* audiences among the Arma, the Askiya lineages and the Timbuktu patricians could no longer treat the *tarikh* texts as statements of a unique kind, and as a feasible political blueprint, and began to treat them instead as just one type of historical record among others.

It is then the notion of genre that gives us the key to what happened. This notion allows us to organise textual traditions into categories of works defined by common properties as to their form, subject matter and strategies for producing meaning. This notion is an essential critical tool, without which proper literary history is impossible. Yet it has not been adequately applied to the Timbuktu *tarikh* works.

Within any given literary tradition, genres have a beginning in time and may come to an end, too. The relationship of a new genre to the tradition within which it emerges is one of rupture, not continuity and accumulation. This is what we have for long failed to consider in our studies of the Timbuktu *tarikh* genre (and when I say 'we', I do include myself in it).

We, and in particular historians, have emphasised continuity between this seventeenth-century genre and what was written in Timbuktu before and after. We have done so in order to bolster our belief that the *tarikh* genre merely reproduced and updated old historical records (and an old interest in the construction of wide historical panoramas and continuous historical narratives) going back over the centuries, and transmitted from generation to generation. It has been in our corporate professional interest, as modern historians, to postulate such continuity, because it supposedly permits us to pronounce authoritatively on the past of the Sahel by quoting the *tarikh* writers' reconstructions of history, which we deem inherited from eyewitnesses positioned in earlier eras all the way back almost to time immemorial.

Hence, to reinforce our own modern-historian authority, we have deprived the *tarikh* writers of their historian status. We have reduced them to 'informants' and providers of supposedly 'raw' evidence. But, in fact, they were not mere informants, but historians like ourselves, and they had their own difficulties in retrieving evidence and reconstructing the past from the point of view of their novel intellectual and political stance – the kind of difficulties modern historians are well acquainted with.

New textual genres are directly or indirectly sponsored into existence by new audiences equipped with new sensibilities, expectations and worldly interests, though these new audiences themselves are also constituted and shaped by the new genres that address them. The process is reciprocal. Hence, if audiences' expectations radically change, the vitality of the textual genre they sponsored may be fatally undermined. *Tarikh* writing went out in Timbuktu when *tarikh* audiences among the Arma, the Askiya lineages and the Timbuktu patricians could no longer treat the *tarikh* texts as statements of a unique kind, and as a feasible political blueprint, and began to treat them instead as just one type of historical record among others.

Figure 7.1 Medieval epigraphic sites in Mali and Niger

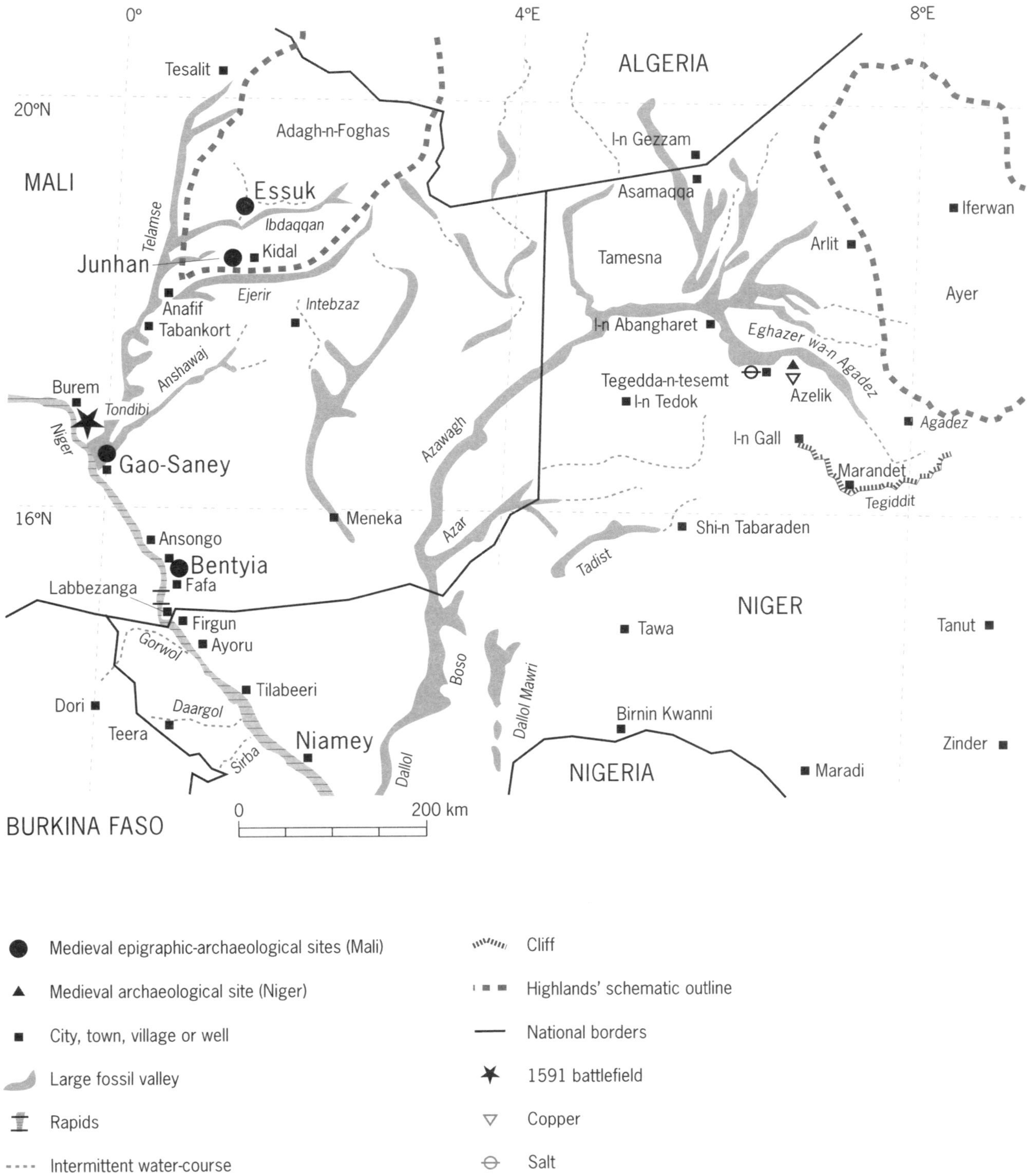

To reinforce our own modern-historian authority, modern scholars have deprived the *tarikh* writers of their status as historians. They have been reduced to 'informants' and providers of supposedly 'raw' evidence. But, in fact, they were not mere informants, but historians like ourselves, and they had their own difficulties in retrieving evidence and reconstructing the past from the point of view of their novel intellectual and political stance – the kind of difficulties modern historians are well acquainted with.

It is then from the notion of literary and political ruptures, and of paradigm shifts, rather than from the notion of continuity, that our analysis must proceed. We must pay special attention to the properties that made the *tarikh* genre different from other genres which preceded and followed it, and which also recorded historical events.

One of those properties is what we may call the 'plenitude effect' imparted by the *tarikh* works to their accounts of dynastic history in the Sahel, all of which culminate in the history of the Askiya dynasty. The purpose of this was to reinforce the symbolic capital of the Askiya lineages who figured among the writers' patrons, and to give those lineages odds in the game of reformed political alliances envisaged by the writers. In practice, it meant constructing narratives of the past that were apparently free of gaps, that is, deploying writing strategies that prevented narrative breaks where evidence was missing. Partly, this 'plenitude effect' was achieved by borrowing stories and characters from Tuareg folklore, and making them pass for historical characters. From Aligurran or Arigullan, a hero of Tuareg lore, the Timbuktu chroniclers fashioned the character they call 'Ali Kulun' or 'Ali Golom', the supposed founder of the Sii or Sonni dynasty of Songhay; and stories associated with the same Tuareg character underlie part of the account of the foundation of the Askiya dynasty provided by the *Tarikh al-Sudan*.[15]

Most of our modern historical reconstructions remain largely based on what the *tarikh* writers said. Given the deceptive fullness of their narratives, we modern historians have so far experienced difficulty in finding, in our own accounts, space to accommodate available evidence which contradicts *tarikh* statements, or to which *tarikh* writers simply did not have access. Yet such evidence exists, and offers support to a new critical approach to the work of the seventeenth-century Timbuktu historians.[16]

I shall now show some of this evidence, which in this particular case comes from Arabic epigraphy rather than from Tuareg oral tradition. The evidence originates in Gao and Bentiya, two of the most important medieval epigraphic sites in the territory of the Republic of Mali (see Figure 7.1 on page 99). It consists of one inscription from the Jira Kanje Cemetery (by the side of the mosque known as Askiya Mosque) in Old Gao, and two from Bentiya's Larger Cemetery. These three inscriptions prove the unreliability of fundamental aspects of the historical reconstructions provided by the seventeenth-century Timbuktu chroniclers, and since adopted by most modern historians.

However, as will be seen in the conclusion of this chapter, this should not lead to the dismissal of the Timbuktu chronicles as historical documents. Rather, what is needed is a new mode of investigation and historical appreciation of their texts.

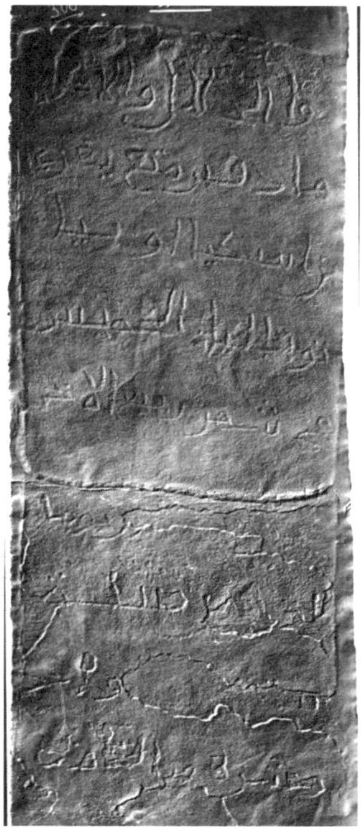

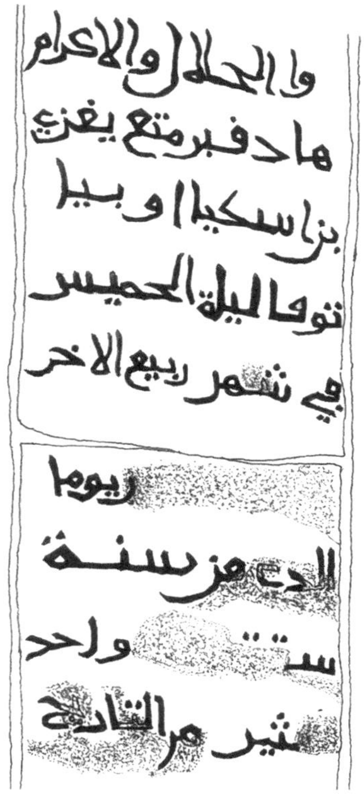

[:1] (ذ) وا [sic:] اَلْجَلاَلِ وَاَلْإِكْرَام

[:2] هَاذَ [sic:] قَبْرُ مُتَغْ [sic:] يغزي

[:3] بْنِ [sic:] اسكيا (أَسكِيَا ؟ إِسكِيَا ؟) اوبيا

[:4] تَوَفَّا [sic:] لَيْلَةَ اَلْخَمِيسِ

[:5] فِي شَهْرِ رَبِع اَلآخِرِ

[:6] .... يَوْمًا

[:7] اَلَّذ(ي) مِنْ سَنَةِ

[:8] سِ(تَّةِ) [sic:] (مِائَةِ) وَأَحَدِ [sic:]

[:9] (وَثَلاَ) ثِينَ مِنَ اَلتَّا(رِيخ)

from left to right:
Figure 7.2 Photo of De Gironcourt's *estampage* 306, done on inscription 62, about the son of an *askiya*, dated 1234, Gao.

Figure 7.3 Moraes Farias's line drawing of De Gironcourt's *estampage* 306.

Figure 7.4 Transcription of the line drawing.

Epigraphic evidence for a new critique of the *tarikh* accounts

The first inscription (see Figures 7.2, 7.3, 7.4) survives only in the form of an *estampage* (paper-squeeze impression) made in Gao at Jira Kanje in 1912, by the French explorer Georges-Reynard de Gironcourt. This *estampage* is now kept in the library of the Institut de France in Paris. The inscription bears the number 62 in the epigraphic corpus published in 2003.[17] Another inscription (number 63), almost certainly from the same cemetery, also contains the title *Askiya*, but its date is no longer readable.

The translation of the surviving part of inscription 62 is as follows:

[…]

[1] Possessed of majesty and bounty [Qur'an 55: 26–27]

[2] This is the tomb of Y.gh.z.y. [Yaghazi? Yaghaziya?]

[3] son of Askiya Aw.b.ya [Awbiyya? Awbaya? 'Uwubiya? Awu-Baya?].

[4] He died on Thursday night

[5] in the month of Rabi' the Last

[6] …days,

[7] which was in the year

[8] s-[-ix hundred] and one

[9] [and thir-]-ty of the [Islamic] Era.

The date of death belongs to the month of Rabi' the Last (the fourth month) of the year 631 of the Islamic calendar, that is, to the period extending between 4 January and 1 February 1234. It is still possible to read this partly erased chronological reference thanks to the diacritical points that have survived.

It shows that the title *Askiya* was in use in Gao no less than 259 years before 1493 (the year of its creation according to the *Tarikh al-Sudan*), and 246 years before the decade beginning in 1480 (from which the *Tarikh al-fattash* appears to date its use). In fact, the title appears to have had a much longer and more complicated history in Gao than the Timbuktu chroniclers ever knew.[18]

The second inscription (see Figures 7.5, 7.6, 7.7) bears the number 226 in the published corpus. It has disappeared from the Bentiya sites and is only known through a De Gironcourt *estampage* (799) preserved in the Institut de France.[19]

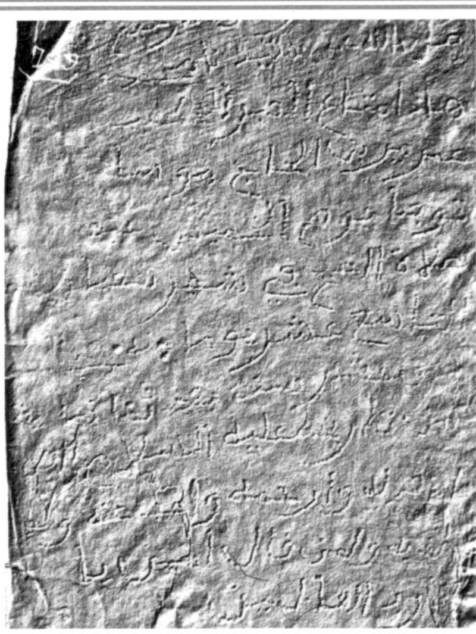

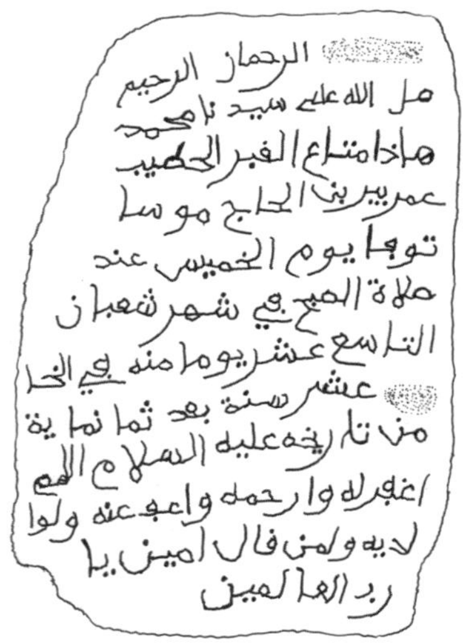

[:1] (بِسْمِ ٱللهِ) ٱلرَّحْمانِ [sic:] ٱلرَّحِيمِ
[:2] صَلِّ [sic:] ٱللهُ عَلَى سَيِّدِنَا مُحَمَّدٍ
[:3] هَاذَا [sic:] مَتَاعُ ٱلْقَبْرِ [sic:] ٱلْخَطِيبِ
[:4] عُمَرِ بِيرِ بْنِ ٱلْحَاجِّ مُوسَا
[:5] تَوَفَّا [sic:] يَوْمَ ٱلْخَمِيسِ عِنْدَ
[:6] صَلاَةِ ٱلصُّبْحِ فِي شَهْرِ شَعْبَانَ
[:7] ٱلتَّاسِعَ عَشَرَ يَوْمًا مِنْهُ فِي ٱلْخَا
[:8] (مِسَ) عَشَرَ سَنَةِ بَعْدَ ثَمَانِمِائَةٍ
[:9] مِنْ تَارِيخِهِ عَلَيْهِ ٱلسَّلاَمُ ٱللَّهُمَّ
[:10] اَغْفِرْلَهُ وَارْحَمْهُ وَاعْفُ عَنْهُ وَلِوَا
[:11] لِدَيْهِ وَلِمَنْ قَالَ آمِينَ يَا
[:12] رَبَّ ٱلْعَالَمِينَ

from left to right:
Figure 7.5 Photo of De Gironcourt's *estampage* 799 done of inscription 226, of a *khatib*, dated 1412, Bentiya.

Figure 7.6 Line drawing of De Gironcourt's *estampage* 799.

Figure 7.7 Transcription of the line drawing.

Here is its translation:

[1] [In the name of God], the Merciful, the Compassionate
[2] God bless our lord Muhammad.
[3] This is the mortal remains [literally: the chattels of the tomb] of the *khatib*
[4] Umar Beere son of al-Hajj Musa.
[5] He died on Thursday at the time of
[6] the dawn prayer, in the month of Sha'ban,
[7] on the nineteenth day of it, in the fif-
[8] teenth year after eight hundred
[9] of his [Prophet Muhammad's] Era, upon him be peace. O God!
[10] Forgive him, and have mercy on him, and absolve him and his par-
[11] ents, and whoever says 'Amen, o
[12] Lord of the Worlds!'

The date of death is the nineteenth day of Sha'ban of the year 815 of the *hijra*, that is, 23 November 1412, which was actually a Tuesday according to the mathematical calendar tables.

The *Tarikh al-Sudan* describes the Kukyia area, which corresponds to the Bentiya sites, as a centre of undiluted 'paganism' from which Pharaoh had recruited sorcerers against Prophet Musa (Moses).[20] Yet the vast Muslim necropolises at Bentiya prove the presence there of a sizeable Muslim community, probably composed of traders, between 1272 and 1489. Actually, the support of this community probably helps to explain the Sonni dynasty's successful bid for power in the fifteenth century.[21] Probably, the office of *khatib* was associated in the Kukyia/Bentiya area not only with the preaching of the *khutba* or Friday sermon, but also with important political functions. It is the only Islamic office known to have existed in Gao under Sonni 'Ali Beeri, the most powerful of the Sonni rulers, who reigned from 1464–65 to 1492. Under the Askiya dynasty, Gao's *khatib* also held the office of *qadi* or judge.[22]

The third inscription (see Figures 7.8, 7.9, 7.10) bears the number 234 in the published corpus.[23] It is still *in situ* at Bentiya's Larger Cemetery. Only part of its text is still readable.

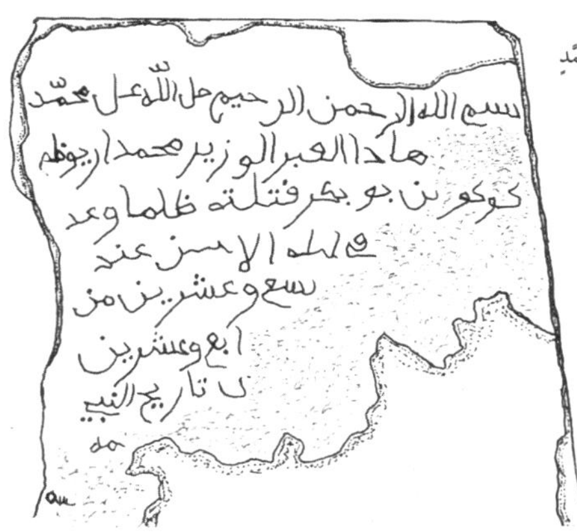

[1:] بِسْمِ ٱللهِ ٱلرَّحْمٰنِ ٱلرَّحِيمِ صَلَّ [sic:] ٱللهُ عَلَ [sic:] مُحَمَّدِ

[2:] .... هَاذَا [sic:] ٱلْقَبْرُ [sic:] ٱلْوَزِيرِ مُحَمَّدِ اريوِ ظَمٌ

[3:] كَوْكَوِ بْنِ بُو[sic:] بَكْرٍ (or: بَكَرَ) قَتَلَتْهُ ظُلْمًا وُغْدَ

[4:] (انْ) .... فِي لَيلَةَ ٱلاثْنَيْنِ عِنْدَ

[5:] .... تِسْعِ وَعِشْرِينَ مِنْ

[6:] .... (ٱلْرَّ) ابِع وَعِشْرِينَ

[7:] .... (مِـ) ـنْ تَارِيخِ ٱلنَّبِيِّ

[8:] .....

from left to right:
Figure 7.8 Inscription 234, of a *wazir*, dated [14]21, Bentiya. Photograph taken in situ.

Figure 7.9 Line drawing of inscription 234.

Figure 7.10 Transcription of inscription 234.

Its translation is as follows:

[1] In the name of God, the Merciful, the Compassionate. God bless Muhammad

[2] ...This is the tomb of the *wazir* Muhammad 'Ariyaw [or: 'Ariyu/'Iriyaw/etc...], praise-named

[3] Kawkaw, son of Bu Bakrin [or: Bubakar]. Ig-[-noble] people iniquitously killed him

[4] ...on Monday night at the time of

[5] ...twenty-nine of

[6] ...[the f-]-ourth and twenty [sic]

[7] ...[o-]-f the Era of the Prophet

[8] ...

The date of death almost certainly belongs to the year 824 of the Islamic calendar, that is, AD 1421.

In addition to preserving a Songhay *zammu* or praise name, inscription 234 confirms the high degree of organisation of the local Muslim community. It is probable that those who held the office of *wazir* mediated between the local trader community and the area's political rulers. The Timbuktu chroniclers had no inkling of such arrangements, hence their depiction of the history of the Kukyia/Bentiya region is highly misleading.

Conclusion

The *Tarikh al-Sudan* of al-Sa'di, the *Tarikh al-fattash* of Ibn al-Mukhtar and the anonymous *Notice historique* aimed at writing up the Sahel of West Africa as a vast geopolitical entity defined by the notion of imperial kingship. It is from them that we have inherited the idea of three great empires (Ghana, Mali and Songhay) succeeding one another in West Africa.

In the texts of the Timbuktu chroniclers, that imperial tradition culminates in the Askiya rulers of Songhay, precisely the dynasty that had lost its political independence at the hands of the invaders who came from Morocco in the apocalyptic year of 1591. Hence the imperial rank of the Askiya needed to be given afresh the highest possible legitimacy.

It is precisely when the Askiya princes had become subordinate to the Arma that the chroniclers rebuilt, and reinforced, the overthrown dynasty's claim to caliphal status. (Significantly, Ahmad Baba, the most famous Timbuktu writer of the preceding generation, had classified the Askiya state as a mere sultanate, not a caliphate.)[24]

At the same time, the meaning of the expression *bilad al-sudan* (land of the black peoples) was continuing to evolve within the *tarikh* genre. As shown by Hunwick, in the *Tarikh al-Sudan*, while al-Sa'di sometimes uses the word *Sudan* with reference to the inhabitants of the region, at other times he uses it in a geopolitical sense to mean the Middle Niger land area.[25] Thus the term *bilad al-sudan* or *ard al-sudan*, which had begun its career as an instrument of otherisation applied from outside the region, was now being taken over by Sudanese insiders and made into a badge of greatness.

The image of the black West African caliphate was meant to rival the caliphal claims put forward from North Africa by Morocco's Sadi dynasty. However, in the immediate context of the Middle Niger region, the function of that image was to persuade the Arma to accept a new social and political pact with the pre-invasion Songhay elites. It was not meant to challenge Arma political leadership.

Two pioneers, DT Niane and Olivier de Sardan, initiated the study of the ideological background of the Timbuktu chronicles.[26] Both these scholars saw the chronicles as celebrations of the social hierarchy that had existed at the time of the pre-invasion Askiya rulers, that is, of the alliance of two traditional ruling classes (the Songhay royal lineages and the literate urban traders), and of the subordination of the slave population and other social classes to those two dominant groups.

But, in fact, one novelty of the *tarikh* genre was its implicit formulation of a blueprint for the future which came to terms with the post-invasion political realities, and hence sought a stable reconciliation with the Arma. The Timbuktu chronicles were far from being a mere exercise in nostalgia. Also, the chroniclers took for granted that slaves and other traditionally subordinate groups should be kept at the lower end of the social hierarchy – this was not the main point of their writing. Rather, their specific aim was a new alliance of elites.

It was this particular political aim that led the *tarikh* writers to engineer a continuous narrative of the region's history, taking in even its remotest periods. Thus, on the same page, al-Sa'di could complain about lack of historical evidence on the Zuwa dynasty, yet claim to provide information about it of which 'those in the know' were well aware.[27]

But, no matter how misleading its accounts of the earliest eras can be, the Timbuktu *tarikh* genre remains a precious source of information about periods chronologically closer to the chroniclers. And, above all, the three great chronicles are invaluable for the light they throw on social relations and politico-ideological issues at the time of their writing.

It must be clear by now that the purpose of this chapter is not to dismiss the Timbuktu *tarikh* texts as historical sources. Rather, the aim is to grasp the *tarikh* writers not as antiquaries, but as senior colleagues in the joint task of producing historical knowledge, and as persons fully engaged in the issues of their own time. Indeed they were highly active historical characters themselves. Their writing was an intervention in their own contemporary history.

NOTES

1 Al-Sa'di (1964); see also the English translation of parts of the text by Hunwick (1999: 1–270); and the excerpts from the work made by the German explorer Heinrich Barth and published by Ralfs (1855).

2 Ibn al-Mukhtar (1964).

3 Anon. A (1964).

4 See Moraes Farias (2003: Chapter 2: 121, 136, 143) – these are references to the numbered paragraphs in Part I and Part II of the book, which have page numbers in Roman numerals.

5 On these forgeries, see Levtzion (1971: 574, 576, 592–593).

6 On these rediscoveries, see Haidara (1997, 1999); Hofheinz (2004); and some of the chapters published in this book.

7 See al-Sa'di (1964: text 1–2, 5, trans. 2–3, 8); Hunwick trans. (1999: 1–2, 6); Anon. A (1964: 327–329); Ibn al-Mukhtar (1964: text 42, trans. 79–80).

8 Anon. B (1966).

9 See Hunwick (1992b: 179).

10 See Abitbol (1982).

11 See Moraes Farias (2003: Chapter 2: 117–120).

12 See Hodgkin (1987).

13 See Moraes Farias (2003: Chapter 2, *passim*).

14 However, an important step toward the analysis of the political motivations behind the writing of *tarikh* works has been taken by Hunwick (1992a).

15 See Moraes Farias (2003: Chapter 2: 165–191; 2006b).

16 On this evidence found in West African oral traditions and Arabic inscriptions, and on the light it throws on the Timbuktu chronicles, see Moraes Farias (1974, 1990, 1993a, 1993b, 1999, 2003, 2006a, 2006b, 2006c).

17 See Moraes Farias (2003: Chapter 2, paragraphs 192–219, and Chapter 6, pages 57–58).

18 See Moraes Farias (2006b).

19 See Moraes Farias (2003: Chapter 3, paragraph 453, and Chapter 9, pages 191–192; 1993b: 58–60).

20 See al-Sa'di (1964: text 4, trans. 6–7); Hunwick trans. (1999: 5–6).

21 See Moraes Farias (2003: Chapter 3: 443–451).

22 See Moraes Farias (2003: Chapter 3: 453).

23 See Moraes Farias (2003: Chapter 3, paragraph 452, and Chapter 9, pages 199–200).

24 See Moraes Farias (2003: Chapter 2: 141–145); and al-Harraq & Hunwick (2000: text 83, trans. 44).

25 See Hunwick (1999: 2, footnote 3).

26 See Niane (1964) and Olivier de Sardan (1975).

27 See al-Sa'di (1964: text 5, trans. 8–9); Hunwick trans. (1999: 6).

REFERENCES

Abitbol M (Ed. and trans.) (1982) *Tombouctou au milieu du xviiie siècle d'après la chronique de Mawlay al-Qasim.* Paris: GP Maisonneuve et Larose

Anon. A (1964) Untitled text known as *Notice historique.* Partial French translation by O Houdas & M Delafosse. Published as the *Deuxième appendice* to Ibn al-Mukhtar, *Tarikh al-fattash*, 326–341

Anon. B (1966) *Tedzkiret en-Nisian.* Edited and translated into French by O Houdas. Paris: Librairie d'Amérique et d'Orient Adrien-Maisonneuve

Haidara ID (1997) *L'Espagne musulmane et l'Afrique subsaharienne.* Bamako: Editions Donniya

Haidara ID (1999) *Les Juifs à Tombouctou.* Bamako: Editions Donniya

al-Harraq F & Hunwick JO (Eds and trans) (2000) *Ahmad Baba's replies on slavery.* Rabat: Université Muhammad V, Institute of African Studies

Hodgkin E (1987) Social and political relations on the Niger Bend in the seventeenth century. PhD thesis, University of Birmingham, Centre of West African Studies

Hofheinz A (2004) Goths in the lands of the blacks: A preliminary survey of the Ka'ti Library in Timbuktu. In SS Reese (Ed.) *The transmission of learning in Islamic Africa.* Leiden/Boston: Brill

Hunwick JO (1992a) Studies in the Tarikh al-fattash (Part 2): An alleged charter of privilege issued by Askiya al-hajj Muhammad to the descendants of Mori Hawgaro. *Sudanic Africa: A Journal of Historical Sources* 3: 138–148

Hunwick JO (1992b) CEDRAB: Centre de Documentation et de Recherches Ahmed Baba at Timbuktu. *Sudanic Africa: A Journal of Historical Sources* 3: 173–181

Hunwick JO (1999) *Timbuktu and the Songhay Empire* (including the English translation, on pp. 1–270, of the Introduction, chapters 1 to 27, and chapter 30, of al-Sa'di, *Tarikh al-Sudan*). Leiden: Brill

Ibn al-Mukhtar (1964) *Tarikh al-fattash.* Edited and translated into French by O Houdas & M Delafosse. Paris: Librairie d'Amérique et d'Orient Adrien-Maisonneuve for Unesco (reprint of the 1913–14 edition)

Levtzion N (1971) A seventeenth-century chronicle by Ibn al-Mukhtar: A critical study of *Tarikh al-fattash. Bulletin of the School of Oriental and African Studies* 34(3): 571–593

Moraes Farias PF (1974) Du nouveau sur les stèles de Gao: Les épitaphes du prince Yama Kuri et du roi F.n.da (XIIIème siècle). *Bulletin de l'Institut Fondamental d'Afrique Noire* série B, 36(3): 511–524

Moraes Farias PF (1990) The oldest extant writing of West Africa: Medieval epigraphs from Essuk, Saney, and Egef-n-Tawaqqast, Mali. *Journal des Africanistes* 60(2): 65–113

Moraes Farias PF (1993a) *Histoire contre mémoire: Épigraphie, chroniques, tradition orale et lieux d'oubli dans le Sahel malien.* Rabat: Université Muhammad V, Chaire du Patrimoine Maroco-Africain

Moraes Farias PF (1993b) Text as landscape: Reappropriations of medieval inscriptions in the 17th and late 20th centuries (Essuk, Mali). In O Hulec & M Mendel (Eds) *Threefold wisdom: Islam, the Arab world and Africa. Papers in honour of Ivan Hrbek.* Prague: Academy of Sciences of the Czech Republic, Oriental Institute

Moraes Farias PF (1999) Tadmakkat and the image of Mecca: Epigraphic records of the work of the imagination in 11th-century West Africa. In T Insoll (Ed.) *Case studies in archaeology and world religion.* Oxford: British Archaeological Reports and Archaeopress

Moraes Farias PF (2003) *Arabic medieval inscriptions from the Republic of Mali: Epigraphy, chronicles and Songhay–Tuareg history.* Oxford/New York: Oxford University Press for The British Academy

Moraes Farias PF (2006a) Barth, le fondateur d'une lecture réductrice des Chroniques de Tombouctou. In M Diawara, PF de Moraes Farias & G Spittler (Eds) *Heinrich Barth et l'Afrique.* Cologne: Rüdiger Köppe Verlag

Moraes Farias PF (2006b) Touareg et Songhay: Histoires croisées, historiographies scindées. In H Claudot-Hawad (Ed.) *Berbères ou Arabes? Le tango des spécialistes.* Paris: Editions Non Lieu

Moraes Farias PF (2006c) À quoi sert l'épigraphie arabe 'médiévale' de l'Afrique de l'Ouest? In C Descamps & A Camara (Eds) *Senegalia: études sur le patrimoine ouest-africain – Hommage à Guy Thilmans.* Paris, Saint-Maur-des-Fossés: Editions Sepia

Niane DT (1964) Mythes, légendes et sources orales dans l'Œuvre de Mahmoud Kati. *Recherches Africaines* [*Études guinéennes*, nouvelle série] 1: 36–42

Olivier de Sardan J-P (1975) Captifs ruraux et esclaves impériaux du Songhay. In C Meillassoux (Ed.) *L'Esclavage en Afrique.* Paris: François Maspero

Ralfs C (1855) Beiträge zur Geschichte und Geographie des Sudan. Eingesandt von Dr. Barth. *Zeitschrift der Deutschen Morgenländischen Gesellschaft* 9: 518–594

al-Sa'di (1964) *Tarikh al-sudan.* Edition and French translation by O Houdas & E Benoist. Paris: Librairie d'Amérique et d'Orient Adrien-Maisonneuve for Unesco (reprint of the 1898–1900 edition)

بسم الله الرحمن الرحيم

ثم الذيب عنه فشاب مازغ زنبر الى اجبنه او بال عزاه ثاو او عتسل او فطيم او تنبر ارا
كل اخشيشر الم تختما شراما اللحم ويال ار ثابو عنه راغ اجدبه زيبا حتى
تم ثابو مانيش البعو اجبه الذيب عنه افيش يشنب مارغ ثال ثابو مو
بابو امشتشنب مدرغ ثال الذيب فشابت مارغ يخشر باقها بيه ثان
ثابو نابغ به يشمحيل ثال الذيب الا امتيب انح اخ يشيكر وانبصد اعليه
وهر اعلى تشه منه اللحم ثال ثابو وانسيه ثاغ ثال الذيب واخيك
بعلشبشبق وحدمن لحيشنز الى خاز غشعو اللحم او كلهم ببشر من تحتيش
شاد ثابو داغ ثال يا محمد وجه الكسول ثال الا انشبه زاب ثال الذيب
ماتل نخجيك فشاني الا يا معا بيده او لا يشبه ثال ثابو لا شو ايسيل داغ
مرابه ثلة ابا طوا عمه نج ثال الذيب او بد اثنه واجب اجدبه الكريم
ورمش [illegible] نجبر الدرام بالحشيشر نجز وامشر اغود للذيب شاد ودر
اباز درارعت اولا جبر غاد الا شايش اوبيشج وارك افششبت الذيب
اثن ما فحل

انتهى

بسم الله الرحمن الرحيم

انشا اعى خالك مه موتت اثلث نسيبه كل اسى اتغيب منها اتنعمش ارا اجلا
اوا اول له منهم واحد وكتسو انهار خلتف فيه صف او جدو افغار بيش اصغار ثاى
بلهف بلمه رمغ عام ولشخصهم ثالهم انتو اشلعنعمر وانتم كل اسى
فزكل انتعمش ازاجل ثالول اشوا نرثا اللهم كلعمر اجيب مركوب ابا يشرمنا لعويشا
وحر وتجر تبا شكات او نسا وده الحيق اقوم انتعمش وامشاو تم مايشيى
البلا البهم وانتمار نشهم الى جا وليكشل ثالولهم ماريتعر ان ازفلابك تنل اشى
نمشى عنا واحد منه اولا ترجع ثالبلهم لكشبل الا اجوى هو ثات ابنا فك امعا
هنر ازماليك مى او لا يرجع انتعش اسى

ثالهم اعطوه واحدا منهم بنا مكوا نعان اتلود ولهم ثالو لهم حنبى زاد وامشاو امطهر الغيل
ثم ماكشبا البا اليهم وانمار انتم الله خاد الكذ فانيس حشه يا شتو امنز هلاذ انو وانشخهم اكور ربيعهم لعنه
نسيع البنا حسن ثاشرا منيش خلانه نعو لواحد من ثاب الغول اثكاد اكرابيت انزاد ح معاكهم عند
الصحى ازرح سابيشع ثال احى اخرى اخبار ازماليكم ثكوال انمداد وثم اكشد عرم انها لامعا
اخمسر رجال بما كماغو شاكد اوجه الكذ فايك هو ثاث عى شادرا ومعبه سا هاذا الكذا
ما نارج نحمير ورمايكم عنه حعبو بالشيع اكنل

CHAPTER 8

Ajami in Africa: the use of Arabic script in the transcription of African languages

Moulaye Hassane[1]

Introduction

Although the script of the Holy Qur'an has played such an important historical role in the transcription of the languages of certain Islamised African peoples, this field has aroused little interest among researchers – because of a lack of sources – and thus remains largely unexamined to this day. However, it is a fundamental facet of Islam's immense cultural contribution to certain African civilisations.

This arises from the fact that before the Islamisation of sub-Saharan Africa, knowledge, behaviour, historical narratives, language in its secret, selected and codified forms – in sum, everything which represents collective memory in its transmission from one generation to the next – all this was passed on orally, just as in pre-Islamic Arabia.

Of course, many older writing systems existed in Africa, of which the best known is that of Ancient Egypt. Hieroglyphics are behind a large part of modern knowledge, and they continue to communicate with us. In the beginning of the fifteenth century (*hijri*) the Bamoum of Cameroon created a somewhat crude writing system based on images. Vai (Liberia) and Ge'ez (Ethiopia) are two slightly more elaborate scripts.[2] The Tifinagh script, a system used to transcribe the Tuareg language, a relative of Berber, is still in limited use in some areas, but is gradually being supplanted by the Qur'anic script.[3]

With the introduction of Islam, a new situation developed in sub-Saharan Africa, where orality continued to be dominant. The new religion was intimately linked to a way of writing (*kitab*), and thus of reading (*al-qur'an*).[4] These writings, which should be read in perfect accordance with the sacred message they bear, had been revealed to the Prophet Muhammad whose mother tongue was Arabic.

Opposite: A folio from Manuscript No. 6113 in the Ahmed Baba Institute. The text is written in Arabic script and the words are a mixture of Arabic and the local Hassani language.

It is thus perfectly natural that this message, which was addressed to humanity and transmitted in Arabic with its specific script, should gradually influence all aspects of the societies which subscribed to it, especially in the sphere of writing.[5] In this way the history of writing certain sub-Saharan African languages will be interdependent with that of Islam.

Historical survey

Islam's 14 centuries in sub-Saharan Africa have been the subject of numerous studies in several languages and the subject is far from exhausted.[6] Considering the vastness of this history, and the position it holds in a modest study such as this one, a reminder of the main points insofar as they impact on the subject will surely help us to understand and delimit our study.

The seventh to fifteenth centuries

The victorious expedition of ʻUqba ibn Nafiʻ al-Fihri in 666 in Fezzan then in the Kawar marks the first military contact of Islam with sub-Saharan Africa.[7] All the same, the possibility that echoes of the new religion reached populations before this historical event should not be ruled out.

Islam thus makes contact with Africa by way of the Sahara, after having crossed the Red Sea (*al-Bahr al-Ahmar*). It crosses Egypt (*al-Fustat*), Cyrenaica (*Tarabulus al-Garb*), Ifriqiya (*al-Ifriqiyya*) and the Extreme Maghrib (*al-Magrib al-Aqsa*). As north–south links across the Sahara Desert were numerous and very old, it was quite natural that Islam should make use of pre-existing caravan routes which linked the different commercial centres of northern Africa with those of southern, eastern and western Africa. Arabs and Berbers are often cited as having played an important part in the first phase of this process.[8] But the diversity of customs linked to the multiplicity of ethnic groups suggests that the pace and means of the process varied in accordance with the political, economic and social history of the ethnic groups.

It thus took several centuries for Islam to gradually spread through the social and religious landscape, a process with two aspects:

- instruction from the Qur'an, of which even partial knowledge is indispensable to all believers in their duty to carry out the five daily prayers, one of the five pillars of Islam;
- education, which is inseparable from instruction in Islam, as the two complement each other. Whilst the first teaches the reading, writing and understanding of the message and the related sciences which popularise it, the second aims to take responsibility for individuals from childhood by giving them the moral and material means for the formation of their personalities with a view to their entry into the community of believers (*umma*), where they will be responsible for further developing the faith.

These basins used for hand washing are typical and distinctive of the West African culture.

The place initially implicated in this fundamental task was the mosque (*masjid*), which served as a place of prayer and debate affecting community life. Some mosques in time became important centres of learning in disciplines other than the religious sciences.[9] These centres served as beacons from which Islamic culture and knowledge were spread throughout sub-Saharan Africa by itinerant scholars and their students. Certain merchants and important rulers began to encourage the scholars and students in their efforts.

The fifteenth to eighteenth centuries

From the fifteenth to the eighteenth centuries these combined efforts began to catalyse a political and economic renaissance which was felt in the emergence of a local lettered class, which extended the work of scholars from the north. After the disappearance of large centres like Awdaghust, Koumbi Saleh and Walata, places such as Niani, Jenne, Timbuktu, Gao, Tigidda and Agadez in turn became very vigorous and prestigious hubs in the cultural and religious spheres. Scholars trained in Fez taught in mosques which had become veritable universities. *Imams*, *qadis* and secretaries (*katib*) were mostly natives of the Ghana Empire and the Mali Empire in the west and of the Kanem Bornu Empire in the east. Islam became a fully fledged African religion and the Qur'anic schools became wholly integrated with African social structures and adapted to their needs.[10]

The nineteenth and twentieth centuries

These centuries were characterised by an Islam that had been re-energised under the banner of reformist Sufi brotherhoods, of which the oldest was the Qadiriyya. This brotherhood emerged in Algeria and then spread into sub-Saharan Africa, firstly to

Timbuktu. Later the Tuaregs and the Moorish Kunta, who were very influential at the time, spread it further south. Its crowning achievement was the creation, in the nineteenth century, of theocratic states like the Dina of Humdallahi, the Sokoto Caliphate and numerous principalities under Islamic *shari'a* law.

The colonial period

Muslim culture had been established in all the large urban centres of sub-Saharan Africa by the time Europeans arrived in these territories. Islamic sciences and Arabic script were fairly widespread but geographically uneven because the importance of the centres of Qur'anic education varied in accordance with the size of the villages where they existed.

Moreover, the pre-eminence of the Muslim religion caused no small concern for the colonial administration, all the more so as the territory to which the latter aspired had been under the influence of Islamic scholars for several centuries. It was at this time that the brotherhoods of Qadiriyya, Tijaniyya, Sanusiyya, Khalwatiyya and their offshoots were busy reinvigorating Islam.[11] Of course, there still existed pockets of ancient or syncretic animist practice. However, in all regions, Islam was present in the systemic machinery of political and social administration and served as a cement to unify ethnic groups who were all the more disparate because of their divergent interests. The predominance of Islam can be seen in the resistance conducted under its banner by some Islamic scholars.[12]

Consequently, it is understandable that in order to establish its policies and realise its occupational ambitions, the colonial administration should devote itself to destabilising the centres which disseminated religious knowledge, centres which it viewed as training recalcitrants hostile to its presence.

To do this, it adopted a three-pronged strategy:

- to undermine the foundations of the religious culture by attacking traditional Qur'anic schools, thus marginalising Arabic as the language of learning, and simultaneously installing its own educational model with an arsenal of accompanying laws and decrees;
- to systematically control anyone considered indifferent towards the colonial administration, in this case marabouts, who were considered charlatans and vagabonds despite their social standing;
- to incorporate anyone who could be considered 'understanding' into the colonial project, and also to reprimand and deport the most openly hostile and resistant elements.[13]

This practice of control and repression nonetheless did not shake the spirit of Islam. Certainly, the level of education declined strongly over time, but for reasons better linked with its own dynamics and the living conditions of Islamic populations than with the success of colonial policy. Thus, during the colonial period it has been observed that religious instruction grew horizontally via the enlargement of its foundations, but declined vertically with the slackening of the brotherhood element.

The Qur'an's linguistic contribution to languages

Islam has been a fully fledged African religion for several centuries. It goes without saying that its message has gradually impregnated the social fabric, beginning with the ancient religious conceptions of communities. Islam has consolidated their existing conception of an omnipotent God who exists above everything else, but whom they used to associate with other secondary deities capable of protecting or threatening the family or tribe. Islam thus recentred belief in 'the only God' by gradually obliterating the idea of secondary gods. I believe it then introduced a new social philosophy by peacefully erasing differences due to linguistic barriers, and promoting the creation of supra-tribal communities (*umma*) inspired by the model of Islam.

The social domain was also reorganised by means of the different Islamic sciences, notably that of jurisprudence (*fiqh*). All social philosophy and traditional practices (marriage, birth, education and instruction) were influenced to differing degrees. Some practices were totally Islamised, others only partially, but the process was under way. If one looks at it closely, this influence was only possible in some cases because of the similarity of the Islamic contribution to the standards in force in certain evolving communities. Even today there exist centres resistant to the Qur'anic message, but a large part of their social practice has been gradually infiltrated by Islamic norms.

The social domain was reorganised by means of the different Islamic sciences, notably that of jurisprudence (*fiqh*). All social philosophy and traditional practices (marriage, birth, education and instruction) were influenced to differing degrees. Some practices were totally Islamised, others only partially, but if one looks at it closely, this influence was only possible in some cases because of the similarity of the Islamic contribution to the standards already in force in certain communities.

The Qur'anic script or *ajami*

The Qur'an did not only contribute to social and religious philosophy; it also affected the field of language which, as we know, continually evolves in accordance with the position of its speakers. The cases of Swahili, Fulfulde, Hausa and Songhay are instructive. Numerous languages of African Muslim communities in West Africa resorted to borrowing Qur'anic terms to express certain previously unencountered situations and ideas, to replace little-used terms, and enriched their vocabulary with new words. The original meaning was kept in some borrowings, but in many other cases was either extended or restricted. Phonetically, furthermore, some borrowings from Arabic remained identical, whereas others underwent the phenomenon of accommodation which allows a language to borrow by integrating suffixes and prefixes, or by bending certain sounds to its own characteristics. This borrowing phenomenon operated directly from Arabic to the African language, and sometimes came via a third intermediary African language.

Scholars eventually resorted to the Qur'anic script in order to transcribe their languages. The adapted Qur'anic script is known as *ajami*; in the Arabic language it is

In order to spread religious knowledge and learning it was thus necessary to find a method that was comprehensible to the believer. Local scholars (particularly those in the brotherhoods) versed themselves in the composition of texts in local languages. To liberate people's minds the Qur'anic script was their only resort. This script was thus utilised in accordance with the uniqueness of each individual language, taking into account those languages that possessed variations in dialect.

a relative term which applies more to the transcribed language than to the script itself. In fact, etymologically *ajami* is used to describe anything modified by incomprehension or 'barbarism' (*'ujma*); thus its application to all languages incomprehensible to the Arabs. The latter contrasted it with eloquence (*fasaha*), which in their opinion was the very characteristic of the Arabic language.

Historically, this idea existed prior to Islam, as it preoccupied poets of the pre-Islamic period. At that time, *ajami* was used more generally for the languages of neighbouring peoples, namely the Persians (*al-furs*) whose language was incomprehensible to the Arabs, and later the Berbers (*al-barbar*) for the same reason.[14] Consequently, one need hardly note that the meaning of the word is dependent on its user and context.

Thus, in the pre-colonial Bilad al-Sudan *ajami* was very commonly used alongside Arabic in all intellectual activities carried out by scholars, and also by the literate masses in particular for correspondence during the colonial period.

With our current knowledge we cannot state with certainty the period in which scholars felt it necessary to resort to this script and to develop this literature in the Bilad al-Sudan. Nor do we have sources allowing us to state if it was in imitation of other Muslim communities (Persians and Berbers) who probably adopted it much earlier than the peoples of Central Sudan.

The hypothesis put forward by oral tradition is that the use of the Qur'anic script is ancient and goes back to the seventeenth century, but only became widespread in the eighteenth century when Islam had gradually spread to the non-literate strata of society. It thus became necessary to find a method of instruction suited to the fact that the majority of believers did not know Arabic, which remained the language of learning.[15]

In order to spread religious knowledge and learning it was thus necessary to find a method that was comprehensible to the believer. Local scholars (more particularly those in the brotherhoods) versed themselves in the composition of texts in local languages. To liberate people's minds the Qur'anic script was their only resort. This script was thus utilised in accordance with the uniqueness of each individual language, taking into account those languages that possessed variations in dialect.

In addition, we also know that the *ajami* literature was methodically used as a means of combat in the religious *jihad* undertaken by Shaykh 'Uthman dan Fodio and in the political consolidation of the Sokoto Empire (see Chapter 9 of this volume).

At first each scholar would have had his own method of transcription, and because some letters – like the 'ayn, sad, sin, dad – did not figure in certain African languages, not all letters would have been retained. Other letters – such as g, p, mb, nd, nh, nj, c, yh – existed in the African languages but not in the Qur'anic set. It was necessary to invent them by adopting similar letters and integrating distinctive markings. But this apparent anarchy in no way constituted a barrier between authors, since they could understand each other intuitively.

Disciplines dealt with in the use of the script

The *ajami* manuscripts bequeathed to us by our predecessors allow us an idea of the disciplines dealt with in this sort of script. Of course, one must be careful of generalising in such a vast and unresearched field but our sample can be considered reasonably representative.[16]

In fact, *ajami* concerned all fields of scholarly activity. We thus find treatises in the following fields:

- *al-tib al-mahali* (the description and traditional treatment of various illnesses);
- *al-saudala* (the properties of plants and ways of using them);
- *'ilm al-asrar* (texts dealing with the field of the occult sciences);
- translations of works and texts from Arabic into an African language;
- numerous texts exist on administrative and diplomatic matters (correspondence between sultans or provincial rulers, and between literate people).

But the script was used primarily for religious matters and includes calls for the purification of the faith, comment on the necessity of strengthening relations between different rural and urban communities, and of developing a conscious Muslim character able to discern social rifts and religious problems. The texts are in prose or in verse (*mandhuma* or *qasida*) and the sources from which they are composed are the Qur'an; the biography of the Prophet (*sira*); educational, historical narratives; extracts from biographies of messengers and prophets (*qisas al-anbiya*); and Prophetic traditions (*hadith*).

In our context, the above disciplines are all the more important as the authors of these texts are addressing believers who in many cases remain attached to ancestral practices which they integrate with Islam. The themes are products of their context and milieu, they keep their didactic characteristics as simplified teaching tools accessible to the public at large. A few key trends can be seen in these texts.

Tawhid

The science of the unity of God (*tawhid*) is one of the disciplines which is dealt with in numerous texts – their aim is to bring syncretist believers to carry out the practices set out in the Qur'an and Prophetic tradition. These texts are written from the observation that, whilst the idea of 'the only God' did not present difficulties for fresh converts who were still attached to ancestral traditions, this was not so in the case of the secondary gods that pervaded everyday life. These gods varied with tradition and were supposed to provide protection from calamities, to intercede with the ancestors to control the ecological environment, and to shield them from famine and epidemics, phenomena which populations experienced cyclically.

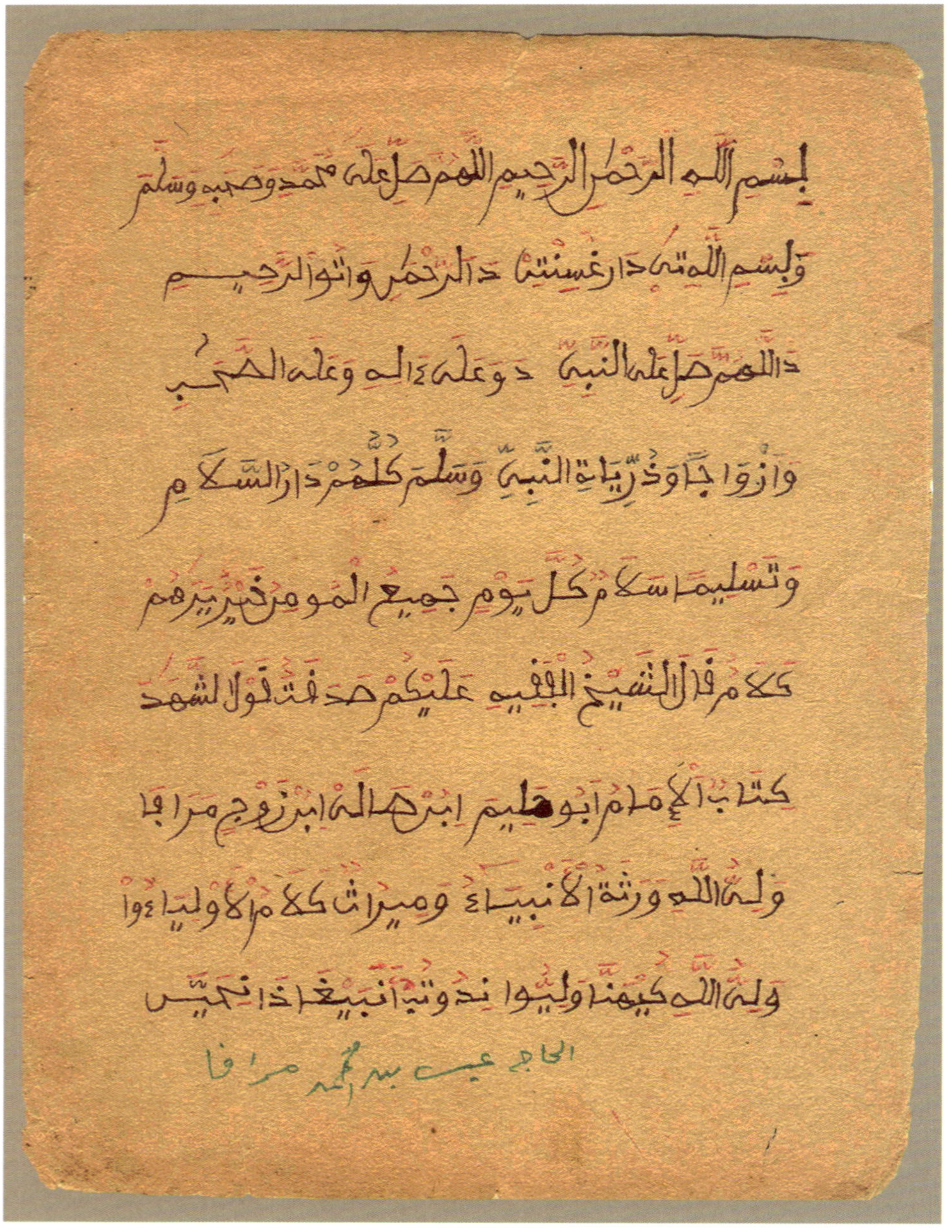

Figure 8.1 A folio from Manuscript No. 3503 in the Institut de Recherche en Sciences Humaines (IRSH/UAM), in Niamey, the capital of Niger. The author is al-Imam Abu Halim b. Sâlay b.Zawji Marafa, and the work is entitled *Manzuma fi al-wa'az wa-l- irshad*. The text is written in Songhay–Zarma (one of the languages spoken in western Niger and the Timbuktu and Gao areas of Mali). It contains extracts from the Qur'an and prophetic tradition, Muslim jurisprudence and biographies of exemplary figures. A literary text which has emerged from the masters of the Sufi schools, it deals with themes ranging from the teaching of religious principles to a behavioural code for believers.

The *tawhid* discipline thus asserts the unity of God, a concept which many believers in West Africa struggled to accept. Certainly the vast majority regularly practised the principles of Islam, but continued to indulge in ancestral religions, forbidden in the Qur'an and in Prophetic tradition.

The authors' descriptions are drawn from those Qur'anic verses that deal with paradise, a reward for the faithful described using Qur'anic imagery which has been carefully adapted to the immediate environment. The authors also use the same methodology to threaten eternal damnation in hell for perverse syncretists. IRSH/UAM no. 3503 (Figure 8.1) gives an idea of the ingenuity of the writers.

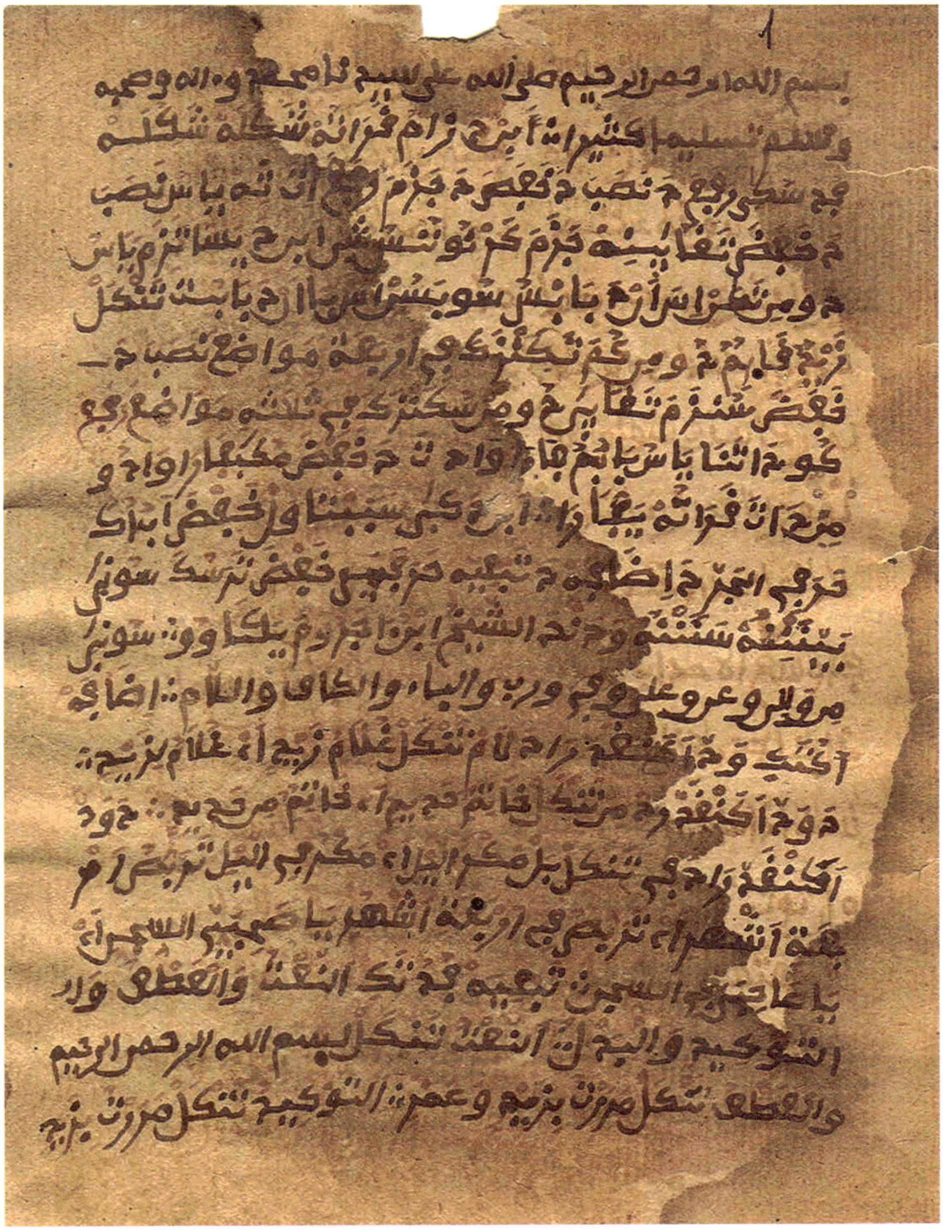

Figure 8.2 A folio from Manuscript No 367 (IRSH/UAM). This is a Hausa version of the work known as *Ajrumiyya*, a text which is particularly valued by beginner learners of Arabic grammar.

Fiqh

Another discipline which is dealt with in numerous texts is Muslim jurisprudence (*fiqh*), whose aim was to explain the wisdom recorded in the Qur'an and in the books of the Maliki jurisconsults (the most widely spread juridical school in western and Central Bilad al-Sudan), particularly the chapters regarding daily life and social relationships between believers. In addition, the authors drew on historical narratives (*qisas al-anbiya*), extracts from Qur'anic commentary, and biblical narratives (*al-israiliyyat*), all mixed with elements of local culture which were not openly contradictory to the above principles. The goal of this discipline was to set out an exemplary model of behaviour

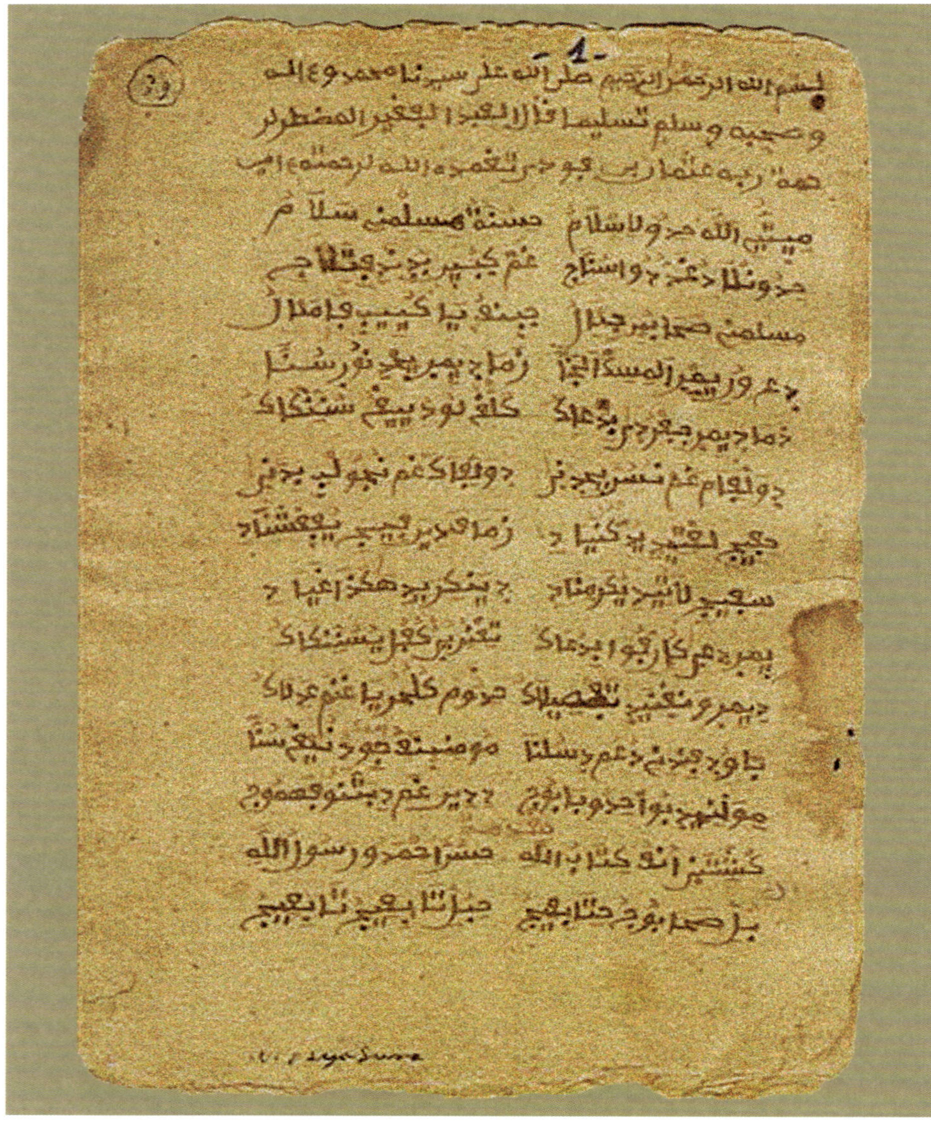

Figure 8.3 A folio from Manuscript No 393 (IRSH/UAM), a series of poems composed in Fulfulde and Arabic by Shaykh 'Uthman dan Fodio in honour of the Prophet Muhammad.

which, if followed, would achieve two objectives: obedience to God resulting in a stable life here on Earth, and salvation in the afterlife which will be realised in paradise. In the Bilad al-Sudan the influence of this discipline over the centuries gradually brought different ethnic groups together, and then unified them to a certain extent. Prior to their unification, these groups of pastoral and nomadic peoples had such divergent interests that serious conflict would often result. One of the most noticeable consequences of this discipline's influence was the linguistic and ethnic mixing between Saharans and Sahelians through intermarriage. Today, community customs continue to be influenced to one degree or another; some have been forgotten, whilst others are disappearing. The fluctuating dynamics of this discipline, fed by a lack of equity in political administration, at times resulted in the demand for the full application of Islamic *shari'a* law by the populations of some ancient religious cities.

Grammar

The Hausa version of the work known under the title *Ajjrumiyya* (IRSH/UAM no. 367; see Figure 8.2) is highly prized in Qur'anic schools in sub-Saharan Africa, particularly by learners beginning Arabic grammar. The author treats the different basic problems of this discipline (of grammar) in several chapters.

Eulogistic poetry

Eulogistic poetry is dedicated to the memory of prophets and messengers, called in Hausa *Yabon Annabi* and in Songhay–Zarma *Annabi Sifey*, but centres on the Prophet Muhammad. By hagiographying persons considered godly and pure, they present models to be imitated in particular ways. Like other original religious compositions from West Africa, this discipline draws on cultural referents specific to the locale, which partly explains its hold over the population. This poetry was first produced orally before being translated into *ajami*.

The poems composed by Shaykh 'Uthman dan Fodio in honour of the Prophet Muhammad are examples of this genre.[17] Composed in Fulfulde *ajami* and in Arabic, these poems contain diverse elements of local culture (see Figure 8.3).

Ajami in the post-colonial period

I have only briefly considered the relationship between the colonial administration and the scholars who held religious knowledge. Whilst it is true that new directions had been taken in the teaching of the Qur'an, notably through the encouragement and promotion of *madrasas*, the administration bequeathed by the colonisers (especially by the French) nonetheless remained mistrustful towards Muslim scholars. Of course, those in power now shared the same background as the scholars and were thus culturally similar, but real power still lay in the metropole. This partly explains why the education policy adopted in the post-colonial state was largely similar to that of the colonisers. It had three main aims:

- creating a secular state in accordance with the political ideals of the colonial power, which had at any rate left its advisers in the chancelleries of the new states;
- taking into account the fact that the majority of the population of Niger was Muslim but avoiding the creation of an 'Islamic state' which would have been considered a failure in their civilising mission;
- privileging relations with Arab countries, especially the wealthiest, to obtain indispensable aid for the economic and social development of the country, thus cutting the ground from under the feet of those who could use the extreme poverty of believers to formulate demands of a political nature under the banner of Islam.

In the realm of education, at the same time as encouraging the creation of *madrasas*, these states above all encouraged the colonial model of education from which local administrative elites had derived. The trend in favour of colonial-style schooling accentuated with independence, and younger generations were completely absorbed into western schools. The rift thus widened between a generation of parents who had grown up in the country in an Islam-influenced traditional culture, and their children, who had become the elite and had grown up in large urban centres which tended to promote western values through school. In less than a century and a half, this colonial model managed by a local administration became a source of inspiration for the class of future decision-makers.

On the other hand, with scholars who had remained attached to a culture largely shaped by Islam, people conversant with *ajami* continued to use it in correspondence, and Qur'anic schools continued to teach from the Qur'an. This duality is one of the characteristics of schooling in Islamic West Africa.

But we are forced to note that today most African languages are transcribed using the Latin alphabet, and linguistics is taught in universities in Romance languages. It seems as if *ajami* will thus be gradually superseded. However, the states of the sub-region (Guinea, Mali, Senegal, Niger and Chad) have put into place national *ajami* literacy programmes with the technical and financial support of the United Nations Educational, Scientific and Cultural Organisation; the Islamic Educational, Scientific and Cultural Organisation; and the Arab League Educational, Cultural and Scientific Organisation. What is more, round-table discussions have been organised with the aim of standardising transcription systems and fine-tuning literary programmes. Preliminary results have produced an operational literacy programme in standardised *ajami*, which will serve as a tool for local community training in line with the mindset of the population.

Conclusion

The long-standing method of transmitting the Muslim community's tradition orally was supplanted by the use of the Qur'anic script which served as a tool for cultural preservation. An inestimable legacy of *ajami* documents in different disciplines has been produced over several centuries. The standardisation of *ajami* is a welcome initiative which will no doubt bring its users closer together. But its use on a grand scale as an effective community literacy tool will pose certain political problems in the current context of competition for linguistic and cultural primacy. Economically disempowered states will need to make political choices, which is why political will is the key factor in this exercise.

As for the relevant populations, they remain firmly attached to the *ajami* script which is tied to the Qur'an, their holy book.

NOTES

1 Translated from French by Simon de Swardt.

2 Ki-Zerbo (1972) – see table of different African scripts in the appendix.

3 Hamani (1988: 79–113).

4 Several Qur'anic verses (59: 21; 12: 2; 39: 28) assert that the Holy Qur'an is a text above all others, uncorrupted by any imperfection. It is designed for the purification of the soul.

5 See Daniel (1970).

6 The most remarkable project remains the *Histoire Générale de l'Afrique* carried out under the aegis of Unesco. The abridged version has been translated into kiSwahili. Hausa and Peule versions are in progress. For the classical period, see Cuoq (1975).

7 Moumouni (1984).

8 Laroui (1970: 218–219).

9 Thus numerous sub-Saharan Africans were trained in the famous university mosques: al-Qarawine in Fez, Zaituna in Tunis, Qayrawan and al-Azhar as-Sharif in Cairo. See El-Fasi & Hrbek (1990: 81–116).

10 Hamani (1981: 26–31). Note that Hamani has drawn up a list of significant scholars who played an important role in intellectual activity. See also Ki-Zerbo (1990: vol. 6, chap. Révolutions Islamiques).

11 For the role played by religious leaders in the face of colonial installation, see Kimba (1981).

12 Salifou (1971: 66).

13 Traoré (1983: introduction).

14 Gibb et al. (1975: 272).

15 Gibb et al. (1975: 272).

16 We have begun on the basis of 70 *ajami* documents preserved in the Département des Manuscrits Arabes et Ajamis in the IRSH. They originate from all parts of sub-Saharan Africa.

17 Manuscripts to be found at the IRSH.

REFERENCES

Batran AA (1990) Révolutions Islamiques. In JFA Ajayi (Ed.) *Histoire générale de l'Afrique* (vol. 6). Paris: Unesco

Cuoq J (1975) *Recueils des sources arabes concernant l'Afrique Occidentale du VIIIe au XVe siècle.* Paris: CNRS

Daniel R (1970) *Croyances religieuses et vie quotidienne. Islam et Christianisme à Ouagadougou, Recherches Voltaïques.* Paris: CNRS

El-Fasi M & Hrbek I (1990) Etapes du développement de l'islam et de sa diffusion en Afrique. In M el-Fasi (Ed.) *Histoire générale de l'Afrique* (vol. 3). Paris: Unesco

Gibb HAR et al. (Eds) (1975) *Encyclopédie de l'Islam* (second edition). Leiden: Brill

Hamani D (1981) *Contribution à l'histoire de l'islamisation des populations nigériennes avant la colonisation.* Provisional document. Université de Niamey

Hamani D (1988) *Les personnalités célèbres dans culture et civilisation Islamiques (le NIGER).* Rabat: ISESCO

Hamidullah M (trans.) (1989) Le Saint Coran et la traduction en langue française. Medina, Kingdom of Saudi Arabia: La Présidence Générale des Directions de Recherches Scientifiques Islamiques, of Ifta, of the Prédication et de l'organisation Religieuse

Kimba I (1981) Guerres et sociétés, les populations du (Niger) Occidental au XIXe Siècle et leurs réactions à la colonisation (1896–1906). *Etudes Nigériennes* 46: 48–49

Ki-Zerbo J (1972) *Histoire de l'Afrique.* Paris: Hatier

Ki-Zerbo J (Gen. ed.) (1990) *Histoire générale de l'Afrique* (nouvelles editions, 8 vols). Paris: Unesco

Laroui A (1970) *Histoire du Maghreb.* Paris: Maspero

Moumouni Z (1984) L'Islam au Niger. *L'Islam Aujourd'hui* 2: 199–206

Salifou A (1971) Le Damagaram ou Sultanat de Zinder au XIXe Siècle. *Etudes Nigériennes* 27: 66

Traoré A (1983) *Islam et colonisation en Afrique, Shaykh Hamahoullah, homme de foi et résistant.* Paris: Maisonneuve et Larose

Samedi 23 janvier

بسم الله الرحمن الرحيم

ثم أمل منا وكيف الذي شاف واحد منهم امر زيتي او عاد
يتغية واتحية مالليل اجنوار التي عادت هي زاد تتغية
اخذناها عند اهله اذور تتعرس دونكاو اهله اعرس وكل
واعطاها يلس حتى امه الاكتيا [illegible] اد خلوه
تحصين لن هو الجمع افلحطب الذي عاد يلس من الحطب
وعاد العصى اكبر اونكب فيه النار والناس شرع
فيه الاكله يعرو حد هاد الناس الذي عاد الغريب
جات لمن كاو واحد وازوده تالت الناس
انت ايد كما عد ابلمن الرابع شالهم اذعو ونشوية
اوفيد النار كالو اعلاه تا الهم مكا تار اتحواما
كات الفمر من النساء ~~Samedi~~ والسلام

30 janvier

جمة اثم ماس الي عيعتل امراد ورتغلب الله يتهي وحد عند ج
والته تغلبه والغلبه وتقعد ويترفد تالت لمرها اذا اشنه
الواسيت اكالة دهه الا بتره الحلاب الرابع
اسبنيه والرابع اعقبه

Samedi le 6 fevrier 1915

Jam

ثم امل ماتنيغ وهوو واحد منهم اسنذ وكن اكبار الي ثم اصاحب
انت واجب اعليد تحتك واندوز ~~[illegible]~~ تكتلك كال اعلاه
واجب تحتلي كا اللوخ وجب مولاي الذي خلفنا كال الوحيد
بابتر مولانا وجب تحتلي كالا اغاو بكي يكحب بالادي

CHAPTER 9

Ajami literature and the study of the Sokoto Caliphate

Hamid Bobboyi

The Sokoto Caliphate (1804–1903),[1] established under the leadership of Shaykh 'Uthman dan Fodio (the Shehu) (1754–1817) with the assistance of his brother, Shaykh 'Abdullahi (d.1829), and his son, Muhammad Bello (d.1837), is reputed to have been one of the most prolific in the Central Bilad al-Sudan, leaving behind a large body of literature which was of immense value in documenting and evaluating the history of the caliphate. The triumvirate itself authored over 250 works and, over the years, their descendants and successors made significant contributions to this veritable intellectual heritage.[2]

Although many of the Sokoto caliphal writings are in Arabic, a significant number of manuscripts, written in the Arabic script, are in local languages, principally Fulfulde and Hausa. The *ajami* literature, despite its potential in broadening our understanding of the history of the Sokoto Caliphate, has been only partially exploited by scholars and, more often than not, for linguistic rather than historical studies.[3] This chapter is an attempt to explore the significance of the *ajami* literature with a view to understanding the role it played in the establishment and consolidation of the caliphate.

Pre-*jihad ajami* literature

Despite the proliferation of *ajami* manuscripts in the late eighteenth and in the nineteenth centuries, the development of *ajami* literature in the Central Bilad al-Sudan before the eighteenth century is difficult to trace with any degree of certainty. John Phillips's assertion that 'the first *ajami* writing for which we have [a] reliable (though not absolute) date is *Riwayar Annabi Musa* by the famous Kano scholar 'Abdullahi Suka which may be seen in the manuscript collection of the Jos Museum'.[4] While 'Abd Allah b. Muhammad b. Salim, known as 'Abdullahi Suka, flourished in the mid-seventeenth century and authored the *Atiyyat al-mu'ti*,[5] there is no firm indication to identify him conclusively as the author of the said Hausa *ajami* manuscript. It is also possible that

Opposite: An example of *ajami* literature, using both African and European languages.

A manuscript at the Ahmed Baba Institute, awaiting restoration and conservation.

both Muhammad b. Masanih (d.1667) and Muhammad b. al-Sabbagh (fl.1640–41) authored some *ajami* manuscripts,[6] but again there is no credible evidence to attribute with any firmness the *Waqar Yakin Badr* to either one of them.

Mervyn Hiskett, who undertook a more extensive work on Hausa *ajami* literature and the development of Hausa Islamic verse, adopted a more cautious approach to the subject.[7] Hiskett drew attention to the existence of two dominant forms of Hausa oral literature: the *kirari* (praise epithets) and *wakar yabo* (praise songs).[8] While these forms could find themselves in lists of kings that ruled and historical chronicles,[9] they remained patently un-Islamic and though they survived they could not be integrated into the mainstream of the Islamic literary tradition. Thus the Hausa 'literate verse' as we know it today, argued Hiskett, was essentially an Islamic creation and possibly an 'innovation' introduced by the Sokoto reformers.[10]

Although the history of the Hausa literate verse could not be fully ascertained before the late eighteenth century, there is some evidence to suggest that some form of Fulfulde *ajami* literature was in existence by the second half of the seventeenth century and that it was coherent enough to have attracted the attention of serious Islamic scholars like Muhammad al-Wali b. Sulayman al-Fallati (fl.1688–89).[11] The latter's *al-Manhaj al-farid fi ma'rifat 'ilm al-tawhid* was an Arabic version of some Fulfulde commentaries on the *Sughra* of al-Sanusi, one of the major texts for the study of *tawhid* in West Africa.[12] How much Shaykh 'Uthman dan Fodio and his colleagues elaborated on the existing literature cannot be fully established, but there was apparently a Fulfulde literary substratum which they could build upon.

The reform tradition

The establishment of the Sokoto Caliphate under the leadership of Shaykh 'Uthman dan Fodio was a gradual process taking several decades to come to fruition. The initial and one of the most crucial stages in this process was that of mobilisation. From 1774, when Shaykh 'Uthman was only 20 years old, he began active teaching and preaching until he established an autonomous *jama'a* (congregation) which was able to begin asserting its independence from the Gobir authorities in 1804.[13] It is within the 'mobilisation framework' of the Sokoto reform movement that we need to locate the significance of *ajami* literature and how it was effectively exploited by the caliphal leaders to establish a substantial presence within the rural and non-literate communities of Gobir, Zamfara and Kebbi. 'Abdullahi dan Fodio (d.1829) was emphatic on the role *ajami* literature played in this mobilisation process when he wrote:

> Then we rose with the Shaikh, helping him in his mission work for religion. He traveled for that purpose to the East and West, calling people to the religion of God by his preaching and his qasidas [odes] in *Ajami* [Hausa and Fulfulde] and destroying customs contrary to Muslim Law.[14]

Ajami literature played an important role during the mobilisation phase of the reform movement, particularly in helping the *jihad* leaders put across their message to their teeming but unlettered followers. It would be difficult to imagine the Sokoto *jihad* emerging as a mass movement without taking into account the effective exploitation of *ajami* to achieve this objective.

Shaykh 'Uthman dan Fodio himself, in emphasising the strategic importance of using *ajami* in his mobilisation efforts, had this to say in his Fulfulde poem titled *Babuwol kire*:[15]

> *Nufare nde am yusbango en baabuwol kire*
> *Mi yusbira ngol Fulfulde Fulbe fu yeetoye*
> *To min njusbiri arabiyya aalimi tan nafi'*
> *To min njusbiri fulfulde Jaahili Faydoye*

> My intention is to compose a poem on the [prostration] of *forgetfulness*
> I intend to compose it in Fulfulde so that Fulbe could be enlightened.
> When we compose [a poem] in Arabic only the learned benefit.
> When we compose it in Fulfulde the unlettered also gain.

The focus of Shaykh 'Uthman dan Fodio and his lieutenants at this stage of the movement appears to have been on developing a conscious Muslim personality, able to discern the social ills of Hausaland and its religious problems and contradictions.[16] This apparent socioreligious protest found expression in several *ajami* poems, particularly those authored by Shaykh 'Uthman dan Fodio. One poem which has enjoyed some popularity in this category is Shaykh 'Uthman's Fulfulde *urjuza*, called *Boneji Hausa* (Ills of Hausaland).[17] This poem admits the many evils prevalent in Hausa society and the conspiracy of silence by leaders of thought which made it difficult to address them in any serious and systematic manner. The poem proceeds to highlight some of these ills:

Goddi boneji mairi bo, bukkaki
Goddi boneji mairi bo, simaki
Goddi boneji maari bo, diccaki
A hinnata goodo e-dou nguski
Goddi boneji mari bo juldo nanngoya
Na yo jeyado, jaggineki tokkoye
Goddi boneji maari shar'u doggata
E mairi jul yimbe mairi ndonnata
Goddi boneji mairi jula nanngata
Zakka mo mashiyaji bo be ittata
Goddi boneji mairi reube njangata
Balli di mabbe bo kurum be cuddata
Wodbe benteje fede sabal sabal
Hayya e be yimbe ngala e dou datal.

Some ills are tattoos on the faces
Others are crying over the dead.
Some ills are the salutations made [during salutations]
'Thou shall not salute while standing'
Some of its ills are the capture of a free Muslim, not a slave.
This action is then followed by enslavement.
From its ills is that the *shari'a* does not prevail.
And many of its people do not distribute estates in accordance with the Law.
One of its ills is performing prayers without ablution.
The *zakat* of their animals they never pay.
Another ill is that women do not learn
Their body they never cover properly
Some of them have their 'bante' aprons loosely blowing 'Sabal Sabal'.
Oh! These people are not on the right path.

Another poem by Shaykh 'Uthman which falls into this category is *Wasuyeji* (Advice), which discouraged social intercourse with oppressive rulers, innovators and other undesirable characters and encouraged keeping the company of the pious, the learned and followers of the Sunna, for the latter, according to the shaykh, was superior to both one's father and mother.[18] Shaykh 'Uthman's Fulfulde poem *Hasotobe* further elaborated on one group of these undesirable characters, the rumour-mongers and hate-mongers who saw nothing good in what the shaykh and his disciples were trying to accomplish.[19]

The second category of *ajami* literature which played an important role during the mobilisation phase of Shaykh 'Uthman's reform movement and subsequently is the *wa'azi* (Hausa) or *waju* (Fulfulde) poetry. *Wa'az*, as Sultan Muhammad Bello b. Shaykh 'Uthman understood it, constituted reminding people about the hereafter, its pleasures and its trials and tribulations with a view to instilling the fear of God into their hearts.[20]

Viewed from the vantage point of available manuscript collections, this category of *ajami* literature appears quite extensive. The main problem, however, is that most of these poems bear no date and it is difficult to assign them properly to this period.

The Fulfulde *qasida* with the title *Duniyayel* (This Miserable World) and attributed to Shaykh 'Uthman dan Fodio falls into this category of *Wa'azi* literature. This and similar poems attempt to underscore the transient nature of this world and to bring home the realisation that it is only the hereafter which is real. The examples *Duniyayel* raises are indeed classic:

> This miserable world is like the snake's body.
> So slippery that anyone getting hold of it will be left empty handed.
> This miserable world is like a shade of cloud.
> The cloud will soon disappear and the shade vanishes.
> This miserable world is like a mirage.
> Those determined to fetch it will find absolutely nothing.[21]

'Abdullahi dan Fodio's Hausa *qasida*, *Mulkin audu*,[22] paints a more graphic picture of the fleeting nature of the world and of the day of resurrection:

> Woe to us on the day it shall be said 'What of so and so? Today he has passed away.'
> Everything of his has passed away
> All the heirs now drink the soup.
> When the day of your death comes,
> You will forget son and grandchild.
> The wealth you have hidden away, will not ransom you, you hear?
> On the Day of Resurrection there will be summons;
> All mankind we shall assemble.
> There will be no waist wrapper, nay, not even a loin cloth;
> there will be none to laugh!
> Judgment will be given, the division will be made;
> every unbeliever will suffer torment.

Shaykh 'Uthman's *Yimre Jahima*[23] extends further the discussion on hellfire by mentioning those who will suffer the torment[24] and seek refuge from the fire of *Jahima* (hell). Finally, the issue of repentance (*tuba*, *tubuye*) brings to a logical conclusion the cyclical discourse of the *wa'azi* literature. Shaykh 'Uthman's *Inna gime* (Mother of Poems)[25] is a good example of a repentance poem, illustrating quite vividly their supplicatory nature.

The third category of *ajami* literature relevant to our understanding of the Sokoto Caliphate at the early stage of its history is the didactic verse that was meant to teach the rudiments of *fiqh*, *tawhid* and *sira*. Muhammad Bello in his *Infaq al-maysur* had shown clearly the importance of these subjects in Shaykh 'Uthman's sermons,[26] and it is very probable that *ajami* was effectively utilised to get the message across to the movement's unlettered followers. I have already made reference to Shaykh 'Uthman's *Babuwol kire or Sujud al-sahwi* (Prostrations on Forgetfulness). This could have complemented other *gime furu'a* which are being transmitted up to the present day.[27] It is also possible that some major works like the *Ihya al-Sunna* (Revival of the Sunna), which the Shehu authored, could have been versified in either Hausa or Fulfulde.[28]

On *tawhid*, one of the extant works is a Hausa composition by one of the disciples of Shaykh 'Uthman, Malam Usman Miga, called *Musan samuwar jalla*.[29] According to Hiskett's analysis, the work was based on *Jawharat al-tawhid* of Ibrahim al-Laqani (d.1668), and *Umm al-Barahin* of Muhammad b. Yusuf al-Sanusi (d.1486).[30] An example of *sira* literature in *ajami* is 'Abdullahi dan Fodio's *Wakar sira*, which gives an elaborate genealogy of the Prophet and various aspects of the Prophet's biography.[31] Related to the *sira* literature but pursued more for spiritual and devotional purposes was the *madh al-nabi* (Praise of the Prophet) literature. This group of *ajami* verse, both in Hausa and Fulfulde, is again quite extensive but could not be accurately dated or firmly attributed to any of the principal actors at this stage of the history.[32]

Hijra, *jihad* and consolidation

The events leading to the *hijra* and *jihad* of Shaykh 'Uthman dan Fodio have been fairly well established. The *Tazyin al-waraqat* of 'Abdullahi dan Fodio and the *Infaq al-maysur* of Sultan Muhammad Bello have given detailed accounts of these momentous events and the resultant consequences. As far as mobilising people for the *hijra* was concerned, once again *ajami* played a vital role. In the words of 'Abdullahi dan Fodio:

> Then our Shaikh 'Uthman – May God perpetuate the glory of Islam through him – when he saw the greatness of the community, and their desire to break away from the unbelievers, and commence Holy War, began to incite them to arms – and he began to pray to God that He should show him the sovereignty of Islam in this country of the Sudan and he set this to verse in his non-Arabic qasida *called Qadiriyya*...[33] (emphasis mine)

It could also be argued that *ajami* literature played an equally important role in mobilising for *jihad* and for understanding how it should be conducted in accordance with the tenets of the *shari'a*. Sultan Muhammad Bello's *urjuza*, titled *Yimre jihadi*, is one of the extant works in this category of *ajami* literature.[34] Closely related to the *jihad* poems is the report of battles and the celebration of the jihadists' victory in them. 'Abdullahi dan Fodio's *Hausa Poem* recounting the Muslim victory at Kalambaina[35] is a good example. In later years Nana Asma'u, the daughter of Shaykh 'Uthman, became one of the principal personalities who gave account of some of these battles, as can be seen from her many poems on the subject. It is, however, important to note that Nana Asma'u was not merely a chronicler of the caliphate's battles and victories. Through her educational activities and vast social network, she greatly enhanced the role of *ajami* in the consolidation of the emerging caliphate. Nana Asma'u and her brother 'Isa translated many of Shaykh 'Uthman's works into Hausa, which made them more accessible to the wider population.[36] She also enriched the *ajami* landscape through her prolific writings and expanded its scope to treat a variety of subjects and issues normally reserved for the classical Arabists.[37]

It is also important to recognise that Nana Asma'u not only witnessed the consolidation of the Sokoto Caliphate but also the demise of almost all those who played pivotal roles in its establishment. The large body of *ajami* literature on eulogies and elegies which Nana Asma'u left us bears testimony to the traumatic nature of these experiences as well as her determination and resilience in ensuring continuity and in helping to restore the emotional balance of society.[38]

Political protest

The last category of *ajami* literature which this chapter will consider is that dealing with political protest. Drastic political change, like that witnessed in Hausaland under the leadership of Shaykh 'Uthman dan Fodio, could only come with huge sacrifices and great expectations. Whenever the leadership failed to meet these expectations, the very instruments used to overthrow the *status quo ante* could also be effectively exploited to subvert the new order. This brings us to an examination of *ajami* as 'subversive' literature.

For the Sokoto Caliphate, however, we need to approach this subject matter with some caution. It could be argued that the radical tradition which was popularised by 'Abdullahi dan Fodio might not have been fully extinguished even after the consolidation of the caliphate. 'Abdullahi dan Fodio, it will be recalled, was disenchanted with the course of the *jihad* as early as 1808:

> When my companions passed and my aims went awry;
> I was left among the remainder, the Liars.
> Who say that which they do not do and follow their desires;
> And follow avarice in everything incumbent upon them…
> Whose purpose is the ruling of the countries and their people;
> In order to obtain delights and acquire rank according to the custom of the unbelievers and the titles of their sovereignty.
> And the appointing of ignorant persons to the highest offices;
> And the collecting of concubines, and fine clothes; and horses that gallop in the towns, not on the battlefield.[39]

Many Sokoto scholars who wrote in *ajami* were not unsympathetic to 'Abdullahi dan Fodio's position and, as the 'transgressions' mounted, these voices became more strident. Malam Muhammadu Na Birnin Gwari (fl.1850) was one of those voices:

Know ye that tyranny will be darkness on the Day of Resurrection;
It is the word of the Messenger of God, Muhammad.
Spread out justice as a carpet in East and West; South and North,
over all, for the community of Muhammad…
Where are the bodyguards, and Harem messengers and concubines;
and the women of the palace? Come listen to what benefits you…
And you, the King's courtiers, stop going round the towns;
confiscating the people's property with unlawful acts.
Riding around on horses in order to peer into the compounds
[to see what to confiscate].[40]

The second voice is that of Muhammad Raji b. Ali b. Abi Bakr (d. after 1865–66). Modibbo Raji,[41] as he was popularly known, wrote a Fulfulde *qasida* which he titled *Alamaaji ngirbuki* (The Signs of Collapse), echoing similar sentiments to those of Muhammadu Na Birnin Gwari:

The signs of collapse are upon us;
The Hadiths of the prophet and the sayings of the righteous point to it…
Tyranny, cheating and injustice are so rampant;
the principal concern being erecting tall buildings
and the abandonment of mosques.
Leaders have become an irresponsible lot, a bunch of dangerous thugs.
You neither find one who does justice nor the one who guides to what is right.[42]

It is interesting that Modibbo Raji, like 'Abdullahi dan Fodio, also expressed immense interest in *hijra*, preferably to Medina, retracing the footsteps of the Prophet:

Had it been that I have where to run to, I would have escaped.
I would then retrace the Prophet's footsteps in Medina.
In reality, the body has remained motionless, unable to commence the journey;
but the mind has eagerly left while the limbs have been stationary.[43]

Concluding remarks

I have in this chapter attempted to explore the significance of *ajami* literature in the study of the Sokoto Caliphate. I have examined the difficulties of tracing the history of the *ajami* Islamic verse in the Central Bilad al-Sudan and addressed the argument that it might have been the Sokoto Caliphate which gave this literature its current identity and character. I have further examined the role that *ajami* literature played during the mobilisation phase of the reform movement, particularly in helping the *jihad* leaders put across their message to their teeming but unlettered followers. It would be difficult to imagine the Sokoto *jihad* emerging as a mass movement without taking into account the effective exploitation of *ajami* to achieve this objective.

Finally, I have examined the role of *ajami* literature during the *hijra* and *jihad* periods as well as during the era of consolidation. The significance of *ajami* as 'subversive' literature during the second half of the nineteenth century was further highlighted, taking cognisance of established trends of radical Islamic thought within the Sokoto Caliphate.

The chapter has also raised the problem of authorship and accurate dating as some of the key problems which make it difficult to take full advantage of the available *ajami* literature. It is my opinion that greater efforts should be made to recover more manuscripts so as to provide a larger and more varied resource pool, which could help clear some of the lingering problems. Researchers should also focus on custodians of oral tradition – older men and women and 'guilds' of the blind who were known for their knowledge of the oral traditions – to get the oral rendition of these documents, as well as information on their authors.

While Hausa and Fulfulde are usually regarded as the two dominant *ajami* languages in Nigeria, we should also explore the availability of *ajami* literature in other 'Islamic languages' including Nupe, Kanuri and Yoruba. This recovery effort will be greatly assisted with better insight into the development of language – specific *ajami* orthography and how this has changed over the centuries.

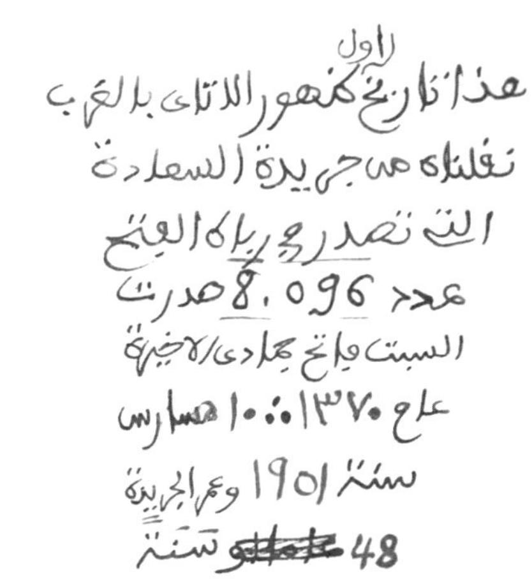

NOTES

1 The period 1804–1903 represents the approximate dates of the existence of the caliphate. Although the *jihad* commenced in 1804, Sokoto was not established until about half a decade later. Secondly, the mobilisation phase started as early as 1774 when Shaykh 'Uthman dan Fodio, the leader of the reform movement, commenced his preaching tours. For a general history of the caliphate, see Last (1977). See also Hiskett (1973) and Fodio (1963).

2 See Hunwick & O'Fahey (1995).

3 See Hiskett (1975) and Furniss (1996). The most useful exploitation of this resource to date remains Boyd & Mack (1999).

4 Phillips (1999: 19).

5 For details on 'Abdullahi Suka see Hunwick & O'Fahey (1995: 32–33).

6 Phillips (1999: 19–20).

7 For a discussion on the issue see Hiskett (1975: 1–11).

8 Hiskett (1975).

9 Hiskett (1975: 2–3) referred to the Kirari in the *Kano Chronicle* as an example of this category of Hausa literature. It is also possible that the Kanuri *girgam* tradition in Bornu could have had its origins in similar circumstances. See Palmer (1936).

10 Hiskett (1975: 18) believes that Islamic verse in Hausa was probably composed during the pre-*jihad* period 'but not to any significant extent, and there is no evidence that it was ever written down'.

11 See Hunwick & O'Fahey (1995: 34–37). It must be pointed out that *al-Manhaj al-farid* is a prose work and not an indication of any 'literate verse tradition'. Though there are references in the field to Fulfulde poems composed by Shaykh Tahir b. Ibrahim al-Fallati (d. after 1745–46), these have not come to light.

12 See Hunwick & O'Fahey (1995: 35).

13 See Last (1977: 3–40).

14 Fodio (1963: 85–86).

15 See Abubakar et al. (2004: 18–25).

16 Sultan Muhammad Bello gave some glimpses into his father's propagation techniques and strategies during this phase of the movement. See Bello (1951).

17 See Saidu (1979: 203–205).

18 See Saidu (1979: 198–199).

19 See Saidu (1979: 201–202).

20 Bello (1951: 91–94).

21 Abubakar et al. (2004: 3–8).

22 Reproduced in Hiskett (1975: 29–31).

23 Saidu (1979: 206–207).

24 Shaykh 'Uthman mentioned the hate-monger, thieves and adulterers, misappropriators of *zakat*, mischief makers, avaricious rulers, corrupt judges, one who defies judgement of the *qadi* and 'the *Mallam* [scholars] who failed to follow what he learnt' (Saidu 1979: 207).

25 Saidu (1979: 197–198).

26 Bello (1951: 74–94).

27 See Abubakar et al. (2004: 18–25). The *furu'* poems which deal with the various branches of *fiqh* abound in the various manuscript collections. However, the problem of dating makes it difficult to attribute them to the period under discussion.

28 A Fulfulde rendering of the *Ihya al-Sunna*, in *urjuza* form, has turned up in the uncatalogued Arabic collection of the Sokoto State History Bureau. The paper is quite old, written by what could be termed a 'steady *jihadi* hand'. It is in fragmentary form and bears neither a title nor a date of composition.

29 Poem quoted by Hiskett (1975: 68–71).

30 Hiskett (1975).

31 Hiskett (1975: 53–58). The Fulfulde *qasida* of 'Abdullahi dan Fodio's *Wakar sira* also appears in Abubakar et al. (2004: 26–67) and is firmly attributed to him. The question immediately arises as to which of the two poems was the original and which one was a translation. This problem may affect many other poems, particularly during the middle period (1840–70) when many of these poems were translated, usually into Hausa.

32 A special mention must, however, be made of Shaykh 'Uthman's *Ma'ama'are* which was rendered into Hausa by his son 'Isa b. al-Shaykh. See Sokoto State History Bureau, mss 4/28/205. Another poem by Shaykh 'Uthman, *Miyetti ya Allah neldo Muhammadu*, can also be found in the John Rylands collection, J9/15.

33 Fodio (1963: 105). A Fulfulde *qasida* titled *Qadiriyya* is available in the Sokoto State History Bureau, 4/15/206, and is very similar in meaning to the poem translated into Arabic by 'Abdullahi dan Fodio.

34 See Abubakar et al. (2004: 71–75).

35 Hiskett (1975: 28).

36 Among other works, Nana Asma'u translated the *Tabbat haqiqa* of Shaykh 'Uthman dan Fodio into Hausa while 'Isa b. Shaykh 'Uthman translated the *Ma'ama'are*.

37 See Boyd & Mack (1999: table of contents, v–viii).

38 Nana Asma'u's poems on these subjects include *Sonnore Abd Allah; Sonnore Bello; Sonnore Mo'Inna; Sonnore Bukhai; Sonnore Gidado; Sonnore Zahra; Sonnore Hawwa; Sonnore Bingel; Sonnore Na'Inna; Sonnore Mustafa; Alhinin Mutawar Modibbo dan Ali; Alhinin Mutuwar Halima.*

39 Fodio (1963: 121–122).

40 Hiskett (1975: 101).

41 Hunwick & O'Fahey (1995: 434–436).

42 Abubakar et al. (2004: 90–103).

43 Abubakar et al. (2004). Compare with 'Abdullahi dan Fodio's poem: 'My heart flew to Madina, dwelling there for years out of desire and it will not return; But my sin kept my body away from it, confused…' (1963: 122).

REFERENCES

Abubakar MB, Tahir US, Hamid B & Dewa S (Compilers and trans) (2004) *Fulfulde poems* (Vol. 1). Yola: Sokoto Bicentenary Committee

Bello M (1951) *Infaq al-Maysur fi tarikh bilad al-Takrur*. London: Luzac

Boyd J & Mack B (1999) *The collected works of Nana Asma'u, daughter of Usman dan Fodiyo (1793–1864)*. Ibadan: Sam Bookman Publishers

Fodio A (1963) *Tazyin al-waraqat*. Edited and translated by M Hiskett. Ibadan: Ibadan University Press

Furniss G (1996) *Poetry, prose and popular culture in Hausa*. Edinburgh: Edinburgh University Press

Hiskett M (1973) *The sword of truth: The life and times of the Shehu Usman dan Fodio*. New York: Oxford University Press

Hiskett M (1975) *A history of Hausa Islamic verse*. London: School of Oriental and African Studies

Hunwick JO & RS O'Fahey (Eds) (1995) *Arabic literature of Africa: The writings of Central Sudanic Africa* (Vol. 2). Leiden: Brill

Last M (1977) *The Sokoto Caliphate*. London: Longman

Palmer R (1936) *The Bornu, Sahara and Sudan*. London: John Murray

Phillips JE (1999) *Spurious Arabic: Hausa and colonial Nigeria*. Madison: African Studies Program, University of Wisconsin-Madison

Saidu AG (1979) The significance of Shehu's sermons and poems in Ajami. In YB Usman (Ed.) *Studies in the history of the Sokoto Caliphate*. Zaria: Department of History, Ahmadu Bello University for the Sokoto State History Bureau

CHAPTER 10

The book in the Sokoto Caliphate

Murray Last

Much has been written on the Fondo Ka'ti, the huge collection of old manuscripts in Arabic now preserved in a library built in Timbuktu with considerable aid from the government of Andalucia.[1] The collection's founder seems to have been a 'Goth' (*al-Quti*) from Granada, who left Spain circa 1468 AD.[2] It is an extraordinarily rich collection, only recently come to public notice. Its very presence in Timbuktu highlights the question not only of personal libraries but also of the way books were made and sold in West Africa's pre-colonial past. Some scholarly communities are relatively well researched: perhaps the most notable are the nomadic Shinqitti scholars of Mauritania, western neighbours of their Timbuktu colleagues; both looked to Morocco and to a lesser extent Algeria for their imports of paper as well as texts.[3]

The focus in this chapter is on manuscripts. Interesting and even more neglected though it is, I have omitted from discussion the trade in printed Arabic books. I do not know what the earliest printed Arabic book in West Africa is. In scholarly Mauritania Shaykh Sidiya's first printed book arrived as late as 1861, reports Charles Stewart.[4] But elsewhere West African scholars in the eighteenth century owned what may have been printed copies of texts by Euclid (obtainable in Mecca), and perhaps also other technical or scientific works. The Sokoto builder, for example, who asked for and got from Clapperton a Gunter's scale, already had all the architectural papers which his father had acquired in Cairo.[5] Similarly, on that second visit to Sokoto in 1826 Clapperton brought out for Muhammad Bello some suitable books printed in Arabic – Euclid's *Elements*, a work by Ibn Sina, and the *History of the Tartars*, along with a Holy Qur'an, the New and Old Testaments, and the Psalms.[6] When 'Fellata' (Fulfulde speaking) scholars returned, from 'Mecca,...the empires of Turkey and Morocco,...Algiers, Tunis and Tripoli, bringing back with them all the Arabic books they were able to beg or buy', no doubt amongst the texts that they brought back were some printed volumes.[7] Bound printed books were presumably cheaper in North African markets and more immediately available than specially commissioned copies to be made by hand. Presses capable

Opposite: Examples of manuscripts enclosed in protective tooled leather wallets which enhanced their portability.

of publishing Arabic texts had been established in the Muslim world by the early sixteenth century (some of the skilled printers being émigrés from Spain), and printed Arabic books exported from Europe for use in the Middle East date from the same period. However, for ostensibly religious reasons no use was made of printing by Muslims till the eighteenth century.[8] Ordinary religious texts could be set in movable type, but so sacred a text as the Holy Qur'an (or the Torah) had to be written by hand, though lithographs of a handwritten text were acceptable. Thus ancient libraries in West Africa are primarily composed of manuscripts.

I want here to look briefly at the problems of manuscript books further to the east of Timbuktu – the Muslim scholarly communities of Hausaland and Borno in modern-day Nigeria – and focus on the pre-colonial period, especially the nineteenth century when the Sokoto Caliphate had succeeded in uniting a larger region than any other independent state in Africa. The state was four months journey west to east, and two months north to south. It was run as a confederation of emirates under the *amir al-mu'minin* in Sokoto with a 'bureaucratic' staff who corresponded by letters written in Arabic in a Maghribi script.[9] The Arabic used was 'classical', not the colloquial speech of North Africa or the Sudan. The language of everyday speech was Fulfulde or Hausa, but neither language was regularly used in writing prose (it was used for verse). Thus the 'common market' here for books was potentially huge, among shaykhs and students alike, and both moved freely around the caliphate.

Books, like letters, travelled too.[10] Of course, many books moved not as a set of pages but as memories in the minds of those who had memorised them. And books were sometimes composed on the move. Scholars on a journey with their books, however, rarely unpacked them en route, it seems. The bibliophile Ahmad Baba, returning home to Timbuktu in 1607 after his release from detention as a hostage in Marrakesh, apologised to the reader of the book he was writing en route – *al-Lam'fi'l-ishara li-hukm tibgh* – for any errors in his quotations (he was writing on the legality of using tobacco, then a new import from the Americas). His books, he said, were all still on his camels as he crossed the wadi Dra'a and so he could not check the accuracy of the citations he was making 'off head'. One exceptional Middle Eastern scholar who was regularly on tour put his library on camelback but ensured his books (and his camels) were kept in alphabetical order.[11] West African scholars were not usually so peripatetic or so well stocked with books (or camels). Shaykh 'Uthman, making his *hijra* from Degel at the start of a risky *jihad* in the late dry season of 1804, packed up his books and had then to borrow a camel from a Tuareg colleague, Malam Agali, to carry his precious library.[12] It is interesting that he chose a camel for the purpose rather than the pack oxen his kinsmen, the pastoral Fulbe, regularly used. Fulbe scholars such as Shaykh 'Uthman had close links to the Berber world of Saharan scholarship, both as students and as copiers of texts only to be found in the Sahara, but he did not speak Tamacheq (his daughter Asma'u did), the common language between scholars being classical Arabic – as Latin could be for Europeans until the 1950s.

To the east of the Sokoto Caliphate was the autonomous state of Borno, for 400 years (c.1400–1800) the dominant Muslim 'empire' in the region. Its staff corresponded with, for example, the ruler of Egypt in such fine Arabic that one letter was preserved as a model in a collection of letters by al-Qalqashandi.[13] Cities then under Borno's hegemony, like Kano, Katsina, Kurmin Dan Ranko and Yandoto, produced scholars who achieved wide fame. Many merchants were also scholars, so travelling (say, to Cairo) was an ordinary part of their lives.[14] The pilgrimage was a special extension of such journeys, especially if the scholar was accompanying his emir on a state visit to Mecca (as interpreter?). I suggest, then, that Borno and Hausaland, while on the margins of the Islamic world, were nonetheless part of it in the way that Scots or Irish or Scandinavian scholars were part of Christendom (for them, of course, Latin was the language of learning). For both Muslims and Christians, the Mediterranean, however distant it was, was central with so many vibrant, creative economies around its shores. While we know much about the book trade and the impact of print in far northern Europe, there is a dearth of knowledge about the far southern end of this single yet divided world. However, the characteristics of the contemporary European book culture were very different, perhaps because paper was introduced about the same time as printing, and together they transformed the European book trade.[15] In West Africa, paper became available to students of Islam some 300 years before the printing press. Indeed, paper was already being widely used in the Muslim world some two or three centuries before Muslims entered West Africa – West African scholarship therefore never had to make and use vellum for its books.

Nonetheless, a recent study of the pre-paper 'Anglo-Saxon Library' is very interesting in that it shows, first, how large libraries in the remote north of Europe could be built up by ambitious abbots travelling down to Rome and bringing back books to their monastic libraries; and second, how easy it was for those same institutional libraries to be broken up and their books lost – this being due not just to raiders but also simply to the decline of learning and scholarship among the monks, not to mention the weeding out of 'obsolete' texts by overzealous librarians.[16] By comparison, being without monasteries and their finances, West African scholars in the 'remote south', the Bilad al-Sudan, were on their own in building up personal libraries (which they might at least pass on to their sons), but they had one other advantage over monasteries: they were not rich, nor did they control treasure that could be looted. They did, however, have families, traditionally unarmed, who could be taken by non-Muslim raiders and sold off as slaves. The survival of book learning thus faced real hazards, both in the north and in the south.

The data on which this chapter is based were initially collected in the mid-1960s when, with the great encouragement of HFC Smith and John Hunwick, I worked for three years (1965–67) on the Northern History Research Scheme at Ahmadu Bello University, Zaria.[17] In all, I catalogued some 10 000 manuscript books, including the entire Arabic manuscript collection (over 3 000 manuscripts) in the National Archives, Kaduna, and photographed rare books in private libraries around the country, among them 100 Fulfulde manuscripts. This was followed by a further period of work from 1978–80 at Bayero

The market for books in pre-colonial West Africa was potentially huge among scholars. Books were often carried around the region on camel back by Tuareg merchants, similar to these men who traverse the desert on camel-back to trade their wares.

University, Kano. Some of my understanding comes from having been in Sokoto as a student of a shaykh who was himself a great bibliophile, and from living among Islamic students (inside Birnin Zaria) within their traditional world of manuscripts at a time when the old 'culture of the book' was still just alive. Since then I have continued to work in northern Nigeria, though not on Arabic manuscripts specifically. No new major collections have come to light, but various researchers over the years have added to public collections and skilfully illuminated our understanding of key texts. However, much remains to be done and it is hoped that this chapter will stimulate students into taking up the subject. The situation is not nearly so dramatic as the Fondo Ka'ti, yet I suggest that it is of real significance to our wider picture of intellectual life in the West African savannah and Sahel.

The context

Hausaland is on the cusp between the western Wangarawa trade system with its book base in Timbuktu and links to Moroccan scholarship, and the eastern Borno-centred system oriented more towards Tripoli and Cairo. Interleaved amidst these two systems were Fulbe scholars and their students. They had connections to the Berber scholars of the Sahel and the Sahara as well as to such a notably scholarly Wangara trade town as Yandoto. They were also connected to the stream of Fulfulde-speaking pilgrims from the far west (the 'Takruri') passing to and fro on the pilgrimage to Mecca, no doubt carrying books, news and ideas in their baggage. But Borno may have been their best source of books – distinguished Fulbe scholars were based there, as were the Tripoli merchants with a tradition of importing Italian paper. This might explain why the majority of texts cited by 'Uthman dan Fodio in his *Bayan wujub al-hijra' ala 'l-ibad*'[18] are post-1600 and Egyptian in origin. But the mid-seventeenth century does seem to have witnessed a major political shift in which the North African merchant houses settled in West Africa significantly lost power or influence – in Timbuktu, in Katsina, in Kano – to be replaced by more military-oriented governments. The shift may reflect the economics of the expanding Atlantic slave trade as much as changes in the balances of power in the Mediterranean.[19]

The scholarly community, in eighteenth-century Hausaland at least, was divided into two intellectual styles: one was a tradition that specialised in preaching (and therefore used local languages). Its skill in Arabic was not especially good, and its need for a range of Arabic books was relatively restricted, with expertise centred around a few key texts. The focus of its teaching was *kalam* (theology, and 'the status of sinners'). Its politics was populist, recruiting runaway slaves to Islam and forming radically Muslim communities. The second tradition was book oriented, with a marked skill required in classical Arabic. Scholars of this tradition taught texts (some also preached) and sought out copies of new books. As exceptional Arabists, it would be they who might be employed as tutors at royal courts. The necessity to be a good Arabist made their circles (*daira*) exclusive, even elitist. The focus was more on jurisprudence (*fiqh*), legal studies requiring the use of a range of books and a greater degree of 'international' sophistication; in addition, Sufism, *tasawwuf*, especially the Qadiriyya, was an important new element for some. *Fiqh* was important for merchants and for the *qadis* who mediated trade disputes – scholars had a role in maintaining social peace[20] – but it also made students increasingly aware of how local Muslim governments were breaking Islamic law and practice. In this sense, this second tradition was potentially revolutionary. The emphasis on literacy meant that local-language poetry was composed and written in *ajami* (that is, local languages written in Arabic script); marginal notes on key texts such as the Holy Qur'an could be written in *ajami* too. This use of local languages gave rise to specific religious dialects, such as Kanembu, alongside the vernacular Kanuri.[21] Religious poetry in *ajami* became a vehicle for popular education and piety, being easily memorable and sung while walking or working.

These two distinct styles of Islamic scholarship persisted into the twentieth century: students enlisted in either one or the other. One was identified with 'Hausa', the other with 'Fulani', but both used Hausa (and Arabic) as the language of instruction. The preaching tradition remains strong and diverse. The most notable now are perhaps the Yan Izala[22] but small, radical groups can often be heard in the marketplaces or on the streets; the preachers also go into villages deep in the countryside.[23] Though the two styles of scholarship are complementary, it is the second tradition, with the importance it puts on books, that is the focus of this chapter. An underlying question, however, is what contribution this bookishness (its lifestyle, its learning) made to enabling a distinct political culture to arise in West Africa, a culture that led to *jihad* and the establishment in the nineteenth century of major Islamic states – those of Sokoto, Masina and Ségou. By contrast, was it the preachers who led to widespread conversion and personal piety but *not* to major political change? Is there something special in an education system centred around rare, much-cherished books – a long apprenticeship with a shaykh to become fluent in Arabic and to read with him a long series of texts alongside his other students; travelling around to various other shaykhs to read further books, and in the process creating a wide network of scholars and student friends, all framed within the organising bond of the Qadiriyya brotherhood and the experience of its joint rituals and discipline? Was there in this long-drawn-out system of book learning and discussion, carried out in minimal comfort, the makings of an Islamic political radicalism? If this is going too far, then I think we can assert that the book trade has indirectly affected Nigerian Muslims' understanding of what a proper Muslim should be; and such key notions as *dar al-islam* and *dar al-harb* (the 'abode of peace' and the 'abode of war' traditionally understood as territories under Muslim and non-Muslim rule respectively) have acquired their significance in Nigeria because they proved very relevant within a distinct intellectual and legal milieu – and this milieu was at least in part formed by what books were available and widely read. In this context, then, the significance of books simply as material objects – the book trade over time – perhaps needs to be examined more closely.

The problem

Although the book trade should be considered regionally, the scale of the problem can be illustrated by taking northern Nigeria as an example. Here one might tentatively estimate that in 1900 (three years before the imposition of colonial rule) there was a book stock of a quarter of a million books, housed in the libraries of individuals with a few really large collections in emirs' palaces and scholarly households. Depending on what is counted as a 'book', the figure might well be closer to half a million. The vast majority of these books are copies, often incomplete, of school texts; almost all are 'religious' books. Locally composed books – 'original' or précis of classical texts – form a small percentage of the total, and are nineteenth century or later in origin. The calculation of the book stock is more of a guess than an estimate, since the crucial problem statistically is how many books were owned on average by each of the vast number of minor scholars, the *malamai*, and by the literate public generally. Paul Marty's figure of three or four each for the Ivory Coast in 1920 seems plausible.[24] Jack Goody quotes that 14 scholars in the important scholarly town of Salaga in the 1960s each had an average of 35 books, but they were almost all new printed texts.[25] In 1962, John Paden reported that the Kano scholar 'Umar Falke left some 1 600 manuscript books (the collection is now in Northwestern University Library). One clearly cannot read these 1960s figures back into the nineteenth century, particularly as it appears that a wealthy and important late nineteenth-century official like the Madakin Kano left on his death only six books;[26] Sokoto's Waziri Gidado in the 1820s had only 'a small collection' of books, of which one was on dreams.[27] Nonetheless, Ahmad Baba lost some 1600 books in Timbuktu in the invasion of 1591.[28] A collection like that in the National Archives in Kaduna was made up of manuscripts bought from *malamai* for very low prices and comprises often rather battered 'school books'. The collection was largely made during the 1950s and early 1960s by touring employees of the National Archives (like Mallam Ilyasu Katsina), when modern paper had been available for 50 years and photocopying machines had not yet been invented. The collection is thus a better indication of the disposable stock of the 'ordinary *mallam*' than are the more selective collections in the Department of Antiquities, Jos (made more professionally by Dr ADH Bivar and Mallam Muntaka Coomassie), or in major emirate libraries such as the Sarkin Kano's library in the old Shahuci judicial school in Kano.

All these are male-owned books; how many women scholars there were, and how many books they owned, is simply an unknown. There were indeed famous women scholars, daughters of famous fathers, and they wrote much poetry. We know that there were, and still are, women Sufis organised into groups – the Yan Taru started by Nana Asma'u in the mid-nineteenth century are well known.[29] But we don't know how many there were or what books they possessed; they may not have had very many. We know, too, that in major scholarly houses the children were taught to read and write, and first learned the Holy Qur'an under the learned women of the house. How many such households there were can only be a matter of conjecture; so too is the number of books, if any, that women owned in their own right – my guess would be a Holy Qur'an (or parts of one), a small book or two of selected prayers (al-Jazuli's *Dala'il al-khairat*, for example), and perhaps some poetry in either Arabic or in *ajami* (Fulfulde or Hausa; perhaps Kanuri in Borno). Books inherited from a father's library would normally be divided up and go to the sons or, in the absence of sons, to male relatives. However, there must have been learned daughters who managed to secure a share and got – or in some way paid for – the texts they most wanted for themselves. No doubt women scholars could borrow books from father or uncle, brother or husband, and have them copied (or copy them themselves), but this is a dimension of scholarly life we as yet know very little about, either in relation to the recent past or the pre-colonial period. Today bookshops, for example in Kano, sell printed texts in Arabic, and many women have gone on the pilgrimage to Mecca, but what books (if any) they bring back with them has not been researched. Shops in cities like London and Paris also offer a range of printed books; it was from these that I bought each year the books I gave to my teacher, the Wazirin Sokoto, books he didn't have in his large collection. But I was never asked by a wife for a book – unsurprisingly.

In short, I suggest there was, around 1900, a potential book-using (and book-making?) clientele comprising 50 000 people who were 'well educated', plus some 35 000 teachers and 165 000 students. Although these figures (derived from the 1921 Nigerian census) are undoubtedly unreliable, it would seem safe to assume there were at least some 250 000 people literate in Arabic or *ajami*, with a much larger number who had had some experience of Qur'anic schools.[30] In addition, there will have been several thousand educated women. What we do not know is the size of the demand for books – for example, how much such students and scholars would be willing to pay for a copy of a book. Paper in the nineteenth century was relatively cheap and available, so a student in need could copy for his own use a text he had borrowed. But did he? Or did he prefer to commit the text to memory, or only such parts of the text that he knew were relevant to him? Since he had probably memorised the Holy Qur'an as a child, his memory was already well trained. Standard, much-cited passages came to mind readily, to be quoted in debate or in court. But full recall requires regular reciting to oneself (the Qur'an takes a month to recite), and few books are so widely valued that they are kept memorised in full; hence, books remain necessary.

How, then, did this vast book stock get produced and distributed? And, given the size of this market, what was the demand for what sort of books, and how was it supplied? Did the book market 'work' and, if not, why not? Let me at the outset reverse normal scholarly procedure and outline for purposes of discussion the broad historical hypotheses I have to suggest.

A possible periodisation: 1400–1900

A schematic historical periodisation of the book trade in West Africa generally might be as follows:

The fifteenth to sixteenth centuries

Initially, books were imported at high prices; before then, books and paper had simply been scarce and unmarketed. The new imports included 'classical' texts (some in new copies?) and a few newly written books available in Cairo or Maghribi bookshops. The date of this importing boom and the particular composition of the stock of books then for sale in northern African bookshops will have largely determined the contents of West African libraries – and also, it could be argued, the shape of West African scholarship. The news of a new book in town was a notable event – for example, in the Kano of both the fifteenth and sixteenth centuries the *Kano Chronicler* reflects the excitement brought by the arrival of specific texts.[31] In the more sophisticated market of early sixteenth-century Timbuktu, Leo Africanus refers to books being the most profitable import there.[32] Fine letter-writing paper, and possibly fine inks, were also early imports for West African royal chanceries; and presumably merchants had some paper for accounts, legal documents and letters.

The sixteenth to seventeenth centuries

In this period, the high prices of books made it profitable to import paper in bulk and to make copies of books locally in West Africa – particularly of books in great demand. Paper was not produced in West Africa owing to the lack of flax and the shortage of linen rags. Cotton was apparently unsuitable for paper and papyrus had gone out of use. The first mention of paper as a standard item of trade to Borno seems to be the précis of a letter sent from Tripoli to Borno (quoted by the late JE Lavers, from his translation of Girard).[33] At the same time, around 1635 AD, Takruri merchants returning from Egypt included paper in their merchandise.[34] The shift to copying may partly explain the otherwise surprisingly wide distribution and popularity of al-Sanusi's *al-'Aqida al-sughra*. Copying was evidently cheap in Timbuktu – for example, supplied with paper, the copyist was paid merely a mithqal per volume for his work, whereas the proof-reader got half a mithqal per volume. Presumably as a consequence, book prices fell to four or five mithqals (or one-fifteenth the value of a slave) by the 1570s.[35] (A mithqal is a unit of weight, equivalent to a little over three-and-a-half grams, used with reference to gold or silver.)

Timbuktu, we know, was rich in books, but what of Borno? I suggest that there the relatively 'trivial' books about Mai Idris Alooma, in which his military campaigns are described, would otherwise stand out as an odd use of paper if paper had been scarce. Similar long, 'secular' texts, however, were being written in paper-rich Timbuktu at about this time – most notably the *Tarikh al-Sudan* and the *Tarikh al-fattash* – so that it is tempting to identify this period as a new phase in the book culture of West Africa, when quantities of paper could be devoted to original compositions on non-religious matters. A question remains why there aren't more such surviving secular texts: must we assume that there were no potential historians (or suitable kings for celebrating) in other states or, alternatively, that all other such 'trivial' texts have been lost without trace? Not being textbooks, were they not copied and re-copied? By contrast, the brief legal documents, the *mahrams* awarding grants to people or places, do survive in Borno; they had at least a monetary value to their owners and were far from 'trivial', so scarcely an extravagant use of paper.

The seventeenth to eighteenth centuries

In the seventeenth to eighteenth centuries, to maintain the copying trade's control over the market, de facto restrictions may have been introduced on the borrowing of books for copying by strangers. As a result, there would have been informal networks of book owners, and these scholarly networks effectively constituted 'schools' noted perhaps as much for their texts (and their commentaries on them) as for their general teaching. Meanwhile, these partial monopolies helped to distort the book market and led to scholars compiling their own précis, with passages or quotations taken from authors considered particularly relevant to the scholar's own teaching. Was this a kind of 'reader' both for his students and, as an *aide-mémoire*, for himself? In short, the trade in rare and recent books was 'privatised', and this only increased the tendency for books to be treated as 'secrets' and for scholars to regard themselves as a closed 'craft'. This would explain the uneven distribution of books (for example, Jenne's riches contrasted with Hamdullahi's poverty nearby in Masina), or the reputation of the Kel el-Souk scholars. I have, however, no specific references to restrictions on book loans – only to those whose generosity in lending a book was notable enough to record. Thus 'Uthman dan Fodio had to travel to Tafadek, north of Agades in the Air mountains, to find a text of Firuzabadi's *al-Qamus al-muhit* which he could copy; presumably he took his supply of paper with him. It was a potentially valuable work: in sixteenth-century Timbuktu a copy had sold for 80 mithqals, more than a slave was worth.[36] But are we to assume that c.1800 there simply was not another more accessible copy in the region, or that Uthman knew that the Tafadek text was 'open' to him? It does suggest that demand, at any rate, was unsatisfied. References to scholars failing to return books they had borrowed are easier to find: for example, my Sokoto colleague Professor Sambo Junaidu tells me Shaykh Uthman (*c*.1800) complained about this in a Fulfulde poem. Sokoto was not unique in this regard; there is a letter in the British Museum by a Sierra Leonean scholar trying to retrieve books he lent to a colleague. Tales about who could not be trusted with a book were commonplace in the twentieth century. Scholars also tended to keep the exact contents of their collections a secret, with good reason. For example, a very rare book, Ahmad Baba's early seventeenth-century text on using tobacco (*al-Lam'fi'l-ishara li-hukm tibgh*), was 'stolen' almost as soon as its location in a library became known in Sokoto. It was, however, eventually 'recovered' through networks of persuasion quite unknown to me. In this context, though scholars tended not to disclose what books they had, they might bring one or two out specially for a particular visitor. A notable instance of this was Alhaji Nasiru Kabara who suddenly one afternoon, after months of talk, showed Professor MA al-Hajj the only known copy of the important seventeenth-century text *Asl al-wangariyyin*. Similarly, I was never allowed direct access to the sultan's library in Sokoto; books from it were always brought out to me by the Alkalin Lardi Yahaya. Hence even the size of large personal libraries is rarely known until the owner's death requires an inventory to be made for the formal purpose of dividing up the inheritance.

The eighteenth and nineteenth centuries

In reaction to these restrictions, the process of import substitution was extended further in the eighteenth and nineteenth centuries by scholars starting to write their own original compositions, sometimes in the local language. The vast majority of early texts were in Arabic. The three leading Sokoto scholars wrote over 300 prose works between them, while a contemporary, the erudite scholar Abd al-Qadir b. al-Mustafa, wrote on a distinct range of secular subjects among his total of 48 works.[37] Local compositions in poetry, some of it in *ajami*, were committed to paper; so too were marginal commentaries in *ajami*. Copying of poetry, especially the shorter poems, was apparently commonplace; it seems probable there was also some trade in at least the more devotional verse. In mid-nineteenth-century Sokoto, poems first written in Arabic were being translated into Fulfulde (and later into Hausa); a new audience, possibly women Yan Taru, would sing them as they walked (I have heard men singing them as they cycle; others while they drive). Fulfulde became increasingly the language of a small elite and of pastoralists. The domestic language of the vast majority was Hausa, the lingua franca used by the newly acquired slaves who might outnumber the free by 30 to 1, or more out on the isolated, slave-run farmsteads. These translations have sometimes survived when the Arabic originals have been lost. Prose in *ajami* Hausa is exceedingly rare; the earliest I know is dateable to around the 1870s or 1880s and is the product of a local, rural religious group. It was the early colonial period that saw the rise of Hausa prose in new compositions which Europeans and the new *boko* (book) schoolchildren and missionaries could read. By the 1950s Arabic prose texts were being translated into Hausa and printed, a process culminating in the rendering of the Holy Qur'an into Hausa in 1982 by Abubakar Gummi.[38]

Other languages were more difficult to read in *ajami*. As already mentioned, Kanembu is found in marginal annotations and there is a body of Kanuri religious poetry in Borno, but I don't think its use was ever as common in Borno as Fulfulde or Hausa became in the Sokoto Caliphate. Heavily tonal languages like Nupe, for example, or Yoruba can be rendered in *ajami* but it is usually only the author that can re-read them; in this sense, such texts in *ajami* become an *aide-mémoire* only for the composer and are not sold. There is a short poem in Nupe *ajami* by the early nineteenth-century reformer Abd al-Rahman Chacha that remains unread; and there are letters in Yoruba *ajami* that date to the 1930s. Presumably other such 'secret' texts remain to be discovered. The language of *jinn* could be written in *ajami*; there is a brief passage in *jinni* prose in a book (*Ishara wa-i'lam*) of Muhammad Bello's, but it is presumably a transcription of spoken *jinni*, a metalanguage one could hear in spirit-possession (*bori*) séances – as one still can today. I have never found evidence of 'automatic writing' using *jinni* – or indeed any more ordinary – language under 'inspiration'.

This new literature, along with the new audiences created by the success of the *jihad* and the establishment of the Sokoto Caliphate, would appear to have stimulated the revival of a local book trade in the nineteenth century. As already mentioned, each of the three main leaders wrote some hundred prose works of varying length but many of these books, unlike others, were widely circulated as guidance to the new generation of emirs and to officials that governed the new state – matters of law as well as practical tips on good governance. Other texts of theirs were works of specialist scholarship. There were also texts on Sufi mysticism for members of the Qadiriyya *tariqa*, which by the mid-nineteenth century was being rivalled by the new Tijaniyya *tariqa* – its shaykhs then produced their own literature in both prose and verse. All these devotional writings needed to circulate among a much wider readership than had existed hitherto.

The late nineteenth century

Finally, in the late nineteenth century, frivolous books of local authorship were composed and committed to writing, as was the lengthy book of doctrine in *ajami* prose mentioned earlier. One such poem, in good classical Arabic and preserved in the Sarkin Kano's collection in the old Shahuci judicial school library (now burned), was strikingly erotic – pornographic even? – and amusing; I remember John Hunwick reading it aloud in December 1961 with much laughter. I don't think we have ever seen its like, but I presume scholars, more often than we now know, did write such *jeux d'esprit* for their own amusement and passed them around among their close friends in the precolonial period. The extent to which there was a market for either frivolous books and *ajami* prose is unclear, but as they are relatively rare, one must assume they did not 'catch on'. Certainly recent scholars, like the late Wazirin Sokoto and the late Wazirin

Gwandu, enjoyed composing Arabic poems as they listened to politicians' interminable speeches or were driven on long car journeys to meetings. These were written down later by friends or even by their drivers who heard them being composed and recited. The poems did not, however, enter the book trade at the time.

To sum up, the main centre for the importation of books during the boom period when prices and demand were highest appears to have been Timbuktu and related markets, with Wangarawa scholar–traders and Fulbe scholars en route to and from Mecca being the main distributors from there eastwards. It seems probable too that Timbuktu, along with Borno, then also pioneered the substitution of bulk paper imports in place of texts. Indeed, their role in the paper trade may have made it easy for scholars in the two places to keep records and write works of local history; elsewhere, the price and scarcity of paper may have inhibited using so much paper for such secular uses.

If, as seems likely, Borno's development later as a centre of the book trade (with Kano as a related market) was built less on importing books than on copying them, it is nonetheless probable that some of the earliest non-Maghribi texts came to Borno from Egypt, Tripoli or Tunis and went into West African circulation from there. But one can draw only very limited inferences of provenance, given the range of contacts available to West African scholars through such less conspicuous merchant networks as the Ibadis and through their own travels, undertaken sometimes in search of a specific book which they needed to copy.

Finally, in the nineteenth century, first the Sokoto Caliphate and then other *jihadi* centres evidently became foci for a regional trade in locally composed texts, and so helped to revive a general market for books which recently, it seems, had come to be found only in private circulation. We know that, once the *jihad* was successful, Sokoto thronged with Arab visitors seeking (and winning) favours; perhaps to gain a good reception these visitors had brought books as gifts. The import trade, however, appears not to have revived. It is for this reason, then, that 'Uthman dan Fodio and his family (especially Muhammad Bello as *amir al-mu'minin* in Sokoto) may have specifically sent out emissaries to buy books in North Africa and Egypt and bring them back. We have no *rihlat* recounting these book-buying expeditions, nor lists of what they brought back; all we know is that Fulbe scholars had indeed travelled for books before the *jihad*. The *jihad*, with all its hasty escapes and raids, may well have disrupted scholars' collections. We know that after at least three attacks pages of books were recorded as lying on the ground, blown about in storms (and presumably damaged drastically by damp). 'Books blowing around' became a figure of speech in recounting attacks ('wrongfully') made by *jihadi* fighters on learned Muslim settlements such as Yandoto or Kalembaina, or much earlier at Gimbana. Zamfara scholars much later said that Muhammad Bello had taken away, as booty, many if not all the books of the region (it was an area noted for its learning). Did Muslim scholars opposed to the *jihad* forfeit their libraries? Did victory hugely augment private collections in Sokoto, Katsina and Kano? If so, nothing is mentioned of all this in the histories. Finally, we know that the loss at the disastrous Battle of Tsuntsua in 1805 of some 1 800 scholars and students who knew the Holy Qur'an by heart represented a huge loss of 'book stock', albeit in this instance kept in the head.[39] But what other books had they memorised? That, intellectually speaking, may have been the more crucial loss. However, books are vulnerable even when left behind in store. Boxes may keep out rain from a leaking roof or a flooded floor, but a worse danger comes from ants and termites whose destruction may continue unseen and unnoticed. Traditionally, books could be kept in a granary, a structure specifically designed to keep ants away from the unthreshed grain stored there as a reserve against famine, often for years on end. Indeed it could be that 'granary' became used colloquially as a metaphor for 'library'.[40] Granaries, however, can burn, and towns were regularly set alight by raiders; residents in panic emptied their rooms of precious items and looting was a problem in the few cases we have any data on.[41] Indeed, Bello's first copy of Euclid had been destroyed in a house fire in 1827. Bound books are relatively hard to burn, but traditionally none of the pre-colonial copies were bound; they were kept as loose sheets between two boards tied with a leather strap. But once the sheets got loose from these boards and the wind caught them, the scattered pages would burn readily. We have no way of calculating the extent of book losses but the danger was real, as the 1960s burning of the emir of Kano's library in the Shahuci judicial school in Birnin Kano testifies. Similarly, there is considerable anxiety now over how the early nineteenth-century library of Muhammad Bello has fared since it was removed from the palace in Sokoto in 1988; the talk is of termites and ants spoiling some books.

Book merchandising

The hypothesis here is that book importing as a business died out at an early date, being replaced on the one hand by personal importing of single texts, and on the other by a local copying industry. Bookselling – if not the business of importing books – only revived in the nineteenth century, and such detail as we have on the local book trade refers to this and the early colonial period.

Apart from the smaller peripatetic dealers in books and pamphlets who had no formal shop, there were retailers who had their own area in the marketplace. Both the two main categories of purchaser, the professional student or scholar and the government official (with the latter being the bigger spender?) were habitually mobile, and this allowed the book trade to be unusually centralised; for example, within the Sokoto Caliphate, bookshops were largely confined to Kano, as indeed was the paper trade. The *waziri* of Sokoto, when he spoke to me about it in June 1983, could not offhand recall the names of any nineteenth-century or early twentieth-century booksellers or copyists in Sokoto. Indeed, the Sokoto caliphal correspondence, preserved in the *waziri*'s house in Sokoto and dating mainly to the 1880s and 1890s, includes a few letters in which paper is being purchased or obtained from Kano. The question remains: were there no paper merchants in Sokoto, or was the *waziri*'s house de facto the source of paper for local scholars? There is no evidence of direct importation of paper into Sokoto on a regular basis, though Sokoto in the 1820s was a much larger centre than Kano. By contrast, Alhaji Mahmudu Koki (1894–1976) recalls his early life as a scholar and copyist in Kano, and gives details of the Kano paper and book trades in the early colonial period.[42] The Tripoli merchants there kept stocks of paper in their houses, from where retailers from the market took their supplies. Writing paper was not, of course, the only type of paper in demand. In the mid-nineteenth century the 'common paper' that Heinrich Barth, the famous German explorer who visited the region in the 1850s, saw in markets was for wrapping the cloth that had been woven or dyed around Kano for export. The wrapping carried the name of the merchant, should the cloth prove faulty and need returning. The wrapping paper was the same brand (*tre lune*) as the better sort of writing paper.[43] The criterion of quality was the paper's degree of absorbency: too absorbent, and the ink spread, making the writing illegible. But if the clothmaker's name was written legibly on the wrapping paper, that quality of paper must not have been very absorbent – or else an area of it was 'sized' first. Almost all writing paper had a watermark, hence our knowledge of the brands used.[44] While writing paper was relatively stiff, it could be folded; it was not brittle like later paper. Letters from the *waziri*'s chancery had a distinct way of being folded, and were carried in pouches of indigo-dyed cloth. Letters were written on the same standard size of paper as books, but book pages were never folded. A torn page in a book could be mended by being carefully sewed along the tear with cotton; some quite ancient books have been repaired in this way, but I don't know of a way to date the repair without scientifically examining the thread to see if it is the old pre-colonial tree cotton. Errors in a text could be corrected by attaching to the page (with a thread) a small supplementary piece of paper. Charms (*laya*) were also a common use of paper; prayers were written upon it, sometimes with small twigs or leaves added. The whole packet was then folded and kept in a small leather pouch for hanging round the neck or waist, especially of young children. There were often many charms on a single cord.

Multiple copies of texts were probably not stocked in bookshops; instead, books were copied on demand and thus required time to organise. Similarly, no doubt because time was not the essence, specific books might have been ordered from Cairo. However, more often individuals returning from pilgrimage must have brought in single copies for their own and their friends' use, in which case copies of these books probably never reached a bookshop and therefore never attained a widespread circulation. Indeed, one suspects that to hand over for public sale a rare book from one's own collection was equivalent to distributing one's assets, just as today there is a clear reluctance on the part of scholars to divulge their total book stock. Nor is there evidence of the old Baghdadi practice of a scholar hiring a bookshop for a whole night to use as a temporary library.[45] To run a bookshop may have been rather trickier than one perhaps imagines. Bookshops presumably provided the 'classics', the local favourites and best-sellers, rather than rare or recently written works. They may have stocked, though, the occasional fine 'presentation' copy, particularly of the Holy Qur'an. Similarly, small books apparently dominated the 'mass' market. Some of Shaykh 'Uthman dan Fodio's books were seemingly designed for this end of the trade. But the bulk of personal libraries (if the National Archives' collection is anything to go by; it is catalogued not by author but by bookseller – 'provenance') must have consisted of poetry, chapters excerpted from books, or simply fragments of larger texts. It seems that the resulting collections were perhaps not unlike students' own 'libraries' of xeroxes today. This then raises the question of what constitutes 'a book'.

From a reader's perspective, a 'book' may be simply the part of a longer work that he uses and needs to have a copy of – in this sense, it is the paper equivalent of the extensive quotation he may have in his head. From the author's perspective, such an excerpt is only part of what he wrote under that title. From the perspective of the executor of an inheritance, a book is not an indivisible whole – it can be divided up among the dead man's inheritors; a book, the executor would say, does not lose its value by being split up. Some scholars disagree and insist that a book is kept in its entirety (after all, no one divides up a horse or a gown), but I think the fact that people can countenance the division of a book into separable parts does suggest that a book need not be considered a single whole. After all, the Holy Qur'an is divided into *suras*, and it is *the* book par excellence. Similarly, many of the books by Shaykh 'Uthman and 'Abdullahi dan Fodio consist of quotations and citations, thus providing the student reader with a very useful selection of sentences to quote in a debate or in making a decision. In a single work, you have a précis of a whole library, many 'books' in one. It may well be that the original, whole book may not exist in any local library, the author having himself taken the quotation from an earlier précis. In short, one cannot tell, merely from the presence of a quotation, that the original work in its entirety was part of the local book stock. Since quite a few 'books' in a collection have no beginning or end, it is not always clear, except to the erudite, where the excerpt comes from. Classics and standard school texts are commonplace and obvious, but a proportion remains listed as 'anonymous' (Bani Ulama-i) in the National Archives in Kaduna. It is a common enough category that has confused researchers unused to the archives' codes: 'BU' has become the archives' most prolific author.

Forgeries pose problems, too. They are mainly of two kinds: books probably composed in the nineteenth century but attributed (wrongly, or should one say 'optimistically'?) to a well-known author; and books wholly concocted in the twentieth century and attributed to a nineteenth-century author. The first is more common, and open to dispute. Frequently the text is about a contested element of Muslim life – such as the Mahdiyya or the Tijaniyya – for which there is evidence that the purported author would not in fact have written in such a manner. This often applies to texts where any authorial name and the conventional opening sentences are absent. A common example is a poem (against the invading Christians) attributed to the last independent *amir al-mu'minin*, Attahiru, but internal evidence makes it clear it was not composed by him personally; it reflects his sentiments, no doubt, but modern researchers seem unworried about accepting a conventional (but inaccurate) attribution. Similarly, some late translations of poems into Hausa are attributed to the author of the early original (Fulfulde) texts, even when we may know the name of the translator. Another important misattribution concerns the *wird* or *Lamma balagtu* which has been printed and widely circulated in a Hausa translation: it is usually said to be by Shaykh 'Uthman, as it describes his vision of the Prophet and Shaykh Abd al-Qadir Jilani *c.*1794 by whom he was given the sword of truth (*sayf al-haqq*). The book is unlike any text that the shaykh ever wrote and has no conventional start. It could possibly be an anonymous disciple's transcription of an oral account that he heard Shaykh 'Uthman give in Sifawa (the shaykh would have been speaking in Fulfulde or Arabic originally), but the one account we do have of the shaykh's oral teaching there has the author's name on it. Again, modern scholars like the late Mervyn Hiskett use it as if it was unproblematic.[46] The text is indeed crucial to our understanding of how the *jihad* was, or could be, legitimated – but does that make it too crucial to dismiss as a possible invention? Should we simply leave it, saying that it may be that the *story* is true but not its status as a formally authored 'book'?

There may well be more forgeries than we know of, but one of the better known is *Kanz al-awlad*, in part a history of the *jihad* purportedly written by Muhammad Sambo b. Ahmed around 1818–19 but actually produced by a scholar in Gusau in the early 1950s. I have seen only two copies (a private one in Kano; Kano has very close connections to Gusau); a copy of the book has now gone into the Bayero University Library. Wazirin Sokoto Alhaji Junaidu knew of the book's existence and said it was fake; Professor MA al-Hajj knew of it too and dismissed it on internal evidence, but recently Professor John Hunwick has included it in his bibliography of Sokoto *jihadi* works as if it was authentic. He adds it 'is not well regarded in Sokoto and has, for this reason, been neglected by scholars';[47] he has not, however, studied the text himself. It may yet gain a life of its own and be cited in doctoral theses as a historical source. Otherwise, forgeries are apparently rare. I have heard the historian DJM Muffet firmly declare an early colonial text to be a forgery, but he had no serious evidence for saying so (except that it went against his general argument). In general, in a culture of hand-copying (as distinct from a bibliographer's culture), a forgery has to be accepted as genuine if many copies are to be made. Might, therefore, wide distribution be one test of a text's authenticity?

My only first-hand evidence for the culture of copying comes from the early to mid-1960s (before 'xerox' machines were available), when one could still 'order' copies of manuscripts from scribes, and the delivered manuscript would then be proof-read by another scholar. The sums paid were very small, but everyone knew whose handwriting was good and whose was not, and who was a really careful copyist. But the real problem lay in ensuring that the master text from which the copy was made was good. Certain scholars were known for never returning the manuscripts they had borrowed for copying. Hence, I took to photographing manuscripts in the house of the books' owner;

it preserved accuracy as well as recorded the actual hand of the original copyist. Early 'classic' hands (that is, *c.*1830 or before) were recognisably different from later hands (*c.*1890 or today): paper was scarcer and handwriting was smaller, neater. I am not sure exactly when the model of good handwriting changed, let alone why – my guess is that it was as late as post-1875. It is indeed tempting to speculate whether the last two pre-colonial *waziris* instituted a regular chancery in their house in Sokoto, with a standardised style of script. Earlier correspondence of this 'standard' type has not been preserved, and one wonders why. Much earlier, more personal letters had been collected into a single book – but they are letters of advice, not short bureaucratic notes to or from an 'office'. A merchant's notebook from 1830s Katsina has survived (in the National Archives, Kaduna), but it is unique: it contains some references to loans and repayments written higgledy-piggledy (and almost illegibly) on pages of a bound journal; it belonged to one of the Wangarawa merchants based there at that time. Much later and more local is a surviving inventory of a recently deceased official's property in Kano,[48] and there is a list of grain brought in to Kano's Nasarawa palace from the emir's slave estates. These suggest an ordinary bureaucratic usage of paper, with texts written in classical Arabic. By contrast, judicial records of the emir's court in Kano were instituted only in the colonial period.[49] Thus only a limited amount of state material, it seems, was regularly committed to writing; the vast majority of paper was used for books. It is possible that an *allo*, a wooden, reusable writing board, was used previously for temporary records and calculations. Primarily made as 'exercise books' for teaching young children how to read and write the Arabic script, they were (and are) ubiquitous and cheap. They last well, too, even if they are bulky to store (and burn easily, it is said). But I have never seen them used as 'notepads'; as students, we used them to make *rubutu*, the tonic medicine people drink made of the ink in which sacred words have been written. Such boards may have been sanctified in a way that paper was not. In this context, stories of how a *mallam*'s *allo* boards were allowed to burn were told to me to illustrate how deeply shocking was the behaviour of a certain notoriously violent district head. Nonetheless, some books are sanctified, most notably the Holy Qur'an – it cannot be placed on the ground, nor can another book be placed on top of it. An urban riot could be set off by a (stereotyped) rumour that a sheet of paper with Arabic on it had been found dirtied and lying on the ground, the suspicion being that some Christian had deliberately besmirched it and so the Christian community needed to be drastically punished. Whatever the case, traditional paper is rarely destroyed deliberately or even simply thrown away.

Although calligraphy was never the exquisite art form it had become in the Middle East (I know of no public 'sign' from nineteenth-century Nigeria, nor were the caliphal seals elegantly complex or beautifully inscribed), nonetheless a fine book-hand for writing was much admired. Borno hands have remained much the most distinguished in Nigeria: Holy Qur'ans copied there are the most prized, and young scholars were sent there to learn that hand (and the Qur'an copyists' trade) – their products were exported in the 1820s to North Africa. Fine copying, with the use of two or three colours, was a source of income that persisted into the twentieth century. One of the most famous copyists, Shaykh Bala, was paid little for an act of skilled reverence (it is said he got £5, c.1959), yet the businessman who commissioned it then had it printed by photo-offset and made a fortune from selling the printed copies at an inflated price; the businessman kept the fortune to himself. The copyist was so disgusted that he never did any copying of texts again. *Mai belt*, as his copy is now called, may be a museum piece, but it stands also for the gross commercialisation of a traditional skill linked to the old-style piety of scholars. Certainly, in the 1960s copyists could be 'bullied' into working for low prices; it was considered not so much a commercial act as a dutiful work of piety. In that way, it resembles bookbinders in the past in Europe: a much underpaid expertise that required a wide range of skills. Bookbinding, I think, was never developed in West Africa, though bound books were clearly known. Books were also stored on their sides, not on shelves on end – this may reflect the relatively small size and personal nature of collections. Public libraries with huge stocks of manuscript books were a late-colonial innovation. As no *waqf* institutions existed in the Sokoto Caliphate – unlike in North Africa – large houses ('lineages') acted as centres of charity and knowledge.

Book production in the nineteenth century

The hypothesis here is that the importation of paper and the copying of (previously imported) books on a large scale date back to the sixteenth century, though the range of titles reproduced narrowed until the late eighteenth and nineteenth centuries, when the revival both in the local authorship and in the local marketing of books led to an increase in copying and book production generally. Again, much of what follows relates to this later period, when the structure of the industry and market conditions had radically altered; for it appears that the nineteenth-century book was relatively cheap to produce.

Paper

Quantities

Imported from Tripoli, the yearly supply in 1767 was some 2 000 reams, equivalent to 4 million folios or 80 camel loads.[50] In Senegambia, paper constituted 3 per cent of imports in 1718 but Curtin does not quote the actual quantities.[51] At 230 folios to a Qur'an, the Tripoli trade was enough to provide paper for some 16 000 Qur'ans. But Tripoli was not, of course, the only North African source, nor was Senegambia the only south-western one. The overall quantity imported must have been substantially greater for West Africa taken as a whole.

Sources

Much of the nineteenth-century imported paper was of Italian manufacture, produced specifically for the Levantine market. The crescent watermark has been common since at least 1320 but was increasingly to be found in North Africa and to the south (for example, Darfur) by the eighteenth and nineteenth centuries. The *tre lune* (three crescents) paper with the names of the various Galvani[52] has achieved a certain fame.[53] It was especially strong, relatively cheap, and of third to fourth quality. 'Crescent' papers were also manufactured in Turkey, but I have not seen figures for the quantities, if any, imported into northern Africa.[54] In short, it may be that 'crescent' paper has to be treated as a type – size and weight – rather than a brand name.

The size of page used for books was, I suggest, a quarter Mansuri (very close to a crown quarto).[55] Because books in West Africa were seldom written in the margins of other books, the folio size half Mansuri was not used as it was in North Africa. An octavo page (one-eighth Mansuri) was used for pocket prayer books. In these formats, no decorations were usually added, either as a border around a page or as part of the title page. Rarely was an ornamental frontispiece or tailpiece included.

Prices

Paper

In 1805 at Sansanding on the Niger River, a ream cost 20 000 cowries. In 1861 at Tripoli it was 12 000 a ream which, given a 100 per cent mark-up (for the costs of transport across the Sahara, etc.), in Kano would come to 24 000 a ream. By 1910 the price in Kano was 26 000 a ream.[56] Sold by the sheet, the profit margin was considerable: 60 cowries bought a sheet of paper, the same price as half a pound in weight of honey. A page was 10 to 15 cowries.[57] In the 1820s, 'writing paper, on which the profit is enormous' was the first item in a list of articles most in demand in Borno[58] – no doubt to be used in the export trade in Qur'ans. Contrary to expectations, therefore, paper seems to have been relatively cheap throughout the nineteenth century, though because of inflation it was even cheaper by the century's end. Yet with a sheet of paper to sell, reported Tomas Edward Bowdich in 1819, an 'inferior Moor' could live a month in Kumasi.[59]

Books

Valuations are found in documents relating to the disposal of property at a person's death. Thus the Madakin Kano's six books were worth only 8 000 cowries, but they were, it seems, only part-books and common ones at that.[60] How these valuations were arrived at in the nineteenth century is not stated, but the values given for books are unlikely to reflect very closely the current price of a new copy. If these old books were disposed of to book dealers, or even to students, they must have undercut the market price. Indeed, the price of books seems to have been relatively low – perhaps 4 000 or 5 000 cowries was average for a standard text (or excerpt?). But a Qur'an might be worth 20 000 – in 1820s Borno, fine Qur'ans were being exported to 'Barbary or Egypt' and selling there 'for 40 or 50 dollars each'.[61] As letter writers, scribes were paid some three or four times the wage of an unskilled labourer. Copyists' labour must have been rewarded in other ways.

Labour

Students

A student's graduation was signalled by his completing a copy of the Qur'an. This was traditionally given to his teacher, who in turn presumably sold it – but not always so: a student might buy himself a big gown and turban from the proceeds of his first Qur'an, says Mahmudu Koki.[62] If we assume 1 per cent of all students in any one year actually finished copying the Qur'an, that implies a production of some 1 600 Qur'ans a year (on my student population estimates given earlier). Borno Qur'ans were of a notably high quality and were exported, and it is possible that demand for Qur'ans was satisfied by Borno's production. Borno attracted students (and therefore cheap copyists?) by its specialisation in Qur'anic studies. Perhaps, then, one should speak of a Borno 'school of calligraphy', since handwriting was the other economic skill which students went there to learn. It is not known which speciality started first – Qur'anic studies or calligraphic copying.

Professional copyists

The value of a book for sale will have depended in part on the quality of the copyist's handwriting. A scholar like 'Abdullahi dan Fodio – so Dr ADH Bivar was told – kept his hand in by doing some copying by the light of a small oil lamp, every single evening, whatever the circumstances. But personal copies, made by less conscientious scholars in their own hand, will have had less resale value. The size of the standard script grew larger as the nineteenth century wore on; the early, *jihadi* hands are much smaller and neater, maybe reflecting personal, rather than professional, styles. Similarly, the various scribes' hands in the Sokoto chancery suggest that an individual's handwriting was more fluid, less formal. But a professional script, let alone the identities of the professional copyists, remains to be established. Nor do we even know if it was always merely a part-time occupation. As in other trades, student labour will presumably have undercut prices for all but the finest work.[63]

The book trade, like religious learning, was probably also subject to certain culturally imposed restraints. Despite being bought and sold in the marketplace, books, by virtue of their also being religious texts, may on occasion have been less liable to direct market forces, with 'alms' replacing price and labour an act of piety. Indeed it seems likely that the writing of charms subsidised scholarly work, in effect paying for the labour expended in book production.

Other costs

Apart from paper, none of the other materials used had to be imported; some were made by the copyists themselves. But books were not usually finished externally with any lavishness, however lovingly the pages might be repaired inside. In short, books were not made specifically to attract the collector.

Inks and pens

All supplies of black, red and yellow inks were manufactured locally, though certain ingredients might be imported for special inks. Inks made from carbon or vegetable tannin (for example, vitex) were used on wooden 'slates', while ferro-tannic inks were used on paper. The carbon and vegetable inks did not stain the wooden writing boards, and could be safely drunk as medicine. Pens, made from cornstalks, were readily available locally, as were erasing materials.

Bindings

The finished book was not usually sewn, though the pages were enclosed within a cover or box of two boards, usually made of goatskin stiffened by cardboard or membrane, and tied together with a thong, as were the earliest Muslim texts. I have seen no reference to why books were not bound in the later Middle Eastern manner, but there seems never to have developed in West Africa a specific craft of elaborate bookbinding such as is found in North African cities. One consequence is that a large number of texts are incomplete, either through loss or through deliberate division of the book when apportioning an inheritance among heirs.[64]

Storage

As with the bindings, so too with storage – the costs were kept low. Books were packed in specially designed goatskin leather bags (*gafaka*) which were sewn smooth side in to a standard format. They could hold more than one book at a time. A special storeroom held the bags of books, and in these conditions books deteriorated little; even dampness does not affect the ferro-tannic inks. Furthermore, as religious books date less rapidly than most commercial items, there was probably little problem over old stock, especially if a common source for the market in books was old texts unwanted by the inheritors of a dead scholar.

Substitute materials

There was apparently no suitable local material to use as a substitute for imported good-quality white paper.

Boards

The most widely used 'substitute' for ordinary paper was the wooden 'slate' or board, used as a school exercise book and no doubt also as 'scrap paper' for trying out compositions. Although there is no fixed size for these boards, the majority take a quarto Mansuri page of text. The width of the board is of course limited by the girth of the tree used, and it is possible this was one factor in helping to determine which page size became standard.

Leather

As far as I know, neither vellum nor parchment was used for books or documents, though there were both sufficient hides and the technology available, at least in the earlier periods, to manufacture either. (A Holy Qur'an written on vellum in Ceuta in northern Morocco, however, is the oldest book in Fondo Ka'ti and dates to AD 1198.[65]) Paper made of bark was not used either, though bark cloth was available locally, if not to an adequately high quality to compete with paper. One characteristic of paper is that it cannot be rubbed down (as vellum can) and reused as a palimpsest; this means we have not lost books due to reuse. Vellum would have been the longer-lasting material, had it not been wholly replaced by paper in the Muslim world at a very early date.[66]

Other papers

Not all paper imported was for writing; wrapping paper was relatively common, especially for the cloth trade in which high-value items like turbans and gowns of beaten indigo might justify the cost of wrapping. Presumably some of this paper was later used by *mallams* to make charms which did not have to be easily legible. Similarly, such paper was used occasionally for some of the early colonial 'treaties'.

Other materials

Small prayers were written on the edges of the large white cotton flags used in *jihad*, but no large-scale inscriptions were put on them or on the later flags made of damask; no stencils were used, either. Nor were there texts on, say, glazed tiles, as used in Middle Eastern buildings. The public display of texts, on walls for example, inside or on the outside of buildings, was not a feature, either. Walls were made of clay (unlike in Timbuktu, no cut stone was ever used) and sometimes plastered, the materials for which could contain impurities like animal urine or dung. Oil-based paint was not readily available and only indigo-blue and white-earth washes were used on walls.[67] Hence in the nineteenth century the paper page was the main medium for decorative work (if any), with coloured inks rather than paint. The calculations done for divination were drawn in sand held within a wooden tray (if in a marketplace) or simply on the ground; the finished squares, however, might be committed to paper. I have never seen pre-colonial maps or diagrams drawn on large sheets of paper except as reproductions of those made specifically for European visitors; again, for simple geographical diagrams, the sand where the discussants sat was used.[68]

Conclusion

This chapter shows how relatively little detailed knowledge we have of Sokoto's book culture – as yet. But by writing about it here not only have I suggested how significant a subject it is, but I trust I might also have persuaded some reader to pursue the whole topic in depth and consider the implications of bookishness. There clearly were boom periods – first the sixteenth then the nineteenth centuries – with different texts coming to hand; different interests too. But I think overall the book trade did not 'work' in West Africa. For example, in 1900 there were, it seems, few if any 'modern' books either available to buy or in circulation in Kano – books on the key Islamist themes that were current in, say, Egypt and causing great debate amongst the scholars of the day as they faced the new Christian colonialism. There was no *waqf*-financed library buying books systematically, no bookseller importing contentious texts for an avid reading public. There undoubtedly were well-read scholars in Sokoto and Kano, but their needs seem not to have been met by the book trade. They relied more on a 'classical' book stock, not a contemporary one. For precedents on how to handle barbarian invaders, they turned to learned discussions that took place at the Mongols' horrific sacking of Baghdad in 1258, when the Tigris was blocked with books and its water was black with ink (and blood). Scholars newly returned from Egypt (like Hamman Joda, the *qadi* at Yola) spoke about the threat from Europeans and must have heard the intellectual ferment in Cairo, but the relevant books did not come back with them, it seems (or, if they did, they remained wholly private copies). One explanation could be that, as people seriously thought the world was nearing its end, it was the core texts of Islam, not modern speculations from abroad, that had priority.

If there was no systematic importation of books (but remember, there was a big book export from 1820s Borno), then the intellectual milieu depended on individual bibliophiles or networks. But it may have been that local scholars, in the main, saw themselves as self-sufficient, and their book stock adequate for their needs. The intellectually curious among them went off to North Africa or towards Mecca, abandoning West Africa as an academic backwater, however good a site it was for *jihad*. It was, after all, a long-standing tradition to seek further education in Cairo, where a place (*riwaq*) had once been maintained for students from Borno (Sokoto seems never to have established such places). Did the local shortage of books lead to a pre-colonial version of the 'brain drain'?

Anyone who has worked in the Nigerian university system over the last 40 years will find echoes of this past history in the state of today's book stock. University libraries no longer systematically buy the latest works, university bookshops have mainly closed down, and such bookstores as do still function stock primarily school books, not the latest monographs or even advanced textbooks. This means that scholars, if they are to be 'up to date', have to have collections of their own, getting books sent out to them or making trips themselves. This results in the average author of an academic article having to write without having first seen the latest research. These authors are stuck in an intellectual time warp dating back to when they last had long-term access to a good library. 'Open access' and the internet now offer to release scholars from their time warps. When that happens, there could be the same excitement over the latest book as Kano intellectuals experienced some 500 years ago. But bookishness needs to be more than an elite obsession. This was realised, I think, by Muhammad Bello and his colleagues in 1820s Sokoto, as they sought to 'modernise' a Bilad al-Sudan that was now more overtly Muslim, and bring it closer to the rest of the Muslim world. Similarly, a century later in the 1930s, young Muslims read avidly in the new literature and sciences now open to them through books (albeit in English) which were readily available in libraries or on loan from teachers and friends. In the last few decades, that window has half closed again as the book market withered. Inevitably in this context, bookishness has also wilted.

Finally, my argument is that our understanding is distorted by focusing just upon 'literacy', as earlier historians have done, let alone by simply contrasting 'oral' with 'the written'. Indeed, studies of the paper trade and even lists of local authors and their works skirt the central problem of 'the book' and the simple facts and consequences of the availability of texts: who had access to what, and when? The size of libraries, the range of texts and their up-to-dateness, the quality of scholars' and students' command of Arabic, are all significant if we are to understand the actual intellectual history of a particular period. Of course, books may not be the only source of ideas, and today there are other media. Admittedly, long conversations with colleagues with excellent memories can be a good substitute. As historians, however, we lack all access to such conversations, unless they were subsequently referred to in a book or a letter. So our intellectual history of a place like Sokoto, so far from the Mediterranean bookstores, can only be very partial. But it does make a proper history of books and the book trade far out on the Islamic frontier especially worth researching. Bookishness in this context required much more toil than in Cairo or Fez – or even Timbuktu – as indeed it still does today. A book 'drought' we know can be devastating; it is essential that we learn to mitigate its effects, and not rely on an imperfect book trade.

ACKNOWLEDGEMENTS

This chapter is a slightly revised version of an article first published in *Studia Africana*, 17: 39–52, Octubre 2006. We thank the Editor for permission to re-publish it here. I would also like to thank colleagues in Sokoto and Kano who read the original text and suggested corrections and additions.

NOTES

1 Hofheinz (2004).

2 Hofheinz (2004: 156).

3 Lydon (2004).

4 Stewart (1970: 243).

5 Denham et al. (1828, 2: 364 [1st journey]); Clapperton (1829: 198 [2nd journey]).

6 These books were chosen with care. Bello had asked for books when Clapperton said goodbye to him in 1824, but we do not know what he wanted. *The History of the Tartars under Tamerlane* may have been the *Shajara-i Turk* by Abu 'l-Ghazi Bahadur, which in a French translation was much used, some 50 years earlier, by Edward Gibbon for Chapter 54 of his *Decline and Fall.* Who printed the Arabic translation is not clear, but it would have been a suitable present after Clapperton's conversations on early Middle Eastern history with Bello during his previous visit. So too would a copy of Ibn Sina's *al-Qanun*, given how actively involved Bello was in medicine and his interest in new approaches – he wanted the British government to post a doctor in Sokoto. Muhammad Bello was, anyway, very widely read: my Sokoto colleague, Professor Sambo Junaidu, reminds me that Bello said he once counted the number of books he had read – they came to 20 300.

7 Clapperton (1829: 206).

8 Krek (1971). The sixteenth-century traveller Leo Africanus reported on the book trade in Morocco and Timbuktu. However, his interest in Arabic book production in Rome, his involvement in the papacy's plans for exporting Arabic books or any other possible links of his with paper makers and printers with connections in the North African trade are more ambiguous – see the new study of him by Natalie Zemon Davis (2006). Ottoman edicts on printing are given in Atiyeh (1995), while comments on early Italian efforts at typesetting the Qur'an are in Mahdi (1995); for a thorough listing, see Abi Farès (2001). In the 1590s, the works of al-Idrisi and Euclid, for example, were printed by the Medicis for export (the Porte having issued import licences). But Arabic translations of Euclid long preceded the advent of printing, and it is

possible that the copy of Euclid Bello first had from Mecca was the Arabic manuscript text, not a printed book. Clapperton found Bello looking at his new Euclid's *Elements*, but tells us nothing more. Why Muhammad Bello was so interested in Euclid is not clear to me; if anything, his uncle 'Abdullah was more of a mathematician – he determined the orientation of new mosques, for example.

9 Last (1967b).

10 There was no formal postal system, but special, professional runners carried the state's letters. Nor were there carts, which meant that any small path was potentially a 'road'. In practice, there were main routes used by caravans between cities, with facilities every 15 miles or so for their beasts (donkeys, camels, oxen, mules, horses) and the porters to feed and rest overnight. So Fulani scholars with a school (*tsangaya*) off the beaten track – as many were, by choice – missed out on the caravan-borne book trade, unless they made a serious effort to keep good relations with colleagues (or rival groups such as the Wangarawa) in the big cities. Isolated groups of scholars deep in the countryside acquired a reputation for serious learning and represented an intellectual life different from the schools in the city, with all its distractions. Professor Sambo Junaidu (2007) has pointed out how many multi-volume books Shaykh 'Uthman and his fellow scholars had memorised by heart before the *jihad*; for some their memory was visual, enabling them to run through the pages of a book to check for a reference.

11 My source for this is Alberto Manguel's *A History of Reading* (1996), where he cites the four volumes of EG Browne's *A Literary History of Persia* (1928–29) (and misspells the scholar–patron's name). Neither Browne nor Browne's main source, Ibn Khallikan (1842–71, 1), quotes this particular story about the alphabetised camels whose owner's proper name is the Sahib Abu 'l-Qasim Isma'il ibn Abi 'l-Hasan Abbad al-Talakani (he died in Rayy in AD 995). Elsewhere, Ibn Khallikan (1842–71, 2: 250) says the *sahib* used to go round with 30 camels (not 400), but later only needed the *Kitab al-Aghani* (of Abu 'l-Faraj 'Ali b. al-Husain al-Isfahani) once he had a copy of it. If the story is not apocryphal, then 30 camels in alphabetical order at least sounds feasible! The 400 camels refer to the number he said he would need to move his library were he to take up the post an emir offered him. At some 300 books per camel, he was overloading his beasts (unless the volumes carried were mainly short books of poetry)! Pedersen (1984: 123) gives the number of camels needed as 100, while the library's catalogue itself took up 10 volumes. The library was finally burned by Sultan Mahmud of Ghazna (Kraemer 1992).

12 A single camel's load would suggest that the Shaykh 'Uthman's library at this time totalled perhaps 100 to 150 books. The number of books a camel can carry depends, of course, on what constitutes a 'book' – a poem would be light compared, say, to the Holy Qur'an (my 'modern' manuscript copy weighs 4.5 pounds), whereas an ordinary nineteenth-century manuscript book I have from northern Nigeria weighs some 2 pounds, including the boards that act as binding (8 sheets = 1 ounce; 128 sheets = 1 pound). A camel can carry a total load of some 300 pounds (more than twice an ox load), divided into two panniers or nets; four boxes containing 50 pounds of books each would allow for a driver or other equipment. Dr Baz Lecocq tells me that, near Timbuktu, the great Kunta Cheikh Baye (d.1927) reportedly carried his 450 books on two camels. In texts like Ibn Khallikan's, it was common to estimate the size of a person's library by the number of camel loads it took to transport it. If, perhaps, Shaykh 'Uthman (and the Kunta) were consciously following this classical, scholarly trope, then the Shaykh's was a modest one-camel collection. My Sokoto colleague, Ibrahim Gandi, suggests however that probably more than one camel was used to carry the Shaykh's books.

13 Al-Hajj (1983).

14 A notable figure in eighteenth-century Cairo, for example, was Muhammad al-Kashnawi al-Danrankawi who lodged with al-Jabarti's father and earned a mention in his history for his powers of magic. Dan Ranko no longer exists as a town. It was a base used by Wangarawa merchants on the kola caravan route between Kano and Gonja (in what is Ghana today), and was sacked by Muhammad Bello shortly after he sacked another, more famous scholarly town, Yandoto. Neither town had been inclined to join the *jihad*. After the sacking of Yandoto, pages of broken books were seen blowing in the wind. The Wangarawa merchants here were serious book owners in the 'western' tradition of Timbuktu (which was their home area), as Ivor Wilks's (1968) work on their kin in Gonja confirms.

15 Eisenstein (1979).

16 Lapidge (2006).

17 Last (1966–67).

18 Uthman b. Fudi (1978).

19 The late sixteenth and early seventeenth centuries saw in the Mediterranean the 'first world war' in which the states of the eastern end of the sea fought the western states; this conflict also involved states in the West African savannah, where it introduced the use of guns. Echoes of the West African conflict are heard even in the contemporary plays of Shakespeare and Marlowe; presumably London audiences recognised the references, which implies that news from Muslim West Africa circulated quite widely.

20 See Brett (1983).

21 Bivar (1960).

22 The Yan Izala or the 'Society for Removal of Innovation and the Reinstatement of Tradition' was the largest Wahhabi Islamic reform movement in West Africa.

23 Kane (2003).

24 Marty (1922: 274–275).

25 Goody (1968: 217).

26 Hiskett (1996: 139)

27 Denham et al. (1828: 365)

28 Saad (1983: 79).

29 Boyd (1989); Boyd & Mack (1997, 2000).

30 Meek (1925). Pre-colonial demography is an even more hazardous topic, but two points should be kept in mind. First, the numbers involved might be relatively small. For example, in the 1820s the population of Kano city was estimated at about 30 000, with Sokoto then about 120 000. But the ratio of slave to free was estimated, by locally resident Arabs at the time, to be 30:1 (Clapperton 1929: 171); and the proportion of 'Fellata' who could read and write was said (snidely?) to be only 10 per cent. In which case, in Kano city there might be as few as 1 000 free-born men, women and children, which means perhaps 250 free adult males and the equivalent number of free adult women – with only 25 to 50 of them seriously literate? Second, this initial population grew hugely in the course of the century as the free men fathered large numbers of children by their concubines; and these children were, of course, born free. Such children from important families were often brought up primarily by slaves, whose interest in Islamic scholarship might be minimal. Hence, scholarly children – boys and girls – of scholarly parents were (and still are) something of an elite. But becoming a 'scholar' could be a way out of lowly slave status, at least in the twentieth century. I have found in villages learned men whose families were once 'royal' slaves – after the end of slavery, they retained an enhanced status by becoming scholars instead. Colonial ('Christian') rule witnessed a boom in Muslim religious education and scholarship.

31 Palmer (1928). In the reign of Yakubu b. 'Abdullahi (c.1452–63), the *Kano Chronicler* reports that 'the Fulani came to Hausaland from Melle, bringing with them books on Divinity [*tauhid*] and Etymology [*lugha*]. Formerly, our doctors had, in addition to the Koran, only the books of the Law [*fiqh*] and the Traditions [*hadith*]'. Then, in 1565–73 it says that the ruler Abu Bakr b. Muhammad Rumfa was the first emir to read *al-Shifa'* of al-Qadi Iyad (d.1149) – it had been brought to Kano by Shaykh al-Tunisi in the previous reign. The emir Abu Bakr also inaugurated the reading of *Jami' al-saghir*, then a relatively new book by al-Suyuti (d.1505) which was brought to Kano, also in the previous reign, by Shaykh 'Abd al-Salam along with copies of 'classics': *Mudawwana* by Sahnun (d.855) and a work by al-Samarkandi (d.983) – probably his major work of *tafsir, Bahr al-'ulum*. At the end of the fifteenth century al-Maghili had 'brought many books' but they are not specified. At the same time, the Wangara scholar–merchant al-Zagaiti initiated the teaching in Kano of the *Mukhtasar* of Khalil ibn Ishaq (he also taught the *Mudawwana* but he did not need a copy – 'he knew it by heart', says the *Asl al-wangariyyin* [al-Hajj 1968: 10]).

32 Africanus (1956: 468–469).

33 Lavers (1979); Girard (1685).

34 Walz (1985).

35 Saad (1983: 80).

36 Saad (1983: 80).

37 Hunwick & O'Fahey (1995).

38 Brenner & Last (1985).

39 Last (1967a: 31).

40 Ba & Daget (1962).

41 Clapperton (1829: 224).

42 Skinner (1977).

43 Kirk-Greene (1962).

44 See Walz (1985).

45 Toorawa (2005).

46 Hiskett (1973).

47 Hunwick & O'Fahey (1995: 231).

48 Hiskett (1966).

49 Christelow (1994).

50 Lavers (1979); he is quoting consul Frazer's report in FO 76/21.

51 Curtin (1975: 246).

52 Valentine Galvani, d.1810 ; Fratelli Galvani, for example Anton, d.1824; Andrea Galvani, d.1855.

53 Eineder (1960); Fedrigoni (1966); Walz (1985).

54 Ersoy (1963). I am indebted to Professor Menage for lending me this book with its reproductions of both Turkish and imported watermarks.

55 The quarter Mansuri was 213 mm by 142 mm. It was, according to al-Qalqashandi in 1412, the 'familiar' size of paper. The variation in page size, and the limited data available on Islamic paper sizes at varying periods, make mine only a speculative suggestion.

56 Park (1816, 1: 464, 2: 218–221); Koki (1977: 32–33). The ream was 500 sheets from which 4 pages were cut per sheet. Usually the number of sheets per ream varied somewhat but data other than for Kano are not available to me (see Walz 1985: 46, notes 40, 43).

57 Koki (1977: 34).

58 Denham et al. (1828 [1st journey]: 189).

59 Goody (1968: 203). Bowdich was a British traveller and scientific writer who, in 1817, completed peace negotiations with the Asante Empire (now part of Ghana) on behalf of the African Company of Merchants.

60 Hiskett (1966: 139). The books were two volumes of the *Sahih* of Bukhari, two volumes of *Dala'il ashfa* (of al-Qadi Iyad?), a part of *Ashfa* again and a part of the *Mukhtasar* (of Khalil) with the *Risala* (of Ibn Abi Zayd?). In the inventory they come low down on the list, alongside 'ten dollars'.

61 Denham et al. (1828 (1st journey), 2: 162). The cost of Qur'ans of course varies with the quality of copying, binding, etc. Compare with the range of values given in inheritance documents from fifteenth-century Turkey (Brusa), quoted by Sahilliogiu (1977). It is hard to estimate what proportion of a book's sale price went to the copyist – perhaps as low as 40 per cent? Five-thousand cowries (or the cost of paper for a Qur'an) is about one-twentieth the value of a slave at this time. Apparently, then, book prices in late sixteenth-century Timbuktu and late nineteenth-century Kano were roughly comparable.

62 Koki (1977).

63 The switch to copying in Timbuktu is a reflection perhaps of the attraction Islamic schooling had for local children. Were the schools 'overproducing' then? The time if not the labour or cost of copying could be reduced either by putting out different sections of the book simultaneously to different scribes for copying (a practice known in medieval Europe as the *pecia*, or quire, system), or by one reader dictating the text to a group of copyists (the scriptorium system). Both systems were used in Sokoto, but apparently it was more usual for a copyist to transcribe an entire book. In Borno, a separate copyist put in the vowelling in coloured ink. The copy would then be proof-read and corrected. How far there was a division of labour in West African book production is not clear – nor, even, what terminology was used, in Arabic or *ajami*. In Sokoto, terms like *warraq* were apparently not used; *k.t.b.* and *n.s.kh.* are both used for copying, while the *katib* was more a scribe than a secretary.

64 'Broken' books, excerpts or parts of a long work, commonly occur in collections elsewhere in the Muslim world. A third of what Shaykh Sidiya bought in Marrakesh was only parts of books (Stewart 1970), and 'volumes' might contain parts of two or three books. The prevalence of 'broken' books, I suspect, was particularly high among 'classics' in private collections and bookshops. In this context, then, will the largest category of complete books have been those locally composed – indeed, perhaps specifically composed to overcome the problems of students having to otherwise work only with scattered excerpts from 'classics'? The commonness of excerpts raises the question again: what constitutes a 'book'? If these excerpts were used, borrowed, re-copied and sold just like books, perhaps we should consider them as books, reissued in effect like part-works, serials and other episodic literature. If so, should we stop referring to them as 'fragments' or 'incomplete'? Was bookbinding therefore unpopular because it made it impossible to split a book up into parts? Even in the first half of the twentieth century, printed classical Arabic books in personal libraries might be kept unbound between boards. One I have seen, a *Mukhtasar* printed in Cairo, was numbered '90' by the owner who was a Native Authority official in Kano, and not a professional scholar.

65 Hofheinz (2004: 165).

66 Bloom (2001); Bosch et al. (1981).

67 Denham et al. (1828: 2).

68 Denham et al. (1828: 2).

REFERENCES

Abi Farès HS (2001) *Arabic typography: A comprehensive sourcebook.* London: Saqi Books

Africanus L (1956) *[Jean-Léon L'Africain] Description de l'Afrique.* Translated by A Epaulard. Paris: Adrien Maisonneuve

Atiyeh GN (Ed.) (1995) *The book in the Islamic world: The written word and communication in the Middle East.* Albany, NY: SUNY Press

Ba AH & Daget J (1962) *L'Empire peul du Macina.* La Haye: Mouton

Bivar ADH (1960) A dated Kuran from Borno. *Nigeria Magazine* 65: 199–205

Bloom JM (2001) *Paper before print: the history and impact of paper in the Islamic world.* New Haven: Yale University Press

Bosch G, Carswell J & Petherbridge G (1981) *Islamic bindings and bookmaking.* Chicago: Oriental Institute, Chicago University

Boyd J (1989) *The caliph's sister: Nana Asma'u, 1793–1865: Teacher, poet & Islamic leader.* London: Frank Cass

Boyd J & Mack B (1997) *Collected works of Nana Asma'u, daughter of Usman dan Fodiyo (1793–1864).* East Lansing: Michigan State University Press

Boyd J & Mack B (2000) *One woman's jihad: Nana Asma'u, scholar and scribe.* Bloomington: Indiana University Press

Brenner L & Last M (1985) The role of language in West African Islam. *Africa* 55(4): 432–446

Brett M (1983) Islam and trade in the Bilad al-Sudan, tenth–eleventh century AD. *Journal of African History* 24: 431–440

Browne EG (1928-29) *A Literary History of Persia.* Cambridge: Cambridge University Press

Christelow A (Ed.) (1994) *Thus ruled Emir Abbas: Selected cases from the records of the emir of Kano's Judicial Council.* East Lansing: Michigan State University Press

Clapperton H (1829/1969) *Journal of a second expedition into the interior of Africa from the Bight of Benin to Soccatoo.* London: John Murray

Curtin P (1975) *Economic change in pre-colonial Africa.* Madison: University of Wisconsin Press

Davis NZ (2006) *Trickster travels: a sixteenth century Muslim between worlds.* New York: Hill & Wang

Denham D, Clapperton H & Oudney D (1828) *Narrative of travels & discoveries in northern and central Africa in the years 1822, 1823 and 1824* ['1st Journey'] (3rd edition, esp. Vol. II). London: John Murray

Eineder G (1960) *The ancient paper mills of the former Austro-Hungarian Empire and their watermarks.* Hilversum: Paper Publications Society

Eisenstein EL (1979) *The printing press as an agent of change.* Cambridge: Cambridge University Press

Ersoy O (1963) *XVIII. ve IX. Yuzyillarda Turkiye' Kagit.* Ankara: Ankara Üniversitesi Basimevi

Fedrigoni A (1966) *L'Industria Veneta della Carta dalla seconda dominazione austriaca all' unita d'Italia.* Torino: ILTE

Girard (1685) *L'Histoire chronologique du Royaume de Tripoly de Barbarie.* Paris, Bibliothèque Nationale

Goody JR (1968) Restricted literacy in northern Ghana. In JR Goody (Ed.) *Literacy in traditional societies.* Cambridge: Cambridge University Press

al-Hajj MA (1968) A seventeenth century chronicle on the origins and missionary activities of the Wangarawa. *Kano Studies* I(4): 7–42

al-Hajj MA (1983) Some diplomatic correspondence of the Seifuwa Mais of Borno with Egypt, Turkey and Morocco. In B Usman & N Alkali (Eds) *Studies in the history of pre-colonial Borno.* Zaria: Northern Nigerian Publishing Company

Hiskett M (1966) Materials relating to the cowry currency of the western Sudan. *SOAS Bulletin,* 29(1): 132–141

Hiskett M (1973) *The sword of truth: The life and times of the Shehu Usuman dan Fodio.* New York: Oxford University Press

Hofheinz A (2004) Goths in the land of the blacks: A preliminary survey of the Ka'ti Library in Timbuktu. In SS Reese (Ed.) *The transmission of learning in Islamic Africa.* Leiden: Brill

Hunwick JO & O'Fahey RS (Eds) (1995) *Arabic literature of Africa: The writings of Central Sudanic Africa* (Vol. 2). Leiden: Brill

Ibn Khallikan (1842–71) *Wafayat al-a'yan.* Translated by M de Slane. Paris: Oriental Translation Fund of Great Britain & Ireland

Junaidu SW (2007) Research methodology among scholars of the Sokoto Caliphate before the British colonial invasion of 1903. Unpublished paper. Sokoto: Usmanu Danfodiyo University

Kane O (2003) *Muslim modernity in postcolonial Nigeria: A study of the Society for the Removal of Innovation and Reinstatement of Tradition.* Leiden: Brill

Kirk-Greene AHM (Ed.) (1962) *Barth's travels in Nigeria.* London: Oxford University Press

Koki M (1977) *Kano malam/Mahmudu Koki*: Edited by Neil Skinner. Zaria, Nigeria : Ahmadu Bello University Press

Kraemer JL (1992) *Humanism in the Renaissance of Islam* (2nd edition). Leiden: Brill

Krek M (1971) *Typographia Arabica.* Waltham, MA: Brandeis University Library

Lapidge M (2006) *The Anglo-Saxon Library.* New York: Oxford University Press

Last M (1966–67) Arabic manuscript books in the National Archives Kaduna. *Research Bulletin, Centre of Arabic Documentation* 2(2): 1–10, 3(1): 1–15

Last M (1967a) 'The Arabic-script literature of the North': i. Arabic prose (pp.31–42); ii. Fulfulde poetry (pp.43–46); iii. Arabic correspondence (pp.47–70). *Second interim report, Northern History Research Scheme.* Zaria: Ahmadu Bello University

Last M (1967b) *The Sokoto Caliphate.* London: Longmans, Green

Lavers JE (1979) Trans-Saharan trade before 1800. Unpublished paper. Kano: Bayero University

Lydon G (2004) Inkwells of the Sahara: Reflections on the production of Islamic knowledge in *Bilad Shinqit.* In SS Reese (Ed.) *The transmission of learning in Islamic Africa.* Leiden: Brill

Mahdi M (1995) From the manuscript age to the age of printed books. In GN Atiyeh (Ed.) *The book in the Islamic world: The written word and communication in the Middle East.* Albany, NY: SUNY Press

Manguel A (1996) *A history of reading.* London: HarperCollins

Marty P (1922) *Etudes sur l'Islam en Côte d'Ivoire.* Paris: Editions Ernest Leroux

Meek CK (1925) *The northern tribes of Nigeria.* Part II. London: Oxford University Press

Palmer HR (1928) *Sudanese memoirs.* Lagos: Government Printer

Park M (1816) *Travels in the interior of Africa* (2 Vols). London: John Murray

Pedersen J (1984/1946) *The Arabic book.* Translated by G French. Princeton, NJ: Princeton University Press

Saad EN (1983) *Social history of Timbuktu.* Cambridge: Cambridge University Press

Sahilliogiu H (1977) Ottoman book legacies. In *Arabic and Islamic garland: Historical, educational and literary papers presented to Abdul-Latif Tibawi by colleagues, friends and students* (197–199). London: Islamic Cultural Centre

Skinner N (Tr. & Ed.) (1977) *Alhaji Mahmadu Koki.* Zaria: Ahmadu Bello University Press

Stewart CC (1970) A new source on the book market in Morocco and Islamic scholarship in West Africa. *Hesperis-Tamuda* 11: 209–250

Toorawa SM (2005) *Ibn Abi Tahir Tayfur and Arabic writerly culture: A ninth-century bookman in Baghdad.* London: Routledge

Uthman b. Fudi (1978) *Bayan wujub al-hijra 'ala 'l-'ibad.* Edited by FH el-Masri. Khartoum: Khartoum University Press

Walz T (1985) A note on the trans-Saharan paper trade in the 18th and 19th centuries, published as The paper trade of Egypt and the Sudan in the 18th and 19th centuries. In MW Daly (Ed.) *Modernisation in the Sudan: Essays in honor of Richard Hill.* New York: L Barber Press

Wilks I (1968) Islamic learning in the western Sudan. In JR Goody (Ed.) *Literacy in traditional societies.* Cambridge: Cambridge University Press

بسم الله الرحمن الرحيم وصلى الله على النبي الكريم شعر لاسماء تانا بنت الشيخ عثمان بن فودي لما تأخر عنها الولادة الى ان مكثت ثلاث عشرة او سبعة عشر سنة بلا ولد فمنّ الله تعالى بهذا الابيات

ڢدا الله نغداني ڢوم ڢذرا … تا ڢو تنر الله ڢما سعرا

اطا انيي اغفت ايو ويدو … كل ڢف كهدا اينونيرا

نى الله ڢميز معك بجا … حبروج دمعك يدو وترا

مغ تشت مكيا الله ولا … دم مر ڢبهلا سوم كبرا

عوز تڢمر يدب الله بهيي … دطام اڢطاني كا تفعرا

الله نرام اتيننه … بعشاغ يدي ڢمايدورا

لاميد نينيد معيغتنا … ڢرو غنت يبيم بجو وبيسرا

ار كصر تجرا يعنجبر … ار يتبتمبز مير تنكيدزا

سيبيتز بجڢار ڢه نصر معا … ينلبعز تدوايم بجو بلابرا

ارد ي بجڢار ڢ مجم مڢر … دم وينن ترز م ڢاكرا

يم د نبد الله يجيج ڢكا … كسطيمقا ڢبو يبيا بيسرا

بين جوم لام بدا ب ذكر … تو با نمتام غنم شكرا

لا عجيم معك تو ادبير … لحليم كلبڢا ڢ يدو ذڢرا

ا بمنت شنيد ب شلمڢيل … برنلاد ڢمتكليڢ ڢا يشرا

تمت بحمد الله وحسن عونه والصلاة
والسلام على رسوله ٢٨ من جماد
الاخيرة ١٣٠٤ من هجرته
صلى الله عليه وسلم بقلم
اسماء تانا بنت محمد
زوجة الحاج بلاري
ب ڢودي ڢغابو
رحم الله الجميع
امين

CHAPTER 11

Muslim women scholars in the nineteenth and twentieth centuries: Morocco to Nigeria

Beverly B Mack

This chapter began as a comparative study of Muslim women's traditional education in the Maghrib, stretching geographically to include Morocco and northern Nigeria, reflecting long historical connections. The reason for interest in this topic was the demonstrated linkages between historic Mauritania (including much of contemporary southern Morocco) and the Islamic intellectual communities of northern Nigeria, indicated in a letter written by nineteenth-century Nana Asma'u in Nigeria to a Mauritanian scholar, with whom she was evidently well acquainted.[1] These connections were made by members of the Sufi Qadiriyya brotherhood in the eighteenth and nineteenth centuries.[2] Sufi devotees were constantly going to and fro between Hausaland and Cairo or Fez and bringing back accounts of wonderful visions experienced by saintly personalities in the metropolises. 'Uthman dan Fodio (the Shehu) had cordial relations with Shaykh al-Mukhtar al-Kunti, the leader of a Sufi community centred around Timbuktu, who also had visions.'[3] People in contemporary Fez know the Fodio family and easily speak of their many written works, while the Tijaniyya brotherhood brings many from Nigeria to Morocco.[4] Nigeria is also connected to Morocco through the Sufi Tijaniyya brotherhood, a more recent moving force in Nigerian experience. Many Tijani adherents in northern Nigeria make pilgrimages to Fez, where al-Tijani's tomb is in the medina.[5]

Underlying these connections is the significance of northern Nigeria in contemporary times as a formidable Islamic region, constituting half of the continent's most populous country. Through sheer numbers alone, Nigerian Muslim women are important to any discussion of Islam in Africa. In a comparative context, the pursuits of women scholars in northern Nigeria are very similar to those of women scholars in Morocco in terms of structure and intention. What remains to be studied are the particular works that are used by Moroccan women in pursuing a course of higher education within the framework of traditional Islamic education.

Opposite: A page from 'So verily…', one of Nana Asma'u's poems, written when her brother, Muhammad Bello, to whom she was very close, left for battle in 1822.

Islamic education in the Maghrib

Recent studies affirm previous perspectives on women's activist roles in the region, especially with regard to education.[6] Mauritanian women's responsibility for educating young children echoes the situation of nineteenth-century Muslim women in northern Nigeria.[7] It remains the same for contemporary families in northern Nigeria, tempered by the addition of daily education outside the home, divided into Islamic and non-Islamic formal education.[8] In addition to providing fundamental education for children they raise, Muslim women in both regions have long been known as teachers of adults in both regions, and significant scholars in their own right. Mauritanian women appear to have kept pace with those of the Fodio family in northern Nigeria in terms of educating both young and old, and producing sufficient numbers of their own scholarly works to generate materials that became part of a growing canon of works for scholars who followed.[9] Thus, the attempt to uncover a canon of works used by Muslim women scholars in the Maghrib requires an overview of traditional materials commonly studied in an Islamic education system, as well as attention to works produced by these women as mnemonic aids in their own teaching professions.

The Qur'an is the foundation of both Islamic thought and literacy. It is impossible to imagine Islamic education without the memorisation of the Qur'an, which begins a Muslim child's education. Islamic education continues to the equivalent of the west's postgraduate level through a complex programme of courses including a wide range of topics like the natural and physical sciences, history, geography, sociology, medicine and mathematics, often at renowned institutions like al-Azhar University in Cairo and the Qarawiyyin *madrasa* in Fez.[10] As library holdings in Mauritania demonstrate, more advanced fields of study included a multitude of topics, such as 'Qur'anic sciences, Arabic language, mysticism (Sufi literature), jurisprudence, scientific manuals (including medicine, astrology and mathematics), general literature...historical accounts (genealogies, biographical dictionaries, chronologies, pilgrimage memoirs), political material...[and] general correspondence'.[11] Nana Asma'u's nineteenth-century collection demonstrates comparable breadth.

Islamic education followed a similar pattern in Kano in the mid-nineteenth century. In Kano, the system of Islamic education begins at age three. For nine years students learn to write and recite the Qur'an, memorising all 114 suras. Following this, they embark on an introduction to various fields: *fiqh*, *hadith*, *tawhid*, *sira* and *nahawu* (grammar). A second reading of the Qur'an follows, assuring a refined facility in comprehension and pronunciation. After the age of about 20, students begin a more advanced study of famous books, reading them for mastery one at a time with the guidance of a teacher. Mastery of a particular work results in their earning a diploma which allows them to teach that work.[12]

Female students and scholars

In addition to providing fundamental education for children they raise, Muslim women in both Mauritania and northern Nigeria have long been known as teachers of adults in both regions, and as significant scholars in their own right.

Although girls begin their Qur'anic education at the same time as boys, they appear to fall away from the system of learning in the adolescent years. The degree to which this is true, or only apparent, is hard to determine. In many cases, especially in urban settings, they are simply not visible. Walking along a street in Fez it is not uncommon to hear a room full of Qur'anic student boys chanting their lessons; upon enquiring why there are no girls, one is assured that the girls are in class at the back of the house, out of public view. In Kano it has been the case that girls were educated by an older generation of learned individuals in their home, leading to the misconception that girls are not educated at all.[13] Nineteenth-century Nana Asma'u and her sisters (especially Khadija, who translated Khalil's renowned *Mukhtasar* into Fulfulde)[14] are not exceptions: Balarabe Sule and Priscilla Starratt's 1991 study of female scholars, mystics and social workers demonstrates that the tradition of Islamic learning is a vital one in contemporary northern Nigeria.[15]

Similarly, in Fez and Meknes women run elementary schools for traditional Islamic education, and Sufi women scholars may opt to continue their post-secondary education in traditional programmes of study rather than at the western-oriented university.[16] In addition, it is not uncommon for those who are more immersed in traditional life to meet regularly (once or twice a week) in study groups at a local *zawiya* for the discussion of a Qur'anic passage or other pertinent commentary on contemporary issues. In each case the *zawiya* gathering is led by a woman qualified to teach, give a sermon and answer questions.[17]

Even apart from formal systems of learning, the idea of the written word preserved in the book is revered in Muslim cultures. The dual founding precepts of Islam – the primacy of the pursuit of knowledge and the confirmation of equity – guide attitudes, and make women's scholarship a likely proposition in cultures that have not been overwhelmed by patriarchal limitations. Even in such cultures, women's insistence upon their rights as set forth in the Qur'an motivates them to pursue their intellectual activities.[18] Furthermore, this is not a new concept. Evidence from tenth-century Andalusia indicates that girls were attending schools with boys then, and women were writing; Wallah, princess-poet, was educated 'in classes including both sexes'.[19]

Traditional influences

The bulk of this study involves attention to works in Nana Asma'u's collection, which include poetic works in large categories. Those works influenced by the Qur'an and the Sunna include mnemonic guides to facilitate memorisation of the Qur'an, stories based on the Sunna, elegies, and poems about medicines of the Prophet. Historical works include influences from the *sira* and eulogies. Works inspired in a Sufi context reflect *khalwa* and *dhikr* experience, an account of Sufi women, and panegyric. Most of these reflect

The dual founding precepts of Islam – the primacy of the pursuit of knowledge and the confirmation of equity – guide attitudes and make women's scholarship a likely proposition in cultures that have not been overwhelmed by patriarchal limitations.

collaborative creativity, but several works best exemplify the collaborative technique with members of the community, and the reworking of poems that were commonly known in the region, some of which are directly related to tenth-century manuscripts, influenced by thirteenth-century panegyric, or focused on Abbasid concepts of state.

Nearly all Asma'u's works testify to direct influence by earlier works; all of them can be understood in the context of her Islamic education, steeped as it was in study of the Qur'an and the Sunna. Thus, a 'canon' of works represents not a static, preserved collection of old works, but a vital collection of materials that includes both the classics and contemporary compositions inspired by both earlier and contemporary works. A single manuscript represents but a moment in the continued variation of materials used for study. Some of these new creations, in turn, became part of a new, ever-changing canon of works in a fluid context of learning.

Beyond examples from Nana Asma'u's works, attention to the materials in use in the region indicates that the exchange of poems and treatises was not only common but also necessary to the advancement of scholarship in Islamic communities. At this point the definition of 'canon' becomes more problematic, because written materials are of only secondary importance to intellectual advancement in Sufi circles. Indeed, in Fez, Sufi scholars express reticence about relying on the written word, or publishing.

Understanding is advanced through contemplation of the spoken word, memorisation of Qur'anic passages and discussion of concepts in a variety of venues, including Qur'anic schools at the lowest to most advanced levels, community study groups in *zawiyas*, and in dedicated affiliation with particular brotherhood study groups. Thus, the 'canon' upon which women scholars in the Maghrib rely includes orally transmitted works, which often are deemed much more valuable than the written ones.

The Fodio community

Nana Asma'u's writings clarify that her education, like that of others of her level of learning, included the study and imitation of classical works as well as collaborative activity among her family members and peers. Her education must have followed the traditional patterns of learning evidenced for others in the region, from Mauritania and Mali to Kano, as her written works reflect familiarity with the topics of such a programme of study. Subsequently, her own written works became part of the corpus of works used in educating, especially in the education of women in the Sokoto Caliphate.

Alhaji Umaru (b.1858 in Kano) knew of Nana Asma'u, and commented in his writings that she was well known in the region.[20] Umaru began Qur'anic school at the age of seven and spent five years learning the Qur'an and Arabic literacy. At the age of 12 he began a programme of advanced learning with several different teachers that was to continue for 21 years, ending in 1891. The areas of study he pursued included Islamic religion, history, law and Arabic language, as well as two years devoted to Qur'anic commentaries and history, and eleven years engaged in the study of religion and language. In addition he studied *hadith* theology, Maliki law historical traditions of Islam, the history of the Prophet's life, world history, West African authorship, Arabic grammar and pre-Islamic and Islamic poetry.[21] It is likely that this course of study was influenced by the intellectual movement that came out of Sokoto and spread throughout northern Nigeria during the nineteenth century in the course of reformation following the Sokoto *jihad*. And although Umaru does not cite works by any of the Fodios, it would not be surprising to find evidence that the poetry and prose produced by the Shehu, 'Abdullahi, Bello and Asma'u was an integral part of the Islamic education system at the end of the century.[22]

Asma'u's early nineteenth-century work, 'The Qur'an', is cited by the late Mervyn Hiskett as a poem of 'little literary interest'.[23] Yet the value of this work is that it compresses into 30 verses the names of every chapter of the Qur'an, rendering it a compact mnemonic device for the teaching of the Qur'an. Any qualified teacher would have been able to unpack each chapter title, teaching the entire chapter over one or more lessons. Asma'u wrote this poem in all three major local languages – Arabic, Fulfulde and Hausa – obviously intending it to have wide audience appeal.[24] This work's value is its efficiency in guiding an organised study of the Qur'an for students at both beginning and advanced levels. Thus, while it is not – to my knowledge – based on an earlier piece, its value in Islamic formal education is clear.

A 'canon' of works represents not a static, preserved collection of old works, but a vital collection of materials that includes both the classics and contemporary compositions inspired by both earlier and contemporary works. A single manuscript represents but a moment in the continued variation of materials used for study. Some of these new creations, in turn, became part of a new, ever-changing canon of works in a fluid context of learning.

Influences on Asma'u's works: Qur'an and Sunna

In *Tanbih al-ghafilin* (The Way of the Pious, 1820) Asma'u has used her brother Bello's *Infaqul al-Maisur*[25] as a model for a discussion of the Shehu's intellectual focus: his teaching methods and materials.[26] This work is imitative of the Sunna, and would have been familiar to anyone raised in the tradition of the *hadith*. Another such work is Asma'u's *Godaben Gaskiya* (The Path of Truth [Hausa], 1842), which advises listeners to follow the path of right behaviour, warning explicitly against sin by describing the pains of hell and explaining the rewards of heaven, as each is set forth in the Qur'an. Thus, it is also imitative of the Sunna, derived directly from the Qur'an,[27] as is *Sharuddan Kiyama* (Signs of the Day of Judgment [Hausa], n.d.). In the latter, Asma'u outlines in graphic detail the punishments of hell as they are described in the Qur'an. In addition, this work allows Asma'u to draw a metaphorical parallel between the price of sin and the cost of disobedience to local authority. The *shari'a* of the caliphate enforced behaviour through statutory punishment, and Asma'u chose to impress upon the masses the importance of obedience at all levels, from civil to spiritual.

Perhaps the most frightening of her works outlining the perils of hell is *Hulni-nde* (Fear This [Fulfulde], n.d.). Written in Fulfulde, it was not meant for the masses, but instead was addressed to her clan. The work's origin is in a poem by Muhammad Tukur; Asma'u added the *takhmis*. Asma'u was also familiar with the Shehu's sermon on the fear of hell, which Bello later incorporated into his own *Infaqul al-maisur surat al-ikhlas*. In each case, these works were demonstrations of the authors' familiarity with the Qur'an's descriptions of hell. They are also implicit examples of collaborative work by the authors.

Several of Asma'u's works are in the classic Arabic poetic mode of elegy; they focus on aspects of character that would be familiar in studies of the Sunna and *hadith*. These include elegies for those well known, like her brother the caliph, Muhammad Bello, as well as for individuals of no historic note. The latter is exemplified by Asma'u's poem *Alhinin Mutuwar Halima* (Elegy for Halima [Hausa], 1844), in which she comments on the virtues of this ordinary woman, a neighbour, who is remembered especially for her patience and mediatory skills among family members.[28] In her 61 collected works, Asma'u includes 15 elegies, and three more that may be considered in this category: two mourn the loss of 'Aisha, a close friend, and one, written the year after an elegy for him, is a deeply felt commemoration of Bello's character. It should be noted that in her remembrance of her brother the caliph, Asma'u noted none of his political or historical achievements. Instead she outlined the moral and ethical qualities that distinguished him as a person who followed the Sunna with his heart.

Asma'u's *Tabshir al-ikhwan* (Medicine of the Prophet [Arabic], 1839) reflects immersion in the *hadiths*. Written in Arabic, it is meant to be appreciated by scholars, especially those who specialised in *tibb an-nabi*, which is understood to be the 'religiously oriented, highly spiritual…healing system of Madina…All the *hadiths* dealing with medicine and related subjects are presented…as an inseparable part of the larger body of the traditions of the Prophet, hence considered genuine and infallible'.[29] This work, like many of her other ones, reflects comparable works by others of her clan. The Shehu mentioned that he felt medical treatment with verses of the Qur'an was Sunna (in his *Ihya al-Sunna* [Revival of the Sunna]), and his brother 'Abdullahi wrote about the conduct of physicians and the procedures they should follow (in his 1827 *Masalih al-insan al-muta'alliqa bi al-adyan* [Benefits for Human Beings Related to Religions] and *Diya al-qawa'id wa nathr al-fawa'id li-ahl al-maqasid* [The Rules for Spreading the Benefits for the People's Goals]). But as with other works, it was her brother Bello who most influenced Asma'u in this piece on medicine. He was noted among writers throughout the Bilad al-Sudan as an authority on medicines.[30] Among Bello's 10 books on medicine is his *Talkhis al-maqasid al-mujarrada fi'l adwiya al-farida* (Summations of Objective Unique),[31] a summation of al-Kastallani's (b.1448 Cairo, d.1517 Mecca) fifteenth-century book on religiously oriented healing. Bello's other works on medicine included one focused on eye diseases (*Tibb al-hayyun* [Remedies for Eye Disease]), purgatives (*al-Qual al-sana' fi wujuh al-taliyan wa'l-tamashshi bi'l-sana*) and piles (*al-Qual al-manthur fi bayan adwiya 'illat al-basur* [Remedies for Piles]). In 1837, in his old age, he wrote *Tibb al-Nabi* (Medicines of the Prophet), a treatise on metaphysical medicine following a visit by Egyptian scholar and Qadiri Sufi Qamar al-Din, who passed his medical knowledge on to Bello.[32] In addition to these works, Asma'u also cites Muhammad Tukur as a source for her own work. Tukur was encouraged by Bello to write a 22 000-word book in 1809, *Qira al-ahibba' fi bayan sirr al-asma*, which explains the medical benefit of reciting the names of God, or Qur'anic verse.[33] His *Ma'awanat al-ikhwan fi mu'asharat al-niswan* (The Means of Helping Brothers Toward Legitimate Social Relationships with Women) focuses on the use of minerals and herbs with prayer for the purpose of curing.[34] In her version, Asma'u focuses on suras 44–108, although it remains to be understood why she did so. In all Bello's works, as in Asma'u's on this topic, the aim was to provide information that could benefit the community.

Historical influences

Another classic Arabic poetic genre, *sira* (biography of the Prophet), is evident in Asma'u's *Filitage/Wa'kar Gewaye* (The Journey [Fulfulde/Hausa], 1839, 1865) – concerning the Shehu's campaigns of reform – and *Begore* (Yearning for the Prophet [Hausa], n.d.). In the first, Asma'u draws clear parallels between the nineteenth-century campaign of the Shehu in reforming Islam and that of the Prophet in establishing Islam in the seventh century. In the second, Asma'u focuses on aspects of the life of the Prophet that can be easily compared with the Shehu's life.[35]

Tabbat Hakika (Be Sure of God's Truth, 1831) harks back to the Abbasid concept of the state (c.750–1258), which was the subject of books by Asma'u's father, the Shehu (*Bayan Wujub* [Communication of What is Necessary Concerning the Hijira], 1806), uncle 'Abdullahi (*Diya al-Hukkam* [The Light for Governors], 1806) and brother Bello (*al-Gaith* [Explanation of the Requirements for the Upright Imam], 1821). Bello's work parallels the seventeenth-century work of the historian Naima (1687) with identical wording concerning the neo-Platonic concept of the 'Circle of Equity', which confirms the need for royal authority.[36] Asma'u's creation relies on the technique of *takhmis*, in which she used her father's work in couplets, adding three lines to each couplet to create a new poem whose running rhyme is the phrase *tabbat hakika* (be sure of God's Truth). The aim of the work is the juxtaposition of earthly and divine truth: truth v. Truth. This functions to raise the metaphorical meaning of the contents to a spiritual level, reminding both listeners and the leader that there is always a higher power than the mortal authority figure who rules.[37]

In addition to *Tabbat hakika*'s focus on the need for rulers to keep in mind divine law, this poem's collaborative nature demonstrates the interdependence practised by Islamic scholars in creating works that are now regarded as having only one author. If Asma'u based her poem on her father's poem in couplets and created a new work in quintains, whose poem is it? A bookseller in Fez showed me many old works of *hadith* and *fiqh*, all attributed to male authors. When I asked if it were possible to find works by women he said it was not, but added that that did not mean that women did not write. He insisted that it was quite common for women to compose, but for propriety's sake they would never sign their own names; they would sign their husbands' names instead.[38]

A bookseller in Fez showed me many old works of *hadith* and *fiqh*, all attributed to male authors. When I asked if it were possible to find works by women he said it was not, but added that that did not mean that women did not write. He insisted that it was quite common for women to compose, but for propriety's sake they would never sign their own names; they would sign their husbands' names instead.

Sufi works

At the end of the eighteenth and beginning of the nineteenth centuries Sufi traffic between Hausaland in northern Nigeria, Fez and Cairo was common. Not only would devotees in Hausaland be familiar with the Qadiriyya brotherhood, but the newly formed Tijaniyya brotherhood (*c*.1780) affirmed a linkage with Fez, where Ahmad al-Tijani is buried in the medina. The Fodio clan's affiliation with Qadiriyya Sufism was pervasive. In addition to Asma'u's involvement in mysticism, the Shehu's wife 'Aisha was a devout mystic, and his wife Hauwa and her daughter Fadima regularly went into retreat.[39] Early in his education the Shehu studied Ibn 'Arabi's *Meccan Revelations* (*al-Futuhat al-makkiyya*, *c*.1238).

Asma'u's *Mimsitare* (Forgive Me, 1833) is written in Fulfulde, thus indicating that it was not intended as a teaching tool for the larger Hausa-speaking audience, but rather was focused toward the Fodio clan. This work, along with *Tawassuli Ga Mata Masu Albarka/Tindinore Labne* (Sufi Women [Hausa/Fulfulde], 1837) and *Sonnore Mo'Inna* (Elegy for my Sister Fadima [Fulfulde], 1838), underlines Asma'u's Sufi activity. *Mimsitare* indicates Asma'u's own entry into *khalwa* (mystical retreat), while the other two works mention Bello's mother Hauwa and her daughter Fadima (respectively) having gone into retreat frequently. Asma'u was 40 when she wrote *Mimsitare*, about the same age as her father when he began to practise *khalwa*, and to have visions establishing his connection to Shaykh 'Abd al-Qadir al-Jilani, founder of the Qadiriyya Sufi order.[40] His recollections about Sufi experiences are related in his *Wird* (Litany).

Her later work, *Mantore di Dabre* (Remembrance of the Shehu [Fulfulde], 1854), is modelled on a work written by the Shehu early in his life, perhaps as early as age 10, in 1765. That poem, *Afalgimi* (Fulfulde), is a simple Sufi litany, whose style she 'copied...from the Shehu' (*Mantore di Dabre* v.10) nearly a century later. Both works appeal to God for strength in following the Sunna and generosity. Asma'u's imitation of her father's early work is meant as an expression of honour to him, following the Arabic poetic tradition of imitating another author's style.

The only poem in which Asma'u mentions her health is one that is clearly in a Sufi context. A mere dozen lines, this piece was untitled but was given a working title in translation: 'Thanksgiving for Recovery' (1839). Although no other known poems concerning recovery exist, this one is linked in context and tone with one by Rabia al-Adawiya of Basra, the eighth-century Sufi of renown. Rabia's poem concerns praying all night and fasting in appeal for the healing of her broken wrist. In Asma'u's work on this same topic she indicates both a reliance on classical sources and creativity in the Sufi mode.

Asma'u's 'Sufi Women' was written with the aim of endowing with respectability the Muslim women of the Sokoto Caliphate, both members in long standing and new converts. The basis of the work was a prose work by Muhammad Bello, *Kitab al-nasihah* ([Book of Advice], 1835), which he asked Asma'u to translate into Hausa and Fulfulde and versify. Its aim was to create a teaching tool with the intention of promoting women's education in an Islamic way of life. To accomplish this, Asma'u crafted a poem that focused on exemplary women in the caliphate community, merging their names and stories with a litany of historically established Sufi women, whose reputations were well known.[41] At the time that Asma'u's collected works were published in translation (1997), it was thought that the earliest manuscript on which Bello's and her works were modelled was *Sifat al-safwat* (c.twelfth century) by Ibn al-Jawzi. However, Rkia Cornell's 1999 translation of Abu 'Abd al-Rahman al-Sulami's tenth-century work, *Dhikr al-niswa al-muta 'abbidat al-Sufiyyat* (Early Sufi Women), demonstrated that al-Jawzi's own work was modelled on the earlier one by al-Sulami.

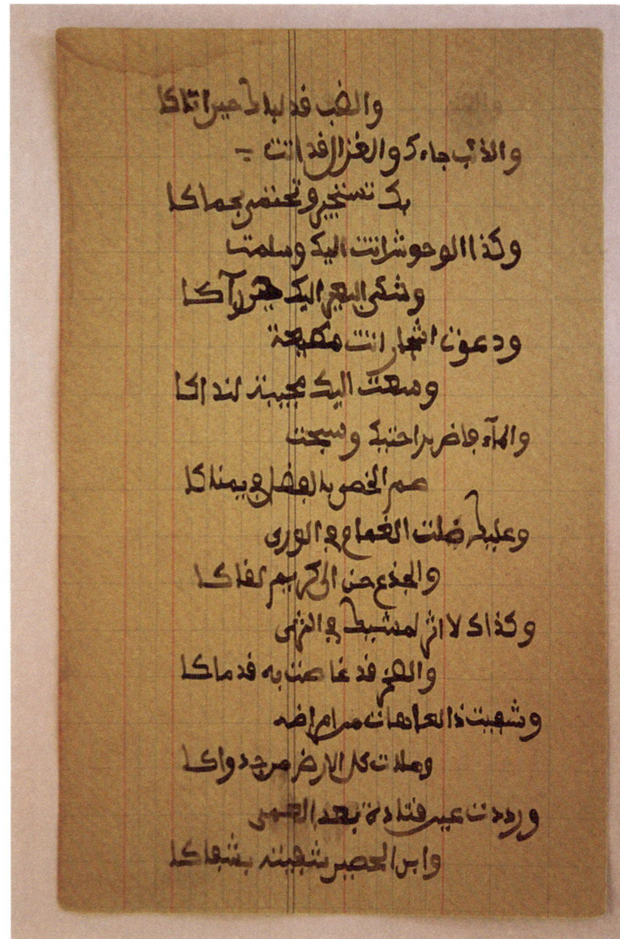

Each poet establishes her own canon by drawing from a vast array of materials that have remained accessible since at least the tenth century. The canon changes with the needs of a particular scholar; the emphasis of works varies according to the needs of the moment. Many of the newer works, created on the foundations of earlier works, become classics for subsequent generations.

Asma'u's poem shares an obvious connection to al-Jawzi's work (and by extension, therefore, to as-Sulami's) because an overwhelming majority of names in the original appear in the same order and with comparable descriptions in Asma'u's poem. Her poem differs from the original, however, in her addition of women from the caliphate to the list of revered Sufi women, thereby elevating their status to that of historical Sufi women. Her poem also differs from Bello's version in that she omitted admonitions to women that he included as a means of trying to control irreverent behaviour. Instead, she focuses on what women have accomplished, and what they are capable of doing to contribute to the Muslim community. This is another example of Asma'u using existing works as the basis for new material honed to a different purpose. In this manner she was able to benefit from the credibility associated with works well established in Islamic intellectual circles, and also revise aspects of the works to convey messages relevant to her place and time. 'Sufi Women' is one of the works used extensively in Asma'u's training of extension teachers for secluded women in the community; thus it provided a window to an Islamic world in which women were recognised as important to the community.

Asma'u's collaborative activities are evident in other works as well.[42] She and other scholars in the caliphate community felt linked to the wider Islamic world. Her father the Shehu wrote only in Arabic. Her uncle 'Abdullahi favoured pre-Islamic poetry, and that of seventeenth-century North African poet Abu 'Ali-Hasan b. Mas'ud al-Yusi.[43] Asma'u's elegies bear striking similarity in tone to those of al-Khansa, a woman poet who was a contemporary of the Prophet,[44] so it is likely that she knew the works of this woman.[45] Asma'u's *Dalilin Samuwar Allah* (Reasons for Seeking God [Hausa], 1861) is rooted in Bello's *Infaqul al-maisur*, which clarifies the content of the Shehu's sermons.

Examples abound of the close collaborative bond among several generations of Fodios, and their reliance on classical works.

Asma'u's *Kiran Ahmada* (In Praise of Ahmada [Hausa], 1839) is a panegyric to the Prophet in the form known as *madih*, which functions to provide an outlet for emotional needs in worship; prophetic panegyric has long been associated with Sufism.[46] Asma'u would have been familiar with panegyrics to the Prophet, which were well known by the thirteenth century, especially al-Busiri's *Burda* (The Cloak), al-Fazazi's *al-Ishriniyyat* (The Twenties), al-Lakhmi's *al-Qasa'id al-witriyya* (Superogatory Odes) and al-Tawzari's *Simt al-huda* (The Necklace of Guidance), all of which were well known in the region. Asma'u's emulation of the subjects and styles of these works is evident in her own poems, so it is known that she was familiar with them.[47] Another example of panegyric is Asma'u's *Mantore Arande* (Remembrance of the Prophet [Fulfulde], 1843). In this work she selected details of the Prophet's life that could be paralleled with those of the Shehu, as she did in 'Yearning for the Prophet'.

Collaboration

Fa'inna ma'a al-'usrin yusra (So Verily… [Fulfulde], 1822)(see page 164) is a prime example of collaborative authorship between Nana Asma'u and her brother Muhammad Bello, to whom she was very close. Her poem is a response to an acrostic poem left for her by Bello as he headed into battle. Each bears the verse *fa'inna ma'a al-'usrin yusra* (Qur'an 94: 5) as the acrostic that runs down the length of their 14 lines, marking the first letter of each line. Bello's poem was written as comfort to a worried sister; hers was composed as a prayer for victory and his safe return. While these works bear no known relation to earlier classical poems, the fact of their close collaboration indicates a style that is representative of Arabic poetry.

Asma'u's *Gawakuke ma'unde* (The Battle of Gawakuke [Fulfulde], 1856) is also highly collaborative. Bello described this battle, as did al-Hajj Sa'id, a follower of al-Hajj 'Umar, and Asma'u would have known those works. Despite its apparent historical theme, this work is actually an elegy describing the character of Bello, his *baraka*, charismatic leadership, and miracle working, setting him in the context of Sufi devotion.[48] By combining these styles and addressing a topic already covered by other poets of her time, Asma'u creates a work of wide appeal at the same time that she paints a political figure with particular Islamic colours.

Contemporary Kano

Sule and Starratt's study of educated women in Kano demonstrates that women's education is a 'widespread urban phenomenon'.[49] They discuss the education of women who came of age during the mid-twentieth century. The pattern of early learning was similar for all: Qur'anic study from a parent during childhood, followed by the study of works on Maliki law and the principles of prayer.[50] Following this stage, they studied various books[51] focused on Maliki law and ritual, panegyric of the Prophet, stories about the Prophet's family, mysticism and Arabic grammar. Their canon of works prepared these women for their roles as teachers and spiritual leaders. It was common for them to teach at several different levels. Many would teach primary school during the day and adult education classes at night. Several ran Islamiyya schools in the neighbourhood, and one was widely known as an expert in the recitation of *tafsir* – she recorded readings for radio and television. In every case women's courses of study continued through successive marriages, establishing the habit of learning as their life's work. In their old age, they continued to teach at a private level, tutoring other women in particular books.

My own experience in close association with women of the Kano palace affirmed that learning for children begins at age four and continues in both the Qur'anic and western mode, as they divided their days between the two schools. There are many options for secondary school, ranging from the School for Arabic Studies to western schools. It is at this stage that women, who marry young, appear to fall away from education, but their retreat into the private milieu of domesticity does not mark the end of education for them. Private tutoring is common and easily suited to a life with domestic demands that militate against sitting in class away from the home. In the 1970s and 1980s, the Kano state government instituted a programme of adult education classes throughout the region. Classes were held during the day and at night to allow for wide attendance. The curriculum was broad, including literacy and numeracy, religious knowledge, childcare and hygiene, and crafts for entrepreneurial skills. At the same time, in the palace several of the emir's wives, with teacher-training certificates themselves, were engaged in tutoring adult women from the royal community and from outside the palace. One of them also established a small primary school class for children in the palace who were unable to attend a formal school. In the trend toward Islamiyya schools replacing Qur'anic schools, Helen Boyle's study in Kano notes that the gender ratio favours girls over boys, 2 to 1.[52] It appears that women in northern Nigeria take very seriously the admonition to 'seek knowledge, even unto China'.

Contemporary Morocco

Several studies of women and education in Morocco have focused on the extent to which girls and women are integrated into public school settings where the genders are mixed.[53] In each case the studies concern the role of literacy as a gauge of empowerment for women functioning in changing socio-economic roles. But none discusses the role and extent of traditional education among women – especially Sufi learning – in Morocco. It is likely that the women who attend *zawiya* discussions on a regular basis, in villages throughout Morocco, have studied works similar to those outlined for Kano – whether

Beyond the collection of written documents, investigation of oral sources is especially central to an understanding of scholarship in Sufi circles. Many Sufis in Morocco note that the most important material is written on the heart, not on paper where it can be destroyed.

in oral or written form.[54] More research is needed to examine the scholarly background of these women and investigate the materials they studied. If the cross-fertilisation of scholarship that appears to be evident for the Maghrib holds, then it may be possible to determine the sources most common to scholarship in the region. Also, it is important to seek further evidence of correspondence between the regions, as shown by Asma'u's letter to the Mauritanian scholar.

In addition to written documents, orally transmitted works are central to an explanation of the works upon which Muslim women scholars in the Maghrib have relied. Helen Boyle's analysis devotes a great deal of space to the concept of the body as a site of cultural production, noting the value of memorisation of the Qur'an in instilling cultural values and understanding. This is particularly relevant to the types of study found among Sufi groups in the region. In discussions at the home of Shaykh Moulay Hassan and his wife in Fez, adherents of a rural Sufi teacher, noted that the works they were taught were conveyed orally. When asked about writing them down, their teacher explained it was preferable to memorise them. Other Sufis discussed the perspective that the written word was a crutch beyond which one needed to move in internalising the word of God. In attempting to understand a canon of works pertinent to women scholars, the importance of the spoken, memorised word cannot be ignored.

Conclusion

In her corpus of works Nana Asma'u relied on both her own educational background in classical Islamic works and her familiarity with works by her kinsfolk for the creation of her own poems. Many of her poems are collaborative works, which honour the poems of her contemporaries by reworking them to her own effect. Echoing a traditional programme of study, her works include descriptions of the Qur'an, panegyric, elegy, and biography of the Prophet. Asma'u transforms some of these into works more pertinent to her own context: her biography of the Shehu parallels her biography of the Prophet; her description of the Prophet's endeavours selects as its focus events that she parallels in her description of the Shehu's campaigns. Asma'u's Sufi devotion is also a formative feature of her works, which include litanies and *dhikr*. Her poem on medicines of the Prophet reflects traditional works on religious-based healing, and her work on Sufi women not only imitates the classic tenth-century work of the same name by al-Sulami, but also weaves into it the names of local women whose status she elevates by their association with historical women of note.

Beyond the collection of written documents, investigation of oral sources is especially central to an understanding of scholarship in Sufi circles. Many Sufis in Morocco note that the most important material is written on the heart, not on paper where it can be destroyed. All Muslims begin with the same source, the Qur'an, whose multivalent nature ensures that it is accessible to all, regardless of their intellectual capability, literacy or talent. Depending on an individual's position in society she will focus on law or history or Sufi concepts or another aspect of interpretation. Thus, an individual's canon will vary depending on her interests and needs, just as one's understanding of the Qur'an depends upon the individual's circumstances.

If 'canon' is to be perceived as an authoritative list, we can begin to collect the names of books common to a region, but because there exist so many classical works, and because the emphasis on one or another would vary from region to region, a canon may not be limited. A fixed canon would militate against the fluidity of learning and composition that is evident in the examples described above. Thus, while it is not possible to establish a static canon of works from which Asma'u – or any other poet – drew inspiration, it is important to confirm that each poet establishes her own canon by drawing from a vast array of materials that have remained accessible since at least the tenth century. The canon changes with the needs of a particular scholar; the emphasis of works varies according to the needs of the moment. Many of the newer works, created on the foundations of earlier works, become classics for subsequent generations, joining the ranks of those that have heretofore constituted the 'canon'. Further fieldwork is needed to investigate the kinds of classical works that constitute the basis for contemporary scholarship.

NOTES

1 See 'Welcome to the Mauritanian scholar' in Boyd and Mack (1997: 282–283). For subsequent references to Asma'u's works, unless otherwise cited, see relevant pages in this source.

2 Asma'u's easy correspondence with the mysterious Mauritanian scholar (Alhaji Ahmed Muhammad al-Shinqiti) implies a longer-standing network of correspondences and familiarity that likely date to at least one if not several previous generations, which would put the connection well into the eighteenth century. More work on the Shehu's writings needs to be done to demonstrate this linkage.

3 Hiskett (1973: 63–64).

4 The erudition of the Shehu 'Uthman dan Fodio, his brother 'Abdullahi, his son Caliph Muhammad Bello and his daughter Nana Asma'u are especially well known, even when their writings are not available.

5 Ahmad al-Tijani, b.1737 southern Algeria, d.1815 Fez, Morocco, established order in 1780.

6 See Mack (2004).

7 Compare Lydon's (2004) observations and those in works on Nana Asma'u – see Boyd (1989); Mack & Boyd (2000); and Boyd & Mack (1997).

8 This was my experience during fieldwork in Kano, Nigeria, 1979–81. In an article in 2005, Margot Badran notes a similar pattern ('Liberties of the faithful', *al-Ahram Weekly*, http://weekly.ahram.org.eg/2005/743/fe2.htm.)

9 Lydon (2004: 48, 68).

10 Fourteenth-century Ibn Khaldun's *Muqaddima* gives a sense of the breadth of traditional Islamic learning.

11 Lydon (2004: 62).

12 Sule & Starratt (1991: 36) – see note 6 for more sources on programmes of study and their appendix, which includes annotated descriptions of the books studied by contemporary Kano women.

13 Galadanci (1971), cited in Sule & Starratt (1991: 37).

14 Sule & Starratt (1991: 36).

15 Note the appendix in Sule & Starratt (1991), which includes a list of traditional books regularly studied by these Kano women scholars.

16 In fieldwork in Fez and Meknes (2002, 2003) I visited these schools and worked with a Sufi woman who had completed secondary school and was immersed in advanced Sufi studies in the medina in Fez.

17 It was my experience that no matter how small the village, these groups of women were devoted to their study sessions: in Tiznit, in south-west Morocco, women meet once a week, while in Tamagroute, at the end of the Marrakesh road, they meet twice a week for sessions of several hours.

18 See Badran ('Liberties of the faithful', *al-Ahram Weekly*, http://weekly.ahram.org.eg/2005/743/fe2.htm) for the confirmation of this perspective, which is also evident throughout my own field notes from Kano in the late 1970s.

19 Nykl (1946: 72), cited in el-Hajj (1996).

20 Pilaszewicz (2000: 86).

21 Pilaszewicz (2000: 10–11).

22 Six other of Asma'u's sisters also wrote: Hadiza, Habsatu, Fadima, Safiya, Maryam and Khadija. Their manuscripts are housed in the family's private collections.

23 Hiskett (1975: 44).

24 It was written in 1829, 1838 and 1850, respectively, appealing (chronologically) to Fulfulde speakers, then the Hausa majority, and finally to Arabic speakers.

25 This title is rendered in English only with difficulty. Neither Jean Boyd nor Murray Last was comfortable with an English translation. Last (1967: xxviii–xxxiii, l) refers to this manuscript as 'the most detailed and factual account of the *jihad'* available. Its availability, however, is moot, considering that several of the Arabic manuscripts of it are in private hands, and the translations by (colonial Resident) EJ Arnett (1920) are unreliable. Boyd adds that: i) Bello gives detailed accounts of the battles they fought on the Gewaye (journey) which need maps. They are not present and without them the text is unfathomable; ii) Arnett did not dissect Bello's words out of quotations from other texts; and iii) It was printed in 1922 on poor paper which crumbled to powder in time. There is also a Hausa translation of *Infakul Maisuri*, trans. Sidi Sayudi and Jean Boyd, Sokoto History Bureau, 1974 (personal communication, 1 October 2006).

26 Sections include attention to: barriers dividing people from paradise; discussion of dangerous habits; redeeming habits; and distinguishing features of those who follow the Sunna.

27 In addition, Asma'u's sense of her authority is clear; she remarks that, 'I, daughter of the Shehu, composed this song – you should follow her…' (v.126).

28 Boyd & Mack (1997: 195–196).

29 Abdalla (1981: 16).

30 Abdalla (1985).

31 127 pages in length.

32 Last (1967), cited in Boyd & Mack (1997: 100). Also noted here is that it was characteristic of both Bello and his sister Asma'u to couch their works in terms of benefit to the masses, a deviation from the focus of classical writers on the topic, who composed their works as gifts to royalty.

33 Abdalla (1981: 158) notes that Tukur's sources for this work 'are not practitioners from the high period of Islamic civilization, but some lesser known Sufis and theologians who flourished in the medieval period'.

34 '…the title translates as "The means of helping brothers toward legitimate social relationships with women" (Alhaji Shaykh Ahmed Lemu, personal communication, 21 September 1994). Abdalla says "in the *Ma'awanat al-ikhwan fi mu'asharat al-niswan* emphasis is placed on *material media* for the treatment of various illnesses and as aphrodisiacs" (1981: 163). As far as we know there is no translation of the work' (Boyd & Mack 1997: 101).

35 Boyd & Mack (1997: 133, 304).

36 See Boyd & Mack (1997: 45–46). 'Abdullahi emphasises the role of a leader in administering justice to the disenfranchised, while the Shehu affirms the role of scholars in enjoining truth, the Sunna, and justice.

37 See Boyd & Mack (1997: 46n) for a discussion of the controversy concerning authorship of this poem.

38 This is perhaps the most extreme form of collaboration.

39 Hiskett (1973: 61–69); Boyd & Mack (1997: 60).

40 Hiskett (1973: 64).

41 Boyd & Mack (1997: 68–72).

42 Boyd & Mack (1997: 133–134) indicate a degree of collaboration that makes tracing an 'original' difficult.

43 Hiskett (1973: 10).

44 Boyd & Mack (1997: 84).

45 The Boyd & Mack (1997: 84) citations include two works by al-Khansa, one cited in Arberry (1965: 38) and one translated by Wormhoudt (n.d.: 96). See also Waddy (1980: 70).

46 'Abdullahi wrote such panegyrics to the Prophet, and the Shehu wrote *Ma'ama'are* (In Praise of the Prophet) in 1805, which 'Isa, Asma'u's brother, translated into Hausa in 1864. See also Hiskett (1975: 43).

47 Hiskett (1975: 43–44, 48–50).

48 Boyd & Mack (1997: 231).

49 Sule & Starratt (1991: 48).

50 *Ahalari* (*al-Mukhtasar al-'alamat al-akhdari fi mathab al-Imam Malik*) by Abu Zaid Abdul Rahman ibn Muhammad al-Saghir al-Akhdari al-Maghribi al-Maliki (Introduction to Maliki law) and *Kawa'idi* (*Qawa'id al-salat*) (principles of prayer).

51 See the appendix in Sule and Starratt (1991).

52 Boyle (2004: 135–136).

53 See Agnaou (2004); Bennouiss (2001); and Boyle (2004).

54 See the appendix in Sule and Starratt (1991).

REFERENCES

Abdalla I (1981) Islamic medicine and its influence on traditional Hausa practitioners in northern Nigeria. PhD thesis, University of Wisconsin

Abdalla I (1985) The *'ulama* of Sokoto in the nineteenth century: A medical view. In B DuToit & I Abdalla (Eds) *African healing strategies*. New York: Trado-Medic Books

Agnaou F (2004) *Gender, literacy, and empowerment in Morocco*. New York: Routledge

Arberry AJ (1965) *Arabic poetry*. Cambridge: Cambridge University Press

Arnett EJ (1920) *Gazetteer of the Sokoto Province*. London

Bennouiss F (2001) *Moroccan female power negotiation*. Fez, Morocco: l'Media

Boyd J (1989) *The caliph's sister*. London: Frank Cass

Boyd J & Mack B (1997) *The collected works of Nana Asma'u, daughter of Usman 'dan Fodiyo (1793–1864)*. East Lansing: Michigan State University Press

Boyle HN (2004) *Qur'anic schools: Agents of preservation and change*. New York: RoutledgeFalmer

Galadanci A (1971) Education of women in Islam with reference to Nigeria. *Nigerian Journal of Islam* 1(2): 5–10

el-Hajj A (1996) Delightful companions: Poetry by women. MA thesis, Indiana University

Hiskett M (1973) *The sword of truth: The life and times of the Shehu Usman dan Fodio*. New York: Oxford University Press

Hiskett M (1975) *A history of Hausa Islamic verse*. London: School of Oriental and African Studies

Last M (1967) *The Sokoto Caliphate*. London: Longman

Lydon G (2004) Inkwells of the Sahara: Reflections on the production of Islamic knowledge in *Bilad Shinqit*. In S Reese (Ed.) *The transmission of learning in Islamic Africa*. Boston: Brill

Mack B (2004) Muslim women's educational activities in the Maghreb: Investigating and redefining scholarship. *The Maghreb Review* 29(1–4): 165–185

Mack B & Boyd J (2000) *One woman's jihad: Nana Asma'u, scholar and scribe*. Bloomington: Indiana University Press

Nykl AR (1946) *Hispano–Arabic poetry, and its relations with the old Provencal troubadours*. Baltimore: JH Furst

Pilaszewicz S (2000) *Hausa prose writings in ajami by Alhaji Umaru from A. Mischlich H. Solken's collection*. Berlin: Dietrich Reimer Verlag

Sule B & Starratt P (1991) Islamic leadership positions for women. In C Coles & B Mack (Eds) *Hausa women in the twentieth century*. Madison: University of Wisconsin Press

Waddy C (1980) *Women in Muslim history*. London: Longman

Wormhoudt A (n.d.) *Diwan al-khansu*. Oskaloosa, Iowa: William Penn College; High Wycombe: University Microfilms

بسم الله الرحمن الرحيم والصلاة والسلام
على نبينا الأمين محمد وعلى آله وأصحابه الأكرمين
ومن تبعهم بإحسان إلى يوم الدين
وبعد فقد سئلت والله المستعان عن امرأة
تشاكت مع زوجها وتخاصمت معه وقالت له
أنت علي حرام كأبي هل يؤثر كلامها هذا في نكاحها
زوجها وهل على الزوج شيء في ذلك وهل
على المرأة نفسها شيء في ذلك فأجيب
والله المستعان أنه ليس على الزوج شيء وكذلك
ليس على المرأة شيء وكلامها هذا يجري في البحر
أو في البر فالمرأة ليس لها تحريم نفسها ولا
تحليلها على زوجها وإنما الطلاق والتحريم
جعلهما الله بيد الزوج لا بيد الزوجة
لقوله تعالى الرجال قوامون على النساء بما
فضل الله بعضهم على بعض وبما أنفقوا من
أموالهم ه فالمرأة لا يؤثر كلامها في تطليق
نفسها أو تحريمها إلا في صورتين
إحداهما أن تنطق بالردة عامدة والثانية
أن يجعل الزوج طلاقها بيدها مع أن هذه لا
تخلو من خلاف عند جمع والظهار إنما يلزم

CHAPTER 12

The Tomb*ouct*ou Manuscript Project: social history approaches

Aslam Farouk-Alli and Mohamed Shaid Mathee

The massive collection of manuscripts produced in West Africa has once again dispelled the notion that Africans were incapable of intellectual work – of reading, writing and scholarly endeavour – before the impact of European colonialism and missionary education. While this dense corpus of writing is a cultural and intellectual legacy that can be used in a variety of ways, we believe it must be claimed as an expression of Africa's intellectual heritage and renewal. In this chapter we begin by briefly sketching the genesis of our research project. We then share some of our prefatory readings, describing the content of selected manuscripts, before exploring possible trajectories for future research through a closer reading of two specific texts. Our excurses into the manuscript corpus divides the material into works of general interest (those that cover a broad range of subjects) and legal texts (more specifically, legal *responsa* or *fatawa*). We begin with the former but pay more attention to the latter, asking what value the legal corpus may have as a source for historical enquiry.

There is presently very little research on the manuscripts for what they can tell us about the social history of that part of Africa over the past centuries: from the fifteenth century when Timbuktu emerged as a centre of learning through to the change of rule from the Mali to the Songhay Empires, through the Moroccan invasion in the late sixteenth century to French colonial domination in the nineteenth century, and from independence to the present.

The Tomb*ouct*ou Manuscript Project

Based at the University of Cape Town, where African history has been taught for many years, Shamil Jeppie conceived of the idea of bringing together expertise in this field and Arabic to work on the content of the manuscripts themselves, thereby extending the sphere of engagement beyond conservation to encompass academic study as well. Funding was sought from the Ford Foundation and was granted, leading to the initiation of a

Opposite: This extract from Manuscript No. 4743, from the Ahmed Baba Institute is an example of a *fatwa*. Legal texts (*fiqh*, *usul al-fiqh* and *fatawa*) are a unique source of social history and also offer insights into juristic reasoning and the ways in which scholars debated their cases in Timbuktu.

The manuscript, *Mawlid al-Nabi* (The Birth of the Prophet) presents a fascinating example of creation myth and salvation history, which centres on the Prophet Muhammad's messengership and on Islam as the last of the revealed religions. More interestingly, it opens a window into the world of inter-religious polemics by way of its descriptions of Christians, Jews and sinful Muslims.

pilot academic project – the Tomb*ouctou*[1] Manuscript Project – within the broader context of President Thabo Mbeki's initiative to safeguard and preserve this legacy.[2]

It was decided to initially concentrate upon a manuscript collection located in the Mamma Haidara private library so as to extend the focus of attention beyond the official Ahmed Baba Institute and to create an awareness of the many other collections in private hands. A selection of legal texts (initially 100 manuscripts of varying size) was digitised at the Mamma Haidara Library in January 2004. Another 60 manuscripts from the Ahmed Baba collection were subsequently also procured. At the very inception of our project it was decided that at least some of the manuscripts digitally captured would be studied in more detail, which included translating them into English. In the course of 2004 we embarked upon the actual study of the digitised manuscripts by producing workbooks comprising selected texts. We held regular reading sessions aimed not only at developing proficiency in reading the various regional scripts – Sudani, Sahrawi, Suqi etc. – but also to familiarise ourselves with their general import, so as to select specific texts for extended study.

Manuscripts of general interest

Manuscript 516 (Catalogue Vol. 1: 287) from the Mamma Haidara collection, for example, provides interesting insight into the socio-political culture of the region. It is a tract of folios written by the reformist 'Abdullahi dan Fodio (d.1829), entitled *Diya al-siyasat wa fatawa al-nawazil* (The Illumination of Legislative Politics and Verdicts on Events). Divided into several sections, it discusses apostasy, highway robbery, hostile combatants and heretics. The manuscript also deals with the issue of politics, which it classifies as either oppressive or just. An outstanding aspect of this work is a deeply philosophical discussion on the six universal elements necessary for existence, that is, life, dignity, wealth, intellect, religion and deterrents from committing sin. Many other interesting themes are also to be found.

In contrast to many of the works in the collection, manuscript 52 (Vol. 1: 28) is a relatively lengthy work of 36 folios. The author and date of the work are unknown, but the colophon clearly states the name of the copyist as Muhammad al-Amin b. Muhammad b. Muhammad Baba b. al-Faqih al-Imaam Guurdu. The manuscript was copied in 1746. The work is simply entitled *Mawlid al-Nabi* (The Birth of the Prophet) but presents a fascinating example of creation myth and salvation history, which centres on the finality of the Prophet Muhammad's messengership and of Islam as the last of the revealed religions. More interestingly, the manuscript opens a window into the world of inter-religious polemics by way of its descriptions of Christians, Jews and sinful Muslims. It also presents a conception of original sin that implicates mother Eve in a manner that is more easily reconcilable with Christian eschatology than with a purely Qur'anic account. This in itself raises the question of the impact of Judaeo–Christian thought upon Islamic thought as expressed in some of these manuscripts.

Manuscript 5292 from the Ahmed Baba collection, entitled *Mu'awana al-ikhwan fi mubshara al-niswan* (Advising Men on Sexual Engagement with their Women), deals primarily with aphrodisiacs and religiously sanctioned sexual activity. It does, however, contain numerous remedies and prescriptions for treating infertility and an array of other ailments, as well as some advice on dealing with disobedient wives, oppressors, enemies and dangerous wild animals. What follows is our paraphrased synopsis of advice on the usefulness of animal body parts and fluids, as well as certain Qur'anic verses for enjoying stimulating, religiously sanctioned sex.[3]

> Drinking cow-milk and mixing the powder from a burned cow horn with food or drink increases sexual potency...For abundant sexual activity and sexual climax a man must drink the dried, pulverised testicles of a bull. If a man suffers from impotence he must take the nail of a cock's right leg, burn it and fumigate himself with the smoke and he will be cured...The dried, pulverised penis of a lizard placed tenderly into honey then licked will let a man experience full sexual desire and satisfaction and will increase his sperm count...To make his wife love him intensely, the husband should wipe both his and his wife's eyebrows and hands with the gall bladder of a fox...By wiping his soles with the head of a bat, a man will see wonderful things when having sex...If a man rubs the blood from a cock's comb onto his penis then has sexual intercourse with his wife, she will only [want to] have sex with him. The blood of a slaughtered black chicken mixed with honey and rubbed on the head of the penis followed by intercourse causes the woman to have an orgasm to the point of madness due to the intensity[4]...If the husband paints his penis and surrounding area with the gall bladder of a male goat he will be extremely powerful during sexual intercourse.[5] In order to strengthen his penis [that is, cure himself from erectile dysfunction] and enjoy sexual intercourse, the husband must recite the following Qur'anic verses: 'Allah is the One Who created you from [your state of] weakness and made out of the weakness strength' [Qur'an 30: 54]; 'Say [O Muhammad] O you disbelievers' [Qur'an 109]; and 'Li Ila fi Quraysh' until its end [Qur'an 106].[6]

The above advice opens a window into the world of ordinary people, showing how they lived and how their scholars, traditional healers and sages sought to guide them. It tells us about how they put to use their resources, their knowledge, technology, tools and instruments. These people were clearly immersed in an Islamic worldview (even if not one exactly in accordance with the normative ideal) as indicated by their almost maverick application of Qur'anic verses as sexual stimulants.

In our contemporary age of Islamic revival, heavily influenced by western modernity, many Muslims would frown upon the use of the Qur'an suggested by the manuscript, regarding it as disrespectful or blasphemous, and they would therefore reject these practices as superstitious and irrational. For a religious society like Timbuktu's, merely broaching a taboo subject such as sexuality was both novel and daring. However, the recourse to and utilisation of Islam's foundational text for treating such afflictions indicates the strong religious orientation of ordinary people in this society. God's name, mercy, permission and blessing are constantly invoked under every circumstance.

Nevertheless, our aim is to look beyond the stories and symbolism of animals and Qur'anic verses – their medicinal value, sexual and otherwise – and to ask questions like: were extramarital affairs a recurrent phenomenon, even if for a limited period and in a limited area? We find the rationale for this question embedded in the manuscript mentioned above on sexual advice, where the author advises a husband who does not want his wife to love another man to dig a hole, kindle a fire with coal and sit over it whilst naked, followed by two units of prayer. The husband must then write the verse 'have you pondered over, and seen the fire that you kindle' (Qur'an 56: 33) 27 times over the ash, mix it with water and then get his wife to wash with it. She will as a result hate all men except him. One wonders why a husband from a traditionally religious community such as Timbuktu would take all these measures in order to have his wife love him alone. Other questions suggested by the manuscript are: was sexual impotence or erection problems commonplace among men at that time? Did women in this society have insatiable sexual appetites? By raising such questions we hope to arrive at – or at least try to identify – behaviour and attitudes indicative of concrete social, moral and lived experiences.

For the contemporary researcher the relevance of the manuscript lies in it 'talking history'. The question, though, is: which history and whose? This question carries added significance when attempting to understand social practice through legal texts in Timbuktu. The history of the ordinary, forgotten people of Timbuktu is concealed in-between the lines of this manuscript and thousands like it. Although ostensibly 'medicinal' or religious in nature, these manuscripts are a powerful resource for reconstructing the 'other' history of Timbuktu. They reveal the agency and thinking of ordinary people by relating 'bizarre' details concerning highly sexed housewives and worried husbands suffering from erectile dysfunction. The contemporary researcher is thereby exposed to a wealth of social historical information.

For the contemporary researcher the relevance of the manuscript lies in it 'talking history'. The question, though, is: which history and whose? This question carries added significance when attempting to understand social practice through legal texts in Timbuktu. The history of the ordinary, forgotten people of Timbuktu is concealed in-between the lines of this manuscript and thousands like it. Although ostensibly 'medicinal' or religious in nature, these manuscripts are a powerful resource for reconstructing the 'other' history of Timbuktu. They reveal the agency and thinking of ordinary people.

Fatwa manuscripts

As mentioned earlier, our readings placed added emphasis on the legal corpus found in the manuscript collection. We provide a brief sample of some of the material we encountered before going on to discuss and analyse a specific text in some detail.

Manuscript 4743 (Vol. 4: 117) from the Ahmed Baba collection is a *fatwa* that was issued in response to a wife who refused to grant her husband conjugal access by telling him that he was now forbidden to her in the same way as her father was. In classical *fiqh* (law) such a phenomenon is known as *zihar*, but it is usually the husband who repudiates the wife by comparing her to the back of his mother. This incident reflects a unique reversal of roles and is possibly revealing of the higher status accorded to women in this region. It is equally possible that this may have been an isolated incident, but the interested researcher is faced with the task of seeking corroborating evidence in the vast collections of juristic rulings available in Timbuktu's manuscript collection.

Manuscript 207, from the same collection, deals with juristic verdicts issued by Qadi Muhammad b. al-Wafi al-Arawani concerning problems related to the sale of slaves and inheritance. The author mentions a dispute between two people regarding the sale of slaves; the import of the manuscript suggests that in Timbuktu buying and selling was in most cases *not* done on a cash basis. The author points out that insistence upon dealing in cash could lead to loss and destruction of the commodity!

Manuscript 1093 from the Mamma Haidara collection is by Shaykh Sayyid al-Mukhtar b. Ahmad b. Abi Bakr al-Kunti al-Wafi (d.1811) and is entitled 'Important Answers to the One who Attaches any Importance to his Religion'. It begins by encouraging us to be of assistance to others and to always offer good advice. Reference is made to the words of sages regarding the importance of the intellect. Talk on the intellect is directed towards the people of Timbuktu who, the author suggests, as inhabitants of the desert pay importance to agriculture and consequently neglect the quest for religious knowledge. In his opinion, this explains their ignorance of many of the tenets of their religion, especially *fiqh*. He therefore sets himself the task, in the form of questions and answers, of educating the people of Timbuktu. Amongst the many questions that he addresses is the question of *zakat* (obligatory alms). The manuscript suggests that the people of Timbuktu considered the giving of alms to be the prerogative of a specific class of people and not in the generally understood sense where anyone who possesses a minimum amount of wealth is obligated to pay *zakat*. The author regards this phenomenon as *bid'a*, a heretical practice that should be rejected. He raises the issue of accepting alms from thieves and oppressors, ruling that it is not permissible to do so as this would be tantamount to assisting them in evil. He concludes by encouraging people to distribute their alms in the manner sanctioned by Islamic teachings.

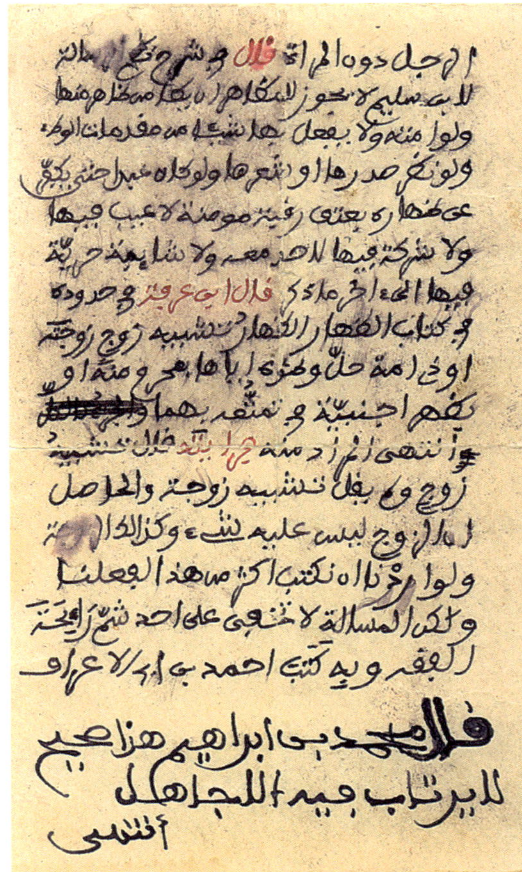

This extract from Manuscript No. 4743 from the Ahmed Baba Institute describes part of a legal ruling issued in the case of a woman seeking to divorce her husband. In classical Islamic law, this is an unusual reversal of roles. Cases like this offer researchers opportunities to try and understand the social context of the ruling, within the vast collection of juristic rulings in the manuscripts.

Fatwas as a historical source

In the course of our research, we have worked with scholars concerned with the history of Timbuktu and its surrounding areas, trying to develop an appreciation for that social milieu and generally exploring multiple aspects of the manuscript heritage. Part of this involved probing the rich *fatwa* legacy as a potential historical source. Legal texts (*fiqh*, *usul al-fiqh* and *fatawa*) offer unique paths into the social history of Timbuktu and the region. While exploring how legal texts act as a major source of social history, we are also beginning to learn a bit more about juristic reasoning and the way scholars debated their cases in Timbuktu.

However, our primary interest concerns whether the Timbuktu *fatwa* manuscripts are able to 'talk history'. Put differently, can they, in addition to telling stories about local actors, tell stories about themselves? If they can, then what kind of history and what types of stories do they relate? We argue that *fatwas* may be seen as a potential source for the history of the region, especially its social history. Thus our project set itself the task of digging beneath the apparent face of events mentioned in the *fatwas* in order to lay bare the human condition as experienced by ordinary people.[7] Even though *fatwas* convey important episodes of Timbuktu's history, they have been neglected and remain an unacknowledged source. For example, Elias Saad's *A Social History of Timbuktu* depends almost entirely on the seventeenth-century chronicles (he dismisses the Timbuktu manuscripts as Arabic sources relevant to the Islamic tradition). In contrast, we choose to see the *fatwa* manuscripts as an important source of social history.[8] Saad was afraid that by approaching Timbuktu through the manuscripts he risked portraying the city as belonging to a realm other than sub-Saharan or black Africa. He is seriously wrong in this claim, precisely because the *fatwas* are rooted in Timbuktu and tell us about all people, not only the scholars and notables emphasised in the chronicles.

Wael Hallaq shows convincingly that *fatwas* originate socially. That many *fatwas* begin with a question, or that many jurists begin their response with 'I have read your question and carefully considered it', is indicative of their social embeddedness. *Fatwas* were thus not just the product of the jurist's imagination or hypothetical adventurism; there is even a dictum that no *fatwa* should be issued about a problem that has not yet occurred in the real world. *Fatwas* involve real persons with real problems and answer questions stemming from the real world, with the names, professions and places of residence mentioned. Any rejection of the worldliness of the *fatwa* genre, Hallaq argues, would make nonsense of both its form and content.[9]

Thus the aim is to see, through these legal manuscripts, how the people of Timbuktu and the broader region made sense of their world by shedding light upon incidental information embedded in these texts. In other words, researching this legacy holds potential for going beyond the legal jargon, the particular religious methodology and the piety; elements that are all fundamental in the issuing of *fatwas*. The manuscripts enable one to walk beside the people who either requested the *fatwa*, or whose doings were the reason for a *fatwa* being issued. Their behaviour and attitudes are far more important than the clear and apparent religiously sanctified or intellectually charged answer of the *mufti*. Aspects of this can be gleaned from the detailed elaboration of one specific text, discussed next.

A more detailed account of a *fatwa* manuscript

Manuscript 354 (Vol. 1: 197) from the Mamma Haidara Library[10] – *Nasran lil-haq wa nushan lil-Muslimin* (In the Cause of Truth and as an Admonishment to Muslims) – is by the late nineteenth-century Timbuktu scholar Qadi Ahmad Baba b. Abi al-Abbas b. 'Umar b. Zayyan al-Sharif al-Hasani. Shakespeare's famous elegiac opening to *Romeo and Juliet* could just as appropriately have been the prologue to this real-life saga of love blossoming in the desert, albeit with a slight change of venue:

> Two households, both alike in dignity,
> In fair Verona [read Arawan], where we lay our scene,
> From ancient grudge break to new mutiny,
> Where civil blood makes civil hands unclean.
> From forth the fatal loins of these two foes
> A pair of star-cross'd lovers take their life[11]

Romeo and Juliet is widely regarded as one of the greatest literary expressions of authentic romantic love,[12] and from this perspective there is a very strong link between the star-crossed lovers and the real-life protagonists we are about to encounter in the late nineteenth-century *fatwa* under discussion. The central distinction is that while all great works of fiction are epiphanies of truth, they are not necessarily constrained by the far harsher realities of everyday existence. In this specific case, the fate of a melodramatic literary death is by no means as daunting as having to face the chief *qadi* of one's village, charged with passing judgment on the legality of one's marriage.

In his short treatise, Qadi Ahmad Baba draws our attention to a *fatwa* issued by the honourable A'li ibn al-Sayyid 'Umar – *qadi* of Arawan – concerning the *faskh* (annulment) of a marriage between a man and a woman deemed foster siblings by virtue of having shared the same wet-nurse. In Islamic law, if the same wet-nurse suckles children from different parents they become legally related through the bond of milk kinship.

Everyone in the village knew the legal status of the couple and their wet-nurse, who was present, identified them as brother and sister. Even though the woman in question was married to another man, her so-called brother maintained close contact with her, enjoying free access to her home under the pretence that he was a legal sibling. Throughout this period, the entire village – except the woman's husband – was aware of the couple's romantic attachment to each other. In fact, the couple did not conceal their love for each other except, of course, from the husband; nor did anyone in the village inform the husband of his wife's affair with her 'brother'. The husband finally suspected his wife's infidelity and divorced her.

For a short time the couple maintained the pretence of being foster siblings, but finally denied it so that they could be legally married. At this point the wet-nurse, along with everyone else in the village, also denied their foster relationship and agreed to their marriage. They were then married by the legal permission of the village's *mufti*, who under the circumstances had no choice but to assent to their marriage.

However, when the honourable *qadi* of Arawan came to know of the incident, he issued an edict annulling the marriage. He refuted the position of the *mufti* who had affirmed the legality of the marriage and marshalled explicit textual proofs, as well as the opinions of classical scholars, as evidence for his judgment.

Thus the aim is to see, through these legal manuscripts, how the people of Timbuktu and the broader region made sense of their world by shedding light upon incidental information embedded in these texts. In other words, researching this legacy holds potential for going beyond the legal jargon, the particular religious methodology, and the piety; elements that are all fundamental in the issuing of *fatwas*. The manuscripts enable one to walk beside the people who either requested the *fatwa*, or whose doings were the reason for a *fatwa* being issued. Their behaviour and attitudes are far more important than the clear and apparent religiously sanctified or intellectually charged answer of the *mufti*.

In the manuscript, Qadi Ahmad Baba continues with an in-depth analysis of the legal verdict, concluding by admonishing all those who colluded in the incident and advising them to faithfully adhere to the ethical teachings of their religion. In so doing he seemingly departs from the institutionalised format of the *fatwa* in Islamic law.

The manuscript is interesting for many reasons, but we will now very briefly explore two interrelated aspects that shed light upon why works in the *fatwa* genre are fundamental sources for the retrieval of social history. The first relates to the genesis of Islamic substantive law and the second deals more specifically with the devolution of the nature of the *fatwa* under the strictures of time and place. It would be more appropriate to begin with the latter aspect and to explain what is meant by devolution.

In its essential form, the *fatwa* is not simply a legal opinion but rather an expression of a divine ethical imperative. From the very inception of Islam, piety-minded Muslims were driven by the desire to live in conformity with the divine will as revealed by the Qur'an. In a recent work on the origins of Islamic law,[13] Wael Hallaq argues that the locus of legal expertise in the formative period did not lie with *qadis* but rather with private individuals motivated to study the law as a matter of piety, that is, solely as a religious activity. A similar observation was made earlier on by Marshall Hodgson, who characterised the early custodians of the law as the 'Piety Conscious'.[14]

It was therefore through the activities of these proto-*qadis* that Islamic law came to be institutionalised. In addition, the responses they provided to questions of faith and religious practice formed the building blocks of Islamic substantive law or *fiqh*. Once again it is Hallaq who convincingly argues that *fiqh* is far more flexible than was earlier suggested. He demonstrates how *fiqh* manuals were continuously updated by new insights brought about through responses to everyday religious concerns.[15] In so doing he also refutes Joseph Schacht's long-standing thesis on the relatively late origins of Islamic jurisprudence.

What is important for our purposes is to make the connection between the *fatwa* and the highly cherished desire of piety-minded Muslims to live in conformity with the tenets of their faith. We know that the colonial enterprise was extremely damaging to the well-established Islamic legal institution in Africa and elsewhere in the Muslim world. However, what can be clearly gleaned from the manuscript under study is that while the institutional edifice of Islamic law may have been relatively easily dismantled, its methodology for coping with the vagaries of time has proven to be far more abiding. In nineteenth-century Timbuktu, we once again find in the Mamma Haidara manuscript the manifestation of the *fatwa* in its essential form – as an expression of an act of submission to the divine will.

It is in similar questions and their responses that one catches glimpses of society that not only fascinate but also humble us by virtue of the insights offered into the common plight of everyday human existence. If the study of history is to be of any value then its purpose must surely be to illuminate, not dominate. Perhaps some redress for the massively neglected stories of ordinary Africans of the past is to be found in the interstices of the manuscripts of Timbuktu.

NOTES

1 The French for Timbuktu is Tombouctou, so as a play on words our project was named 'the Tombo*uct*ou Manuscript Project'.

2 President Thabo Mbeki went on a state visit to Mali in November 2001. His counterpart, President Alpha Konaré, took him on a tour of Timbuktu. The visit to the Ahmed Baba Institute was the highlight of the president's trip and he was so overwhelmed by the manuscript heritage that he pledged to assist the Malians in their conservation efforts. To this effect, a working group was formed comprising a cross-section of government functionaries but also including one academic, Dr Shamil Jeppie, tasked with initiating a project to deliver on the president's promise. The management of the project is based at the Department of Arts and Culture. Training of Malian conservators in appropriate conservation procedures began in 2003, led by conservators from the National Archives of South Africa.

3 This particular usage stands contrary to the pietistic notion that sees the Qur'an as purely the foundational text and guide for Muslims on theological matters and legal issues. In this instance, the Qur'an is seen as equally potent in matters that would easily be described as blasphemous or at least disrespectful by adherents to the pietistic and rational trend.

4 Geertz (1974) shows how, in Balinese culture, cocks are masculine symbols par excellence and the language of everyday moralism is shot through, on the male side of it, with roosterish imagery. *Sabung*, Balinese for cock, is used metaphorically to mean hero, warrior, man of parts, ladykiller, bachelor, dandy, political candidate, champion or tough guy. Similarly, Darnton (1984) shows how in seventeenth-century France cats were viewed as agents of witchcraft, useful for medicinal purposes and as sex symbols.

5 The author warns that the above-mentioned measures should not be resorted to excessively as they may cause infection of the woman's sexual organs – in the same way that modern pharmaceutical companies issue warnings about side effects pertaining to the usage of their medication.

6 Implementation of this cure requires these verses to be recited three times for a period of seven days (from Sunday to Saturday), every morning and evening, over leaves (usually seven) from particular trees soaked in water. The water should then be drunk and poured over certain foods.

7 By ordinary people we mean those who were not rulers, notable merchants or from the intellectual and religious elite. Darnton (1984: 252–253) suggests that historians can benefit much from anthropology in order to understand 'the otherness' of previous eras.

8 Saad (1983) focuses on the role of wealthy scholarly elites and not on the lives of ordinary people (the subaltern) of Timbuktu.

9 Hallaq (1994: 38).

10 Sayyid (2000–03).

11 Shakespeare (2000: Act 1, Prologue).

12 Bloom (1998).

13 Hallaq (2005).

14 Hodgson (1974).

15 Hallaq (1994: 38).

REFERENCES

Bloom H (1998) *Shakespeare and the invention of the human.* New York: Riverhead Books

Darnton R (1984) *The great cat massacre and other episodes in French cultural history.* London: Penguin Books

Geertz C (1974) *Myth, symbol, and culture.* New York: Norton

Hallaq W (1994) From fatwa to furu. *Islamic Law and Society* 1(1): 29–65

Hallaq W (2005) *The origins of Islamic law.* Cambridge: Cambridge University Press

Hodgson MGS (1974) *The venture of Islam.* Chicago: University of Chicago Press

Saad E (1983) *A social history of Timbuktu: The role of Muslim scholars and notables, 1400–1900.* Cambridge/New York: Cambridge University Press

Sayyid AF (Ed.) (2000–03) *Catalogue of manuscripts in Mamma Haidara Library* (4 vols, prepared by Abdel Kader Haidara). London: al-Furqan Islamic Heritage Foundation

Shakespeare W (2000) *Romeo and Juliet.* Edited and with an introduction by H Bloom. Philadelphia: Chelsea House Publishers

PART III

SCHOLARS OF TIMBUKTU

1

بسم الله الرحمن الرحيم صلى الله على سيدنا محمد وآله وصحبه وسلم تسليما
قال الشيخ العارف الرباني القطب الكامل الفرد الذي إنسان
عين الحقائق الصمدانية ولسان شخص الدقائق القدسية العرفانية
مجمع بحري الشريعة والحقيقة وحامل راية السنة البيضاء والطريقة
إمام الأئمة وخاتمة خلاصة الأمة في الأسرار والأنوار شيخنا وسيدنا
المختار بن السيد أحمد بن الشيخ أبي بكر الكنتي ثم الوافي حفظه ورعاه الواحد
الصمد العلي آمين
الحمد لله جاعل قلوب العلماء مفاتيح لحل أقفال المشكلات وماحي الريبات
ومحيي الأموات ومنشئ العظام الرفات والصلاة والسلام على منبع الرحمات
وعلى آله وأصحابه البررة الهداة بعد وإنه عن لي أن أجيبك أيها الأخ الزكي
عما طلبته مني بعض الفتاح العليم الهادي بمنه إلى الصراط المستقيم فيما
نصه قولك قد عظم احتياجنا إلى مختصر جامع للقدر الذي تدعو الحاجة إليه مما
يشترك في الانتفاع به الحر والعبد والمرأة والصبي لسهولته وبيانه مع الإيجاز
والاختصار من توحيد الله تعالى المبلغ إلى معرفته والتشبث بأذيال أنبيائه وأوليائه
عار عن الغلو والتقصير لأن الغلو في الدين كالتقصير منه وقد قلت إنه قد كثر خوض جملة
الناس في هذا القدر الذي هو التوحيد وشاع تكفيرهم لعوام المسلمين من أمة محمد صلى
الله عليه وسلم فالجواب أنه لا يعذر بالجهل في موجبات الكفر وموجبات الكفر هو
إنكار ما يعلم من الدين ضرورة أو تكذيب نص الكتاب العزيز أو إنكار صفة من صفات الكمال
أو تكذيب الرسل أو بعضهم أو القول بقدم العالم ولا يكفر مؤمن بمطلق الجهل
لأن الجهل لازم أصول البشرية روي عن إمامنا مالك رضي الله عنه أنه قال الجهل
ببعض الصفات لا يوجب الكفر وإنما يوجب الكفر عناد الحق واعتقاد الشرك
واختيار الكفر على الإيمان مستدلا بالحديث الوارد في الصحاح عن النبي صلى الله عليه وسلم
أنه قال كان رجل ممن قبلكم أسرف على نفسه فلما حضرته الوفاة جمع بنيه وقال
لهم ألست قد أحسنت أن يتبعكم قالوا بلى قال لهم إن كنتم تطلبون بري والإحسان الذي
بلغ امتثالهم فاحرقوني ثم انسفوني وأذروا رمادي الخافي سحقوه كذا سمعنا ثم إذا ادروها
فلئن قدر الله علي ليعذبني عذابا لم يعذبه أحدا من العالمين ففعلوا ما أمرهم به فأمر
الله الريح بجمعه في الهواء ثم رد إليه روحه فقال له يا عبدي ما حملك على ما صنعت
قال أي رب خوفك وخشية عقابك والحياء منك فقال الله تعالى له اذهب فقد غفرت
لك وأدخلتك الجنة برحمتي فهذا العبد غير عالم بتمام قدرة الله حيث يقول لبنيه ليس

قدر

CHAPTER 13

The life of Shaykh Sidi al-Mukhtar al-Kunti

Yahya Ould el-Bara[1]

The knowledge we have about the Islamisation of the populations of the Saharan and sub-Saharan west is sometimes confused and lacking in historical rigour, for the beginnings of Islam in Saharan Africa are known only in their broadest outlines.[2] The Islamisation of these populations seems to have been slow and progressive.[3] It began with missionaries and merchants who were probably Ibadites (Kharijite)[4] and was completed by the Almoravid movement (eleventh century AD). It was shaped into its definitive form in the cradle of the Sanhaja society.

Beginning with this Almoravid movement, Islam began to play a decisive role in the cultural, social and political sphere of the western regions of Saharan and sub-Saharan Africa. It created a shockwave that deeply affected the region, and became implanted in the behaviour, lifestyle and culture of the people. The Malikite rite, the Junaydite order, and the Ash'arite dogma[5] represented the principal reference points of this Islam. All three delineated the general framework of the religious life of the people.

However, to talk of Islam as a religious law requires us to differentiate between three components which are clearly distinct according to the field of religion dealt with. The first component, *'aqida*, studies the precepts of faith based on logical and rational arguments and proofs; the second component, *fiqh* (law), considers rituals, transactions and contracts; and the third component, *tasawwuf*, considers questions of relevance to mysticism, namely how to devote oneself to the adoration (*'ibada)* of God, to turn away from the vanities of this world, and to renounce (*zuhd*) the satisfactions one can find in pleasure, wealth or social status.

Each of these three branches is represented by movements or schools founded by the great religious figures of Islam's first centuries. These leaders distinguished themselves by the nature of their interpretations and their conceptual and methodological tools. In this way, in the area of faith we find the currents of Mu'tazila, Ash'ariyya, Maturidiyya, Muhadditha, and so on; in the area of *fiqh* the schools of Hanafites,

Opposite: The first folio of the *al-Minna* manuscript composed by Shaykh Sidi al-Mukhtar al-Kunti.

The legitimacy of each brotherhood is assured by a chain of mystical transmission (*silsila*) from the founder of the order to the Prophet. Followers believe that the faith professed by their brotherhood is the esoteric essence of Islam and that the rituals of their order possess the same degree of importance as the canonical obligations. The brotherhoods were introduced south of the Sahara from the fifteenth century and spread like a tidal wave across all regions and classes of society. They first became visible in the cult of saints, namely men – living or dead – who possessed *baraka* or supernatural powers.

Malikites, Shafi'ites, Hanabalites, etc.; and in the area of *tasawwuf* the brotherhoods Qadiriyya, Shadhiliyya, Naqshabandiyya and Tijaniyya.

The institutionalisation of *tasawwuf* (formation of brotherhoods)

Learned followers of the different brotherhoods affirm that *tasawwuf* was born at the same time as Islam,[6] and that its doctrine is based on the words of the Prophet who, as a contemplative, was the first master of *tasawwuf*.

However, it seems useful to examine the process by which the first forms of saintliness and ascetic practice slowly developed into more organised groups and into an esoteric instruction focusing on a doctrine which became more structured and institutionalised, and which came to be described as Sufism. This development is still not entirely clear.

If one is to believe certain men of letters, from the very earliest times a concentration of the spititual way around *siyyaha*[7] (mystical states) can be noticed. But it is from the beginning of the seventh century that some Muslim ascetics (*zuhhad*), steeped in piety, began to feel a need to devote themselves to this divine adoration. These *zuhhad* observed the behavioural code known as *adabi*; they also observed rituals which occupied a vital place in their way of living and behaving.

Sufism thus began as a mystical, philosophical and intellectual movement, but one should not forget that the resulting fraternalism (*turuqiyya*) constitutes a form of sociability with its own way of functioning, and its own social and political action. It is important to remember that it is principally as a form of sociability that Sufism manifests its relationship with history and with past and present societies.

The legitimacy of each brotherhood is assured by a chain of mystical transmission (*silsila*) from the founder of the order to the Prophet. Followers believe that the faith professed by their brotherhood is the esoteric essence of Islam and that the rituals of their order possess the same degree of importance as the canonical obligations (*wajibat*).

The affiliation of each Sufi to his order is carried out by means of a pact consisting of a profession of religious faith and vows which vary according to the different brotherhoods. Total submission to the master is a necessary condition for spiritual allegiance. In this sense the famous Islamic historian Ibn Khaldun wrote: 'The disciple must be in the hands of a shaykh, as the body is in the hands of the corpse-washer, or the blind man stepping towards the ocean is in the hands of his guide.'[8]

The different leaders of the orders of brotherhoods known in the Sunni world observe the path of al-Junayd (d.909). This famous Sufi, originally from Baghdad, should be considered the great inspiration for a moderate version of Sufism. Avoiding the doctrinal excesses of mystics such as Abu Yazid al-Bastami, Du al-Nun al-Misri and al-Hallaj, who frightened and distanced orthodox believers, he laid the foundations upon which the great Sufi systems would be built.[9] On these grounds he appears in the *silsila* of all the large and well-known Sunni brotherhood orders.

The brotherhoods were introduced south of the Sahara from the fifteenth century and spread like a tidal wave across all regions and classes of society. They first became visible in the cult of saints, namely men – living or dead – who possessed *baraka* or supernatural powers.[10]

With time, a standard organisation developed around this cult; its essential elements were the *zawiya* (place of residence of the saint or his spirit), the saint or his lieutenant (generally a descendant) and the *murids* (disciples or aspiring followers).[11]

The religious orders or brotherhoods that developed widely south of the Sahara are one aspect of the cult of saints. These orders were organised and hierarchical and some of them extended their branches into a large proportion of the Muslim world.

In the society of the time, the saint was vital as a protector and saviour. His place of residence became not only a sanctuary and religious centre, but a social and political centre too.[12] The *zawiya* was the centre of the cult of the saint, which practised the *dhikr* ceremony – tireless repetition of a certain prayer, in an appropriate manner, until the achievement of a state of grace where one entered into contact with the divine. However, the role of *zawiya* was not limited to mystical instruction (*tarbiyya*); it filled numerous social functions and was responsible for the redistribution of worldly possessions to all those in need – the poor, fugitives and foreigners in transit.[13]

Despite the traditional hostility of the *fuqaha* (jurists) towards those who claim direct access to God through saintliness (*walaya*) outside societal norms, religious brotherhoods developed so rapidly in the sub-Saharan region that belonging to one of the brotherhoods became an important part of carrying out religious duties.[14]

The most important of the religious brotherhoods which spread through the sub-Saharan region are:

- The Qadiriyya (referring to Sidi 'Abd al-Qadir al-Jilani), especially in its two branches: al-Bakka'iyya (referring to al-Shaykh Sidi A'mar ould al-Shaykh Sidi Ahmad al-Bakkay, d. sixteenth century) and al-Fadiliyya (referring to al-Shaykh Muhammad Fadil ould Mamin,[15] d.1869–70).
- The Shadhiliyya (referring to Abu al-Hasan al-Shadhili, d.1169) in its two branches: al-Nasiriyya (referring to Muhammad ibn Nasir al-Diri, d.1626) and al-Gudfiyya[16] (referring to al-Shaykh Muhammad Lagdaf ould Ahmad al-Dawdi al-Jaafari[17] d.1802).
- The Tijaniyya (referring to al-Shaykh Sidi Ahmad al-Tijani, d.1815) with its two branches: al-Hafiziyya (referring to al-Shaykh Muhammad al-Hafid ould al-Mukhtar,[18] d.1831) and al-Hamawiyya[19] referring to al-Shaykh Hamah Allah[20] (d.1943).

As *hadarat*, these brotherhoods constituted organisational and political frameworks greater than the tribe or the family. These Sufi *hadarat* are social and religious institutions centred on the person of the shaykh (educator), who draws his authority from a chain of transmission which traces back to Muhammad and thus guarantees the shaykh's legitimacy.[21]

The success of these brotherhoods in the sub-Saharan world must be considered in the light of several factors. It can be explained by the fact that material life was becoming more difficult, and disasters like droughts, epidemics and wars were increasing. There was also widespread weakening of the central authorities (Almoravid, Mali, Wolof) and growing insecurity, aggravated by the strengthening of tribal ties which occurred throughout the zone.[22]

There is another explanation for the extraordinary success of the brotherhoods: they 'recuperated' and mobilised former pre-Islamic practices and beliefs. It goes without saying that these orders, from the very fact of their extraordinary success with the masses, ended up having very little to do with the Sufi or mystic ideal.

The Qadiriyya

This mystical brotherhood is spread out all over the world and takes its name from its founder 'Abd al-Qadir al-Jilani (d.1167), an Iraqi originally from Naïf, south of the Caspian Sea. Early on he acquired the rudiments of Arabic in his native village before going to Baghdad to pursue studies in Islamic law and theology with various doctors from different schools – Hanbalite, Shafi'ite, and so on. He was initiated into Sufism by Shaykh Abu al-Khayr Muhammad ibn Muslim al-Abbas (d.1131).[23]

Shaykh 'Abd al-Qadir was the most influential scholar of his time in the science of *shari'a* (religious law) and the disciplines related to *haqiqa* (divine truth). His reputation in the sciences of Sufism and *shari'a* was such that he eventually became known as the most learned man of his time (*qutbu zamanihi*).[24]

This great Sufi master built a *zawiya* which quickly became famous for the quality of its written and oral teachings. These instructions centred on the total renunciation of worldly life and the obligation to devote oneself constantly to exercises of piety, to live for God alone, to renounce the pomp and ceremony of this world, to retreat from society, to devote oneself to devotional practices, and to in no way seek the pleasure, riches and honours that most men seek.[25]

The main ideas of 'Abd al-Qadir's new order are grouped in two works entitled *al-Ghunya li-talibi tariqi al-haqq* (Sufficient Provision for Seekers of the Path of Truth) and *al-Fath al-rabbani* (The Sublime Revelation), where he expounds the themes of his mystic philosophy.

The Qadiriyya order only spread into the world many years after the disappearance of its founder,[26] towards the end of the twelfth century AD, thanks to the dynamism of his children, grandchildren and followers. Abu Madyan (d.1198) played an important role in the expansion of this mystic order in all regions of the Muslim west.[27]

The three determining elements for the diffusion of the Qadiriyya into the Sahara and in the countries of Bilad al-Sudan were the caravan trade, the sermons of al-Maghili[28] (d.1504) and the flight of the Tuat Kunta on the arrival of the Beni Hassan in their country.

Qadiriyya south of the Sahara

Many Muslim West African populations think that belonging to a *tariqa* is a religious obligation. This is the reason many adults belong to a brotherhood from a young age, and this membership is generally automatic.

The vast majority of sub-Saharan African populations think that belonging to a *tariqa* is a religious obligation. This is the reason many adults belong to a brotherhood from a young age, and this membership is generally automatic.

In the sub-Saharan region the Qadiriyya order was introduced by Muhammad ibn Abd al-Karim al-Maghili.[29] Sidi Ahmad al-Bakkay,[30] the son of Sidi Muhammad al-Kunti (born at the beginning of the sixteenth century) was, it seems, the first to join, but it doesn't appear that he worked towards the popularisation of the movement.[31] It was his son, Shaykh Sidi A'mar, a faithful disciple and travelling companion of al-Maghili, who became a keen propagator of the Qadiriyya order, and the great master of this order[32] after al-Maghili's return to the north. It was by means of this grouping of mystics that the Qadiriyya order entered the Sahara. (Chapter 14 of this volume provides more detail on the history of the Kunti family.)

Shaykh Sidi A'mar was succeeded by his eldest son Ahmad al-Fayram (d. *c.*1553). Ahmad al-Fayram was succeeded by his eldest son al-Shaykh Sidi Muhammad al-Raggad (from whom the Rgagda tribal group's name is derived). He was a great scholar and died in 1577. Shaykh al-Raggad was succeeded by his son al-Shaykh Sidi Ahmad (d.1652), who constructed the *zawiya* in Tuat.

Shaykh Sidi Ahmad was succeeded by his son Sidi 'Ali, the *qutb* or pole of saints and master during his reign (1652–89) and whose marvels were widely known.[33] Sidi 'Ali was succeeded by two nephews, the sons of Sidi A'mar ibn Sidi Ahmad: first al-Shaykh Sidi Ahmad al-Khalifa (d.1693), then al-Shaykh Sidi al-Amin Bou Ngab, the 'Man in the Veil' (d.1717).[34]

After Sidi al-Amin the *khilafa* (mastery) of the Qadiriyya left the tribe and passed to a sherif of Takrour whose name was Sidi 'Ali b. al-Najib b. Muhammad b. Shuayb (d.1757). It was at Taghaza that he received his mystical initiation from Sidi al-Amin.[35] After Sidi 'Ali, mastery of the *tariqa* came back to the Kunta tribe, yet this time not to the Rgagda tribal group, but to the Awlad al-Wafi tribal group. This is where al-Shaykh Sidi al-Mukhtar al-Kabir plays his part.

Al-Shaykh Sidi al-Mukhtar and his enterprise

Al-Shaykh Sidi al-Mukhtar was the second last of the children of Ahmad ould Abu Bakr ould Sidi Muhammad ould Habib Allah Wuld al-Wafi ould Sidi Amar al-Shaykh ould Sidi Muhammad al-Kunti, the eponymous forebear of the Kunta tribe.[36]

The nomadic, Arabic-speaking Kunta formed a complex of independent family groups. They were gifted merchants, which allowed them to form a veritable economic empire stretching over a huge territory, from the Atlantic Ocean to Aïr, from Morocco to black Africa.

This nomadic tribe, which roamed from Timbuktu to Ifoghas Adrar, Dinnik and Gourma, and occasionally into the Hodh, is undoubtedly one of the most important Moorish maraboutic tribes (Bidane). It is a product of the population distribution of the south-west Sahara. In fact, it only crystallised into its current ethnic configuration at the end of the seventeenth century.[37]

The nomadic, Arabic-speaking Kunta formed a complex of independent family groups. They were gifted merchants, which allowed them to form a veritable economic empire stretching over a huge territory, from the Atlantic Ocean to Aïr, from Morocco to black Africa.

The Kunta were propagators of the Qadiriyya order south of the Sahara. They have identified themselves with (and been identified with) this order to such an extent that their names have become synonymous. West African Qadiriyya is often called Bakkaiyya – from the name of the Kunta ancestor al-Shaykh Sidi A'mar ould al-Shaykh Sidi Ahmad al-Bakkay who spread the order in the sixteenth century – or Mukhtariyya, from the name of Sidi al-Mukhtar al-Kunti who restored the order at the end of the eighteenth century and into the nineteenth century.

Al-Shaykh Sidi al-Mukhtar was born in the north-east of Araoun in Azawad (a region in the north-west of Mali) between 1729 and 1730. He lost his mother when he was four or five years old and his father when he was ten. His elder brother Muhammad became his guardian, although it seems he was strongly influenced by his maternal grandfather Beddi ibn al-Habib, who had a strong affection for him.[38]

Raised by scholarly marabouts of high distinction, and gifted with intelligence, it is not surprising that from his first years Shaykh Sidi al-Mukhtar developed rapidly in the paths of piety and Islamic science.

At the age of 14 he left his guardians in search of divine wisdom, knowledge and guidance. His first masters were Tuareg scholars of the Kel Essouk group. He then continued his studies of Islamic law and in particular of Khalil's *Mukhtasar* with another Tuareg tribal group (the Kel Hourma), where he studied with several scholars .[39]

Convinced he should go deeper into his studies, he turned towards Timbuktu where he stopped for a while only to continue his search for his master of choice, al-Shaykh 'Ali ibn Najib, a great sage and an illustrious master of Qadiriyya. At his school he was instructed in the science of Qur'anic exegesis, the science of tradition, the life of the Prophet (*sira*), theology (*'aqida*), jurisprudence (*fiqh*), grammar, recitation of the Qur'an (*qira'a*) and philology.[40]

After having acquired mastery of 13 disciplines relating to religious law and its associated sciences, he turned towards the spiritual path under the guidance of this same shaykh.[41] He practised extremely harsh exercises of piety to prepare himself for the mystical order. Through this process his shaykh inculcated a powerful mystical education in him and initiated him into the Qadiriyya as well as giving him the power to confer it.[42] It was this consecration that would make al-Mukhtar the successor of Shaykh 'Ali ibn al-Najib in the leadership of Qadiriyya.

According to his biographers, he spent four years with his shaykh and then moved to settle in Walata, in present-day Mauritania, near the tomb of his ancestor Sidi Ahmad al-Bakkay. Later he moved to Tagant, where his fame began.[43] From 1756 he took the title of shaykh of the Qadiriyya order, thus affirming his superiority over all the other Qadirite masters' *wirds* (litanies) which existed in the Sahara and especially in the Tuareg and Moorish areas.

Although eminent amongst the great Sufi saints and nicknamed the master of the time (*sahibu al-waqt*) – that is, the outstanding figure of his epoch (the eighteenth century) – al-Shaykh Sidi al-Mukhtar was also one of the most illustrious theologians of the west Sahara and of Bilad al-Sudan. His teachings attracted students of every kind to his place of residence and he authored a large number of works.

Teaching and works

Although eminent amongst the great Sufi saints and nicknamed the master of the time (*sahibu al-waqt*) – that is, the outstanding figure of his epoch (the eighteenth century) – al-Shaykh Sidi al-Mukhtar was also one of the most illustrious theologians of the west Sahara and of Bilad al-Sudan. His teachings attracted students of every kind to his place of residence and he authored a large number of works, including:

- *Tafsir al-fatiha* (commentary on the *fatiha*);
- *Tafsir al-Qur'an* (commentary on the Qur'an);
- *al-Shumus al-muhammadiyya* (Muhammadan Suns – a work of theology);
- *al-Jur'a al-safiyya* (The Pure Mouthful);
- *Kashf al-labs fi ma bayna al-ruh wa al-nafs* (Clarification of Ambiguity in the Difference Between the Spirit and the Soul);
- *Hidayat al-tullab* (The Conversion of Students; three volumes);
- *al-Minna fi i'tiqad ahl al-sunna* (Favour in Orthodox Belief);
- *al-Burd al-muwwashsha* (The Many-Coloured Garment);
- *Kashf al-gumma* (The End of Doubt);
- *al-Ajwiba al-labbatiyya* (Replies to the Questions of Labbat);
- *Fada'il ayat al-Kursi* (The Virtues of *ayat* al-Kursi);
- *al-Albab fi al-ansab* (Hearts Concerning Genealogies);
- *Sharh al-ism al-a'zam* (Commentary on the Great Name of God);
- *Junnat al-murid* (The Follower's Shield);
- *Jadwat al-anwar fi al-dabbi 'an awliyya Allah al-akhyar* (The Brand of Light for the Defence of God's Finest Saints);
- *al-Kawkab al-waqqad* (The Shining Star).

Social and political role

Al-Shaykh Sidi al-Mukhtar played one of the most important roles in Saharan and Sahelian life in the last part of the eighteenth century and the first decade of the nineteenth. He gave an important spatial, religious and political dimension to the Qadiriyya order. In addition, the career of al-Shaykh Sidi al-Mukhtar, as with that of his successor,

One of the important aspects of the career and activity of the saint was this interaction between the tribal and religious concerns in all stages of his life. Religious prestige, which was expressed in the formation of a *tariqa*, was quick to transform itself into political leadership. In fact, in the region of the Moorish tribes the founders of the brotherhoods were often leaders of tribal bodies.

confirms the thesis that the religious man is a pacifying mediator whose goal is the maintenance of balance in a society permanently threatened by destabilising conflict.

Relationships between saints (who hold power over the invisible) and sultans (whose power is limited to this world) were always uncomfortable, but they usually ended in mutual acknowledgement and in favour of the saint, who would be solicited to provide protection for the political leader. Each thus bowed before the other, which amounted to mutual recognition of authority and legitimacy.[44]

One of the important aspects of the career and activity of the saint was this interaction between the tribal and religious concerns in all stages of his life. Religious prestige, which was expressed in the formation of a *tariqa*, was quick to transform itself into political leadership. In fact, in the region of the Moorish tribes the founders of the brotherhoods were often leaders of tribal bodies.

Al-Shaykh Sidi al-Mukhtar died on 29 May 1811 at the age of either 84 or 91, leaving more than 8 children. He was buried in Bulanwar in the north of Mali.

Al-Shaykh Sidi al-Mukhtar and the order (al-Bakka'iyya)

Al-Shaykh Sidi al-Mukhtar is incontestably the most renowned representative of the mystical al-Qadiriyya order in the southern outskirts of the Sahara. From within the original brotherhood (Qadiriyya), he managed to found his own brotherhood, known as al-Bakka'iyya (referring to al-Shaykh Sidi A'mar ould al-Shaykh Sidi Ahmad al-Bakkay, d.1590).

The founding of Bakka'iyya took place within the framework of rejuvenating the religion and the brotherhoods. This renewal (*tajdid*) was experienced all over the Muslim world at the end of the eighteenth century and in the nineteenth century.

According to al-Shaykh al-Mukhtar, the *wird* of Bakka'iyya is the most illustrious; it holds pride of place over all others and cannot be replaced by any other.[45] He who possesses it dies only in the best possible conditions.[46] This *wird*, which is strictly obligatory, is composed of a certain number of *dhikr* that disciples must accomplish after every prayer:

- God provides us with everything, what an Excellent Protector (200 times).
- I ask forgiveness from God, the Immense (200 times).
- There is nothing but God, the King, the Truth, the Evident (100 times).
- The prayer for the Prophet (100 times).[47]

In addition to this *wird*, the follower must recite a certain number of extra prayers of which the *wadhifa* is the most important.

Al-Shaykh Sidi Muhammad's *Kitab al-taraif wa al-tala'id* lists certain proscriptions imposed on followers of the Qadiriyya Bakka'iyya order. In this regard he wrote: 'Contrary to what happens in other brotherhoods, it is forbidden to us to abandon ourselves to games, conspicuous displays of ascetism, fainting, dance, or exaggerated shouting to praise God. On the other hand, many of our shaykhs do not forbid or condemn singing. We must not wear rags or special garments.'[48]

This tendency of the Bakka'iyya order to conform to religious orthodoxy (always underlined by disciples of al-Shaykh Sidi al-Mukhtar) is confirmed elsewhere by a renowned scholar and Sufi of Shadhili allegiance. Muhammad Salim ould Alumma (d.1963) reports that al-Shaykh Sidi al-Mukhtar al-Kunti often defined *tasawwuf* by saying:

> *al-sufi man labissa al-sufa 'ala al-safa*
> *wa ittaba 'a tariq al-mustafa*
> *wa qthaqa al-jassada ta 'm al-jafa*
> *wa kanat al-dunya minhu ala qafa.*[49]
>
> The Sufi is he who wears wool on top of his purity,
> follows the way of the Prophet, endures bodily punishments,
> dedicates his life to adoration and
> withdraws from this worldly life, abandoning all earthly things.

Shaykh Sidi al-Mukhtar was a veritable religious conqueror whose miracles are so numerous they can scarcely be counted.[50] His disciples were missionaries who spread through all the countries of West Africa.[51] He made the Kunta into Islamisers and spiritual directors of the tribes of the Sahel and the Sahara. Thanks to the charisma and dynamism of its disciples, this *tariqa* took root in all the countries of West Africa and became the most important brotherhood from the end of the eighteenth century.

Outside the Moorish and Tuareg tribes, the spirituality preached through the Qadiriyya found fertile ground in African populations. Its memory is deepest in Senegal, Guinea, northern Ivory Coast and in the Islamised Sudan. All the black peoples who consider themselves adherents of Qadirism come under the affiliation and discipleship of al-Shaykh Sidi al-Mukhtar.

Paul Marty, the renowned French scholar of the region, claims that the Bakka'iyya order is practised by:

- all Kunta tribal groups from Mali, Algeria and Mauritania;
- the *zawiya* of al-Shaykh Sidiyya al-Mukhtar and in particular all the attached Moorish and black branches;
- the Mourides group of al-Shaykh Ahmadou Bamba in Senegalese Baol and its dependants;
- the Bou Kunta in Senegal and all the attached branches;
- the Fulani, Songhay and Igellad group of the Middle Niger region (Goundam);
- the Fulani and Marka group from Masina (Jenne, Dia);
- the Malinka group from upper Guinea (Kouroussa, Kankan, Beyla);
- all the Diakanke groups and their subsidiaries from Guinea (Touba, Bakadadji, Bissikrima, Kindia, Conakry) and upper Senegal (Bafoulabé, Kita);

Shaykh Sidi al-Mukhtar made the Kunta into Islamisers and spiritual directors of the tribes of the Sahel and the Sahara. Thanks to the charisma and dynamism of its disciples, this *tariqa* took root in all the countries of West Africa and became the most important brotherhood from the end of the eighteenth century.

- the Simono and Marka group from Banmana (Koulikoro, Ségou, Sansanding);
- the Fadiliyya brotherhood created by al-Shaykh Muhammad Fadil (*c*.1797–1869);
- the dan Fodio from the north of Nigeria;
- the Masina Fulanis.[52]

Particularities of Bakka'iyya

Apart from the erudition of the masters of the Bakka'iyya order and their recitation of a combination of *dhikr* and *wird* composed by the founder al-Shaykh Sidi al-Mukhtar, the particularity of this order is the special interest it takes in occult knowledge – study of the secrets of letters, talismans, astronomy, exorcism, interpretation of dreams etc. – and in the teaching and propagation of this knowledge.

This interest in occult knowledge of Bakka'iyya merits particular attention. This occult knowledge is formulated in the Moorish saying *'al hikmatou kuntiyyatun aw futiyyatun'* (wisdom/occult knowledge belongs to the Kunta and Futa) and has caused long polemics between the *fuqaha* of the region. For this reason, in what follows we will describe in detail justification for the usage of occult knowledge in the Bakka'iyya, taking as a foundation the *fatawa* of the great founding father of the Bakka'iyya order, al-Shaykh Sidi al-Mukhtar al-Kunti.

It is important to underline that despite the assimilatory force of Islam in sub-Saharan Africa, it has not entirely superseded traditional beliefs, which still persist. If these beliefs are no longer directly known to us, their rites nonetheless persist – at times solemnly displaying their pagan colours – surviving side by side with the orthodox beliefs or incorporated into the Islamic rites.

With Islamisation, this occult and mysterious power became largely the privilege of scholars and saints, and particularly the most charismatic amongst them. The power of these men was no longer formulated in terms of magic but in terms borrowed from the new religion – they could act on nature by virtue of the Holy Word rather than through magical practice. From then on, the emphasis was placed on the proximity of these men to divinity (the notion of holiness) or on the gifts that divinity had granted them (the notion of *baraka*).

In talismanic art, it is difficult to make the distinction between what is legal and part of secret science (*sirr*) and what is prohibited because it is part of magic. Besides, in all Muslim societies sorcery, although separated from religion, tends to reintegrate with it by means of talismanic art. This is why, in Ibn Khaldun's opinion, Islam makes no distinction between *sirr* and talismanic arts, and in *al-Muqaddima* he places them both in the only chapter on prohibited practices.[53]

Without doubt, Islam is hostile to occult practices and conceptions for they can conceal animist syncretism, which had a large hold on the local population. The *fatwa* of al-Maghili (d.1461), in reply to the questions of Askiya Muhammad (1493–1528), the ruler of Mali, confirms this sentence for the use of magic:

> Be they condemned to death any sorcerer or sorceress or whosoever who claims to create wealth, divert armies, or perform other actions of this type through talismans, magic formulas or other procedures. Whosoever amongst them returns to their senses should be left alone. Whosoever, on the other hand, refuses must be killed. Whosoever pretends to write the words from the Book of God or holy words in this goal or in other goals of like genre should not be believed. He is but an impostor. He must be driven out.[54]

In fact, the Qur'an, which represents the first fundamental source of Islamic law, contains no information concerning esoteric therapeutic practices. On the other hand, prophetic tradition or the Sunna, the second fundamental source of Islamic law, contains numerous *hadiths* which explicitly refer to treatments of an esoteric nature.

The use of therapeutic incantation (*ruqa*) by the Prophet and his companions is reported in several anthologies of *hadiths*, including the two authentic anthologies of al-Bukhari and Muslim. The legality of incantation is unanimously approved of by theologians and the life of the very earliest Muslims bears witness to this.

In a famous *hadith* the Prophet says: 'For every illness, God has provided a cure.'[55] The recognition by the Prophet himself of the therapeutic value of the *fatiha* (the first *sura* of the Qur'an) is for Muslim theologians the most important argument for the legality of incantation.

The Prophet himself opened the way to treatment of illnesses and problems by means of esoteric procedures. The signs of particular immediate power accorded to the Qur'an are manifest even in the lifetime of the founder of Islam. In this regard, the use of the *sura fatiha* by one of the Prophet's companions as an incantation to heal snake bites is highly instructive. Citing Abu Sa'id al-Khudri, al-Bukhari reports:

> We were on a journey and we halted when a woman accosted us and informed us that the chief of her tribe had just been bitten by a snake and that her men folk were absent. She asked, 'Is there amongst you an incantatory healer (*raqi*)?' A man who had no reputation in the field as far as we knew stood up, accompanied her and made incantations in aid of the chief who was soon healed. As recompense the chief gave him 30 sheep, and milk to drink. When our man returned we asked him, 'Are you an incantation specialist or a confirmed practitioner?' and he replied, 'Not at all, I practise incantation solely with the mother of the book (*fatiha*).' We decided to talk no more of this before consulting the Prophet. On our return to Medina we told him the story and he exclaimed, 'How did he know that it (*fatiha*) has incantatory power? Share the spoils amongst you and put my share to one side.'[56]

The discreet presence of the Arabic root word *raqa* with its incantatory content in the Qur'an certainly contributed to the success of the use of incantations, even if the success was ascribable to prophetic practice, amply relayed by traditionists.

As can be expected, the science of secrets incited lively polemics amongst the theologians of the region. Some think that the use of magical formulas for dispelling evil is nothing but a way of thwarting divine will, or a form of belief in a supernatural power which may even intervene against fate. They see, therefore, nothing but a magical practice rigorously proscribed by Islam, for the power to act on natural forces is analogous to the power of the magician, which is vociferously condemned in the Qur'an. Moreover, these esoteric formulas can contain 'associationist' (polytheistic) statements or vows in contradiction with the fundamental precepts of Islam.

In this vein, Sidi 'Abd Allah ould al-Haj Ibrahim (d.1817) wrote:

> Religious law does not distinguish between magic, talismans and illusionism: it puts them all in the same category of forbidden objects. These sciences are forbidden because they turn the soul towards the stars or other objects rather than towards the Creator. The Lawmaker has only allowed us actions in accordance with our religion, which assures us happiness in the afterlife (*akhira*) and well-being on earth (*dunya*). Outside of these two legitimate preoccupations, everything harmful is forbidden in proportion to the amount of harm it can do.[57]

Likewise, Muhammed Fal ould Muttali (d.1870) said in a poem (prose translation follows):

> Citing Ibn Arafa, al-Sa'idi says that the practice of incantation using hermetic words or expressions is rigorously forbidden, even if effective. Their authors may even be subjected to the death penalty.[58]

The major argument of these *fuqaha* is the reply that Malik (d.795) gave to someone who asked him if the use of non-Arabic Names of God (*al-asma al-ajamiyya*) in their original form for esoteric ends is authorised by Islam. He replied, 'Who tells you that it is not infidelity (*kufr*)?'[59]

For al-Shaykh Sidi al-Mukhtar, Malik's answer is not as cutting as it appears. In fact, it is rather ambiguous for it lends itself to differing interpretations. One interpretation would, for example, lift the ban in the case where the user of these formulas made sure of the non-existence of elements opposed to the monotheistic spirit.[60] Infidelity is thought of as the association of other deities or elements with the One God; if one were to make sure the other names referred only to Allah, one would still fall within monotheism.

Al-Shaykh Sidi al-Mukhtar considers that the science of the secret is authorised on condition it obtains good results. The prohibition rests on the results of the incantation. If these are positive, the prohibition is lifted; if not, it remains in place. This position is based on ethical considerations inspired by the Prophet's *hadith*: 'Do not hesitate to come to the aid of your brother in Islam.'[61]

Al-Shaykh Sidi al-Mukhtar puts forward a second argument, that the incantation of incomprehensible phrases is well known in prophetic tradition.

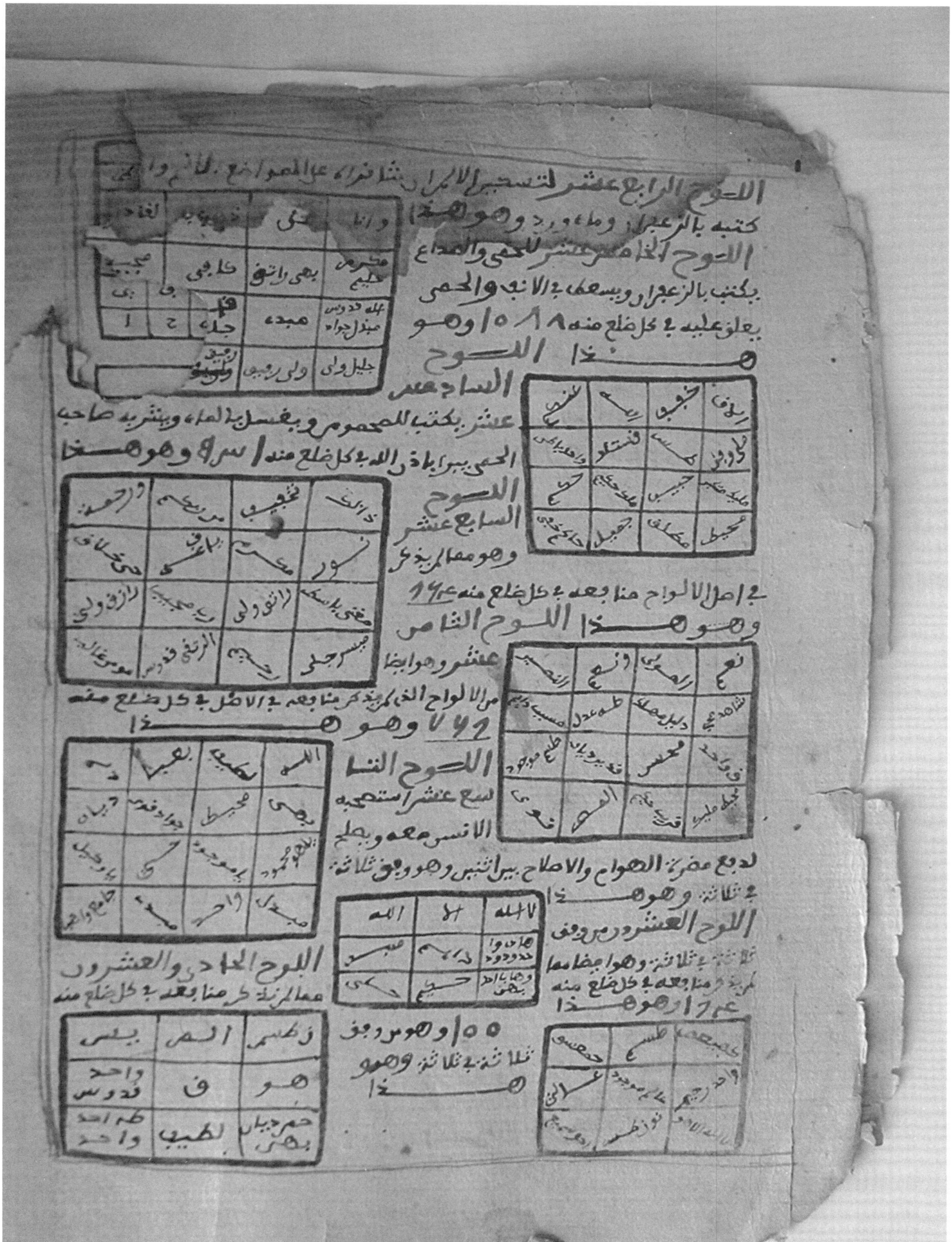

This manuscript shows examples of incantations and esoteric healing practices.

> One finds esoteric incantations recounted by traditionists whose meaning is not clear. Al-Hafid Abu Nuaym reported that the Archangel Gabriel taught the Prophet to recite a particular phrase to heal snakebites. The phrase goes '*Praise to God. Shajjatun, qarniyyatun, matiyyatun, bahr qafla*'[62] and then the healer blows seven times on a wooden knife which he sticks into the sand.[63]

Theologians who authorise the 'black arts' refer to the above *hadith* and its hermetic formulas. As noted concerning the differing interpretations of Malik's words, the hermetic character of an incantatory phrase should not be a handicap for its use towards therapeutic ends. The continuity between pre-Islamic Arabic practices and Qur'anic practices is clearly evident in the example of incantation.

On the other hand, al-Shaykh Sidi al-Mukhtar thinks that incantation or any other therapeutic formula is only effective if its user is pious and possesses *baraka*, for the esoteric force of the incantation is directly linked to the socioreligious status and charisma of the user. He writes in this regard:

> Abu Hamid al-Ghazali leads us to understand moreover that the effectiveness of the incantation resides as much in the saliva as in the magical formula itself. This is why it is often said of the users of unsuccessful incantations that they lack 'the spittle of Sahnun'.[64]

This famous phrase was pronounced by a great Islamic saint when various complaints about one of the disciples of Sahnun (d.854) were being addressed to him. The disciple wanted to continue the tradition of his master in the healing of diverse illnesses through the recitation of the *fatiha*. Although the disciple in question repeated the same incantation as his master, his patients never managed to recover. They lodged a complaint against him with a holy man of the time who called him in and interrogated him on his manner of treating his patients. The healer replied that he acted just as his master Sahnun had done – he repeated the *fatiha* and spat lightly on his patients. The holy man replied, 'Indeed the *fatiha* is incontestably an effective incantation for healing all sorts of illnesses as the Prophet said, but does your spittle have the same power as that of Sahnun?'[65]

In the last two centuries the region has known continual theological quarrelling over this matter. The climax of these polemics occurred in 1996. It is illustrated by an anecdote over which much ink has been spilled, and which has re-ignited the debate with greater fervour.

It is the story of a woman who was bitten by a snake in a small village situated in the Mederdra department of Mauritania. Following the bite the woman's foot swelled up and the first signs of poisoning began to show. Her husband, a Salafite trader, refused the intervention of a Qadirite cousin, although well known in the area for his mastery of these sciences. The husband began to make *fatiha* incantations himself in accordance with the prophetic tradition. This procedure was utilised by the Prophet's companion Abu Sa'id al-Khudri and consecrated by the Prophet in the famous *hadith* mentioned above.

After reciting *fatiha* for several hours the state of the woman did not show signs of improving. Rather, it was deteriorating to the point that oedema had reached her thorax and she was in agony. At this point the woman's parents began to worry that she would die and they thus went in search of the healer whom the husband had turned away earlier.

Despite the reticence of the husband, the local *qadi* judged that the woman's situation required urgent attention and ordered the healer to be summoned. When he began his incantations there was an immediate improvement in the woman's condition. He breathed several formulas from the so-called black *gabza* into his turban, with which he fanned the bitten limb. The patient vomited straight away and began to feel better. Several people who came to enquire into the state of the woman declared that the husband had nearly killed his wife with the recitation of the *fatiha*.

These words were reported to other people in the village of Salafite allegiances, and they automatically considered them as a declared heresy – they were considered heresy since they claimed that the *fatiha*, in other words the Word of God, had almost killed someone. The problem became rather serious and was put for arbitration before the *qadi* of the village. He cut the debate short by saying that these words were not aimed at the Qur'an but rather at the user of the incantation, who apparently did not possess the famous spittle of Sahnun. The *qadi* viewed the healer as a Muslim who had used his words to save the life of a person in danger. His words had had the desired effect; all this was considered as lawful in Islam.

This debate illustrates the controversial aspect of incantation and of the sciences of knowledge. From it we can draw several lessons, in particular that Qadirite populations neither reject nor hesitate to use even the most hermetic and unintelligible occult formula. The story and the debate that accompanied it had the effect of encouraging this sort of practice and reinforced arguments in favour of the positive effects of the occult sciences.

This is also why there is a strong tendency in this society to have greater faith in the virtue of so-called black practices than in so-called white practices. Many people believe that the use of white incantatory practices requires a now rare degree of piety and even perhaps intrinsic or hereditary aptitudes in the practitioner, whilst black incantations require neither great erudition nor, generally speaking, any natural disposition. Mastering them can be achieved with a short training period and initiation.

Just as the shaykhs of Bakka'iyya see nothing wrong with the use of knowledge (secrets of letters and geometric forms), nor do they see anything wrong with its ensuing remuneration. In this regard, al-Shaykh Sidi al-Mukhtar wrote:

> The legitimacy of remuneration for the practice of *ruqya* (kind of talisman) is explicitly recognised by the Prophet when his companions decided to consult him over the spoils from the incantation in Medina. He ordered them to share out the spoils. The remuneration always exacted by practitioners, which is on occasion considerable, finds in this *hadith* a legal justification.[66]

The founding saint always managed to put into place a dynastic strategy based on ancestral status. By this process he assured the continuity of the direction of *tariqa* in his direct descendants. Spiritual legitimacy became linked to genealogical legitimacy, which made the power of the brotherhood dependent on the power of the tribe. However, the more the designated chief became involved in social affairs, the more he lost control of the *tariqa* and his spiritual authority.

Succession

Shaykhs normally name their *khalifa* (successor) through the gift of a string of beads, a prayer mat, a staff or some similar object. It was thus that Shaykh Sidi al-Mukhtar al-Kabir chose his successor by giving his beads to his son al-Shaykh Sidi Muhammad just before his death.

Indeed, the founding saint always managed to put into place a dynastic strategy based on ancestral status. By this process he assured the continuity of the direction of *tariqa* in his direct descendants. It was also this mechanism which modified the meaning of the symbolic links of the foundation of the *tariqa*: in this foundation the succession of a shaykh was not necessarily given to his family but to a spiritually qualified master; this then was changed to family succession. Spiritual legitimacy became linked to genealogical legitimacy, which made the power of the brotherhood dependent on the power of the tribe. However, the more the designated chief became involved in social affairs, the more he lost control of the *tariqa* and his spiritual authority.[67]

Al-Shaykh Sidi Muhammad was born in 1765. He too was famous for his immense learning, his austerity, his ascetism and his power of attraction through speech and visions. He was incontestably the greatest representative of the Bakka'iyya order after the disappearance of his father and he distinguished himself from his other brothers by his reputation as a mystic. His many miracles contributed to creating this image of him in the eyes of his followers.

This great Sufi of the Bakka'iyya was useful to his contemporaries. He saved the town of Timbuktu from total destruction by Cheikhou Amadou's Fulanis in around 1825–26. His intervention stopped the pillage and arson, and led to the organisation of a regular governmental mission of Fulanis to Timbuktu.

During the life of his father, al-Shaykh Sidi Muhammad undertook several missions of a political nature to the tribes and authorities of the region – all activity, albeit perceived as religious, had a political and social dimension. He was in a sense the manager of the political and social affairs of his father, and thus became very experienced in these matters. He distinguished himself through the strategies he used to give his group social standing in his negotiations over territorial issues.

He died in 1826, and continuing his work became the major preoccupation of his family. As with any organisation based mainly on personal charisma, the disappearance of the founding fathers changed the nature of charismatic domination in the brotherhood.

Al-Shaykh Sidi Muhammad was succeeded by his two eldest sons: first Sidi al-Mukhtar al-Sagir (d.1847), then al-Shaykh Sidi Ahmad al-Bakkay (d.1865).

NOTES

1 Translated from the French by Simon de Swardt.

2 Ould Muhammad Baba (1996–97: 6).

3 Cuoq (1984: 56–57).

4 Cuoq (1984: 61).

5 The Malikite *madhhab* is one of the four schools of jurisprudence that developed in the Sunni world; the Junaydite order is a branch of *tasawwuf* (Sufism); and the Ash'arite dogma is the most common theological school in Islam.

6 Al-Shaykh Sidi al-Mukhtar al-Kunti, *al-Kawkab al-waqqad fi fadail al-ashyakh wa al-awrad* (manuscript), page 46, Institut Mauritanienne de Recherche Scientifique.

7 See Muhammaddou Ould Aghrabatt, *al-Radd 'ala Ould Hanbal al-Hasani* (manuscript), Institut Mauritanienne de Recherche Scientifique.

8 Ibn Khaldun (1985: 87).

9 Ibn Khaldun (1985: 88).

10 Ould Shaykh (1991: 201).

11 Ould Shaykh (1991).

12 Boubrik (1999: 76).

13 Ould Shaykh (1991: 209).

14 Ould Shaykh (1991: 210).

15 A great Sufi of the Qadiriyya order from the Mauritanian east, founder of the Fadiliyya order and father amongst other masters of al-Shaykh Malaynin and al-Shaykh Sad Buh.

16 Gudfiyya is a religious brotherhood whose followers have been accused of committing unorthodox practices. See Beyries (1935) and Laforgue (1928: 658).

17 Great saint and Sufi Shadhili from the Hodh region.

18 Great Sufi and scholar of the Idawali (Trarza). He was the first propagator of Tijaniyya in western Africa.

19 For detailed information on this order, see Traoré (1983).

20 Ahmadu Hamah Allah, better known under the name of al-Shaykh Hamah Allah, is from the tribe of Ahl Muhammad Sidi (Shurufa of Tichitt). After brief religious studies, the missionary of Tlemcen Lakhdar identified him as caliph of Tijaniyya. His influence was considerable in the western Bilad al-Sudan; the veneration which he received was extraordinary. He died during his internment at Montluçon (France).

21 Ould Cheikh (1991: 234).

22 Ould Cheikh (1991).

23 Holland (1997).

24 Ibn Khaldun (1985: 56).

25 Holland (1997).

26 Mu'nis (1997: 12–14).

27 Mu'nis (1997).

28 Muhammad ibn 'Abd al-Karim al-Maghili was originally from the village of Tlemcen. He was a theologian who had a strong influence on the Tuwat region and beyond, right up to the Songhay Empire and Hausa countries. He is known as a defender of strict orthodoxy, as his famous answers to the questions of Askiya Muhammad bear witness.

29 This *wird* transmission, and thus the transmission of the Qadiriyya via this route, seems unlikely.

30 The nickname 'Bakky' (the Tearful) was given to the shaykh by his contemporaries to honour his piety. It is reported that he once missed prayers in the mosque. The guilt immediately caused him to weep abundantly and he never again stopped crying or, at the very least, having watery eyes.

31 Marty (1920: 123).

32 His name is to be found in the mystic transmission chain of Qadiriyya immediately after al-Maghili, who was himself a disciple of Jalal al-Din al-Suyuti.

33 Wuld Hamidun (1987: 41).

34 Marty (1920).

35 Marty (1920).

36 Ould Cheikh (2001: 139).

37 Marty (1920).

38 Marty (1920).

39 Al-Cheikh Sidi Muhammad, *Kitab al-taraif wa al-talaid min karamat al-shaykhayn al-walida wa al-walid* (manuscript), Institut Mauritanienne de Recherche Scientifique.

40 Marty (1920).

41 Marty (1920: 56).

42 Marty (1920: 57).

43 Al-Shaykh Sidi Muhammad, *Kitab al-taraif.*

44 See Weber (1995: 45).

45 Al-Shaykh Sidi al-Mukhtar al-Kunti, *al-Kawkab al-waqqad,* page 67.

46 Al-Shaykh Sidi al-Mukhtar al-Kunti, *al-Kawkab al-waqqad.*

47 Al-Shaykh Sidi al-Mukhtar al-Kunti, *al-Kawkab al-waqqad.*

48 Al-Shaykh Sidi Muhammad, *Kitab al-taraif.*

49 Ould Hamidun, *al-Masouaa* (manuscript), Institut Mauritanienne de Recherche Scientifique.

50 Ould Hamidun, *al-Masouaa.*

51 Amongst his disciples who became great masters and founders of *zawiya*s can be mentioned: al-Shaykh Sidiyya ould al-Mukhtar ould al-Hayba (Awlad Abyayri); al-Shaykh al-Qadi ould al-Haj Atfaga (Idaydba); al-Shaykh al-Mustafa ould al-Haj Atfaga (Idaydba); al-Shaykh Ahmed ould A'waysi (Idaynnib); al-Shaykh ould Animanni (Anwazir); al-Shaykh Baba al-Hay ould Mahmud ould al-Shaykh A'mar (Abdukkal); al-Shaykh al-Mukhtar (Awlad Bisba'); al-Shaykh al-Mustaf ould al-'Arbi (Awlad Abyayri); al-Shaykh Muhammad al-Amin ould Abd al-Wahhab (Leglagma); al-Shaykh Abbata ould al-Talib Abd Allah (Idagjmalla).

52 Marty (1920: 98).

53 Ibn Khaldun (1985: 87).

54 Cuoq (1975: 28).

55 Ibn Anas Malik (1977: 342).

56 al-Bukhari (1947: 123).

57 al-Fatawa, in Ould el-Bara (forthcoming).

58 al-Fatawa, in Ould el-Bara (forthcoming).

59 al-Fatawa, in Ould el-Bara (forthcoming).

60 al-Fatawa, in Ould el-Bara (forthcoming).

61 al-Bukhari (1947: 89).

62 Muslim (1954: 4/54).

63 al-Fatawa, in Ould el-Bara (forthcoming).

64 al-Fatawa, in Ould el-Bara (forthcoming).

65 Al-Shaykh Sidi al-Mukhtar al-Kunti, *al-Kawkab al-waqqad.*

66 al-Fatawa, in Ould el-Bara (forthcoming).

67 Gellener (1970).

REFERENCES

Beyries J (1935) Notes sur les Ghoudf de Mauritanie. *Revue d'études Islamiques* 1: 52–73

Boubrik R (1999) *Saints et sociétés, anthropologie historique d'une confrérie ouest saharienne.* Paris: CNRS editions

al-Bukhari (1947) *al-Jami al-sahih* (Vol. 2). Cairo: al-Babi al-Halabi Press edition

Cuoq J (1975) *Recueil de sources arabes concernant l'Afrique occidentale du VIIIéme au XVIème siècle.* Paris: CNRS editions

Cuoq J (1984) *Histoire de l'islamisation de l'Afrique de l'Ouest des origines a la fin du XVIème siècle.* Paris: Librairie Orientale Paul Geuthner

Gellener E (1970) Pouvoir politique et fonction religieuse dans l'Islam marocain. *Annales* May–June: 699–713

Holland M (trans.) (1992) *al-Fath al-rabbani* (Dar al-Albab, Damascus, n.d.). Houston: Al-Baz Publishing

Holland M (trans.) (1997) *al-Ghunya li-talibi tariq al-haqq* (Dar al-Albab, Damascus, n.d.). Fort Lauderdale: Al-Baz Publishing

Ibn Anas Malik (1977) *al-Muwwatta.* Cairo: Dar al-Kutub al-Misriyya edition

Ibn Khaldun (1985) *al-Muqaddima.* Beirut: Dar Sadir edition

Laforgue P (1928) Une secte hérésiarque en Mauritanie 'les Ghoudf'. *Bulletin du Comité d'études Historiques et Scientifiques de l'AOF* 1: 654–665

Marty P (Ed.) (1920) *Etude sur l'Islam et les tribus du Soudan: Tome premier les Kounta de l'Est-les Berabich-les Iguellad.* Paris: Ernest LeRoux

Mu'nis H (1997) *Tahqiq kitab watha'iq al-Murabitin wa l-Muwwahidin.* Cairo: Dar al-Ma'arif

Muslim AH (1954) *al-Jami al-sahih.* Cairo: Matbaat al-Babi al-Halabi edition

Ould el-Bara Y (forthcoming) *al-Majmoua al-Kubra al-Chamila li fatawa wa nawazili wa ahkami Ahl Garb wa Janub Garb al-Sahra*

Ould Muhammad Baba A (1996–97) Le contexte tribal du mouvement Almoravides. PhD thesis, DEA University CA Diop, Dakar

Ould Cheikh AW (1991) La tribu comme volonté et comme représentation. In P Bonte (Ed.) *Al-Ansab: La quête des origines.* Paris: Maison des sciences de l'Homme

Ould Cheikh AW (2001) La généalogie et les capitaux flottants: al-Saykh Sid al-Mukhtar et les Kunta. In *Emirs et présidents: figures de la parenté et du politique dans le monde arabe*, (collective authorship, under the direction of P Bonte, E Conte & P Dresch). Paris: CNRS editions

Traoré A (Ed.) (1983) *Islam et colonisation en Afrique: Cheikh Hamahoullah: homme de foi et résistant.* Paris: Maisonneuve & Larose

Weber M (1995) *Le savant et le politique.* Paris: Plon

Wuld Hamidun M (1987) *Hayat muritaniyya (la vie intellectuelle), al-dar al-arabiyya li al-kitab* (Vol. 3). Tunis, Tripoli: no publisher

منزلة الطالع
وان تريد
معنا
دائرة البروج والمنازل والحروف وبدن الانسان
معنا عا سم وهو مربع ضربناه في عه وزدنا عليه هش هذا
النشر ثم نقصنا من جملة العدد ثمانية ونزلنا ما بقي في الوفق وان
كان الخير فتزيد على جملة برم وهما ٧٥ لا وان كان للشر
فانقص من جملة الوفق سيطا وهما ٨٥ وتنزل ما بقي في الوفق
الربع وهو عه في عه وهو اذا جمعته جملة عدد الخمس وما
تريد ان تفعل بعض من الشر فاضرب جملة ذلك العدد في عه وزدنا
عليه هش وهما ٥ ببا واسقطنا من جملة العدد سيطا وهما
٨٥ ونزل ما بقي من العدد في بيوت الوفق في طالع دبر وان كان
العمل الخير فتزيد على جملته برنه وهما ٧ مب ولا تنقص من الجملة
شي ونزلها في الوفق في طالع سعيد والله اعلم وهذا الوفق فيه الحروف

CHAPTER 14

The works of Shaykh Sidi al-Mukhtar al-Kunti

Mahamane Mahamoudou[1]

In the name of Allah, Most Beneficent, Most Merciful,
May His salutation and peace be upon the noblest of all prophets.
May the peace of Allah be upon you, and His mercy and blessings.

Al-Shaykh Sayyid al-Mukhtar ibn Ahmad ibn Abi Bakr ibn Habib Allah ibn al-Wafi ibn Umar al-Shaykh ibn Ahmad al-Bakkay ibn Muhammad al-Kunti, known as al-Shaykh al-Kabir, was born Arawan in 1729 and settled in Timbuktu in his youth. He died in 1811 in Bulunwar, which is over 100 kilometres from Timbuktu. The shaykh belonged to the Kunt, a famous tribe in the region known for its knowledge and piety and which traced itself back to 'Uqba ibn Nafi' – a companion of Prophet Muhammad and an Arab general who began the Islamic conquest of North Africa; he died in 683.

The shaykh studied all the Islamic disciplines, including its fundamental principles, its branches and its arts, such as jurisprudence, grammar, morphology, prophetic traditions, Qur'anic exegesis, astronomy, philosophy, internal sciences, external sciences,[2] and so on. He became skilful in all of these. Ahmad al-Bakkay, one of his grandsons, describes him thus in a poem: 'He read the *Khulasa* [The Summary] of Imam Malik before the obligatory fasting of the month Ramadan [meaning that he had not yet reached the age of puberty when religious duties become obligatory for a Muslim – he was between seven and twelve years old]; his grandfather taught it to him and he was the shaykh of the path.'[3]

He was brought up in a Sufi environment under the tutelage of al-Shaykh Sayyid Ali ibn al-Najib and from him he took the Qadiri Sufi path. He renewed the Qadiri path, building many *zawiyas* and adding to it a number of prayers, litanies and other devotions. He was a pious and righteous teacher and had a relationship with all the scholars of the region, who flocked to him from all areas and tribes. He was also a skilled politician, clear in word and action, with good insight into matters. Tribal instability was very common in his time and he played an exemplary role in striving towards

Opposite: A folio from a manuscript on astrology. Shaykh Sidi al-Mukhtar al-Kunti discussed the stars and what was said about them in the Torah: the 12 towers and their division into 28 stations; every tower having two-and-a-third stations, and these towers being divided into 360 degrees; every tower having 30 degrees; that the sun passes once every year and by this an orbit is completed; and the moon completes a cycle in 28 days.

reconciliation and peace. In short, he was a wise teacher, general, judge, father and protector of those who sought refuge.

He spent his life admonishing, guiding, improving and educating all classes of people in Timbuktu and its surrounds. One of his students, the great shaykh, jurist and pious saint al-Shaykh Muhammad Abd Allah Su'ad, alluded to this in a poem praising Timbuktu:

> Timbuktu was surrounded by safety
> and abundance when he came to it
> He resided in it with security
> and he lead it to its guidance
> It prospered and they too prospered
> and those who came to it prospered[4]

Al-Shaykh al-Kabir's son wrote a biographical account of the shaykh's life in a huge volume which he did not complete and which he named *Kitab al-tara'if wa al-tala'id fi dhikr karama al-walida wa al-walid* (The Exquisite and Rare Regarding the Miracles of the Mother and Father).[5] A brief synopsis of the volume follows.

INTRODUCTION: The appearance of a *karama* and its conditions and the difference between it and a *mu'jiza* and other unusual events and the refutation of those who reject the occurrence of a miracle.

CHAPTER 1: The birth of the two shaykhs (that is, Sayyid Mukhtar and his wife), their age at their death, their lineage and the beginning of their lives (how they started out and reached the status that they had); how the shaykh sought knowledge, his travelling for it and how he persevered in seeking it; those who studied under him.

CHAPTER 2: His piety and ascetic qualities while still being wealthy; his perseverance, respect, forgiving nature and courage; his politics.

CHAPTER 3: His knowledge, virtues and methods of teaching.

CHAPTER 4: His interaction with people: oppressors, leaders, 'ordinary' people, students, neighbours, relatives, friends and so on.

CHAPTER 5: Unusual deeds which are agreed upon as the pearls of his everlasting supernatural activities, that is, his miracles since he was considered a saint.

CHAPTER 6: Consensus of the entire nation, whether Bedouins or city dwellers, regarding his grand status, his leadership, his knowledge of the Qur'an and the prophetic tradition, his influence in *tasawwuf* and internal disciplines; people seeking his authorisation and travelling to him in the quest for knowledge.

CHAPTER 7: His bequests and correspondence, which are no less important than his other profound writings and great poetry; his death and the period just prior to it.

CONCLUSION: The unusual miracles of the *shaykha*, the mother (Sayyid Mukhtar al-Kunti's wife), her life history, her moral values, her love for her Lord, her chastity, her perseverance and polite nature, her generosity and compassion to all creation, her humility and the care that she offered to the poor and weak, her fear of her Lord and how she wept and cried, her honourableness and high aspirations.

Al-Shaykh al-Kabir's works

The shaykh was famous for his abundant writings and his beautiful style. He was very concerned about the condition of the community, and these thoughts are quite visible in his writings, which articulate his role, his activities and his diverse responsibilities. His writings portray his formulation of ideas and recommendations, as well as his successful analysis and treatment of problems. He left behind more than 100 important and diverse treatises dealing with a range of disciplines, such as history, *tasawwuf*, Islamic law, belief in the oneness of Allah, the Qur'an, *hadith*, *jihad*, politics, medicine, science, geography, poetry, astronomy and so on. A brief discussion of some of his most important works follows.

The shaykh was famous for his abundant writings and his beautiful style. He was very concerned about the condition of the community, and these thoughts are quite visible in his writings, which articulate his role, his activities and his diverse responsibilities. He left behind more than 100 important and diverse treatises dealing with a range of disciplines, such as history, *tasawwuf*, Islamic law, belief in the oneness of Allah, the Qur'an, *hadith*, *jihad*, politics, medicine, science, geography, poetry, astronomy and so on.

Works at the Ahmed Baba Institute and the Mamma Haidara Library

Fath al-wahhab 'ala hidaya al-tullab

THE AID OF THE GIVER FOR THE GUIDANCE OF THE SEEKERS

In this four-volume manuscript[6] on Maliki jurisprudence, each volume exceeding 700 pages, al-Shaykh al-Kabir expounds on numerous legal and academic issues. I have researched the volumes since 1980:

- Volume 1 was copied from the original by Muhammad al-Mustafa ibn 'Umar ibn Sayyid Muhammad Ashiyya, and completed on 13 November 1853.
- Volume 2 was copied from the original in 1853 by al-Mustafa ibn 'Umar for Isma'il ibn 'Abd Allah.
- Volume 3 is in the handwriting of Baba ibn 'Abd al-Rahman ibn Sinb al-Hartani for Isma'il ibn 'Abd Allah.
- Volume 4 was copied by Muhammad al-Mustafa ibn A'mar on the order of al-Shaykh ibn Mawlay Isma'il ibn Mawlay 'Abd Allah in 1854. The volume was completed by Muhammad al-Mustafa in 1855.

Al-minna fi i'tiqad ahl al-sunna

THE GIFT IN EXPLAINING THE CREED OF AHL AL-SUNNA
(FOLLOWERS OF ORTHODOX SUNNI ISLAM)

This 519-page manuscript[7] was copied from the original in 1859 in a beautiful, clear Sahrawi script. The manuscript consists of Islamic creed and touches upon many academic issues. The author was asked to:

The following topics are also covered in the manuscript: types of faith and believers, the nourishing of faith and the benefits of *istighfar* (seeking forgiveness); the infallibility of the prophets; major sins and how they are distinguished from minor sins; predestination; the unbelief of all nations except the Islamic nation; the invalidity of fire worshipping; the glorification of mountains and birds and the signs of the last hour, such as the descending of 'Isa (Jesus) and the coming of *dajjal*; the letters that were revealed at the beginning of the Qur'an.

> compile a brief but comprehensive book as the need may be, so that all can benefit from it, whether he be a free person or slave, woman or child, because of its easiness and its concise explanation on the unity of Allah which leads to knowing Him, and the clinging to the tails of His messengers and saints, and it should be free from fanaticism and negligence, both being a defect in religion, and I have said that many ignorant people entered upon the discussion of this discipline, i.e. the unity of Allah, and their branding of ordinary Muslims of the *umma* of Muhammad [saw] as non-believers.[8]

Al-Shaykh al-Kabir explains the origin and meanings of the word *tawhid* – knowledge that is a gift that must be tasted and that isn't acquired through research and studies – and also what is contained in *Sura al-Ikhlas* (Chapter 112 in the Qur'an). He deals with this in detail, using proof from the Qur'an, prophetic traditions, stories and other texts. He also speaks about his preference for some parts of the Qur'an over others, the interpretation of *ayat al-kursi*,[9] the different types of *shafa'a*, the Prophet being the best of prophets, and gives an overview of the science of astronomy.

The following topics are also covered in the manuscript: types of faith and believers, the nourishing of faith and the benefits of *istighfar* (seeking forgiveness); the infallibility of the prophets; major sins and how they are distinguished from minor sins; predestination; the unbelief of all nations except the Islamic nation; the invalidity of fire worshipping; the glorification of mountains and birds and the signs of the last hour, such as the descending of 'Isa (Jesus) and the coming of *dajjal* (the Antichrist); the letters that were revealed at the beginning of the Qur'an; different types of proofs and admonitions; a description of the throne of Allah; the debate of the Prophet with the delegation of Najran[10] concerning the oneness of Allah; the saints, signs of sainthood, miracles of the saints and types of *awliya*; a biography of Abu Bakr and those who came after him, such as 'Umar; the keys to and treasures of paradise; the people of the allegiance of *al-ridwan*;[11] the innocence of 'Aisha and the virtues of 'Aisha and Khadija; the student of knowledge and the virtue of seeking knowledge; the virtues of the household of the Prophet; important admonitions uttered by al-Hasan ibn Ja'far; the virtues of people of honour, such as Abu Madyan; ascetic saints that lived in seclusion in mountains and caves, worshipping Allah; things that prevent a response to *du'a* (supplication); the virtue of those who have knowledge of Allah; al-Maghili's poem when he reached the *rawda* (sacred area) in Medina; a discussion of al-Maghili and the fall of the Askiya Empire; the burial of Sayyid 'Umar al-Shaykh in the land of Aff Sus; the story of a Christian; the children of 'Abd al-Rahman al-Barabish and a historical overview of his family; mention of al-Shaykh Sayyid Ahmad al-Fayram, al-Sayyid Muhammad al-Ruqad and al-Sayyid Ahmad ibn al-Sayyid Muhammad al-Ruqadi; an overview of the history of the Bilad al-Sudan and its empire until Ghana; a biography of Muhammad ibn Muhammad known as Babaku; information about al-Shaykh Sayyid

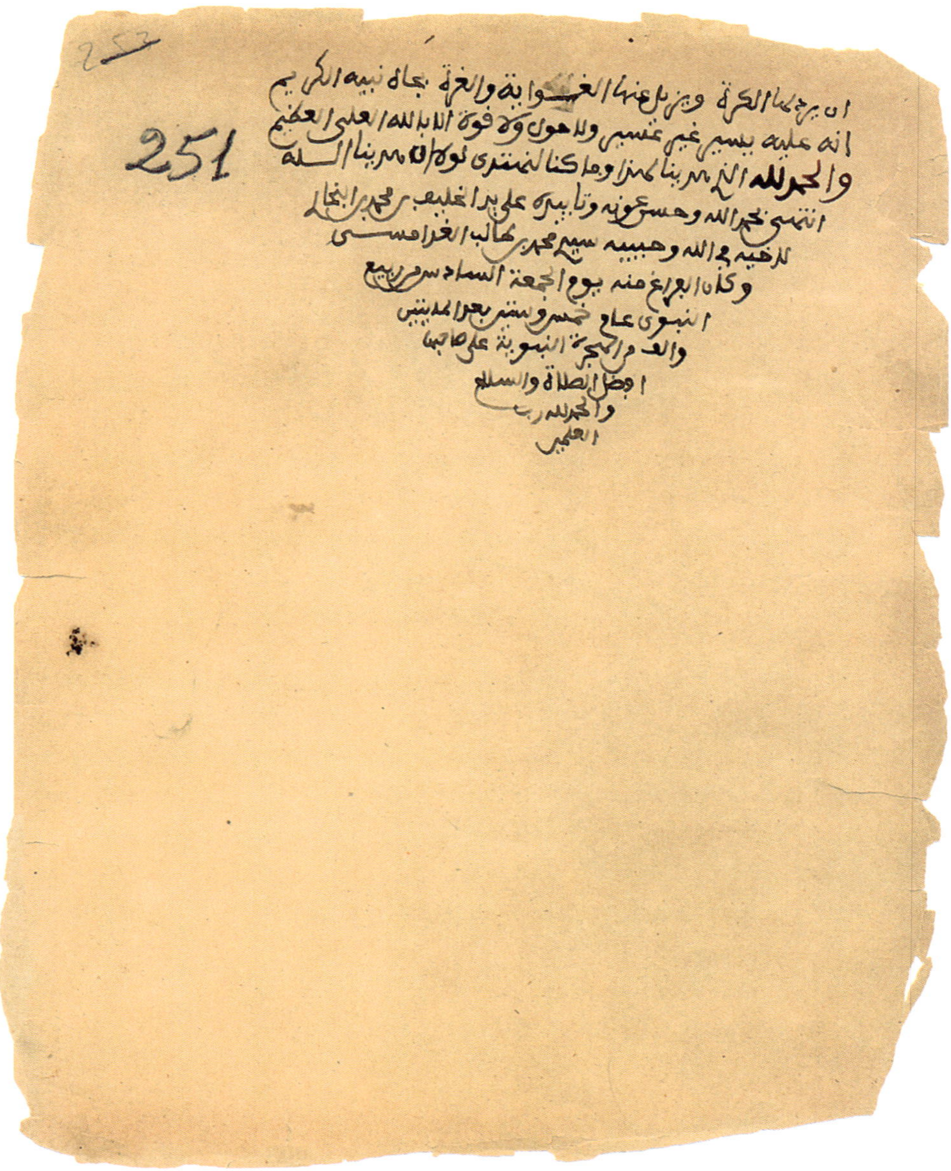

The final page of *al-Minna fi i'tiqad ahl al-sunna* by Sayyid Mukhtar al-Kunti.

al-Mukhtar and his travels and visits to Walata; the fruits of knowledge; statues; the four mosques; the parables used by Allah; types of glorification of the angels; the glorification of inanimate objects; the remembrance of Allah after prayers; a compendium of remembrance and numerous invocations; the names of the satans (the devils) and how they mislead people; the performance of righteousness; the wisdom of recurring and extraordinary events; Allah's words: 'Allah did not make for man two hearts in his chest'; the necessity of believing in the night journey of the Prophet; the virtue of seeking forgiveness; the virtue of certain *adhkar* and *adhkar* to be said in the mornings and evenings; the virtue of beneficial knowledge and that which follows it; the reality and nourishment of faith; types of humility; the validity of the faith of the follower.

Al-Jar'a al-Safiya wa al-nafha al-kafiya

THE PURIFIED DOSAGE AND SUFFICIENT FRAGRANCE

The compilation of this six-chapter manuscript[12] was completed in June 1793. Al-Shaykh al-Kabir called it by this title because, according to him, it was based on the Book (*al-Qur'an*), prophetic tradition and stories of the prophets and saints. The work was also abridged under the title *al-Rashfa al-shafiya min al-jar'a al-safiya* (The Curing Gulp of the Purified Dosage).[13]

In the introduction al-Shaykh al-Kabir mentions all the books that he used as references, such as the six primary sources in *hadith*, *al-Targhib wa al-tarhib* (The Encouragement and Discouragement), *'Amal al-yawm wa al-layla* (Rituals for the Day and Night), *al-Rawda* (The Garden of the Seekers) of al-Nawawi, *al-Irshad* (The Guidance), *al-Rawd al-aniq* (The Eloquent Training), al-Samarkandi's book, al-Quti's book *al-Lubab* (The Core), *Sunan al-salikin* (The Ways of the Travellers), *al-Ashwaq fi masarih al-'ushaq* (The Yearning of the Lovers) and the book (title not mentioned) of Ibn al-Khatib.

He alludes to many topics, including *khalwa*, special characteristics of the Prophet, the seeking of knowledge, remedies for ailments of the heart, intermediation, well-known *awliya*, refutation of the claims of some Islamic sects, recommendation of seclusion with Allah, the divisions of the inner self, types of disciplines, the meaning of linguistics, evil scholars and *dajjal*, the realities of *dhikr* and the relationship of love, Allah does not occupy a particular direction,[14] the blameworthiness of arguing, general ethics, interaction with people, the usage of tobacco, corruption, spreading mischief, killing, and doing good towards the family and women and the punishment of those who degrade them.

Kashf al-lubs fi ma bayn al-ruh wa al-nafs

REMOVING THE CONFUSION REGARDING THE DIFFERENCE BETWEEN THE SOUL AND THE INNER SELF

In this 12-chapter manuscript,[15] which was not completed, the shaykh points out that the *nafs* (ego) tries to overwhelm knowledge with ignorance and incompetence and, no matter how hard you try to repel it, the soul or human desires are always able to deceive you. And if you try to perceive and understand it, it defies you by being invisible. The shaykh portrays the *nafs* as a petite body that clings to the limbs, just like water clings to a green plant. He also alludes to the benefits of the *nafs*, the hardness of the heart, cleansing of the outer and inner self, and consciousness of one's self publicly and privately. He states that religion only becomes victorious through the pious *awliya*, and discusses the world of spirits and souls, its strengths and weaknesses, its delicateness and heaviness and how to bring harmony between the two. He explains that sins are to the heart like poison is to the body, causing harm on various levels. Then he uses parables and stories to explain the results of committing sins and the harm it brings. Some of the outcomes of sin are the prevention of the light of knowledge, the prevention of sustenance and obedience, loneliness, difficulty of affairs, darkness in the heart, minimising the lifespan, expulsion of blessings, and baseness and contamination of the intellect. Sins bring about factors of destruction in this world and in the hereafter, as well as the wrath of Allah and cursing by the animals.[16]

Al-Shaykh al-Kabir also speaks about *tawhid* and its divisions, such as the unity of Allah's qualities, names and actions. He extracts all the creeds from the chapter *al-Ikhlas* (Chapter 112 of the Qur'an) and explains the status of spirituality, as well as the great name of Allah. He discusses when the reality of faith is realised in a person, and whether spiritual 'essence' and the nature of a person are physical or abstract.

Then he returns to a discussion on seeking knowledge and things that bring about *taqwa* (consciousness of Allah) consciousness of Allah, things that impede the process of *taqwa*, types of innovations, the heart being the container of every presence, and conditions and ailments of the heart and the limbs. He also discusses in detail division and sectarianism according to *ahl-al-kalam*.

Fiqh al-a'yan fi haqa'iq al-Qur'an
THE SPECIFIC JURISPRUDENCE REGARDING THE REALITIES OF THE QUR'AN

or

Lubb al-albab fi haqa'iq al-sunna wa al-kitab
THE CORE OF ALL CORES REGARDING THE REALITIES OF THE PROPHETIC TRADITION AND THE BOOK

The shaykh wrote this two-volume manuscript[17] after some of his students asked him to clarify the phenomenon of rain clouds, which form part of the hidden things.[18] He responded by adding all realities and precisions required from such a work in clarifying the realities of the rain clouds, rain, lightning, thunder and the land of the unseen, and refuting the ideologies of those who go astray.[19]

In the first volume he embarks on a 245-page discussion of clouds, their meanings, their formation, the time of their formation and people's fears and apprehensions when they don't come in time. Then he speaks about storms and water and their benefits, the *jinn* and their existence, and what is specific to this *umma* regarding the criteria of *hadith* and its narration. He also discusses the similarities between humans and animals, the difference between internal and external waters, different types of earth, types of inspiration, and types of speech (essential, explicit and implicit).

He discusses the stars and what was said about them in the Torah, the 12 towers and their division into 28 stations, every tower having two-and-a-third stations, and these towers are divided into 360 degrees, every tower having 30 degrees that the sun passes once every year and by it an orbit is completed, and the moon completes a cycle in 28 days, and why they are called towers.[20] He also speaks about the bee and how nectar is used, as well as about the objectives of the Qur'an and the sciences extracted from it.

In the second volume of 467 pages he concentrates on the rights of scholars, their high positions, their different types and levels and what their rights are as well as their duties and obligations. Then he speaks about the striving of the inner self and what the seeker is in need of, the conditions of desire and its obstacles, fear and hope and its realities, what affords the seeker true perception and what takes it away from him, the ailment of self-appraisal, enlightenment, obstacles and strategising in the repelling of Satan, taste and its meaning, the difference between love and intimacy, the virtue of travelling, prophetic medicine, the principles of virtue and interest, fairness towards spouses, the wisdom of neglecting the two meanings of *al-Ikhlas* and the causes that inspire writing.

Al-Burad al-muwasha fi qat' al-matami wa al-rusha

THE EMBELLISHED GARMENTS IN THE ERADICATION OF GREED AND CORRUPTION

This manuscript[21] consists of two volumes. In the introduction to the first volume the shaykh points out the reason for writing the work. He then starts by speaking about two litigants who appear in front of a judge; the second litigant has no evidence. The judge passes a verdict while his eyes are – metaphorically – tightly shut against the facts. The shaykh then goes on to describe types of bribery, the person who pays it, the one who accepts it and its danger to society; the judiciary and what the responsibility of the community is when a judge is unjust; trust keeping and what it entails; ignorance; the prohibition against plundering; giving gifts to witnesses; and the four conditions pertaining to appearing in front of a judge: equality between the two litigants; equality in intention, stopping greed that is current and that can occur in the future; and making a firm decision. Some narrations mention a fifth condition (which is unknown).

He also discusses the principle of *halal*; the prohibition against consuming people's wealth wrongfully; the reality of *fiqh*; charging a fee for work done; justice and its conditions; innovations; types of intuition; the role played by the heads of a tribe in a community; mocking religious ordainments such as usury;[22] acceding to oppression; taking bribes; fanaticism and deceit; breaking or violating trust; the consequences of certain calamities, especially the calamity of fanaticism that may destroy a village. Here he explains that Allah gave a dispensation for everything except four things: *dhikr*; fulfilling a trust; justice; and honouring agreements. He discusses this extensively, so much so that he goes into a discussion of certain doubtful areas such as the use of tobacco. Then he discusses involvement with that which is abominable; attaching importance to responsibility; taking care of subordinates; the just ruler and calamities that can be anticipated when a ruler is unjust; protecting the youth by establishing workshops for artisanship; showing compassion to all creation; and punishments and beating.

In the second volume he discusses what is recommended for rulers, leaders, governors and judges; electing ministers; affording good, sincere advice and counselling; and having good employees who are pious and truthful. Then he discusses the crime of false testimony and different trades such as tailoring, agriculture, horsemanship, well digging, script copying, metal work, weaving, butchery and tanning. A discussion follows on the acquisition of wealth and its importance; what is necessary for the seeker of knowledge; exceeding the bounds during debates; an encouragement of travelling in the quest for knowledge; the virtue of listening to *hadith*, and being in the company of scholars and honouring and respecting them; the virtue of knowledge and remembrance of Allah; piety in religion; deceit in religion and swearing a false oath; usury and contracts; that which causes the contamination of the intellect; that which leads to failure; good character, charity and its acceptance; saving the one who wants to destroy; consequences of affording a guarantee; to hit a woman means to do so with a handkerchief and not with a stick; marital rights; *halal*; and *haram*, which is built upon two things: filth and corruption.

Kashf al-niqab al-asrar fatiha al-kitab

THE UNVEILING OF THE MASK PERTAINING TO THE SECRETS OF THE OPENING CHAPTER OF THE BOOK (THE QUR'AN)

This manuscript[23] discusses *sura al-fatiha* (Chapter 1 of the Qur'an) – what it contains, its titles, its disciplines, sciences extracted from it, and so on. The shaykh explains that *sura al-fatiha* consists of various subjects such as *tawhid*, the greatness of the names and qualities of Allah, the secrets of the letters,[24] special features of the names and shapes in the Qur'an, historical knowledge and legal rulings. Then he discusses the *fatiha* and its correct articulation in detail: truthfulness and its signs; confronting Satan and his assistants; the best charity is the charity of water; discussion on usury; ignorance is the gravest sin; the rights of relatives; the meaning of worship; praiseworthy and blameworthy innovations; the meaning of success; humility in prayer; humility of the limbs; and a chapter on what is indicated in the *fatiha* pertaining to the names of Allah.

Fath al-wadud fi sharh al-maqsur wa al-mamdud

THE AID OF THE BELOVED IN ELUCIDATING THE SHORTENED AND THE LENGTHENED POEM

This manuscript[25] is a commentary on the poetic treatise *al-Maqsur wa al-mamdud* (The Shortened and the Lengthened Poem), written by Imam Muhammad ibn Malik, author of the well-known *al-Alfiyya* (The One Thousand), a didactic poem with 1 000 couplets on Arabic grammar. The poem consists of 157 verses without any introduction. It is an unusual and profound poem, each verse consisting of four words, two with short vowels and two with long vowels. All the words have a similar pronunciation but different meanings. It is eloquently written and structured and contains deep Sufi thoughts – only those who are deeply rooted in the Arabic language and its literary styles will be able to interact with this poem.

Shaykh Sayyid al-Mukhtar mentions the following in the introduction to his commentary on *al-Maqsur wa al-mamdud*:

> With the praise of Allah and His assistance in accomplishing our objectives, the book *al-Maqsur wa al-mamdud* has increased in beauty and splendor with this

commentary, because I have surpassed its order in a way that my ocean covers his river, my fruits overwhelm his flowers, though we are in different eras, him having the virtue of precedence and I having the advantage of following [many other scholars]...And I have added to his book verses of revelation, I have beautified it with the strangeness of the language, I have brought forth in it great admonitions, strange questions, stories of notables, notes on literature and poets, stories of the prophets and saints, issues such as staying away from oppression and hatred and the calamities they cause, encouragements and discouragements, strange legal issues, rational theories...So it became sweeter than honey...

The manuscript was completed in 1786 and contains approximately 200 pages. It was printed for the first time in the kingdom of Saudi Arabia and edited by Dr Mamun Muhammad Ahmad.[26]

Al-'Ilm al-nafi'

THE BENEFICIAL KNOWLEDGE

This manuscript[27] speaks about the conditions of the heart; devotion to *dhikr*, benefits and types of *dhikr*; honouring agreements; the benefits of advice; intention; gratitude; the actions of the limbs;[28] the consequences of bad character; a discussion of the prophetic saying 'Religion is advice'; and the grand status of the saints.

Jadhwah al-anwar fi al-dhabb al-manasib awliya Allah al-akhyar

ILLUMINATION ON REFRAINING FROM DISRESPECTING THE STATIONS OF THE CLOSEST FRIENDS OF ALLAH

This manuscript[29] is a refutation of al-Mukhtar ibn Bawn Sahib al-Ihmirar, who rejected the miracles of the saints (the shaykh had also refuted Ibn Bawn in several other poems before he wrote this manuscript[30]). The manuscript looks critically at the reality of a friend of Allah (a saint), who he is, how he became a saint, the saint's miracles, and the difference between these unusual events and *istidraj* (something unusual committed by a sinful person). The manuscript contains many examples of the miracles of the prophets and the companions, and the shaykh gives an in-depth explanation of these using Qur'anic proofs, prophetic statements and convincing Sufi expressions. It is worth mentioning that he was able to convince Ibn Bawn to such an extent that the two of them exchanged brotherly letters and poems of love. Ibn Bawn repented and took back everything he had rejected pertaining to the miracles of the saints.

Nuzhah al-rawi wa bughyah al-hawi

THE WALK OF THE NARRATOR AND THE DESIRE OF THE CHARMER

This is a very valuable manuscript[31] about *tawhid* and prophetic history. It deals with the following topics: the oneness of Allah and understanding this without exaggeration or negligence; the beginning of time; astronomy; the birth of the Prophet; the beginning of revelation and the night journey (*al-isra'*); the special features given to the Prophet above all other prophets regarding the unseen world from the time that he became a prophet until the final hour, that is, the end of time;[32] the miracles that he shared with all other prophets; that which is specifically for him in bringing together all aspects and positions of previous religions;[33] information regarding the monks, priests, fortune-tellers, bad *jinns* and glad tidings; information about the nearness of his prophethood and birth to the end of time; explanations of *halal*, *haram* and *shubha*; paradise and hell; divine wisdoms and prophetic expressions; medicines for the heart and body from plants, minerals and gems; the Prophet's special features and his *umma*; the non-prophet status of the sons of Ya'qub except for Yusuf; the Prophet's acts of worship; the beginning of the holy sanctuary, its sanctity, status and some of the traces of its inhabitants; the virtue of Medina and of the companions; ethics, advice and *tasawwuf*.

It is worth noting that in this manuscript Shaykh Sayyid al-Mukhtar al-Kunti summarised an entire library in one volume.

The commentary on *al-Maqsur wa al-mamdud* is eloquently written and structured – only those who are deeply rooted in the Arabic language and its literary styles are able to fully interact with this poem.

Al-Nasiha al-shafiya al-kafiya

THE CURING AND COMPREHENSIVE ADVICE

This manuscript[34] – in the handwriting of Nuh ibn al-Tahir and his brother – discusses the following topics: admonitions; guidance; cleanliness; beautifying and showing compassion to the self; sincerity; complete covenants; people of patience and righteousness at the time of a calamity; honouring agreements; brotherhood in Islam; types of bounties; extravagance; eagerness; moderation; guiding the foolish; goodness toward neighbours; the reality and etiquette of supplication; the danger of free mixing between men and women; miserliness; the unjust ruler; the sin of a scholar; seeking of knowledge; the importance of the remembrance of Allah; an explanation of how Allah mentioned the five daily prayers in a single verse (Qur'an 30: 17–18: Glory be to Allah when you enter into the night and into the morning…); and Allah's greatest name.

Al-Irshad fi masalih al-'ibad

THE GUIDANCE IN THE INTEREST OF THE SERVANTS (OF ALLAH)

This two-volume manuscript[35] admonishes and reminds religious fanatics of the truth and refutes those who brand Muslims as unbelievers. It also includes information on the different religious sects and alludes to numerous arguments between these sects.

Al-Kawkab al-waqqad fi dhikr al-mashayikh wa haqa'iq al-awrad

THE PIERCING STAR IN MENTIONING OF THE SCHOLARS AND THE REALITIES OF THE LITANIES

This manuscript[36] explains the meaning of a *wird* and its linguistic and technical origin, discusses revelation and inspiration, and presents proof that shows that the litanies are taken from the Qur'an and prophetic statements. Other topics covered are: supplication and its etiquette; the miracles of the saints; honouring and respecting scholars, and the conditions for becoming a scholar; the reality of light, fear and hope taken from his book *Nudar al-dhahab*; the origin of midnight prayers (*tahajjud*); the signs of sainthood; an explanation of the word *shaytana* (to acquire Satanic qualities); the distinction between the Satan of *jinn* and Satan of mankind; the difference between the knowledge of the worshipper and that of the Worshipped; issues regarding the remembrance of Allah, its times, its abridgement, what must be done if it is missed, adding to it and what to do if the time is too short to perform it; the difference between the person who negates and what is being negated; the difference between the one whom Allah grants completion in knowledge and action, and acting without knowledge;[37] neglecting the self; the meaning of *al-huyuli* (Greek philosophical term for matter); prophetic traditions and their interpretation; and prophetic supplications for certain occasions. He ended the manuscript with accounts of the prophets and pious scholars.

Al-Tadhyil al-jalil al-'adim al-mathil

THE GRAND APPENDIX AND THE IDEAL NON-EXISTENCE

This manuscript[38] describes a shaykh who guides (*al-murabbi* – the spiritual master who initiates and guides the seeker into the spiritual path and quest). It is very similar to *al-Kawkab al-waqqad*, and is in fact found as an attachment to that manuscript.

Ajwiba Labat

THE RESPONSE OF LABAT

One copy of this manuscript[39] can be found at the Ahmed Baba Institute; another is held by al-Sayyid Bad ibn Muhammad al-Kunti in Amkawal. The manuscript is also called *al-Ajwiba al-Labatiyya* (The Labati Responses/Answers). It contains answers to some questions that were posed by his student Shaykh Labat, and gives information about kinds of medicine and medicines suitable for specific ailments, the virtue of marriage, the etiquette of husband and wife, the evil person, predestination, remembrance and its etiquette, the ruling of some thoughts of the heart (i.e. how one will be judged for one's secret thoughts), the etiquette of a follower (*murid*), the virtue of knowledge, trust in Allah and perseverance.

Nafh al-tib fi al-salah 'ala al-nabi al-habib

THE PERFUMED FRAGRANCE OF SALUTATIONS TO THE BELOVED PROPHET

This manuscript[40] contains numerous formulas of salutation on the Prophet. The shaykh's son wrote a commentary on this manuscript which he named *al-Rawd al-khasib fi sharh nafh al-tib* (The Fertile Garden on the Elucidation of the Perfumed Fragrance). The commentary was published a few years ago (exact date unknown) by Bamawi ibn Alfa Mawi al-Jinnawi, principal of the school in Bobojolaso.

Sullam al-ridwan bi dhawq halawa al-iman

THE LADDER OF SATISFACTION IN TASTING THE SWEETNESS OF FAITH

This manuscript[41] contains answers concerning the ethics of the teacher and of teaching and learning. It also discusses these topics: the words of the Qur'an; that which the teacher instructs the student pertaining to cleanliness, prayer, names (such as the names of the months); the ruling of dry ablution used for the recital of the Qur'an;[42] and the ruling on following the actions of a scholar. The shaykh explains that it is permissible for a legally responsible adult to leave off the learning of the individual obligations[43] only in order to learn the Qur'an, and then discusses the prophetic saying, 'There is no prayer for the neighbour of the mosque except in the mosque.'

Qasida fi al-nasiha wa al-irshad wa al-tawassul

POEM ON ADVICE AND GUIDANCE AND INTERMEDIATION

This manuscript[44] consists of a poem of approximately 304 verses. In it the shaykh mentions the names of some of the prophets, saints and pious people and their effects. He uses them as intermediaries to Allah. The poem starts like this:

> Is it from His secret towards the callers that He moves,
> Be kind to us and replace the difficulty with ease,

And ends like this:

> So ask Allah for His assistance towards god-consciousness,
> And for the flock that You have made our responsibility of freeman or slave,
> Then the salutations of Allah and His peace,
> Upon the selected one, the chosen of all people.

Al-Ajwiba al-muhimma liman lahu bi 'amr al-din himma

THE IMPORTANT ANSWERS FOR THE ONE WHO ATTACHES IMPORTANCE TO THE ISSUES OF RELIGION

This manuscript[45] is different to the other legal works because it is not arranged according to the chapters of Islamic law, as was the norm. It covers approximately 45 issues pertaining to education, the acquisition of wealth, marriage, teaching, the etiquette of a man towards his household, the reality of brotherhood, ascetism, paying alms, the judiciary, leadership, laws of commerce, advanced trade, seclusion, supplication of decision,[46] the status of the purity of the water that comes from a well and other important issues.

Other titles at the Ahmed Baba Institute

The following titles may also be of interest to researchers:[47]

- *al-Mir'ah al-maymuna* (The Blessed Mirror).
- *Matiyya al-khalas fi kalima al-ikhlas fi sha'n al-mu'allim wa al-muta'alli* (The Tools of Deliverance in a Sincere Word in the Relationship of Student and Teacher).
- *Manzuma li asma Allah al-husna* (A Didactic Poem on the Beautiful Names of Allah). This poem is *lamiyya*, each verse ending with the letter lam.
- *Maqala fi al-awliya wa karamatihim* (An Essay Regarding Saints and their Miracles).
- *Manzuma fi al-dhat al-ilahiyya* (A Didactic Poem on the Divine Essence). Many scholars have written commentaries on this poem.
- *Fatwa fi al-amwal al-ma'khudha min al-lusus wa al-muharibin* (Fatwa on Wealth Taken from Thieves and Combatants).
- *Manzuma fi madh al-Suqiyyin* (A Poem in Praise of the Suqiyyin [a tribe]).
- *Manzuma fi madh 'ashiratihi wa al-difa' anha* (Poem in Praise and Defence of his Clan).
- *Fatwa fi sha'n al-damm al-mustaqirr fi al-jawf ba'd al-dhabh* (Fatwa on Blood that Remains Inside an Animal After its Slaughter).
- *Manzuma fi al-istisqa'* (Didactic Poem on Praying for Rain).
- *al-Muthallath al-Kunti* (The Kunti Triangle). This triangle – an esoteric triangle used in Islamic numerology/astrology – was commented upon by Shaykh Sayyid Muhammad al-Kunti, who is also the compiler.
- *al-Manzuma al-musamma bi al-siham al-musaddada* (A Didactic Poem Called the Accurate Arrows). This is a very useful supplication as a defence against enemies.
- *Qasida sard al-masaha* (title not translatable into English). Some say this poem is by Shaykh Sayyid Muhammad.
- *Qasida li al-shaykh Sayyid al-Mukhtar al-Kunti fi al-wa'z wa al-irshad wa tarbiya al-awlad wa huquq al-azwaj* (A Poem of Sayyid al-Mukhtar al-Kunti Pertaining to Advice, Guidance, Rearing of Children and the Rights of Spouses). Its beginning reads: 'When will you wake up and your heart is disillusioned? And you will gain in years and months.'
- *al-Jadwal al-Kunti fi al-fa'l bi istikhraj al-ayat al-qur'aniyya* (The Kunti Table of Luck Through an Extraction of Certain Qur'anic Verses). This is a table consisting of 12 columns and rows. Six Qur'anic verses are placed in it and they are used in *istikhara*. Another table consisting of 12 columns and rows is also used for the placement of Qur'anic verses or messages that will guide you.[48]
- *al-Ism al-a'zam* (The Greatest Name [of Allah]). He taught and dictated this manuscript to his son Shaykh Sayyid Muhammad ibn Shaykh Sayyid al-Mukhtar al-Kunti. The manuscript is about the sublime position of the most sublime name of God, namely Allah.
- *Fadl al-kilab 'ala akthar mimman yalbas al-thiyab* (The Preference of Dogs Above Most of Those Who Wear Clothes i.e. humans) I haven't seen this manuscript, but

its title has been mentioned in various oral reports. According to these reports, the manuscript contains a discussion about dogs. It claims the dog is a very tame and friendly animal and it shows this through its different movements, aimed at acquiring friendship and love. It is also known for its loyalty and protectiveness. It amuses people with its bark and people become afraid of it.

The successful preservation and protection of these manuscripts cannot take place unless attention is given to the cultural, educational and administrative aspects related to their safeguarding. Cultural centres and manuscript libraries need to be equipped with the necessary resources and staff in these centres should receive continuous training. The preservation of these manuscripts will be to the benefit of the whole world.

Letter held by Muhammad Ould Ham

Risalah min al-shaykh Sayyid al-Mukhtar ila tilmidhihi Nuh ibn Tahir al-fullani (Letter from Shaykh Sayyid al-Mukhtar to his student Nuh ibn Tahir the Fullani) is in the collection of Muhammad Ould Ham in Amman. It consists of advice and reconciliation between him and Ahmad ibn Muhammad Lubbu.

Titles held by Bad ibn Muhammad al-Kunti

The following manuscripts are in the possession of the family of Bad ibn Muhammad al-Kunti in northern Bram in Amkawal:

- *Zawal al-ilbas fi tard al-waswas al-khannas* (The Dissipation of Confusion Through the Chasing Away of the Devil's Whispering).
- *al-Qasida al-jami'a bayn al-shari'a wa al-haqiqa* (The All-Encompassing Poem on [a Juxtaposition] between the Law and Reality).
- *Risala min al-shaykh Sayyid al-Mukhtar fi ikhmad al-fitan bayn al-qaba'il* (A Treatise of Shaykh Sayyid al-Mukhtar in Extinguishing the Infighting Between the Tribes).

Titles held by Bubakr ould Hammad

The following manuscripts are in the possession of Bubakr Wuld Hammad in Akmahur, northern Baran:

- *Wasiyyah li al-shaykh Sayyid al-Mukhtar fi ahwal taqallub al-zaman* (Exhortation by Shaykh Sayyid al-Mukhtar on the [Adverse] Conditions of the Vicissitudes of Changing Times).
- *Khitaf al-ghawwas fi lujaj al-makr li al-khawwas wa 'irfas 'iras al-dukhrus al-'usnus al-akhyas al-ruqas wa hays bays 'ala maslub al-naja wa mukharmis al-kharnus 'an thalb awliya Allah dhi al-makri wa al-adha* (this title speaks of a treatise in defence of the saints and refutes those who try to harm or disrespect them). Interpretation: *al-'iras* – unstable difference, *al-dukhrus* – the one who enters, *al-'usnus* – the weak, *al-akhyas* – a goat with a broken horn, *hays bays* – it is said of someone who tries to narrow a path or opportunity, *al-mukharmis* – the one who dismisses, *al-kharnus* – baby swine. Only the first page of this manuscript is in the possession of Bubakr Ould Hammad. It is said that the manuscript belongs to Shaykh Sayyid al-Mukhtar al-Kunti, and also that it is written in Spanish.

Conclusion

In summary, the works of this great scholar and wise man are important not least because of the extensive variety of subjects they address. However, many of these valuable works are being neglected and exposed to destructive conditions. In some cases, different sections of the same manuscript are held by different people in different places.

The successful preservation and protection of these manuscripts cannot take place unless attention is given to the cultural, educational and administrative aspects related to their safeguarding. Cultural centres and manuscript libraries need to be equipped with the necessary resources and staff in these centres should receive continuous training. The preservation of these manuscripts will be to the benefit of the whole world.

NOTES

1 Translated from Arabic by Ebrahiem Moos and Mohamed Shaid Mathee.

2 External sciences, i.e. the exoteric; internal sciences, i.e. the esoteric sciences (spirituality, gnosticism, etc.).

3 Unpublished and uncatalogued manuscript in the Mamma Haidara Library.

4 Unpublished and uncatalogued manuscript in the Ahmed Baba Institute.

5 Unpublished and uncatalogued manuscript in the Ahmed Baba Institute.

6 Unpublished and uncatalogued manuscript in the Ahmed Baba Institute.

7 Manuscript number 415 at the Ahmed Baba Institute and number 515 at the Mamma Haidara Library.

8 *Al-Minna fi i'tiqad ahl al-sunna*, manuscript number 415 at the Ahmed Baba Institute and number 515 at the Mamma Haidara Library.

9 Chapter 2 Verse 255 of the Qur'an, a very famous verse often recited by Muslims.

10 Najran was a city in Yemen in southern Arabia. The people were called Bani Najran (children of Najran). They were Christians with whom the Prophet Muhammad debated regarding the nature of Jesus and the oneness of Allah.

11 *Ridwan* means satisfaction; Allah was satisfied with the believers for swearing this allegiance with the Prophet (see Qur'an 48: 18).

12 Manuscript number 500 at the Ahmed Baba Institute.

13 Manuscript number 1657 at the Ahmed Baba Institute and number 137 at the Mamma Haidara Library.

14 Allah does not take up space or place, i.e the debate whether God is in a particular space or place cannot be attributed to him since this is a quality of created beings and not the creator.

15 Manuscript number 3616 at the Ahmed Baba Institute.

16 God and animals curse the sinner; all creatures despise a person who sins and disobeys the commands of his Lord.

17 Manuscript number 2854 at the Ahmed Baba Institute.

18 The functioning of the clouds and how they work is not fully comprehended by humans; it is one of the secrets of Allah.

19 Meaning those disbelievers or sceptics who deny or doubt God's power to bring the clouds and therefore rain, especially because Timbuktu is a semi-desert/desert area.

20 This is a complex concept in Islamic astronomy/astrology.

21 The first volume is recorded under manuscript number 10215 and the second volume under number 10216, both at the Ahmed Baba Institute.

22 Meaning those who regard interest on money loaned as permissible. In Islam interest is an abomination and totally forbidden.

23 Manuscript numbers 10222-1418-1699-2479 at the Ahmed Baba Institute and number 4550 at the Mamma Haidara Library.

24 The letters of the alphabet; all have special spiritual features and secrets.

25 Manuscript number 2035 at the Ahmed Baba Institute and number 562 at the Mamma Haidara Library.

26 Publication details for this book are unknown.

27 Manuscript number 10219 at the Ahmed Baba Institute.

28 All those actions that involve your limbs, such as using your hands in prayer or to hit someone, your tongue in speaking good things or for slandering someone, etc.

29 Manuscript number 3111 at the Mamma Haidara Library (also held at the Ahmed Baba Institute).

30 One of the poems is listed under number 2046 at the Ahmed Baba Institute and another important essay on the miracles of the saints under number 2284.

31 Manuscript number 3076 at the Mamma Haidara Library (as above).

32 God granted Prophet Muhammad certain special gifts not given to the rest of the prophets, such as the night journey into heaven and standing in God's celestial court.

33 Islam is the final religion; all other religions are subsumed under Islam.

34 Manuscript number 1538 at the Ahmed Baba Institute.

35 The first volume is recorded under manuscript number 1834 and the second volume under number 1835, both at the Ahmed Baba Institute.

36 Manuscript number 1608 at the Ahmed Baba Institute.

37 One may have knowledge and not act on it and, in contrast, one may do things without knowledge.

38 Manuscript number 1805 at the Ahmed Baba Institute.

39 Manuscript number 1258 at the Ahmed Baba Institute.

40 Manuscript numbers 1607 and 1614 at the Ahmed Baba Institute.

41 Manuscript number 713 at the Ahmed Baba Institute.

42 In the absence of water, ablution is made with dust.

43 Things that every individual is personally required to know and enact.

44 Manuscript number 338 at the Ahmed Baba Institute.

45 *Al-Ajwiba al-muhimma liman lahu bi 'amr al-din himma*, manuscript number 1093 at the Mamma Haidara Library.

46 A prayer that is made before making any important decision in one's life, thereby seeking God's guidance.

47 *Al-Mira al-maymuna*, manuscript number 1814; *Matiyya al-khalas fi kalima al-ikhlas fi sha'n al-mu'allim wa al-muta'allim*, manuscript number 1821; *Manzuma li asma Allah al-husna*, manuscript number 1254; *Maqala fi al-awliya wa karamatihim*, manuscript number 2284; *Manzuma fi al-dhat al-ilahiyya*, manuscript number 2983; *Fatwa fi al-amwal al-ma'khudha min al-lusus wa al-muharibin*, manuscript number 2716; *Manzuma fi madh al-Suqiyyin*, manuscript number 2649; *Manzuma fi madh 'ashiratihi wa al-difa' 'anha*, manuscript number 1752; *Fatwa fi sha'n al-damm al-mustaqirr fi al-jawf ba'd al-dhabh*, manuscript number 1766; *Manzuma fi al-istisqa'*, manuscript number 2372; *al-Muthallath al-Kunti*, manuscript number 9590; *al-Manzuma al-musamma bi al-siham al-musaddada*, manuscript number 2349; *Qasida sard al-masaha*, manuscript number 2701; *Qasida li al-shaykh Sayyid al-Mukhtar al-Kunti fi al-wa'z wa al-irshad wa tarbiya al-awlad wa huquq al-azwaj*, manuscript number 4888; *al-Jadwal al-Kunti fi al-fa'l bistikhraj al-ayat al-qur'aniyya*, uncatalogued, author's own; *al-Ism al-a'zam*, manuscript number 413.

48 Through consulting these verses that speak of happiness and paradise or that speak of God's punishment and hell, one will get an order or advice regarding how to proceed with doing something (such as a job) or to desist from doing it.

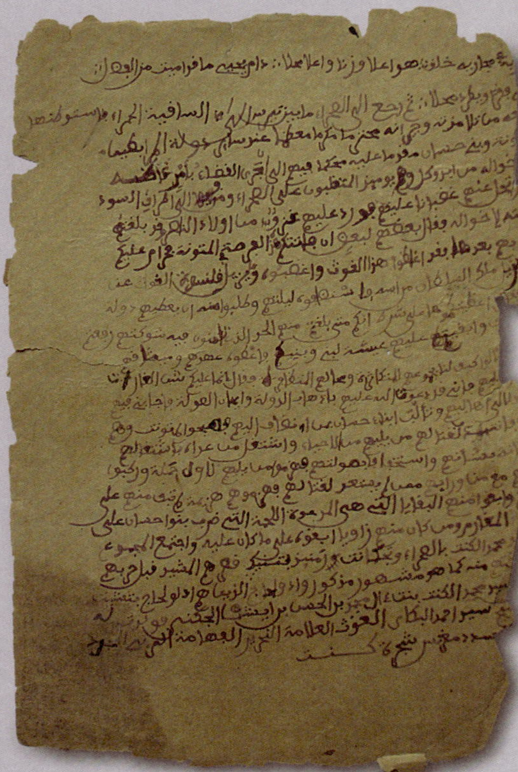

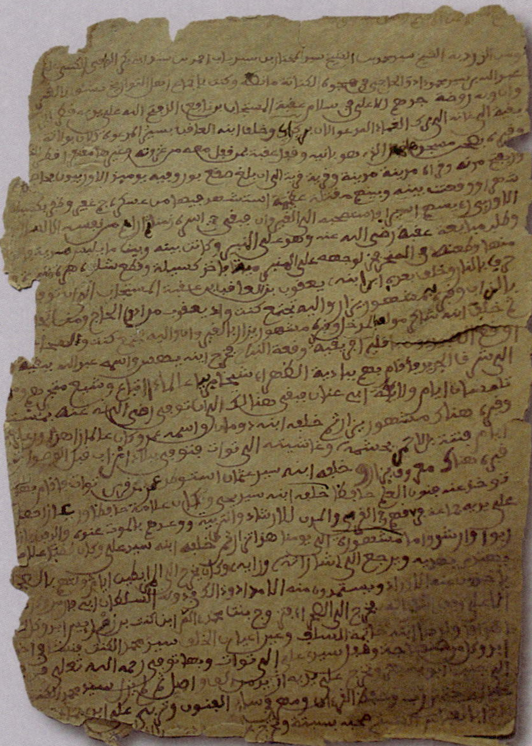

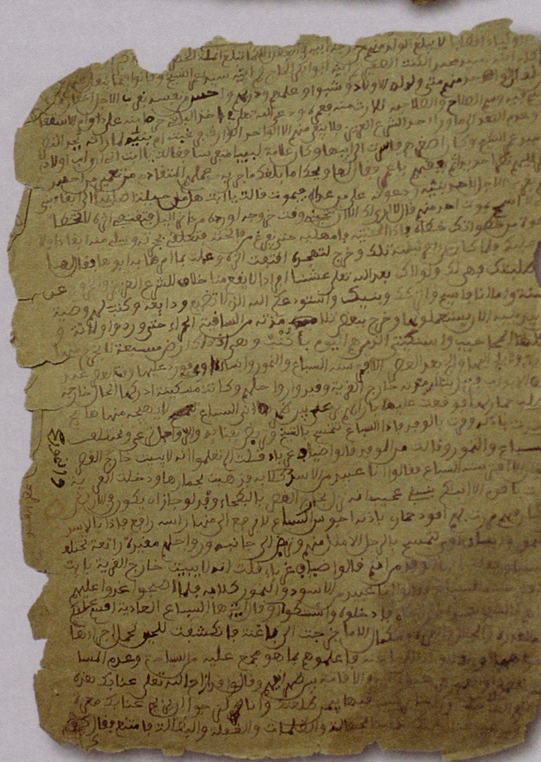

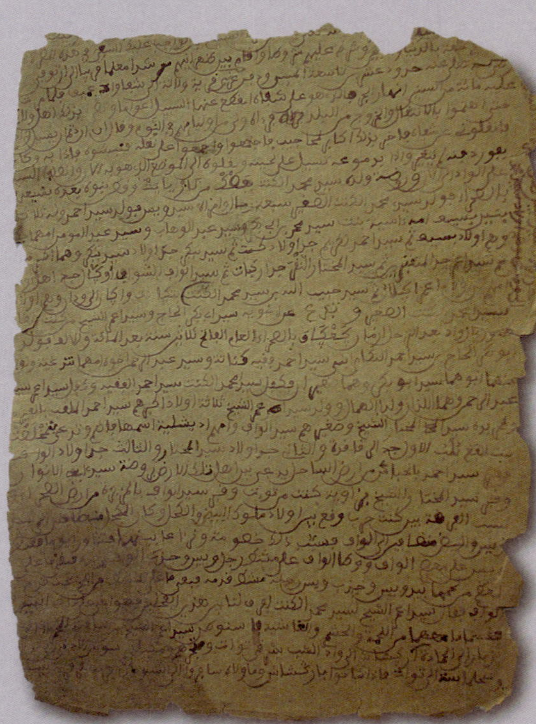

CHAPTER 15

A man of letters in Timbuktu: al-Shaykh Sidi Muhammad al-Kunti

Abdel Wedoud Ould Cheikh[1]

Shaykh Sidi Muhammad left behind a considerable number of writings that have largely remained unpublished, most of which consist of his many letters offering theological and political advice to the leaders of his day.

As has become clear in Chapters 13 and 14, the Arabophone *qabila* (tribe) of the Kunta were present from at least the sixteenth century in a large section of the western and Central Sahara – from the Wadi Dar'a region in Morocco to the Taganit in Mauritania, and from the Al Tuwat in Algeria to the upper Niger River basin – and played a significant role in the religious, economic and political history of Timbuktu and its hinterland.

The Kunta, largely involved in trans-Saharan trade (they controlled the Idjil saltworks in Mauritania[2]), were a strong presence in caravans circulating between Taoudenni, Arawan and Timbuktu.[3] Due to their mobility, they were essential in the transmission of the propagation of the Qadiriyya brotherhoods throughout the Sahelo–Sahara, having been involved in a large number of regional 'tribal' and 'political' conflicts. The Kunta were spiritual mentors, chaplains and mediators to the principal groups (Tuaregs, Peuls, Arma, Moors) involved to various extents in the public biography of Timbuktu, and even appeared to exercise a quasi-sovereignty (at least spiritual) over the city at the time of Sidi Ahmad al-Bakkay (d.1866). Between Sidi Ahmad al-Bakkay and his grandfather, al-Shaykh Sidi al-Mukhtar (d.1811) – the true initiator of Kunta 'wealth' in the Timbuktu region – was al-Shaykh Sidi Muhammad (d.1826), the father of al-Bakkay and chronicler of the family.

Shaykh Sidi Muhammad left behind a considerable number of writings that have largely remained unpublished, even if they nourished many works devoted to the religious and political history of the region.[4] To my knowledge, the only fairly significant university work written about him is the doctoral thesis presented in 1977 by Abdallah wuld Mawlud wuld Daddah, at the Université de Paris-IV Sorbonne.[5]

In this chapter, I will first provide a brief overview of the Kunta and then deal more specifically with the religious, intellectual and political role of Shaykh Sidi

Muhammad, whose influence was widespread in Timbuktu and its region, extending from the Atlantic to the Chad–Nigerian borders in the east and from the Wadi Dar'a and the Touat in the north to the depths of the African Sahel.

The Kunta and Timbuktu

The earliest written references that we have of the Kunta and of their presence in north-west Africa date back to the middle of the fifteenth century,[6] but the traditions of this Saharan tribe endeavour to connect it with a distant and prestigious Arabic origin, specifically the descendants of 'Uqba ibn Nafi' al-Fihri.[7]

An epistle written by Shaykh Sidi Muhammad in 1824 called *al-Risala al-ghallawiyya* provides a kind of reference 'visiting card' of the Kunta, describing their genealogy, their historical journey across the whole of the western Sahara and their division. We also find scattered and widespread details on the history and genealogical organisation of this *qabila* in various other sources: other texts of Sidi Muhammad (in particular in his *Kitab al-tara'if* [The Book of the Rare (Knowledge)] which will be dealt with further on, as well as in his many letters), those of his father Sidi al-Mukhtar (*Kitab al-minna* [The Book of the Accomplished Desire]), and even in the writings of their disciples.[8]

Let us briefly summarise the account provided by *al-Risala al-ghallawiyya*, without being overly concerned about the uncertainties and contradictions affecting its historical content. The important thing is that it provides the foundations of legitimacy, the 'explanation' of the genealogical and geographic subdivisions of the Kunta and the journey that led a large number of them to settle in the hinterland of Timbuktu.

According to *al-Ghallawiyya* the Kunta had a single ancestor, 'Uqba ibn Nafi', the Muslim conqueror of North Africa and the founder of Qayrawan. Still according to this source, 'Uqba conquered Ghana and seized the town of Biru – the future Walata, well-known centre of trans-Saharan trade and one-time rival of Timbuktu – where two major ancestors of the Kunta were buried (al-'Aqib, son of 'Uqba, and Sidi Ahmad al-Bakkay al-Kabir). The Tuwat is presented as an essential point of reference in the movement south-west of the ancestors of the Kunta. *Al-Ghallawiyya* repeatedly cites the tombs of the Kunta's ancestors along their journey until the tomb of Sidi Muhammad al-Kunti al-Kabir, who was buried, according to this account, in Fask in the north-west of present-day Mauritania. It seems that it is from Sidi Muhammad al-Kunti al-Kabir that the *qabila* gets its name (Kunta), which he owes to his maternal grand-father – Alam b. Kunt – from the Sanhaja tribe of the Abdukkil to which the name 'Kunt' belonged.

It is nonetheless from Sidi Muhammad al-Kunti al-Kabir, and mainly from his son, Sidi Ahmad al-Bakkay, whose death is recorded in the epistle of Shaykh Sidi Muhammad as being in 920 *hijra* (about 1514), that the story of the Kunta began to shift from myth to plausible genealogical and factual consideration.

The three sons of Sidi Ahmad al-Bakkay – Sidi 'Umar al-Shaykh, Sidi Muhammad al-Kunti al-Saghir, Sidi Abu Bakr al-Haj – are given as the basis for the entire geological structure of the Kunta.[9] The same account tells us that from the beginning of the eighteenth century a territorial separation came between the descendants of Sidi Muhammad al-Kunti al-Saghir, the Kunta ancestor in the west who settled in the Taganit, Agan and Adrar in Mauritania, and the Kunta of the Azawad, who mostly came from Sidi 'Umar al-Shaykh.

The reason given by Shaykh Sidi Muhammad[10] for this separation was a conflict which broke out between the Awlad Malluk al-Bid and the Awlad Malluk al-Kihil and which gradually mobilised the whole tribe into two rival groups around Sidi Ways, the son of Sidi Muhammad al-Kunti al-Saghir (ancestor of the Awlad Bu-Sayf), and Sidi al-Wafi, the son of Sidi 'Umar al-Shaykh (ancestor of the Awlad al-Wafi, to which Shaykh Sidi Muhammad belonged, hence the *nisba* of 'al-Wafi'[11] he sometimes gave himself).

For fear that the rivalry between these two camps would degenerate into a civil war with unforeseeable consequences, a territorial divide was decided upon. 'Sidi 'Umar al-Shaykh and his descendants travelled from the Sagya al-Hamra' and its Atlantic shore (Zbar) to the Hmada and to the Argshash, as far as Wadi al-Shabb in the east of Tuwat. They devoted themselves to trade in the lower Sus, the Dar'a and the Tuwat as far as Sijilmasa. When they settled in the Argshash and its vicinity, they organised caravans to the country of the blacks (*al-sudan*), some of them going to Timbuktu and to the 'black Sudan' (*al-sudan al-kihil*): Katsina, Gobir and Hausa.[12] The descendants of Sidi Muhammad al-Kunti al-Saghir settled around the southern border of the Sagya al-Hamra', in Tiris and in the Adrar, as far as the Taganit and the Agan.

The Kunta of the east, particularly the Awlad al-Wafi to which the family of Shaykh Sidi Muhammad belonged, were naturally the most directly involved in the economic, cultural and political life of Timbuktu, even if on the surface the movement of the tribal '*asabiyya* networks and their interweaving quickly spread alliances, enmities and exchanges throughout the Kunta world wherever its Saharan fabric was involved. The spread of the economic and religious influence of the Kunta within the hinterland of Timbuktu, and their increasing hold over the trade of salt from Taoudenni, did not fail to produce clashes. The 'diplomatic' ability of the initiators of their regional wealth – Sidi al-Mukhtar, Sidi Muhammad, al-Bakkay – which was mostly based on their 'scientific' and religious authority, enabled them to successfully face their adversaries. Committed to defending the interests of their close community and to preserving what they believed to be the good of the whole Muslim *umma*, the shaykhs of the Kunta also deployed a large-scale activity of intercession and mediation within the groups which exercised some form of influence in the region of Timbuktu and in both its nearby and remote hinterland.

Having mostly been educated in Tuareg camps and introduced to the Qadiriyya by a noteworthy religious scholar belonging to this community (Sidi 'Ali b. al-Najib[13]), Shaykh Sidi al-Mukhtar, and his son Sidi Muhammad after him, also became involved

A contemporary Tuareg man preparing tea outside his tent. The Kunta were spiritual mentors, chaplains and mediators to the Tuaregs, Peuls, Arma and Moors, all the principal groups involved in the biography of Timbuktu.

in the internal affairs of the Tuaregs (intertribal wars, inheritance disputes, etc.), as well as in their relationship with Timbuktu and with the groups that had formed part of its history, especially the Arma–Songhay and the Peuls.

The Tadmakkat Tuaregs were held in a position of quasi-vassalage by the Arma for a long period of time but they managed to reverse the power relationship in their favour beginning with the harsh defeat inflicted on the Arma in Taghia in May 1737.[14] From this date, and for several decades, they asserted themselves as major participants in the politics and military life of Timbuktu and its hinterland in the upper Niger River basin. The assassination of their chief, Ughmar, by the Arma resulted in the siege of Timbuktu in 1755. Shaykh Sidi al-Mukhtar successfully assisted the Tadmakkat in lifting the siege. He had intervened in the inheritance disputes that arose after the deaths of Ughmar and his son and successor Abtiti, and for this reason Sidi Muhammad's *Kitab al-ṯara'if* presented him as the true orchestrator of the complicated system of successions within the Iwillemmeden (the different Tuareg tribes). Sidi Muhammad also credited Shaykh Sidi al-Mukhtar with a decisive influence over the devolution of the chieftainship among the Brabish, with whom the Kunta sometimes had a difficult relationship, mainly because of the 'tax' pressure they placed on trade to Timbuktu.

The Tuaregs were not always peaceful and intense friction existed, particularly with the Kal Antasar, well after the death of Shaykh Sidi al-Mukhtar and the accession of Shaykh Sidi Muhammad. It was with the latter that the Kunta's contacts with the other ethno-cultural communities of the region, particularly with the Peuls of Macina, experienced their most significant development. The Peuls were more distant geographically than the nearby Tuaregs but this did not prevent Shaykh Sidi Muhammad from interceding with the leaders of the Peul *jihad* at the beginning of the nineteenth century – the *jihads* took place in Sokoto and Macina – in order to respond to legal concerns they raised, to pacify a conflict involving his customers or disciples, or to advise them. Thus, in the work entitled *al-Futuhat al-qudsiyya bi al-ajwiba al-Fullaniyya* (The Blessed Triumphs or the Fulani Responses), written in response to 24 questions asked by Ahmadu Lobbo, Sidi Muhammad provided the outline for a kind of Islamic constitution for the Peul state that was being established. These letters to influential lineage chiefs such as Hammadi Galadio and Nuhum Tahiru (Nuh b. at-Tahir) regarding their disputes with Ahmadu Lobbo demonstrate the extent of his influence, and the importance of the mediation activity he conducted among the Peul groups gravitating around the armed preaching of the founder of the Peul Islamic state of Macina. The

Books formed a crucial item of trade throughout West Africa. This highly annotated manuscript would have been greatly prized.

letter that Shaykh Sidi Muhammad sent to the leaders of the Sokoto, with whom he also seemed to have had a relationship, will be discussed later in the chapter.

This chapter will not, however, explore the many occasions on which the Sidi al-Mukhtar family became involved in disputes between the Kunta and the western Moorish world – where certain of their disciples played a significant role[15] – due to the relative geographical distance of this area from Timbuktu. We turn instead to some considerations regarding the life of Shaykh Sidi Muhammad and his works.

Al-Shaykh Sidi Muhammad: the man and his works

The complete education of Shaykh Sidi Muhammad, and significant moments in his career, took place behind the scenes and under the supervision of his father, Shaykh Sidi al-Mukhtar. While it was traditional in this area for young students to take a long journey to visit the most well-known teachers and schools in the region and to make the pilgrimage to the holy places of Islam, gleaning lessons and *ijazat* along the way, Sidi Muhammad never seems to have left his native Azawad and the only teacher he recognised was his father.

Even if we do not have any accurate information on his curriculum, it was most probably based on that of his father, of which he gives us an ample description at the beginning of the monumental biography he wrote on him. These were the studies recommended by all the Saharan–Sahelian schools of the time: science of the Arabic language (grammar, lexicography, metrics, rhetoric, literary history); the Qur'an and its interpretations; the *hadith*, taught mainly around six *sihah* (authentic compilations of prophetic traditions) in the Sunnite tradition; Malikite Ash'arite *fiqh*, based on classic works (mainly the *Mukhtasar* of Khalil b. Ishaq and the *Risala* of Ibn Abi Zayd) and their commentators; and the history of 'classical' Islam, where the *sira* plays a prominent role. Sufism and the works of the great inspirers of brotherhood movements (al-Junayd, Ibn 'Arabi, al-Ghazali, al-Suhrawardi, etc.) also formed a part of the education of Shaykh Sidi Muhammad, whose father was responsible for introducing the Qadiriyya into Saharan–Sahelian Africa. Works on *adab* and on wisdom, elements of arithmetic, logic, medicine and astronomy completed an education that was in full compliance with the educational heritage of his pious ancestors.

But the most precious education that Sidi Muhammad received from his father was undoubtedly the practical side of managing a brotherhood establishment, the learning of patience and wisdom and also the mindfulness to be used when conducting the many mediation sessions and interventions required of brotherhood leaders in a particularly unstable universe that mostly escaped the power of any centralised authority.

The works of Sidi Muhammad largely reflected the place that the aforementioned political and ethical concerns took in his life. The most significant part of the legacy written by Shaykh Sidi Muhammad consists of the monumental hagiographic biography he dedicated to his father, *Kitab al-tara'if wa al-tala'id min karamat al-shaykhayn al-walida wa al-walid* (The Book of Original and Inherited Knowledge on the Miracles of Two Shaykhs, My Mother and My Father). This work, which appears incomplete, aimed mainly at establishing the moral example of Shaykh Sidi Muhammad's father and his concern for the 'public' good. As far as the rest of his work was concerned, and apart from a few very traditional exegeses,[16] most of the writings of Shaykh Sidi Muhammad consist of his many letters about refutation or combat aimed at establishing legitimacy from a theological[17] or, more frequently, from theological and political points of view.[18]

Abdallah ould Mawlud[19] provides a succinct description of these letters, collected by al-Shaykh Sidiyya al-Kabir. I am using the same corpus, which consists of 47 letters copied by, or at the request of, this eminent disciple of Shaykh Sidi Muhammad, and the original of which is preserved in the manuscript library of Ahl al-Shaykh Sidiyya in Boutilimit.

These letters, very rarely dated but all probably chronologically situated between 1811 (the date of his father's death) and 1826 (the date of his own death), are varied in length and in subject matter. They range in length from half a page, in which a disciple is asked to hasten the return of an expected caravan, to a 60-page treatise on power in which the shaykh provides an explanation to his addressee on the proper code of behaviour that a Muslim emir should observe. An appreciable number of these letters were sent to high-ranking Peuls, especially to Ahmadu Lobbo, the founder of the Muslim state of Macina. In a long epistle (23 folios) sent to Lobbo in 1823, Shaykh Sidi Muhammad pretended to be an enthusiastic defender of the *jihad* which would soon cause the partisans of Lobbo to seize the upper Niger River basin and Timbuktu.[20] In other instances, Shaykh Sidi Muhammad wrote to Lobbo asking him to enforce the judgment of a *qadi* in favour of one of his Peul disciples regarding the sharing of a controversial inheritance, and to attempt mediation in favour of his politico-religious client, Galadio.

He also wrote to noteworthy Tuaregs for various reasons: to al-Nur, sultan of Kal Away', for instance, to request the return of plundered property, and a long epistle sent to the 'sultan' of the Iwillemmeden, Kawa b. Amma b. Ag ash-Shaykh b. Muhammad al-Bashir and his *qadi*, al-Salih b. Muhammad al-Bashir, to alert them to the machinations of al-Jaylani – a religious agitator who appeared among the Kal Dinnig in around 1800[21] – and his claims that he was the long-awaited *mahdi*.

The close and distant relatives of the shaykh, particularly his brother Baba Ahmad, who left to settle among the Moorish tribes of the Hawz, were also largely involved in his epistolary activity. These tribes, and the many disciples that the shaykh included in them, also received a significant number of his letters. Shaykh Sidi Muhammad thus wrote a very long letter to the *jama'a* (congregation) of the Aghlal of the Hawz to denounce the aggression of Ahl Sidi Mahmud, together with the Idaw'ish, against his

The covered courtyard of Jingerey-Ber Mosque.

Kunta cousins in the Tagant. In this letter he developed his vision of the history of the Kunta, and energetically denied the claims attributed to the chief of Kunta's adversaries – 'Abd Allah wuld Sidi Mahmud (d.1839) – to make himself *imam*, at the same time specifying what qualities a candidate for the imamate should have, as well as the essential prerequisites for the legitimacy of his candidature. He also wrote to the *jama'a* of the Funti,[22] within the framework of the same conflict, to request their intervention on the side of the Kunta. Still in the interest of the factions of his tribe that migrated west of the Azawad, he wrote a long letter to the *jama'a* of the Ahl Buradda to refute their claims to monopolise the control of these regions to the detriment of the Kunta.

Al-Shaykh Sidi Muhammad took over from his father as the head of the *zawiya* Qadiriyya that his father had created in the Malian Azawad, around the wells of al-Mabruk and Bujbayha, some 300 kilometres north-east of Timbuktu. Trans-Saharan trade was essential to the survival of this undertaking. The political autonomy given to him by his position, unusual in relation to all the powers that exercised some form of influence in the region, gave his *zawiya* a role of intercession and mediation which, in addition to the moral obligation connected with his spiritual vocation, would constitute, together with actual teaching, one of Shaykh Sidi Muhammad's main concerns. The power of influence that he endeavoured to generate and maintain was aimed mainly at individuals with power, tribal chiefs or founders of states such as Ahmadu Lobbo in Macina or 'Uthman dan Fodio within the present-day Niger–Nigerian borders. To give an idea of his position as moralist and adviser to the prince, I will look specifically at one of his texts, addressed to 'Uthman dan Fodio, to his brother 'Abdullahi and to his son, Muhammad.

Moralist and adviser to the prince

The position of shaykh of the *tariqa* al-Qadiriyya, passed on by Shaykh Sidi al-Mukhtar to his son Shaykh Sidi Muhammad, conferred on the latter the status of moral priest in his own community of disciples. It obliged him, on many occasions, to intercede with all the close and distant authorities he felt the need to influence in order for them to reconcile their behaviour with the higher interests of the Muslim *umma* and, secondly, with the interests of the shaykh himself and of his community. A letter addressed to the leaders of the Sokoto, one which features among the body of letters mentioned earlier, will enable me to illustrate this aspect of the intellectual and political activity of Shaykh Sidi Muhammad.

It is a document of 28 folios. It is handwritten in an elegant, narrow Maghribi script and has 30 lines per page, in a 16 cm x 11 cm format. It is undated but our guess is that it was probably written between 1811, when Sidi Muhammad took the reins of the brotherhood establishment created by his father, and 1817, the year of the death of his principal addressee, 'Uthman dan Fodio.

As in all the other writings of Sidi Muhammad, this letter reflects a sound knowledge of the history of classical and even contemporary Islam, from which he took his examples and found his models for political and moral behaviour. However, he failed to display the least originality in relation to the literature dealing with the same themes – 'the mirrors for princes'[23] – and from which he borrowed all his *topoi*.

Moderation and balance, associated with the fundamental values of fairness (*'adl*) and compassion towards the weak and oppressed, within the framework of a strict adherence to legal standards defined by Sunnite Islam, is the dominant tone of this document, which is completely marked by the Islamic duty of sound advice (*nasiha*).

The letters addressed to dan Fodio, to his brother 'Abdullahi and to his son Muhammad, just like the classical texts that inspired them – particularly *al-Tibr al-masbuk fi nasa'ih al-muluk* (The Found Pure Gold or The Wise Advice Given to the Kings) of al-Ghazali, *al-Ahkam al-sultaniyya* (The Government Rules) and *Adab al-dunya wa al-din* (The Right Behaviour in Mundane and Religious Affairs) of al-Mawardi and *Siraj al-muluk* (The Kings' candelabra) of al-Turtushi – first insist on the duty of *nasiha*, which is incumbent on the *'alim* (scholar) towards the prince and towards the *emir*. The celebration of knowledge and scholars and of their role among

The celebration of knowledge and scholars and of their role among the leading political authorities of a Muslim state goes hand in hand with a respect for the role of each of the two 'guilds' – the *'ulama* and the *umara* – in the Muslim city, and of the rules of behaviour that each group should ideally adopt towards the other. The ideal is that the princes seek the good advice and the company of the *'ulama* when necessary, rather than the other way around. A *hadith* quoted by Shaykh Sidi Muhammad says, 'The best (*khayru*) sovereigns (*al-umara*) are those who frequent scholars (*'ulama*); the worst scholars (*sharru al-'ulama*) are those who frequent sovereigns.'

the leading political authorities of a Muslim state goes hand in hand with a respect for the role of each of the two 'guilds' – the *'ulama* and the *umara* – in the Muslim city, and of the rules of behaviour that each group should ideally adopt towards the other.

The epistle then continues with canonical examples of a good ruler/prince taken from the tradition of certain venerable figures of the political past of the Muslim world (the Prophet himself, the *rashidun* – specifically 'Umar b. al-Khattab, 'Umar b. 'Abd al-'Aziz, etc.), and goes on to reveal a collection of commonalities in the paradigmatic vision of the ideal Muslim political authority and its methods of intervention as elaborated by both the scholarly and the popular traditions of Muslim societies.

I wrote elsewhere[24] of this vision of legitimate political authority and of its methods of legitimising the 'sultanic culture' in Islamic countries. By this I refer to something that goes beyond politics and religion and encompasses the entire scope of norms and values of the societies concerned, as it is reflected mainly in the proverbs, tales, poetry, works of ethics and wisdom, and so on. I would even suggest that this scope contains a certain unity, of which the text by Shaykh Sidi Muhammad, who mentions the predecessors cited earlier, shows the continuity. The unity in question is particularly expressed in a collection of commonalities (the rules of good princely behaviour) that has been repeated indefinitely since at least the eighth century,[25] the model for which is provided by the Qur'an, the canonical collections of *hadith*, the accounts of the edifying and marvellous lives of the 'great beings' before Islam (somewhat mythical and individualised giants, genies, kings and 'elders' of long ago), prophets and legendary figures from the Old and the New Testament, and from Islam ('companions', caliphs, viziers, generals, recognised interpreters of the dogma, mystics and aesthetes of renown), and tales and legends (*Kalila wa dimna*, the *1001 Nights*). The 'lesson' that Shaykh Sidi Muhammad teaches his correspondents of Sokoto falls completely within this heritage.

The letter addressed to dan Fodio mentioned earlier thus opens very classically with a development devoted to the theme of the relationship between 'scholars' and 'princes', around the duty of giving the sort of advice that would lead to, or revive, good Muslim behaviour. Sidi Muhammad refers to the *hadith* which says that 'religion is sound advice' (*al-din al-nasiha*). Leaders are reminded to 'return' the good that Allah gave them when he gave them power, by treating the 'flock' (*ra'iyya*) he entrusted to them with fairness. And al-Shaykh Sidi Muhammad specifies that it is the *'ulama's* duty to fulfil their religious obligation by reminding the leaders of the advice above.

The ideal, however, is that the princes seek the good advice and the company of the *'ulama* when necessary, rather than the other way around. A *hadith* quoted by Shaykh Sidi Muhammad says, 'The best (*khayru*) sovereigns (*al-umara*) are those who frequent scholars (*'ulama*); the worst scholars (*sharru al-'ulama*) are those who frequent sovereigns.' So the good *'alim* should flee the court and its 'corruption' and the good sultan is he who continues to hire the scholar and imitate him in his quest for (religious) knowledge and its rigorous application. The figure of the pious sovereign, a contradictory character, who should in some way shift his focus away from this role (as pious *'alim*) in order to fulfil his fundamental vocation as instrument of the law, is presented as a possible point of synthesis between the antithetical requirements managing men. This goes hand in hand with the responsibility of sovereignty, on the one hand, and with the ascetic and unselfish quest for actual knowledge of the *'alim*, on the other.

This aporia leads al-Shaykh Sidi Muhammad to celebrate the figure of the sovereign 'in spite of himself', of the legitimate heir of power with a passion for study and complete devotion to his pious practices who, against his will, as it were, must confront his 'curse' (*baliyya*) represented by the exercise of power. Mawlay Sliman, the 'alawite contemporary sovereign of Sidi Muhammad, and particularly reputed to favour brotherhood movements, is given as an example of a position of this kind, and to which the *rashidun* and 'Umar b. 'Abd al-'Aziz supply his initial models. The pious sovereign, annoyed by the impossibility of escaping his royal responsibility, may, following the example of Mawlay Sliman, continue practising his pious exercises in secret, away from the greedy and corrupt eyes of the courtesans.

The exercise of power, wrote Shaykh Sidi Muhammad to his Peul readers, is not merely laying down a set of pernicious restrictions with necessarily disastrous moral consequences. In principle, it is an ambiguous activity, which can be both a source of perdition and/or a channel for exceptional moral elevation. This is because power is both useful and dangerous. The 'general nature' of the sovereign's mission – in other words, the responsibility he exercises towards his subjects – makes him an operator of accumulation, of summation, of virtues and of vices which he contributes towards promoting among these subjects. Because, as Shaykh Sidi Muhammad says, quoting an old Arabic–Muslim refrain, 'subjects take on the behaviour of the prince'.[26] The sultan is the moral seat of authority, directly accountable for the behaviour of his subjects; he multiplies his own wrongs by favouring their bad behaviour and, in reverse, increases his merits if he encourages them to adopt proper behaviour. Hence the celebration of the fair sultan (*'adil*) and of historical characters whom he is supposed to incarnate: 'Umar b. al-Khattab and 'Umar b. 'Abd al-'Aziz, in particular. Al-Shaykh Sidi Muhammad repeats that after the various 'mirrors for the prince' that inspired him, there is no higher moral position or greater proximity to Allah – apart from the prophets and angels – than that of sultan *'adil*. A *hadith* he quotes compares the efficiency of the fair sovereign to that of the Qur'an: 'Allah separates (*yazi'u*) with the sultan [that] which he does not separate (*ma la yazi'u*) with the Qur'an.'[27]

The considerable privilege and dignity conferred on the fair prince through his upright behaviour and the rewards in the afterlife to which they are supposed to open the way, have their opposite in the terrible threats weighing down on the iniquitous sovereign who allows himself to be guided in his behaviour by his bad tendencies, his instincts for pleasure or, even worse, by the pernicious advice from people in his court. Here Shaykh

'The exercise of power', wrote Shaykh Sidi Muhammad, 'is not merely laying down a set of pernicious restrictions with necessarily disastrous moral consequences. In principle, it is an ambiguous activity, which can be both a source of perdition and/or a channel for exceptional moral elevation. This is because power is both useful and dangerous. The "general nature" of the sovereign's mission – in other words, the responsibility he exercises towards his subjects – makes him an operator of accumulation, of summation, of virtues and of vices which he contributes towards promoting among these subjects. Subjects take on the behaviour of the prince. The sultan is the moral seat of authority, directly accountable for the behaviour of his subjects; he multiplies his own wrongs by favouring their bad behaviour and, in reverse, increases his merits if he encourages them to adopt proper behaviour.'

Sidi Muhammad, quoting another cliché from sultanic literature, reminds those to whom he addresses his epistle that all *umara* – be they fair or tyrannical – will arrive in chains on the day of the final judgement and the iniquitous among them will be fed to snakes as big as dunes and to scorpions as big as mules.

Moreover, this danger (abundantly illustrated) is presented as almost inevitable given the progressive exhaustion of virtue in the world, especially since the demise of the first of the Prophet's companions. The theme of millenarianism is associated here, as it was elsewhere in sultanic literature, with the indirect exercise of power by the *imam*, now a sultan, and with the benefits of public levies to individuals of doubtful origins (*a'jam*, mainly, and other *mamalik* [slaves; in Muslim history the white slaves and elite soldiers who ruled Egypt and parts of Syria from 1252 to 1517]) and morals. The increase in the number of iniquitous sovereigns is itself given as a sign of the 'end of time', of the 'coming of the hour' of which the Sokoto leaders are invited to take heed. The 'hour is coming', writes Shaykh Sidi Muhammad to impious sovereigns (*fajara*).[28]

Shaykh Sidi Muhammad advises the princes to refuse luxury and ostentation and to mistrust their entourages. He denounces, as did those who inspired him from the 'mirrors of princes', *tahajjub* (hiding away), or the temptation to remove themselves from the sight of their subjects/dependants (*ra'iyya*), at risk of becoming the prisoners of the chamberlains and other not always reliable intermediaries.

And if the sultan is 'the shadow of God on earth' – another *topos* of the sultanic vision of the world – it is because he imposes a cosmic order where people are merely indirect agents. In places, sultanic literature – in whose wake Sidi Muhammad speaks to the emirs of Sokoto – suggests a proto-Hegelian way of reading history, around the themes of imminent justice and of the history of the world as the trial of the world. It suggests that, after all, people ordinarily only have the governments they deserve. Kings are independent of people and are instruments in the hands of Allah, 'sovereign of sovereignty'. A *hadith* of the Prophet attributed to Malik b. Dinar and quoted by Shaykh Sidi Muhammad says:

> I am the king of kings (*malik al-muluk*). I hold the hearts of kings in my hand (*qulub al-muluk bi-yadi*). If you obey me, you invite mercy (*ja'altum 'alaykum rahma*), if you disobey me, you bring punishment on yourselves (*niqma*). Do not busy your tongues with abuse against kings, but instead repent before Allah, he will 'fold' them (*yu'tifuhum*) over you.[29]

People may certainly play a part in the 'softening' that Allah, the only holder of power, wishes to imprint in the heart of the princes governing them, but they have no direct influence over their management of 'public' matters, if this adjective has meaning in this context.

Somewhat linked to the 'supervision' of kings by God, who features as a divine concession to the exercise of a sultanic authority that is partly outside divine action, is the affirmation, fully developed by Shaykh Sidi Muhammad and the works that inspired him, of the 'rotating' nature, necessarily limited in time, of the maintenance of the power of a given group or individual. This is not an internal restriction, connected with some form of institutional regulation, but the inexorable precariousness, the transitory way of manifesting all the things of this base world (*dunya*), in contrast to the permanence and the inalterability of pleasures and beings of the afterlife (*al-akhira*). The sultan's court is the place par excellence where the infidelity of time, the ruthless blade of fate, plays its 'tricks' and transforms the blind waltz of individual itineraries into a kind of universal lottery.[30]

Shaykh Sidi Muhammad advises the princes to refuse luxury and ostentation and to mistrust their entourage. He denounces *tahajjub* (hiding away), or the temptation to remove themselves from the sight of their subjects (*ra'iyya*), at risk of becoming the prisoners of the chamberlains and other not always reliable intermediaries.

Alongside this divinely inspired model is the model of royal wisdom, of time immemorial, the wisdom of the 'guild' of the *salatin* or *muluk* (*diwan al-muluk*), which exemplifies a 'moderate' art of good governance across time and countries and on which time has no hold. Solomon and Alexander the Great, the kings of pre-Islamic Persia, of China and of India provide him with his heroes and legendary figures.[31]

The 'secular' theme of *'adl*, of fairness, an essential theme throughout sultanic literature as well as in the epistle of Shaykh Sidi Muhammad, is more specifically linked to this timeless power of the sultan, to the perpetuity of this power, regardless of the religious nature of the person exercising it. It is expressed, with variations, in the following circular expression, written by Shaykh Sidi Muhammad:[32]

> No *sultan* without an army (*jund*), no army without resources (*mal*), no resources without taxes (*jibaya*), no taxes without prosperity (*'imara*), no prosperity without justice (*'adl*), no justice without a *sultan*. Justice thus appears as the foundation of all foundations (*asas li-jami' al-usus*).

Hence celebration in all its forms, directed at the addressees of the shaykh, of the *fair sovereign*, be it a Muslim leader or a prince of another denomination. Hence the intimate association established between his physical and moral state and the good health and balance of the world. A true shaker of the cosmos, the ideal sovereign of the sultanic representation of power is both the moral sum of all the princes of the world before him and a physical centre of the universe of which he adjusts the rhythm of time. After so many others, Shaykh Sidi Muhammad wrote *al-Sultan al-zaman* (The Sultan is the Age),[33] to mean that history is subject to the behaviour and good will of the sovereign of the moment. The theatre of the state of which he is both the great impresario and the only star, and the celebrations and commemorations he organises, aim to tune the ('public' or 'private') events of his life to match the cosmic deployment of the universe. The epistle of Shaykh Sidi Muhammad offers a metaphor of the world as a human organism of which the sultan would be its 'brain'; the vizier, 'the heart'; the vizier's subordinates, 'the hands'; and the masses (*al-ra'iyya*), 'the feet'; with fairness (*'adl*) making up its 'soul'.[34] It is not surprising that the sultan is presented as the operator of the failure or of the universal ruin of his time, the guarantor of the fertility or the channel of the misery of his kingdom.

The sultan's mind is therefore not only the essential mediator of the *'adl*, it is also his entire body.[35] The sultan is the emanation of an arbitrary and invisible power; he must remain visible and his body, the physical seat of fairness, must remain accessible to the *ra'iyya*. Hence, another commonplace of sultanic literature: the denunciation of the *'ihtijab* (concealed), of the confinement of the prince by the viziers and the chamberlains, which is compared to a divine prerogative because God alone may escape the eyes of his creatures. Yet, and for the same reasons, according to the clichés of the same literature quoted by Shaykh Sidi Muhammad, his duties include omniscience and omnipresence, which makes him similar to a celestial authority. This is the theme of the 'unremarkable sovereign'[36] and of incognito: the sultan is a night wanderer or lost hunter taken in by humble folk, far from his retinue and his palace, and hears truths hidden from him by his entourage; he assesses his image rating among his *ra'iyya*, and in the making of startling decisions, demonstrates his generosity and his sense of *'adl* (extravagant gifts to the needy or admirers, spectacular promotions of an anonymous 'fair man', or the brutal and sudden punishment of those failing to obey sultanic 'laws'). Ideally, he should be able to say to each of his subjects: I know what you ate last night and how you obtained the clothes you wear.[37]

As in all sultanic culture, the epistle of Shaykh Sidi Muhammad shows the sultan's periodic incursions into the world of ordinary people in the form of a duplication of the sultan himself, appearing as a kind of Janus of the social condition, leading a luxurious public life among the 'important people' of his court, and an ascetic and parsimonious private life on the underside of this gleaming decor, where he sometimes takes on small jobs to earn an honest living without violating the resources of the 'treasury chamber' (*bayt al-mal*).[38]

The image of the pastorate, combining the idea of belonging to the flock and the shepherd's intimate knowledge of it with the shepherd's responsibility to show it the right way without denying himself the use of its products, summarises a large part of this vision of power, and it also returns like a leitmotif in sultanic literature. Shaykh Sidi Muhammad quotes a well-known *hadith*:[39]

> You are all shepherds (*kullukum ra'in*) and all accountable for the object of your protection (*wa kullukum mas'ul 'an ra'iyyatih*): the *imam*, who is the shepherd of men (*'ala al-nasi ra'in*) is accountable for this 'sheepfold' (*ra'iyya*); a man is the shepherd (*ra'i*) of the members of his family (*ahla baytih*) and he is accountable for his 'sheepfold'; the woman is the shepherdess (*raa'iyya*) of the members of her husband's household (*ahla bayti zawjiha*) and of her children (*waladiha*) and she is accountable for it (*wa hiyya mas'ula 'anhum*); a man's slave (*'abd al-rajul*) is the shepherd (*ra'i*) of his master's property and he is responsible for it. You are certainly all shepherds and are all accountable for your sheepfold.

Here, as in other passages in the epistle of Shaykh Sidi Muhammad and of the 'mirrors' before it, the pastoral theme becomes intermingled with household management and the hierarchy of sex, age and ranking within the family, which is an extension of the smooth running of public matters by the sultan/shepherd.

As a shepherd, the sultan must naturally endeavour to protect his 'flock' against predators. And, of course, the herd will be on the road to ruin if – an assumption explicitly envisaged by Sidi Muhammad – its care falls into the hands of 'wolves';[40] in other words, if the sultan himself and his subordinates become agents of the destruction of the *ra'iyya*. This is because salvation cannot come from the flock and no effective resistance can come from it; the flock is the obedient and passive instrument of its shepherd.

In succinct form, the above were some of the essential lines of the letters written by Shaykh Sidi Muhammad to the emirs of Sokoto. The political moral it presents may not be original in relation to the whole of what we have called sultanic literature, but it nevertheless demonstrates both the scope of the Qadiri master's knowledge of this literature and the position of *murshid* (guide) and of *nasih* (one who gives advice) which, in compliance with the clichés of this literature, the good *'alim* must portray towards princes who are likely to hear his advice and take his recommendations to heart.

كملت هذه النصيحة بحمد الله
وحسن عونه وصلى الله على سيدنا
محمد وعلى آله وصحبه
وسلم تسليما

NOTES

1 Translated from French by Davina Eisenberg.

2 MacDougall (1980).

3 Genièvre (1947).

4 In particular Hamet (1910); Marty (1920–21); Batran (1971); and the thesis by Wuld Mawlud (1977).

5 wuld Mawlud (1977).

6 The earliest mention of the Kunta made available by sources is a letter from the ruler of Borno dated February 1440 and sent 'to all the *murabitun*, to the descendants of al-Shaykh al-Mukhtar and Sidi 'Umar al-Shaykh and to their brothers among the Darma'aka' (or Dirim'ka, according to Norris) in the Tuwat and quoted by Martin (1908: 122–123). Compare with Batran (1971: 54). In a second work by Martin (1923: 33–34), quoted by Batran (1971: 56), the year 1551 is given as the date of the arrival of a Kunta army in the Tuwat which forced a tribute of 100 *mithqal* on the inhabitants of Timmi. Norris (1986: 130) evokes the problems raised by the information provided by Martin when they are confronted with the historical and genealogical traditions of the Kunta from Shaykh Sidi al-Mukhtar.

7 With telescoping between the latter and another 'Uqba, known as al-Mustajab al-Jahmi, a 'companion' who died in Cairo. Compare Norris (1986) with Wuld Mawlud (1977): genealogical discrepancies claimed from the same ancestor – 'Uqba – one leading towards the Banu Umayya, the other towards the Fihrites. The claim of descent from the founder of the Qayrawan is commonplace among the Saharan–Sahelian populations (Peuls, Moors, Tuaregs, etc.).

8 Withcomb (1975) gave a critical assessment of these different sources.

9 Sidi Muhammad, *al-Risala al-ghallawiyya* (manuscript), page 59, personal copy.

10 Sidi Muhammad, *al-Risala al-ghallawiyya* (manuscript), page 66, personal copy.

11 These Awlad al-Wafi of the Azawad are not to be confused with the Awlad Sid al-Wafi of the Mauritanian Taganit.

12 Sidi Muhammad, *al-Risala al-ghallawiyya* (manuscript), page 66, personal copy.

13 Compare with Sidi Muhammad, *Kitab al-tara'if wa-t-tal-a'id min karamat al-shaykhayn al-walida wa al-walid* (manuscript), personal copy.

14 Wuld Mawlud (1977: 90).

15 I refer here particularly to Shaykh Sidiyya b. al-Hayba al-Intisha'i. See in particular Stewart (1973) and Ould Cheikh (1992) on this character and his influence.

16 A commentary from the *fatiha*, an exegesis of the *waraqat* of al-Juwayni, and so on. These texts remained unpublished to date.

17 Particularly its text entitled *al-Sawarim al-hindiyya fi hasm da'awi al-mahdiyya* (*c.*1811/1226), aimed at the notable monk of the Kal Dinnig, al-Jaylani who, at the turn of 1800, claimed to be the *mahdi*.

18 See, in particular, his *Risala al-ghallawiyya*, in which he defends the Kunta of the Tagant against the Ahl Sidi Mahmud and their chief 'Abdallah w. Sidi Mahmud, to whom he attributes the claim of wanting to make himself *imam* of Moorish communities of the region concerned.

19 Wuld Mawlud (1977).

20 Brown (1969).

21 On al-Jaylani and the politico-religious context and its preaching, we can particularly look at the details provided by Nicolas (1950: 56–59).

22 Part of the warrior tribe of the Awlad Mbarik, made up between the regions of ar-Rgayba (present-day Mauritania) and the Bakhounou of Mauritania–Mali. This is the 'Lucama kingdom' (deformation of the name of their chief at the time, A'li wuld A'mar) of Mungo Park.

23 'The mirrors for princes' is literature dealing with the qualities, attributes and education of princes/rulers in the Islamic world.

24 Ould Cheikh (2003).

25 See the edition by Muradi (1981) for the main references in Arabic on the subject.

26 *'Al-Ra'iyya 'ala din al-malik.'* My copy of the manuscript, folio 13, 1.

27 *'Inna Allah yazi'u bi-s-sultan ma la yazi'u bi al-qur'an.'* My copy of the manuscript, folio 16, 2.

28 My copy of the manuscript, folio 12, 1.

29 My copy of the manuscript, folio 21, 1.

30 The millennialist theme which feeds this rolling representation of 'fortunes' is sometimes associated with the theme of the *circle* and the *cycle*, which in Ibn Khaldun (1981) takes the form of a biogenesis or the birth and youth of dynastic education, followed by periods of maturity, which in turn precede senility and death.

31 Note the places of the epistle of Sidi Muhammad where they are evoked. See al-Muqaffa (1982).

32 My copy of the manuscript, folio 8, 2.

33 My copy of the manuscript, folio 10, 1.

34 My copy of the manuscript, folio 10, 2.

35 Compare with the story told by Shaykh Sidi Muhammad about a 'Chinese' ruler who lost his hearing and whose subjects were upset, as was he, because he could no longer hear their complaints and bring them justice. He ordered that from then on all those who had a complaint to lodge should dress in red and he travelled around to see the complaints of all who he could no longer hear. Manuscript, folio 14, 1 and 2.

36 Expression used by Dakhlia (1998).

37 My copy of the manuscript, folio 12, 1.

38 My copy of the manuscript, folio 9, 1.

39 My copy of the manuscript, folio 5, 2.

40 Sidi Muhammad quotes the following line: 'The shepherd protects his beasts against wolves. What would happen if the sheep were entrusted to the wolf keeper?'

REFERENCES

Batran AA (1971) Sidi al-Mukhtar al-Kunti and the recrudescence of Islam in the western Sahara and the Middle Niger *c.*1750–1811. PhD thesis, University of Birmingham

Brown WA (1969) The caliphate of Hamdullahi *c.*1818–1864. PhD thesis, University of Wisconsin, Madison

Dakhlia J (1998) *Le divan des rois.* Paris: Albin Michel

Genièvre J (1947) *Les Kounta et leurs activités commerciales* (no. 1240). Paris: Mémoire du Centre des Hautes Etudes d'Administration Musulmane

Hamet I (1910) Littérature Arabe saharienne. *Revue du Monde Musulman et de la Méditerranée* 12: 194–213, 380–398

Ibn Khaldun A (1981) *al-Muqaddima.* Beirut: Dar al-Fikr

MacDougall EA (1980) The Ijil salt industry: Its role in the precolonial economy of the western Sudan. PhD thesis, University of Birmingham

Martin AGP (1908) *Les oasis sahariennes.* Alger: Adolphe Jourdan

Martin AGP (1923) *Quatre siècles d'histoire marocaine.* Paris: Alcan

Marty P (1920-21) *Etudes sur l'islam et les tribus du Soudan.* Paris: Leroux

al-Muqaffa A (trans.) (1982) *Kitab kalila wa dimna.* Beirut: Mu'assasat al-ma'arif

Muradi M (1981) *Kitab al-ishara ila adab al-imara.* Edition by R al-Sayyid. Beirut: Mu'assasat al-ma'arif

Nicolas F (1950) *Tamesna: Les Ioullemmeden de l'Est ou Touareg (Kel Dinnik).* Paris: Imprimerie Nationale

Norris HT (1986) *The Arab conquest of the western Sahara.* London: Longman

Ould Cheikh AW (1992) *al-Ansab: La quête des origines. Anthropologie historique de la société tribale arabe.* Edited by P Bonte. Paris: Editions de la Maison des sciences de l'homme

Ould Cheikh AW (2003) La science au(x) miroir(s) du prince: Savoir(s) et pouvoir(s) dans l'espace arabo-musulman d'hier et d'aujourd'hui. *Revue du Monde Musulman et de la Méditerranée* 101/102: 129–155

Stewart CC (with Stewart EK) (1973) *Islam and social order in Mauritania: A case study from the nineteenth century.* Oxford African Affairs Series. Oxford: Clarendon Press

Withcomb T (1975) New evidence on the origins of the Kunta. *Bulletin of the School of Oriental and African Studies* 38(2): 403–417

wuld Mawlud A (1977) Shaykh Sidi Muhammad wuld al-Mukhtar al-Kunti: Contribution à l'histoire politique et religieuse de Bilad Shinqit et des régions voisines, notamment d'après les sources arabes inédites. PhD thesis, Université de Paris-IV Sorbonne, Paris

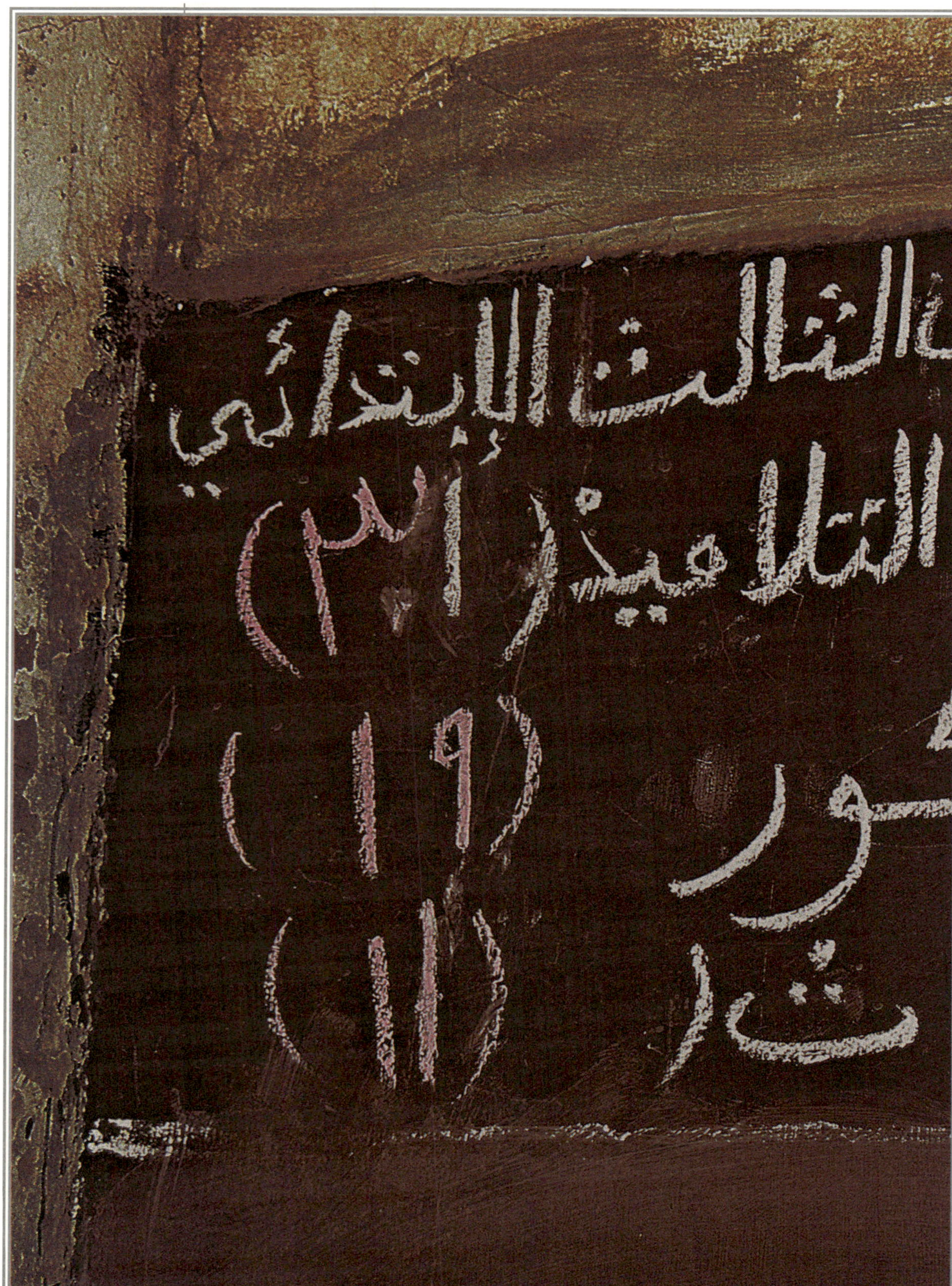

الثالث الابتدائي
التلاميذ (٣٦)
(١٩)
(١١)

CHAPTER 16

Al-Shaykh Abu al-Khayr: illustrious scholar and pious friend of God

Muhammad Diagayete[1]

The city of Timbuktu is regarded as one of the most prominent centres in West Africa for the diffusion of knowledge by virtue of the attention and patronage that its scholars received from some of its rulers. This diffusion of knowledge saw periods of change that oscillated between growth and decline. However, Timbuktu remained a pioneer in the transmission of knowledge due to the prominence and status of its scholars, whose fame spread far and wide.

In this chapter I address one of the luminaries of Timbuktu and Arawan – Shaykh Abu al-Khayr ibn 'Abd-Allah al-Arawani al-Timbukti. He, as with many other scholars, has not enjoyed any serious and scientific study except for a few general biographies. It is hoped that this chapter will whet the appetite of researchers and encourage them to embark upon a serious study of the shaykh (and other neglected scholars) to highlight his prominent role in, and contribution to, Islamic civilisation. I will introduce the shaykh by undertaking a study of his life and his activities, as well as a discussion of his written works.

Abu al-Khayr: lineage, education and knowledge genesis

Shaykh Abu al-Khayr[2] ibn 'Abd-Allah ibn Marzuq ibn al-Hill, follower of the Maliki legal school and adherent of the Qadiri,[3] Dardayri and Shadhili[4] Sufi orders, was born in Arawan at the turn of the fourteenth century of the Islamic *hijri* calendar[5] and died there in 1397 (AD 1975). He was buried in the mosque of Sayyid Ahmad ibn Salih ibn al-Wafi ibn Ad (d.1772).

Not much is known about Shaykh Abu al-Khayr's early childhood or of his youth except that he hails from a scholarly family that instilled in him a love of knowledge and learning. He began the recitation of the Qur'an at the hands of his brother 'Ali ibn

Opposite: Chalkboards like this one have been used by generations of students to practice writing in Arabic.

‘Abd-Allah ibn Marzuq ibn al-Hill (d.1944), an illustrious shaykh among those who taught the recitation of the Qur’an in Arawan. He then read under the tutelage of Shaykh al-Talib al-Habib (d.1972), who was a witty scholar and well versed in the science of the correct rendition of the Qur’an, its calligraphy, the perfection of its ruling and rendition of its different modes of reading. He was arguably the greatest scholar of the sciences of the Qur’an of his time.

Abu al-Khayr memorised the Qur’an in his early childhood with Shaykh al-Talib al-Habib after only one reading, with no revision. It was a feat which many of the *‘ulama* found hard to believe and they therefore doubted his retention of the holy book. However, when the *‘ulama* of Mauritania came to Arawan to test him, they found him fluent and erudite not only in his rendition[6] of the Qur’an but in his writing of it as well. He read the *Khazrajiyyah*[7] under the tutelage of Abu al-‘Abbas Ahmad ibn al-Salih al-Suqi, which the latter in turn began reading with his shaykh ‘Amar al-Ruqadi. He then read under him the *Alfiyyah* of al-‘Iraqi,[8] a work on the science of prophetic traditions (*‘ulum al-hadith*). Abu al-‘Abbas Ahmad ibn al-Salih al-Suqi then gave him permission to narrate and teach.[9] After memorising the Qur’an and mastering its rulings and the art of its rendition, he studied Islamic substantive law, source methodology in jurisprudence, prophetic traditions, grammar, linguistics, Arabic literature, rhetoric, logic and other disciplines under the tutelage of the jurist Shaykh Ahmad ibn Babakr ibn al-Sayd (d.1921)[10] in Arawan.

Abu al-Khayr memorised the Qur’an in his early childhood with Shaykh al-Talib al-Habib after only one reading, with no revision. It was a feat which many of the *‘ulama* found hard to believe and they therefore doubted his retention of the holy book. However, when the *‘ulama* of Mauritania came to Arawan to test him, they found him fluent and erudite not only in his rendition of the Qur’an but in his writing of it as well.

Shaykh Abu al-Khayr had many students, including: Mawlay Ahmad Babir al-Arawani (d.1997);[11] Mawlay al-‘Arabi ibn Mawlay Hashim; Mahamane Mahamoudou,[12] popularly known as Hamu, who at the time of writing is still alive;[13] Muhammad ‘Abd-Allah ibn Ahmad ibn Abu ‘l-‘Araf al-Takni;[14] al-Shaykh ‘Umar Nasiri from the village of Tayi next to the city of Jenne; Sidi Muhammad al-Rahmah (d.2004); Sidi Ould al-Qadi, who at the time of writing is still alive; Bu ‘Ali ibn Sidi Bubakr; al-Shaybani ibn Muhammad al-Mukhtar; and Imam Ansunughu.

The shaykh’s activities

Shaykh Abu al-Khayr shuttled between Arawan and the city of Timbuktu, spending six months of the year in each. He devoted his life to worship and learning. His typical day, even in his old age, began after the dawn prayers with a complete reading of a fifth of the Qur’anic exegetical work of *al-Jalalayn*,[15] and a complete reading of al-Jazuli’s *Dala’il al-khayrat* (The Proofs of the Good). He then undertook the rest of his worship activities and mundane tasks.

After sunrise he taught *hadith*, *tafsir*, *fiqh*, *mantiq* and other sciences. A group of *‘ulama* used to attend these gatherings, where each took his lost gem,[16] gaining knowledge in Qur’anic exegesis, prophetic traditions, substantive law, syntax and the other sciences. These gatherings were forums for disseminating knowledge, characterised by silence

At Sankore Mosque in Timbuktu.

and the absence of polemical debates except when the *'ulama* asked the shaykh something.[17] His ethic was that of al-Imam al-Shafi'i (d.820 *hijri*): 'A scholar, unless asked, remains silent.'[18]

During the day he also passed judgment in disputes and attended to the giving of legal verdicts (*ifta*). At times he simply sent his rosary (*sibhah*) to the litigants (specifically the Bedouins) for them to reconcile and they willingly accepted his call for peace and reconciliation. Thus he solved problems and complexities which his peers among the *'ulama* and other notables were unable to solve. For example, the people of Mauritania invited three scholars – two from Mauritania and one from Mali – to solve the problem of Basikunah (a dispute concerning the rights of usage of a certain well which a few tribes in Mauritania were fighting for). However, it was when Shaykh Abu al-Khayr dealt with the issue that the Mauritanians unanimously agreed that he alone was able to solve the problem, which he did with cogent proofs that all the disputants accepted.

It would appear that Shaykh Abu al-Khayr's role in giving legal verdicts caused him tremendous worries, not merely because he was a 'lone orphan' among ignorant people but also because of the confusion that pervaded scholarly circles – the contradictory views and verdicts that left a *mufti* (jurisconsult) perplexed as to which standards he should use to judge by.[19] In a letter to Muhammad Yahya ibn Salim al-Wallati (1851–1936),[20] Shaykh Abu al-Khayr raised the following issues:

His typical day, even in his old age, began after the dawn prayers with a complete reading of a fifth of the Qur'anic exegetical work *al-Jalalayn*, and a complete reading of al-Jazuli's *Dala'il al-Khayrat* (The Proofs of the Good). He then undertook the rest of his worship activities and mundane tasks.

> As for what follows: from the writer to the great illustrious scholar, the pious jurist, the pure God-fearing one, the aware and cleansed, our master and pole of our age Muhammad Yahya ibn Salim. The purpose of my writing to you is to ask about that wherein lies my salvation for the day when [people] will be seized by the feet and foreheads. Times have coerced me to fulfilling the duty of *ifta'* as I am one and alone among ignoramuses except for a few by the grace of God, therefore enrich me with a verdict that will free me. The matter has become complicated due to the proliferation of differences between the views of the scholars (May God be pleased with them and us). Is it then not permissible or necessary for any one of us to issue *fatwas* except in accordance to the well-known [views] stated in the books of the [Maliki] school? Or do we have the right to practise *ifta'* taking into account every strong [opinion] in the *madhhab* or not? And is it permissible for us to give verdicts subject to the prevailing customs (*'urf*) of our time knowing that we are ignorant regarding its reality, condition, and who instituted it? The establishment of all that is an almost impossible task. And can the intentions and aims of the people of our time in their [practice of] divorce and giving oaths be regarded as custom? And should custom, where it contradicts an explicit text of Malik [ibn Anas], be discarded and given no consideration as al-Zurqani said or not? And what if it [the *'urf*] contradicts a Qur'anic text, or prophetic tradition, and the majority opinion of the school? Give us an answer wherein there is a soothing for our chests. Or is it preferred to discard the institution of *ifta'* in our time? And with the scarcity or even the non presence of [true] scholars who should sit, or be appointed, for *ifta'*?[21]

At night he resumed his educational sessions. None of this prevented him from reading the *al-Shifa'* of al-Qadi al-'Ayad (d.1145) and spending much of his night in additional acts of worship.

Allah had blessed Shaykh Abu al-Khayr with a bright and luminous intellect and a retentive memory, which he used to memorise the books of jurisprudence and law, and which granted him a deep understanding of them. He was well acquainted with all the commentators on these works and even memorised the *tafsir al-Jalalayn*. As with many of the scholars of his day, he was a walking encyclopaedia, carrying his knowledge with him wherever he travelled. He was brilliant in *tafsir* and *hadith*, excelling in both. The author of *al-Sa'adah al-abadiyya* aptly described him thus:

> Our jurist *shaykh*, the standard bearer, the master of the art, the exegete, the unrivalled scholar of Takrur,[22] its jurist, teacher and *mufti* whose only concern is how to benefit from knowledge and benefit others...he reached the pinnacle in the science of *tafsir* and *hadith* in which he was unequalled.[23]

Likewise, his student Mahamane Mahamoudou, known as Hamou Muhammad Dedeou, described him in these words:

> 'Abu al-Khayr was a scholar, a retainer [of texts], the proof of trustworthy reliability, the master who was depended on to respond with religious guidance to incidents and

A modern-day scholar teaching at a school in Timbuktu.

events and in the issuing of *fatwas*. He was a luminary in the sciences of *hadith* and all its techniques; completely capable in discerning authentic traditions and spurious ones, its paths and its finer hidden points. He was a genius in the knowledge of the rulings [deduced] from prophetic tradition and its meanings as well as its complications. He was strong and well versed in the knowledge of its vocabulary specifically the difficult ones, a master in the biographies of its narrators, the precise form of their names – including titles, patronyms, etc. – their deaths, births, information, tales, and holy acts (*karamat*). He was an *imam*, an authority, a firm foundation [of knowledge], a judge, pious, thorough and meticulous in his views and actions; what he said, ruled or commanded was not marred by hesitation or mixed feelings. He was a paragon of patience, tranquillity, clemency and endurance.[24]

Muhammad al-Khalifa ibn al-Mustafa, one of Shaykh Abu al-Khayr's contemporaries, not only acknowledged the shaykh's virtue, testified to by his many visits to him in order to be blessed, but declared him the undisputed master for solving problems and

Shaykh Abu al-Khayr composed a poem in praise of the wealthy Ahmad bin Abi 'l-'Araf, describing him as one inspired with intense love for the collection of manuscripts and books, and who spent all his wealth and valuables to possess them, thereby preserving this priceless Islamic heritage.

complex questions at the end of the fourteenth century *hijra* in the land of Takrur. In this regard he composed a poem wherein he made a supplication to God for the benefit of the shaykh. The poem extolled the virtues and the status of Shaykh Abu al-Khayr and the esteem in which people, both scholars and laity, held him.

The shaykh's poetry

Shaykh Abu al-Khayr and other early scholars were polymaths and not limited by specialisation in certain disciplines only. It is thus no wonder that the shaykh composed beautiful poetry that evoked and awakened sentiments. Most of his poems were commendations, encouragements and eulogies.[25] One poem in didactic form lauds the didactic poem of Ibn Salim al-Wallati, in which the latter summarised the *Mukhtasar*[26] of Khalil (d.1365). In the poem Abu al-Khayr compares this work of Ibn Salim to the sun and the moon in its illumination and clarity. He also composed a poem in praise of the wealthy Ahmad ibn Abi 'l-'Araf (1864–1955),[27] describing him as one inspired with intense love for the collection of manuscripts and books, and who spent all his wealth and valuables to possess them, thereby preserving this priceless Islamic heritage. In another poem, which was an addition and decoration to a poem by al-Shaykh al-Tijani ibn Sayyid Muhammad, he eulogises the great and erudite scholar Ahmad ibn Abi Bakr ibn Muhammad al-Sayd (d.1921).

The shaykh's contemporaries

Shaykh Abu al-Khayr was a contemporary of many scholars and a significant number of jurists. His relationship with most of them was good. The few sour relationships that did exist sprang from jealousy, rancour and rivalry. Among his contemporaries were al-Shaykh Bhai ibn Sayyid 'Amar al-Kunti (1865–1929), with whom he corresponded on matters of *ifta* and the judiciary; Shaykh Muhammad Yahya ibn Salim al-Wallati, who acknowledged the virtue of and his preference for Shaykh Abu al-Khayr to the extent that he became the only one allowed to write the prefaces to his books and book collections; and Shaykh al-Tijani ibn Muhammad al-Amin (d.1947) – Shaykh Abu al-Khayr's teaching colleague in Arawan – who said to his students regarding Shaykh Abu al-Khayr: 'Do not ask me [about anything] as long as this jurist is among us for indeed we found our shaykhs acknowledging his virtue and superior knowledge.'[28] Also among his contemporaries was Shaykh Muhammad al-Salik ibn Khayyi al-Tanwajiwiyy, the pious scholar who wrote more than 20 books. He heaped endless praise on Shaykh Abu al-Khayr in the prefaces of some of his books.

Then there was Shaykh Antat or Antut (d.1946), the jurist and scholar acknowledged by the scholars of his day as the authority in syntax and who wrote a commentary on the *Manzuma* of Ibn Salim, commented upon by Abu al-Khayr. Other contemporaries were Shaykh Muhammad ibn Ibrahim ibn 'Abidin, second only to Shaykh Abu al-

Khayr in the passing of *fatwas*, and Muhammad al-Amin and his brother Muhammad Tahir titled Addah. Between them, these scholars ran quite a few schools in substantive law and source methodology in jurisprudence. There was also the great shaykh 'Alin ibn Muhammad ibn Ahmad ibn Muhammad ibn Muhammad Ber al-Arawani (d.1921), who used to revoke his *fatwas* in favour of those of Shaykh Abu al-Khayr. Then there were Shaykh Akk Halawin, his friend and colleague in executing the office of *ifta*; al-Shaykh ibn al-Zayn al-Jabhi; Shaykh Muhammad Mahmud ibn Shaykh al-Arawani (1910–72); Shaykh Muhammad al-Tahir ibn Sharaf; al-Qadi Baba ibn Sidi; Muhammad Yahya wuld Yakan al-'Ayshi; and, finally, 'Abd-Allah ibn Badi ibn al-Munir al-'Alawi, the master scholar of morphology (*sarf*) who, whenever he did commentary on any verse of the Qur'an, did so only after applying all the rules of morphology and those of many other pious scholars.

In summary then, Shaykh Abu al-Khayr enjoyed a strong relationship with many people: black and white, of the desert and of the Niger Bend. The gatherings to discuss Qur'anic exegesis and prophetic traditions, and the celebration of the Prophet's birthday, were all occasions when the ties of love, solidarity and mutual care were strengthened and consolidated.

Written works

Tarikh Arawan wa Tawdeni

THE HISTORY OF ARAWAN AND TAWDENI

The manuscript[29] consists of four folios written in a modern Sudani script. Sidi ibn Muhammad al-Rahim and 'Abdan al-Sultan started writing the manuscript. It was completed by Shaykh Abu al-Khayr who also collated it in 1962. Two pages on the history of Tawdeni are attached to the manuscript. The manuscript deals with the history of the establishment of the city of Arawan, transmitting Sidi 'Urwah's knowledge of when Arawan was established, by whom, and its subsequent growth and development. Sidi 'Urwah clarifies that Ahmad ibn Add ibn Abi Bakr built Arawan after he left al-Suq, one or two years before the latter's destruction. Ahmad ibn Add travelled to numerous places such as Adrar, Tadararat and Talik before finally settling in what became Arawan. There he married a woman called Fatima bint al-Firdaws from the Amaqsharan tribe, who owned the land. However, the Amaqsharan quarrelled amongst themselves over land rights, so Shaykh Ahmad ibn Add 'cursed' them and they dispersed into splinter groups.

The manuscript also refers to those families that came and settled in Arawan, such as the Wasratawhu from al-Kabal, al-Wali al-Hashimi al-Mukhtar, the grandfather of Idwa'il, the family of Bu 'Aliyu, Ahmad al-Sa'ih and the Barabish. Construction in Arawan reached its peak with the arrival of Lahib ibn Sidi ibn Muhammad ibn 'Ammam, as many of his devoted followers joined him so as to receive his *baraka* (blessings) as well as those of his predecessors. Assisted by the shaykh of the Barabish, Ahmad La'bid, they built houses and dug over 140 wells. The many traders from Ghadamis who descended upon Arawan and Tuwat revived the city with commerce, trading in different commodities. Cows, sheep, oil and other merchandise came from Timbuktu in the south.

The epilogue of the manuscript is an exhortation to the inhabitants of Arawan to follow and obey their rulers.

Maktub fi al-waqf

TREATISE ON ENDOWMENTS

This manuscript[30] is a treatise on religious endowments and consists of four folios written in small but clear script. Some parts of the manuscript have been water damaged. Shaykh Abu al-Khayr mentions the numeric value of the letters of the Arabic alphabet (for example, the *alif* [corresponds to the sound 'a'] equals 1, the *ba* ['b'] equals 2, the *waw* ['w'] equals 6, the *ha* ['h'] equals 5), delineating the difference in calculation between the Islamic West[31] and the Islamic East. For example, in the word *ayqash* the last letter (the shin ['sh']) equals 1 000 in the Islamic West whilst in the Islamic East the letter *ghayn* ('gh') – not *shin* – equals 1 000, hence the word *aykagh* instead of *ayqash*.

Then, he deals with Indian numerology whose calculation of the value of letters was similar to that of the Arab West (Maghribi) calculation. He also dwells upon the benefit of *Sura al-Ikhlas* (the Qur'anic chapter on the uniqueness of God) and how to employ it in order to procure one's wishes and desires.

Fath al-karim 'ala' manzuma Muhammad Yahya ibn Salim al-musammah nahwi shahrayn

THE NOBLE ACCOMPLISHMENT ON (ELUCIDATING) THE DIDACTIC POEM 'TOWARDS TWO MONTHS' OF MUHAMMAD YAHYA IBN SALIM

Classical Muslim scholars had the habit of stating their motive for writing a text, a practice which Shaykh Abu al-Khayr upheld. Regarding his writing of *Fath al-karim*,[32] he says:

> Some brothers requested me to write a lucid and clear commentary on the didactic poem by the ascetic and famous servant of God Muhammad Yahya ibn Sidi Muhammad ibn Salim on the science of Arabic [language]. This in order to analyse its words and complexity, to clarify its ambiguous meanings in the best possible manner in a commendable and pleasant style that pleases the loving, affable author and offends the jealous wrongdoer. I, given the meagre resources and my ill qualification in this art, responded to this request because of the reward in that and the great virtue, requesting from Allah acceptance and guidance and to lead me to the straightest path.

The manuscript consists of 86 folios and is original, that is, written by the author in the Sahrawi font. The date of its authorship and copying is not mentioned nor, as far as I know, has it been printed. The manuscript contains most if not all the rules on the precepts of the Arabic language, such as the particles (prepositions, particles of accusativeness, particles of abrogation, etc.) and nouns (definite and indefinite, masculine and feminine, etc.). It also discusses verbs and their different cases, such as plain (root) and derived forms. Thus the manuscript is an invaluable commentary for anyone wanting comprehensive knowledge of the precepts of the Arabic language. One criticism that can be directed against it is the illegibility of the handwriting on some pages. In spite of this, the manuscript remains a source worthy of attention, reading and study.

Al-jawab al-muskit fi radd hujjaj al-mu'tarid 'ala 'l-qa'ilin bi nadbiyya al-qabd fi salah al-nafl wa 'l-fard

THE IRREFUTABLE REPLY IN REBUTTING THE CLAIMS OF THE OBJECTOR TO THOSE WHO ARGUE FOR THE PREFERENCE OF FOLDING THE ARMS IN OBLIGATORY AND SUPEROGATORY PRAYERS

This accredited manuscript[33] consists of ten folios of which the last two are a commentary and reiteration of the authenticity and correctness of the proofs that Abu al-Khayr forwarded to Muhammad ibn Khayy al-Tinwaji al-Tinbukti and Muhammad ibn Ibrahim ibn 'Abidin ibn al-Tahir al-Kunti. Abu al-Khayr wrote the manuscript in 1952 and Muhammad al-Tahir, called Sharaf Baba, copied it in a beautiful Sahrawi script. In it Abu al-Khayr deals with an issue – the practice of dropping the hands or folding them during prayers – that divided Muslims (and still does), splitting their unity, leading at times to infighting and conflict. The author states that the folding of hands is narrated in authentic prophetic traditions and is obligatory. He addressed this question in order to convince those scholars who rejected the particular *hadith*s on the practice of folding the hands saying:

> When we saw the views of some of the learned people of our day and gauged from their views the same objection to the authentic, straightforward, beautiful *ahadith* going back in a continuous chain to the Prophet regarding the folding of the hands in prayers and we being commanded to do so we, with certainty, saw it as our obligation to defend the *sunnah*, ourselves, our dignity and our actions in prayers.

Abu al-Khayr demonstrated that the prophetic traditions on folding the hands during prayers are authentic and sound, and mentioned in all the primary *hadith* compilations such as al-Bukhari, Muslim, the *Muwatta* of Malik, *Sahih* of Ibn Khuzayma, al-Nasa'i, al-Tabrani in his *Kabir*, Ibn Hiban in his *Sahih*, al-Tirmidhi in his *Jami'*, Abu Dawud, Ahmad ibn Hanbal in his *Musnad*, and others.[34]

Therefore, he claimed, most of the companions of the Prophet who resided in Medina, as well as the sucessors,[35] only reported the practice of the folding of hands. As for the practice of the people of Medina[36] (which those who object to the folding of hands in prayers cite as proof), it was not established as a normative practice and subsequent source of legislation during the era of the Rightly Guided Caliphs,[37] but came into effect only after their death and after the end of the era of the companions.

His compilations

Shaykh Abu al-Khayr wrote on almost all subjects, from law (more than 30 works), jurisprudence and history to literature. Although the shaykh was a great exegete and scholar of *hadith*, we have not seen any work by him on Qur'anic exegesis nor have we come across many authorisations granted by him to his students.[38] Among his many written works are *Miftah al-falah fi adhkar al-masa' wa 'l-sabah*[39] (The Key to Success in the Remembrance of Morning and Night). He wrote the following poems: a eulogy,[40] a praise of Yusuf[41] and a condemnation of the world.[42] In one treatise he responds to a question about sleeping in the mosque;[43] in another he mentions some of the virtues of Abu 'l-'Abbas Sidi Ahmad ibn al-Salih al-Suqi.[44] There are written authorisations (*ijazat*) that he gave to Muhammad ibn al-Siddiq[45] and Alfa Salim Baber al-Timbukti,[46] and a single authorisation in *hadith*.[47] There are numerous letters: a letter to the judge Muhammad al-Amin ibn Ahmad Baba ibn Abi 'l-'Abbas al-Hasani;[48] a letter to the judge Ahmad Baba b. Abi 'l-'Abbas b. 'Umar b. Zayan al-Hasani;[49] a rebuttal of the view that regarded the wealth of those Muslims who accepted and dealt with the colonialists as permissible;[50] a letter on agency;[51] a letter to Muhammad Yahya ibn Muhammad Salim al-Wallati;[52] a response to doubt around the mandatory waiting period for women after divorce in the instance of remarriage; a letter on the selling of meat in exchange for stitched skins (leather);[53] questions; and a *fatwa*.[54] Among the many *fatwa*s there is one directed to Ahmad ibn Abi Bakr ibn al-Sayyad;[55] one on secret marriage;[56] another on *zakat* (alms);[57] and others on *hiba* (gifts)[58] and the issue of *imama* (delivering the sermon and leading of prayers) of the two festivals (*al-'Idayn*).[59] Then there are *fatwa*s on what transpired between the desert dwellers with regard to their trading in sheep;[60] on reconciliation;[61] on bartering and commercial trade;[62] on inheritance;[63] on delegation of power and authority;[64] and on agency.[65] There is a *fatwa* that addresses the problem that transpired between the children of Buhan and the children of 'Imran around the well called al-Hass al-Abyad.[66] There is also a set of *fatwas*[67] and responses,[68] and the responses of Muhammad Yahya ibn Salim to the questions of Abu al-Khayr.[69] There is a commentary by Ibn 'Ashir on the *Ajrumiyya*[70] and a commentary of *Maraqi al-su'ud*[71] which he did not complete. He also gives information about *munawala*,[72] and many other *fatwa*s on incidents that transpired.[73]

It is clear that Shaykh Abu al-Khayr was not only an active scholar, but also an exemplary personality in the peaceful resolution of disputes. His death left a vacuum in the region, specifically in Timbuktu and Arawan.

NOTES

1 Translated from Arabic by Mohamed Shaid Mathee.

2 Ahmad ibn Abi 'l-'Araf al-Takni calls him Abu 'l-Khayrat (the father of all goodness), indicating that he was alive in 1935. He wrote a rather short biography of him which barely whets the appetite. See al-Takni (2000: 67). In this chapter I too am unable to give an elaborate biography of him with regards to his lineage, as he himself mentioned no one higher than his immediate great-grandfather in all of his writings that I was able to read.

3 He received the Qadiri order (its rendition) from al-Shaykh al-Ghawth al-'Azam al-Shaykh al-Tarad ibn Abi 'l-'Abbas Muhammad Fadil ibn Mamin al-Na'mawi al-Wallati, whom he used to be in correspondence with and whose advice and counselling he sought. See al-Takni (2000: 99).

4 I do not think it far-fetched to suggest that al-Shaykh Abu 'l-Khayr was a Tijani as well, since he expressed his desire and wish to belong to the order with the following words: 'Let it come to your knowledge dear *faqih* that I am a devoted adherent of the Shadhili order and the Order of al-Shaykh Mawlaya 'Abd al-Qadir al-Jaylani and should I be granted the opportunity to combine between them through the Tijani Order [I would]. So please do give me the permission to do so as I wish for you to be one of my *ashyakh* [leaders/guides in Sufism] so that I am with your group and holding fast to your side, and Salam to you.' This he wrote in a letter to Muhammad Yahya ibn Salim al-Wallati. See manuscript number 5828 in the Ahmed Baba Institute.

5 Although researchers agree that the date of the demise of Shaykh Abu al-Khayr is 1975 they disagree on his date of birth. John Hunwick holds that he was born at the beginning of the fourteenth century of the Islamic calendar: 'He was born in the early years of the 14th century of *hijra*' (2003: 155). Hunwick does not give a source for this view, although I am certain that he depends on Mahamane Mahamoudou (known as Hamou Muhammad Dedeou) – the only possible source, according to my knowledge, who possesses an almost complete biography of Shaykh Abu al-Khayr. Hamu says in his manuscript entitled *Nawazil al-Shaykh Abi al-Khayr ibn 'Abd-Allah al-Arawani* (The Verdicts of al-Shaykh Abi al-Khayr ibn 'Abd-Allah al-Arawani), 'He was born in the beginning of the 14th century *hijri*,' without giving an exact date.

6 Al-Arawani, Muhammad Mahmud ibn al-Shaykh. *Kitab al-tarjuman fi tarikh al-Sahra' wa 'l Sudan wa balad Timbukt wa Shinqit wa Arawan wa nabdh min tarikh al-zaman fi jami' 'l-buldan* (The Book on the Narrating of the History of the Sahra and the Sudan, the Land of Timbuktu, Shinqit and Arawan and a Synopsis on the History of the Time of all Countries), Ahmed Baba Institute, manuscript number 762, page 25.

7 This is a book in prosody (*al-'arud*), a science that studies the endings and rhymes of verses in Arabic poetry, by Abd Allah ibn Uthman al-Khazraji.

8 He was 'Abd al-Rahim ibn al-Husayn b. 'Abd al-Rahman Abu 'l Fadl Zayn al-Din, known as al-Hafiz al-'Iraqi (d.1404). The poem is called *alfiyya* which literally means 'the thousand' as it refers to a didactic poem with a thousand verses or couplets. The *Alfiyya* in this case is a work on the science of the prophetic traditions in the form of a didactic poem.

9 Al-Arawani, Abu al-Khayr. *Maktub fi dhikr fada'il al-Shaykh Abi 'l-'Abbas Sidi Ahmad ibn al-Salih al-Suqi* (A Treatise on Enumerating the Virtues of Shaykh Abi 'l-Abbas Sidi Ahmad ibn al-Salih al-Suqi), Ahmed Baba Institute, manuscript number 1034.

10 He is the judge (was the Chief Justice), the erudite and intelligent scholar Sidi Ahmad ibn Bubakr ibn al-Sayd ibn al-Faqih Sulayman ibn Taliban ibn al-Faqih Sulayman ibn Muhammad Aghan ibn al-Shaykh Sidi Ahmad ibn Add (d.1921). He also composed impromptu poetry.

11 He is the author of the book *al-Sa'ada al-abadiyya fi ta'rif bi 'ulama Timbukt al-bahiyya* (The Perpetual Bliss in Introducing the Scholars of Glorious Timbuktu).

12 It is apt here to mention that Shaykh Mawlay al-'Arabi is Hamu's actual and direct teacher. However, his teacher taught him that everyone who learned at the hands of Shaykh Abu al-Khayr would be blessed in his knowledge and therefore Mawlay al-'Arabi used to 'coerce' Shaykh Abu al-Khayr to teach some works to his student Hamu.

13 Hamu is an able copyist and an illustrious scholar who read the *Risala* of Ibn Abi Zayd al-Qayrawani and some of the books of *hadith* at the hands of Shaykh Abu al-Khayr.

14 Abu 'l-'Araf was accepted by the *'ulama* of his day as the undisputed authority in Arabic grammar.

15 This exegetical work was compiled by the famous fifteenth-century scholar 'Abd al-Rahman al-Suyuti and his teacher Jalal al-Mahalli.

16 A weak prophetic tradition recorded by al-Tirmidhi (1991: 301, *hadith* number 2611) and by Ibn Majah (1996: 205, *hadith* number 4159). In full it reads the word of 'wisdom is the lost property (gem) of the believer, wherever he/she finds it he most deserves to take it'. 'Lost gem' is a metaphor for knowledge that a Muslim must look for and, upon finding it, take it. In this case, Shaykh Abu al-Khayr's knowledge was that gem.

17 Translator's note: It is not clear whether it was only when the shaykh asked or when anyone else asked.

18 Ibn al-Qayyim al-Jawziyyah (1999: 168).

19 Translator's note: This issue around confusion and ignorance reveals the important epistemological reality in which the Muslim world finds itself at all times, specifically in the era of European colonialism and post-colonialism.

20 Muhammad ibn Yahya ibn Muhammad ibn Salim, born in Walata and lived and died in Na'ma. Of his more than 70 compilations are *al-Taysir fi ahkam al-tanzil* (The Rulings of the Revelation [the Qur'an] Made Easy), in which he mentions the rulings of the Qur'an; a beautiful synopsis of *Sahih al-Bukhari*; a synopsis of Malik's *Muwatta* and others. See the biography of Muhammad Yahya by al-Takni (2000: 132–141). Ahmed Baba Institute, manuscript number 9207.

21 See Ahmed Baba Institute, manuscript number 5828, titled *Risala 'ila Muhammad Yahya b. Salim al-Wallati* (Epistle to Muhammad Yahya ibn Salim al-Wallati).

22 Takrur was originally a kingdom in Senegal that was a kind of successor 'empire' to the great Ghana Empire after the collapse of the latter. However, later it was used to designate the whole of black Africa, specifically sub-Saharan West Africa, and thus came to be used interchangeably with Bilad al-Sudan (Sudanic Africa).

23 See Ahmed Baba Institute, manuscript number 2752, titled *al-Sa'ada al-abadiyya fi 'l-ta'rif bi 'ulama Timbukt al-bahiyya* (The Perpetual Bliss in Introducing the Scholars of Glorious Timbuktu), pages 58–59.

24 Mahamane Mahamoudou, *al-Nawazil*, page 4 (unpublished paper in author's personal collection).

25 Due to insufficient time I was unable to collect and collate all his poetry.

26 The *Mukhtasar al-Khalil* is a standard text in the Maliki legal school and one of its most referred to sources. It was written by Ishaq ibn Khalil.

27 Ahmad ibn Ambarak b. Bark ibn Muhammad, called Abi 'l-'Araf – from the tribe of Takn, born and reared in Kalmim (Morocco) from the district of Sus and Wadanun, settled in Timbuktu. He was born into a family of knowledge, judiciary and commerce. He studied in his village then moved to the Shinqit then to Timbuktu, where he stayed most of his life. He established a library that played a pioneering role in the preservation of manuscripts, whether through copying, purchasing or exchange. See '*Khazzanah Ahmad bib Abi 'l-'Araf*, an unpublished and uncatalogued manuscript in the private collection of Mahamane Mahamoudou. See also al-Takni (2000: 6–8, 81).

28 Oral information passed on by Hamou, Abu al-Khayr's student, who heard it directly from a student of Shaykh al-Tijani ibn Muhammad al-Amin.

29 Copied by Sidi Muhammad and 'Abd al-Rahman ibn al-Sultan, Ahmed Baba Institute, manuscript number 621.

30 Al-Arawani, Abu al-Khayr. See Mamma Haidara Library, manuscript number 2264.

31 The term *al-Maghrib al-Islami* refers geographically to that area which today stretches from Libya to Morocco, including Mali and Mauritania. This is in contrast to the *al-Mashriq al-Islami*, which refers to the eastern Islamic and Arab lands such as the Levant (*Bilad al-Sham*), the Arabian Peninsula, Iraq, etc.

32 Al-Arawani, Abu al-Khayr ibn 'Abd-Allah ibn Marzuq, in Ahmed Baba Institute, manuscript number 419, and Mamma Haidara Library, manuscript number 3247.

33 Al-Arawani, Abu al-Khayr, in Ahmed Baba Institute, manuscript numbers 632 and 2812.

34 In these works are collected the traditions ascribed to the Prophet and at times to the companions. *al-Bukhari, Sahih Muslim, Jami' al-Tirmidhi, Sunan Abi Dawud, Sunan ibn Majah* and *Sunan al-Nasa'i* are known as the six canonical books of *hadith* compilations, although the others – numbering at least 15 – are regarded as reliable sources.

35 The second generation of Muslims that came after the generation of the companions; they saw, met and lived with those who were companions of Prophet Muhammad.

36 In the Maliki school the living practice of the people of Medina was regarded as a source of law and part of the legal epistemology of that school. The Malikis argue that since the Prophet – and most of his companions – lived in Medina, it stands to reason that their practice would best reflect that of the Prophet.

37 The era of the Rightly Guided Caliphs refers to the first four caliphs after the demise of the Prophet from the eleventh year of the Muslim calendar until the year forty (AD 632–660), that is, roughly a period of 30 years.

38 Authorisation (*ijaza*) is the phenomenon where the expert teacher in Islamic scholarship – specifically in the science of prophetic traditions and other sciences, as well as in the recitation of the Qur'an – gave students permission to teach those sciences from his books and ideas.

39 Manuscript numbers 8368 and 9530, Ahmed Baba Institute.

40 Manuscript number 9533, Ahmed Baba Institute.

41 Copied by the author, al-Arawani, Abu al-Khayr. See manuscript number 3085, Ahmed Baba Institute.

42 Copied by the author, al-Arawani, Abu al-Khayr. See manuscript number 4730, Ahmed Baba Institute.

43 Copied by the author, al-Arawani, Abu al-Khayr. See manuscript number 1034, Ahmed Baba Institute.

44 Manuscript number 1033, Ahmed Baba Institute.

45 Manuscript number 3442, Ahmed Baba Institute.

46 Manuscript number 6355, Ahmed Baba Institute.

47 Manuscript number 3930, Ahmed Baba Institute.

48 Manuscript number 3728, Ahmed Baba Institute.

49 Manuscript number 3884, Ahmed Baba Institute.

50 Manuscript number 5286, Ahmed Baba Institute.

51 Manuscript number 5609, Ahmed Baba Institute.

52 Manuscript number 5828, Ahmed Baba Institute.

53 Manuscript number 650, Ahmed Baba Institute.

54 Manuscript number 1545, Ahmed Baba Institute.

55 Manuscript number 1546, Ahmed Baba Institute.

56 Manuscript number 3959, Ahmed Baba Institute.

57 Manuscript numbers 2623 and 2624, Ahmed Baba Institute.

58 Manuscript number 3443, Ahmed Baba Institute.

59 Manuscript number 3247, Ahmed Baba Institute.

60 Manuscript number 3533, Ahmed Baba Institute.

61 Manuscript number 5918, Ahmed Baba Institute.

62 Manuscript number 5962, Ahmed Baba Institute.

63 Manuscript number 5981, Ahmed Baba Institute.

64 Manuscript number 5991, Ahmed Baba Institute.

65 Manuscript number 7953, Ahmed Baba Institute.

66 Manuscript number 8047, Ahmed Baba Institute.

67 Manuscript number 10, Mamma Haidara Library.

68 Manuscript numbers 8, 3245 and 3268, Mamma Haidara Library.

69 Manuscript number 5113, Ahmed Baba Institute.

70 This is a work in Arabic grammar.

71 There is an original copy in the hands of al-Shaybani, the *imam* of Ansongo (a village near Gao). He was the student of Shaykh Abu al-Khayr.

72 *Munawala* refers to a certain method or form in the way the student receives (called *tahammul* in Arabic) prophetic traditions from the teacher or the one who knows the particular prophetic tradition(s). See al-Takni (2000: 67); Mahamane Mahamoudou, *al-Nawazil*, page 4; Ahmed Baba Institute, manuscript number 2752, titled *al-Sa'ada al-Abadiyya fi 'l Ta'rif bi 'Ulama' Timbukt al-Bahiyya*, page 59.

73 Hamu (Shaykh Abu al-Khayr's student) has thus far compiled the 35 *fatwa*s under the title *Nawazil al-Shaykh Abi 'l-Khayr bin 'Abd-Allah al-Arawani* (The Verdicts of Shaykh Abi 'l Khayr ibn 'Abd-Allah al-Arawan). He is continuing in this task.

REFERENCES

Hunwick JO & RS O'Fahey (Eds) (2003) *Arabic literature of Africa: The writings of western Sudanic Africa* (Vol. 4). Leiden: Brill

Ibn al-Qayyim al-Jawziyyah (1999) *Ilam al-Muwaqiin* (Vol. 4, second edition). Beirut: Dar al-Kutub al-Ilmiyyah

Ibn Majah A (1996) *Sunan ibn Majah* (Vol. 12). Beirut: Dar al-Maarifah

al-Takni A (2000) *Izala al-rayb wa 'l Shakk wa 'l-tafrit fi dhikr al-mu'allifin min ahl al-Takrur wa 'l-Sahra' wa ahl 'l-Shinqit.* Edited by al-Hadi al-Mabruk al-Dali. Zawiya, Libya: al-Hadi al-Mabruk al-Dali

al-Tirmidhi M (1991) *Jami' al-Tirmidhi* (Vol. 9). Beirut: al-Maktab al-Islami

PART IV

THE TIMBUKTU LIBRARIES

CHAPTER 17

The state of manuscripts in Mali and efforts to preserve them

Abdel Kader Haidara[1]

This chapter explores the state of manuscripts in Mali, specifically in Timbuktu and the adjacent region, and the history of the manuscripts from before their 'disappearance' (concealment) until their resurfacing. The chapter also discusses Savama-DCI (Sauvegarde et Valorisation des Manuscrits pour la Défence de la Culture Islamique), a consortium of private libraries established in 1996, which is committed to the preservation of manuscripts in Timbuktu.

The state of the manuscripts

The city of Timbuktu is an authentic and original Islamic space that illuminated the paths of knowledge[2] and learning for students and researchers. It is rich in the art of building, and boasts an abundant literary heritage and well-stocked manuscript libraries. There are about 408 private manuscript collections in Timbuktu and the surrounding areas (and there are other collections not included in this count).

These manuscripts reflect our civilisational legacy in general but, more specifically, our recorded and written heritage. It is a legacy filled with tremendous gifts and abundant benefits. The manuscripts carry the collective memory of our ancestors, proof of their identity, their thoughts, and a summary of their experiences. They are rich in thought and scientific content and highlight the constructive role played by our predecessors and the undeniable contributions they made to the growth of Islamic civilisation.

The manuscripts deal with all kinds of knowledge and disciplines, including the Qur'an and its sciences, Qur'anic exegesis, prophetic traditions, Islamic substantive law and source methodology in jurisprudence, theology, Sufism (gnosticism), philosophy, psychology, biology, geometry, logic, rhetoric, grammar (syntax), Arabic language, travel, geography, history, politics, arithmetic, astronomy, astrology, medicine, chemistry, physics, meteorology, botany, music, methods of teaching, biographies and

Opposite: Many of the manuscripts have been damaged by insects, neglect, moisture and inappropriate storage.

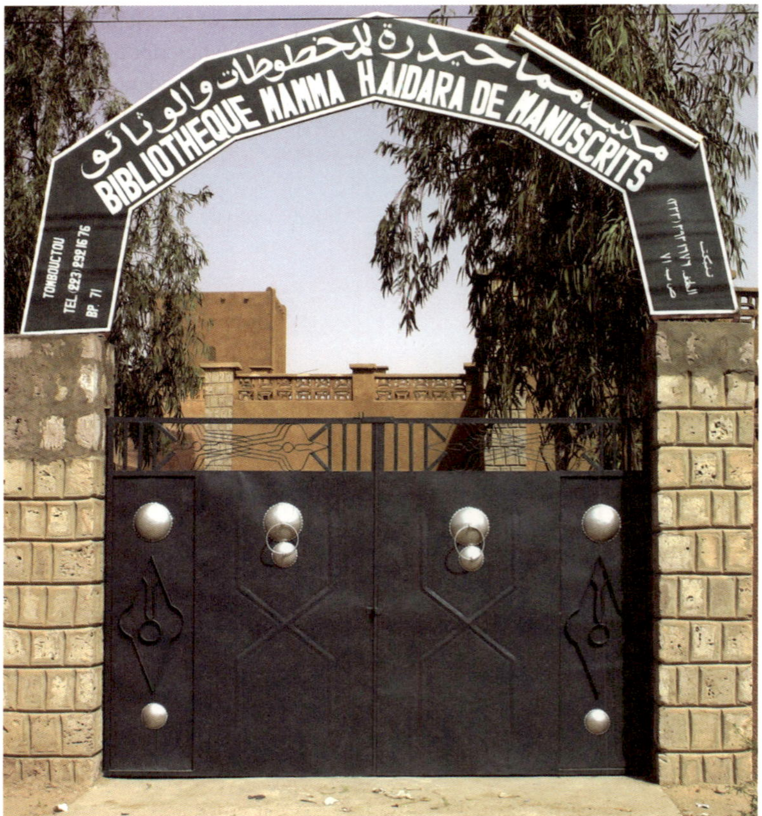

The entrance to the Mamma Haidara Manuscript Library in Timbuktu.

how to deal with disputes. They also deal with issues such as tolerance in Islam, the rights of women and children, the rights of orphans, the rights of workers, and human rights in general.

There are various kinds of documents – administrative, scientific, commercial, political; personal correspondence (letters); manuscripts on the relationship between tribes, peoples, cities and countries; *fatwas* (religious verdicts) on all issues; and so on.

However, the manuscripts are generally in a very bad state and many have been damaged by termites and other insects, human neglect, moisture in the air, inappropriate storage methods and so on. If not for these things, the estimated number of manuscripts in Timbuktu and its surrounding areas would have been in the millions. However, according to the latest estimates, there are about one million manuscripts in Mali, distributed between state, private (owned by an individual) and family libraries and collections. For example, in counting the manuscripts in some of the collections and libraries of the province of Timbuktu (not only the city), we found a total of 101 820 manuscripts. It is possible that a like number can be found in Ségou, Gao, Kaye, Mopti and Kidal.

The 'disappearance' of the manuscripts

There is no doubt that the manuscripts were concealed for a substantial period of time – a period that lasted a full century or more. The proof for this claim lies in the fact that no reference was made to the existence of the manuscripts by researchers who visited the region during the colonial era and thereafter. And so it was taught in schools and universities that Africa had no recorded (written) history, but only an oral tradition. However, the works of travellers who visited the area before the arrival of European colonialism mention the presence of priceless manuscripts. Ibn Battuta – the well-known traveller who visited the region in the pre-colonial era – and al-Hasan al-Wazzan (better known as Leo Africanus) – who visited the region in the seventeenth century – both spoke of the presence of manuscripts in the region of Timbuktu, and of those who worked on the manuscripts.

There are many factors that led to the 'disappearance' of the manuscripts and their subsequent reappearance. Perhaps one of the greatest causes was the clashes and

Custodian of the Mamma Haidara Manuscript Library, Abdel Kader Haidara.

disputes between African Islamic scholars and colonialists who, soon after their arrival, began systematically plundering the manuscripts and moving them to European cities. For example, all the manuscripts in the collection of the illustrious scholar Shaykh 'Umar Tal (d.1865) were taken to France and are still kept there in the French National Library in Paris. The manuscripts of other scholars were moved to different European capitals and major cities. Because of these developments, African Islamic scholars began to hide whatever manuscripts they had. Some placed the manuscripts in leather bags and buried them in holes; others left them in abandoned caves in the desert; and yet others sealed up the doors of their libraries with mud to conceal them.

Reasons for the reappearance of the manuscripts

With the end of colonialism, the people of the region turned their attention to the hidden and buried manuscripts. In 1964 the United Nations Educational, Scientific and Cultural Organisation held an international conference in Timbuktu to discuss the issue of African world heritage. They turned their attention to the African manuscripts and agreed on the establishment of various centres: the Institut Fondamental de l'Afrique Noire (IFAN) Dakar; a centre for researching, collating and recording oral history narratives in Niamey, the capital city of the Republic of Niger; and another centre for the search and preservation of old manuscripts based in the Malian city of Timbuktu.

Many small private collections of manuscripts are kept in homes in and around Timbuktu. Stored in trunks or cupboards, these precious family treasures are very vulnerable to decay.

As a result of this, the Ahmed Baba Institute – adopting the name of Ahmad Baba al-Sudani al-Timbukti, one of Timbuktu's greatest scholars during the sixteenth and seventeenth centuries – was opened in Timbuktu in 1973 (see Chapter 20 for more on the Ahmed Baba Institute). The staff at the Institute conducted awareness campaigns and encouraged people to bring out the manuscripts they and their forebears had concealed. They assured people that their reasons for collecting the manuscripts were to protect and preserve them from theft and further plundering. They also assured the owners that the manuscripts would remain under their control should they want to benefit from them in reading or doing research. In this manner the collection of some manuscripts was gradually undertaken and completed, thanks to the efforts of – and huge costs borne by – the Ahmed Baba Institute and its staff.

In spite of these tremendous efforts, though, most of the manuscripts were collected only after 1991. This coincided with the election of a new government that returned to the citizens their democratic rights, among which was the right to establish foundations, companies and private societies. Owners of manuscripts grabbed the opportunity and established a society for the preservation and evaluation of these manuscripts. Another awareness campaign was launched, explaining the scientific and civilisational value of the manuscripts and urging people to hand them over to the public manuscript library, the Ahmed Baba Institute.

The first private library to open its doors to the public was the Mamma Haidara Library, which obtained funding from the Andrew Mellon Foundation in New York. After this many other private libraries opened their doors. Today Timbuktu has 21 private libraries and many manuscripts are seeing the light after their concealment under the ground.

Savama-DCI

Savama-DCI, a non-governmental organisation based in Timbuktu, was established in 1996 for the protection and evaluation of manuscripts in defence of Islamic heritage. It entered into a contract with the Malian government in 2005. A partnership with the Ministry of Culture resulted in the construction of a general library made up of a number of smaller libraries in the city of Jenne. The ministry has financed the construction of this library, which commenced in 2005.

Savama-DCI has also signed an agreement with the Ford Foundation, which by the time of writing had committed itself to donating more than half a million US dollars for the period 2005–08. With this monetary assistance, three private libraries have been established and/or renovated:

- the Mamma Haidara Library (renovations);
- the Imam al-Suyuti Library, situated next to the Jingere-Ber Mosque;
- the Wangari Library.

All three libraries were inaugurated in April 2006. Savama-DCI has additionally pledged to achieve the following by the end of 2007:

- indexing (cataloguing) the information in 500 manuscripts from each of the 3 libraries;
- conserving and preserving 500 manuscripts from each of the 3 libraries;
- training youth in the art of indexing;
- training about 50 women in the art of conserving manuscripts;
- continuing the search for manuscripts in remaining private collections;
- translating 10 manuscripts on topics such as dealing with wars, tolerance in Islam and women's rights;
- organising an international meeting in Timbuktu on the African manuscripts at the end of 2008.

All of these activities have been made possible by virtue of funding from the Ford Foundation.

NOTES

1 Translated from Arabic by Mohamed Shaid Mathee.

2 Translator's note: I translate the Arabic word *'ilm* as 'knowledge' instead of 'science' so as not to give the impression that natural science (physics and chemistry) or social science – as they are defined in modern universities – was meant.

مكتبة القوطي
المكتبة الأندلسية في تمبكتو
Biblioteca Andalusí de Tombuctú

CHAPTER 18

The private libraries of Timbuktu

Ismaël Diadié Haidara and Haoua Taore[1]

The creation of private libraries is a relatively new phenomenon in the cultural life of Timbuktu. Libraries in the modern sense of the word are places where anyone can go to consult books, in this case manuscripts, open to the general public. The Timbuktu libraries are probably better referred to as private collections gathered by individuals or families who use them for educational purposes or their own private reading.

Since 1996, however, 21 of Timbuktu's private collections have been opened to the public (listed in Table 1). This number does not include libraries outside the city limits and there are many important ones, such as those in Arawan and Bujbeha in the Sahara Desert, and those located along the river in Diré.

Within Timbuktu, the Sankore district has eight libraries (38%); Badjindé has seven (33%); Sareikeyna and Sareyk have four (19%) and Jingarey-Ber has two (9%). Thus, of the seven administrative areas of the city, four contain private libraries and essentially the libraries are concentrated in the old sections of the city.

No one has yet researched the emergence of private collections over time, but a study of this kind would begin to explain their location in the older parts of Timbuktu as they proliferated between the sixteenth and nineteenth centuries. As early as the second half of the sixteenth century Ahmad Baba (and Moroccan and Spanish authors) began to mention the existence of these private collections. The *tarikhs* of the seventeenth century mention the purchase of manuscripts by different scholars, as well as copies of manuscripts commissioned by the *askiyas* for scholars in Timbuktu. Many of those opening their libraries today are descendants of these scholars.

The first private library was opened to the public in Timbuktu in the twentieth century by a Moroccan bibliophile called Ahmad Boularaf. He was born in about 1864 in Morocco, and first lived in Shinqit in Mauritania. He opened his library in Timbuktu in about 1907 and employed transcribers to copy the manuscripts that enriched his

Opposite: Ismaël Diadié Haidara, custodian of the Fondo Ka'ti Library.

Table 1 Private libraries in Timbuktu

Family custodian	Name of library	Location
Imam al-Aqib	Sankore Mosque	Sankore
Adil Muhammad Mahmud	Qadi Muhammad Mahmud	Sankore
Mahmud M Dedeou	Cheihkna Bulher	Sankore
Sidi al-Wafi	Qadi M Ahmad Baber	Sankore
San Chirfi Alfa	Alfa Salum	Sankore
Mahmud Alfa	Alfa Ibrahim	Sankore
Sidi Lamine	Sidi Gumo	Sankore
Mahamane Arbijé	Alfa Baba	Sankore
Imam Hasey/Mukhtar	al-Wangari	Bajindé
Hamdi Salum	Boularaf	Bajindé
Baba Sidi Baba	Qadi Ahmad Baba II	Bajindé
Chirfi	Mawlana Abdalrahman	Bajindé
Sumayla Hammu	Hammu	Bajindé
Abdalrahman Haman	Alfa Haman Sidi	Bajindé
Alfadi Ahmed Bano	Ahmed Bano	Bajindé
Imam Sidi Alfa Umar	Alfa Umar	Sareikeyna
Abdel Kader Haidara	Mamma Haidara	Sareikeyna
Ismaël Diadié Haidara	Fondo Ka'ti	Sareikeyna
Abdelhamid Maiga	Cheibani Maiga	Sareikeyna
Imam Soyuti/Sane	Jingere-Ber Mosque	Jingere-Ber
Imam Suyuti	Suyuti	Jingere-Ber

collection. In 1945, Boularaf's collection consisted of 2 076 manuscripts but by 2002 this number had dwindled to 680, as many of the manuscripts were donated to the Ahmed Baba Institute, a public library owned by the Malian government. When the owners of other private collections saw the decline of the Boularaf Library, they decided to open their private libraries to the public.

Of the 21 libraries listed in Table 1, only five are easily accessible to the public. These five libraries collectively house just over 20 000 manuscripts (see Table 2) and they generally experience similar problems around preservation.

Table 2 Private libraries easily accessible to the public

Library	Opened	Approx no. of manuscripts
Mamma Haidara	1996	9 000
Fondo Ka'ti	1999	7 026
al-Wangari	2003	3 000
Imam Soyuti	2004	800
Jingere-Ber	2004	500

Damage to manuscripts

Factors that result in damage to manuscripts include environmental factors, the components of paper and ink, and human greed, neglect or ignorance.

A technical study of buildings in Timbuktu would have to be done for an accurate picture to be given of the environmental factors involved in preserving manuscripts in this city. The private libraries are often housed in rooms that are exposed to the same environmental factors as any other building in Timbuktu, such as dust, light, highly variable climatic conditions and space constraints. The manuscripts are usually stored in tin trunks or on low tables called *koma*. These storage methods crush the manuscripts, prevent air from circulating between them, and promote the development of micro-organisms, including moulds and bacteria. Dust is one of the most significant causes of damage.

With the electrification of Timbuktu, the population rapidly moved from using oil lamps to gas lamps, and then to electric lamps. There has also been a shift from using fibre bulbs to neon bulbs, which consume less electricity but which contribute more actively to the discolouration of paper and ink.

Without an analysis of Timbuktu's rainfall levels combined with its temperature gradients it is impossible to accurately determine the effects of the climate on manuscripts. However, on average, during winter, the temperature oscillates between 5 and 12°C, and in summer it is between 45 and 52°C. The average difference in temperature between seasons is thus about 40 degrees, which obviously impacts on the manuscripts. Hot, dry air makes the manuscripts brittle, causing them to disintegrate, and the short rainy season causes humidity, which promotes moulds and bacteria. Other environmental factors that damage the manuscripts include pollution, floods, fires, earthquakes and the collapse of houses.

The materials from which the manuscripts are made are another source of deterioration and make their preservation problematic. In the private libraries of Timbuktu, manuscripts are generally made of parchment and paper. As far as I am aware, there is only one Qur'an from the twelfth century, which is made of vellum. Manuscripts dating from the thirteenth to the fifteenth centuries are in better condition since paper was then made using linen and cotton fibres. From the sixteenth and seventeenth centuries, the quality of the paper declined considerably. Chemical elements used for bleaching the paper and acidic gumming methods have accelerated the chemical degradation of paper, which becomes brittle, yellow and acidic. Many of the Timbuktu manuscripts are from the sixteenth and seventeenth centuries, and electronic pH measuring, as well as urgent de-acidification, has become necessary.

The ink used, mainly from the sixteenth century, was often metal based. Moisture has increased the ink's acidity levels and caused the ferrous content to damage the paper. In some cases, ink has eaten deep into the paper, the text has become illegible and the fragile paper has disintegrated.

Elements to be taken into consideration when examining the human factors responsible for the deterioration of the collections of manuscripts, and the manuscripts themselves, include:

- the closure of many libraries due to political reasons;
- dispersion of manuscripts/libraries' contents through inheritance;
- mishandling of manuscripts;
- unsuitable storage methods, for example when manuscripts are piled up in chests;
- theft of manuscripts for resale on the black market;
- breaking up manuscripts into separate sections;
- owners throwing away or destroying damaged manuscripts.

The factors discussed above have been largely responsible for the destruction of manuscripts in private collections in Timbuktu. If these manuscripts are to be preserved, the following conditions will have to be met: suitable buildings need to be constructed to house the manuscripts and equipped with restoration, digitisation and storage facilities; the manuscripts must be restored and digitised; and catalogues of each library's manuscripts must be compiled and published.

The Fondo Ka'ti Library

What is today the Fondo Ka'ti Library was begun when the Islamicised Visigoth Ali b. Zyad al-Kunti left Toledo in Spain in 1469. He went into exile with a sizeable collection of manuscripts, and ended up in Goumbou, in the Soninké region of present-day Mali. The collection was enriched in Goumbou with the manuscripts of Askiya Muhammad and Alfa Kati Mahmud b. Ali b. Zyad (d.1593). Ismael b. Alfa Kati then took charge of the collection in Tindirma, until 1612. The manuscripts were then moved to Bina, under the guardianship of Mahmud Kati II (d.1648), and after that the collection was passed on to his son, Mahmud Kati III, and moved to Goumdam. The collection was then passed on to Ali Gao, then to Mahmud Abana b. Ali b. Mahmud Kati II and finally to Alfa Ibrahim b. Ali Gao b. Mahmud Kati III, under whose guardianship the library was dispersed. In 1999 the collection was brought together again, and manuscripts, which had been dispersed among the different branches of the family who lived in various villages along the Niger River, were brought to Timbuktu.

There are 7 028 manuscripts in this collection which represents the whole compendium of medieval Islamic knowledge: Qur'an and Qur'anic traditions; law and the foundations of the law; theology and mysticism; history and genealogy; philology and grammar; logic and philosophy; poetry and metre; astronomy and astrology; medicine and pharmacopoeia; and mathematics and physics. Some of the manuscripts are juridical consultations or juridical Acts dealing with a variety of subjects such as: the life of the Jews and Christian renegades in Timbuktu; the sale and freeing of slaves; marriage and divorce; coinage and its uses; the commerce of books, salt, gold, fabrics, cereals, spices and cola nuts. Others are letters from rulers or merchants from both sides of the Sahara.

Many of the foundational works are annotated by the learned men of Cordova and Granada, Fez and Marrakesh, Qayrawan and Tripoli, Cairo and Baghdad. Others are put into verse and annotated by the learned men of Timbuktu, Jenne, Shinqit, Wadan and Walata. Many of the manuscripts are signed or annotated by Mahmud Ka'ti or his descendants.

Many of the manuscripts contain watermarks which identify the origin of the paper. Calligraphic styles range from Andalusi, Maghribi, Saharaoui, Suki, Sudani and Sharqui scripts. Their formats vary from 6 to 7 centimetres or 22 to 29 centimetres and many are covered in tooled leather. They date from the twelfth to the nineteenth centuries.

Today the manuscripts are generally in quite bad condition due to the multiple factors discussed earlier. The conservation of the manuscripts is imperative and will hopefully be achieved soon through restoration and digitisation. There are also plans for the publication of the library's catalogue.

NOTE

1 Translated from French by Davina Eisenberg.

CHAPTER 19

Shaykh Baghayogho al-Wangari and the Wangari Library in Timbuktu

Mukhtar bin Yahya al-Wangari[1]

In the name of Allah, Most Gracious, Most Merciful
The most excellent of Creators brings salutations upon the best of creation.

The city of Timbuktu was built in the latter part of the fifth century *hijri* (AD 1100) by the Tuareg of Maghsharan. They first used it as a station to move their livestock to during the winter season when they came from Arawan, a city of knowledge, pious people, saints and judges. They also stored grain and other goods there, and dug a number of wells. Timbuktu's unique location in the region attracted merchants who met and sometimes rested there. In time the city transformed into a market for Saharan traders and caravans (from Egypt and the oases of Aujalah, Ghadamas, Fazan, Tuwat, Tiflalit, Fez, Sus and Dar'a) en route to the market in Walata.

Towards the end of the eleventh century, Timbuktu replaced Walata as the destination of the trade routes. Timbuktu became an important centre for meeting and trading in West Africa. Trade in salt, wheat, slaughtered camels and gold nuggets occurred between the cities of the Bilad al-Sudan and the cities of the northern Sahara. In this way Timbuktu became a dominant centre for traders passing between Jenne and Walata. The city also became famous for its river fishing and port facilities. The importance of the Niger River for Timbuktu is illustrated in the fact that the city is located near to the river, which dominates a large part of West Africa. This gave Timbuktu, the largest commercial centre, a huge advantage over the neighbouring markets – the river was an indispensable medium for transporting merchandise and people to places such as Gao and Mopti. Trade in these neighbouring markets started to decline around the end of the fourteenth century, in part due to Timbuktu's suitable geographical location, but also because the town became the centre of learning and so attracted numerous scholars, many of whom came from patrician families.

Opposite: Inside the al-Wangari library in Timbuktu's Bajinde district, South Africa's deputy minister of arts and culture is shown the collection of manuscripts on display, and meets several of the *imams* and scholars of the city.

Thus it was not strange that a flourishing trade brought with it economic and cultural prosperity, as well as 'civilisation'. One of Timbuktu's architectural relics from the earliest days of the city's existence is the minaret of the Sankore Mosque, located in the northern area of the city. According to the historian 'Abd al-Rahman al-Sa'di (d. post 1656) in his *Tarikh al-Sudan*, it was built by the generosity of a wealthy woman of the Aghlal tribe.[2] Sankore's intellectual and cultural character developed from very early on through the co-development of the architectural movement with the construction of mosques and schools, on the one hand, and the arrival of groups of scholars, professors and students, on the other. This conferred upon the city the cloak of fame, honour and historical immortality until it was regarded by the Muslims of the region as on a par with other great Islamic centres of learning and knowledge, such as Ishbiliyah (Seville) and Granada. This reality is attested to by 'Abd al-Rahman al-Sa'di:

> Thus did they choose the location of this virtuous, pure, undefiled and proud city, blessed with divine favour, a healthy climate, and [commercial] activity which is my birth place and my heart's desire. It is a city unsullied by the worship of idols, where none has prostrated save to God the Compassionate. A refuge of scholarly and righteous folk, a haunt of saints and ascetics, and a meeting place of caravans and boats.[3]

Historians further extol the status of the city when they describe its inhabitants as people who revered knowledge and who invited scholars and the most famous jurists from as far afield as Egypt, Morocco, Iraq and Spain to teach at Timbuktu's Sankore University.[4] Al-Hasan al-Wazzan, better known as Leo Africanus, described Timbuktu as a city swarming with numerous judges, men of letters and propagators. They were spread all over the city with their manuscript libraries as a result of the flourishing of the sciences (knowledge) that were taught at the Sankore University and the numerous other circles of knowledge.[5] Trade in books, more than in any other commercial goods, became the most lucrative source for profits. The public libraries that were owned by the scholars were open to all who wanted to borrow or read books.

Education in Timbuktu

The curricula in Timbuktu's centres of learning, specifically at Sankore, included all the Islamic disciplines known and taught in the other universities in the Islamic world at that time, such as al-Azhar University in Cairo, al-Qarawiyyin in Fez and al-Qayrawan in Tunis. These disciplines included theology, Qur'anic exegesis, prophetic traditions, substantive law and the rational sciences such as syntax, morphology, rhetoric, logic, history, geography and other sciences which at that time constituted the fundamental pillars of the Islamic sciences.

The Sankore Mosque was also famous for the teaching of the Maliki legal school of thought, taught by scholars thoroughly proficient in their subject, whether they were natives of Timbuktu or from other places. This was indicative of the cultural and educa-

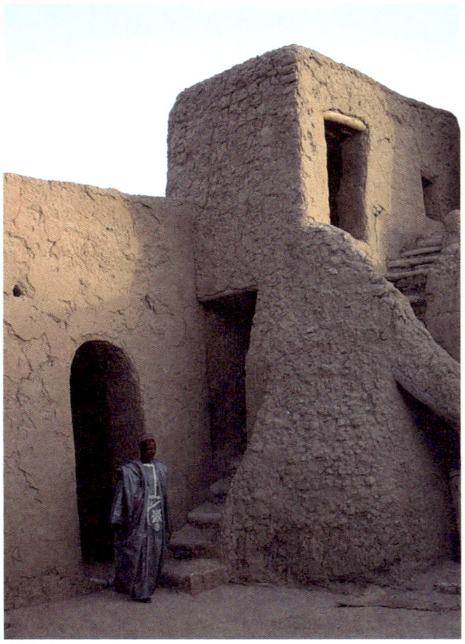
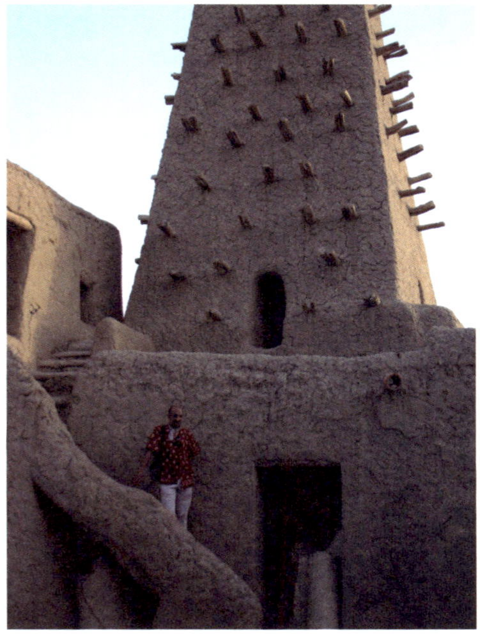

The Sankore Mosque, famous centre of learning in Timbuktu since the earliest days of the city's existence.

tional links between Timbuktu and the most famous Islamic centres of knowledge on the African continent: the cities of Qistat and Qayrawan in Tunisia and Fez in Morocco.

The eminent scholar al-Qadi Muhammad al-Kabari said:

> I was the contemporary of righteous folk of Sankore, who were equaled in their righteousness only by the Companions of the Messenger of God – may God bless him and grant him peace and be pleased with all of them.[6]

Among them were the jurist al-Hajj, grandfather of Qadi 'Abd al-Rahman b. Abi Bakr b. al-Hajj; the jurist 'Abu Abd Allah Anda Ag-Muhammad b. Muhammad b. 'Uthman b. Muhammad b. Nuh al-Sanhaji; the jurist al-Mukhtar b. Muhammad b. al-Faqih (meaning the jurist) al-Mukhtar al-Nahwi; Abu Muhammad 'Abd Allah b. al-Faqih Ahmad Buryu; the three grandsons of Anda Ag-Muhammad in the female line: the jurist Abd Allah, the jurist al-Hajj Ahmad, and the jurist Mahmud; sons of the jurist 'Umar b. Muhammad Aqit; al-Sharif Sidi Yahya; Qadi 'Umar b. al-Faqih Mahmud; Abu 'l-Abbas Ahmad b. al-Faqih Muhammad b. Said; Abu Bakr b. Ahmad Ber; the jurist Muhammad Baghayogho al-Wangari and his brother the jurist Ahmad Baghayogho and many others.[7]

Muhammad Baghayogho al-Wangari

Muhammad b. Mahmud b. Abi Bakr al-Wangari at-Timbukti al-Jinnawi, known as Baghayogho (b.1523–24, d.1594), was a distinguished shaykh and jurist. Al-Sa'di describes him thus in the *Tarikh al-Sudan*:

> He was a source of blessing, a jurist, an accomplished scholar, a pious and ascetic man of God, who was among the finest of God's righteous servants and practising

> scholars. He was a man given by nature to goodness and benign intent, guileless, and naturally disposed to goodness, believing in people to such an extent that all men were virtually equal in his sight, so well did he think of them and absolve them of wrongdoing. Moreover, he was constantly attending to people's needs...becoming distressed at their misfortunes, mediating their disputes, and giving counsel. Add to this his love of learning and his devotion to teaching, in which pursuit he spent his days...his lending of his most rare and precious books in all fields without asking for them back again...Sometimes a student would come to his door requesting a book, and he would give it to him without even knowing who the student was...doing this for the sake of God.[8]

Ahmad Baba al-Sudani (d.1627) said: 'One day I came to him asking for books on grammar, and he hunted through his library bringing me everything he could find on the subject.'[9] This anecdote sheds light on Baghayogho al-Wangari's library in Timbuktu and the distribution of his manuscripts across the city. Ahmad Baba himself had a library whose books were confiscated by the Moroccan army after their occupation of Timbuktu in 1591: 'I had the smallest library of any of my kin, and they [the soldiers of the invading Moroccon army] seized 1 600 volumes.'[10] Ahmad Baba further says about his shaykh, Muhammad Baghayogho al-Wangari:

> He had enormous patience in teaching throughout the entire day, and was able to get his matter across to even the dull-witted, never feeling bored or tired until those attending his class would grow fed up without it bothering him. I once heard one of our colleagues say: 'I think this jurist drank Zamzam water [water from the Zamzam well in Mecca] so that he would not get fed up during teaching.'[11]

Ahmad Baba also remarked on the shaykh's perseverance and adherence to worship, his good intentions and aversion to bad characteristics, and his positive approach to all people, even oppressors. He was chaste and humble and carried the flag of righteousness with tranquillity, respect and good character. Everyone loved and praised him and it was agreed that he guided people's tongues. He was very spirited in his teaching and was never harsh to beginners or to slow learners.

He devoted his entire life to teaching, even while faithfully attending to the needs of the general public and to judicial matters. Once the sultan invited him to accept appointment as *qadi* of Gao, the seat of the Songhay Empire, but the shaykh refused the offer, holding himself aloof from it. He devoted himself to teaching, particularly after the death of Qadi Sidi Ahmad b. Muhammad b. Said (there is no apparent reason for this). Ahmad Baba al-Sudani says:

> When I first met him he was teaching various classes at the beginning of his day from the hour of the early morning worship until mid-morning. Then he would return to his house and perform the mid-morning prayer (*salah al-duha*), remaining a while and after that sometimes going to the *qadi* (the judge), to plead for people or to effect a reconciliation. During the noon hour, he would teach in his house and lead the

people in the noon prayer and then teach again until the time of the afternoon prayers. After this, he would go out to teach in some other place until dusk or thereabouts. He then performed the *maghrib* prayers (a few minutes after sunset), then continued his teaching in the great mosque until the *isha* prayer (evening prayers) and then finally returned home. I heard that he always used to spend the last part of the night engaged in prayer and devotions.[12]

Al-Imam Baba Mahmud, a descendant of Muhammad Baghayogho al-Wangari and present *imam* of the Sidi Yahya mosque in Timbuktu.

Baghayogho al-Wangari's education

The shaykh studied Arabic and Islamic law under his father, al-Qadi Mahmud, and his maternal uncle, al-Faqih Ahmad. He then travelled to Timbuktu with his brother, the jurist al-Faqih Salih Ahmad. There they studied Ahmad b. Muhammad b. Said's teaching of the *Mukhtasar* of Khalil. Together they then travelled to perform the pilgrimage with their maternal uncle and met with al-Nasir al-Laqani, al-Tajuri, al-Sharif Yusuf al-Urmayuni, al-Barhamtushi al-Hanafi, Imam Muhammad al-Bakri and other scholars.[13]

On their return from the pilgrimage and on the death of their maternal uncle, they settled in Timbuktu and, under Ahmad b. Muhammad b. Said, studied jurisprudence and *hadith*. With him they also read the *Muwatta*, the *Mudawwana*,[14] the *Mukhtasar* and other works, following his teaching devotedly. Under Ahmad Baba al-Sudani's father they studied source methodology in jurisprudence, rhetoric and logic, and read with him the *Usul*, that is, the jurisprudential work of the Egyptian scholar al-Subki, and the *Talkhis al-miftah*. They also attended the spiritual retreat of Shaykh al-Khunaji whilst remaining committed to their reading, thereby gaining abundant knowledge until Muhammad Baghayogho became the unparalleled shaykh of his age in the various branches of learning.[15] Ahmad Baba al-Sudani says:

> I remained with him [Baghayogho al-Wangari] for ten years, and completed with him the *Mukhtasar* of Khalil in my own reading and that of 46 others some eight times. I completed with him the *Muwatta*, reading it for comprehension, as well as the *Tas'hil* of ibn Malik, spending three years on it, in an exhaustive analytical study. I also studied the *Usul* of al-Subki with al-Mahalli's commentary exhaustively three times, the *Alfiya* of al-'Iraqi with the author's commentary, the *Talkhis al-miftah* with the abridged [commentary] of al-Sa'd, which I read twice or more, the *Sughra* of al-Sanusi and the latter's commentary on the *Jaza'iriyya*, and the *Hikam* of ibn 'Ata' Allah with the commentary of Zarruq; the poem of Abu Muqri, and the *Hashimiyya* on astronomy together with its commentary, and the *Muqaddima* of al-Tajuri on the same subject, the *Rajaz* of al-Maghili on logic, the *Khazrajiyya* on prosody with the commentary of al-Sharif al-Sabti, much of the *Tuhfat al-hukkam* of ibn 'Asim and the commentary on it by his son; all the above were in my own reading. I read exhaustively with him the entire *Far'i* of Ibn al-Hajib, and attended his classes similarly on the *Tawdih* missing only from [the section on] 'deposited goods' to [the section on] 'judgments'; also much of the *Muntaqa* of al-Baji, the *Mudawwana* with the

commentary of Abu 'l-Hasan al-Zarwili, and the *Shifa* of Iyad. I read with him about half the *Sahih* of al-Bukhari and listened to it in his reading; similarly the whole of the *Sahih* of Muslim and parts of the *Madkhal* of Ibn al-Hajj and lessons from the *Risala* of Abi Zaid al-Qayrawani, and the *Alfiyya* and other works. I undertook exegesis of the Mighty Qur'an with him to part way through Surah al-'Araf (the eighth chapter of the Qur'an), and I heard in his delivery the entire *Jami al-mi'yar* of al-Wansharishi (d.1508), which is a large work, as well as other works of his. We discussed the finer points of these works at length and I went over with him the most important matters in them. In sum, he is my teacher; from no one else did I derive so much benefit…[as] I did from him and his books. May God shower him with mercy and recompense him with paradise. He granted me a licence in his own hand [writing] for everything for which he had a licence and for those works for which he gave his own [in order to teach and deliver texts, etc]. I drew his attention to one of my writings, and he was pleased with it, and wrote praise of it in his own hand; indeed he wrote down portions of my scholarly research, and I heard him quoting some of it in his classes, for he was fair-minded and humble, and ready to accept truth from wherever it came. He was with us [his students, fellow scholars and friends] on the day of the tribulation [Moroccan conquest of Timbuktu in 1591], and that was the last time I saw him. I heard later that he had died on Friday 19 Shawal 1002 (8 July 1594). He wrote some comments and glosses in which he pointed out the errors made by commentators on [the *Mukhtasar* of] Khalil and others, and he went through the large commentary of al-Tata'i [on the *Mukhtasar*], pointing out most valuably the errors of that author, as well as those al-Tata'i transmitted from others. I [Ahmad Baba] gathered these together in a small [independent] work – May God shower him with mercy.[16]

The library of Baghayogho al-Wangari

The library was established some time between Shaykh Muhammad Baghayogho's arrival and settling in Timbuktu and his death in 1594. The first person who undertook to preserve and protect the library was his third son, Imam Ibrahim al-Wangari, in the mid-seventeenth century. After his death it was in the care of Ahmad al-Wangari, then al-Imam Sidi Mahmud, then Alfa Aba Bakr al-Wangari, then his son Muhammad al-Mustapha al-Wangari, then al-Imam Muhammad al-Wangari, called Baniyu, and then his son al-Imam Baba Alfa 'Umar al-Wangari.

One of the great-grandchildren of the founder of the library, namely al-Imam Mahmud al-Wangari (Hasi), deserves all praise for collating and preserving the manuscripts after the library was dissolved and its manuscripts scattered in various places amongst family members in Jenne, Gundam and Timbuktu. He collected whatever manuscripts he could get from family members and kept them in one place. However, despite these efforts of al-Imam Mahmud al-Wangari, many of the manuscripts remained scattered all over until al-Sayyid Sidi Mukhtar Katani b. Sidi Yahya al-Wangari[17] started an earnest search for all the contents of the library of Shaykh Muhammad Baghayogho.

I depended on oral testimony and information found in documents (manuscripts, authorisations, letters, correspondence, etc.). I then requested a meeting with the entire family to discuss the construction and arrangement of the library. All of them agreed and thanked me for the initiative and the excellent idea which would restore to the family its status and honour in the Timbuktu community, which in turn would be nourished by the knowledge and culture offered by the library.

The entrance to the Wangari Manuscript Library in Timbuktu.

Al-Imam Baba Mahmud, the *imam* of the Sidi Yahya Mosque, who is responsible for family heritage and customs, instructed me to put all our manuscripts in one of our homes. I then organised the library, naming it the Wangari Manuscript Library. It is a private library and its doors are open to all who desire to do research and seek knowledge. The first to officially recognise the library was the municipal mayor of Timbuktu, who supported us and granted us permission to open on 26 September 2003.[18]

We received a firm commitment from all those members of the family who possessed manuscripts to hand them over until we had collected a large number of the scattered manuscripts, especially the ones in Timbuktu and Gundam. Over 1 500 manuscripts were collected at the time, although it is possible that we have more than that number. We are therefore revising the count as well as continuing the search for other manuscripts. All the manuscripts that we have thus far collected make up the contents of the Wangari Library. The library contains many works written by Moroccan and Sudanese scholars.[19] The oldest manuscript in the library, comprising parts of the Qur'an in the *riqqa*[20] script that belonged to Muhammad Baghayogho al-Wangari, was copied in 1107 *hijri*. The library also contains some important historical documents.

The current condition of the manuscripts is not good given the difficult conditions and meagre resources of this town. The manuscripts are in dire need of restoration and binding. Also, the special room in which they are stored is small and unsuitable. We therefore hope for extended assistance in order to put in place the best conditions for the preservation of the manuscripts. We have suggested to potential donors and officials that the house of Shaykh Muhammad Baghayogho al-Wangari be repaired and renovated and that it be registered on the list of national and international heritage sites, as the manuscript heritage played an important role in the dissemination of the Arabic language and Islamic culture throughout all the regions of the western Bilad al-Sudan.

The most important manuscript libraries – with all of which the Wangari Library has excellent relationships – in Timbuktu and surrounding areas are: the Ahmed Baba Institute, the Mamma Haidara Library, the Nadi Shaykh Sidi al-Mukhtar al-Kunti Library, the Fondo Ka'ti Library, the Arawan Library, the Boudjbeha Library, the al-Shaykh al-Tijan Library, the al-Shaykh Sidi Alin Library, the Muhammad Mahmud b.

al-Shaykh al-Arwani Library, the Imam al-Suyuti Library, the Qadi Ahmad Baba Abi 'l-Abbas Library, the Muhammad al-Tahir Sharaf Library, the Alfa Baba Library, the Abul Araf al-Takni al-Timbukti Library, the Qadi wa 'l-Imam al-Aqib Library, the Alfa Salim al-Lamtuni Library, the Muhammad Yaish al-Kaladi Library, the Ababa al-Bakri Library (in Gundam), the Mawlay Ali al-Shaykh Haidara Library, the Sidi al-Makki Library, the Sharaf Alfa Ibrahim Library, the Ahmad Badiji Library, the Shaykh Almin Iji Library, the Mawlay Ahmad Baber Library, the Abd al-Qadir b. Abd al-Hamid Library (in Kulanji, Senegal), the al-Kitani Library (in Fez, Morocco), the San Sharfi Library, the Ahmad Baniyu al-Wangari Library and the Baba Alfa Umar al-Wangari Library.

The legacy of the manuscripts

Throughout the past 14 centuries, Arabs and Muslims have made a huge contribution to the development of the sciences, culture and knowledge, resulting in the modern civilisation that the world is benefiting from today. They were able to spread their culture to many nations greater than them in number and stronger in resources. They manufactured the best paper, the best quality ink, and the choicest leather for manuscripts. Their books were widely available at a time when the use of paper was still underdeveloped in Europe.

Comparatively few Arabic manuscripts remain, as many were burned in the courtyards of Cordova during the time of the tragedy of Spain, or destroyed in the Tigris River during the Mongolian wars,[21] or buried in graves and walls during communist rule in central Asian Muslim countries during the twentieth century. Whatever manuscripts remain fall into one of two categories: those that found their way to Europe; and those that are still in Arab countries, many of the latter having been lost or damaged. The time has come for us to salvage what can be salvaged. We should train a capable group of people to protect and safeguard these Arabic–Islamic manuscripts, thereby assuring their preservation and creating the opportunity for researchers to benefit from them.

After conducting a study in conjunction with the Ahmed Baba Institute in 1967, the United Nations Educational, Scientific and Cultural Organisation indicated that there are over one million manuscripts in Mali. Our view as curators of the private libraries is that between the eleventh and seventeenth centuries there were more than a million manuscripts scattered between the old Sankore Mosque, other mosques, private Islamic schools and family homes. We believe that many manuscripts were taken to Morocco following the Moroccan invasion and occupation of Timbuktu in 1591.

The authors and copiers of the manuscripts – some of whom were women – were Arabs from Morocco, the East, Spain and western Arawan. Many were Africans, specifically from Timbuktu, Walata and Jenne. Some of these authors wrote in African languages like Tamasheq, Hausa, Songhay, Wolof, Fulfulde and Bambara, but all were in Arabic script. There are entries in the margins of some of the manuscripts to indicate who the original owners were, who bought the manuscript and for what price, which fluctuated between money and gold.

The manuscripts deal with the sciences of the Qur'an; Qur'anic exegesis; *hadith*, including its sciences; Islamic law; jurisprudence; *sira*; *tawhid*; morphology, linguistics, grammar, prosody, rhetoric, logic and expression; philosophy; travel; medicine and physiology; chemistry; engineering; astrology; design; inheritance; herbology; Arabic poems, documents and correspondence; slave trading; occult sciences; *fatwas*; and the discussions of the scholars. These scholars from Timbuktu and other areas exchanged knowledge and Islamic research. There were great intellectual riches in this exchange of opinions and ideas, which echoed through to the regions of the Niger River and the shores of the Arabs.

NOTES

1 Translated from Arabic by Nurghan Singh and Mohamed Shaid Mathee.

2 The author used a manuscript copy of the *Tarikh al-Sudan* as his reference but since the translators have used John Hunwick's translation of the work, from here on we will cite the translation as reference. See Hunwick (1999: lix).

3 Hunwick (1999: 29).

4 Translator's note: Hunwick cautions against applying the term 'university' to Sankore or Timbuktu as it amounts to facile comparisons. He says: 'What was taking place in Timbuktu should be viewed within the cultural context of Islamic civilization, rather than being associated conceptually with a European institution' (1999: lviii).

5 Translator's note: In addition to the Sankore Mosque there were other, albeit smaller, centres of learning.

6 *Tarikh al-Sudan*, manuscript copy.

7 Hunwick (1999: 38–49).

8 Hunwick (1999: 62–63).

9 Hunwick (1999: 63).

10 Hunwick (1999: 315).

11 Hunwick (1999: 63).

12 Hunwick (1999: 64).

13 Hunwick (1999: 65).

14 Translator's note: these two works are the earliest works of Maliki jurisprudence.

15 Hunwick (1999: 65).

16 Hunwick (1999: 65–68).

17 The author of this chapter, henceforth referred to in the first person singular (I).

18 Under the licence number 12/CUT/2003, dated 26 September 2003.

19 Translator's note: not Sudan the country, but Sudan in Arabic meaning 'black Africa'.

20 Translator's note: this is one of the many calligraphic fonts or scripts in which Arabic, specifically the Qur'an, was written.

21 Translator's note: the first incident refers to just after 1492 when Christians in Spain regained control over the whole of the Iberian Peninsula and began the Inquisition against Muslims and Jews. Thus there was a campaign to destroy all traces of Islam – through conversion to Christianity, executions or removal of people from the Peninsula, destruction of books and manuscripts, taking over of Islamic architecture such as mosques and turning them into churches, etc. The second incident refers to around 1250 when the Mongol forces swept across the world, sacking and destroying Baghdad in 1258. It is reported that their pillage lasted for around 40 days, during which time close to a million people were killed and many books were dumped in the Tigris River.

REFERENCE

Hunwick J (1999) *Timbuktu and the Songhay Empire: al-Sadi's* Tarikh al-Sudan *down to 1613 and other contemporary documents.* Leiden: Brill

CHAPTER 20

The Ahmed Baba Institute of Higher Islamic Studies and Research

Muhammad Ould Youbba[1]

The Republic of Mali is a vast country extending over 1 204 000 square kilometres. It is one of the largest countries in West Africa and one of the most widely open to the Arab world, bordering as it does on Algeria and the Islamic Republic of Mauritania. It has close ties with the Arab world, namely, Morocco, Libya, Tunisia, Egypt, Saudi Arabia and Sudan, as evidenced in manuscripts at the Ahmed Baba Institute of Higher Islamic Studies and Research (formerly the Ahmed Baba Centre or Cedrab [Centre de Documentation et de Recherches Ahmed Baba]).

Founded by the Imagharen Tuareg at the beginning of the twelfth century, Timbuktu was, at the outset, a mere watering place where, according to local legend, a woman named Bouctou had settled. These same Tuareg entrusted their heavy baggage to her when they had to travel. Tombouctou, or Timbuktu, means 'property of bouctou' in Kel Tamasheq.

Timbuktu made its debut in history with what would thereafter be its essential characteristics: a multiracial and multi-ethnic society where observance of the same religious faith (Islam), as well as a pronounced liking for business on the part of the inhabitants, were to be the principal factors in development and intermingling. A trading point for goods coming from the Maghrib and the Mashreq via Teghaza, Arawan, Biru (Walata) or Al Suq and from the south via Jenne, Timbuktu soon became the rallying point for people of diverse races, ethnic groups and cultures. Its commercial calling resulted from a series of factors which harmoniously took over from one another in space and time: the complementarity between the Maghrib and the Bilad al-Sudan, the switch of Saharan trade routes from west to east following the destruction of Ghana by the Almoravids, the Islamisation of the population and, lastly, Timbuktu's situation on the Niger River.

Opposite: Architect's model showing plans for the construction of the Ahmed Baba Institute building in Timbuktu. Construction is expected to be completed in 2008.

As to its Islamic calling, this dated back to the time of its foundation. It did not have to overturn its gods in order to embrace another faith. Did not al-Sa'di write: 'It is a city unsullied by the worship of idols, where none has prostrated save to God the Compassionate'?[2]

An ideal trading place between the Maghrib and the Bilad al-Sudan, Timbuktu soon became a coveted city. Thus it passed successively under the domination of the Mandingo Empire (after 1325), the Songhay Empire (after 1468), the king of Morocco (from 1591), the Peul Kingdom (1826–62), the Toucouleur Kingdom (1862–63), the Kunta (1863–65) and, finally, French colonial rule (1893–1960).

From August to September 1966, an international committee of experts convened in Abidjan to finalise a project on the general history of Africa. In accordance with the committee's recommendations, the general conference of the United Nations Educational, Scientific and Cultural Organisation (Unesco) adopted a resolution[3] pertaining to the study of African cultures. In terms of this resolution, Unesco organised a meeting of experts in Timbuktu on the use of written sources of African history in 1967. The idea of creating a regional resource and research centre for historical studies in the Niger valley was proposed at this meeting.

In the minds of its promoters, this centre would cover the basin of the Niger in the general sense of the word, that is, the Sudano–Sahelian zone stretching from Mauritania to the edges of Lake Chad, including Mali, Niger and Burkina Faso as well as the Saharan regions of North Africa.

In line with these suggestions, on 23 January 1970 the Mali government passed a decree[4] providing for the creation of the Ahmed Baba Resource and Research Centre (Cedrab). It was opened on 8 November 1973. The aims of Cedrab were to:

- organise the search for and collection of documents written in Arabic and African languages about the history of Africa;
- classify, microfilm and catalogue the documents;
- ensure the preservation of the manuscripts using modern, scientific methods;
- try to publish some of the catalogues and manuscripts in books and journals;
- diffuse African culture in the Arabic language, using historical manuscripts;
- strive for the development of Arabic–Islamic culture, of which Timbuktu represents one of the largest centres;
- become a central point for the exchange of information, a reception centre for researchers, a point of union for cultural relationships between Mali and the Arab world and all other countries interested in African civilisations and cultures.

The Ahmed Baba Institute of Higher Islamic Studies and Research

Following Act 00–029, Cedrab became the Ahmed Baba Institute of Higher Islamic Studies and Research (IHERI-AB) on 5 July 2000. Since then it has been a financially independent, national establishment of a scientific, technological and cultural nature.

It must, however, be emphasised that the Institute is not yet fully functional. A number of departments have experienced difficulties getting started, one problem being that of human resources. In fact, it is practically impossible to find the specialised professors needed by the Institute in order for it to function, and the only solution is to request technical assistance from other Islamic countries and organisations whilst waiting for nationals to be trained to fill the posts. For example, the Institute proposes technical assistance in the form of tripartite co-operation between Mali, which will be responsible for the visiting professors' accommodation costs; institutions such as the Islamic Educational, Scientific and Cultural Organisation and the Islamic Development Bank; countries such as Libya, Kuwait and the United Arab Emirates, which will pay the professors' salaries; and countries such as Mauritania, Morocco, Egypt and Sudan, which have sufficient human resources to supply professors and take charge of their transport.

Other problems include the facilities, notably the lack of classrooms and equipment, especially in the publishing domain. The manuscript room does not meet the scientific norms for preservation and the current library will have to be enlarged. We hope that with the co-operation of the Republic of South Africa, these problems will be solved.

It is estimated that the Institute has a manuscript collection of more than 20 000 documents, thanks to support from the national budget and the subsidies granted by the kingdom of Saudi Arabia. This figure, which makes the Ahmed Baba Institute the largest Arabic manuscript documentation centre in black Africa, represents only a fraction of the manuscript resources available in Timbuktu and its region. However, it must be noted that, despite our selective treatment of manuscripts in private libraries, the manuscripts remain exposed to damage and destruction by water, insects, fire and other factors.

Part of the Institute's collection is indexed in bilingual catalogues (Arabic–French) of 1 500 titles each, completed with the assistance of the al-Furqan Foundation of London. The Institute is looking for a partner for the Arabic edition of the remaining volumes and for the English version of the entire collection.

The Institute is collaborating with several countries, including:

- Norway – the Saumatom project (Salvaging the manuscripts of Timbuktu) is financed by Norad (Norwegian Agency for Development Cooperation);
- South Africa – for the training of persons skilled in restoration, and the construction of the Institute's new headquarters;

Left: Sign above the entrance to the existing Ahmed Baba Institute.

Right: Director of the Ahmed Baba Institute, Dr Mohammed Gallah Dicko.

- Luxembourg – which is intervening via Unesco to take responsibility for training personnel, educating those persons in possession of manuscripts, digitising manuscripts, etc.

All these projects reinforce the activities connected with electronic filing, preservation, research and training, originally undertaken with the Arelmat project (Electronic Filing of the Manuscripts of Timbuktu), financed by the Ford Foundation for one year in 2000.

The Institute inherited from the Ahmed Baba Centre a scientific journal named *Sankoré* which has experienced publication problems, but at the time of writing its fifth issue was in the process of being published. Thanks to the funds at its disposal for research, the Institute can undertake two study projects every year from now on. For example, in 2004 it launched the study project on traditional education in Timbuktu and another on the 333 saints of Timbuktu.

To summarise, the Institute has constraints on two levels, namely: a shortage of personnel, aggravated by the departure of staff due to retirement; a shortage of financial means for the acquisition of manuscripts disposed of by private persons who are no longer able to keep them in their homes. Project funds do not extend to the collection of manuscripts, which is one of the Institute's basic missions, and this constitutes a real problem for the Institute. Admittedly, the Institute's share in the national budget has been revised upwards since 2004 but this does not enable it to carry out its activities.

The Institute's statutes and structures

The Institute is a state institution, incorporated into the Ministry of Education. It has three departments: education and research, information and publishing.

The education and research department is responsible for undergraduate and post-graduate education and research. It has five sections dealing with Islam; history; social anthropology; Arabic–African linguistics and literature; and Arab–African medicine and pharmacopoeia. The information department is responsible for finding, collecting and digitising manuscripts written in Arabic and other languages; classifying and cataloguing the collection and ensuring its preservation; and promoting information about African culture and the use of Arabic through the manuscripts. The publishing department is responsible for publishing and distributing the products of the Institute's research.

The Institute's objectives and some difficulties

The overall aims of the Institute are to:

- collect and purchase manuscripts;
- educate and inform those in possession of manuscripts;
- determine the state of the localities in which the collections are held;
- make an inventory of the manuscripts;
- draw up a map of private libraries in Mali.

The results expected include digitising the private libraries (and so enriching the Institute's databank) and making the manuscripts' contents available to researchers. However, the transport available to the Institute is inadequate, so hindering its ability to successfully carry out its mission to collect, inventory and classify ancient manuscripts from all of the eight regions of Mali, covering a surface area of over one million square kilometres. At present personnel travel to the depots that they are able to reach with the means at their disposal. Nevertheless, the most remote places that cannot be reached are those most rich in manuscripts. The Institute is planning a large public awareness campaign in these zones. Clearly, this will be impossible without suitable transport. (In 2007, new vehicles were donated to the Institute.)

A possible spin-off which could guarantee the viability of the above-mentioned projects is tourism. As more tourists are attracted to Timbuktu, so more money will come into the city and thus the government can invest more money in making the project more attractive for tourists and researchers to visit.

In close collaboration with the Ministry of Tourism, such a programme would consist of exhibiting manuscripts at the Institute. The programme could also be widened to include the exhibition of private collections and other museum structures containing manuscripts in Mali. Note, however, that for maximum profitability, all facets of the tourism industry would need to be embraced, including accommodation, catering and transport. Tourism would not prove viable if it were limited to revenue collected from guided tours only.

South African archivist, Mary Minicka, studying watermarks on a manuscript at the Ahmed Baba Institute.

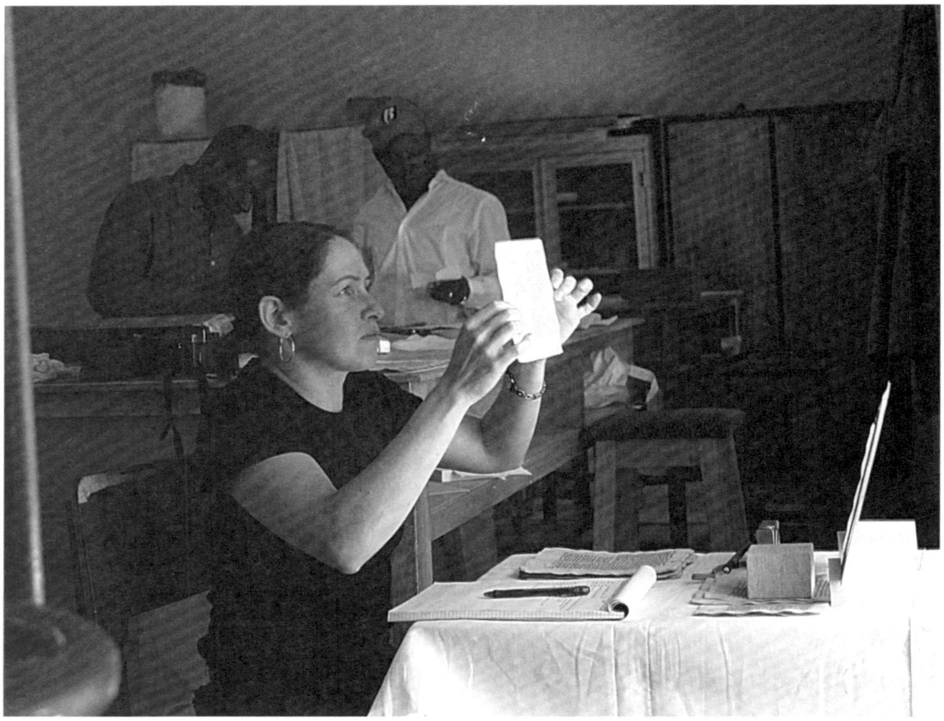

The history of Mali's manuscripts

As has been noted, the presence of manuscripts in Mali is linked to the Islamisation of the country. The use of Arabic in diplomatic relations with the contemporary Arab–Islamic empires, Almoravids, Merinides and so on contributed to the development of this language. The pilgrimages of Emperor Mansa Musa in the fourteenth century and Emperor Askiya Muhammad in the fifteenth century were just as instrumental in bringing this part of Africa into contact with the Arab–Muslim world of the Maghrib and the Middle East. Between the first half of the eighteenth century and the first half of the nineteenth century a plethora of erudite persons from the north of Timbuktu rose to prominence, amongst which were the Kunta, Ansaré, Suqi and Arawani peoples. The Peul and Toucouleur Islamic revolutions also fuelled a wealth of literature in Arabic and Fulani.

Colonisation dealt a hard blow to the legacy left by these people. Many collections were burned, looted or taken away. As a result of the droughts in the early twentieth century, many who possessed manuscripts got rid of their patrimony by burying it in the sand or entrusting it to neighbours before emigrating in large numbers to other countries. Despite these vicissitudes, West Africa – and Mali in particular – still harbours many unlisted, unidentified manuscripts and, even today, many families still jealously hide their collections. Those who are searching for manuscripts are denied access to them, as there is fear of a repetition of the requisitioning and pillaging which occurred during the colonial era. The Ahmed Baba Institute has embarked on search missions in the regions of Timbuktu, Gao and Mopti. The objectives of these missions are to educate and inform those persons possessing manuscripts about their importance, to locate the manuscripts, microfilm them or even negotiate their possible surrender to the Institute, as it is a national institution.

The Institute envisages proceeding with these missions in other regions of the country in order to enable it to draw up a map of existing private libraries, to find out about the state they are in and to propose a comprehensive strategy which would serve as a plan of action for the preservation of the manuscripts.

Content of the manuscripts

Those at the Institute understand the word 'manuscript' to refer to all works handwritten in the Arabic script by Malian and foreign writers of past centuries: literary books, legal agreements, correspondence and other documents. The manuscripts occupy a special place in our culture, otherwise considered to be for the most part oral. They have in fact contributed to the cultural development of our country across time and space, and are preserved in family collections throughout the country.

Apart from those belonging to the Institute, the manuscripts generally enjoy private legal status, for they are bequeathed to their owners, from father to son, down through the generations, sometimes for several centuries. Despite their legal status as private property, the manuscripts form part of the national written heritage, which is why the Institute is seeing to their proper preservation, giving assistance to educate and inform their owners and sometimes intervening in the treatment of the manuscripts. The importance of the manuscripts lies in their quantity, the quality of their contents and the owners' attachment to them. The manuscripts represent a patrimony bequeathed by forebears and are therefore of great spiritual and moral value to the owners. For them the manuscripts are a sacred legacy, and it is as difficult to sell them as it would be to exchange their father's cap for money. Family pride is largely the reason. Unfortunately, most of those who possess manuscripts are no longer in a position to preserve their collections due to a lack of means and expertise.

The manuscripts are bequeathed to their owners, from father to son, down through the generations, sometimes for several centuries. The manuscripts represent a patrimony bequeathed by forebears and are therefore of great spiritual and moral value to the owners. For them the manuscripts are a sacred legacy, and it is as difficult to sell them as it would be to exchange their father's cap for money. Family pride is largely the reason. Unfortunately, most of those who possess manuscripts are no longer in a position to preserve their collections due to a lack of means and expertise.

Furthermore, there is the problem connected with the contents of the manuscripts themselves. The manuscripts deal with all manner of topics and recount facts relating to all aspects of life: historical, political, social and private events. The nature of some of these events, which happened a very long time ago, may have serious repercussions on current social life. For example, among the manuscripts there are commercial deeds and legal transactions which may compromise families who are well placed in the social hierarchy by recounting all sorts of unfortunate events or despicable acts involving their ancestors. There are some which mention a family's debt with regard to another family or unjustly acquired wealth (land, house) by a certain family.

Whether the manuscripts are of a legal or commercial nature or mere correspondence, they contain countless details. We find documents originating from kings, princes and

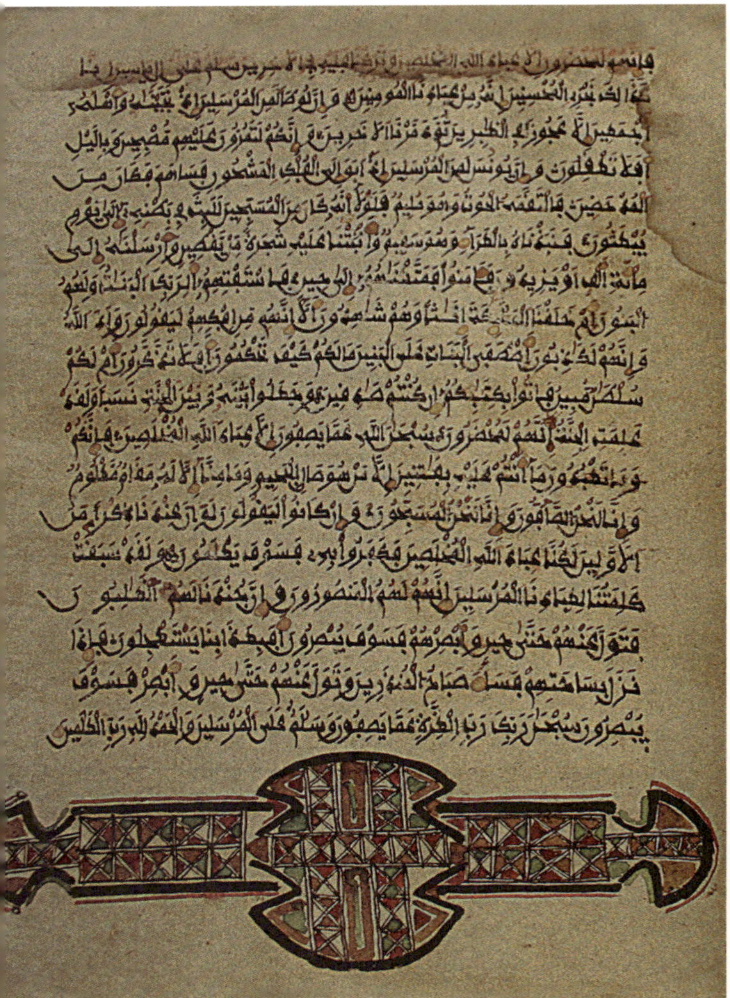

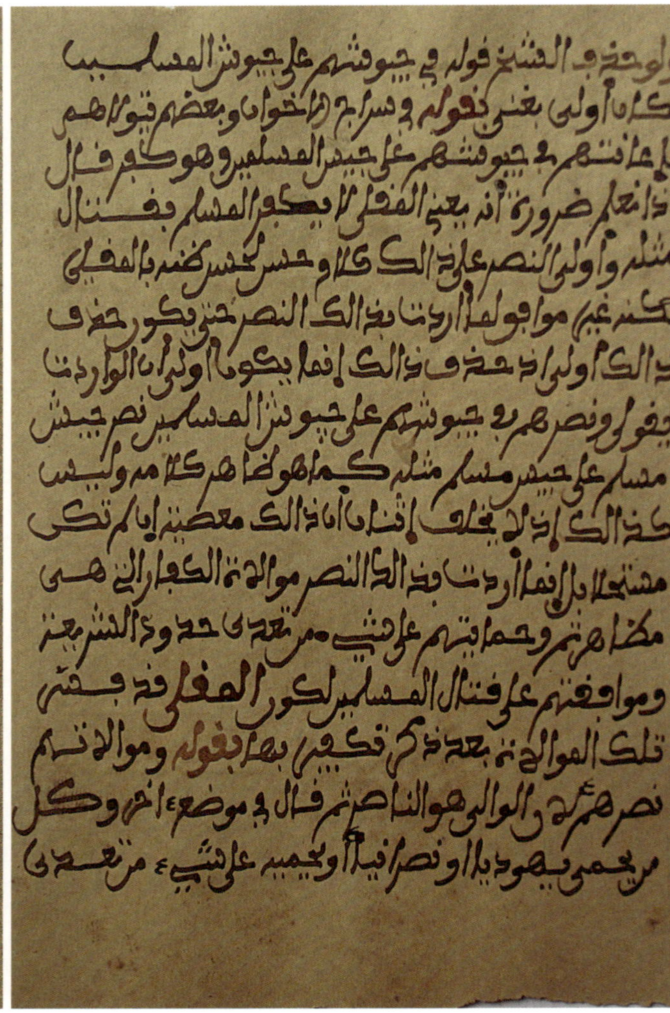

political figures whose writings give us detailed information about the period in question. They also cover all domains, namely history, literature, Islamic sciences, commercial deeds, law, stories about travel, trans-Saharan commerce in particular, *fatawa*, panegyrics, scientific treatises, pharmacopoeia, correspondence and so on. A distinction should be made here between these manuscripts and those imported from the Maghrib and the Middle East which, for the most part, are fundamental works on the *fiqh*, apart from a few scientific treatises.

Manuscripts produced in Timbuktu and its surrounds consist of correspondence, poems, *fatawa* and the *tawhid* treatises which fuelled conflicts between the religious brotherhoods of Qadiriyya and Tijaniyya in the eleventh century *hijri*.

The topics dealt with in the manuscripts at the Institute can be categorised as follows: *Fiqh*, including *fatawa* (28%); correspondence (24%); history (20%); panegyrics (10%); grammar (10%); Qu'ran and exegesis on the Qu'ran (4%) and science (2%). Approx-

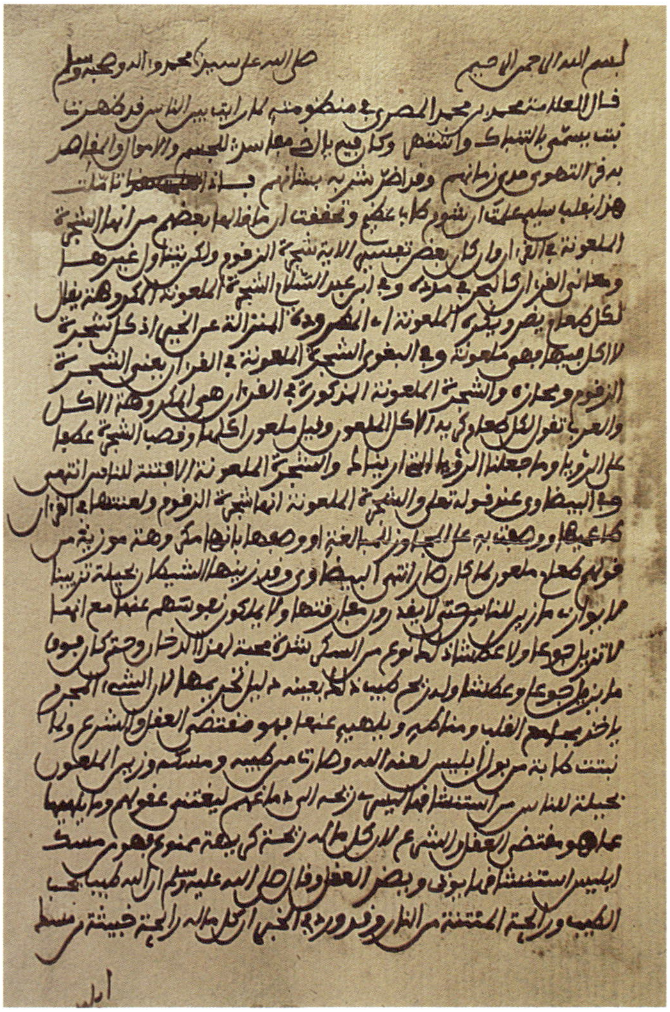

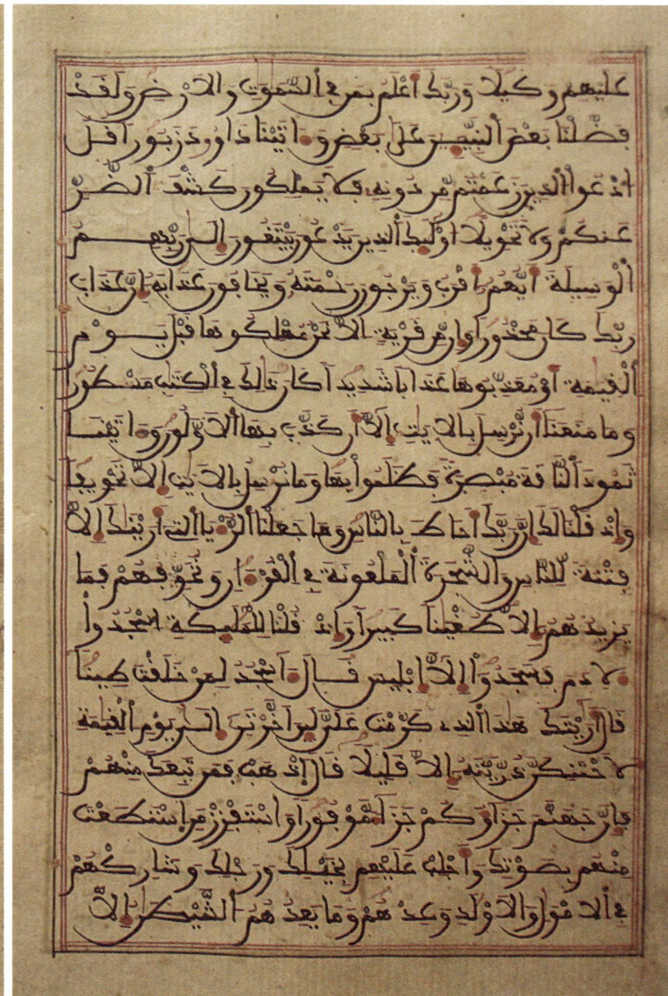

imately 2 per cent of the manuscripts are *ajami* and have not yet been sorted according to these categories.

The manuscripts constitute for Timbuktu and Mali a source of justifiable pride, a jealously guarded treasure. Among our populations, anything written in Arabic script assumes a sacred character because this script is also that of the Holy Qu'ran.

The calligraphy of the manuscripts

To date, very little work has been done on the calligraphy used in the manuscripts, despite its importance in the written heritage, and practically no study has been made of the writing tools and the inks used. This nevertheless constitutes an interesting field of research. According to Ibn Khaldun, the calligraphy in African manuscripts derives from Andalusian calligraphy, whence the introduction of Andalusian books in our subregion. (Also see Chapter 5 of this volume.)

Different calligraphic styles found in manuscripts in Timbuktu. From left to right, these are examples of Suqi, Sudani, Sahrawi and Maghribi script.

The principal forms of calligraphy used in the manuscripts at the Institute are:

- the eastern form, which is characterised by the simplicity of the letters and the absence of embellishment;
- the African form, used by the Peuls, Toucouleurs, Soninkés, Hausa and Wolofs. The letters are thick and solid, particularly those used by the Hausa. This form is thought to originate from the Maghribin writing;
- the Sanhajan form, prevalent among the Berber tribes, thought to be a local creation and related to Tafinagh, like the Suqi form.

After independence, the eastern calligraphic forms imposed themselves with the arrival of academics from countries like Egypt and Arabia, giving the local forms of calligraphy an archaic connotation. The Institute is currently trying to revive these forms of writing by revitalising the copyist profession.[5]

The writing tool used in West African manuscripts in general, including those at the Institute, was the calamous, varying in length from 12 to 16 centimetres and made from the branch of a local shrub or a bird quill. The ink container, shaped like a small bottle, was made locally from leather or wood from the calabash tree.

The most common colours of ink used were black and then red. Other colours used were brown, yellow and blue. Inks were made from charcoal and gum arabic, but sometimes other products were added to make them brighter (gelatine) or indelible (iron rust). These products are very acidic and, with time, rot and perforate the paper.

Preserving the manuscripts

Preservation involves the set of techniques and processes intended to halt or retard the progressive deterioration of the organic, material components of the manuscripts. These components (parchment, paper, ink, etc.) are subject to ageing.

It is an undeniable reality that the manuscripts are in a state of deterioration. Nature has endowed us with a warm, dry climate suitable for the preservation of paper, but that does not mean that our manuscripts are secure from all danger. There are many other harmful factors, such as biological (insects), chemical (acidity, humidity), natural (fire, water, wind, dust) and human (careless handling, theft, fraudulent sales, etc.). To guard against this threat, the Institute clears the depots of dust and regularly fumigates the manuscripts. In spite of this, most of our manuscripts are in a serious state of deterioration and show signs of irreversible damage caused by water, insects and the incorrect preservation methods to which they were subjected before reaching us. They are faded and discoloured, which often renders the texts illegible.

The room in which the manuscripts are stored at the Institute is also inadequate. It is cramped and poorly equipped, with a shortage of glass cabinets – currently the preferred storage space. The increasing number of manuscripts – 20 000 in a room designed for

5 000 – has resulted in the manuscripts being stacked one on top of the other, which is detrimental to their preservation as they are old and their own weight is crushing them. The library has no ionometer to measure the acidity of the paper and of consumables such as glue and leatherette.

With the aid of partners, the Institute today possesses the equipment necessary to cope with the problem of preservation and restoration, as well as a large amount of computer hardware and consumables for both preservation and digitisation. In the workshop where the binding and restoration is carried out, modern equipment is used to make the covers for the documents and to bind and restore the manuscripts. Restoration is a highly technical profession which necessitates the completion of a training programme, and is not to be confused with binding. Nowadays preservation and restoration techniques are highly developed, with continuous research in the domain, and those involved must keep abreast of developments in research.

Physical preservation is an essential aspect of the safe keeping of the manuscripts and, cognisant of this, the Ahmed Baba Institute equipped itself with a restoration–preservation unit in 2000. Those employed in this unit include local artisans and graduates from the National Arts Institute of Mali.

The work in this unit consists of clearing the manuscripts of dust, regenerating the inks or restoring those manuscripts which are deteriorating before making the protection boxes to ensure more long-term preservation. Prior to being restored, the manuscripts undergo the following procedure:

1 Transport from the storage room to the workshop.
2 Recording the details of the file containing the manuscripts: number of manuscripts; number of folios; dimensions; identification of the type of binding.
3 Assessment of each manuscript's state of preservation.
4 Identification of the destructive elements (acidity, mould, fungus etc.).
5 Filming the manuscripts before preservation work is undertaken.
6 Determination of the work to be done on each manuscript.

The manuscripts are scanned again after the preservation work has been carried out. At present the construction of the protection boxes for the manuscripts constitutes the unit's principal activity. The technique used consists of assembling several pieces of cardboard, previously cut up according to the dimensions of the manuscript to be protected. Once assembled, the pieces of cardboard are then wrapped in a neutral (acidless) fabric which is in turn covered with leatherette of different colours – the latter for purely aesthetic reasons. The finished product is a simple box with a lid facilitating the opening and closing of the cover for the documents without damaging the manuscript or manuscripts. The boxes are designed to hold one or several manuscripts, depending on the volume of manuscripts. All the boxes are numbered. All the materials used – glue, paper, leatherette – are acid free. Thus protected, the manuscripts have a longer preservation period.

At present the construction of the protection boxes for the manuscripts constitutes the unit's principal activity. The technique used consists of assembling several pieces of cardboard, previously cut up according to the dimensions of the manuscript to be protected. Once assembled, the pieces of cardboard are then wrapped in a neutral (acidfree) fabric which is in turn covered with leatherette of different colours - the latter for purely aesthetic reasons. The finished product is a simple box with a lid facilitating the opening and closing of the cover for the documents without damaging the manuscript or manuscripts. The boxes are designed to hold one or several manuscripts, depending on the volume of manuscripts. All the materials used - glue, paper, leatherette - are acid free. Thus protected, the manuscripts have a longer preservation period.

Digitisation in progress at the Ahmed Baba Institute.

The role of the South African specialists who have worked in Timbuktu to train local conservators has been invaluable.

Digitisation

This is one of the sections most recently created by the Institute in collaboration with technical and financial partners. It was created out of concern for safeguarding the original manuscripts and facilitating their accessibility to a maximum number of researchers, by making the written documents available in another medium. At the time of writing, 55 500 pages of 325 manuscripts had been digitised.

Digitisation work consists of digitising (scanning) each manuscript page by page. The work is carried out on the software Adobe Photoshop. The resolution used is 150 PPP (Point-to-Point Protocol). The Tiff format is used for registering the back-up of a maximum amount of data, as the JPEG format only accepts part of the image. The digitised pages are then codified for consultation and identification. The digitisation work is carried out using a flat, cold-light scanner (CanoScan FB1210U). On average, 100 pages are digitised daily. The Institute has three functional scanners. Following this, the manuscript is saved on to CD with its identification sheet.

Digitisation is important for the preservation of the manuscripts: it allows for minimum handling of the original documents by researchers, documents which are often fragile on account of their age, and protects them from further deterioration; the CDs containing the manuscripts constitute a very useful form of safeguarding and preservation; the Zoom Tool or the colour level can be used to render legible those manuscripts which have deteriorated; the digitised documents will also form a virtual library on the internet (the manuscripts digitised as TIFF files will be converted to JPEG).

However, there are some problems: the Institute's computing equipment is getting older and older and the computers do not have a large capacity, hence the problem of image storage. The dimensions of the scanners prevent certain manuscripts from being properly digitised and the digitisation process is very slow.

Cataloguing

Cataloguing is an important aspect of the work done on manuscripts. It allows for the identification and indexing of the documents. This work consists of reading the document meticulously and selecting 33 items of information from each manuscript. This information is then entered on a data identification sheet together with the number of the manuscript, the identity of the author and the document, its physical condition, a summary of the document and the bibliographic sources referred to in the document. After this, the data identification sheets are captured on MS Word software. Depending on the volume, the condition and the theme of the manuscript, each researcher processes an average of one manuscript per day.

This work is important because it identifies each manuscript and gives some idea about its content. The data identification sheet is a useful tool for researchers who may work with the manuscript. The identification sheet also accompanies the digitised manuscript on CD. It will consequently enable us to develop a manuscript database and thereby facilitate accessibility on intranet or internet once the Institute is connected, thus opening up access to the manuscripts to the outside world. It will also play a part in publishing a catalogue of the manuscripts for the Institute. At the time of writing, 2 224 manuscripts had been processed, catalogued and captured on MS Word.

Some of the difficulties encountered by those cataloguing the manuscripts are:

- the advanced state of deterioration of certain documents, rendering the text illegible;
- difficulty in identifying the types of calligraphy used;
- no recorded authors for certain manuscripts;
- manuscripts having several authors and therefore not knowing who wrote what;
- difficulty in identifying the make and quality of the paper;
- the absence of coordination and contact with those working on the cataloguing in other countries;
- the need for further education to raise the skill level of those working in the libraries and doing the cataloguing.

Training

In order to keep up to date in matters of preservation and restoration, the Institute attaches much importance to training. The Institute has initiated a training workshop in restoration and preservation, conducted by trainers from the Institute, for the benefit of library workers at Timbuktu's private libraries.

The Institute receives international experts – chosen by Unesco and the Institute – to supervise its activities and provide training (Hubert Emptoz for digitisation and Jean-Marie Arnoult for preservation).[6] Each year, training over a period of two to four months is given to library workers in Bamako and in Timbuktu, as well as in other countries, for example France.

Within the scope of its collaboration with the Institute, South Africa receives library workers each year for a series of training courses at the National Archives of South Africa. Some of the difficulties encountered in the training process are:

- the size of the Institute's premises, which were originally designed for a limited number of workers and are too small to host more training staff;
- the high cost of importing consumables and other materials needed in the training courses, and that are not available on the Malian market;
- the shortage of equipment such as presses and cutters (at present there is only one press available at the Institute);
- the lack of measuring equipment and apparatus;
- the lack of documentation in matters relating to restoration and preservation.

Training of personnel is imperative as much for the Institute as for the private libraries. However, manuscript libraries are currently not sufficiently well established to generate funds with a view to professionalising their personnel. For this reason it is important to consider creating a course in library science at Bamako University. Efforts in training will come to naught, though, if other incentives are not given: financial, material and legal protection of the manuscripts in order to create professions for the trainees to move into.

NOTES

1 Translated from French by Verity Newett.

2 See Hunwick (1999: 29).

3 Resolution number 3324.

4 Decree number 12/PGRM.

5 The profession of copying manuscripts and reproducing them was common in the Islamic world before the popularisation of the printing press and was the way manuscripts were propagated and preserved.

6 Professor Hubert Emptoz from the Laboratoire d'Informatique en Images et Systèmes d'information (LIRIS), Lyon, France. Jean-Marie Arnoult, General Inspector of Libraries, French government.

REFERENCE

Hunwick J (1999) *Al-Sa'di's Tarik al-Sudan down to 1613 and other contemporary documents.* Leiden: Brill

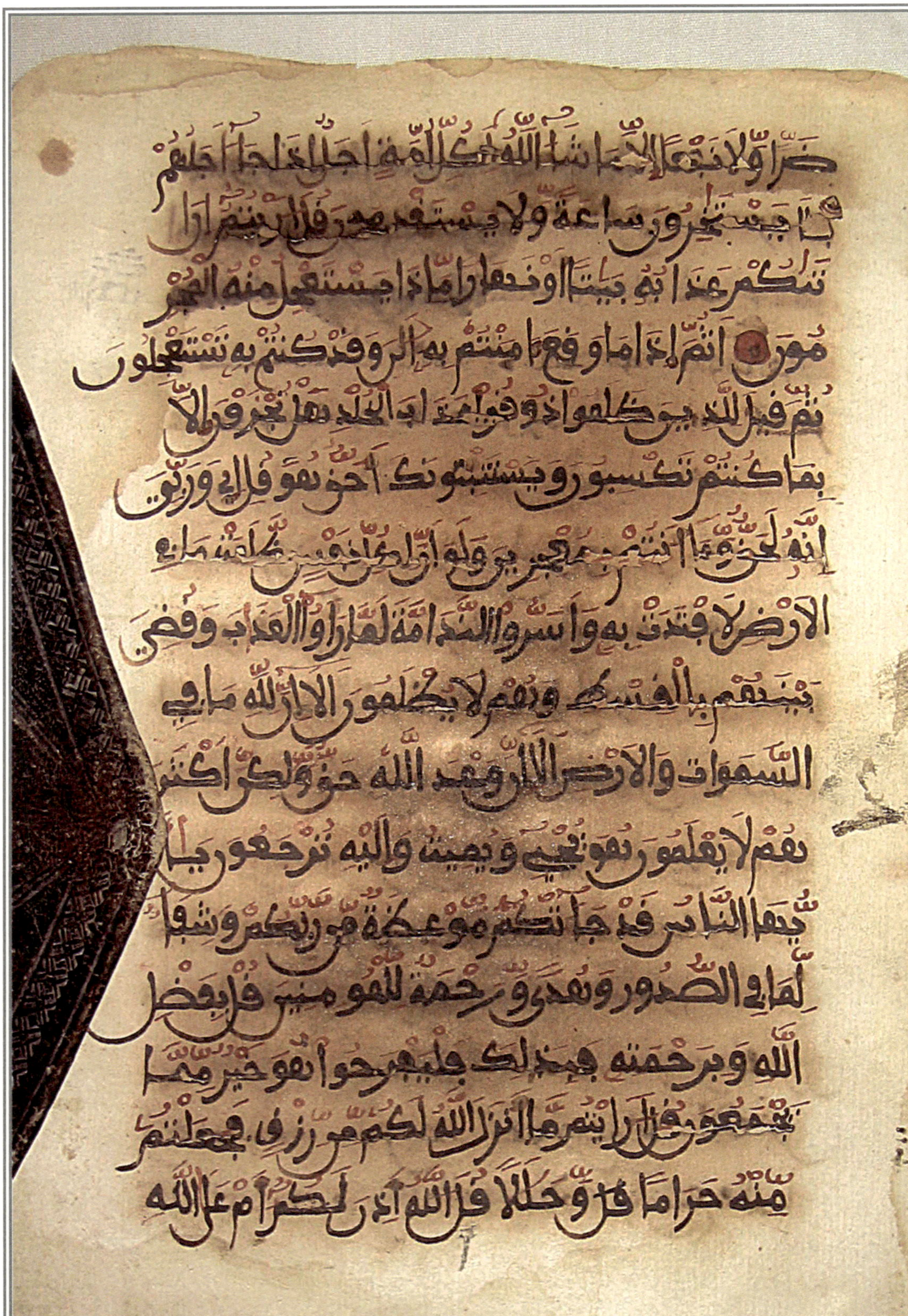
ضرا ولا نفعا الا ما شاء الله لكل امة اجل اذا جاء اجلهم
فلا يستاخرون ساعة ولا يستقدمون قل ارءيتم ان ا
تيكم عذابه بياتا او نهارا ماذا يستعجل منه المجر
مون اثم اذا ما وقع ءامنتم به ءالان وقد كنتم به تستعجلون
ثم قيل للذين ظلموا ذوقوا عذاب الخلد هل تجزون الا
بما كنتم تكسبون ويستنبئونك احق هو قل اي وربي
انه لحق وما انتم بمعجزين ولو ان لكل نفس ظلمت ما في
الارض لافتدت به واسروا الندامة لما راوا العذاب وقضي
بينهم بالقسط وهم لا يظلمون الا ان لله ما في
السموات والارض الا ان وعد الله حق ولكن اكثر
هم لا يعلمون هو يحيي ويميت واليه ترجعون يا ا
يها الناس قد جاءتكم موعظة من ربكم وشفا
ء لما في الصدور وهدى ورحمة للمومنين قل بفضل
الله وبرحمته فبذلك فليفرحوا هو خير مما
يجمعون قل ارايتم ما انزل الله لكم من رزق فجعلتم
منه حراما وحلالا قل الله اذن لكم ام على الله

CHAPTER 21

The Arabic Literature of Africa project

John Hunwick

The origins of the Arabic Literature of Africa project go back almost 40 years, though its inspiration originates even before that. In 1964 at the University of Ibadan, Nigeria, I initiated a project called the Centre of Arabic Documentation. The objective of the project was to microfilm Arabic manuscripts from northern Nigeria, and to catalogue and analyse them. As part of the project I started in the same year to publish a journal called *Research Bulletin* through the university's Institute of African Studies. In the third issue of the journal, in July 1965, I announced in the introduction that a project had been conceived to assemble biographical information about authors of Arabic writings and the works they had written, based on existing sources, and supplemented by information arising from the manuscripts that had been microfilmed. The eventual aim was to bring all this information together and publish it in a bio-bibliographical volume on West African Arabic writers. The model for this volume was the celebrated multi-volume work by the German scholar Carl Brockelmann, *Geschichte der arabischen Literatur*: two original volumes (later revised and updated) and three supplementary volumes all published in the 1930s and 1940s. These volumes covering Arabic writing tradition from Morocco to India comprise a total of 4 706 pages, but have only four pages referring to Arabic writings in sub-Saharan Africa. Certainly, before the 1950s little was known about the Arabic writings of Africa south of Egypt and the Maghrib, although one or two collections of such manuscripts did exist in Europe – most notably the library of al-Hajj 'Umar b. Sa'id al-Futi and his descendants, seized by French colonial forces in Ségou in 1890 and preserved in the Bibliothèque Nationale in Paris, but left uncatalogued for almost a century.

Certainly, before the 1950s little was known about the Arabic writings of Africa south of Egypt and the Maghrib, although one or two collections of such manuscripts did exist in Europe – most notably the library of al-Hajj 'Umar b. Sa'id al-Futi and his descendants, seized by French colonial forces in Ségou in 1890 and preserved in the Bibliothèque Nationale in Paris, but left uncatalogued for almost a century.

The *Arabic Literature of Africa* series

In view of the absence of any guide to sub-Saharan Arabic writings, and the evident richness of such a tradition in West Africa, the idea of creating such a guide for West Africa grew in my mind, though at that time I thought that it would all be contained

A manuscript ready for restoration, digitisation and conservation.

in a single volume. One just could not imagine how much Arabic writing there had been, or the huge number of hidden manuscripts that would eventually come to light. The map on page 308 shows where some of the larger manuscript and archive collections from West Africa are currently held.

For the next 25 years I continued to gather information about the titles and locations of West African Arabic manuscripts, recording it all, before the existence of computer technology and its public availability, on card indexes. In 1980 (whilst at the American University in Cairo) I discussed the project with Professor Sean O'Fahey of the University of Bergen, Norway, whose greatest area of interest and knowledge, as regards Arabic sources, was the Nilotic Sudan and East Africa. O'Fahey immediately offered collaboration to expand the project from West Africa to include the whole of sub-Saharan Africa. We decided that we would, as it were, divide the continent between ourselves. Whilst I would focus on Africa west of Lake Chad, O'Fahey would work on Africa to the east of Lake Chad, covering the Sudan, the Horn of Africa, and East Africa. The first product of this enterprise was a journal called *Arabic Literature of Africa: A Bulletin of Biographical and Bibliographical Information*, of which three issues were published through the Program of African Studies at Northwestern University between 1985 and 1987.

In the early 1990s we began to plan publication of a series of volumes of such information, and in 1994 and 1995 the first two volumes were published by Brill Academic Publishers of Leiden, Netherlands, the original publishers of Brockelmann's series.[1]

Volume 1, *Arabic Literature of Africa: The Writings of Eastern Sudanic Africa to c.1900,* was compiled by O'Fahey. He was assisted by two Sudanese scholars, Muhammad Ibrahim Abu Salim and Yahya Muhammad Ibrahim; two German scholars, Bernd Radtke and Albrecht Hofheinz; and a Norwegian scholar Knut Vikør who, together with O'Fahey and myself, had in 1990 launched at the University of Bergen an annual journal called *Sudanic Africa: A Journal of Historical Sources*, in which much information on African Arabic writings has since been published, as well as short Arabic documents in their original Arabic text with English translations.

All volumes of *Arabic Literature of Africa* were planned to refer to 'Sudanic Africa', a term primarily referring to the Sahelian region, known in medieval Arabic as the *Bilad al-Sudan* (land of the black peoples), but also to include the rest of 'sub-Saharan Africa'.

Volume 1: Eastern Sudanic Africa

The first volume – on eastern Sudanic Africa – dealt with the area that now comprises the Republic of the Sudan, covering the seventeenth, eighteenth and nineteenth centuries. The information in this volume, and all others since, was divided into chapters according to periods of time and/or the interrelationship of the authors and their writings, for example members of a Sufi 'brotherhood' (*tariqa*). In fact, some of the richest chapters in Volume 1 deal with Sufi *tariqas*. Among these was that of a Sufi shaykh, who originated from and initially functioned outside the Bilad al-Sudan, but whose teachings later had much influence on it and on the Horn of Africa. This was Ahmad b. Idris, who was born in Morocco in 1750 and died in the Yemen in 1837. Such an inclusion is justified in the introduction to the chapter, which reads as follows:

> We have grouped here the Sufi traditions that derive from Ahmad b. Idris, his son 'Abd al-'Ali, and his Sudanese student Ibrahim al-Rashid. This tradition includes the Idrisiyya (variously called Ahmadiyya Idrisiyya, or Ahmadiyya), Rashidiyya, Sahiliyya and Dandarawiyya *tariqas*, that were to spread to Egypt, Ottoman Turkey, the former Yugoslavia and Albania, Syria, Somalia, East Africa, and southeast Asia.[2]

One other *tariqa*, originating from a disciple of Ahmad b. Idris, forms another separate chapter. This is the Sanusiyya, founded by Muhammad b. 'Ali al-Sanusi, who was born in Mustaghanim in Algeria in 1787 and set up his *tariqa* in what is now eastern Libya, eventually spreading it through southern Libya and Chad, with branches of it going as far east as Darfur in the Sudan and as far west as Kano in Nigeria.

Another major chapter deals with the writings of the Sudanese Mahdi Muhammad Ahmad, who took over the area from the Turco–Egyptians in 1884, and his successors, beginning with the *khalifa* 'Abd Allahi.

O'Fahey and Hunwick will draft a follow-up to this volume in the coming years, with some Sudanese and European collaborators, dealing with Arabic writings of the West Africa in the twentieth century, including material outside the 'intellectual tradition', such as the writings of the famous novelist al-Tayyib Salih. This will constitute Volume 5 of *Arabic Literature of Africa*.

Volume 2: Central Sudanic Africa

Hunwick compiled Volume 2 with the assistance of three Nigerian scholars (Razak Abu Bakre, Hamidu Bobboyi and Muhammad Sani 'Umar), as well as two German scholars (Roman Loimeier and Stefan Reichmuth). It was published in 1995 with the subtitle 'The Writings of Central Sudanic Africa'. Central Sudanic Africa is defined principally as Nigeria, but the volume also includes material on parts of Cameroon, Chad and Niger.

The volume starts off with a chapter entitled 'The Central Sudan before 1800', beginning with a poet called Ibrahim b. Ya'qub al-Kanemi, who died around 1212 and is known to us through poems he composed when he was in Morocco and Spain (Andalusia), parts of which were recorded in writings by Arabic authors of those regions. He was certainly the earliest known West African writer, but by the sixteenth century many more writers emerged, not only in northern Nigeria (Bornu and Hausaland), but also in the Timbuktu region. Perhaps the most important chapters in that volume deal with a family whom I call the Fodiawa. The primary scholar of that family was 'Uthman b. Muhammad Fodiye, also usually known as 'Uthman dan Fodio (d.1817), the Islamic regenerator (*mujaddid*) and creator of an Islamic state, generally known nowadays as the Sokoto Caliphate. He was a Fulani whose origins were in Futa Toro (Senegal), from where ancestors of his migrated to Hausaland in the fifteenth century. He was a note-worthy scholar who wrote at least 100 works in Arabic, plus numerous poems, mainly in Fulfulde. Other members of his family whose works are listed include his brother 'Abdullahi ('Abd Allah; d.1829), who wrote 88 works in Arabic and 6 in Hausa; dan Fodio's son and political successor Muhammad Bello (d.1837), author of 175 works, including 70 Arabic poems; and dan Fodio's daughter Nana Asma'u (d.1864), who wrote 9 poems in Arabic, 42 in Fulfulde and 26 in Hausa. In another chapter, the volume includes writings of other relatives of Shaykh 'Uthman, his brother 'Abdullahi and his son Muhammad Bello, as well as the viziers who served Shaykh 'Uthman and his successors, right down to the *wazir* Junayd (d.1992), who assembled a great library of manuscripts and himself wrote some 50 works and a *diwan* of poetry, and to whom Volume 2 was dedicated. Other chapters deal with writers of other areas such as Kano, Katsina and Bornu, with two chapters recording writings of scholars of the Yoruba-speaking region of south-western Nigeria (Ilorin, Ibadan and Lagos), both compiled by Stefan Reichmuth. A final chapter focuses on polemical literature for and against Sufism, chiefly compiled by Muhammad Sani Umar.

Volume 3: Ethiopia, Eritrea and Somalia

Volume 3 is currently being compiled by O'Fahey in two parts: 3A, covering Ethiopia, Eritrea and Somalia, already published in 2003; and 3B, covering the Swahili region of East Africa, hopefully to be published in 2008. Both volumes include writings in African languages in the Arabic script, especially 3B, in which the majority of writings are in the Swahili language. Volume 2 included some writings in Hausa and Fulfulde, if the author also wrote in Arabic. Later, I hope it will be possible to produce a volume uniquely focused on Hausa and Fulfulde writings from Nigeria, Niger and Cameroon.

Volume 4: West Africa

Volume 4, compiled by myself, was published in May 2003. This volume, totalling 814 pages, deals with Mali, Senegal, Guinea, the 'Greater Voltaic Region' (that is, Ghana and parts of Ivory Coast and Burkina Faso), and a chapter of information on a part of Niger.

Manuscript collections of West Africa

How, one may wonder, is information obtained about manuscript copies of all these writings? First of all, there are now numerous collections of manuscripts that have been catalogued, both in African countries and in Europe – although far more collections exist and still need to be catalogued. Foremost among such catalogued collections are two Malian collections: one in Timbuktu and one in Paris. One is the Ahmed Baba Institute

(see Chapter 20 in this volume) collection of Timbuktu, which has so far been only half catalogued in Arabic – only 9 000 out of some 20 000 manuscripts through the al-Furqan Islamic Heritage Foundation in London.[3] The Paris collection referred to is the library of al-Hajj 'Umar and his descendants, seized in Ségou by French colonial forces in 1890 and two years later deposited in the Bibliothèque Nationale. Finally, in 1985 a catalogue was published, entirely in French, with the title *Inventaire de la Bibliothèque 'Umarienne de Ségou*.[4] It contains some 700 works by a wide range of authors, both West African and from elsewhere in the Muslim world. Other catalogued collections in Africa include both public and private collections catalogued by the al-Furqan Foundation: in Nigeria part of the Arabic collection of the National Archives, Kaduna has been catalogued, as well as the University of Ibadan library collection, whilst those of the Jos Museum and the important collection of the late *wazir* of Sokoto, Junayd b. Muhammad al-Bukhari, are in preparation. The research and documentation centre of Ahmadu Bello University, known as Arewa House (located in Kaduna), is run by Hamidu Bobboyi, who recently negotiated agreements with the sultan of Sokoto and the emir of Kano to undertake cataloguing of their manuscript collections, which will most likely contain documents of historical interest as well as works of the Islamic intellectual tradition.

As regards Mauritania, the al-Furqan Foundation has published a catalogue of 12 private collections (6 in Shinqit and 6 in Wadan), with a total of over 1 100 manuscripts; and Charles Stewart of the University of Illinois has catalogued, and made available through his university, the private collection of the family of Shaykh Sidiyya of Boutilimit. In Senegal, too, several private collections have been catalogued by Ousmane Kane.[5] These include the libraries of Serigne Mor Mbaye Cissé of Diourbel, of the late Shaykh Ibrahim Niasse of Kaolack, and of al-Hajj Malik Sy of Tivaouane, all of which contain large numbers of manuscripts of writings by Senegalese authors, including the library owners themselves. Ousmane Kane has examined several other collections, whilst the archives of IFAN (the Institut Fondamental [formerly Francais] d'Afrique Noire) at the Université Cheikh Anta Diop in Dakar contain hundreds of Arabic manuscripts by Senegalese authors, plus Fulfulde manuscripts from Guinea.

Elsewhere in West Africa there are collections of reproductions of manuscripts, the originals of which were retained by their owners, whose personal collections have never been preserved or catalogued. At the University of Ibadan, manuscripts from Nigerian collections were microfilmed in the 1950s and 1960s by the main library and, after 1964, by the Centre of Arabic Documentation in the Institute of African Studies, totalling some 700 items. At the University of Ghana in Legon a different method was used in the 1960s and 1970s. Manuscripts were borrowed from Muslim scholars and xeroxed in multiple copies. The originals were then returned to their owners together with a number of xerox copies, so that they could share their collections with other scholars. Whilst at least two xeroxed copies of every manuscript were held at the University of Ghana in its Institute of African Studies, it was permissible for any scholar who needed

LOCATION	INSTITUTE	FOR AN OVERVIEW OF THE COLLECTION
ACCRA	National Archives of Ghana	
ABIDJAN	Institut d'Histoire, d'Art et d'Archéologie Africaines	
ALGIERS	Fonds Ben Hamouda, Bibliothèque Nationale d'Alger	
BOUDJBEHA	Private library of Shaykh Bay b. Zayn b. 'Abd al-'Aziz of Boudjebeha	See ISESCO (1988)
CAIRO	Arab League/Jami'at al-duwal al-'arabiyya: Ma'had al-makhtutat	See Sayyid (1954–63)
	al-Azhar University Library	See al-Azhar University Library (1949)
	Dar al-Kutub al-Misriyya	See Dar al-Kutub al-Misriyya (1924-42)
DAKAR	Institut Fondamental d'Afrique Noire, Université Cheikh Anta Diop	See Diallo et al. (1966); Mbaye & Mbaye (1975); Mbacké & Ka (1994)
DIOURBEL	Maktabat Serigne Mor Mbaye Cissé	See Kane (1997)
EVANSTON	Northwestern University	
	• Louis Brenner's collection of xerox copies of Arabic books published in Africa	Catalogue in situ
	• 'Umar Falke collection	Database catalogue in situ
	• Hiskett Legacy collection	Catalogue in situ
	• John O Hunwick collection	
	• John Naber Paden collection	Catalogue in situ. Also see Saad (1980)
	• Ivor G Wilks' Field Notes (copies available at the Institute of African Studies, University of Ghana, and Rhodes House Library, Oxford)	
FEZ	Library of Al-Qarawiyyin	See Bel (1918); al-Fasi (1979)
THE HAGUE	See Voorhoeve (1980)	
JOS	Nigerian National Museum	See Arif & Hakima (1965)
KADUNA	National Archives of Nigeria	See Muhammad (1995); Last (1966, 1967); and index in situ
KAOLACK	Maktabat al-Hajj Ibrahim Niyas	See Kane (1997)
LEGON	Institute of African Studies, University of Ghana. Copies available at the African Studies Library, Northwestern University, Evanston, Illinois	See Boyo et al. (1962); Martin (1966); Odoom & Holden (1965, 1967, 1968)
LONDON	British Library	See card index in situ
	School of Oriental and African Studies, University of London	See Gacek (1981)
MARRAKESH		See bin al-'Arabi (1994)
MEKNES	Maktabat al-Jami' al-Kabir	See Dilayru (1977)
	al-Khizana al-'amma	See Dilayru (1977)

LOCATION	INSTITUTE	FOR AN OVERVIEW OF THE COLLECTION
NEW HAVEN	Malian Arabic Manuscript Microfilming Project. Sterling Library, Yale University	See Nemoy (1965)
NIAMEY	Institut de Recherche en Sciences Humaines	Cyclostyled list in situ. Also Kani (1984)
PARIS	Bibliothèque de l'Institut de France	See Smith (1959a); Hunwick & Gwarzo (1967)
	Bibliothèque Nationale,	See Ghali et al. (1985); Vajda (1950); Smith (1959b); Sauvan & Vajda (1987)
	Musée des Arts d'Afrique et d'Océanie	See Adnani (2000–01)
RABAT	Khizanat Mu'assasat 'Allal al-Fasi	See al-Harishi (1992–1997)
	Al-Khizana al-'amma	See al-Tadili & al-Murabiti (1997); al-Tumi (1973). Also card indexes in situ
	Al-Khizana al-Hasaniyya (Bibliothèque Royale)	See al-'Arbi al-Khattabi (1980–1987) and catalogues in situ
	Ma'had al-Dirasat al-Ifriqiyya, Jami'at Muhammad al-Khamis (Institut des Etudes Africaines, Université Mohammed V)	No published catalogue
	Bibliothèque Générale et Archives du Maroc	See Unesco (1962)
SALÉ	al-Khizana al-'ilmiyya al-Subayhiyya (Subayhiyya Library)	See Hajji (1985/1405)
SHINQIT	Private libraries of Ahl Habut, Ahl Ahmad Sharif, Ahl Hamanni, Ahl 'Abd al-Hamid, Ahl Luda' and Ahl al-Sabt	See Yahya (1997)
TAMGROUT	Library of the Nasiriyya zawiya	See al-Mannuni (1985)
TIMBUKTU	Ahmed Baba Institute	See Ahmed Baba Institute (1995-98)
	Mamma Haidara Manuscript Library	See Sayyid (2001)
TETUAN	Al-Khizana al-'Amma (General Library of Tetuan)	See Al-Khizana al-'Amma (1981)
	Maktabat al-Jami' al-Kabir (Bibliothèque de la Grande Mosquée, Tetuan)	See Dilayru (1977)
TIVAOUANE	Maktabat al-Hajj Malik Sy	See Kane (1997)
TUNIS	Dar al-Kutub al-Qawmiyya (National Library of Tunisia)	See Mansur (1975)
	Maktabat al-'Abdaliyya	See Maktabat al-'Abdaliyya (1908–11)
	Bibliothèque de la Mosquée de Zeitouna	
WADAN	Private libraries of Ahl Muhammad b. al-Hajj, Ahl al-Kitab, Ahl Dahi, Ahl 'Idi, Ahl Yaya Buya and Ahl Ahmad Sharif	See Yahya (1997)
YALE	See Nemoy (1965).	
ZARIA	Northern History Research Scheme, Department of History, Ahmadu Bello University	See al-Bill (1967–87); and card index in situ

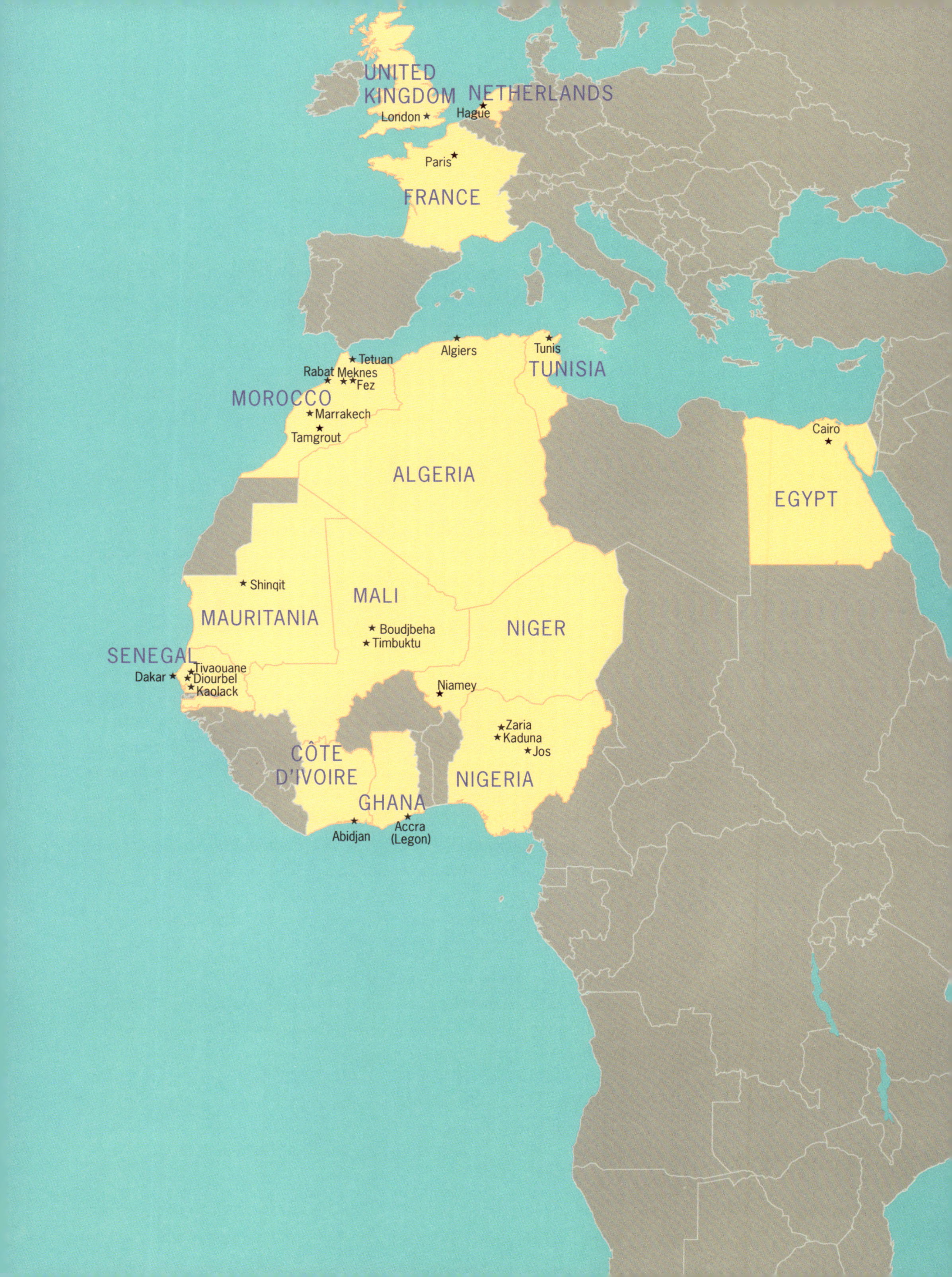
UNITED KINGDOM
London
NETHERLANDS
Hague
Paris
FRANCE
Tetuan
Algiers
Tunis
TUNISIA
Rabat
Meknes
Fez
MOROCCO
Marrakech
Tamgrout
ALGERIA
Cairo
EGYPT
Shinqit
MALI
MAURITANIA
Boudjbeha
Timbuktu
NIGER
SENEGAL
Tivaouane
Dakar
Diourbel
Kaolack
Niamey
Zaria
Kaduna
Jos
CÔTE D'IVOIRE
NIGERIA
GHANA
Abidjan
Accra
(Legon)

an item to purchase a xerox copy. As a result of this accessibility policy, Professor Ivor Wilks – the leading expert on the history of Muslim communities in Ghana, and a director of the project – purchased copies of every manuscript, and later donated this collection to Northwestern University. The Arabic collection in Northwestern University's Africana Library also contains a collection of some 3 000 manuscripts obtained through the sons of a deceased Tijani scholar of Kano, called Umar Falke (d.1962), and some 500 items obtained by Professor John Paden in Nigeria. This latter collection not only contains original manuscripts, but also locally published reproductions of some Arabic (and Hausa) writings by Nigerian scholars. These published versions, which I have designated as 'market editions' since they are openly sold in marketplaces, have been added to by myself (over 400 items), first from Nigeria and later from Senegal, where such a manuscript publication method is also popular.

The richest West African private libraries so far known to me are the two famous ones of Timbuktu – first of all the Mamma Haidara Memorial Library, organised and run by Abdel Kader Haidara (see Chapters 17 and 18 in this volume). This contains some 5 000 manuscripts, just over 3 000 of which are already described in a catalogue published by the al-Furqan Foundation, with a volume of the remainder still awaiting publication. They are stored in a well-designed building, but are awaiting scientific conservation and digitisation. They consist of a wide range of writings, both in topic and origin of author, although a considerable number are by authors of the Timbuktu region. The other important private library is the so-called Fondo Ka'ti, a collection of some 3 000 manuscripts belonging to members of a clan descended from the famous sixteenth-century historian Mahmud Ka'ti, author of the *Tarikh al-fattash*. The collection is now located in Timbuktu (with many more items still with family members in the village of Kirshamba, about 161 kilometres to the west of Timbuktu) and is under the direction of Ismaël Diadié Haidara and his brother Ousmane Haidara. This extraordinary collection contains some manuscripts whose creation goes back to the sixteenth century, whilst within it is a beautiful copy of the Qur'an copied in Turkey in 1420. Unfortunately the manuscripts have not yet undergone scientific conservation, but recently a building was constructed where they can be safely housed. Now that this has been done, it will be possible to catalogue them, although in 2001 the German scholar Albrecht Hofheinz put together a draft catalogue on behalf of the Institute for the Study of Islamic Thought in Africa (Isita).

Other major libraries include the remainder of the library of Boularaf, a man of Moroccan origin who settled in Timbuktu early in the twentieth century. Following his death in 1955, the majority of his manuscripts were inherited by a son of his and given, after 1970, to the Ahmed Baba Institute. The remainder of the collection is looked after by his grandsons, but is neither conserved nor catalogued. Also important is the library of Houmal, the *imam* of Jingere-Ber Mosque, which was for years buried below ground and is now being removed and is in urgent need of conservation and cataloguing. There are many other libraries in Timbuktu – Abdel Kader Haidara, in an article published in 1999 (in

Revue Anthropologique[6]), lists a total of 30 private collections within the city, and approximately 100 in the rest of the Middle Niger region of Mali (also see Chapter 18 in this volume). A major manuscript library is the Wangari Library, originated by Muhammad Baghayogho (d.1594), but mainly containing items (said to be a total of 8 000) obtained by his descendants (see chapter 19, this volume). There are important libraries in southern Saharan locations such as Arawan and Boudjebéha, which were both, prior to the twentieth century, recognised centres of Islamic scholarship. In Boudjebéha mention should be made of the library of Shaykh Bay, who inherited it from family members. Shaykh Bay himself is a leading scholar of the region, and has devoted much energy to retaining his family library. Containing many fine and valuable manuscripts, it greatly deserves conservation and cataloguing.

There are many libraries in Timbuktu – Abdel Kader Haidara lists a total of 30 private collections within the city, and approximately 100 in the rest of the Middle Niger region of Mali.

Elsewhere in West Africa there are important public and private collections. In Niamey, the capital of Niger, there is a large public collection at the Institut de Recherche en Sciences Humaines (IRSH). Originally, it was assembled by the scholarly president of the Assemblée Nationale of Niger, the late Boubou Hama, but later handed over to the University of Niamey, which incorporated it into IRSH. There are more than 3 200 manuscripts, with no scientific conservation, but recently catalogued.[7] Although many of the manuscripts are by authors from Niger, there are also many by authors from Mali and some by authors from what are now Ghana and Burkina Faso. They are stored in a room without any sort of climate control, and some of them are in a fragile condition. This is a major West African collection that is easily accessible. A description of the collection was written in 1984 by the Sudanese–Nigerian scholar Ahmad Kani and published in the *Bulletin d'Information* of the Fontes Historiae Africanae project (then directed by me). He made this interesting observation:

> Overall, the IRSH collection covers a wide geographical area, stretching from the old Kanem-Bornu region across Hausaland, through the Niger Bend, and northwards to Air and the Saharan regions, and ranges chronologically from the 14th century to the present day. Materials relating to state formation, interstate and external relations, are contained in the collection. The collection also houses important material on various Islamic sciences such as *fiqh* (jurisprudence), *tasawwuf* (Sufism), *tawhid* (theology), *tafsir* (exegesis), and related disciplines. A great deal of literature of North African and Middle Eastern origin is included within the IRSH collection. The Western Sahara is another area of provenance of mss in the IRSH collection. The Shinqit region in particular has a long-standing tradition of literary activity. The IRSH possesses a photocopy of a manuscript in the author's handwriting of the *Izalat al-rayb wa'l-shakk wa'l-tafrit fi dhikr al-mu 'allifin min ahl Takrur wa'l-Sahra' wa-ahl Shinqit* by Ahmad Abu'l-A'raf [Boularaf] – a work written in 1941–42, a biographical dictionary of *'ulama'* of 'Takrur' and the Sahara. Perhaps the most interesting aspect of the IRSH collection, and one which distinguishes it from other collections in West Africa is its holdings of works by West African Sufi shaykhs of the eighteenth and nineteenth centuries (especially writings of the Qadiri shaykh al-Mukhtar al-Kunti).[8]

Overall, the IRSH collection covers a wide geographical area, stretching from the old Kanem-Bornu region across Hausaland, through the Niger Bend, and northwards to Air and the Saharan regions, and ranges chronologically from the fourteenth century to the present day. Materials relating to state formation, interstate and external relations are contained in the collection. The collection also houses important material on various Islamic sciences such as *fiqh* (jurisprudence), *tasawwuf* (Sufism), *tawhid* (theology), *tafsir* (exegesis) and related disciplines.

The xeroxed collection of the Institute of African Studies of the University of Ghana has already been mentioned, but there are many other private collections in different parts of that country. The al-Furqan Foundation has recently published a catalogue of 15 such libraries, with a total of over 3 000 manuscripts, including numbers of items on medicine (20), history (80), geography (11), philosophy (17), and astronomy and mathematics (32), as well as the traditional Islamic sciences such as Qur'anic study.

Some Nigerian manuscripts exist elsewhere in Africa. One set of Arabic manuscript collections in the Sudan belongs to descendants of the sultan of Sokoto's family and associates, who fled from the British conquest of Hausaland in 1903. They eventually settled in and around a place known as Mai Urno to the south of Khartoum. With them are numerous manuscripts of works by Sokoto writers, and the main collections have been examined by Muhammad Sharif, an African-American student and digitiser of manuscripts (to form a basis for cataloguing). Likewise, many Timbuktu manuscripts are now in public collections elsewhere in Africa, principally in Morocco. Some are in Algeria, brought there by an Algerian who in the early twentieth century taught in a Timbuktu school.[9]

The Arabic Literature of Africa project was one of the foundation stones of Isita, set up by myself in the Program of African Studies at Northwestern University (Evanston, Illinois) in collaboration with O'Fahey in 2001. The objectives of Isita include identification and analysis of Arabic manuscript collections, and the translation and publication of manuscripts dealing with African history and aspects of Islamic thought in Africa. One of our ultimate aims is to map Arabic manuscript libraries in various countries of Africa and to analyse their content. Also, I still plan to undertake more work on *Arabic Literature of Africa*. Volume 6 on western Saharan Africa (Mauritania) is one I shall work on myself, together with Ulrich Rebstock, the prominent German scholar on Mauritania – and hopefully with more help from Charles Stewart, who has catalogued a private manuscript collection in Boutilimit in Mauritania. If Muhammad Sani Umar becomes available – which I hope he will – I would wish him to compile a volume on Hausa and Fulfulde (Fulani) writings of Nigeria and Cameroon,[10] together with Hamidu Bobboyi and perhaps with Ibrahim Mukoshy who, in the 1960s, was my assistant in the Centre of Arabic Documentation in Ibadan, and is now a professor of Nigerian languages at the University of Sokoto.

An overview of West African Islamic and scholarly traditions

Western Sudanic Africa constitutes a large and diverse region. *Arabic Literature of Africa* Volume 4 only attempts to cover certain parts of it – those where sufficient research has been done, and where a strong manuscript tradition exists. To a large extent this also reflects the areas where Islamic scholarly and literary traditions have been most prominent.

One of the key centres of Islamic scholarship, from a millennium ago right down to the twentieth century, has been Timbuktu, and not only the city itself – though this was the inspirational heart – but also the neighbouring regions of Azawad (the semi-desert region to the north of the Middle Niger) and the western reaches of the Niger Bend from Gimbala down to Masina. As Timbuktu established itself as a centre of commercial interchange between tropical Africa and Saharan and Mediterranean Africa during the fourteenth century AD, it began to attract men of religion as well as men of business – the two categories sometimes overlapping. The city was early settled by members of the Masufa tribe of the Sanhaja confederation following the apparent dissolution of the Almoravid movement in sub-Saharan Africa. To what extent they brought with them the Maliki juristic tradition is not clear. When Ibn Battuta visited Timbuktu in 1352 he noted the predominance of the Masufa, but had nothing to say about Islamic learning there. A century later, however, a Masufa clan – the Aqit – migrated to Timbuktu from Masina, and they clearly brought with them a deep tradition of learning, especially in the sphere of *fiqh*. Muhammad Aqit's descendants, intermarried with another Berber and possibly a Sanhaja family, provided the *qadi*s of Timbuktu over the next century and a half.

But such Saharan peoples were not the sole source of Islamic knowledge in Timbuktu at that period. In fact, the most celebrated member of the Aqit clan, Ahmad Baba (1556–1627), had as his principal shaykh a Juula scholar from Jenne, Muhammad Baghayogho. The Juula were undoubtedly among the first West Africans to acquire Islamic knowledge, being originally a merchant group who traded gold with North African merchants in Ancient Ghana. They may well have been influenced eventually by Almoravid Maliki teachings. At some point in time (perhaps after the break-up of Ancient Ghana), some of them settled in the Masina region. By the fifteenth century they had opened up a trade route southwards from Jenne for acquiring gold that was being mined in the Akan forests of what is now the Republic of Ghana. Some also moved into the central Niger Bend region, especially Timbuktu, whilst others moved eastwards to Hausaland. They played a significant role in bringing Islam to areas of what are now the Ivory Coast and southern Burkina Faso. Another group of them, originally settled in Diakha in the Masina region, dispersed westwards and became celebrated as proponents of Islamic knowledge under the name Diakhanke (that is, people of Diakha), better known as the Jahanke.

Timbuktu distinguished itself from the sixteenth century onwards as a centre of study which attracted students from many parts of West Africa, and scholars of Saharan oases from Walata to Awjila, and also from North African cities. The city's educational reputation has led some people to speak of a Timbuktu university, beginning with Felix Dubois, who wrote of the 'University of Sankore'.[11] While the Sankore quarter in the north-east of Timbuktu certainly was an area which attracted many scholars to live in it, there is nevertheless no evidence of any institutionalised centre of learning. Teaching of some texts was undertaken in the Sankore Mosque, and also in the Sidi Yahya Mosque and the Great Mosque – Jingere-Ber – but teaching authorisations (*ijazat*) always came directly from the individual shaykhs with whom the students

Pedagogical writings arise from the need for students to have textbooks. Whilst texts from outside West Africa circulated within the region, teaching shaykhs often abridged some of them, wrote commentaries on them, or versified them so as to make them easier for students to memorise.

studied. Much of the teaching was done in the scholars' homes, and individual scholars had their own personal research and teaching libraries. In terms of writings, Timbuktu was noted for its *fiqh* works right into the twentieth century and, apart from anything else, there is a rich *fatwa* literature in the Timbuktu region. Timbuktu is also noted as a source of historical writing. One of the earliest such works, the *Jawahir al-hisan fi akhbar al-Sudan*,[12] was a product of the sixteenth century written by one Baba Guru b. al-Hajj Muhammad b. al-Hajj al-Amin Ganu. Nothing is known about him and his book has never come to light, but it is known of since it was a source for the celebrated *Tarikh al-fattash*, written by members of the Ka'ti family. A twentieth-century scholar, Ahmad Baber (d.1997), wrote a book with the same title designated to take the place of the lost sixteenth-century work. The other great chronicle of Timbuktu and the Middle Niger region, the *Tarikh al-Sudan* of 'Abd al-Rahman al-Sa'di[13], was written at about the same time as the *Tarikh al-fattash* (mid-1650s), while roughly a century later an anonymous chronicle, *Diwan al-muluk fi salatin al-Sudan*, recorded the history of Timbuktu and its region under the rule of the Moroccan forces from 1591 onwards. The Timbuktu chronicle tradition appears to have spread far and wide over West Africa. In what is now the Republic of Ghana there has been a strong chronicling tradition, beginning with the *Kitab ghanja* in the early eighteenth century. Following the Moroccan conquest of Timbuktu in 1591, many of the city's scholars dispersed and it is known that some went as far south as the Volta River basin. That region[14] was also a meeting point for scholars from east and west. From the west came Juula scholars from the time of the establishment of the trade route from Jenne, leading down to the town of Begho just north of the Akan forests. Others established themselves in towns of the northern Ivory Coast such as Bonduku, Buna and Kong, and eventually in Ghanaian polities such as Wa and Gonja. From the east, in the late seventeenth century, Hausa merchants from what is now northern Nigeria began to pursue their trading activities in the Greater Voltaic basin, while in the late nineteenth century such activity brought in trader–scholars such as al-Hajj 'Umar b. Abi Bakr, originally from Kebbi, who settled and made his scholarly reputation in Salaga.

In a very broad sense, Arabic writings of western Sudanic Africa may be classified under four headings: historical; pedagogical; devotional; and polemical. Historical writings help Muslim communities to establish and confirm their identities, a necessary exercise for those living in remote areas surrounded largely by non-Muslim peoples, but also valuable in terms of community solidarity for those dwelling in recognised centres of Islam, such as Timbuktu, Arawan and Jenne. Only occasionally, starting in the twentieth century (and under the influence of European colonial administrators), do we find a broader and what might be called more 'secular' approach to history. A notable example of this is the celebrated *Zuhur al-basatin* (Plants of the Gardens) of the Senegalese writer Musa Kamara (d.1943 or 1945), a broad history of the lands and peoples of Futa Toro and its neighbours; some writings of al-Hajj 'Umar b. Abi Bakr of Kete-Krayke in Ghana (d.1934) also fall into this category. Kamara also wrote works in verse that are of historical significance, including an account of the 1892 civil war in Salaga and commentaries on colonial intrusions into the Volta region. The historical writing tradition of what is now the north of the Republic of Ghana is very rich. As Bradford Martin once wrote: 'If this material could be used for research it would contribute very greatly to a rewriting of the history of this region, which is so badly needed.'[15]

Pedagogical writings arise from the need for students to have textbooks. Whilst texts from outside West Africa circulated within the region, teaching shaykhs often abridged some of them, wrote commentaries on them, or versified them so as to make them easier for students to memorise. This was especially true in great educational centres such as Timbuktu, but is also characteristic of the Greater Voltaic region where, no doubt, copies of texts from elsewhere were rather more difficult to obtain due to the remoteness of the region from the trans-Saharan trade networks. Noteworthy among such teachers was al-Hajj Marhaba (d.1981), who wrote treatises on aspects of the Arabic language, but who was also noteworthy for his writings on Muslim communities of the region.

Devotional writings are common throughout West Africa, written both in Arabic and in local languages such as Fulfulde. Both al-Mukhtar al-Kunti (d.1811) and his son Muhammad (d.1825–26) wrote a considerable number of prayers which have been preserved and re-copied over the past two centuries. Al-Mukhtar also wrote a major work on devotion for the Prophet, *Nafh al-tib fi 'l-salat 'ala 'l-nabi al-habib* (The Spending of Goodness in Prayer Upon the Beloved Prophet), which was commented on by his son, who himself wrote a collection of panegyrics of the Prophet, *al-Sitr al-da'im li'l-mudhnib a1-ha'im* (Prayers for the Prophet).[16] Poems in praise of the Prophet, and seeking his intercession, are indeed a popular form of writing. Ahmadu Bamba (d.1927), the Senegalese Sufi leader, wrote dozens of such poems and these are recited by members of his *tariqa* in chanting fashion rather like the singing of hymns in Protestant Christian communities. Paper copies of many of these are available in the form of market editions reproduced in Dakar. In the other widespread Sufi *tariqa* of the Senegambia region, the Tijaniyya, there is a considerable volume of writing, especially poetry, in praise of the originator of the *tariqa*, Ahmad al-Tijani, and beseeching him to bless and intercede on behalf of his adherents. The most famous writer of such works was the Senegalese Tijani leader Ibrahim Niasse (d.1975), whose *al-Kibrit al-ahmar fi'l-tawassul bi-awa'il al-suwar wa-bi-uruf al-ayat al-ghurar* is in his *Jami' jawami' al-dawawin*,[17] which is made up of such poems.[18] He also wrote and published a collection of six *diwans* totalling nearly 3 000 verses, but these were in praise of the Prophet Muhammad. Ibrahim Niasse himself became an almost legendary figure in West Africa, and was regarded as a saint by many of his numerous followers. As a result, many writers in the region wrote poems honouring him.

As for polemical writing, that is mainly a feature of the rivalry between the Qadiriyya and the Tijaniyya *tariqas*, which surfaced in the mid-nineteenth century or, under the influence of Wahhabi teachings, attacks on Sufism as a whole, generally in the second half of the twentieth century, as the Saudi Arabian impact on Muslim Africa increased. In the nineteenth century the Kunta scholar Ahmad al-Bakkay (d.1865) was a leading anti-Tijani polemicist, not least because his authority over the Timbuktu region was challenged by the Tijani conqueror al-Hajj 'Umar (d.1864). Some of his sharpest conflict was with a Qadiri 'convert' to the Tijaniyya, generally known as Yirkoy Talfi (or in Arabic [translation] Wadi'at Allah), whose strong response was to 'make al-Bakkay weep'– *Tabkiyat al-Bakka'i*. Ahmad al-Bakkay not only attacked local Tijanis, but even entered into polemic with a Moroccan Tijani, Muhammad b. Ahmad Akansus (d.1877), to whom he addressed the treatise *Fath al-Quddus fi 'l-radd 'ala Abi 'Abd Allah Muhammad Akansus* (Introduction of the Most Holy [God] in response to Abu Abdullah Muhammad Akansus) as a rebuttal of the latter's *al-Jawab al-muskit* (The Denied Response). In the twentieth century a leading early figure in such polemics was 'Abd al-Rahman b. Yusuf al-Ifriqi (d.1957), a Malian scholar who studied in Saudi Arabia and who wrote *al-Anwar al-rahmaniyya li-hidayat al-firqa al-Tijaniyya* (Merciful Lights for Guidance of the Tijaniyya Group), an attack on the Tijaniyya and encouragement to its adherents to abandon it. Even in the 1990s in Senegal there was sharp controversy over Sufism. Muhammad Ahmad Lo, a scholar with Saudi connections, published his *Taqdis al-ashkhas fi 'l-fikr al-Sufi* (Dedication of Persons on Sufi Thinking) in Riyadh in 1996, to which Shaykh Tijan Gaye wrote as a response *Kitab al-taqdis bayn al-talbis wa'l-tadlis wa'l-tadnis* (Book of Dedication Between Deception, Deceit and Pollution). In 1997 Muhammad Ahlmad Lo published (evidently in Saudi Arabia) his doctoral thesis with the title *Jinayat al-ta'wil al-fasid 'ala 'l-'aqida al-Islamiyya* (Perpetration of the Corrupt Interpretation on the Islamic Doctrine), which constitutes an attack on many interpretations of Islam, including both Twelver and Isma'ili Shi'ism, and Islamic philosophers, and culminates with an attack on Sufism. Western Sudanic Africa is not, of course, the only locus of such polemics. Anti-Sufi writing and responses thereto are also to be found in Central Sudanic Africa, specifically Nigeria.[19]

In addition to the abundant Islamic literature written in Arabic in western Sudanic Africa, there are also Islamic literatures in African languages. The best known of these (and perhaps the most abundant) is the Fulfulde literature of Futa Jallon in Guinea.[20] Fulfulde was also written in Futa Toro in Senegal, but little is known of it other than the famous *qasida* of Muhammad 'Ali Cam (or Mohammadou Aliou Tyam), a supporter of al-Hajj 'Umar, whose poem is about the latter's life and work. In Senegal there is also writing in Wolof, using the Arabic script (see, for example, Serigne Musa Ka), but it has not been possible to incorporate much of that literature into Volume 4 of *Arabic Literature of Africa*. In Mali, the Songhay language has also been written in Arabic characters and some Songhay devotional poems are preserved in the Ahmed Baba Institute in Timbuktu, but again, it has not been possible to list such material. Finally, it must be pointed out that some Muslim writers of the twentieth century have composed works in French, or translated some of their Arabic writings into French. Noteworthy among such writers is Sa'd b. 'Umar b. Sa'id Jeliya (known as Saad Oumar Touré), director of a school in Ségou, who has written 5 works in French as well as 21 in Arabic. The Senegalese founder of the Union Culturelle Muslumane, Shaykh Touré (b.1925), has written mainly in French – 8 books and some 20 articles. The practice of writing in English in an anglophone country such as Ghana appears to be less common. The only clear example is a bilingual work by Muhammad Mustafa Kamil (b.1936), a disciple of Ahmad Babah al-Wa'iz and director of the school he founded in Kumasi. That work is his *Bayan nisab al-zakat al-hawli li'l-dhahab wa-qimat rub' al-dinar al-shar'i fi 'umlat sidi al-ghani. Notes on Zakat and Dowry in Islam*, a bilingual publication on the minimum amount of capital upon which *zakat* is to be paid, calculated in Ghanaian cedis, and the lawful minimum dowry payment in cedis.

Conclusion

The future may well see an increase in the amount of bilingual Islamic literature in both francophone and anglophone countries as the *madrasa* system continues to expand. More and more Islamic schools are being established, many of them combining traditional Islamic teaching in Arabic with elements of 'western' disciplines, taught in either French or English. What will be interesting to see is the extent to which more Islamic literature is written and published in African languages – a phenomenon that certainly grew during colonial rule in Guinea. Some authors, however, even use traditional Arabic verse styles to deal with contemporary political (even non-Muslim) figures, or to comment on modern issues. Prominent among these is the Senegalese scholar and Arabic schools inspector Shaykh Tijan Gaye, who has written poems about President Léopold Senghor and Nelson Mandela, and another poem on Islam and humanitarian organisations.

NOTES

1 Brill has been a publisher of Oriental Studies for 220 years, and has produced some of the most celebrated writings on Islamic religion and culture – one of the most famous of which is the *Encyclopedia of Islam*, the second (and most recent) edition of which consists of 12 volumes (published between 1960 and 2003 – to which I have personally made a number of contributions dealing with sub-Saharan Africa). The academic quality of Brill's publications, and its splendid publication appearances, make it literally a 'Brill-iant' publisher. I now edit Brill's new Islam in Africa series, and Sean O'Fahey assists in editing the Oriental Studies series.

2 Hunwick & O'Fahey (1994: 123).

3 Currently, a new full cataloguing is taking place, plus digitalisation of the manuscripts.

4 Volume 2 of the *Subsidia Bibliographica* of the Fontes Historiae Africanae. See Ghali et al. (1985).

5 Formerly of Saint-Louis University, Senegal, and now of Columbia University, New York. Kane provided information for *Arabic Literature of Africa* Volume 4.

6 Also published in Gaudio (2002).

7 The al-Furqan Foundation published the catalogue in late 2004.

8 Kani (1984: 41).

9 This refers to the Fonds Ben Hamouda in the Bibliothèque National d'Alger, in Algiers.

10 Although such writings are obviously not 'Arabic Literature' (of Africa), they were written in those languages in the Arabic script, and their topics are similar to those of the Arabic language writings of the area.

11 Dubois (1897: 275).

12 See Hunwick & O'Fahey (2003b: 62).

13 Called in Chapter 12 of *Arabic Literature of Africa* the 'Greater Voltaic Region'.

14 See Martin (1966: 83).

15 See Hunwick & O'Fahey (2003b: 112).

16 Published in Cairo in 1979.

17 See Hunwick & O'Fahey (2003b: 284).

18 See Hunwick & O'Fahey (1995: Chapter 13).

19 See Hunwick & O'Fahey (2003b: Chapter 10).

REFERENCES

Adnani J (2000–01) Inventaire des manuscrits du Fonds Archinard de la Bibliothèque du Musée National des Arts d'Afrique et d'Océanie. *Islam et Sociétés au Sud du Sahara* 14/115 (15): 3–75

Ahmadu Bello University (1967-1987) *Interim Reports* (Second, Third, Fourth, Fifth and Sixth). Zaria

Ahmed Baba Institute (1995–98) *Fihris makhtutat markaz Ahmad Baba li'l-tawthiq wa'l buhuth al-tarikhiyya bi Tinbuktu / Handlist of manuscripts in the Centre de Documentation et de Rechercher Historiques Ahmed Baba* (5 Vols). London: Al-Furqan Islamic Heritage Foundation

Arif AS & Hakima AM (1965) *Descriptive catalogue of Arabic manuscripts in Nigeria: Jos Museum and Lugard Hall Library, Kaduna*. London: Luzac & Co.

al-Azhar University Library (1949) *Fihris al-kutub al-mawjuda bi'l-Maktaba al-Azhariyya*. Cairo

Baber A (2001) *Jawahir al-hisan fi akhbar al-sudan*. Edited by al-Hadi al-Mabruk al-Dali. Benghazi: n.p.

Bel A (1918) *Catalogue des livres de la bibliothèque de la Mosquée d'El-Qarouiyine*. Fez: n.p.

al-Bill 'U (1984) *Index of Arabic manuscripts of the Northern History Research Scheme*. Khartoum: Khartoum University Press

bin al-'Arabi S (1994/1414) *Fihris makhtutat khizanat Yusuf bi-Marrakesh*. Beirut: Dar al-Gharb al-Islami

Boyo OE, Hodgkin T & Wilks I (1962) *Check list of Arabic works from Ghana*. Legon: Institute of African Studies

Brockelmann C (1937–43) *Geschichte der arabischen Literattur* (2 Vols & 3 Supplementary Vols). Leiden: Brill

Dar al-Kutub al-Misriyya (1924–1942) *Fihris al-kutub al-'arabiyya al-mawjuda bi'l-Dar li ghayat sanat 1932*, Vols 1–8. Cairo

Diallo T, M'Backé MB, Trifkovic M & Barry B (1966) *Catalogue des manuscrits de l 'IFAN*. Dakar: Institut Fondamental (formerly Français) d'Afrique Noire

Dilayru (1977) Qa'ima awwaliyya bi 'l-makhtutat min mu'allafat al-ashiqqa' al-Muritaniyyin wa-jumla min al-Ifriqiyyin al-ukhar fi 'l-maktaba al-maghribiyya. Communication presented to the Arab League Educational, Cultural and Scientific Organization conference on Arabic manuscripts in Africa, Nouakchott

Dubois F (1897) *Timbuctoo the mysterious*. London: William Heinemann

al-Fasi MA (1979) *Fihris makhtutat khizanat al-Qarawiyyin* (4 vols). Casablanca: al-Dar al-Bayda'

Gacek A (1981) *Catalogue of the Arabic manuscripts in the Library of the School of Oriental and African Studies, University of London*. London: SOAS

Gaudio A (Ed.) (2002) *Les bibliothèques du desert*. Paris: L'Harmattan

Ghali N, Mahibou M & Brenner L (1985) *Inventaire de la Bibliothèque 'Umarienne de Ségou*. Catalogue. Paris: CNRS editions

Gibb HAR et al. (Eds) (1960–2004) *Encyclopaedia of Islam* (12 vols). Leiden: Brill

Haidara AK (1999) Bibliothèques du désert: Difficultés et perspectives. In *Revue anthropologique*. Paris: Institut International d'Anthropologie

Hajji M (1985/1405) *Fihris al-khizana al-'ilmiyya al-Subayhiyya bi-Sala/Catalog of Subaiheyya Library in Sala*. Kuwait: The Arab League Educational, Cultural and Scientific Organization

al-Harishi 'A (1992–1997) *al-Fihris al-mujizl li-makhtutat Mu'assasat 'Allal al-Fasi*. Rabat

Hunwick J (1965) Introduction. In *Research Bulletin* 3. Nigeria: University of Ibadan, Institute of African Studies

Hunwick J & Gwarzo HI (1967) Another look at the De Gironcourt papers. *Research Bulletin: Centre of Arabic Documentation* 3(2): 74–99

Hunwick JO & O'Fahey RS (Eds) (1985–87) *Arabic literature of Africa: A bulletin of biographical and bibliographical information* (Issues 1–3). Evanston, Illinois: Northwestern University, Program of African Studies

Hunwick JO & O'Fahey RS (Eds) (1994) *Arabic literature of Africa: The writings of eastern Sudanic Africa* (Vol. 1). Leiden: Brill

Hunwick JO & O'Fahey RS (Eds) (1995) *Arabic literature of Africa: The writings of Central Sudanic Africa* (Vol. 2). Leiden: Brill

Hunwick JO & O'Fahey RS (Eds) (2003a) *Arabic literature of Africa: The writings of the Muslim people of northeastern Africa* (Vol. 3A). Leiden: Brill

Hunwick JO & O'Fahey RS (Eds) (2003b) *Arabic literature of Africa: The writings of western Sudanic Africa* (Vol. 4). Leiden: Brill

ISESCO (Islamic Educational, Scientific and Cultural Organisation) (1988) *Culture et civilisation Islamiques: le Mali.* Rabat: ISESCO

Kamara M (1998) *Zuhur al-basatin.* Florilege au jardin de l'histoire des Noirs; sous la direction et avec une introduction de Jean Schmitz, avec la collaboration de Charles Becker et al.; traduction de Sai'd Bousbina. Paris: CNRS editions

Kane O (1997) *Fihris makhtutat al-shaykh Mor Mbay Sisi wa-maktabat al-hajj Malik Si wa-maktabat al-shaykh Ibrahim Niyas fi Sinighal.* London: al-Furqan Islamic Heritage Foundation

Kani A (1984) A new source on the literary activity of the 'ulama' of the Central and western Sudan: The Niamey collection. *Bulletin d'Information* 9/10: 41–48. Fontes Historiae Africanae project. London: The British Academy

Ka'ti M (1964) *Tarikh al-fattash.* Edited and translated by O Houdas & M Delafosse. Paris: E. Leroux [1910–11] 1913; repr. Paris: Librairie d'Amérique et d'Orient Adrien-Maisonneuve

al-Khattabi M (1980-87) *Faharis al-khizana al-malikiyya / Catalogues of Al-Hassania Library* (6 Vols). Rabat

al-Khizana al-'Amma (General Library of Tetuan) (1981) *Fihris al-makhtutat-Khizanat Titwan.* Tetuan

Last M (1966) Interim report by the Research Fellow in Nigerian History with a short catalogue of Arabic texts preserved on microfilm at Ahmadu Bello University. In *Northern History Research Scheme: First interim report.* Zaira

Last M (1967) The recovery of the Arabic script literature of the north. In *Northern History Research Scheme, Second interim report.* Zaira

Maktabat al-'Abdaliyya (1908-1911) *Barnamaj al-Maktaba al-'Abdaliyya* (4 Vols). Tunis

Mamma Haidara Manuscript Library (2000) *Catalogue of manuscripts in the Mamma Haidara library* (3 Vols). Compiled by Abdel Kader Haidara and edited by Ayman Fuad Sayyid. London: Al-Furqan Islamic Heritage Foundation

Mansur AH (Ed.) (1975) *al-Fihris al-'amm li'l-makhtutat.* Tunis: al-Ma'had al-Qawmi li'l-Athar

al-Mannuni, M (1985) *Dalil makhtutat Dar al-Kutub al-Nasiriyya bi-Tamgrut.* Rabat

Martin B (1966) Arabic materials for Ghanaian history. *Research Review* 2. Institute of African Studies, University of Ghana

Mbacké K & Ka T (1994) Nouveau catalogue des manuscrits de l'IFAN. *International Society for the Systems Sciences* 8: 165–199

Mbaye ER & Mbaye B (1975) Supplément au catalogue des manuscrits de l'IFAN. *Bulletin de l'IFAN* 37: 878–895

Muhammad BY (1995) *Fihris makhtutat dar al-watha'iq al-Qawmiyya al-Nayjiriyya bi-Kaduna, al-Juz' al-Awwal.* Edited by JO Hunwick. London: al-Furqan Islamic Heritage Foundation

Nemoy L (1965) *Arabic manuscripts in the Yale University Library.* New Haven: Connecticut Academy of Arts and Sciences

Odoom KO & Holden JJ (1965) Arabic Collection, *Institute of African Studies: Research Review* 4(1)

Odoom KO & Holden JJ (1967) Arabic Collection, *Institute of African Studies: Research Review* 4(1): 30–73

Odoom KO & Holden JJ (1968) Arabic Collection, *Institute of African Studies: Research Review* 4(2): 66–102

Roper G (Ed.) (1992–95) *World survey of Islamic manuscripts* (4 Vols). London: al-Furqan Islamic Heritage Foundation

Saad E (1980) The Paden collection of Arabic materials from Kano. *History in Africa* 7: 369–372

al-Sa'di A (1964) *Tarikh al-sudan.* Arabic text edited and translated into French by O Houdas with E Benoist. Paris: Adrien-Maisonneuve for Unesco (reprint of the 1898–1900 edition)

Sauvan Y & Vajda G (1987) *Catalogue des manuscrits arabes.* Index (n. 6836–7214). Paris: Bibliothèque Nationale

Sayyid AF (Ed.) (2001) *Catalogue of manuscripts in Mamma Haidara Library* (3 Vols, prepared by Abdel Kader Haidara). London: al-Furqan Islamic Heritage Foundation

Sayyid F (1954–63) *Fihris al-makhtutat al-musawwara* (3 Vols in 8 parts). Cairo: n.p.

Smith HFC (1959a) Source material for the history of the western Sudan. *Journal of the Historical Society of Nigeria* 1(3): 238–247

Smith HFC (1959b) Arabic manuscript material bearing on the history of the western Sudan: The archives of Segu. *Historical Society of Nigeria Supplementary Bulletin of News* 4(2)

al-Tadili S & al-Murabiti S (1997) *Manshurat al-Khizana al-'Amma li'l-kutub wa'l watha'iq.* Rabat

al-Tumi M (1973) *Fihris al-makhtutat al 'arabiyya al-mahfuza fi 'l-khizana al-'amma li'l-kutb wa'l-watha'iq,* (Vol. 1, 3ème series 1954–57) Rabat

Unesco (1962) *Liste de manuscrits selectionés parmi ceux qui sont conservés a la Bibliothèque Générale et Archives du Maroc, reproduits par l'Unité Mobile de Microfilm de l'Unesco.* Rabat: Mission de l'Unesco

Vajda G (1950) Contribution a la connaissance de la littérature arabe en Afrique occidentale. *Journal Société des Africanistes* 10: 229–237

Voorhoeve P (1980) *Handlist of Arabic manuscripts in the Library of the University of Leiden and other collections in the Netherlands* (2nd English edition). Leiden/Boston: Leiden University Press/Kluwer Boston

Yahya A (1997) *Fihris makhtutat Shinqit wa-Wadan.* Edited by U Rebstock. London: al-Furqan Islamic Heritage Foundation

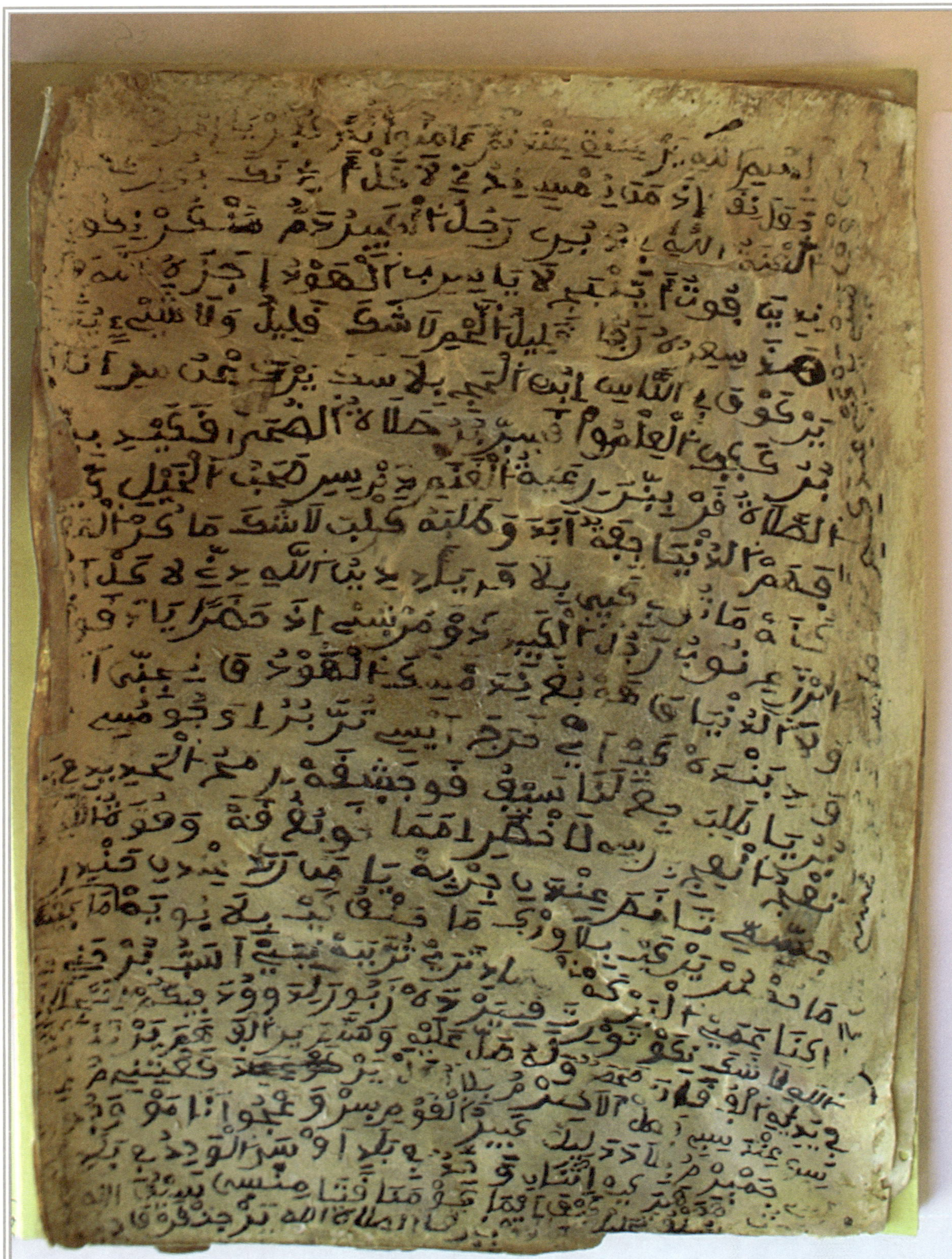

CHAPTER 22

A West African Arabic manuscript database

Charles C Stewart

Nearly 15 years ago I had an opportunity to microfilm a private library of Arabic materials in Boutilimit in southern Mauritania built, initially, by a scholar who had spent a dozen years studying under Kunta tutelage in the Timbuktu region, 1812–24. This project led to my developing the first version of a bilingual manuscript catalogue database and search engine to record the roughly 110 000 folios of material.[1] That particular effort was written up and hard copies of the collection description were subsequently made available to a number of libraries, as was the national collection at the Mauritanian national repository for Arabic manuscripts when the software became available in 1991. Subsequent to entering those two collections, others were added in the early 1990s before the project nearly came to a halt while my attentions were focused elsewhere. Only in November 2006 was the material transferred to a new platform, an easily accessible, internet-based site with an enhanced search engine. In this database we have amassed the largest single collection of titles and authors (over 20 000 extant Arabic manuscript sources) from West African collections, focused in the main on the libraries in and around Timbuktu. This chapter will propose that this database be utilised as a beginning for a universal, online resource for Sahelian Arabic-script manuscript identification.

One of the challenges of identifying local manuscript fragments, and of gaining some relative sense of the value of particular collections, is our lack of more than a notional feel for what constitutes standard (not to mention extraordinary) scholarly activity in particular collections.

The literary heritage of Timbuktu has been greatly celebrated in recent conferences, on websites, and by the generous subvention by organisations like the al-Furqan Foundation for preserving and cataloguing existing libraries in that region. From my own experience, one of the challenges with identifying local manuscript fragments, and of gaining some relative sense of the value of particular collections, is our lack of more than a notional feel for what constitutes standard (not to mention extraordinary) scholarly activity in particular collections. Indeed, how to assess the Arabic literary heritage of pre-colonial West Africa remains elusive in the absence of a comparative base for evaluating individual collections, complicated even further by the recent (near exclusive) attention that has been heaped on Timbuktu's rich heritage at the expense of scholarly activity to the west and east of the Niger Bend. In effect, the West African Arabic manuscript database provides an anecdote for these problems and moves us forward in our efforts to identify partial records and author names. As other document collections are added to it – and this chapter serves as an invitation for additional materials to be so contributed – its value as a 'baseline' for assessing Arabic scholarship not only in Timbuktu but across the West African Sahel will be enhanced.

The database presented here began with the first version of our Arabic Manuscript Management System (AMMS), created in 1987 as a finding aid for an Arabic manuscript microfilm project that preserved over 100 000 folios of material from the private library of Haroun ould Sidiyya in Boutilimit, Mauritania.[2] Our object then was to produce a bilingual hard-copy finding aid for that collection, which consisted of diverse types of material ranging from letters and notes to local histories and classical treatises in the Islamic sciences. Our goal was a simple and quick computer-generated entry system using untransliterated Latin letters alongside Arabic entries that could be equally accessible to readers (and input specialists) using either Arabic or English. Our end product was a bilingual catalogue with indices that would be user-friendly in both languages. The original AMMS program was written using an early Arabdos software to create 31 possible fields for entries about each manuscript and with an indexing capability to cross-reference and locate up to three fields in either language. Two years later the same software was employed to input a finding aid and generate indices for the Mauritanian national manuscript collection at the Institut Mauritanien de Recherche Scientifique (IMRS).[3] The possibility of expanding the number of entries to include other West African collections prompted a second version of AMMS, on the same platform, with the capability of merging files into a single database. Subsequently, in the early 1990s other published catalogues and hand-lists from West African collections housed in Niger,[4] Paris,[5] Timbuktu[6] and Evanston, Illinois,[7] were entered in the database. Taken together, over 19 000 records from these 6 collections were recorded in the AMMSvers.2 database, possibly a majority of the extant titles for the West African Sahel (excepting correspondence) at the time.

The research potential of a union index of authors, nicknames, titles and subject matter in these collections of West Africa's Arabic literary heritage, with the capability of expansion as other collections are uncovered, became obvious. AMMS provided us with a mechanism to reunite a literary tradition represented by tens of thousands of Arabic documents across the West African Sahel that has been largely unknown beyond the work of a small band of local scholars and an even smaller cohort of western-trained Arabists. Even where these materials were accessible to researchers in public repositories, the importance of this literary tradition has been well masked by the disparate systems used to record it and the dispersal of individual collections in Africa, Europe and North America. The AMMS project seeks to bring together, in a single database, a sizeable cross-section of these Arabic materials, despite their imperfect annotation and documentation, to provide us with an index to roughly 200 years of Sahelian literary activity. It was at this point, in the early 1990s, that the work of editing over 19 000 entries for consistent orthography and subject identification foundered on the magnitude of that task, an increasingly fragile software platform, and difficulties in disseminating an unwieldy end product. One positive result of my inattention to the project for nearly a decade is that these problems have now been largely resolved, thanks to advances in computer technology. In 2002 all of the 19 778 records were ported onto a Windows platform, the screen was redesigned and, most significant, a search engine was created that overcame many of the previous difficulties that had arisen from the inconsistency of our input parameters. The present AMMSvers.3 allows for easy addition of new material, internet access to these collection entries, and an opportunity to finally reunite an impressive quantity and range of Arabic writing representative of a broad sweep of intellectual life in Sahelian West Africa in, mainly, pre-colonial times. During the decade this project was on hold, new finds of manuscripts in private libraries in Mauritania and Mali continued apace, and the numbers of additional manuscripts now catalogued from 'new' collections may have eclipsed the number of initial entries in AMMSvers.2; we welcome the addition of these new entries into the AMMSvers.3 database to build this resource for future generations of scholarship.

The AMMS project seeks to bring together, in a single database, a sizeable cross-section of these Arabic materials, despite their imperfect annotation and documentation, to provide us with an index to roughly 200 years of Sahelian literary activity.

The database is, purposely, a low-tech, simple program designed to be easily accessible by users who may not have either sophisticated machines or detailed knowledge of (or concern with) refined transliteration systems. The principle at work here is that once enough data have been entered about specific manuscripts, it should be possible to establish comparisons across the database and resulting identifications or likely identifications with like works, thanks to a powerful search engine. At present the input screens provide space for a title (in Arabic only), the form the work takes (generally, poetry or prose with subsets of descriptors if available), subject matter (in Latin characters and Arabic), author name, *nisba*, and familiar name in both scripts, date of composition and author's dates, copyist's name and, for correspondence, additional identifiers, all in both scripts. Two larger fields at the close of each record allow for additional information in Latin script and Arabic. Currently, we are consolidating some of the lesser-used fields and adding fields for inputting the first lines of individual manuscripts and an additional field to identify variants on the author name. But the important thing is that these fields cover the basic identifiers traditionally used in manuscript documentation and the search engine will function equally well in either script or a combination of them.

The manuscript collections that form the base for this database are representative of the Sahel region, thus allowing researchers a glimpse into the intellectual traditions represented by five centres beyond the Niger Bend as well as Timbuktu. Early indications suggest subtle differences in the literary heritage across the breadth of the Sahel, but for the purpose of simply identifying major influences and contextualising the

Timbuktu tradition of scholarship, this database allows us to easily compare individual manuscripts as well as whole collections for the first time. A summary of the collections that have been entered follows, in the order in which they were added.

The 'Boutilimit' entries in AMMS

The manuscripts that make up the Boutilimit collection come from the private library amassed by Haroun ould Sidiyya Baba (1917–78) who spent the last 30 years of his life reconstituting the library and letters of his great-grandfather, the Moorish savant Shaykh Sidiyya (d.1868), as well as his wider family's literary record – from Sidiyya's mentors in Timbuktu (Sidi al-Mukhtar al-Kunti and his son Sidi Muhammad), Sidiyya's son, Sidi Muhammad (d.1869), and his son, Sidiyya Baba (d.1926). At his death Haroun left over 100 000 folios of manuscript material that was microfilmed and catalogued in 1987–88 (the beginning of the AMMS project). The description of that process can be found in the introduction to the catalogue as well as several journal articles that focused on the construction of our bilingual, computer-based finding aid.

Contents

The significance of this collection lies, first, in its very breadth – roughly 100 years of book collecting (*c*.1810–1910), interspaced with letters and treatises from and about Shaykh Sidiyya, his son, grandson and two of his great-grandsons. This representative work of four generations of scholars within the same family includes 700-odd pieces of their correspondence, in addition to the literary works they consulted. Second, this four-generation 'slice' of intellectual life is linked to one of West Africa's premier scholarly lineages, the Kunta savants in the Timbuktu region where Shaykh Sidiyya studied for 12 years (1810–23), and includes over 130 letters Sidiyya copied from his Kunta mentors.

Access

One copy of the film is available for consultation at the University of Illinois Library Archives, filed under 'CC Stewart Collection'; two other copies of the film were returned to Mauritania in the care of Baba ould Haroun, custodian of his father's collection, for deposit in an appropriate national repository. The originals of these manuscripts remain in Boutilimit in the care of Baba ould Haroun.

The 'Nouakchott' entries in AMMS

The manuscripts that make up the Nouakchott collection were recorded in the AMMS in 1988–89 from the hand-list of the national repository for Arabic manuscripts at the IMRS in Nouakchott. The IMRS began purchasing Mauritanian libraries and individual manuscripts in 1975 and by the late 1980s had acquired over 3 100 items entered in AMMS. A separate project at IMRS focused on the preservation of poetry and is not included in this list that primarily focuses on major literary works rather than on ephemera (correspondence, individual legal decisions, etc.). The manuscripts in this collection bear comparison to two other hand-lists of Mauritanian work by Mokhtar ould Hamidoun and Adam Heymowski in 1964–65, and Ulrich Rebstock's microfilmed selection of 2 239 manuscripts (including over 600 from the IMRS collection) in 1985.

Contents

At the time this listing was compiled the IMRS collection was made up of manuscripts from 72 libraries, mainly from the region of Trarza in the south-west quadrant of the country and with a focus on manuscripts of local authorship. The AMMS listing includes a number of items (493) that had not been identified at that time, but the number of multiple copies in this collection points to the possibility that the contents may be broadly representative of scholarly activity in the region adjacent to the right bank of the Senegal River.

Access

The IMRS provides access to its collection by bone fide researchers who make application through the Bibliothèque Nationale in Nouakchott.

The 'Ségou' entries in AMMS

The manuscripts that make up the Ségou collection were recorded in the AMMS in 1988–89 from the catalogue prepared in 1985 by Ghali, Mahibou and Brenner, *Inventaire de la Bibliothèque 'Umarienne de Ségou* (Inventory of the 'Umarian Library at Ségou). The collection has been variously called the Ahmadou Library and Fonds Archinard (the latter after the French officer who seized the manuscripts at the time of conquest in 1890). References to these manuscripts had appeared previously but incompletely in a 1925 catalogue of Arabic manuscripts at the Bibliothèque Nationale, and in a 1976 catalogue based on a selective inventory of the collection done in 1947–52. These efforts both omitted much material of interest to West African historians, which led to the entire collection being re-catalogued and microfilmed between 1979 and 1982; the inventory cited above was published three years later.

Contents

The Ségou collection is from the library of Ahmadu Seku, son of al-Hajj 'Umar, who inherited his father's conquests and ruled a territory increasingly under siege from 1864 until the French conquest in 1890. It contains numerous fragments and single-page items and a large, valuable body of correspondence. Its disparate make-up lends it a certain air of authenticity as a working library, a repository of day-to-day writings not filtered by an owner self-conscious of his scholarly image.

Access

The Ségou collection is available at the Bibliothèque Nationale de Paris, Section des Manuscrits Orientaux. Xerox copies and/or microfilm of the collection are available at Yale University Library, Africana Collection, and at the Ahmed Baba Institute in Timbuktu.

The 'Timbuktu' entries in AMMS

The manuscripts that make up the Timbuktu collection were recorded in the AMMS in 1990–91 from a photographed copy of the hand-list maintained at Cedrab, made available for this project by the then director Mahmoud Zoubair. At that time 5 640 manuscripts had been recorded at Cedrab, a compilation of locally gathered materials that has since grown to over 16 000 holdings. The al-Furqan Islamic Heritage Foundation began printing a series of catalogues for Cedrab in 1995 with rather more attention to individual manuscripts than was possible for us as we worked from the hand-list, and although the numeration of the first 5 640 items in AMMS.3 roughly corresponds to the printed volumes, there is some discrepancy and researchers will need to confirm the record numbers for the Timbuktu collection that are cited in AMMS.3 entries with the official published volumes.[8]

The order in which manuscripts are listed in these catalogues and the AMMS.3 numeration are not always exact and the online description of this collection explains where these discrepancies appear.

Contents

The Timbuktu collection was built from various individual collections in northern Mali beginning in the late 1970s. Among the most important local libraries that were incorporated into the Cedrab collection was that of Ahmad Boularaf, a Timbuktu bibliophile of Moroccan ancestry. By the early 1990s, Cedrab had become the major Arabic manuscript repository in West Africa, recipient of Unesco (United Nations Educational, Scientific and Cultural Organisation) and al-Furqan funding and with facilities for researchers and manuscript preservation that are unparalleled across the Sahel. Its early accessions reflect the bias found in other national repositories towards classical works and major local authors, although more recent acquisitions (as reflected in the published catalogues) include a large amount of correspondence and lesser works, perhaps more reflective of the locally produced literary record of the region. This first online version of AMMS.3 has not been coordinated with the additional data relative to individual entries that appear in some of the published catalogues, and it must therefore be used as a rough, and partial, guide to the Cedrab collections. We hope, in the short term, to reconcile this early listing of Cedrab materials with the published record and add those materials that had not yet been catalogued in the early 1990s.

The 'Kano' entries in AMMS

The manuscripts that are listed under 'Kano' are drawn from three collections housed at the Africana Library at Northwestern University that were entered in the AMMS by staff there in 1990–91. While they are not exclusively drawn from Kano, they are indicative of northern Nigeria's rich literary heritage. AMMS entries 2 055–2 614 come from the Paden collection, acquired by John Paden for Northwestern in the 1970s; AMMS entries 2 615–5 948, labelled 'Falke', come from the 'Umar Falke Library, also acquired by Northwestern in the 1970s; and AMMS entries 2 949–6 263, identified as 'Hunwick', come from Professor John Hunwick's collection.

Contents

The 'Kano' collections have been surveyed by Muhammad and Hay,[9] and the Paden collection by Saad.[10] By comparison to the compilations of manuscripts from 'national' collections that appear in AMMS and which feature heavy concentrations of classical texts, the Paden and Falke private libraries tend to privilege contemporary, twentieth-century material heavily influenced by writings associated with the Tijaniyya *tariqa*. Saad estimated that about one-half of the Paden accessions were privately printed pamphlets and books from Kano, Zaria and Cairo. Like the private library that makes up the Boutilimit collection, the Falke entries hold special interest as the library of an individual bibliophile.

The Timbuktu collection was built from various individual collections in northern Mali beginning in the late 1970s. Among the most important local libraries that were incorporated into the Cedrab collection was that of Ahmad Boularaf, a Timbuktu bibliophile of Moroccan ancestry. By the early 1990s, Cedrab had become the major Arabic manuscript repository in West Africa, recipient of Unesco and al-Furqan funding and with facilities for researchers and manuscript preservation that are unparalleled across the Sahel.

AMMS subject rubrics

Titles, authors and discrete collections aside, it has been the subject headings for entries that have attracted our greatest attention. As an indicator of where we have arrived, to date, in this ongoing process of identifying manuscript entries, I refer readers to the AMMS website homepage (see endnote 1) under 'subject headings', where the complete listing of our current classification system is available, in both Arabic and English. The range of subject headings used in AMMS expands upon the subject headings developed for the Boutilimit and Nouakchott collections, but in cases where there is a minimal level of detail annotated, the subject headings have been reconstructed from titles where these are available.

The subject headings that identify the AMMS entries were developed from the content of individual manuscripts identified by cataloguers of manuscripts cited in AMMS, rather than from an externally imposed set of classifications. The rubrics represent an editing of those subject entries, their consolidation and standardisation, but occasionally the same or similar material may appear under more than one general rubric, following the best judgement of different cataloguers. Cross-references in the subject headings noted above draw attention to the most common of these overlapping references; references that appear in italics (as in *see Belief: theology*) indicate the rubrics under which that particular material can be located, and so on.

The principal subject categories in AMMS
(with numbers of records, effective 30 September 2003)

Arabic language (1 258)
Belief (1 936)
Biography (213)
Conduct (105)
Devotional (1 632)
Economy (554)
Education (174)
Esoteric sciences (455)
Ethics (424)
Geography (20)
Hadith (516)
History (488)
Jurisprudence (3 934)
Literature (1 841)
Logic (107)
Medicine (99)
Politics (572)
Prophet Muhammad (480)
Qur'an (854)
Reform (44)
Science (231)
Social matters (159)
Sufism (731)

The AMMS search engine is sensitive to individual words, irrespective of their placement in subcategories in this listing. For example, a subject search for the word 'caths' will identify manuscripts in two different secondary headings under jurisprudence as well as under politics; a search for 'conundrums' will identify records under Arabic language, jurisprudence, literature and Qur'an; 'genealogy' appears under three different rubrics; 'slaves' and 'captives' appear under four different rubrics, and so on.

Currently, AMMS is under contract with the al-Furqan Islamic Heritage Foundation to incorporate listings of manuscripts from seven of the West African catalogues published by the Foundation. We welcome additional material as well as suggestions for refinements.

NOTES

1 See http://www.westafricanmanuscripts.org/.

2 This project was described in Stewart & Hatasa (1989).

3 Published by xerography. See Stewart et al. (1992).

4 *Liste des manuscripts en langues arabe et ajami a l'Institut de Recherche en Sciences Humaines, Niamey – Niger.* Niamey, Institut de Recherche en Sciences Humaines, 1979, no author listed.

5 Ghali et al. (1985) manuscripts seized by the French at the time of occupation of Ségou, conserved at the Bibliotheque Nationale.

6 Based on the first 5 640 entries in a hand-list filmed at the Centre de Documentation et de Recherches Ahmed Baba, Timbuktu (Mali) in 1991.

7 Three collections, labelled as 'Paden' (from a purchase by John Paden), 'Falke' (the 'Umar Falke Library) – both from Kano, Nigeria – and 'Hunwick', the collection of Professor John Hunwick.

8 See Ould Ely & Johansen (1995: records 1–1 500); 'Abd al-Muhsin al-'Abbas (1996: records 1 501–2 999; 1997: records 3 001–4 500; 1998: records 4 501–6 000); and al-Furqan Islamic Heritage Foundation librarians (1998: records 6 001–9 000).

9 Muhammad & Hay (1975).

10 Saad (1980).

REFERENCES

'Abd al-Muhsin al-'Abbas (Ed.) (1996) *Handlist of manuscripts in the Centre de Documentation et de Recherches Historiques Ahmed Baba, Timbuktu, Mali, Volume 2.* London: al-Furqan Islamic Heritage Foundation

'Abd al-Muhsin al-'Abbas (Ed.) (1997) *Handlist of manuscripts in the Centre de Documentation et de Recherches Historiques Ahmed Baba, Timbuktu, Mali, Volume 3.* London: al-Furqan Islamic Heritage Foundation

'Abd al-Muhsin al-'Abbas (Ed.) (1998) *Handlist of manuscripts in the Centre de Documentation et de Recherches Historiques Ahmed Baba, Timbuktu, Mali, Volume 4.* London: al-Furqan Islamic Heritage Foundation

al-Furqan Islamic Heritage Foundation librarians (Compilers and eds) (1998) *Handlist of manuscripts in the Centre de Documentation et de Recherches Historiques Ahmed Baba, Timbuktu, Mali, Volume 5.* London: al-Furqan Islamic Heritage Foundation

Ghali N, Mahibou M & Brenner L (1985) *Inventaire de la Bibliothèque 'Umarienne de Ségou.* Paris: CNRS editions (Fontes Historiae Africanae, Subsidia Bibliographica)

Muhammad A & Hay R Jr (1975) Analysis of a West African library: The Falke collection. In B Mittman *Personalized data base systems.* Los Angeles: Melville Publishing Company

Ould Ely SA & Johansen J (Compiler and ed.) (1995) *Handlist of manuscripts in the Centre de Documentation et de Recherches Historiques Ahmed Baba, Timbuktu, Mali, Volume I.* London: al-Furqan Islamic Heritage Foundation

Saad E (1980) The Paden collection of Arabic materials from Kano. *History in Africa* 7: 369–372

Stewart CC & Hatasa K (1989) Computer-based Arabic management. *History in Africa* 16: 403– 411

Stewart C, Salim A & Yahya A (1992) *General catalogue of Arabic manuscripts at the Institut Mauritanien de Recherche Scientifique.* Urbana: University of Illinois at Urbana-Champaign

PART V

BEYOND TIMBUKTU

CHAPTER 23

Arabic literature in the eastern half of Africa

R Sean O'Fahey

Undoubtedly the oldest Arabic documents concerning sub-Saharan Africa are those excavated at Qasr Ibrim on the Egypt–Sudan border. These go back to the tenth and eleventh centuries (with some items from the ninth century) and throw light on relations between Muslim Egypt and Christian Nubia in the Fatimid period (909–1171). Unfortunately, they have yet to be published.

The following gives a brief survey of what is known about the situation concerning Arabic literature in north-eastern and eastern Africa, beginning with the Sudan.

The modern Sudan republic has a very rich manuscript tradition, still largely unexplored. The various public, and some private, collections are described in the *World Survey of Islamic Manuscripts*.[1] Here some 30 collections are listed. The oldest manuscript so far located is a commentary on the *Mukhtasar* of Khalil b. Ishaq by al-Jundi, dated 963 *hijra* (c. AD 1555), and there are others from the sixteenth and seventeenth centuries. The largest public collection is located in Khartoum's National Records Office (NRO)[2] which, in addition to pre-colonial and colonial administrative records (numbering over 20 million items), houses about 15 000 literary manuscripts. The NRO possesses one collection which is unique in an African Islamic context, namely the administrative and judicial records of the Mahdist state (1882–98), estimated to comprise some 250 000 items. Although much has been written on the Mahdist state, this mass of documentation, particularly relevant for social and economic history, has hardly been exploited. Additionally, the University of Khartoum houses several collections totalling some 3 000 manuscripts; these include an extremely valuable collection of medical manuscripts organised by the late Dr Tijani al-Mahi, as well as a small collection of manuscripts from Mauritania.

None of these collections is properly conserved or catalogued. However, *Arabic Literature of Africa* (Vol. 1)[3] provides a preliminary survey of the writings of the nineteenth century and before.

No attempt has ever been made to survey private manuscript holdings along the Nile or in western or eastern Sudan. Given the exceptionally dry climatic conditions and the existence of numerous Sufi centres, it is very probable that there are many more manuscripts to be found.

In striking contrast to the detailed archaeological surveys that have been made of the Nile Valley, where, for example, over 40 archaeological sites have been excavated in Lower Nubia alone, no attempt has ever been made to survey private manuscript holdings along the Nile or in the western or eastern Sudan. Given the exceptionally dry climatic conditions (in this respect, similar to the savannah and Sahelian regions of West Africa) and the existence of numerous Sufi centres, particularly in Omdurman, Shendi, al-Damir, Berber, Dongola and elsewhere, it is very probable that there are many more manuscripts to be found. I would guess that there are as many manuscripts in private ownership in Omdurman as there are in the public collections. To give only one example, one Sufi leader in Omdurman has produced privately a work of over 300 pages on his manuscript collection.[4] If the current negotiations to end the conflict in the Sudan are successful, it may prove possible to find funding to make a start on such a survey.

Additionally, it should be mentioned that there is a collection of about 5 000 or more xerographic and photographic copies of manuscripts and documents from the Sudan deposited at the Centre for Middle Eastern and Islamic Studies, University of Bergen, Norway. These include some thousand items from the various Sufi orders present in the Sudan, particularly the various branches of the Idrisiyya tradition, judicial documents and land charters from the Darfur sultanate, and the commercial records of a prominent nineteenth-century Sudanese family of traders. A catalogue of this collection is in progress.

Moving eastward to consider Eritrea, Ethiopia and Somalia, our information is very patchy and uneven. However, one contrast with other areas of Muslim Africa is that north-eastern Africa has received the attention of a number of distinguished orientalists. Thus Enrico Cerulli has written with great authority on the Arabic writings of Somalia while Ewald Wagner has comprehensively catalogued, described and analysed the indigenous writings, in Arabic, Harari and Silte, of the city state of Harar.[5] More recently, researchers such as Hussein Ahmed (Addis Ababa), Scott Reese (Northern Arizona University), Alessandro Gori (Naples) and Jonathan Miran (Michigan State University) have been actively engaged in mapping and cataloguing in the region. What is known to date of the Islamic writings of north-eastern Africa is brought together in *Arabic Literature of Africa* (Vol. 3A), entitled *The Writings of the Muslim Peoples of Northeastern Africa.*[6]

East Africa (here meaning Kenya, Uganda and Tanzania), particularly the coastal region, is home to a literary tradition that is unique in Islamic Africa, namely a highly developed literature in a living African language, Swahili, written for centuries in the Arabic script. Swahili is the most widely spoken African language in Africa with an estimated 100 million speakers. Swahili is also the Islamic African language with the most highly developed literary tradition, inviting comparison, particularly in regard to its poetry, with Farsi (Iran), Urdu (India) and Turkish. Presently, how old the Swahili poetic tradition is, is difficult to say. Here a distinction needs to be made between the physical survival of manuscripts and the longevity of the poetic tradition. The damp, humid conditions along the coast have meant that, in contrast to Sudanic Africa, both west and east, few old manuscripts have survived – the earliest we have are from the late seventeenth century. However, the poetic tradition, which may well incorporate pre-Islamic elements, must, on linguistic grounds, be much older. Such poetic cycles as Fumo Liongo (see later) – comparable to the Sunjata cycle[7] in West Africa – probably have their roots in the thirteenth and fourteenth centuries. Characteristic of Swahili literature are the *tendi* – epics, often of 5 000 quatrains or more, on themes drawn from episodes in early Islamic history, themes common to several cultures around the Indian Ocean, reflecting Swahili's unique position as Africa's only urban maritime culture. The longest *tendi* is that on the last moments of the Prophet Muhammad, which comprises 45 000 quatrains. Some 300 *tendi* from the eighteenth century to the early twentieth century are known, but of these only 6 have been properly edited and translated.

East Africa, particularly the coastal region, is home to a literary tradition that is unique in Islamic Africa, namely a highly developed literature in a living African language, Swahili, written for centuries in the Arabic script. Swahili is the most widely spoken African language in Africa with an estimated 100 million speakers. Swahili is also the Islamic African language with the most highly developed literary tradition.

Swahili is also exceptional in another sense: it is the one African Islamic literary tradition, apart from those in Ethiopia and Somalia, that has a history of over 100 years of study within an orientalist paradigm. German orientalists such as Van Velten and Ernst Dammann, the Dutch scholar Jan Knappert, French and British missionaries and scholars such as Edward Steere, Father Charles Sacleux and JWT Allen have contributed much to the study of Swahili both as a culture and literature. Dammann's catalogue of the Swahili manuscripts in Germany,[8] together with that of Wagner for Ethiopia,[9] have set a standard of scholarship that needs to be emulated in other parts of Islamic Africa. While much of this scholarship may be regarded as uneven, it has nevertheless laid the foundation for the further study of Swahili literature.

The study of Swahili in the immediate post-colonial period became subsumed under concerns of nation building and language planning, particularly in Tanzania, under the influence of President Julius Nyerere. In recent years the situation has changed with the enthusiastic adoption of Swahili, and Swahili poetic forms, by poets far from the coastal area. This has led to an efflorescence of interest in classical Swahili poetry and, with it, a concern with the preservation of existing manuscript collections. The largest of these is to be found at the University of Dar es Salaam, preserved in the Institute of Kiswahili Research. This collection of about 4 000 items was made by the late Dr JWT Allen in the late 1950s and early 1960s; there exists a preliminary checklist by Allen,[10] but the collection is badly in need of conservation and cataloguing to professional standards. It is hoped that a Norwegian aid agency will fund a programme to make a start in this area. In addition to the Dar es Salaam collection, there is a small but very rich collection of Arabic and Swahili manuscripts (the earliest from the late seventeenth century) held at the departments of Antiquities, Archives, and Museums in Zanzibar, comprising some 600–700 manuscripts. Outside Africa, there are major collections of Swahili manuscripts in Germany (see Dammann's catalogue) and at the School of Oriental and African Studies (Soas) in London. The Department of African Languages at Soas has recently received a very substantial grant to prepare a proper catalogue of the collection at the school.

This has been something of a Cook's tour of the region and its Islamic intellectual heritage. The important point to emphasise is that this is very much a living tradition. The facility and rapidity with which poets coming out of a non-Swahili and, in many cases, a non-Muslim background, have adopted and adapted the classical Swahili poetic forms of *tendi*, *nyimbo* and *shairi* to local concerns emphasises that the literary tradition of Swahili is very far from being moribund. One recent survey reckons there are 2 000–3 000 'Swahili' poets active as far afield as Rwanda, the Congo and Zambia. This I hope will be apparent when *Arabic Literature of Africa* (Vol. 3B), entitled *The Writings of the Muslim Peoples of Eastern Africa*, hopefully forthcoming soon, is published. But it cannot be emphasised enough how much more there is to do in terms of research. Islamic north-eastern and East Africa are still very much terra incognita in terms of their intellectual, literary and artistic traditions.

Overview of *Arabic Literature of Africa: The Writings of the Muslim Peoples of Northeastern Africa*

The modern states and near-states that make up the region here defined as north-eastern Africa comprise Eritrea, Djibouti, Ethiopia and Somalia. Although in terms of population the area is predominantly Muslim, leaving aside numerous small sultanates, either tribal or urban in origin, the major state-forming tradition in the region is Christian. The size and strength of Ethiopia has waxed and waned over the centuries, but its existence has defined much of the experience of Muslims within its borders, or in countries neighbouring it. Likewise, real or putative conflict between Muslims and Christians tends to dominate (perhaps overly) surveys, for example by Trimingham,[11] of Islam and the Muslim presence in the region. This is not to say that war and polemic between Christian and Muslim have not happened, but the complexities of coexistence have been understudied (Ahmed[12] is a beginning).

Within the wider context of Muslim Africa, both north and south of the Sahara, the region has a unique position within Islamic history, featuring as it does in the *sira* of the Prophet. In about 615 the first *hijra* took place, when several small groups of Muslims took refuge in the court of the Negus, assumed to be the ruler of Axum, in what is now northern Ethiopia.[13] The details of this episode or its historicity do not concern us here, but its consequences, or rather the imagined recollection of its consequences, do. A *hadith* is reported thus, 'Leave the Abyssinians in peace so long as they do not take the offensive.'[14] From this tradition arose an ambiguity among the Muslim learned class about the status of Christian Ethiopians within the Islamic *Weltenschauung* (world view) that was embodied in a distinctive literary genre, the *fada'il al-habash* or *hubshan* (The virtues of the Ethiopians) which, in an indirect way, goes back to the 'Blameless Aethiops' of Herodotus. This is no antiquarian issue; in modern times, the status of Axum as a place sacred to both Christian and Muslim has been, and still is, a contentious issue between the two communities. Two political examples of overarching ambiguity in the region are the membership of Somalia in the Arab League and the 'Arabism' debate concerning Eritrea's identity in the 1960s and 1970s.[15] In this respect, both Eritrea and Somalia have affinities with the Republic of Sudan, which has its own ambiguous relationship to the Muslim Arab world.

In this respect, Ethiopia and its environs mark themselves off from much of the Muslim Africa recorded in the volumes of the *Arabic Literature of Africa* series in that they partake of some of the issues that mark the complex multi-confessionalism of the Middle East and, for example, Muslim Spain. *Jihad* and counter-*jihad* there certainly were, but there was also a scholarly polemic, exemplified in the writings of Enbaqom and Zakaryas. Little of this is found elsewhere in Muslim Africa, although there are some traces of it in the Christian–Muslim encounters of the late nineteenth century in East Africa (see, for example, 'Ali b. Muhammad b. 'Ali al-Mundhiri in *Arabic Literature of Africa*, Vol. 3B).

It is not possible here to give a detailed ethno-history of the Muslims of north-eastern Africa. Crudely, the Muslim communities of the region may be characterised as nomadic, for example the Somali and Beja; settled agriculturalists, as in Wallo in Ethiopia; or dwelling in small urban coastal settlements such as Masawwa', Zayla', Harar, Mogadishu or Brava, the latter two being extensions northwards of the Swahili urban environments that dominated the East African coast, and whose writings will form the bulk of *Arabic Literature of Africa* (Vol. 3B), while the former form part of a nexus of maritime city states that rim the Red Sea (including Jidda, al-Lith, al-Hudayda and al-Mukha on the northern coast, and Sawakin on the southern coast) and which have their roots in Graeco–Roman times.

It is from one of these cities, Zayla', that the first Islamic writings come, namely the scholarly production of a group of émigré Zayla' scholars, largely based in Cairo in the fourteenth century. Their surviving writings are recorded in Chapter 2 of *Arabic Literature of Africa* (Vol. 3B). This tradition continued with the presence in Cairo of Ethiopian Muslims, somewhat later designated as Jabart, and concretised by the establishment of a *riwaq al-jabartiyya* or hostel (literally 'corner') for the maintenance of Jabarti Muslim students at al-Azhar. The most famous Jabarti was undoubtedly the Egyptian chronicler 'Abd al-Rahman b. Hasan al-Jabarti, whose writings fall outside our purview, but whose family had a long connection with the *riwaq*. The longevity and complexity of Islamic connections in the region are well illustrated by the fact that the *riwaq al-jabartiyya* was to have an important role in the formal establishment in July 1960 of the Eritrean Liberation Front, which in turn led to an Eritrean state in 1991. The Islamic strand in the emergence of a distinctive Eritrean nationalism is a complex and ambiguous one.

The sixteenth and seventeen centuries were the high point of the Muslim–Christian confrontation between the Christian highland empire of Ethiopia and the largely lowland Muslim cities. Here, for the first time – unless one includes the period of Abraha, the Sassanian Persian and Byzantine involvement in the region at the time of the birth of the Prophet – the region becomes the scene of a semi-global geopolitical involvement, pitching alliances between Ethiopia and the Portuguese against the city states of the Hawash Valley, and their largely Somali nomadic rescuers under Ahmad Gran, backed to a degree by the Ottomans. The *Futuh al-Habash* is the major record of this struggle. The geopolitical scene moved on; the Christians fell out among themselves as Portuguese Jesuits failed to win over orthodox Ethiopia, while the Ottomans consolidated their control of the coast.[16] It was only in the nineteenth century that confrontation resumed, with the wars between the Mahdist Sudan and a resurgent Ethiopia under Johannes and Minilik.[17]

It is very hard to generalise about the character of Islamic writings. In one sense, they differ little from what will be found elsewhere in Muslim Africa. At one end of the spectrum are the commentaries and super-commentaries on approved texts of *fiqh*, here largely from the Shafi'i school which dominates the region. But it is clear that both in Wallo and Somalia, from the late eighteenth and early nineteenth centuries onwards, there were winds of change in the form of greater *tariqa* activity, an activity that may very loosely be described as 'neo-Sufi'. This activity was characterised by the establishment of communities[18] of adherents to specific Sufi traditions – in our region mainly Qadiriyya, Sammaniyya, Tijaniyya, Salihiyya, Dandarawiyya and Idrisiyya – and who were often recruited from hitherto marginalised groups. Other new trends appear to include the production of *manaqib* (virtues; praises) literature centred on both 'international' and local saints (Harari writings are rich in this category), and the production of popular poetry, either in Arabic or in various vernacular languages; these two categories obviously overlap. Here one can usefully compare the careers of Muhammad Shafi b. Muhammad with that of Uways b. Muhammad al-Barawi, the one from central Ethiopia, the other from southern Somalia. One research area that is still in its infancy is the study of the links in the late eighteenth and early nineteenth centuries between the Muslim communities of north-eastern Africa and those of the Islamic heartlands, in particular the Hijaz and the Yemen.

Popular Islamic poetry, whether in Arabic or in vernacular languages, is to be found throughout the region. Research on the various traditions in the region is very uneven. The work of Cerulli and Wagner on Harari writings and, more recently, Samatar, building on Andrzejewski and Jammac 'Umar Ciise on the Somali male poetic tradition, and Kapteijns on Somali-sung women's poetry, only highlight how much more there is to be done. There are interesting comparisons to be made here in terms of themes and the influence of classical Arabic prosodic forms both with Sudanese popular poetry (see *Arabic Literature of Africa*, Vol. 1, Chapter 3) and the complex prosodic developments of Swahili poetry (which is documented in *Arabic Literature of Africa*, Vol. 3B).

Another area that deserves investigation is the creation of literacy in vernacular languages, whether through the adaptation of the Arabic script to the needs of local languages, whether Oromiñña, Harari or Somali, or through the creation of new scripts, for example Abu Bakr b. 'Uthman Oda's invention of a script for Oromiñña and the complex history of the Osmania script in Somalia. This is a complex theme in the region; one example is the contemporary debate among Ethiopian Muslims, not on whether to translate the Qur'an into Amharic, but whether to print it in *ajami*, that is, the Arabic script, or in the Ethiopic alphabet. These debates have their echoes both among the Hausa and others in West Africa, and among the Swahili of East Africa. But it is, I think, true to say that the orthographic debate is more complex in north-eastern Africa than anywhere else in Muslim Africa.

The Islamic literatures of north-eastern Africa thus represent and reflect a variety of different impulses. Proximity to the Middle East – but not simply proximity, since there is also the imperialist intervention of Ottoman Turkey and Khedivial Egypt to consider, plus the Islamic policies of Italy and later Britain in Eritrea – means that the nature of the relationship of north-eastern Africa with the Islamic heartlands was different in kind from, for example, West Africa. In intellectual terms there were, indeed, the traditional patterns of 'shaykh seeking', of the transmission of *isnads*, both in *fiqh* and *tasawwuf*, both from within the region and from without, the writing of commentaries and the like, and the coming of new Sufi affiliations, especially in the nineteenth century. But, because of the involvement of the region in both local and regional conflicts that consciously or unconsciously cut across the religious divide, whether it be Turk versus Portuguese, British and Italian against the Mahdists of the Sudan with reverberations in Eritrea and western Ethiopia (see Talha b. Ja'far), or 'Abdille Muhammad Hasan versus the British, Italians and Ethiopians in Somalia, the nature of Muslim/non-Muslim interaction was qualitatively different in north-eastern Africa by comparison with most of the rest of Muslim Africa. North-eastern Africa is not quite Africa, nor is it quite the Middle East; it partakes of both, but is not quite either, and this is reflected in the complexities of its Islamic intellectual traditions.

Overview of *Arabic Literature of Africa* (Vol. 3B)

The study of Swahili

No other living Islamic African language, including Arabic,[19] has had such a long and complex pedigree of scholarship brought to bear upon it as Swahili, both as a language and a culture.[20] In the western scholarly tradition, the first generation was represented by Ludwig Krapf, J Rebmann, WE Taylor, Edward Steere and Charles Sacleux – all Christian missionaries, as were several key figures of a later generation such as Ernst Dammann and Roland Allen.

But Krapf (d.1887) was not the first outsider to take an interest in Swahili. Rather, it was a Muslim scholar from Oman, Nasir b. Ja'id al-Kharusi (d.1847) who wrote at least two works comparing herbal medicine as practised in Oman and Arabia with that among the

Swahili. A tradition of interest in and, increasingly, the practice of Swahili, especially poetry, grew among the Omani and Hadrami *'ulama* of the coast and islands, as they interacted in various complicated ways with the local scholarly and literary elites. This tradition was to intersect in various ways with the Christian missionary tradition.

Christian missionary interest in Swahili was essentially utilitarian, a way into the community, and eventually a means of proselytisation. The Universities Mission to Central Africa, based in Zanzibar, was prohibited by the sultans from missionary activity directed towards Muslims, but they were allowed to proselytise among freed slaves. There was some tension between Muslim and missionary, which Bishop Edward Steere (d.1887) helped to provoke by holding public sermons in the slave market, by the side of which the Anglican Cathedral was built. The famous Zanzibari scholar 'Abd al-'Aziz b. 'Abd al-Ghani al-'Amawi wrote a response to Steere, which unfortunately appears not to be extant. However, one response has survived, namely a defence of Islam entitled *Jawab 'ala 'l-Risala al-mansuba ila al-Masih b. Ishaq al-Kindi al-Nasrani* by the Ibadi scholar 'Ali b. Muhammad al-Mundhiri. However, the exchanges between the missionaries and the *'ulama* seem to have been essentially gentlemanly; al-'Amawi helped Steere with the latter's work in translating the Bible into Swahili.

Relations between WE Taylor (d.1927) and many of the local scholars in Mombasa seem to have been especially cordial, even if Taylor seems to have harboured ambitions of converting Swahili Muslims to Christianity. This cordiality had important consequences for Swahili literature, in that the friendly collaboration between Taylor and Muhammad Sikujua led to the recording for posterity of much of the poetic production of Muyaka b. Haji al-Ghassaniy, an outstanding poet of *mashairi* of a generation before them. Without Sikujua and Taylor, Muyaka would be a lost voice. In Mombasa, and to a lesser extent in Zanzibar and Lamu, there appears to have been an interaction between two scholarly traditions that were able to respect each other.

In Lamu, the role of Muhammad Kijumwa – poet, calligrapher, wood-carver and dance master – as an interlocutor with several researchers, among them Alice Werner, W Hichens and Ernst Dammann, was of profound importance to Swahili studies.

In several respects the missionaries, and later colonial officials and nationalist language-planners, had a specific agenda. One aspect was the romanisation of Swahili. As Frankl has noted, there is no particular reason to romanise Swahili; the language is no easier or more difficult to read in either script.[21] The administration of German East Africa, throughout its duration, regarded Arabic script as normal (Swahili: *Kiarabu*), and made no effort to change it. Although nowhere explicitly stated, the 'decoupling' of Swahili from the Arabic script may be regarded as a way of 'de-Islamising' the language.

Decisive in this was the Interterritorial Language Committee's decision to adopt Kiunguja (the dialect of Zanzibar, which was never an acceptable form in classical Swahili literature) as 'standard' Swahili,[22] in preference to Kiamu (the dialect of Lamu) or Kimvita (the dialect of Mombasa), both of which are the preferred forms for classical Swahili writing.[23] Wilfred Whiteley, who was actively engaged in the enterprise, sums it up thus: 'In Swahili…the standardization [was] effected on a non-literary dialect during a period of Colonial administration. Inauspicious augury for a national language.'[24] Whiteley does not explain why Kiunguja was chosen. RA Snoxall, author of a Swahili/English dictionary and member of the Interterritorial Committee, offers an explanation:

> First of all [at a conference meeting], I was asked why had Kiunguja or Zanzibar dialect of Swahili been chosen for standardisation rather than the other forms, such as Kimvita, which I had mentioned. I replied that it was because it was more used in commerce than the other forms and its commercial value really dictated its being chosen as the standardised form of the language.[25]

If one is talking of the late 1920s, when Mombasa was becoming the major port for East Africa, this does not seem to be a very persuasive argument.

Questions of definition

Swahili literature poses a major challenge in terms of defining boundaries. For example, much of the *tendi*, or epic poetry writing in Swahili, was, and is, produced within an Islamic milieu. However, a number of *tendi* are on modern secular themes. Many of these have been included, either for the sake of their form or because they were written by people from a Muslim background. Again, transitional writers – that is, writers emerging from a Swahili Muslim background, but who increasingly wrote on 'national' or secular themes (Shaaban b. Robert is an outstanding example) – are generally included.

The problem of boundaries is compounded by contradictory definitions of 'secular' and 'Islamic'. Ibrahim Noor Shariff argues that 'at every stage of history, the Swahili have produced a far greater volume of secular poetry than of homiletic verse', but continues that 'Swahili society has traditionally attached great importance to the *preservation* [Shariff's emphasis] of religious verse for posterity'.[26]

In other words, although at any given time more non-religious verse was being composed, much less of it has survived. This is probably true of any literate Islamic society. But here one must be careful to distinguish between 'secular' in the sense of not being about overtly religious topics, and 'western-influenced' or 'modern'. Indeed, Muyaka b. Haji al-Ghassaniy, for example, wrote verse on secular topics, but did so within the context of a Muslim community.

Shariff further argues that western scholars of Swahili have compounded the problem by overemphasising the Islamic nature of Swahili culture and literature. He quotes Knappert: 'Swahili literature is entirely Islamic from its inception in 1728 [the date of the *Hamziyya*] until the advent of German administration in 1884.'[27] If Knappert is defining 'Islamic', in a generalised cultural context, as the literary production of a Muslim society, then it seems to be an unexceptional generalisation. This alleged bias is de facto, based on problems of source criticism. It is understandable that Knappert chose, as a scholar, to concentrate on Swahili Islamic poetry, in as much as there were available some general yardsticks by which to analyse it. Thus in researching *tendi*, recounting episodes in the life of the Prophet, or the early years of the Islamic era, Knappert was able to build upon the research of Rudi Paret[28] on the *maghazi* (genre of prophetic biography in Islamic literature) legendary found throughout the Muslim world.[29] Shariff argues that there is another reason for this overemphasis on the religiosity of Swahili literature, quoting Lyndon Harries: 'There are hundreds of short Swahili poems in the Library of the School of Oriental and African Studies, which still defy interpretation, partly because no one is able to provide the context in which the poem was written.'[30] A look at Professor Abdulaziz's admirable study[31] of Muyaka's *shairi* will confirm Harries's point. The problem is a continuing one: there are many poems, particularly in the very rich and varied collections at the Soas (London) that are of such a specific and occasional nature that their interpretation has probably been lost forever. This is not a problem peculiar to African literatures.

Following this line of argument further, Shariff continues by contending that the sophistication of Muyaka's verse – and that of his contemporaries – is such 'that it could not have been invented by Muyaka or his contemporaries'.[32] The argument is analogous to that used in the study of classical Greek literature: that Homer is too sophisticated to have stood at the beginning of a literary tradition.

I argued above that the secular quota of literature (not necessarily in writing), in most Islamic societies, was probably greater than what has survived until today. Indeed, this is probably true of the pre-modern literatures of all the monotheistic religions. What was written down and has survived is what the people of the time thought important, and they tended to give priority to religious or homiletic literature. 'Secular' literature was transient, or survived for non-literary or marginal or ironically religious reasons; the Arabic poetry of the *jahiliyya* ('the ignorance') that is, the pre-Islamic period, survived in part for its importance to the canons of Arabic style, essential to an understanding of the sacred book.

Arabic Literature of Africa (Vol. 3B) is intended to be a record of what exists (or is reported to have once existed) in the way of writings of a primarily Islamic character in the region, although some discussion of oral forms will be included. Thus, no attempt is made to engage in the debate about the identity of the Swahili people, their origins, or the degree to which their literature is Islamic or secular – themes on which there is already a large and often polemical literature.[33]

Rollins notes:

> Between the years 1900–1950, there were approximately 359 works of prose published in Swahili; 346 of these were written by Europeans and published mainly in England and Germany.[34]

He continues by noting that, overwhelmingly, this literature was Christian, and that it tended to impose a Euro–Christian norm on the language. Needless to say, this literature is not included here. To the present compilers, very striking is the degree to which European scholars of Swahili have indulged in aesthetic and other value judgements about the literature they are studying – to a far greater degree, for example, than western scholars of Arabic literature.

When the time comes to write a general history of Swahili literature, to which hopefully *Arabic Literature of Africa* (Vol. 3B) will be a useful contribution, the complex interaction between 'orientalist', colonial administrator, Christian missionary and indigenous (however defined) writers will present an analytical problem of the greatest complexity.

On the periodisation of Swahili poetry

Before the twentieth century, Swahili literature seems to be primarily poetry. There is little or no evidence that the language was used to write prose, except for the odd letter, some of which survive from the early eighteenth century. Arabic was used for prose; there are parallels here with Farsi and Urdu.

Swahili poetry is at once oral, sung and written; the complex interaction between the three is beyond the scope of this overview.

Despite the pioneering research of Taylor, Dammann, Harries, the Allens (father and son) and Knappert, our understanding of this tradition is still fragmentary. There is much basic philological, lexicographical and textual work to be done before any reliable overview can be given. No one has been more assiduous in warning against premature generalisations than Jan Knappert in his various surveys. The comments that follow must be seen in this context.

In presenting a very preliminary periodisation, one must begin with the poetic cycle by, or about, the northern Kenyan coastal 'culture hero', Fumo Liongo, a figure of anywhere between the seventh and seventeenth centuries, who may have existed or not, and who may have written some, but surely not all, of the poetry ascribed to him. What might be essayed at this stage is the assertion that it is within the Fumo Liongo cycle complex that the origins of *tendi* as a poetic tradition may be found.

This latter point raises again, for the moment, the unanswerable question as to the transmission of 'popular' Islamic themes that were later transmuted into Swahili in epic forms. Again, there is an ambiguity here, in that the earliest, physically surviving long poem, the translation dated by Knappert to 1652 of the *Hamziyya* by Bwana Mwengo, is a rendering into Swahili of a well-known Arabic literary text. What we know of the *Hamziyya* points to a Pate origin, and the scanty evidence we have of the origin of *al-Inkishafi* (The Soul's Awakening), possibly the greatest of Swahili *tendi*, suggests a very sophisticated poetic milieu in that city in the eighteenth century. The earliest manuscripts are epics, *chuo* or *tendi*, for example the *Chuo cha Herkal* (Epic of Herkal), one manuscript of which is dated 1141 *hijra* (AD 1728–29).

At this stage in our knowledge, about the only safe generalisation one can make is that poems such as *al-Inkishafi* were not the products of a young untried tradition, but rather the productions of a very refined and sophisticated poetic tradition. How literary, or how oral, this tradition was in its inception is an open question.

A further question for consideration in exploring the history of Swahili poetry is the extent to which the forms and content of the poetry reflected the changing socio-political realities along the East African coast.

Again, generalisations are probably premature, but one might argue that the post-Portuguese period (effectively after about 1700) saw a certain political hegemony in Pate/Lamu, the area that, in the eighteenth and early nineteenth centuries, produced some of the classics of Swahili literature like *al-Inkishafi* and *Mwana Kupona*. This political hegemony may be related to patterns of trade on the Benadir coast in Somalia before the coming of the Omani hegemony, that is, in a northerly direction.

In mid-nineteenth century Mombasa, under an assertive Mazrui clan fighting against the inroads of Sa'id b. Sultan of Oman and Zanzibar, there emerged new poetic forms, supremely espoused by Muyaka b. Haji, namely the *shairi*, intimate, dialogic and polemical. In terms of what has survived, it is the nineteenth-century dialogue/polemic poetry that is the most substantial, if one accepts that most of the epics we have today, outside the so-called 'classical' corpus of *tendi*, are de facto modern. The bulk of the Taylor (Soas) and Dammann (Berlin) collections comprise this genre. But this is essentially 'occasional' poetry where, as Harries reminds us, the occasion of its composition is often beyond recovery. However, its recovery and interpretation are a challenge to future historians of Swahili literature. This dialogic tradition, *kujibizana*, about which Ann Biersteker has written much, has reinvented itself in the twentieth century in the newspapers. It seems not unreasonable to see a continuity between Muyaka b. Haji and Moza binti Mi, writing on the topics of the day in the Zanzibari newspaper *Mwongozi*. While some poets will hail the coming of the East African shilling, or the birthday of King George V, others deal with much more enduring themes.

Once established, the writing of *tendi* became an integral part of Swahili literary culture. *Arabic Literature of Africa* (Vol. 3B) documents in detail the enormous range and variety of the Swahili poetic epic tradition. Less well known is the writing of poetry of a didactic character by, for example, the Brava poetess Dada Matisi, and Muhyi 'l-Din al-Qahtani. Here one is at a meeting point between the past and modernity; Matisi and al-Qahtani used Swahili (or in the former case, Cimini) to present Islamic teachings in the vernacular. Out of this was to grow indigenous (as opposed to missionary-inspired) Swahili prose literature.

Swahili prose writing

In the nineteenth century and before, Muslim scholars of the coast and islands wrote prose in Arabic and poetry in Swahili (although some, such as al-Qahtani, wrote poetry in both languages). Swahili prose writing emerged approximately in the 1920s.

The pioneers here were Muhammad al-Amin al-Mazrui and his brother-in-law, Muhammad Qassim. The Mazruis and their Zanzibari counterpart, 'Abdallah Saleh Farsy, produced a very considerable body of Swahili Islamic prose literature, which is duly recorded in *Arabic Literature of Africa* (Vol. 3B). Most of this literature is didactic in nature, essentially pamphlets or booklets giving elementary information on a variety of Islamic topics. More ambitious are the various translations, beginning with the *Ahmadiyya* version, of the Qur'an.[35] The production of such literature has vastly increased in recent years and there are few mosques that do not have a bookseller outside their doors. There is some reason to believe that much of this literature is directed towards women, who are becoming an increasingly visible element in Muslim public life.

From the 1930s there has developed a tradition of writing fiction in Swahili. Many of the leading exponents of fiction writing write out of an Islamic milieu. The most influential figure was Shaaban b. Robert, whose father converted to Christianity, but who himself returned to Islam. Bin Robert is a transitional figure in the emergence of Swahili as a national language.

Arabic writings

The earliest Arabic writing, apart from the classical Arab geographers, that throws light on Islam on the East African coast is *al-Sira* or *al-Maqama al-Kilwiyya* (The Story of Kilwa) by Muhammad b. Sa'id al-Qalhati. It is an Ibadi polemic written around 1116 (*hijri*) by two brothers living at Kilwa, 'Ali b. 'Ali and Hasan b. 'Ali, who were actively propagating Ibadi Islam in the Kilwa region.

The earliest indigenous Arabic writing is the Kilwa chronicle entitled *al-Sulwa fi akhbar Kilwa* (The History Book Concerning the Pleasure of Kilwa). The original version was written by an unnamed author who was born on 2 Shawwal 904 (13 May 1499). The antiquity of this chronicle, the oldest in sub-Saharan Africa, is confirmed by the fact that Joao de Barros (1496–1570) quotes a partial translation in his *Da Asia* (Of Asia), first published in 1552.[36]

Little in Arabic has survived before the nineteenth century except for some Ibadi texts dating from the seventeenth and eighteenth centuries, brought to Zanzibar under the sultanate. In 1880 Sultan Barghash (r. 1870–88) established a printing press in Zanzibar and embarked on an ambitious programme of printing Ibadi works of theology and jurisprudence, involving a network of scholars from the Wadi Mzab (Algeria), Cairo, Oman and Zanzibar (see Chapter 2 of *Arabic Literature of Africa*, Vol. 3B).

Since the dominant *madhhab* in East Africa is Shafi'i, much of the Arabic writing concerns that school's jurisprudence.

NOTES

1 Roper (1994: 129–154).
2 National Records Office, PO Box 1914, Khartoum.
3 O'Fahey & Hunwick (1994).
4 Hasan b. Muhammad al-Fatih b. Qarib Allah; see O'Fahey & Hunwick (1994: 113).
5 Wagner (1997).
6 O'Fahey & Hunwick (2003).
7 Sunjata Keita was the founder of the Mande Malian Empire and much poetry was written about him, referred to as the Sunjata cycle.
8 Dammann (1993).
9 Wagner (1997).
10 Allen (1963).
11 Trimingham (1952).
12 Ahmed (2001).
13 Trimingham (1952: 44–46).
14 Abu Da'ud, quoted in Trimingham (1952: 46).
15 See Erlich (1994: 151–164).
16 Orhonlu (1969).
17 Emperor Johannes IV (r. 1868–89) and Emperor Minilik II (r. 1889–1913).
18 *Jama'a* in Arabic, *camaa* in Somali.
19 Brockelmann has some eight pages devoted to Africa in his five volumes published between 1937 and 1949. By the 1940s the study of Swahili was nearly a century old.
20 See further Miehe and Mohlig (1995).
21 See Frankl (1998).
22 The Interterritorial Language Committee was established in 1930. See Whiteley (1969: 79–95) on the promotion of 'standard' Swahili.
23 This is not to overlook the body of poetry in Chimini or Chimbalazi, the Swahili dialect of Brava in southern Somalia.
24 Whiteley (1969: 94). What is striking is that Whiteley never really explains the rationale behind the decision. The whole episode invites further investigation.
25 Snoxall (1984).
26 Shariff (1991: 41).
27 Knappert (1971: 5).
28 See Paret (1927–28).
29 See Gibb et al. (1960–2004: 2, v, 1161–1164).
30 Harries (1962: 2).
31 Abdulaziz (1994).
32 Shariff (1991: 43).
33 See, for example, the polemic against the western 'orientalist' imposition of an Arab–Muslim identity upon the Swahili and their literature in Mazrui and Shariff (1994).
34 Rollins (1985: 51).
35 I exclude from consideration here the translation of the Qur'an by the missionary Godfrey Dale.
36 See Freeman-Grenville (1962: 34).

REFERENCES

Abdulaziz MH (1994/1979) *Muyaka, 19th century Swahili popular poetry.* Nairobi: Kenya Literature Bureau

Allen V (1963) *A catalogue of the Swahili and Arabic manuscripts in the library of the University of Dar es Salaam.* Leiden: Brill

Brockelmann C (1937–49) *Geschichte der arabischen Literattur* (2 Vols, 2nd edition 1943–49; 3 Vols Supplement, 1937–42). Leiden: Brill

Dammann E (1993) *Afrikanische handschriften* (Vol. 1): *Handscriften in Swahili und anderen Sprachen afrikas.* Stuttgart: Franz Steiner

Erlich H (1994) *Ethiopia and the Middle East.* Boulder, CO: Lynne Rienne Publishers

Frankl PJL (1998) Review of *Tarjama ya al-muntakhab katika tafsiri ya qur'ani tukufti. British Journal of Middle Eastern Studies* 25: 191–193

Freeman-Grenville GSP (1962) *The medieval history of the coast of Tanganyika, with special reference to recent archaeological discoveries.* Berlin: Akademie Verlag

Gibb HAR et al. (Eds) (1960–2004) *Encyclopaedia of Islam* (12 Vols). Leiden: Brill

Harries L (1962) *Swahili poetry.* Oxford: Clarendon Press

Hussein A (2001) *Islam in nineteenth-century Wallo, Ethiopia: revival, reform, and reaction.* Leiden: Brill

Knappert J (1971) *Swahili Islamic poetry.* Leiden: Brill

Mazrui AM & Shariff IN (1994) *The Swahili: Idiom and identity of an African people.* Trenton, NJ: Africa World Press

Miehe G & Mohlig WJ (1995) *Swahili handbuch.* Cologne: Rudiger Koppe Verlag

O'Fahey RS & Hunwick JO (Eds) (1994) *Arabic literature of Africa: The writings of eastern Sudanic Africa to c.1900* (Vol. 1). Leiden: Brill

O'Fahey RS & Hunwick JO (Eds) (2003) *Arabic literature of Africa: The writings of the Muslim peoples of northeastern Africa* (Vol. 3A). Leiden: Brill

O'Fahey RS & Hunwick JO (Eds) (in press) *Arabic literature of Africa: The writings of the Muslim peoples of eastern Africa* (Vol. 3B)

Orhonlu G (1969) *Habesh eyalati.* Istanbul: n. p.

Paret R (1927–28) Die arabische Quelle der Suaheli-Dichtung Chuo cha Herkal. *Zeitschrift der Deutschen Morgenlandischen Gesellschaft* 1: 241–249

Rollins JD (1985) Early 20th century Swahili prose narrative structure and some aspects of Swahili ethnicity. In E Breitinger & R Sander (Eds) *Towards African authenticity, language and literary form.* In *Bayreuth African Studies* 2: 49–68

Roper G (Ed.) (1994) *World survey of Islamic manuscripts* (Vol. 3). London: al-Furqan Islamic Heritage Foundation

Shariff IN (1991) Islam and secularity in Swahili literature: an overview. In KW Harrow (Ed.) *Faces of Islam in African literature.* London: J. Currey

Snoxall RA (1984) The East African Interterritorial Language (Swahili) Committee. *Swahili Language and Society* 22: 15–24

Trimingham JS (1952) *Islam in Ethiopia.* London: Frank Cass

Wagner E (1997) *Afrikanische handschriften* (Vol. 2): *Islamische Handschriften aus Athiopien.* Stuttgart: Franz Steiner

Whiteley W (1969) *Swahili: The rise of a national language.* London: Methuen

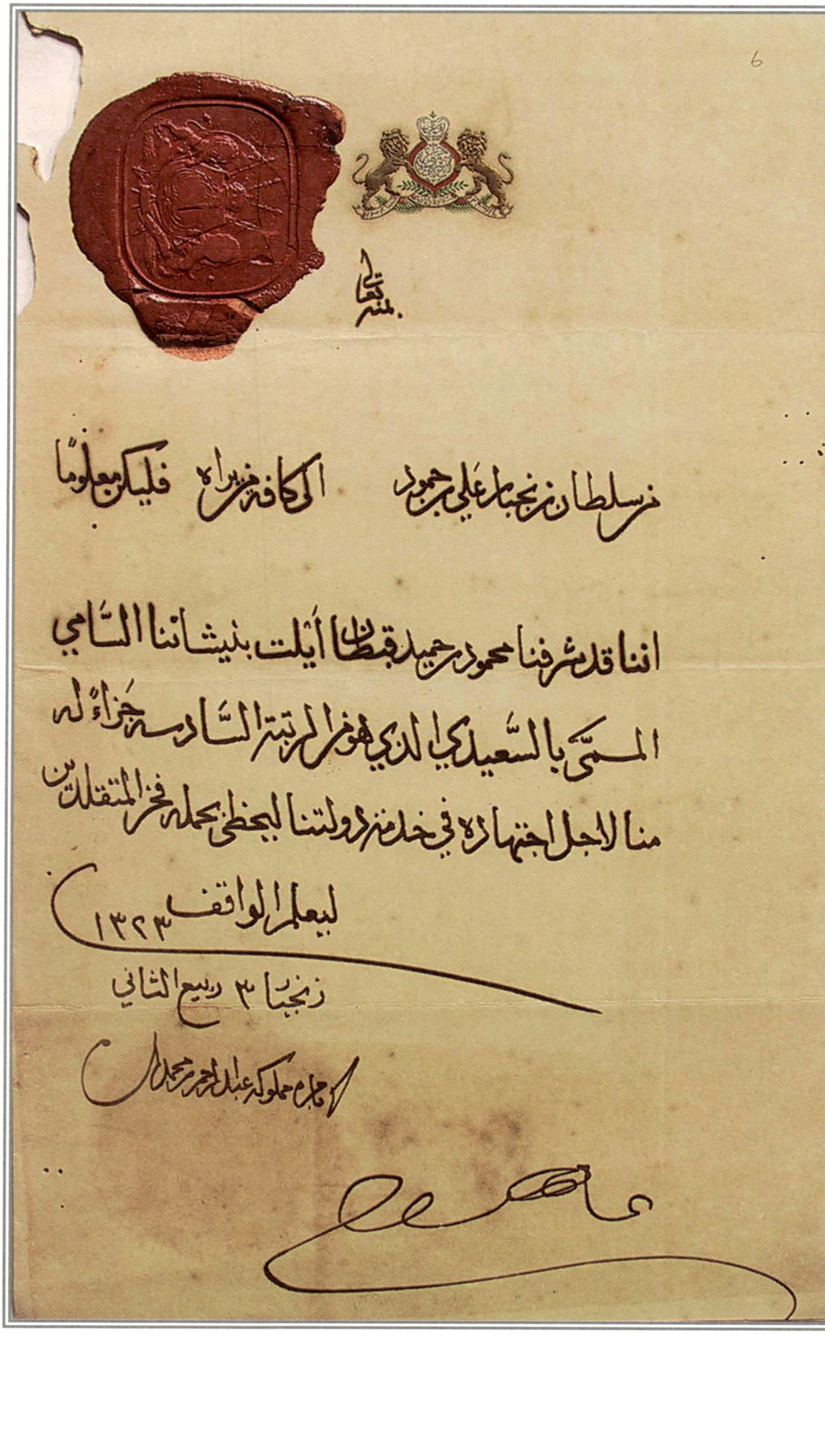

6

بسمه تعالى

من سلطان زنجبار علي بن حمود الى كافة من يراه فليكن معلوما

اننا قد شرفنا محمود بن حميد قبطان أيلت بنيشاننا السامي

المسمى بالسعيدي الذي هو من الرتبة السادسة جزاء له

منا لاجل اجتهاده في خدمة دولتنا ليحظى بحمله فخر المتقلدين

ليعلم الواقف ١٣٢٣

زنجبار ٣ ربيع الثاني

كتبه مملوكه عبد الله بن محمد

CHAPTER 24

Textual sources on an Islamic African past: Arabic material in Zanzibar's National Archive

Anne K Bang

The Zanzibar National Archives (ZNA) in the Kilimani district outside Zanzibar Stone Town is home to a rich collection of material in Arabic and also a number of documents in Swahili in the Arabic script.[1] This material dates from the Omani era of East African history (*c*.1800–90) as well as from the period of the British protectorate (1890–1963). Among these is a large collection of Arabic manuscripts originating from Zanzibar itself, from East Africa, Oman as well as the Middle East. There is also a rich collection of Arabic correspondence deriving from the sultans of Zanzibar with contemporaries in Africa, the Middle East and Europe, as well as *qadi* (*shari'a*) court records, title deeds and *waqf* files. The Islamic presence in East Africa has been both extensive and diverse, and this is reflected in the collection held in the ZNA. The richness and variety of the collection recently led it to be nominated for the United Nations Educational, Scientific and Cultural Organisation's Memory of the World Register.[2] In the past decade, several researchers – African, western and Omani – have started to use this wealth of material as direct sources for historical research. The nature of the manuscripts and documents is almost exclusively Islamic, that is, a combination of manuscripts deriving from all Islamic sciences, legal handbooks and rulings, poetry and correspondence.

Challenging statements by earlier scholars of Islamic Africa, Scott Reese has pointed out that texts of a religious nature are in themselves of historical value, in so far as they demonstrate a level of knowledge, interconnectedness and technology at a certain place at a certain point in time. Secondly, the texts themselves do contain valuable historical information given that social and political issues of the day frequently tended to be played out precisely within religious discourse.[3] In other words, the documents housed in the ZNA provide not only phenomenological knowledge about Islam, but also concrete and direct historical evidence on a range of issues pertaining to East

Opposite: An East African Arabic manuscript dated 7 June 1905. It is interesting to note how much the calligraphic styles vary between East and West African manuscripts.

African society. Finally, as archive files, they constitute not only a piece of Islamic heritage but also a substantial part of the East African literary corpus.

What will be presented here is thus a broad overview of the content and recent research conducted on the non-colonial records held at the ZNA. I draw on the work of several of my colleagues as well as that of the staff at the ZNA who have, at times against heavy odds, managed to preserve a collection which adds greatly to the literary heritage of sub-Saharan Africa.

This chapter will outline the historical background to the existing collection, and discuss historical topics and themes that have been studied and may be pursued further with reference to the material. Finally, a note is added on the state of preservation in the ZNA, including suggestions for its improvement.

Background: the Omani (Bu Sa'idi) rulers of East Africa, *c.*1830–90

The new sultan of Oman, Sayyid Sa'id b. Sultan al-Bu Sa'idi turned his attention towards East Africa upon his ascent to power in 1804. At that time, Omani (and general South Arabian) migration to East Africa had been an ongoing process for centuries, dating back to at least the twelfth century. Clans of South Arabian origin, such as the Mazruis and the Nabhanis, the al Shaykh Abi Bakr b. Salim and the Jamal al-Layl had spread throughout the coast and merged with the existing population to form a coastal urban aristocracy, centred on cities like Lamu, Mombasa and Kilwa. Ties with their clansmen in South Arabia may have been weakened but were nevertheless called upon in times of distress, such as during the Portuguese era.

Sayyid Sa'id turned to Zanzibar, which he made his new capital in 1832. This shift was not only a reactivation of previous and long-standing trade and tribal relations. It was also a completely new form of direct Omani rule, which was aimed primarily at creating a trade depot for the vast riches of the African mainland (slaves, spices, ivory and copra, to name but a few).[4] The 'new Oman', as represented by its new rulers, the Bu Sa'idis, was maritime and mercantile, and able to subjugate the previous leaders of the coastal towns. Direct Omani overlordship was not always welcomed, not even by clans of Omani origin – hence, for example, the long-standing feud between Sayyid Sa'id and the Mazrui clan of Mombasa during the 1820s and 1830s. Nevertheless, upon the death of Sayyid Sa'id in 1856, the Omani Empire included all of Oman, as well as the coast of Africa from Guardafui to Cape Delgado.

Despite its massive commercial expansion, the Omani transoceanic empire stood little chance of surviving the emergence of Great Britain as the main naval power in the Indian Ocean. Internal Bu Sa'idi rivalry and direct British involvement led to a division of the Omani Empire in 1861. The East African part of the possessions were headed by Sayyid Sa'id's son Majid, while his brother Thwayni became sultan of the Omani mainland.

In political and economic terms, the Bu Sa'idi Empire of East Africa was already in decline by the time Sayyid Barghash b. Sa'id was pronounced sultan in 1870. British influence was mounting and the abolition of slavery led to a shortage of manpower and eventually to the impoverishment of the landowners. By the 1880s, the Arab plantation owners were in reality deeply indebted to the Indian merchant class. Nevertheless, the era of Sayyid Barghash (r. 1870–88) has been called the 'golden age' of the Zanzibari Bu Sa'idi sultanate. The 'golden age', however, must be understood in cultural terms. Material innovations were many during the reign of Barghash: palaces were built, electricity introduced to Zanzibar Town, and water supply systems constructed. Finally, and most importantly from the point of view of scriptural heritage, Barghash's reign saw a steep rise in scholarly activities. *Ribat*s (religious schools) were endowed by *waqf* funds, scholars were supported and books from overseas were imported to Zanzibar at an unprecedented rate.

Last but not least, Barghash brought a printing press from Syria along with experienced printers, very much inspired by the spirit of reform then current in the Arab world. The press was active from 1879 and launched an extensive programme of printing key Omani legal texts written in North Africa and preserved as manuscripts in Oman.[5] Its most ambitious project was the printing of the 90-volume *Kitab qamus al-shar'iyya* (Book/Dictionary on *shari'a*) by the Omani scholar Jumayyil b. Khamis al-Sa'idi. Unfortunately, printing ceased after 19 volumes. As far as can be ascertained on the basis of the holdings in Zanzibar, the only work printed by a contemporary Zanzibari was by the *qadi* and major intellectual Nasir b. Salim (known as Abu Muslim) al-Rawwahi (d.1920). In 1898 the Sultanic Press published an account of a tour by the young crown prince in East Africa.

Interestingly, the Sultanic Press is also listed to have published a travel account by al-Rawwahi concerning a journey to South Africa. This is one of the publications that cannot be found.

The issue of scripturalism: Omani rule and the production of text

While earlier scholars such as JS Trimingham[6] tended to view East African Islam as mainly a function of oral transmission within the urban aristocracy, more recent research has tended to emphasise a combination of two strands: an oral poetic tradition transmitted in KiSwahili and a tradition of Islamic learning transmitted in writing and in Arabic.[7]

The emergence of the Omani sultanate in the nineteenth century tipped the scale in favour of the written, Arabic-based strand of the tradition. By the 1850s, state-appointed *liwali*s (appointed executive of law and order) made Omani power apparent on the local level, and *qadi*s were appointed by the state rather than brought forth locally within the community. In addition, the economic powerbase of the Bu Sa'idis was new-style plantation owners rather than a redistributive, local aristocracy. They could afford to sponsor scholars, establish schools and encourage literacy, the prime example being Sayyid Barghash's founding of a printing press in Zanzibar Town.

The Omani sultanate also meant that access to authority came to be regulated by the central government rather than by the traditional patricians. In the same process, Islamic knowledge was reinterpreted to mean a set of literary tenets that could be checked, controlled and debated according to books.[8] It can be argued that the process opened up East African scriptural Islam to the wider Islamic world, in so far as writings deriving from other parts of the Islamic world (of all Islamic sciences, including Sufism) became known, copied and, in turn, discussed in writing by the new corps of highly literate East African scholars. There emerged a new class of *'ulama* whose outlook transcended the local to an extent which had not been the case in the eighteenth century. The body of material today kept in the ZNA is evidence of this process.

Although the Barghash era was marked by a strong emphasis on the Ibadi sect (the dominant school of Oman),[9] the Shafi'i Sunni community of East Africa was also marked by the same upsurge in scriptural learning. This was a surge most decisively linked to the emergence of organised Sufism on the coast, associated with the orders of the Shadhiliyya, Qadiriyya and the 'Alawiyya. Sufi manuals and poetry were copied from their Middle Eastern originals and in turn commented upon by scholars fully versed in scriptural Islamic scholarship. This development, too, is very much in evidence in the Zanzibar archives.

The ZNA collection: overview of the Arabic material

Books and treatises

The manuscript collection of the ZNA consists of about 800 manuscripts, the majority originally held by the sultanic palace and transferred following the revolution of 1964. In addition, about 100 items were added in 1999, transferred from the collection gathered under the auspices of the now defunct Eacrotonal.[10] The earliest documents date from the late 1700s, while the latest date from the early twentieth century. The collection reflects the penchant of the East African scholarly class for collecting, copying, commenting upon and writing books.

Part of the collection consists of copies of works of non-East African origin, in some cases with commentaries added by local scholars, thus adding a local point of view on matters of Islamic scholarship. The majority of works, however, are of Omani/East African provenance and thus make a very substantial contribution to the literary heritage of the region, as well as serving as a demonstration of Zanzibar's important role as a seat of learning.

The collection includes treatises on Islamic disciplines such as law, theology, *hadith*, *fiqh*, grammar, poetry and rhetoric. In addition, the collection includes valuable works

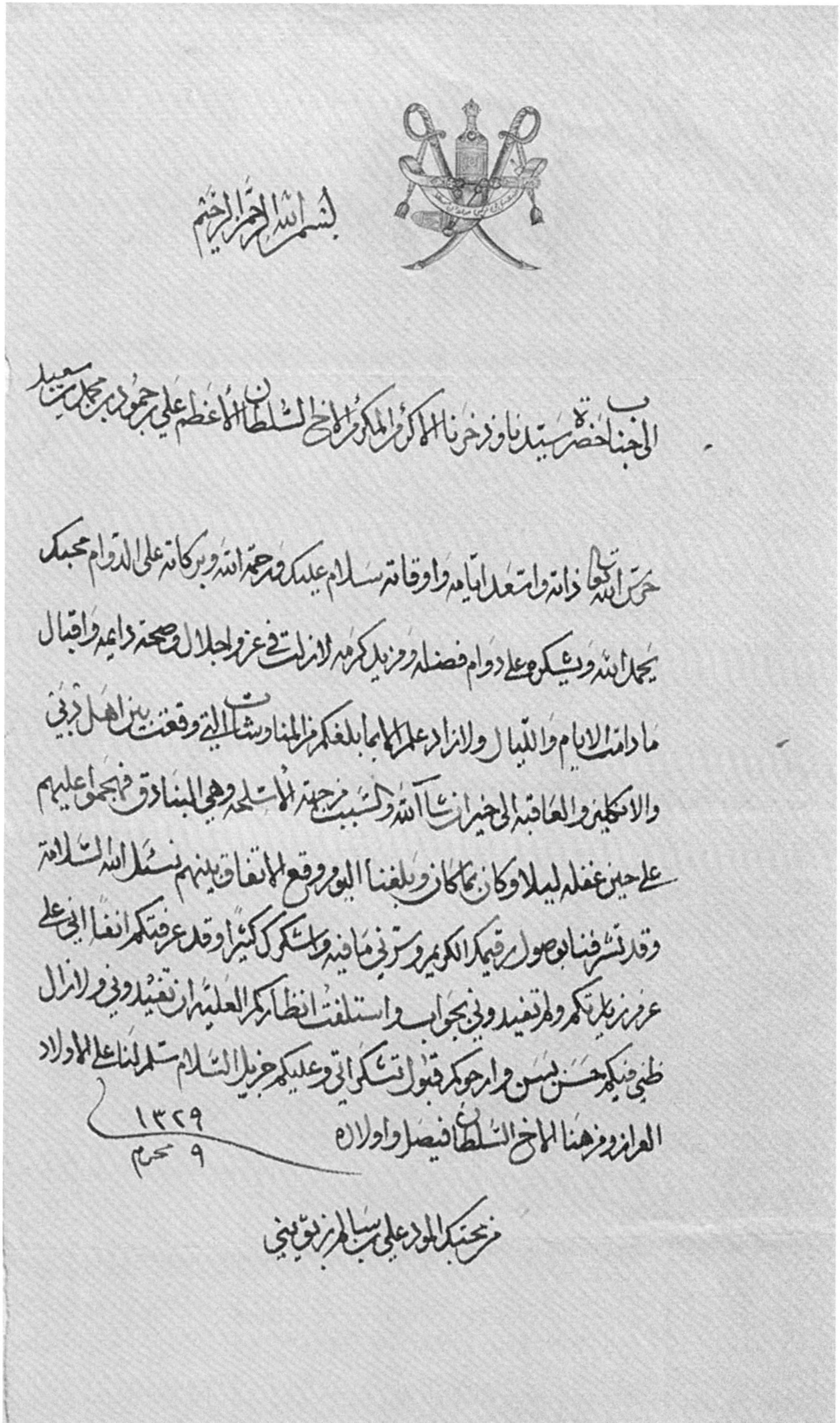

بسم الله الرحمن الرحيم

الى جناب حضرة سيدنا وذخرنا الاكرم المكرم الاخ السلطان الاعظم علي بن حمود بن محمد بن سعيد

حرس الله تعالى ذاته واسعد ايامه واوقاته سلام عليكم ورحمة الله وبركاته على الدوام محبكم
بحمد الله ونشكره على دوام فضله ومزيد كرمه لا زلت في عز واجلال وصحة دايمة واقبال
ما دامت الايام والليال والاراد علم الهمام بلغكم من المناوشات التي وقعت بين اهل دبي
والانكليز والعاقبة الى خير ان شاء الله والسبب من جهة الاسلحة وهي البنادق فهجموا عليهم
على حين غفلة ليلا وكان ما كان وبلغنا اليوم وقع الاتفاق بينهم نسئل الله السلامة
وقد تشرفنا بوصول رقيمكم الكريم وسرني ما فيه واشكركم كثيرا وقد عرفتكم انفا ابي على
عزم زيارتكم ولم تفيدوني بجواب واستلفت انظاركم العلية ان تفيدوني وان لا زال
ظني فيكم حسن [illegible] وارجوكم قبول تشكراتي وعليكم جزيل السلام سلموا لنا على الاولاد
العزاز ومن هنا الاخ السلطان فيصل واولاده

١٣٢٩
٩ محرم

من محبكم المود علي بن سالم بن ثويني

Letter dated 10 January 1911 to the Sultan Sayyid ʻAli b. Hammud al Bu Saʻidi in Zanzibar.

on medicine (herbal and prophetic medicine), magic, astronomy, navigation and travel accounts (*rihlat*).

In terms of authors, the collection includes many Omani authors, especially within the field of *fiqh*. In addition, the collection includes original copies by famous East African scholars as well as by lesser-known authors. Several of the works of the famous *qadi* and Qadiri Sufi 'Abd al-'Aziz b. 'Abd al-Ghani al-'Amawi (1832–96)[11] are included in the collection.

The sultanic correspondence

An important part of the collection is the body of correspondence deriving from the Bu Sa'idi sultans of Zanzibar. Although the letters are generally dated more recently than the manuscripts, as a total they make up a cohesive and substantial historical source for the era of Bu Sa'idi rule, both before and after the British colonial intervention. The collection consists of approximately 2 600 letters, the earliest dating back to the 1840s and the reign of Sayyid Sa'id b. Sultan and the latest to the 1940s and the reign of Sayyid Khalifa b. Harub.

Roughly one-sixth of the collection derives from Sayyid Sa'id, one-sixth from his successors Majid and Khalifa, and one-sixth from Sayyid Barghash. The bulk – approximately half – of the collection[12] derives from Sayyid Hammud b. Muhammad and his son and successor 'Ali b. Hammud, that is, from the period 1896–1911. This part of the collection is also the most varied, containing everything from details on expenditure on dinner parties, letters from editors in the Middle East, and notes on the plague to wedding cards and family letters from the Omani branch of the family (including letters from female family members). All in all, the collection is an invaluable source which gives insight into the Bu Sa'idis' relations with their East African cadre of bureaucrats and landowners, their subjects, their Indian money lenders, their family in Oman and, not least, with rulers, intellectuals and reformers in Africa, Arabia and the Middle East. It thus constitutes a vital source for both East African and Omani history. It has yet to be fully used as a source for historical research.

Legal records, *sijillat*, deeds and *waqf* documents

During the Bu Sa'idi era, a corps of specially appointed *qadis* would hear cases and record deeds and *waqfs* according to the system prevailing in most Islamic societies. It is likely that each *qadi* kept his own record rather than there being a central state system where all cases were kept. For this reason, we have only very few legal records deriving from the pre-colonial Bu Sa'idi era. There are, however, some exceptions. The ZNA is also home to a number of *sijillat* dating from the 1880s to the 1920s, 'record books' where brief summaries of each case were noted. Some 42 books have been preserved and these contain detailed information on each case, including its outcome.

In addition, *waqf* records pre-dating the British Protectorate can be found in cases where they were safeguarded in anticipation of later disputes over the *waqf*, or reproduced as evidence in cases where problems arose concerning its administration or distribution.[13] Several such cases are held in the ZNA, with original *waqfiyyas* dating back to the time of Sayyid Barghash, which was a particularly active period for *waqf* endowments. Some of the more substantial *waqfs*, endowed by the Zanzibar sultans, were published by the Sultanic Press and are presently held by the ZNA. As for title deeds and sale contracts, about 200 are included in the sultanic correspondence.

However, from the period after the British Protectorate, the picture is very different. The ZNA houses a large collection of criminal and civil cases[14] that date from the period following the legal reform of 1908. In this collection, the outline of the cases is in English but the *qadi*'s deliberation is in Arabic, at least up to the 1940s or 1950s.

Also for *waqf* records, the collection is very substantial from the period after the establishment of the British Wakf Commission.[15] These records have been thoroughly indexed and fed into a database.

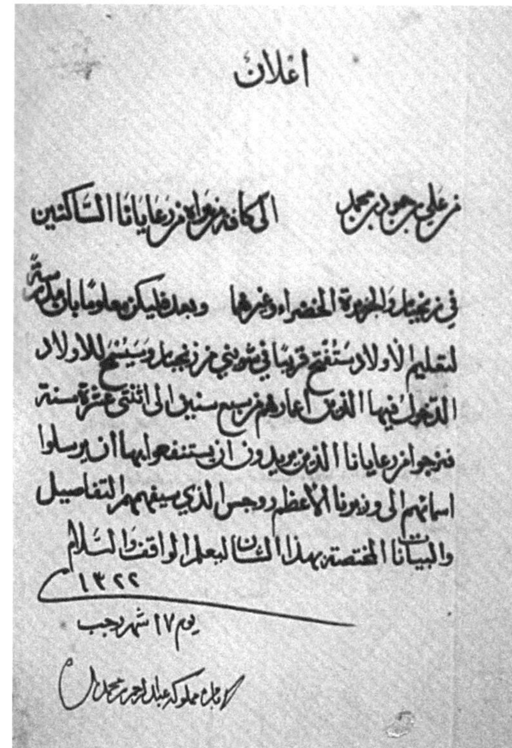
اعلان
من علي بن حمود بن محمد الى كافة من يراه من رعايانا الساكنين
في زنجبار والجزيرة الخضراء وغيرها وبعد فليكن معلوما بان مدرسة
لتعليم الاولاد ستفتح قريبا في شوني من زنجبار وسيسمح للاولاد
الدخول فيها الذين اعمارهم من سبع سنين الى اثنتى عشرة سنة
فنرجو من رعايانا الذين يريدون ان يستنفعوا بها ان يرسلوا
اسمائهم الى وزيرنا الاعظم روجرس الذي سيفهمهم التفاصيل
والبيانات المختصة بهذا الشان بالعلم الواقف والسلام
١٣٢٢
يوم ١٧ شهر رجب

Public announcement dated 27 September 1904 announcing the opening of public schools for children in Zanzibar aged between 7 and 12.

The scriptural–literary heritage of East Africa and the collection of the ZNA: issues and fields of study

Setting aside the academic debate as to whether transmission of knowledge in East Africa has been primarily oral (understood as 'African') or scriptural (understood as 'Middle Eastern'), it seems clear that the corpus of text held by the ZNA demonstrates an at least 200-year-old tradition of production of text as a medium for transmission. The fact that the texts are primarily in Arabic does not detract from their importance as a part of the scriptural heritage of the region. As historical sources, the 'Arabness' of the material rather illustrates that the East African *'ulama* of the day were conversant with intellectual developments overseas and able to express their opinions in a language that could also be read outside the region. Furthermore, it does not mean that oral transmission in the vernacular did not take place, continuously and on all levels, from the most basic Qur'anic schools to learned exegesis among the advanced scholars.[16]

Rather, our focus should be on what these documents can tell us about the intellectual tradition evolving on the coast and the political and social circumstances in which it emerged. Here, a number of interesting issues can be explored.

East African Islam in context

Although, as stated at the outset of this chapter, several studies have now been conducted on the basis of Islamic writings of East Africa, much still remains to be done. The corpus of documents held at the ZNA constitutes a very important source in this regard. How was Islamic reform formulated? How did it interact with other reformist movements of the age? What did the *'ulama* read and who did they refer to in their own writing?

How were Islamic practices of a more popular nature (divination, astrology, spirit possession remedies, dream interpretation) fused with the more *shari'a*-based aspects of the faith?

Inter-African intellectual ties

The correspondence of the Zanzibar sultans and the output of the Sultanic Press demonstrate not only the close ties between East Africa and Arabia but also between Zanzibar and other parts of Islamic Africa. One example can be found in the network of Ibadi scholars, closely connected on the axis Algeria–Zanzibar. The greatest reformer of Ibadism in the late nineteenth century was Muhammad b. Yusuf Attafayyish (1820–1914) of Wadi Mizab in southern Algeria. His works on *tafsir*, *fiqh*, *hadith*, logic and literature were influential both in Oman and in Zanzibar. Attafayyish's long-standing ties with the Zanzibari sultanate can be cited as an example of inter-African intellectual relations. For a period, Attafayyish was financially supported by Sayyid Barghash himself and later kept up close connections with his successors. Several of his works were printed by the Sultanic Press in Zanzibar and distributed widely in Algeria, Egypt and Libya, as well as Oman.[17]

Corresponding evidence of intellectual ties for the Shafi'i Sunni population is likely to be found among the documents held in the ZNA.

The study of East African medicinal history

A not insignificant proportion of the manuscripts held by the ZNA deals with issues of medicine in one form or another. Little academic work has been conducted on these documents, which constitute a rich source on the history of medicinal practices.[18]

There are books on herbal recipes and on magic, and books outlining the tradition known as *tibb nabawwi* (prophetic medicine). At least three copies of classics are included in the collection, indicating that there was awareness and usage of them in East Africa.[19] The book *Kitab al-rahma fi al-tib wa al-hikma* (Book on the Mercy in Prophetic Medicine and Wisdom) by Jalal al-Din al-Suyuti (d.1505) may be placed in the latter category. The copy in Zanzibar dates back to 1728 and is thus the oldest copy manuscript in the archive and an example of the awareness of the Zanzibari scholars of previous knowledge. The *Shajarat al-arsh* (The Tree of the Throne) is an example of a locally produced treatise on medicine, the copy in the archives dating from 1936. This treatise was written by the adviser of Sayyid Sa'id b. Sultan, Nasir b. Ja'id al-Kharusi (1776–1847). It describes roots, plants and herbs used for medicine and magic.

Most of the books, however, date from the mid-to-late 1800s and have yet to be surveyed beyond their index entries.

Astronomy/navigation

Not surprisingly, given East Africa's close dependence on long-distance seafaring, a number of the manuscripts in the collection deal with issues of astronomy and navigation. Many of Zanzibar's most renowned Islamic scholars devoted at least one of their works to this topic. Earlier scholars like RB Serjeant have done some work on the navigational poetry and methodology of South Arabia, but much has yet to be done on the material deriving from East Africa.

The study of Muslim–Christian relations

The period from which most of the documents of the ZNA derives was also the time of missionary expansion into the Bu Sa'idi dominions. Where Islam formerly had been the sole point of cultural and civilisational reference for the educated population, Christianity made numerous converts among the slave (and later ex-slave) population and could not be disregarded.

Among the documents most directly dealing with Muslim–Christian relations is a *risala* dating from 1891 in defence of Islam by 'Ali b. Muhammad al-Mundhiri (1866–1925). The Mundhiri family were Ibadis of Omani origin and were closely connected with the Bu Sa'idis as scholars and *qadis*. When the missionary presence became paramount in Zanzibar during the 1880s, the '*ulama* engaged in debate – both verbally and, like al-Mundhiri, in the form of writing. The text itself is a response to a document known as 'The Apology of al-Kindi in Favour of Christianity over Islam', originally composed around 830 by a Christian Arab upon an invitation to embrace Islam. In the nineteenth century, the document (although clearly not in its original form) was used by missionary organisations working in Islamic societies.[20] In his response, which is preserved in original in the ZNA,[21] al-Mundhiri displays considerable familiarity with Christian tenets and the historical context of the Christian gospels as he refutes the arguments of al-Kindi by discussing such topics as the Trinity and the divinity of Christ.

The state of preservation at the ZNA

It is important to note that a substantial proportion of the Arabic material in Zanzibar still remains in private hands, as collections in private homes or as *waqf* property in mosques or religious associations. Due to mistrust of the government or for other reasons, individuals have been reluctant to part with originals for storage in the archives.

Concerning the private collections, it is of some urgency that these be registered and restored. They are in danger of rapid deterioration due to exposure to humidity and ants, and of being sold to wealthy buyers arriving from Gulf states.

Special case: the collection of sultanic correspondence

Despite being both substantial and unique, the sultanic correspondence collection held at the ZNA is not preserved in a manner optimal for its safe keeping, or for use by the public. This is due partly to a lack of funds for material improvement and partly to a lack of skills among the staff, such as knowledge of Arabic and competence in modern conservation methods. In other words, it is important that the sultanic correspondence collection at the ZNA be catalogued and conserved in such a manner that it may be a fully functional research collection. This effort should include both material conservation as well as efforts to raise skills among the staff.

Given the finite size of the collection and its nature (mostly one- or two-page documents), it should ideally be stored as a database where the documents are scanned and accessible online, either on-site or from anywhere in the world. This would save the documents from the wear and tear of handling. An urgent project would thus be the indexing, scanning and material conservation of the correspondence. In addition, such a project would have to include competence-raising components, especially on the part of the archive staff.

At present, the archives do not have staff qualified in Arabic, Swahili and English. If funding could be found, staff could be recruited from the State University of Zanzibar or from private colleges such as the Muslim Academy, which produces candidates knowledgeable in all three languages. Secondly, the conservation staff at the ZNA have not received training in conservation since the 1980s. It is thus proposed that they receive in-house training on the most recent conservation methods from an expert from either India or Europe. It is also proposed that one of the staff members responsible for indexing receive training in either Khartoum or Bergen. This is necessary because although the person may be conversant in Arabic, Swahili and English, they are unlikely to be familiar with the process of transliteration of Arabic script into Latin characters. In order to create an index useful to researchers, this is absolutely essential. Finally, the technology necessary for the project would have to be provided, including scanners, digital cameras and computers sufficiently powered to run a large database.

NOTES

1 Gratitude for information presented in this chapter is due to the staff of the ZNA, its director Hamadi Omar, its former senior archivist Khamis S Khamis and its Arabic reader Omar Shehe, and to Professor Abdul Sharif, Director of the Department of Museums, Zanzibar. Furthermore, thanks are extended to Lorenzo Declich and Friedhelm Hartwig, both of whom have worked extensively on the collection.

2 See http://portal.unesco.org/ci/ev.php?URL_ID=12543&URL_DO=DO_TOPIC&URL_SECTION=201&reload= 1062662650.

3 Reese (2004).

4 For the economic background to the Omani expansion, see Sharif (1987).

5 On the impact of the Matba'a al-Sultaniyya (Sultanic Press) founded by Barghash, see Sadgrove (2004).

6 Trimingham (1964).

7 Purpura (1997) has argued that the two strands of the East African intellectual tradition formed part of an integrated whole until the emergence of the Omani sultanate in the nineteenth century. Only then, she argues, did the tradition split into two distinct parts: an oral one associated with KiSwahili and a written one associated with the Omani state.

8 This process also opened up new avenues of social mobility, especially for recent arrivals from Arabia who were already fluent in Arabic and conversant with the literary tradition of Islam. A clear example of this was the scholar and *qadi* Ahmad b. Sumayt, portrayed in Bang (2003).

9 As a distinctive branch of Islam, the Ibadiyya traces its roots to the Kharijiyya secessionists of early Islam, from which it eventually broke in 685. As the founding element of the Omani imamate – and later the Bu Sa'idi dynasty – it has been marked by a tendency towards tolerance of other sects. By the nineteenth century, the main areas of Ibadism were Oman, Zanzibar (and, by extension, the Omani/Bu Sa'idi strata of East Africa), southern Algeria and pockets of Libya.

10 Eastern African Centre for Research on Oral Traditions and African National Languages. See the original checklist of the Eacrotonal collection completed in 1988. Apparently, some 30 of the manuscripts were lost before or during the transfer. This, however, will be clear once the collection is fully indexed within the ZNA. For an overview of the Eacrotonal collection, see Khamis (2001) (Archives, Manuscripts and Written Historical Sources, Oral history, Archaeology).

11 Originally hailing from Brawa, 'Abd al-'Aziz al-'Amawi was appointed *qadi* of Kilwa at the tender age of 16. After a few years there, he returned to Zanzibar where he served as *qadi* until his retirement in 1894. A study of the works of 'Abd al-'Aziz is presently being prepared by Professor Valerie Hoffmann, University of Champagne-Urbana, USA.

12 Files AA5/8 and AA5/9.

13 This is the reason why the texts of the original *waqfiyya*s of Sayyid Hammud b. Ahmad al-Bu Sa'idi were reproduced in court. He was a close companion of Sayyid Barghash who endowed a number of very substantial *waqf*s in the 1870s. His endowments were subject to the efforts of the British-established Wakf Commission to regulate proceeds from the *waqf*s, and in this case the original documents were reproduced and are kept with the court records: ZA-HD6/55 and ZA-HD3/12.

14 Records indicated as HC.

15 Records indicated as HD.

16 Abdallah Saleh Farsy (1989), our most direct source on the life of the East African '*ulama*, repeatedly refers to sessions of *tafsir*, etc. taking place orally in the various classes of the shaykhs.

17 For an overview of Attafayyish's works printed at Zanzibar, see Sadgrove (2004).

18 One exception is Declich (2001, 2004).

19 Declich (2001, 2004).

20 For background on the al-Kindi apology and al-Mundhiri's response, see Hoffmann (2004). See also O'Fahey & Vikør (1996).

21 ZA 8/10. The version held by the ZNA is 316 pages long but, according to V Hoffmann, apparently incomplete.

REFERENCES

Bang AK (2003) *Sufis and scholars of the sea, family networks in East Africa*, 1860–1925. London/New York: RoutledgeCurzon

Declich L (2001) The Arabic manuscripts of the Zanzibar National Archives: Sources for the study of popular Islam in the island during the 19th century. In BS Amoretti (Ed.) *Islam in East Africa: New sources*. Rome: Herder

Declich L (2004) Zanzibar: Some nineteenth-century Arabic writings on healing. In S Reese (Ed.) *The transmission of learning in Islamic Africa*. Leiden: Brill

Farsy AS (1989) *Baadhi ya wanavyoni wa kishafi wa mashariki ya Afrika/The Shafi'i Ulama of East Africa, ca.1830–1970: A hagiographical account*. Translated, edited and annotated by RL Pouwels. University of Wisconsin, African Primary Text Series, III

Hoffmann V (2004) al-Mundhir and the defence of Ibadism in Zanzibar. Unpublished paper, MESA, San Francisco

Khamis KS (2001) The Zanzibar National Archives. In BS Amoretti (Ed.) *Islam in East Africa: New sources*. Rome: Herder

O'Fahey S & Vikør K (1996) A Zanzibari *waqf* of books: The library of the Mundhiri family. *Sudanic Africa* 7: 5–23

Purpura P (1997) Knowledge and agency: The social relations of Islamic expertise in Zanzibar Town. PhD thesis, City University of New York

Reese S (2004) Introduction. Islam in Africa: challenging the perceived wisdom. In S Reese (Ed.) *The transmission of learning in Islamic Africa*. Leiden: Brill

Sadgrove P (2004) From Wadi Mizab to Unguja: Zanzibar's scholarly links. In S Reese (Ed.) *The transmission of learning in Islamic Africa*. Leiden: Brill

Sharif A (1987) *Slaves, spices and ivory in Zanzibar*. London: James Currey

Trimingham JS (1964) *Islam in East Africa*. New York: Books for Libraries

Picture credits

Cover manuscript: An example of North African script from the Ahmed Baba Collec-tion, catalogue no. 557, *Tanbih al-Anam fi bayani ulumi maqami nabiyina Muhammad*, by Abdul Jalil b. Azum Al-Qayrawani. D. 971 *hijri*. Image supplied by the SA–Mali Project

Cover photograph: DHK Architects

Maps: Adapted from authors' versions by Jenny Young

pp. xvi, 5, 8, 18, 20, 28–29, 33, 34 36, 77, 92–93, 111, 124, 135, 137, 190–191, 234, 235, 240, 249, 251, 253, 262–263, 256, 268, 270, 277, 279, 281, 283, 290, 292, 298, 302, 304, 305, 309, 321, 332: The South Africa–Mali Project

Endpapers and contents pages, pp. 25, 41, 45, 47, 94, 109, 123, 171, 180, 185, 192, 205, 213, 217, 230, 240, 294, 295: manuscripts from the Ahmed Baba Institute, Timbuktu, images supplied by the Tombo*uct*ou Manuscript Project

pp. xiv–xv, 6, 77, 286, 330: DHK Architects

p. 25: manuscript from the Mamma Haidara Library, Vol. 1, 52

p. 53, 54, by Jonathan M Bloom

p. 58: Leeds University, Ms. 301, fol. 3a, after Brockett 1987: fig. 2, supplied by Sheila S Blair

p. 62: after *Quaritch* 1995: 73, supplied by Sheila S Blair

p. 63: after Brockett 1987: fig. 1, supplied by Sheila S Blair

p. 65 (left): Bibliothèque Nationale, Arabe 402, slide purchased and supplied by Sheila S Blair

p. 65 (right): after Blair 2005: fig. 12.15, supplied by Sheila S Blair

p. 67: British Library 1405, after Blair 2005: fig. 12.16, supplied by Sheila S Blair

p. 68: Fondo Ka'ti Library, supplied by Sheila S Blair

p. 71: after Safwat 2000: no. 72, supplied by Sheila S Blair

pp. 99, 101, 102, 103: map, photographs, line drawings, and transcriptions of Arabic inscriptions from *Arabic Medieval Inscriptions from the Republic of Mali: Epigraphy, Chronicles, and Songhay-Tuareg History*, by PF de Moraes Farias (2004), published by Oxford University Press and The British Academy, reprinted here with kind permission of The British Academy

pp. 116, 117, 118: IRSH/UAM, images supplied by Moulaye Hassane

p. 164: supplied by Jean Boyd and Beverly Mack

pp. 266, 267: courtesy of Abdel Kader Haidara and supplied by the Tombouctou Manuscript Project

p. 283: supplied by Mukhtar b. Yahya al-Wangari

p. 348: Zanzibar National Archives, ZA-AA5/27 (1), Photographed by Friedhelm Hartwig

p. 353: Zanzibar National Archives, ZA-AA5/27 (2), Photographed by Friedhelm Hartwig

p. 355: Zanzibar National Archives, ZA-AA5/8-98, Photographed by Anne K Bang

Contributors

Anne K Bang
Research Fellow
Norwegian Research Council/
University of Bergen, Norway

Sheila S Blair
Norma Jean Calderwood University
Professor of Islamic and Asian Art,
Boston College, and
Hamad bin Khalifa Endowed Chair
of Islamic Art
Virginia Commonwealth University, USA

Jonathan M Bloom
Norma Jean Calderwood University
Professor of Islamic and Asian Art,
Boston College, and
Hamad bin Khalifa Endowed Chair
of Islamic Art
Virginia Commonwealth University, USA

Hamid Bobboyi
Director
Arewa House Centre for
Historical Documentation and Research
Ahmadu Bello University, Nigeria

Timothy Cleaveland
Associate Professor
African Studies Institute
University of Georgia, USA

Muhammad Diagayeté
Researcher
Ahmed Baba Institute of Higher Islamic
Studies and Research, Mali

Souleymane Bachir Diagne
Professor
Department of Philosophy
Northwestern University, USA

Paulo F de Moraes Farias
Honorary Senior Research Fellow
Centre of West African Studies
University of Birmingham, UK

Aslam Farouk-Alli
Political Counsellor
Department of Foreign Affairs and
Former Researcher
Tombo*uctu* Manuscript Project
University of Cape Town, South Africa

Abdel Kader Haidara
Director and curator
Mamma Haidara Memorial Library, Mali

Ismaël Diadié Haidara
Director and curator
Fondo Ka'ti Library, Mali

Moulaye Hassane
Head of the Department of Arabic
and Ajami Manuscripts
Human Sciences Research Institute
Abdou Moumouni University of Niamey,
Niger

John Hunwick
Professor Emeritus and
Director
Institute for the Study of
Islamic Thought in Africa
Northwestern University, USA

Shamil Jeppie
Senior Lecturer and Director
Tombo*uctu* Manuscript Project
Department of Historical Studies
University of Cape Town, South Africa

Murray Last
Professorial Research Associate
Centre of African Studies
School of Oriental and African Studies
University of London, UK

Beverly B Mack
Professor of African Studies
University of Kansas, USA

Mahamane Mahamoudou
Pedagogical Advisor
Pedagogical Animation Centre of Timbuktu,
Director
ISESCO-AMAI Library, and
Teacher of Islamic Sciences, Mali

Mohamed Shaid Mathee
PhD student and Researcher
Tombo*uctu* Manuscript Project
University of Cape Town, South Africa

Roderick J McIntosh
Professor of Anthropology
Yale University, USA, and
Visiting Professor of Archaeology
University of Pretoria, South Africa

R Séan O'Fahey
Professor of non-European Studies
University of Bergen, Norway, and
Adjunct Professor
Northwestern University, USA

Yahya Ould el-Bara
Professor
Department of Arabic and Islamic Studies
Zayed University, United Arab Emirates

Abdel Wedoud Ould Cheikh
Professor of Anthropology and Sociology
University of Metz, France

Mohammed Ould Youbba
Adjunct Director-General
Ahmed Baba Institute of Higher Islamic
Studies and Research, Mali

Charles C Stewart
Interim Associate Provost for
International Affairs and
Professor
Department of History
University of Illinois, USA

Haoua Taore
Assistant Curator
Fondo Ka'ti Library, Mali

Mukhtar bin Yahya al-Wangari
Director and curator
Al-Wangari Library, Mali

Editorial notes

Transliteration

Arabic names and titles are transliterated broadly as suggested in *The Chicago Manual of Style (15th Edition)*. We have tried to simplify the transliteration as much as possible, using no diacritical marks, except for the *hamza* (') and the *'ayn* ('). We have kept the definite article al joined to the noun with a hyphen and without indication of the elision before the sounds *d, n, r, s, sh, t,* and *z* (e.g. *Tarikh al-Sudan* not *as-Sudan*). Since the Arabic alphabet does not distinguish between capital and lowercase forms, we have only capitalized proper nouns and the first word in a sentence or in a transliterated title of a book or manuscript. Personal names in African languages are spelt in a way that approximates to their actual pronunciation when it is known, or as they have been vowelled in the manuscripts. Muslim names of Arabic origin are transliterated accordingly, though local pronunciations vary considerably (for example, Amadu for Ahmad, Usman for 'Uthman). We have tried to maintain consistency in spellings but have also included spellings as commonly used in Francophone Africa, thus the Ahmed Baba Insitute is spelled thus because of its usage in Mali but we have used Ahmad Baba to refer to the scholar as this is consistent with our transliteration method.

Dates

Correspondence of *hijri* and Gregorian dates was calculated using Faik Resit Unat's *Hicri tarihleri miladi tarihe cevirme kilavuzu* (Ankara: Turk Tarih Kurumu Basimevi, 1994). If unstated, the date is from the Gregorian calendar; we have only indicated both dates when the original date in a manuscript is *hijri*. Some minor divergences might exist since months are set according to the sightings of the new moon. The order of the months in the *hijri* year is as follows: *Muharram, Safar, Rabi' I, Rabi' II, Jumada I, Jumada II, Rajab, Sha'ban, Ramadan, Shawwal, Dhu al-Qa'da, Dhu al-Hijja.* The months are of either 29 or 30 days, and a complete year is 355 days. A *hijri* (lunar) century is approximately 97 Gregorian (solar) years.

Glossary

'abid	a devout servant of God
abu shibbak	a thick brown or cream-coloured paper
adab (adj. *adabi*)	etiquette or literature
'adil	a just person
'adl	justice; fairness
aflak	astronomy/astrology; the study of celestial bodies
ahl-al-kalam	scholars of theology
ajami	non-Arab, i.e. Turk, Persian, African etc; non-Arabic languages written in Arabic script
akhira	afterlife
'aqida	dogma; creed
askiya	title used by the rulers of the Songhay Empire
awliya	saints; friends of Allah
balad	village or town; district
baraka	blessings, supernatural powers
bihari	from Bihar; a distinctive calligraphic style used in India
Bilad al-Sudan	the Saharo–Sahelian land across middle Africa from the Atlantic to the Red Sea
dajjal	anti-Christ
diwan	register or poetry collection
dhikr (pl. *adhkar*)	remembrance of Allah; repetition of a prayer
dunya	earth; refers to the world as lower and temporary and deceptive
emir (pl. *umara*)	prince; commander, political leader
falsafa	philosophy
faqih (pl. *fuqaha*)	jurist
fatiha	opening chapter of the Qur'an
fatwa (pl. *fatawa*)	legal opinion, response
fiqh	Islamic substantive law, jurisprudence
hadarat	a Muslim person of high spiritual status or an elderly person; any person who is present; a manner of addressing a respected person
hadith	prophetic tradition
hajj	the ritual pilgrimage
halal	that which is wholesome and permissible
hamziyya	A poem where each stanza ends with the letter hamza
haqiqa	truth, divine reality (used in Sufism)
haram	that which is prohibited
hijra	migration
hijri	The Muslim calendar
ifta	the act of issuing religious–legal verdicts
ijaza (pl. *ijazat*)	teaching authorisation
ikhlas	sincerity

'ilm	knowledge
imam	religious or political leader; prayer leader in a mosque
isnad	chain of narrators in prophetic traditions
jahiliyya	pre-Islamic era
jama'a	congregation
jihad	exertion in the way of God; in certain contexts it refers to holy warfare in support of Islam
jinn	spirits
kalam	theology
karama (pl.)	miracle, holy act
khalifa	caliph; deputy, successor
khalwa	mystical retreat; seclusion
khatib	one who delivers sermons on Friday and other occasions
kitab	book
madhhab	school of jurisprudence in Islam, of which there are four in the Sunni world
madrasa	school
Maghrib	north-west Africa
mahdi	the Guided one; refers to the saviour who will come to fill the world with justice and equity
mallam (pl. *malamai*)	minor scholar
mansaya	monarchy
mantiq	logic
mufti	jurisconsult
muluk (sg. *malik*)	kings
murabit (pl. *murabitun*)	tenth-century Muslim movement that established a state in North Africa and Spain
murid	disciple, follower
nafs	ego, self
nasiha	advice
nisba	ascription to place, tribe etc.
qabila	tribe
qadi	judge
qasida	ode
qutb	chief of saints; learned man (lit. 'magnetic pole')
ra'iyya	the masses
rashidun	rightly guided; refers to the first four caliphs of (Islam after the Prophet's demise (632–660)
ribat	religious school
ridwan	satisfaction, pleasure
rihla (pl. *rihlat*)	journey; account of one's travels
risala	the message of Islam; treatise; correspondence
sajda	prostration
salah	ritual obligatory prayers five times a day as well as superogatory ones
shairi, mashairi	intimate, dialogic and polemical poetry
shari'a	Islamic law
shaykh (pl. *ashyakh*)	male scholar of Islam or head of the tribe
silsila	chain of mystical transmission
sira	biography of the Prophet; the study of the life of the Prophet
Sunna	prophetic normative tradition
sura	Quranic chapter
tafsir	Qur'anic exegesis
takhmis	a classical Arabic poetic process rather than a genre per se; its a five-line verse amplification of a pre-existing couplet by a master
tarikh	chronicle
tariqa	brotherhood
tasawwuf	Sufism; spirituality
tawhid	Islamic theology; the concept of Oneness; the unity of Allah; unity; monotheism or unity of; Islamic creed
tendi	epic poetry writing
'ulama (sg. *'alim*)	scholars; intellectual authorities
umma	nation; the Muslim global world
urjuza	poem in the rajaz metre
usul al-fiqh	source methodology in jurisprudence
wa'azi	genre of literature; admonishing talk, exhortation to do good and discard bad
waqf	pious foundation, endowment
waqfiyya	case concerning a waqf
wazir	minister, vizier
wird	litany
zakat	alms
zawiya	place of residence of the saint or his spirit; Sufi centres

Index

Given the dificulty of alphabetising Arabic names, the following conventions are used: people who have clear family names such as al-Kunti, al-Arwani, etc. are listed under their family names; and people whose names do not give full lineage, are abbreviated, or contain titles by which they have become known, are listed according to their first name, for example, Ahmad Baba, Nana Asma'u, Sonni 'Ali.

C

D

M

... اسبيت فتله الكاهية محمد
... وهو اول من قتله بالعنبج
... وانه سبع واربعين رقبة
... رهم وغيرهم نسئل الله
السلامة والعافية وفاهت العشنة
... الرماة والتوار فاي موتا
... عام اربع وثمانين بيوم
... ثالث من جماد الاولى
الباشا بعد موته كبير رحمه
... مع علي وخالف الرماة
... بعد نحلم وبرز الرماة
... فحصر تيباي بجهة النوار
... المقتلة ويوم السابع عشر
بيوم الاربعا جمع جلالو
... الباشا نوح وضربوا للنوار

... فتقتلوا مع التوارق من ...
التبعلالة وجمع عنه الباشا نوح خلق
كثير وقامت الجموع في اهل تنبكت
في حصر التوارق اهل تنبكت لا
يخرج احد ولا يدخل احد الا ...
في ثالث رمضان يوم الجمعة خرج
الباشا من القصبة لزيارة صلحاء
تنبكت فتلاقي الباشا مع التوارق
في ابراز حتى اروضة دبير محمود
ومع الباشا ثلاثة رجال الكاهية
داهر والباشا نوح وعبد الرحمن اخ
الباشا ... فقاتلوا مع التوارق
جرح الباشا وضربا الباشا ...
التوارق على اهل سنكري ونهبوا
... دار دبير سنكري دبير محمد بن عبد
وقاتل اهل سنكري مع التوارق وقتل

27

... من رجال اهل سنكري
... جمعهم وخلوا وسط تنبكت
من التوارق وفي اخر شوال بعث الباشا
ولد ... صلحاء تنبكت خبر ...
... كلهم نحو اربعة عشر
يوما الناس داخلين وخارجين وفي
الرابع عشر من القعدة غار هبيدي
على ... وقتلوا من قتلوا واسروا
من اسروا وذلك يوم الاحد وتولى هبيدي
... حاجب لخيل التوارق الذي ...
مات وفي ... توفي الامام عثمان
بن عثمان امام جامع الطيب وتولى
... بن الشيخ عبد العزيز بعده وفي
... خامس وثمانين بنى اهل سنكري
حصنهم ... بالبناء ...
رجع اهل سنكري ... وفي ... الضحى

... ربيع الاول توفي عبد ...
... وفي هذا العام توفي جامع
الهنا عبد الرحمن ... بابا بن ... وفي
العام توفي الامام المصطفى ولد ...
وضريب جامع الهنا وجامع القصبة ...
هلم جرا وفي ... العشنة ...
عبد الكريم ... قبضة ...
... ومشى به الى ...
... الاول ...
... وحيث توفي ...
عثمان ... وتولى الامام ...
بن عتيق ... في الامامة ...
وعشرين سنة ...
... المختار ... وفي اخر السنة ...
ربيع الانور وصلح الباشا ...
... الباشا احمد ...
... من الخيل ...
... من الباشا ...

29

... عبد الله نصيبه وان يقبض
... مصيبة ...
... الاول رمضان وفي العام
... توفي الفقيه يحيى بن ...
... الغاية المصطفى بن عبيد
... رجع نصيبه
المصطفى الحاج عبد الرحيم الحكومة
... عنه كتب خبر الى عمار بن
... سعيد وهو في ...
... وغضب وخرج في ...
... وحصل في ... سبع
... الباشا ... الغلاء
... اهل الغوارب ...
... اهل الغرابة على الراي
... وبعثوا عبد ...
... محمد احمد ...

32

تنبكت ... واجبر الباشا وجمع
الباشا اهل تنبكت ... وفقها
... والقاضي والكاهية ...
الباشا عبد الله ...
... القاضي الى عنه عمار ...
طبيب وفي اخر ... دار الكاهية
... بعدما ... عبد الله
وبعث ... مولاي عمر ...
ومولاي محمد ومحمد بن القاضي احمد وامام
جامع ... الى ...
ثمانية وثمانين ستة ايام من صفر
توفي زوجة الباشا ...
بنت ... محمد بن ... وفي ...
عشر من الشهر توفيت ام الباشا
... العباس وفي ...
عشر ... ربيع النبوي توفيت ام
الكاهية ... بنت الفقيه محمد
رحمة الله عليهما وفي العاشر جماد الاخر

ليلة الخميس توفي الكاهية يحيى بن ...
... موت ... في ... حومة
... وفي شهر ذي القعدة غار
التوارق ... ووجد الحال
محمد الكاهية ... في البلاد
... منهم الامر ... الله على ...
... ليلة ... وتوفي
الباشا ... وفي ... الاول
... خامس من الشهر توفي الباشا
... بعد ما مكث في الكاهية
تسعة اعوام وفي ليلة الرابع و...
والعشرين ... توفي محمد العربي
... السلامة والعافية وتوفي الباشا
... جمع الجيش ...
من ... الله ...
... عني ...

... الكاهية ... وهو في ...
وحصر حصروا ... الكاهية
باشا حتى يعلموا الخبر ورد الكاهية
... الجيش ...
الباشا ... على ...
... يقبلونه وجمع الجيش
في جامع ... الكاهية على
الحاكم عبد الله ... بن محمد و...
... الجيش ... عليه
... الكاهية عبد ... وفي ...
رجب جاء خبر موت العشنة عبد الله
... وتولى الامامة عبد الرحمن اماما
في جامع الهنا ...
... العشنة ... الكاهية ...
والكاهية باشا ...
واحدة في شهر جماد الاول رحمه الله ...

34

... وفي شهر رجب تسع
... توفيت ... الرحمة بنت
... وفي شعبان ...
... ابكر ومكث في القضاء
عشرة اعوام وفي ثمانية وعشرين ...
... القعدة توفي ...
... ليلة الاحد توفي
... العباس و...
... المصطفى بن القايد
... على مفتاح دار ...
... ودخلوا اهل ...
... الليلة وفي الرابع و...
... من جماد الاولى ...
... القايد ... ومكث
... الشهر وفي ...

من شهر شوال توفي مولاي محمد بن ...
... عام خامس ... عشر ...
... توفي ... زوجة الكاهية
... وفي شهر رجب بيوم
الجمعة ستة وعشرين وخمسة توفي
رقية زوجة العربي الجزار وفي
يوم التاسع والعشرون من رمضان
توفي القايد ... بن الكاهية
... وفي عام ... وقعة
... وفي اول يوم من ... القعدة ...
... على اهل ... وقتل
... ولد ... وابنا ...
... ليلة الاحد ...
وفي ... يوم الاثنين توفي ...
... بن القايد ...

وفي شهر رجب جاء خبر موت القايد باشا
توفي في ... وفي شهر شعبان جاء
خبر موت عمار ولد ... توفي في ...
وفي شهر رمضان جاء خبر موت
... في شهر ...
موسى ... خبر وصل ...
توفي ... وتسعين ... اخر يوم
من ربيع الاول عشية الجمعة
توفي ... بن القايد ... وفي
شهر شعبان ثلاث عشر من ...
يوم الجمعة توفي الكاهية ...
بن ... خامس من شعبان
توفي ... وبنوته ...
... تسع ... يوم تاسع ...
المحرم توفي الامام ... بن ...
... عبد الرحمن رحمة الله عليه وهو
... الذي ...

... الرسول وتولى الامامة ابنه الفقيه
الامام ... جامع ...
الامامة ... سعيد المذكور ...
اعوام وفي ربيع الثاني ...
... وحل ... قبض ...
بن القايد ... عبد الله ...
... وعدوا ... من ...
... الامامة ...
... جمع جلال واسهم ...
... وقتلوا البدو ...
وعدد ... القاتل والمقتول
... محمد الباشا احمد ...
... من ... محمد ...
... مع ... عنه ...
المقتولين ... الادية ...
... وفي يوم الثالث ...
... والغعير ...

كتاب في الحوادث والوفيات التي جرت في تنبكت وحولها من 1748م - 1800 تقريبا ويتناول أيضا تاريخ جلوس كل باشا على عرش التنبكتية في تنبكت

3315

الثاني وفيه أخبر موت عبد الله
بعده علي بن [illegible] يجتمع عليه
[illegible] قتلوا عددا [illegible]
وعدوا [illegible] أمواله ومكث
الباشا في توليته خمسة أشهر
وعزل في العاشر من شوال في هذا
العام تولى بكر بن الفع مصور باشا
ومكث فيه ثلاثة أشهر وفي
[illegible] وقتل [illegible] القايد [illegible]
ابن أخته القايد عبد الغفار في
ابراز الثاني وستين ومائة وألف
توفي القايد بابا سيد [illegible]
[illegible] وتوفي [illegible] الرزاق
[illegible] عبد الرحمن بن سنبير

بن الإمام سعد ويسمى [illegible] العام
[illegible] وفي ذلك العام توفي الإمام
ابراهيم بن عبد الله إمام جامع
سنكري [illegible] وتولى إمامة
الجامع ابن عمه الإمام ابراهيم
بن أحمد سبعة عشر سنة ومات
في ذلك العام خلق [illegible] لا يحصى
الثالث والستين ومائة وألف
تولى بكر بن الفع مصور أيضا باشا
باشا من صفر ومكث في
الرئاسة ثلاثة عشر شهرا و
وعزل [illegible] باب القايد ابراهيم
وفي يوم [illegible] ذي القعدة في
شهر شوال في هذا العام توفي

القاضي باب المختار وتولى بعده
القضاء القاضي باب بن ولاة البلد
المذكور ومكث في الولاية ستة
أعوام عام الرابع والستين وما[illegible]
وفي [illegible] القايد سعيد بن [illegible]
أحمد عزوزة وفي رجوعه [illegible]
توفي إمام جامع القصبة [illegible]
الله بن الإمام عثمان وفي [illegible]
شوال يوم الثامن وعشرين من
الشهر توفي الإمام عتيق [illegible]
جامع الكبير يوم الأحد وتو[illegible]
الإمام [illegible] عبد الله بن الحاج الإمام
ومكث في الإمامة ثمانية أعوام
[illegible] الخامس والستين ومائة وألف
[illegible] القايد عبد الغفار الى [illegible]

وفي السادس والعشرين من رمضان
يوم الجمعة توفي الإمام باب
الفقيه محمد بغيغ وتولى بعده
أخوه الإمام محمود بن محمد بغيغ
ومكث بعده في الإمامة
عشرين أعواما وتولى بعده
في الجامع الإمام باب سعيد
بن الحاج عبد الرحمن وفي المحل
عام سبعين توفي مولاي سعيد
مولاي محمد بن محمد الحسني
وفي التاسعة عشر من جمادى
في [illegible] عام سبعين [illegible]
[illegible] سعيد بن سنبير [illegible]
تعزية موت عمار [illegible] رجع
[illegible] موته [illegible]

6

رمضان [illegible] العافية وتوفي [illegible] سعيد [illegible]
[illegible] يوم الاثنين الثاني والعشرين
من الشهر وفي يومه توفي [illegible]
بن بكر ولد [illegible] في ليلة الأربعاء ال[illegible]
الرابع والعشرين من الشهر
توفي القايد بن القايد سنبير وفي
ليلة النصف من شعبان توفي
[illegible] سالم وفي يومه توفي
القايد علي بن عبد الرؤوف باشا
وهو الذي تولى القاضي محمود
القضاء بن القاضي أحمد وولي البلد
[illegible] في موضع أركي سالم وهو
الذي [illegible] بن الطيب [illegible]
وعزل يوم الأحد عاشر رمضان
وفي ذلك اليوم [illegible] القايد [illegible]

بن أحمد توفي في [illegible] ولا رجع في
يوم عزله عبد [illegible] توفي محمد [illegible]
وفي الثاني والعشرين من ذي القعدة
في [illegible] وحمل جنازته إلى [illegible] وفي
في جامع [illegible] ويوم [illegible] خبر من
[illegible] من ذي الحجة ليلة الجمعة
توفي الحاج عبد الرحمن بن علي
الغنام وفي عام الحادي وسبعين
توفي مولاي عبد الرحمن وفي
[illegible] خمس وعشرين من شعبان
من ذلك العام سالم بن [illegible]
الكاهي محمد [illegible] وفي خامس
رمضان توفي محمد زوي بن الفقيه
[illegible] شوال [illegible] في
شهر شوال ثم تولى الباشا علي
بن [illegible] في شهر

8

ذي الحجة بعد العيد في آخر [illegible]
[illegible] وسبعين العام الثالث
وسبعون في شهر صفر توفي
كبير [illegible] باب القايد ابراهيم
ثامن عشر من الشهر وفي
ربيع الثاني توفي مولاي [illegible]
وفي يوم السابع يوم الثلاثاء
طلع الباشا إلى كبر مع الجيش
وبات في كبر وفي غده يوم
الأربعاء [illegible] تنبكت
على التوارق [illegible] واقتتل
مع التوارق قتالا أشد بدا وغلب
التوارق وقتل يومئذ القايد
علي بن عبد الرؤوف والشريف
مولاي الشريف بن مولاي [illegible]
وقتل الباشا وماتت العامة

9

العلاتيبيا [illegible] ومكث في [illegible]
شهرين ومعه في محلته محمد
[illegible] بعض التوارق بكل
من معه من التوارق وفي [illegible]
ذي الحجة رجع محمد المختار [illegible]
التوارق وبعده رجع [illegible] الباشا
إلى [illegible] يريد [illegible]
[illegible] وجد الماء [illegible]
وفي [illegible] الحجة غار العلاتيبيا
على محلة الباشا وقتل في [illegible]
[illegible] وقتل بن الله وكبير [illegible]
بن [illegible] وعمار ولد [illegible] ورجع
الناس [illegible] بالله
تنبكت [illegible] الكاهية محمد والقايد
منصور ومكث الباشا [illegible]

14

ثلاثة أشهر ثم رجع الناس إلى
تنبكت ليلة الثامن عشر من
ربيع النبوي في العام الخامس
وسبعين عزل الباشا في ذي الحجة
الشهر ومكث في [illegible] ثلاثة
إحدى عشر شهرا وفي ليلة
استهلال ذي القعدة آخر
العام خامس وسبعين توفي
الفقيه الجليل العالم العلامة
سعيد بن محمد بغيغ رحمه الله
في شهر [illegible] توفي [illegible] عمار
رابع من الشهر السادس و
سبعين توفي القايد بكر بن
الفع مصور وفي ليلة رابع عشر
من صفر توفي الكاهية منصور بن الفع

15

بن سنبير بن [illegible] وحمل جنازته من كواسيكي
وفي [illegible] بن [illegible] بلقاسم التواتي
وتوفي [illegible] سنبير ولد [illegible]
ليلة الأحد ثاني من شوال
توفي القايد عبد الغفار بن
الكاهية سلامه وفي صبيحة
الاثنين ثالث شوال السادس
وسبعين توفي الإمام عمار إمام
جامع القصبة وتولى الجامع
بابا بن الإمام عتيق وفي ليلة
الخميس ثاني عشر من ذي القعدة
توفي [illegible] بن الحسن [illegible]
[illegible] في إقليم
السودان من تنبكت وتسمى
تلك [illegible] عام سابع و
وسبعين توفي مولاي سنبير [illegible]

16

[illegible] كواسيكي وفي آخر [illegible] توفي الشيخ [illegible]
الله بن الشيخ عبد العزيز [illegible]
وسبعين يوم الأربعاء [illegible]
ربيع الثاني تولى القايد علي [illegible]
[illegible] وخالف أهل [illegible] بكبير [illegible]
[illegible] كبير [illegible] ولم [illegible]
عزل الباشا وولي في داره ومكث
في الولاية خمسة أشهر وفي آخر
العام جاء خبر موت القايد [illegible]
من [illegible] العام الثامن وسبعين
قتل [illegible] الشيخ عبد الرحمن
بن المختار الشيخ أولاد أحمد [illegible]
[illegible] وجاء أولاد أحمد [illegible]
وقتلوا في [illegible] وماتت خلق كثير
[illegible] في جمادى الآخرة [illegible]
من الشهر توفي الكاهية علي بن الكاهية

17